Writing Home

Writing Home

A Quaker Immigrant on the Ohio Frontier

The Letters of Emma Botham Alderson

EDITED BY DONALD INGRAM ULIN

LEWISBURG, PENNSYLVANIA

Library of Congress Cataloging-in-Publication Data

Names: Alderson, Emma Botham, 1806–1847, author. | Ulin, Donald Ingram, editor.
Title: Writing home : a Quaker immigrant on the Ohio frontier; the Letters of Emma Botham Alderson/ edited by Donald Ingram Ulin
Description: Lewisburg, Pennsylvania : Bucknell University Press, 2020. | Includes bibliographical references and index.
Identifiers: LCCN 2019059111 | ISBN 9781684481965 (hardcover) | ISBN 9781684481989 (epub) | ISBN 9781684481996 (mobi) | ISBN 9781684482009 (pdf)
Subjects: LCSH: Alderson, Emma Botham, 1806–1847—Correspondence. | Alderson, Emma Botham, 1806–1847—Family, | Howitt, Mary (Mary Botham), 1799–1888—Correspondence. | Quaker women—Biography. | Frontier and pioneer life—Ohio. | British Americans—Biography. | Warsaw (Ohio)—Biography.
Classification: LCC F495 .A44 2020 | DDC 977.1/77 [B]—dc23
LC record available at https://lccn.loc.gov/2019059111

A British Cataloging-in-Publication record for this book is available from the British Library.

www.bucknelluniversitypress.org

Distributed worldwide by Rutgers University Press

Manufactured in the United States of America

Contents

PART II
A Home of Their Own: First Years at Cedar Lodge

PART III
The Final Years

Illustrations

Preface

Work on this book was, as they say, something of a journey home to a place I'd never been before. I grew up in the 1960s and 1970s attending Mount Toby Monthly Meeting of the Society of Friends (Quakers) on the outskirts of Amherst, Massachusetts. In "first-day school" (the Quaker term for Sunday school, arising originally out of a reluctance to name pagan deities), we sang songs about saving the whales and organized relief efforts for victims of the 1976 Guatemalan earthquake. Conversations and activities promoted what we came to recognize as Quaker values, like peace, simplicity, equality, and social justice. We learned that, from the days of the earliest Quakers, who refused to remove their hats, use honorific titles, or otherwise recognize class difference, Friends had always been in the vanguard of every progressive social cause from penal reform to women's and civil rights to the abolition of slavery. This particular narrative is not entirely wrong, but I was to learn in later years that the actual story was a great deal more complicated. From what I understood of it, however, the Society of Friends was an organization to which I was proud to belong.

I say "organization," because I could see little if any similarity between Quakerism and the more theocentric outlook that I associated with the term "religion." I understood that, historically at any rate, Quakerism was a Christian denomination, but there was more talk of George Fox, Quakerism's founder, than of Jesus. The emphasis on values, right living, and social action rather than metaphysics or doctrine defined Quakerism for me. The truth was to be sought not in scripture or in church teachings, but in something Quakers mysteriously (to me at least) referred to as the "inner light": that infallible guide in each of us, if only we would listen to its advice. The beauty of Quakerism, it seemed to me, was that the inner light made all outward authority, including that of my parents, the police, the Bible, and even God, irrelevant. I would later learn that the inner light is not so much a matter of personal inclination as a manifestation of divine "leading," but at the time my youthful understanding (or perhaps misunderstanding) of Quakerism corresponded nicely with prevailing counterculture ideals of doing one's own thing while saving the earth. It seemed self-evident to us that, from Woodstock to the antiwar rallies, my generation was enacting the vision of George Fox, right down to the description of him in his "old leather breeches" and his "shaggy, shaggy locks" from the popular Quaker song, "Walking in the Light."

I had heard of others who called themselves Quakers but whose practices and beliefs differed significantly from the Quakers I knew. Their meetings were more like church services than our entirely unprogrammed gatherings, in which anyone might speak out of the silence on whatever topic was foremost on his or her mind. These other Quakers more closely approximated what I understood as Christianity but (perhaps for that very reason) struck me as pretenders to the name "Quaker." Richard Nixon had called himself a Quaker and attended Whittier College, a Quaker-affiliated college, where his name is now attached to an endowed chair and an annual scholarship. Smugly, if unconsciously, I came to imagine two sorts of Quakers: those whose progressive views and eschewal of any fixed or metaphysical doctrines marked them as the real Quakers, and those, like Nixon perhaps, who had fallen back into the kind of Christianity that Fox had rejected, with its rigid hierarchies, official doctrines, and conservative attitudes.

After high school, I drifted away from the Society of Friends and no longer attended meeting, but in graduate school at Indiana University, my doctoral research on representations of the English countryside introduced me to the work of William and Mary Howitt, liberal activist Quakers of the mid-nineteenth century. My own identity as a Quaker was rekindled by my admiration for their advocacy for reform, women's suffrage, abolition of slavery and of the death penalty, and other liberal causes, as well as their (especially his) disdain for most forms of organized religion. Together they published prolifically and traveled in international reform circles with the likes of Frederick Douglass, William Lloyd Garrison, and Lucretia Mott. As an American Quaker (though I had let my formal membership lapse) and now scholar, I was drawn to a book of Mary's called *Our Cousins in Ohio* (1849), based on the journals of her sister Emma Botham Alderson, who had emigrated to America in 1842 and died in 1847. Mary Howitt's Quaker activism and her correspondence with her sister in America seemed an ideal opportunity to align my adult professional work as an American scholar of Victorian studies with the Quakerism that had remained central to my identity since childhood.

My work on producing a new edition of *Our Cousins in Ohio* (out of print since 1866) was put on hold when the missing correspondence on which that book was based resurfaced at the University of Nottingham. When I traveled to Nottingham to select a few letters for inclusion in the book, I discovered a richer and more complex picture of a young woman struggling to find her identity as a woman, mother, Quaker, and Anglo-American. My aim shifted from an edition of *Our Cousins* with a few sample letters to a fully edited collection of the letters themselves. Thus began my relationship with Emma Alderson and her family.

But family relations are notoriously strained by individual growth and the discovery of unexpected differences. Emma's letters to her two sisters (Anna Harrison and Mary Howitt) and her mother (Ann Botham) hint at such strains and at efforts to overcome them, both within their family and within the larger "family" of the Society of Friends. As my work progressed, similar strains and a comparable process of healing defined the kinship I had come to feel with the Alderson family. My research took me beyond the naively binary view of Quakerism I had held as an adolescent to an understanding of the real differences that strained and sometimes even split the family of Quakers, and often individual Quaker families, in the nineteenth century: the Hicksites and the Orthodox, the Gurneyites and the Wilburites, and other groups fiercely divided by divergences in their divine leadings. What's more, I learned that Emma's husband, Harrison, was an ardent minister (there were no ministers that I was aware of in the Quakerism of my youth) and that the family's Quakerism was firmly rooted in the evangelicalism then sweeping Britain and America. Missionary work, Bible societies, and a loving but sternly superintending God operated in the Aldersons' lives with an urgency that I had only ever associated with non-Quaker denominations, or maybe those Nixon-Quakers. I was still interested in her letters, but without the same sense of identification that had fired my enthusiasm at the beginning.

As I continued working through the correspondence and researching the contexts, something else happened. I began to see how Emma and her two sisters (especially Mary) and their mother, Ann Botham, navigated their own differences in faith while seeking and affirming their common ground across an ocean and much of a continent. I watched Emma struggling to reconcile her commitment to the Society of Friends, even as her own divine leadings prompted resistance to some of its leaders' positions, especially their reluctance to take a more aggressive stance against slavery. What I saw everywhere was a faith in what Quakers call "discernment," the practice of testing, individually and collectively, one's inner leadings, to discriminate between those that derive from purely personal motivations and those that derive from something higher, transpersonal, and even divine. Discernment is demanding work, requiring deep and honest reflection, tested perhaps against one's reading of the Bible, or works by Friends or other inspirational writers.

Decisions among Friends on anything from the purchase of new carpeting for the meeting-house to collective statements on the morality of slavery or war require not only consensus, but something called "clearness." This is the point at which individual egos have yielded to what Howard Brinton calls "the deepest self, . . . that self which we share with all others, . . . of which we are all branches."[1] It can be a slow and sometimes frustrating process, but it is premised on a faith in everyone's capacity to discern what is right (a capacity associated with what Fox called "that of God in everyone") and on a recognition of the liability of individuals and even of a majority to be waylaid by ego in their search for the truth. Whereas consensus may be generated within a group through debate and compromise among its members, clearness entails discernment: a communal discovery of truths beyond the collective egos of the group. This was vastly different from the purely individualistic "inner light" I had imagined as an adolescent. Many meetings and even families in the nineteenth century were split over their divergent leadings, but those that held together maintained a faith in a process of discernment made stronger by the sincere differences within a group of Friends collectively seeking to know the truth.

I also came to recognize a more complex and less binary relationship between social and theological positions. Growing up, I had identified with the so-called Hicksite Quakers, who had separated in 1827 over their abiding reliance on the inner light as the one sure source of truth, and I had identified that religious position with the progressive politics of my own Quaker connections. Now I found that they had been no less divided on the question of progressive political action than Alderson's so-called "Orthodox" Quakers, with their greater reliance on scripture and the professions of recorded ministers. Among both groups could be found committed activists on behalf of a better society as well as those who associated direct action with temporal rather than divine leadings or worried that engagement with "the world" would threaten their unique Quaker spirituality.

What I came to see was a Society of Friends wrestling with its differences while struggling to discern its path. The schisms were real and remain so to this day, but though we might disagree, family is family, as they say. In these letters we witness the loving reconciliation of Ann Botham's conservative, quietistic tradition, Mary Howitt's liberal activist version of Hicksite Quakerism, and Emma Alderson's more evangelical but no less politically committed orthodoxy. Liberal, Hicksite, and Orthodox Friends shared commitments to peace and social justice. Just as my own Quaker community had opposed the war in Vietnam and organized relief for earthquake victims in Guatemala, Alderson wrote against America's war with Mexico and organized relief efforts for the victims of the famine in Ireland. In the end, I came to feel like a part of a greatly extended family, whatever our differences on various theological and political matters.

When I first boarded the plane to England to examine Alderson's correspondence, I had no idea how many different directions this work would take me in. Trained as a Victorianist and, perhaps secondarily, as a British Romanticist, I found myself digging into the fields of botany, religious studies, transportation, postal history, American history, and American studies of all kinds. Without the help, large and small, of innumerable individuals and organizations, Alderson's voice would most likely still be buried in the archives of Nottingham.

Funding for the work has come in part from grants and two sabbaticals from the Office of Academic Affairs and Vice President Steven Hardin at the University of Pittsburgh at Bradford and from two Hewlett Grants from the University Center for International Studies of the University of Pittsburgh. The staff of Hanley Library, including Marietta Frank, Jean Luciano, Kim Bailey, and Mary Ellen Brooks, helped me out repeatedly with locating and retrieving materials I needed. No less important has been the support and encouragement of numerous colleagues, including Nancy McCabe, James Baldwin, Tammy Haley, Paula Closson-

Buck, and my department chair, Jeffrey Guterman. Students, too, have participated in and advanced this project at various stages; they include Laura Grise Patterson, Jesse Patterson, Alana Eastman, and Isaac Payne. During the final weeks of this project, Amy Wilcockson and Charlotte May of the University of Nottingham provided invaluable services collecting physical data about the letters, proofreading transcriptions, and taking photographs.

The University of North Carolina at Chapel Hill welcomed me for a year in its research collections, where I benefited from the help of librarian Tommy Nixon. Of course, a great debt is owed to the staff in Special Collections at the University of Nottingham, for so many things: for their foresight in purchasing, preserving, and cataloging Alderson's writings; for their unflagging assistance in locating manuscripts; for their extra eyes when I needed help deciphering some word or passage; and for their general encouragement in this work. In particular, I have to thank Linda Shaw, Hayley Cotterill, Marie Hague, Nick Dewhurst, and Caroline Kelly, some of whom are no longer employed there.

In coming to understand the complicated history of the Society of Friends, I have received invaluable assistance from librarians and archivists at various Quaker archives, including John Anderies at Haverford College; Gwendolyn Erickson at Guilford College; Josef Keith and Joanna Clark at the library of Friends House in London; and Lee Bowman, Jean Mulhern, and Patti Kinsinger at the Watson Library of Wilmington College. Above all, I want to thank Thomas Hamm for his unstinting generosity in sharing his encyclopedic knowledge of Quaker history and helping me locate certain important documents.

A project like this one has necessarily and delightfully taken me outside of the halls of academia to draw on expertise of all kinds. Richard Burkert of the Johnstown Area Heritage Association and Greg Zaborowski at the Allegheny Portage Railroad Historic Site helped me understand the Allegheny Portage Railroad, traversed by the Aldersons on their way from Philadelphia to Pittsburgh. Peter White of the North Carolina Botanical Gardens as well as Valerie Pence and Olivia Lantry of the Cincinnati Zoo worked with me to sift through Alderson's numerous botanical references. J. E. Roberts-Lewis, librarian at the Royal & British Numismatic Libraries, explained some of the nuances of currency and the nature of the "tea token."

Much of my work has taken me into the labyrinths of genealogical websites and historical societies, where I received tips and information I could not have found elsewhere. In particular, my work benefited from correspondence with Jo Skelton, Mark Simpson, and Richard Scott of the Alderson Family History Society; with Harold Sampson and Agnes Sawyer, grandchildren of Alderson's niece and correspondent Margaret Ann Harrison; with Sabrina Darnowsky, who has meticulously documented the history of Cincinnati Monthly Meeting; and with Merle Rummel, Elder and historian of the Church of the Brethren in eastern Indiana.

Of course I must also thank Greg Clingham, former director of Bucknell University Press, who first took this project under his wing, and his successor, Suzanne Guiod, who saw it through; and Mary Ribesky of Westchester Publishing Services, who oversaw the book's production. Near the end, copyeditor Anne Healey's eagle-eyed, if often humbling, corrections and suggestions made this a far better volume than it would have been otherwise.

Assistance comes, too, from sources closer to home. My mother, Priscilla Ulin, my sister, Marjorie Ulin, and my niece, Maya Ulin-O'Keefe lent their exceptional editing skills to the improvement of this manuscript. Above all, I am indebted to the patience, encouragement, and assistance of Jessica Kubiak, whose uncountable hours helping with transcriptions, proofreading, and editorial decisions represent only the beginning of the support she has given me through this long process.

Abbreviations

ANBO	*American National Biography Online*
Howitt Corr., UNMSC	Correspondence of Mary Howitt (1799–1888), Manuscripts and Special Collections, University of Nottingham
DQB	*Dictionary of Quaker Biography*
ITSG	Amice Macdonell Lee, *In Their Several Generations*
OCO	Mary Howitt, *Our Cousins in Ohio*
ODNB	*Oxford Dictionary of National Biography*, online edition
OED	*Oxford English Dictionary*

Writing Home

Introduction

We are lying off the Black Rock probably till tomorrow, thinking mournfully of the dear, dear Friends we have left; may the Almighty bless you. Farewell.
—*E. A. [written a mile from the Liverpool dock on the edge of new life]*

On September 17, 1842, a Quaker family of seven stepped off the *Shenandoah* at Philadelphia, having left Liverpool six weeks earlier. Emma Botham Alderson, age thirty-six, had grown up in the village of Uttoxeter, in the Midlands county of Staffordshire, the daughter of a land surveyor and the youngest of three sisters. Having lived under the shadow of her sister Mary Howitt, one of the day's most popular writers, Alderson was finally setting off to make a new life of her own. Her husband, Harrison Alderson, age forty-two, had been born to a farming family in Yorkshire but, like so many other farmers' sons, had left the countryside to find work in the city. After an apprenticeship to a grocer and a few years in the tea trade, he had met Emma. Together they had returned briefly to farming before making the momentous decision to seek a new life in North America. With Harrison and Emma Alderson were three children: the infant Anna Mary, only eight months old; two-year-old Agnes; and four-year-old William Charles. Harrison's thirty-four-year-old sister, Elizabeth Alderson, and fourteen-year-old nephew, Richard Alderson, completed the party.[1]

One might consider them typical in many ways of the 22,000 British immigrants arriving that year in the United States: a young family filled with a mixture of hopes and fears, seeking new opportunities in a new land. Times were hard in Britain as the social and political infrastructure failed to keep pace with the rapid shift toward an industrial economy. In contrast to Britain's starkly limited economic opportunities and growing political unrest with little prospect of relief in the foreseeable future, America seemed a land of almost unlimited possibility and an escape from the grinding industrialism of the Old World. The year 1842 was a peak year for British immigration to the United States, but the numbers continued to climb dramatically through the 1840s as conditions in Britain worsened and the American frontier continued to expand. The number of English and Welsh immigrants arriving in the United States tripled from the 1820s through the 1830s and then more than tripled again in the 1840s.[2]

In other ways, the Aldersons stood out among those immigrants as more likely prospects for success in the New World. It has been well established that in general English immigrants to the United States were not seeking an escape from intolerable financial situations at home so much as opportunities for improvement for themselves and their children, and possibly protection against further declines in their fortunes in England.[3] Nevertheless, the Aldersons' ability to emigrate together and then to purchase a good home on cleared land indicates that they must have had a financial advantage over many other families who had to immigrate serially and to undertake the much more arduous task of clearing their own land. In comparison to other parents of English immigrant families, Harrison and Emma were somewhat older than the averages of 34.1 years for male heads of household and 30.9 years for their wives.[4]

To speak of averages or typicality, however, is to risk overlooking the distinctiveness of every individual experience and thus to misunderstand the experience of the immigrants themselves. They were farmers, tradesmen, craftsmen, laborers, and domestic servants. In the ships' passenger lists, many reported no occupation, but of those who did, farmers figure the most prominently for the 1840s and 1850s, a response, perhaps, to the growing mechanization of agriculture and a general shift in the economy from agriculture to industry. The vast majority were middle-class, nonconformist Protestants. There were individuals, both married and single, traveling alone; couples; and whole families. Some viewed their decision as permanent; many others expected to return to their homes and families once they had saved enough money in that land of milk and honey. The unique history and circumstances of each immigrant made the actual experience of immigration as much an individual experience as a collective one.

Emma Alderson's own experience was short—just over five years from her arrival in America to her death in December 1847—but in that time, she left for future generations one of the most detailed records we have of a woman's life on the frontier during this period, consisting of several hundred pages of letters and journals.[5] This correspondence is addressed mainly to her mother, Ann Botham, and her two sisters, Anna Harrison and Mary Howitt. Sometimes they are addressed to her brothers-in-law, Daniel Harrison and William Howitt, or her nieces Margaret and Mary Ann Harrison and Margaret Howitt. (Readers may want to refer to the family tree; see figure 4.)

The letters are about raising children and running a farm, about the relationship between a frontier city and its more rural environs. They catalog—sometimes with scientific rigor, other times with poetic enthusiasm—the flora of her new landscapes and the customs of her new neighbors. They also recount many of the great events of the day, including the abolition movement, the Mexican-American War, westward migrations, and presidential elections. Her impressions of life in her new world are those of a committed Quaker, while her experience as an immigrant to that world just as surely shaped her understanding of Quakerism as that denomination struggled with its own schisms. An avid reader of travel narratives, Alderson demonstrates a keen awareness of the power of topographical description layered with personal narrative (so much so, in fact, that in one early letter, the description suggests the Alps or the Andes, with "deep valleys and frightful precipices all around, mountains over mountains, most sublimely beautiful," as much as it does the Alleghenies) (see page 70). But Alderson's letters are not so much a travel document as a settling document: they are about making a home in a new place. What is striking, and a kind of counterpoint to Alderson's story of settlement, is the number and variety of characters who travel *through* that place: traveling Quaker ministers, slaves on their way to freedom, Mormons on their way to Utah, soldiers on their way to Mexico, passenger pigeons on their way north and then south again. Threaded through the commotion is a vivid and highly personal account of one woman's experience of finding her own place—emotionally, spiritually, and culturally, as well as geographically—in that new land.

Alderson's correspondence has provided the basis for two published accounts of her life, both in the voices of others. The first, Howitt's *Our Cousins in Ohio*, went through a series of editions and reprintings from 1849 to 1866 as a "companion volume" to *The Children's Year* (1847), an account of a year in the life of Howitt's own two youngest children.[6] *Our Cousins* follows the correspondence very closely, but the place and personal names are changed (at Alderson's request) and the details and chronology are altered to fit Howitt's narrative.[7] Howitt offered the story of her sister's family as a complement to that of her own children—in other words, to that of the English "us" implied in the title's pronoun "our." The voice, too, is significantly different: the voice of the book is the confident, authorial voice of the older, famous sister, near the peak of her career.[8] The voice in the letters, by contrast, is sometimes confident and even ebullient in its enthusiasm for the landscapes and lifeways of this new country, but it is more truly the voice of the immigrant as it modulates through anxiety, sadness, curiosity, and even anger at some of what Alderson saw around her. This correspondence also contributed to the most complete account we have of Alderson's life, in a chapter of Howitt's great-niece Amice Macdonell Lee's 1956 family biography.[9] Lee's chapter on Alderson's life retains all the actual names, but it is brief, highly selective, often inaccurate, and still very much in the authorial voice of a published relation.

In *The Extraordinary Work of Ordinary Writing*, Jennifer Sinor asks us to recognize and honor the resistance to conventional forms that is posed by diaries and other forms of "ordinary writing": "The decision that a text cannot stand on its own, that it lacks context, or that it is unreadable spurs the need for a mediator, the presence of one who can bear the story." Faced with the raw text of her sister's letters and journals, clearly Howitt acted on her perception of that need. Sinor argues that only by allowing such texts to stand on their own can we begin to see the complexity and depth in the voices that have produced them: "Turning our attention away from our accountability in making sense out of a text that seems limited or empty and toward the writer's agency in producing the text in the first place not only complicates the site of ordinary writing but also the subject position of the ordinary writer."[10] Alderson's letters and journals, written with a more-than-ordinary understanding of writing as a public act, complicate Sinor's distinction between the ordinary and the extraordinary, but only if, following Sinor's recommendation, we allow Alderson's own language to stand as much as possible on its own.

Our Cousins was then and is still today a compelling account of domestic life on the American frontier,[11] and so this project began with my own interest in publishing a new edition of that book. My research took me to the University of Nottingham, where the original correspondence had, for the first time, been made available to the public. There I found a far richer account, less polished and internally consistent than the sister's published version, told in a voice that rose and fell in confidence but grew gradually stronger as the years went by. This was Alderson's own story told in her own voice, modulated in subtle ways to address three different recipients; more than a story, it is the firsthand record of the first five years in the making of an American immigrant. Statistics and generalizations are helpful in understanding social trends, but they do little to help us understand the lives that make up those trends. Alderson's writings, presented in her own voice and sustained over a period of five years, offer one of the clearest firsthand accounts in existence of immigrant life and thus a unique window onto the world within which her life and others like hers were taking shape.

Friends and Family

Harrison must try what he can do with W[illiam Howitt] to make him a good orthodox friend. I hear he has been writing about the society in Tait's; . . . but after all I fear he has not "rightly represented" us by identifying us with Elias Hicks.

—Emma Alderson to Mary Howitt, May 6, [1836][12]

Emma Alderson and all of her extended family were closely connected with the Religious Society of Friends (or Quakers), a name drawn from Christ's words to his apostles, "You are my friends if you do what I command. I no longer call you servants, because a servant does not know his master's business. Instead, I have called you friends, for everything that I learned from my Father I have made known to you" (John 15:14–15). Any understanding of Alderson's motivations, outlook on life, and relationship to her family must take into account her (and her family's) involvement with a denomination in the throes of significant doctrinal tensions and even schisms throughout much of the first half of the nineteenth century. Over two-thirds of the English immigrants to the United States from 1845 to 1855 were nonconformists, and roughly two-thirds of those were Methodists, with Congregationalists and Baptists making up most of the rest.[13] Having already broken with the established church, nonconformists were a step closer to emigration than Anglicans in England or Presbyterians in Scotland.

The actual number of Quaker immigrants was not large relative to the immigrant population, but Quakers, with their distinctive speech and dress and strict prohibition against exogamy (until 1860), had knit themselves together more closely than most other denominations by the first part of the nineteenth century. More-

Figure 1. Engraving of Mary Howitt, from a portrait by Margaret Gillies. The portrait and any information about its creation appears to have been lost. Courtesy of Carl Woodring.

over, between 1675 and 1715, following the restoration of the monarchy, some 23,000 Quakers had sought religious freedom in the colony granted to William Penn.[14] Thus, for some 150 years, a "dense network of relatives among the Quaker bourgeoisie" and a tradition of supporting one another had contributed to a growing prosperity among English Friends relative to other religious groups.[15] With emigration, that network extended overseas to the benefit of travelers and new immigrants, who frequently found old friends and readily made new ones. Thus, when Alderson writes to her mother and sisters about Quaker neighbors or visitors, she does so with a familiarity surprising, perhaps, in a correspondence conducted over such a great distance; yet many of these individuals were already well known to the letters' recipients. Such contacts provided a quick network of support in the new land and also a common ground through which relationships with relatives

Figure 2. Statue of William and Mary Howitt. Bronze bas relief on granite pedestal (1901) by Sir George (James) Frampton (1860–1928). Originally created for display at Nottingham Castle, the statue was moved in 2019 to Newstead Abbey.

and mutual friends back in England could be sustained. Visitors carried news, letters, gifts, and greetings both ways across the Atlantic, and in her own letters to England, the immigrant could send news of the traveler's safe passage and share her joy in having spent time with these mutual friends.

For all the support that religion may have provided for English and immigrant Quakers, however, changes taking place in the Society of Friends (or sometimes the apparent lack of change) created tensions as well, which led many to leave the denomination and, in America especially, produced permanent schisms among those calling themselves Friends.[16] Alderson's extended family remained closely knit, even through their great physical separation, but they were not immune to those tensions insofar as nearly every form of Quakerism found its adherents among one or more members of that family.

After their emergence in the second half of the seventeenth century, when Quakers struggled unremittingly to publish their "Truth" in the face of brutal persecution, Quakers settled into a more conservative period in the eighteenth century, shifting their energies from religious outreach to the maintenance of their so-called

Figure 3. Portrait of Anna Harrison, from Amy Greener, *A Lover of Books: The Life and Literary Papers of Lucy Harrison* (London, 1916).

peculiarities of speech, dress, and manner as a way of setting themselves apart from the rest of the world. Members of the Society of Friends were prohibited from taking oaths, removing their hats in deference to social rank, paying tithes and church rates, wearing any but the plainest clothes, marrying outside of the society, or employing a clergyman to officiate at a marriage. Music, dancing, and imaginative

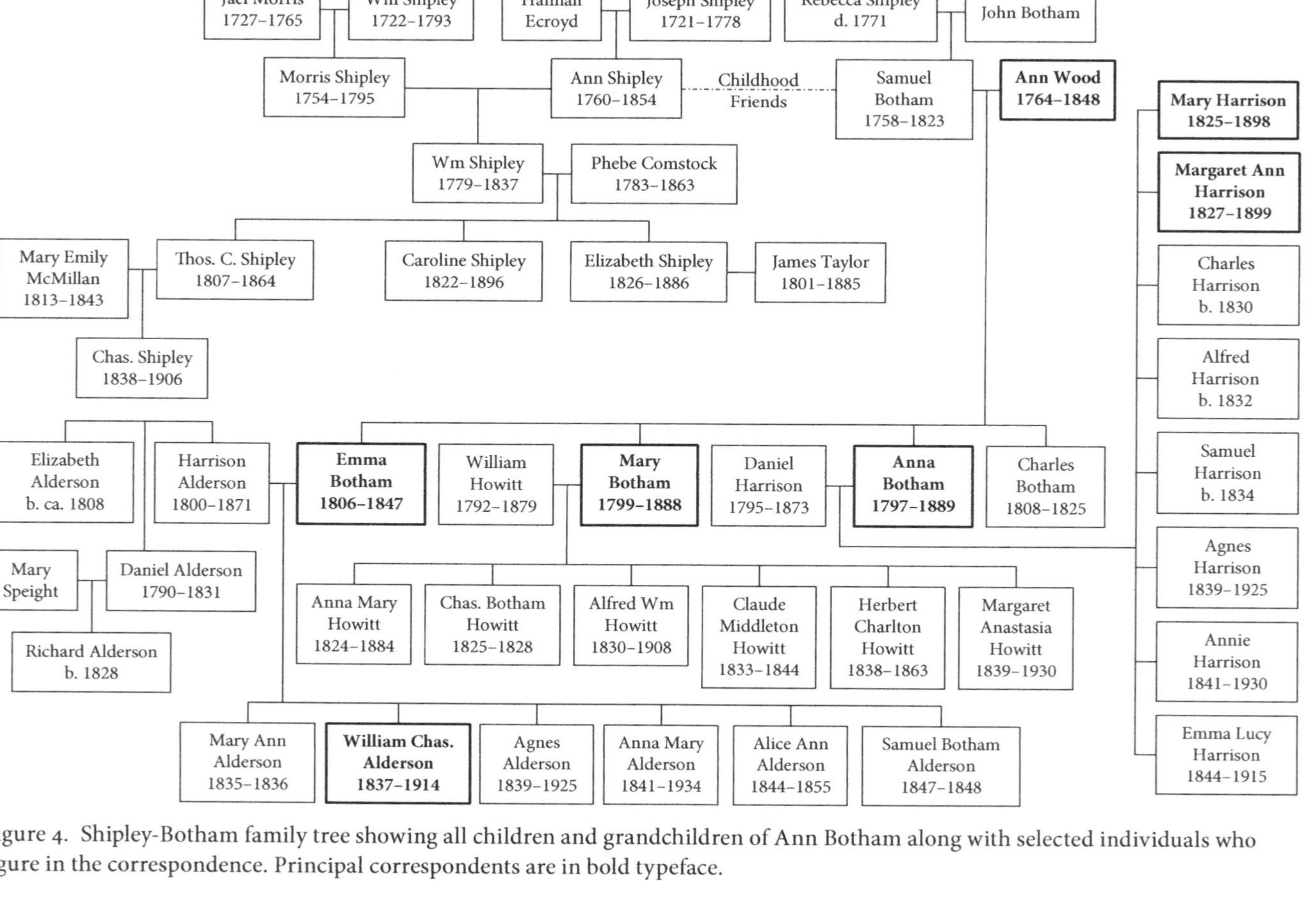

Figure 4. Shipley-Botham family tree showing all children and grandchildren of Ann Botham along with selected individuals who figure in the correspondence. Principal correspondents are in bold typeface.

literature were all strongly discouraged as cultivating too great a love of this world. Strict rules regarding marriage led to many resignations and many more expulsions, or "disownments," as they were called among Quakers, so that the number of Quakers dropped steadily through the nineteenth century, from about 20,000 in 1800 to fewer than 14,000 in the 1860s, when these restrictions were eased and eventually eliminated. By the end of the century, the number had grown again to a little over 17,000.[17]

The first great shift in the Society of Friends came about with the rise of evangelicalism in England. While traditionalists, or what we now call "Conservative" Friends, clung to the Quaker peculiarities and to the silent worship punctuated spontaneously by the "vocal ministry" of any member led by the divine spirit to speak, others saw the charismatic ministry of the evangelicals as an answer to the long, drowsy meetings of their ancestors. It may be, too, that in that age of revolution and uncertainty, Friends were drawn to the more precisely defined doctrines of the evangelicals. Historically, Friends had put their faith in the idea of continuing revelation, the idea that to the patient and receptive individual, God might speak today with as much authority as he had through Moses or Paul. Most of the controversies that have racked Quakerism since its beginnings have turned on the relative authority of the scriptures versus that of the "inner light," or what Quakers call "that of God in each of us."

Like many of the new Christian sects that emerged out of the Reformation, Quakerism had been essentially an inward and, in many ways individualistic, faith. Early Quakers believed in the possibility of individual perfection, universal salvation, and the imminent realization of the kingdom of God on Earth. In these end times, there was no need or time for outward rituals and sacraments, as each member sought within and collectively for salvation. Evangelicalism forever altered both the cultural and the theological terrain of Quakerism. While silent worship and inward searching still retained an important place in the tradition, a new emphasis emerged on the fallen nature of man, the atonement by a historical Christ for the sins of Adam and Eve, and salvation of the individual through the acceptance of Christ's sacrifice. Quakers had long spoken of a baptism in the spirit; now some went so far as to advocate baptism by water, rejecting the traditional Quaker suspicion of all outward rituals.

With this new turn in Quaker doctrine and practice came an opening of communication and cooperation between Quakers and other denominations. Although Friends of all sorts supported various liberal social movements—such as the abolition of slavery and the death penalty, prison reform, and improvement in working conditions—Conservative Friends were wary of so much involvement with the world, fearing the erosion of their community and distinctive practices. They were concerned, too, that actions arising from rational deliberation and open debate with those unacquainted with Quaker faith and practice might be motivated more by temporal and political concerns than by the inner voice of the divine spirit. One of the most dramatic instances of this tension occurred in 1843 in the Aldersons' own Indiana Yearly Meeting when Levi Coffin, one of the principal figures in the

Underground Railroad, led a schism of "Anti-Slavery Friends" who resented the refusal of the Yearly Meeting to act more firmly.[18] Although Quakers shared a common belief in the possibility of a kingdom of Heaven on earth, where peace would reign and poverty, suffering, and inequality would be overcome, they were not in agreement about how much their own worldly activity ought to contribute to bringing about that kingdom of Heaven. Both groups—those committed to waiting and those committed to acting—are found among evangelical as well as the more theologically traditional Quakers, although in the first half of the nineteenth century, activism was embraced more consistently by the evangelicals.

Quaker history has tended, for good reason, to focus on the leaders of these various movements: Elias Hicks, whose testimony on behalf of the authority of the "inner light" above that of the literal scripture helped pave the way for the Hicksite separation in America in 1827; Isaac Crewdson, the staunchly evangelical Friend whose *Beacon to the Society of Friends* catalyzed the Beaconite separation in Manchester in 1831; the Conservative John Wilbur and the evangelical Joseph John Gurney, whose antithetical views on Quakerism led to the second major schism in the 1840s; and Levi Coffin and Charles Osborn, who led the separation of the Anti-Slavery Friends in 1843. What is missing from such accounts, however, is a consideration of the ways in which individual Friends responded to these movements within the faith to which they claimed their allegiance. Due to Quakerism's relatively nonhierarchical administrative structure and a belief in the individual's access to divine revelation, Friends (women as much as men) were encouraged more than in most denominations to take a direct interest in questions of church practice and doctrine. The works and lives of ordinary Friends, therefore, deserve more attention than they have received.

Readers looking in Alderson's letters for a systematic or close examination of Quakerism will be disappointed, since the bulk of the material reflects family life, travel, and daily events. That material, however, is thoroughly infused with a spiritual investment in Quakerism, including its commitment to peace, equality, and integrity, three of the so-called testimonies by which Quakers have historically sought to live. Historically, the ideas of Quakerism have been circulated and debated more often in "lower" genres such as tracts, epistles, minutes, and journals than in the more elevated genres of sermons and treatises. In one of his most-quoted passages, George Fox (1624–1691), the founder of Quakerism, wrote, "When all my hopes in . . . men were gone, so that I had nothing outwardly to help me, . . . I heard a voice which said, 'There is one, even Christ Jesus, that can speak to thy condition,' and when I heard it my heart did leap for joy. . . . Thus when God doth work, who shall let [i.e., hinder] it? *And this I knew experimentally.*"[19] Although Alderson's life and letters are less permeated by Quaker faith and practice than, for example, those of more famous Quakers such as John Woolman (1720–1772) or George Fox, her dedication to maintaining a regular correspondence reflects the high value that Quakers have historically placed on personal life writing as an expression of indwelling divinity and an experimentation in its daily practice.

From its inception, Quakerism was notable for its recognition not only of women's spiritual gifts but of their role in the public sphere. Women traveled in the ministry, spoke publicly, and even (though perhaps to a lesser degree than men) published their views, often to the outrage of establishment church leaders. Alderson never achieved the public profile of many other Quaker women before and during her time—women such as Elizabeth Fry (1780–1845), Lucretia Mott (1793–1880), Margaret Fell (1614–1702), and Elizabeth Margaret Chandler (1807–1834)—but these women represented a tradition within which the value of women's writing and self-expression had been recognized for nearly two centuries.[20] She often chafed against the burdens of a woman's life on the frontier, but she never saw her domestic obligations as otherwise antithetical to more public pursuits. "I believe women may be intelligent & have intellectual tastes & pursuits," she wrote, "& yet be actively domestic" (see page 196). Alderson played an active role in the affairs of the two Monthly Meetings to which she belonged in America and seemed to look forward to participating more as her children grew older and more independent.

Emma, with her sisters, Mary and Anna, had grown up in a fairly strict, Conservative Quaker household. Their father, Samuel Botham (1758–1823), a land surveyor, was descended from a long line of Quakers and farmers in the northern moors of Staffordshire. His father, John Botham, had moved to Uttoxeter in southern Staffordshire in 1750 and married Rebecca Shipley (d. 1771), a widow with two sons and a malting business of her own. In 1758, Samuel was born, the second son and child of John and Rebecca. As a child, Samuel played a good deal with his cousin, Ann Shipley (1760–1854), who would later be a close friend and something of a surrogate mother to Alderson in Ohio.[21] Their mother, Ann Wood (1764–1848), by contrast, was descended from François Dubois, a Huguenot who fled in 1572 from France to Shrewsbury, where he anglicized his name to Wood. Out of a line of manufacturers, Ann Wood's most noteworthy (or notorious) ancestor was her grandfather, William Wood (1671–1730), holder of the patent for producing coinage for Ireland and colonial America beginning in 1722.[22] The American coinage was a success, but the Irish coinage raised an uproar (due, perhaps, to the Irish never having been consulted) that elicited a scathing satire from Jonathan Swift and finally led to tremendous financial losses when the currency was withdrawn. In Ireland, Wood's effigy was dragged through the streets and burned.[23]

William Wood's son Charles, Alderson's maternal grandfather, was one of fifteen children. Appointed assay master in Jamaica by Sir Robert Walpole, Charles Wood became a proficient metallurgist and is credited with having introduced platinum to Europe in the 1740s. After returning from Jamaica a widower, Wood married Jemima Brownrigg, widow of a Mr. Lyndon, who had captained the slave ship *Dolphin*. Wood built Lowmill ironworks near Whitehaven, where his six children were born, before moving to Merthyr Tydvil, where he established Cyfarthfa ironworks. Wood's innovations in using coal to fuel the smelting gave the British iron industry its greatest boost in the eighteenth century.[24] It is ironic that Wood's methods made possible the rapid production of British cannon to put down the American Revolution, for in Jamaica he had become a passionate advocate of political and personal liberty, including that of the American colonists, and a staunch opponent of slavery. According to Mary Howitt, all of these ideas made a deep impression on his daughter Ann and served to develop a bond between father and daughter, especially since those sympathies were not shared by his wife or his other daughters.[25]

After her father's death, Ann moved through a few governess positions, including one with George Horne (1730–1792), dean of Canterbury and later bishop of Norwich,[26] before settling with her wealthy cousin, another William Wood, in Hammersmith near London. From that busy and glamorous life, Ann was called back to South Wales to live with her mother when her sister left home to be married. Feeling isolated and without direction, she began a spiritual quest, which led her briefly to Catholicism and then, for the first time, to Quakerism. Learning then that, on his deathbed, her father had requested that any of his children who wished to join the Society of Friends be permitted to do so, she began attending meeting and soon became a member.

In 1795, Ann met Samuel Botham; the next year they were married and moved to a small house in Uttoxeter, where they lived with Samuel's father, John, an herbalist whose "peculiar temper, ignorance of life outside his narrow circle, and inability to allow of dissimilarity of habits and opinions" made Ann's life difficult.[27] In 1797, Anna was born; two years later Mary followed. Howitt remembers her grandfather as a stern and traditional man:

> His features were good, but his countenance severe; over his very grey hair he wore a grey worsted wig, with three stiff rows of curls behind, and was attired in a dark-brown collarless suit of a very old-fashioned cut, wearing out of doors a cocked hat, also of an old Quaker type, a short great-coat or spencer, and in winter grey-ribbed worsted leggings, drawn to the middle of the thigh. Although a stickler for old customs, he was one of the very first in the Midland Counties to use an umbrella.[28]

Fortunately, John Botham did not stay with them for long: sometime after 1802 he accidentally wounded the baby Anna with the scissors he used for preparing herbs. Mortified by his own action, he moved out to live in a cottage on the edge of town.

The Quakerism of Samuel and Ann Botham's household was of the most traditional type: strict in its adherence to Quaker peculiarities of dress and speech; careful to avoid the contamination of literary, musical, or other influences from the fallen world; and sure in its conviction "that Christ, the true inward light, sends to each individual interior inspirations as their guide of Christian faith, and that His Spirit, being free, does not submit to human learning and customs. . . . So fearful were they of interfering with [the inner light] that they did not even teach us the Lord's Prayer."[29] Instead, they were given the writings of the early Quaker theologian Robert Barclay, whose reliance on the inner light above any holy texts would later be repudiated by Quaker evangelicals. To the girls Anna and Mary and later to their younger sister, Emma, such a life could be intolerable. "It is impossible to give an adequate idea of the stillness and isolation of our lives as children," writes Howitt.[30] It was a life of "Puritanical rigidity" in which "the very mention of a play, a dance, or a horse-rider's exhibition was forbidden."[31] Meetings for worship, which they had to attend twice on Sunday and once on Thursday, tended to be silent, tedious affairs except when some visiting minister brought a little more excitement. Once Emma confided to Mary that she "was sure the apostles did not have drowsy silent meetings."[32]

Anna and Mary at least had each other and the attention of two able-bodied parents. Following the birth of her son, Charles, in 1809, Ann Wood was ill for several years, leaving the two younger siblings to be cared for by Anna and Mary, along with their nurse, "Nanny." It was in these years that the three sisters developed the bond that would survive their later separations. Anna and Mary had had the benefit of schooling and private tutors; under the family's more straightened circumstances, they would be Emma's teachers and guides in life. Thus, when Mary left in 1821 to marry William Howitt, and Anna married Daniel Harrison two years later, Emma's loneliness and frustration only increased to the point of depression. With characteristically unorthodox vocabulary and syntax, she wrote to Mary that

> My heart is bursting with love. Thee and my Lady have turned your backs on me. I'll rin wood; such barbarity dearest Polly; I want thy instruction and advice. . . . it makes me miserable to think what a poor ignorant useless creature I am, a down right chip in porrige, neither do myself or anybody else ~~any~~ good and not much more religion than a hottentot to my shame be it spoken. I look upon thee & william as monsters of perfection and a word of encouragement from either of you would [be] like the dew of heaven on the parched ground.[33]

The Howitts were already establishing what would grow to be a formidable literary reputation, while Emma saw herself languishing alone now in a provincial backwater.

In 1823, their father died, alleviating somewhat the strictness of the Quaker prescriptions regarding dress and appearance[34] but also leaving an emotional gap in Emma's life and a further straightening of financial circumstances. So began what was clearly a difficult time for Emma, as she struggled to find her own identity amid the limitations imposed on a young Victorian Quaker woman. In 1823, she wrote again to Howitt, "I am lonlier than ever. . . . Can poor little dwarfish Emma Botham drag through a long solitary winter, to sleep solus and to wake to worse than widowhood?"[35] The next year Charles began an apprenticeship in Liverpool, but within a year he left unexpectedly and enlisted as a sailor. An injury incurred during his first voyage worsened after they landed in Quebec, and Emma was home alone when word arrived that he had died on November 3 in Hôtel Dieu Hospital, at just sixteen years old.[36]

Emma was not one to feel sorry for herself for very long, however, and soon (sometimes to the consternation of her family) she was exploring new possibilities of religious, professional, and romantic sorts. Her reading turned for a time to educational theory. (She was impressed by Andrew Bell, who ran the Madras Orphan

Asylum, and by the Quaker Joseph Lancaster, who put Bell's ideas into practice in a charitable school in Lancashire.[37]) She wrote to Howitt with her ideas, including a rough business plan for a school of her own, but there are hints of family disapproval, and the scheme was never realized. Dissatisfied with the dullness of silent Quaker worship, Emma began attending church instead for a time. Of most concern to her family, however, were Emma's romantic adventures. We know nothing from her own letters, but the letters between her two older sisters indicate a concern both for Emma's reputation and for their mother's possible embarrassment. "She is a most saucy damsel and barely thanks a man for his graces," Mary told Anna, who was quick to agree: "I could tell thee of someone else who was more than half smitten, but what with dreams, poetry and sentimentalism he almost put Emma out of conceit with all Irishmen."[38] As antidote, Mary offered what she knew best: literary work. First she suggested that Emma write a "Life of Christopher Columbus for Children" and later a "record of death-bed scenes of all kinds, good and bad."[39] The exemplary death-bed scene was a popular genre for early Victorian Quakers—the Society of Friends' *Annual Monitor*, published by William Alexander of York, had been making it a staple since 1813—but neither project seems to have materialized. At last, due perhaps to the sisters' and mother's exasperation over Emma, or perhaps to financial considerations, or even simply to a longing for family, Emma and her mother let the house in Uttoxeter and moved to Preston in Lancashire, nearer to the home of Daniel and Anna Harrison.

The tensions evident in this early correspondence between Alderson and her mother give way entirely to an agonized longing in her letters from America, perhaps an indication of remorse for the difficulties she had caused her mother growing up. Knowing of her dissatisfaction with life in Uttoxeter, one can only wonder at Alderson's recollection later of a time "when my mother's house was the very pleasantest spot on earth to me and she the sovereign blessing for whom my heart felt daily, hourly thankful" (see page 130). Yet there may have been a sincere deepening of that relationship, either in spite of or due to the great distance between them. When Ann Botham died in the spring of 1848, the *British Friend* attributed her death to the shock of having just lost her daughter in America, "to whom she was more than ordinarily attached."[40]

It was in Lancashire in 1832 that Emma met Harrison Alderson, and the next year they were married. The family must have been pleased: Alderson was Daniel Harrison's first cousin and as sober a Quaker as one might hope to find. Formerly a lover of music and an acclaimed player of the pipes, Alderson decided to guard himself against such vanity: one day he walked out into the fields, played through his favorite tunes, and then threw away the pipes, never to play them again.[41] Emma's stern father would have been pleased had he lived to witness the match.

Like the Bothams, the Aldersons were an old family of northern Quakers. Harrison Alderson had grown up in the remote village of Stone House in Dentdale, now in Cumbria inside the boundaries of the Yorkshire Dales National Park, but at the time a part of the West Riding of Yorkshire. It was here that Quakerism had its birth, and the Aldersons might well have been in the audience in 1652 when

George Fox visited Stone House to gather converts. In any case, the Aldersons were among those early converts, and some of the first Quaker meetings were even held in the home of James Alderson, perhaps an ancestor of Harrison.[42] Succeeding generations of Aldersons all seem to have included at least a few "ministering Friends" (including Harrison's grandfather John Alderson and great-grandmother Alice Burton Alderson), but by the early nineteenth century, the small but vibrant meetings in this rural area were on the decline as Friends migrated to urban areas.[43] As a young man, Harrison had followed that trend, moving to Lancaster, where he apprenticed with the grocer William Crossthwaite and maintained membership in Lancaster Monthly Meeting. At the end of his apprenticeship, he moved to Blackburn, transferring his membership to the nearby Preston Monthly Meeting and going to work as a tea merchant.

Harrison's Quaker severity might seem an unlikely attraction to a young woman who had chafed for so long under a similar severity in her parents' home and who now seemed to be leaving Quakerism behind, going so far as to attend church on occasion. One explanation might lie, ironically, in the similarity between Harrison Alderson and Samuel Botham, who had died shortly after Emma's seventeenth birthday. At sea in her own self-doubts and uncertainties about her future, did she find in Harrison a substitute for the father who had left her just as she was leaving girlhood behind? If so, she must also have welcomed one striking difference between the two men: both practiced an almost puritanical severity in their religious lives, but while her father's severity grew out of a conservative Quaker inwardness, her husband's was of the more evangelical variety. Perhaps Emma was willing to renounce some of the worldly pleasures she had begun to enjoy as long as she could at the same time give up those "drowsy, silent meetings" for the more charismatic ministry of people like Harrison. Emma had always yearned to reach beyond the limits prescribed for the traditional Victorian Quakeress; flirtation might have been one reaction to those limits, but her earlier school scheme reflected her real desire to work for the benefit of the larger world. Quaker evangelicalism represented just such a movement within the Society of Friends as a whole. Although the evangelical wing of Quakerism today tends to be the more politically conservative wing, early-nineteenth-century evangelicalism made it possible for Quakers to join with others to promote secular as well as religious reforms around the world. Such an outlook must have offered Emma the outlet her energies had long desired without the renunciation of her family's faith.

The three sisters' religious lives took very different paths. Anna had married Daniel Harrison, whose family had been Quakers for many generations but whose liberal views and love of more worldly pleasures gave the girls' father cause for concern.[44] Around 1843, Daniel and Anna Harrison moved from Liverpool to Birkenhead, where they came to know the Reverend Joseph Baylee of Trinity Church. Formerly a Quaker, Baylee led Anna to a conviction of the value of the sacraments, especially baptism and the Lord's Supper (or Eucharist). She had been a committed Quaker for most of her life and had held various offices in the Liverpool Monthly Meeting, but for some years, doubts about Quaker doctrine had led her on a spiritual search through such theologians as Thomas Dale and F. D. Maurice. In 1843 or 1844, Anna left the Society of Friends to join the Church of England. Unable to follow his wife, Daniel remained a Quaker. Although at first such a separation must have caused tremendous pain to both, Anna and Daniel's daughter Mary reports that in the end, the deep self-reflection occasioned on the part of both parents by this separation "deepened and widened their intercourse, and in later years it was their habit for some hours of the afternoon to read aloud and discuss a number of books which must have discovered their intellectual differences of opinion."[45]

The Howitts had also been moving away from the Quakerism of their childhoods, but toward a more liberal Unitarian, even Universalist, faith. Through their books and articles and their management of the *People's Journal* and then *Howitt's Journal*, the Howitts had placed themselves in the center of the mid-nineteenth-century reform movement. William had written on the history of Quakerism for *Tait's Magazine* and for the seventh edition of the *Encyclopaedia Britannica*. For the Howitts, Quakerism was essentially democratic and nonhierarchical, constantly evolving through the doctrine of "continued revelation," and committed to bringing about God's kingdom on earth through social as well as religious reform. Evangelicals were similarly committed to reform, but their deference to the word of scripture infringed upon the authority of the inner light as much as Anglicanism might with its prescribed prayers and rituals. Conservative Quakerism of the kind practiced by Samuel Botham deferred appropriately to the inner light but was exceedingly cautious about the pursuit of social, political, or missionary work, even when consistent with the leadings of that inner light. The Howitts began attending Unitarian services, and in August 1847 Mary wrote to her sister Anna,

> Thou wilt be glad to hear that we have drawn up our resignation of membership, signed it, and when thou readest this, it will be noised abroad that we are no longer Friends. Strange as it may seem to thee, I have an old love of the Society. I know that the majority of Friends are narrow-minded, living as much in the crippling spirit of sectarianism as any denomination whatever; and I know that they and I never could assimilate; yet I do love them all, with an ingrained sentiment, which makes me feel as if somehow they were kindred to me. It is strange, perhaps, but there is not one so-called religious body that I could conscientiously connect myself with. There is, to my feelings a want of real spirituality, a want of a real, child-like, living trust in them all.[46]

Much later in life, Mary Howitt moved toward Anglicanism, and a few years before she died, she converted to Roman Catholicism.

Thus the three sisters and their mother, though united in a common faith, were also divided along the same lines that divided Quakerism in the nineteenth century. By the late 1840s, Alderson, the daughter who had during her youth probably caused her mother the greatest anxiety, was the only one of the three who, like her, remained a Quaker. The correspondence gives no sign of tension between Emma Alderson and Anna Harrison over changing religious beliefs, while between Alderson and her mother we find a deep spiritual unity made more poignant by frequent recognitions of the tensions that had strained their relationship during the years in Uttoxeter. Between Alderson and Howitt, we find the most explicit expression of religious difference, especially regarding the Wilburite-Gurneyite division in the 1840s, when Alderson came down strongly on the side of the evangelical Gurneyites and Howitt seems to have been more sympathetic to John Wilbur. Confrontational and frequently abrasive, William Howitt gave the family the greatest cause for concern. But, as Emma's strong relationship to her husband and Mary's continued affection for the Society of Friends show, none of the sisters was dogmatic to the point of intolerance. In 1836, Emma had invited Mary to visit them, adding that "Harrison must try what he can do with W[illiam] to make him a good orthodox friend. I hear he has been writing about the society in Tait's; we are going to read his paper but after all I fear he has not 'rightly represented' us by identifying us with Elias Hicks. Now remember I have not read his paper so I only speak from hearsay, but I could go to the stake in maintenance of our being neither Hicksites nor Beaconites."[47] Years later in America, Alderson would break at least privately with the wisdom of her own Yearly Meeting when she took the side of the activist Levi Coffin and the "Anti-Slavery Friends" who had been forced to secede for their aggressiveness in combating slavery.

Final Years in England

We know very little of the precise motivations or the deliberation that lay behind the Aldersons' decision to emigrate. It seems to have happened quickly, and when Mary Howitt heard the news, she remembers, "it went to my heart like a dagger."[48] The prospect of her sister's emigration to America may have revived memories of her brother Charles's fate seventeen years earlier. But friends and relatives had already emigrated to America, including Samuel Botham's cousins Morris and Ann Shipley and Daniel Harrison's brother Thompson. As thousands of their countrymen continued to do so, it might have seemed to the Aldersons a natural step.

Times had been hard for the Aldersons, as they had been for the country at large. For the first four or five years of their marriage, the couple lived in the small industrial town of Blackburn on the outskirts of Lancaster, where Harrison worked in the tea trade. Their first child, Mary Ann, was born there in 1835 but the next year became ill, died on December 20, and was buried on Christmas day.[49] A letter to her sister Mary Howitt describing the event shows Emma coping with the trauma of losing her first-born child, as she alternates poignantly between the reassurance of religious faith and the outpourings of grief that inevitably follow such a tragedy:

> Though the trial is indeed a hard one, yet our consolations abound: a strong and blessed certainty of immortality supports my mind & I have been enabled to rejoice continually in the rememberance of a Saviour's love. I feel assured & the thought often passes through my mind, she is as much ours now as she ever was, she is only in another & a better place far beyond the reach of the pain & weariness & sin of this troubled scene. . . .

> Dear dear child we nursed her night & day for a fortnight & saw her suffer so much as made me ready to profess I should be thankful to see her released, but when I saw her lovely form, a lifeless corpse wasted by pain and so changed by suffering as to be scarcely recognized, the anguish of heart is not to be told. It was a melancholy pleasure to lay her out & do for her the last sad office & to gaze upon her beautiful countenance, so placid & so sweet in death. The room in which she lay was full of holy influence & a peace beyond the silence of the tomb was there, but dear Mary when it came to closing the cofin & losing forever in the solid the sight of her dear, dear face, I felt overwhelmed; my last earthly consolation seemed withdrawn & I could have clung with wild agony to the little that was left me. Oh it was a bitter moment & nature seemed as if she would have her way, but I thank God that calmer & better moments have succeeded & he who wept over the tomb of Lazarus & reproved not the sorrow which he often witnessed would pardon that natural twist of feeling.—and now his blessed will be done.[50]

By March, Alderson was pregnant with her second child, but the shadows of financial distress along with cholera, influenza, and typhus hung over England's urban areas. In May, Alderson wrote to her sister Mary Howitt, then living far away in the relatively pastoral serenity of Esher, ten miles outside of London:

> We have had dismal weather again of late & times too are very bad. The poor, as is always the case, feel it first & most severely & what is worst there seems little prospect of improvement. . . . It seems as if things wore a gloomy aspect: the untoward season, the hard times, which all more or less feel, the desolation there has been in families by death, especially amongst children, whereby many a hearth is lonely and silent & many a heart aching which before was happy in an abundance of joy. I do think they are serious awful times and I wish, if intended for our correction & improvement individually & collectively, that we may not harden our hearts, but seek with humble feelings to be more worthy of the innumerable blessings which yet remain to us.[51]

In both of these letters, Alderson demonstrates her capacity to confront and articulate her own deepest emotions while holding firmly to a belief in the operation of forces much more than personal. That same ability to understand one's life both personally and transpersonally would be evident in the years to come as she managed the further trauma of separation from the rest of her extended family.

On November 5, William Charles was born, and soon after that Emma and Harrison gave up the smoky town of Blackburn to follow their dream of farming and country life. Two more children followed—Agnes in 1839 and Anna Mary (Nanny) in 1841—but times were as hard in the country as they had been in the city. Emma's sisters, too, had experienced their own difficulties that had reduced family contact. By 1839, Daniel Harrison, also in the tea business, had done very well financially and, at the age of forty-four, was already planning a retirement in the country, leaving the day-to-day management of his business in the joint care of his partner and his youngest brother. The Harrisons were ready to buy land and begin building a new home when Daniel's business partner committed the firm to what his daughter describes only vaguely as "a most disastrous speculation which he feared would have the result of ruining them both."[52] Anna had to give up plans to visit Mary, and the family had to give up their home in Liverpool for a greatly reduced lifestyle in the nearby village of Birkenhead. Though these were difficult years, they seem to have rekindled in Anna a love for botany and the natural world that had occupied her and Mary as girls in Uttoxeter and that would form an important bond among the sisters, as the three shared botanical information and even seeds across the Atlantic.

Life was changing for the Howitts as well. About the time of the Harrisons' financial crisis, William and Mary Howitt took their family to Germany, where they could live less expensively while learning German in hopes of embarking on a series of translations. Heidelberg offered some of the same pastoral simplicity that Anna Harrison had found in Birkenhead and that others were seeking through emigration to America: "The life seemed simpler, the habits easier and less expensive, than in England. There was not the same feverish thirst after wealth as with us; there was more calm appreciation of Nature, of music, of social enjoyment."[53] From her condition of relative happiness and prosperity, Howitt wrote to Harrison that she had been reading in the papers

> doleful accounts from England, . . . people starving, the manufactures sinking, and Sir Robert Peel laying on an income-tax to cure all! How dark and fearful seems the future! I do not wonder at Harrison and Emma determining to leave England. Although of this I am sure, that if they go to America with Utopian notions of finding human nature much better there than in England, they will be mistaken. But this I can well believe: they will live calmer, and be surrounded by better subjects of contemplation. They will find the perfect simplicity of life congenial to them, and will have the pleasure of seeing their children growing up healthy, hopeful-minded men and women. All is struggle, fever, and delirium in England. There is no room for the coming-up generation.[54]

The Aldersons left no such clear statement of their motivations to emigrate, but Howitt's assessment no doubt contains a good deal of the truth. Indeed, as Charlotte Erickson argues, some version of that "agrarian idyll" (often without Howitt's qualifying reminder about human nature everywhere) formed the principal motivation for nineteenth-century emigration. To many if not most immigrants, the New World seemed to offer economic stability, independence from wage labor (or even from the cash economy altogether), increased leisure, and closer family ties.[55] Probably as important as the economic reasons, however, was Harrison's commitment to the ministry. Although recognized as a minister in England, he hoped for a wider scope in America, and after they arrived there he lost no time in establishing himself as a key figure in the Monthly Meeting, first in Westland, Pennsylvania, and then in Cincinnati.

Unlike the great number of emigrants who believed from the beginning that they would return to Europe after a few years, the Aldersons seem to have been fully committed to making a permanent home in America. They were more fortunate than many of their fellow immigrants, whose limited resources required that one family member go ahead to raise enough money for the others to follow. Such arrangements were difficult emotionally as well as financially, especially for farmers, for whom the extra hands might make the difference between success and failure. It is doubtful that the Aldersons would have emigrated under such conditions, but in any case, they were at a great advantage in being able to come as a family. Like all immigrants, they struggled with obstacles they could not have foreseen—from difficult weather to a shortage of domestic help—but with perseverance, a strong network of social support, adequate financial resources, and a certain amount of luck, their condition improved and justified the great decision to emigrate. Another source of support was the network of Friends, many of them directly related. Cousins William and Alice Mason and brother Ralph Alderson helped establish them the first year in Pennsylvania, while their entry into Cincinnati must have been eased by their connection to Ann Shipley (Samuel Botham's cousin) and her family.

After landing in Philadelphia in September 1842, the Aldersons traveled to Westland, just southwest of Pittsburgh, where they spent their first winter. A recession in the United States had forced many ambitious landowners to sell at a loss, so the following spring, they were able to buy a farm at a discount in Warsaw, Ohio, west of Cincinnati on the other side of Mill River (see figures 18 and 19). Buying improved land saved the Aldersons from an obstacle that broke so many immigrant farmers, namely that of clearing forested land in preparation for the plow. The Cedars, as their new home had been called, had already been cleared, plowed, and planted. The Aldersons renamed it Cedar Lodge.

But success in the new land, as in the old, was often met with terrible reversals of fortune. Financially, the Aldersons continued to prosper, but following the birth of Samuel in December 1847, Alderson developed complications. What might have been a simple infection, treatable today with antibiotics, was made even more serious by heavy rains that flooded the roads from Warsaw to Cincinnati, delaying medical help for a few days. Their physician and good friend Joseph Taylor arrived before the end, but there was nothing he could do, and in the evening of December 16, Emma Alderson died, leaving her husband with four young children and a newborn baby named after her father, Samuel Botham.

Putting Pen to Paper

The life of an immigrant farmer was a busy one, and that of the Aldersons was no exception. The letters document an almost constant stream of activities, including agricultural work, making family clothes, preserving food for the winter, teaching the children, and more. Alderson writes little about her own direct involvement with the Society of Friends, but the minutes of the Cincinnati Monthly Meeting list her as a member of various committees, showing that she must also have been a regular attender of meetings for worship and business.

As immigrants often note in their correspondence, servants in America were hard to find and expensive to keep, making the maintenance of a large middle-class household much more difficult than it would have been back in Europe. Some of the time, Alderson could count on her sister-in-law, Elizabeth, who had come with them, but more often than not the letters point to interpersonal conflict, Elizabeth's dissatisfaction with life in the New World, and Alderson's dissatisfaction with Elizabeth's company.

Writing under such conditions must have been difficult, and it was made more so by a recurring problem with her eyesight that sometimes made close work difficult or impossible. Nevertheless, she somehow found time for a prodigious literary output. Like many of the immigrant writers whose correspondence we now have access to, Alderson frequently apologizes for lapses in communication but just as frequently chides the recipients (her sisters, never her mother) for failing to keep up their end of the correspondence. But correspondence was her lifeline to family, and so time had to be made. Although she was a regular attender of the Cincinnati Monthly Meeting, Alderson often notes in her letters that Harrison and the children had gone to meeting. Perhaps illness or some other factor had kept her home, but clearly these were precious opportunities, to be grasped whenever they arose.

Among the collections of immigrant correspondence discovered and published in recent years, Alderson's is exceptional for a number of reasons. Above all, there is the density and consistency of the record itself. Perhaps because their authors were too busy or perhaps because they were waiting until they could justify their emigration to family back home, most extant collections of immigrant correspondence commence some years after the writer's arrival in the new country. The volume of Alderson's writing increases in later years, but there are no large gaps anywhere.

Furthermore, although women obviously kept journals and wrote to relatives, the vast majority of immigrant correspondence available from this period is written by men.[56] Women may have been too busy through a longer portion of the day, or perhaps literacy was lower among women. It might be that their letters were less often preserved by family and future generations, to whom the daily routines of keeping house and raising children may have seemed of less relevance than the public activities of their husbands.[57] Whether we attribute her writing to the tradition of publicly active Quaker women, to the model Alderson had in her sister Howitt, or to some other cause, the record she left offers a uniquely rich window into the life of a middle-class Quaker woman on the Ohio frontier.

Equally remarkable is the survival of the letters themselves. Like most immigrant correspondence, Alderson's is one-sided, with little or nothing to show for the letters she must have received. Sadly, we have to infer the contents of those letters from Alderson's replies. Although hundreds of pages of her own writing remain in relatively good condition, there might have been more were it not for at least two unfortunate incidents. Sometime around 1845 in a moment of depression, Anna Harrison burned a collection of letters, drawings, and manuscript poems. Another time, a boy the Howitts had hired to look after William's study was caught selling manuscripts and correspondence to a scrap dealer, but not before a great deal had already disappeared.[58] How much of what was lost came from Alderson we will never know, but we are fortunate to have been left with such a complete account in the letters that remain.

Letters, Authorship, and Transnational Modernity

> *The author's name manifests the appearance of a certain discursive set and indicates the status of this discourse within a society and a culture. . . . A private letter may well have a signer—it does not have an author.*
>
> —*Michel Foucault, "What Is an Author?"*[59]

Michel Foucault's point, as I understand it, is that, while an author's name signifies a book's position within a publicly held system of values and meanings, the signature on a letter points directly and quite privately to the actual person whose words appear above it. Certainly there is an intimacy, even a physicality, in letters that does not feature in other genres. For the immigrant, especially, separated indefinitely from friends and family, the letter offered a surrogate embodiment of intimate relationships. As David Gerber notes, "The letter has been touched by the other writer, whose handwriting is a material mark of a physical presence. When we are told that letters have been kept under the pillow, or carried in the bosom and near the heart, we are being given explicit avowal of this physical presence and the evocation of intimacy."[60] Thanking her mother for a parcel, Alderson's comments dwell as much on the symbolic intimacy as on its contents: "It seems as if every thing was sanctified by thy touch; the very stitches on the wrappers are endeared to us" (see page 251). In another letter to her mother, Alderson describes her pleasure in writing as a "pleasure of holding converse with thee" (see page 257). In contrast to the author's name, with its marketability and its accessibility as a public signifier, the signature of the letter writer is hardly a signifier at all insofar as it directs the reader unequivocally and intimately to a single individual, shutting out the messy marketplace of language and promising an essentially private, if textual, experience.

Such is the fiction of epistolarity that has informed our reading of letters since the eighteenth century. The epistolary novel mobilized that fiction in the interest of its own fictions of intimacy, naiveté, and emotional transparency (as if the language of the letters themselves were incidental). As Elizabeth Heckendorn Cook writes, "while keeping its actual function as an agent of the public exchange of knowledge, [the letter] took on the general connotations it still holds for us today, intimately identified with the body, especially a female body, and the somatic terrain of the emotions, as well as with the thematic material of love, marriage, and the family."[61] These connotations have helped marginalize the personal letter in relation to the traditional master narratives of literature and history, while obscuring the vast array of subgenres and modes we encounter within the personal letter. However, resistance and innovation arise mainly from the margins, and the availability of letter-writing to those, such as women and the working class, whose voices were excluded from the more public forms of communication, meant that this vast body of literature has only recently come to the attention of historians and literary scholars.

By the 1920s, revisionist historians were urging the use of immigrant correspondence as the basis for a new U.S. history to challenge the elite history of white, Anglo-Saxon men.[62] One of the earliest and most influential works was the five-volume *The Polish Peasant in Europe and America* (1918–1920) by sociologists William I. Thomas and Florian Znaniecki.[63] The material from letters, they believed, provided the qualitative data necessary to put the study of Polish immigrant culture on a positivist, empirical footing. More recently, attention has turned to letters by women, a trend that has likewise opened history up to a greater diversity of voices and experiences.[64] Henry Louis Gates Jr. has devoted much of his career to a similar case for serious recognition of the slave narrative in English and African American studies departments.

In much of the early work on life-writing from outside the dominant culture, the texts themselves were assumed to speak directly to the conditions of immigrants, women, African Americans, and others in the authentic, unmediated voices of the people themselves. Necessary as it is that we hear those voices, however, we should be wary of what Amanda Gilroy and W. M. Verhoeven describe as the "trope of authenticity and intimacy, which elides questions of linguistic, historical, and political mediation."[65] Responding to the debates over authenticity that have surrounded the use of slave narratives as historical documents, Charles T. Davis and Gates open their introduction to *The Slave's Narrative* with a reminder that "no written text is a transparent rendering of 'historical reality.'"[66] Organized into three sections—the slave narratives themselves, "Slave narratives as history," and "Slave narratives as literature"—their work aims at treating the texts seriously "as narrative discourses as important to criticism for their form and structure as they are important to historiography for the 'truths' they reveal about the complex workings of . . . 'the slave community.'"[67] In attending to the formal and rhetorical elements in an immigrant's or an ex-slave's narrative, we must abandon the myth of the naively transparent correspondent; in doing so, we may learn more about that writer's world than we will by considering too narrowly the authenticity or accuracy of its content.

Giving up conventional investments in the immediacy or naiveté of epistolary content, we can more productively face the complexity of immigrant correspondence, deepening our understanding not only of the texts' own origins but also of the categories through which textual production and consumption in general have been understood: public/private, literary/nonliterary, and even our definition of authorship. In her study of epistolary form in Samuel Richardson's 1748 novel *Clarissa*, Christina Marsden Gillis cautions against too easy an acceptance of the idea of the letter as a transparent "window into the heart," finding instead a "peculiar ambiguity between private and public."[68] By the end of the eighteenth century, the personal letter had been thoroughly incorporated into public discourse. Manuals abounded on style and etiquette for letter writers, and the novel—that first truly commercial literary form—had taken the personal letter as one of its principal modes of expression. And just as the public novel owed much of its form to the personal letter, personal letters inevitably drew heavily on public discourse—not just the eighteenth-century letter-writing manuals, but travel narratives, poetry, oratory, journalism, and more. Alderson's extensive reading of travel narratives clearly informed much of her description of her new country. Alongside such descriptive material, letters by Alderson and others are filled with journalistic accounts of contemporary events, snatches of poetry, and domestic advice, suggesting the sort of "heteroglossia" that Mikhail Bakhtin associates with the novel form.[69]

In one of the more insightful treatments of early modern epistolarity, James How examines the "epistolary spaces" that were opened up in 1650 by the creation of the English post office: "'public' spaces within which supposedly 'private' writings travel."[70] For centuries, letters and messages had traveled by private courier, but "imaginations of epistolary spaces only became fully possible with the continuity brought about by an organized postal system. What the Post Office did was to bring about a whole new level of connectivity."[71] With an act of Parliament, a new virtual social space was created—akin, perhaps, to contemporary cyberspace—where private lives and relationships might be nurtured. Yet privacy itself seemed to disappear in the public post, where private letters jostled promiscuously together and were liable to be opened by government inspectors or meddling officials, or they might miscarry and be delivered into the wrong hands or lost altogether. The proliferation of letter-writing manuals testifies to the novelty of epistolary space and the need for an equally novel discourse capable of meeting the demands of that curiously public-private space.

Epistolary spaces have to be imagined by a corresponding public in much the same way that nations have to be imagined by those living within a certain geographic boundary. Benedict Anderson describes the modern nation as an "imagined community," a political entity that comes into being through a collective act of imagination in what he calls (following Walter Benjamin) the "chronotope" of "empty, homogeneous time."[72] Emblematic of that chronotope is the novel, a record of events that can be mapped within an entirely rational (but otherwise empty) Cartesian time-space. Citizens of a nation cannot come together in physical community, but they may imagine a community of citizens operating simultaneously within a chronotope like that of the novel. Although How writes only of epistolary *space*, a comparable shift in our understanding of *time*, with the rhythms of sending and receiving information, or the "dailiness" identified by Sinor as fundamental to ordinary writing, would have been necessary to the imagination of that "space."[73]

Epistolary space as How describes it is significantly different from Anderson's homogeneous chronotope insofar as "it had burgeoning London always at its centre: a vortex at the heart of epistolary space to which all letters and the thoughts of all their writers and readers gravitated."[74] In this regard, early modern correspondence suggests more the residual formation of the city-state than the emergent formation of the modern nation-state. Cook's assessment of correspondence at the end of the eighteenth century would also seem to place epistolarity and nationalism on opposite sides of an epistemic divide, with the "loss of an enlightenment faith in correspondence" leading to "the decline of the Republic of Letters under the pressures of a developing nationalism."[75] According to Cook, the shift from public criticism to private subjectivity at the end of the eighteenth century spelled the collapse of a transnational public sphere, and therefore "the rupture of the correspondence between Europe and America."[76] Certainly correspondence continued across the Atlantic, but correspondents now wrote as individualized national subjects and no longer as rational citizen-critics in that supranational Republic of Letters.

Perhaps because her conception of epistolarity is limited to that ideal of the disinterested public citizen, Cook's narrative of "the end of epistolarity" oversimplifies both national identity and its relation to letter writing. Writing about Howitt's *Our Cousins in Ohio*, Linda H. Peterson calls our attention "to those who, from more private spaces, also help to construct national identity."[77] "Replicating the form of *The Children's Year*," she argues, "*Our Cousins* . . . is based on—indeed seeks to extend—certain British social, cultural, and political values."[78] Howitt's text, based on Alderson's letters, participated in the formation of national identity in two countries: in America it made claims for a transplanted Englishness against the claims of German and other non-English settlers; in Britain it invoked images of a British diaspora to reaffirm the centrality of domestic production within British national identity.

When we move from Howitt's nonepistolary account of the Aldersons' lives in Ohio back to the letters themselves, multinationalism comes to look more like transnationalism, complicating Cook's thesis further. The act of emigration and resettlement involved not merely a move from one part of the world to another, but a transformation in one's very relationship to space and time. David A. Gerber notes the "compression of space and time" that occurred with the rapid improvements in transportation for both people and mail.[79] Distance was no longer the obstacle it had been a generation earlier. With the advent of transatlantic steam packets in 1842, a voyage that had once taken six weeks now took only two. A family whose native shores had until recently formed the farthest edges of its imaginable territory could now seriously entertain a voyage to the other side of the world. The vastness of America likewise suggested a very different world conceptually from the Old World left behind. Interpersonal relationships operated differently in the New World and, even more dramatically, in that "transnational social space" to which the immigrant now belonged.[80] Drawing on Anthony Giddens, Gerber describes the "disembedding" of identity from local contexts and "distanciation," or "spreading out of social relations across time and space."[81] In this context, immigrant writing had far more to do than merely relate news and send affection. Relationships to friends, family, and places might not have been dissolved by emigration, but if they were to persist, they would have to be reformulated to operate according to the time-space fabric of that new transnational culture in which they now existed, a task to be undertaken almost entirely through the personal letter.

The notion of immigrant correspondence as a series of naive and unselfconscious effusions thus assumes both too much and too little about those immigrant writers: too much insofar as it posits a clarity and single-mindedness unlikely in even the simplest circumstances, too little insofar as it fails to account for the complexity of the demands placed on the immigrant writer. As Gerber has argued, immigrant correspondence served both a conservative function, maintaining family ties and shared traditional values, and a radically innovative function insofar as, through that correspondence, a wholly new form of social and familial space had to be invented. As we have already seen, the letter writer, alone with paper and pen, sought to reproduce an experience of intimacy denied in its physical form by the distance separating the two correspondents. Far more important than the exchange of information, Gerber argues, was the attempt at recovering that often mythical "sense of continuity in relation to people and place" that had seemingly been lost due to emigration.[82]

Yet even as immigrant correspondents struggled conservatively to maintain or reestablish that sense of continuity, their engagement with the new systems and technologies of postal communication (and perhaps the impossibility of reestablishing some lost or mythical community) involved them in the exploration of radically new forms of social space. Ironically, having rejected the industrial modernity of their old country, these agrarian idealists became, as Gerber writes, "pioneers on the frontiers of global modernity."[83] Letters had always had their place in public discourse; new in the nineteenth century was the vastly expanded network of correspondents and the transnational nature of the sphere in which that discourse was taking place. The letters and voices of "private" individuals were taking complicated routes across vast spaces and political boundaries. They were the interpreters of a new culture to the old one left behind and pioneers of an even newer culture in which personal and familial relationships might be maintained textually in diaspora.

Although she would hardly have thought of herself in such terms, Alderson's writings are exemplary of the forms of communication and interpersonal relations emerging within this new transnational social space. Indeed, through her relationship to the famous Mary Howitt, Alderson's writing would almost inevitably engage more pluralistic modes of identity and authorship than those conventionally associated with the solitary author writing within a homogeneous tradition or the solitary letter writer pouring her heart out to some intimate acquaintance. As Peterson has noted, Howitt was among the first to take a truly "*familial* approach to professional artistic production."[84] Not only did the material for her publications often grow out of domestic situations or begin as stories told to her children, but also the production of those works frequently involved collaboration with her husband, William, and daughters, Anna Mary and Margaret.

Engaging more family members over far greater distances than any other of Howitt's works, the collaborative production of *Our Cousins*, beginning with Alderson's letters, offers a remarkable test case of the extent to which such collaborative authorship might be taken. In 1847, Howitt's introduction to *The Children's Year* noted that this project had begun as an "experiment of keeping for one whole year an exact chronicle, as it were, of the voluntary occupations and pleasures, and of the sentiments and feelings, as far as I would gain an accurate knowledge of them, of my two youngest children."[85] Even before that book had appeared on the shelves, Howitt and Alderson were corresponding about the possibility of producing what Howitt would call a "companion volume" detailing the life of those children's cousins on the Ohio frontier.[86] Once again the private domestic sphere would furnish the basis for a public and commercial enterprise, only this time the labor of book production itself would take a domestic form, including material by William Charles Alderson and illustrations by Anna Mary Howitt. If Howitt's work in general "re-envision[s] the family's work as collaborative life writing,"[87] the evolution of this particular project goes further by remodeling the family's workshop according to the logic of a modern global social space.

David A. Gerber and Charlotte Erickson have done the most to dispel the myth of the naive or unselfconscious immigrant writer and to establish the competence demanded by such writing. Although immigrants' writing skills were typically less polished than those of the published author, they nevertheless demonstrate an understanding of, and an ability to navigate, this new, virtual social space, establishing new identities and defining new forms of relationship through their writing. Alderson's writing is technically idiosyncratic, with unorthodox and inconsistent spelling and punctuation and almost no sentence or paragraph breaks. Furthermore, the frequent expressions of sorrow at her separation and longing for reunion would suggest something more nostalgic and naive than self-consciously modern. Yet as a constitutive element of the modern condition, nostalgia should not necessarily be taken literally as a rejection of her new circumstances. Furthermore, as Gerber has argued, nostalgia may function positively in immigrant letters as "an adaptive mental strategy for negotiating continuity and change."[88] Writing to at least five named individuals, often about the same events, Alderson demonstrates a clear understanding of audience and of the power of writing to define the relationship between writer and audience.

Emma Alderson wrote at a time when, like the Internet in our own time, letter-writing (especially transatlantic correspondence) was coming into its own as part of the fabric of everyday life. New conditions of living and new opportunities for communication led to dramatic increases in the use of the postal service during the early 1840s by a widening cross-section of the population in Europe and America. Among the causes of that rise were growing literacy rates among women and the working classes, increasing movement of individuals around America and overseas, reductions in postal rates, and improvement in the reliability of the postal service. The volume of mail carried by the British postal system had been increasing steadily, but with the introduction of the penny post, the number of

Paid
Paid 25
Danl Harrison
Temple Place
Liverpool
Old England
Ann Botham

Figure 5. Letter #8 to Ann Botham via Daniel Harrison. Ht/7/2/9, Correspondence of Mary Howitt (1799–1888), Manuscripts and Special Collections, University of Nottingham.

letters more than doubled from 76 million in 1839 to 169 million in 1840.[89] Until that time, the high costs and unreliability of regular mail meant that writers frequently used private couriers. Before the introduction of the postage stamp, the cost was generally borne by the recipient, making writers reluctant to burden family members with letters on any but the most important matters. Increased reliability, lowered costs, and the simplicity of the postage stamp made writers more willing to pay in advance to send more mail than they would have otherwise; with the cost of letter writing shifted to the sender, the act of sending a personal letter became a more unequivocally generous act, one to be undertaken more frequently and with less reserve. As volume rose, so too did postal revenue, leading to further improvements and growth in the postal system. For women, especially those engaged in a public enterprise such as publishing or reform work, the rise of a cheap and reliable postal service created powerful opportunities for networking in place of the clubs, universities, and other institutions that were still largely restricted to men.

For Alderson in America, the situation was more complicated. Farther out on the frontier, even getting paper, pens, and ink could be difficult, though near Cincinnati, Alderson seems to have had a ready supply of these things. Her letters were usually written on both sides of a large sheet of paper with room left for an address. In lieu of an envelope, the paper was then folded into a packet and sealed with wax so that the address showed in the center of one side (see figures 5, 7, and 12). Letters

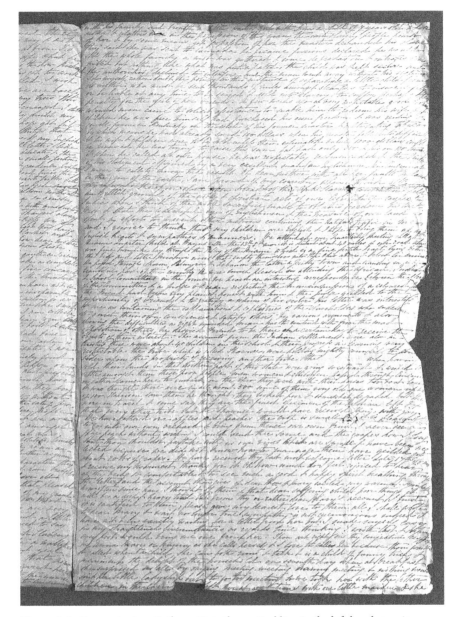

Figure 6. Letter #12 to Ann Botham. Note the vertical line in the left-hand margin, presumably Mary Howitt's marginalia from her preparation of *Our Cousins in Ohio*. Ht/7/2/12, Correspondence of Mary Howitt (1799–1888), Manuscripts and Special Collections, University of Nottingham.

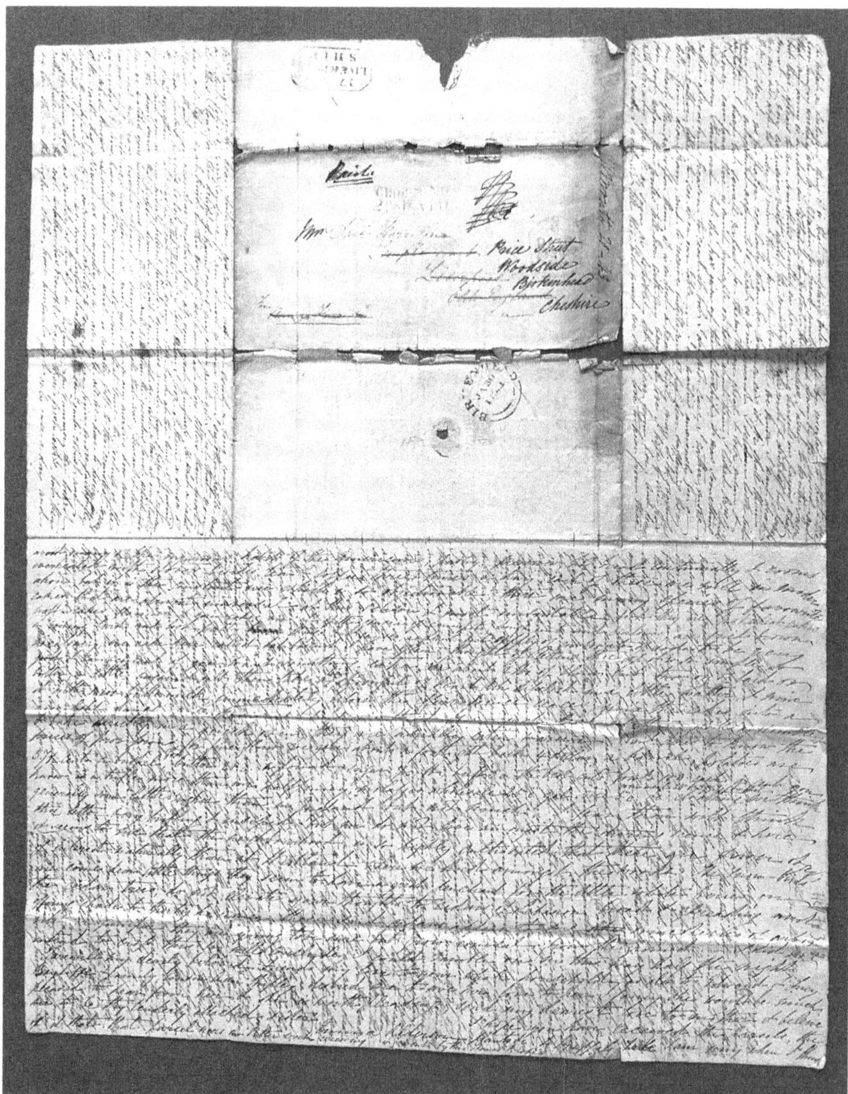
Paid.
Woodside
Birkenhead
Cheshire

Figure 7. Letter #15 to Anna Harrison, showing the use of cross-writing to save on paper and postage. Note, too, the readdressing of the letter and the multiple postmarks, evidence of the many hands through which a letter might pass. Ht/7/3/2, Correspondence of Mary Howitt (1799–1888), Manuscripts and Special Collections, University of Nottingham.

were frequently damaged in transit or when they were opened by the recipient, but envelopes were rare because they involved higher postage costs. Another means of economizing on paper and postage was cross-writing, the practice of filling the page once, then rotating it 90 degrees and continuing the letter across what had already been written (see figures 7 and 13). Sometimes, on especially thin paper when the ink has bled through, a reader has to contend with cross-writing from

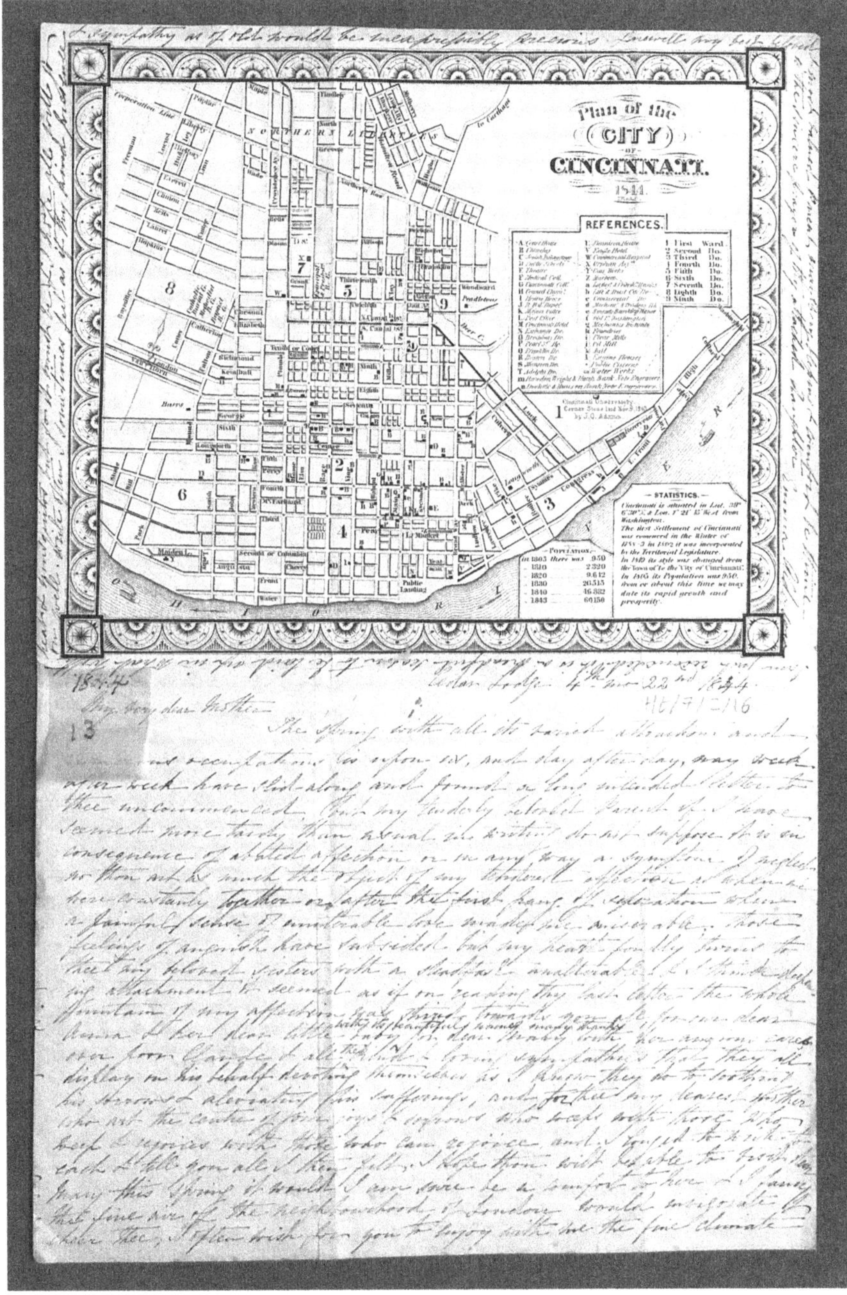

Figure 8. Letter #18 to Ann Botham on stationery with an engraving of a street plan of Cincinnati. Ht/7/2/16, Correspondence of Mary Howitt (1799–1888), Manuscripts and Special Collections, University of Nottingham.

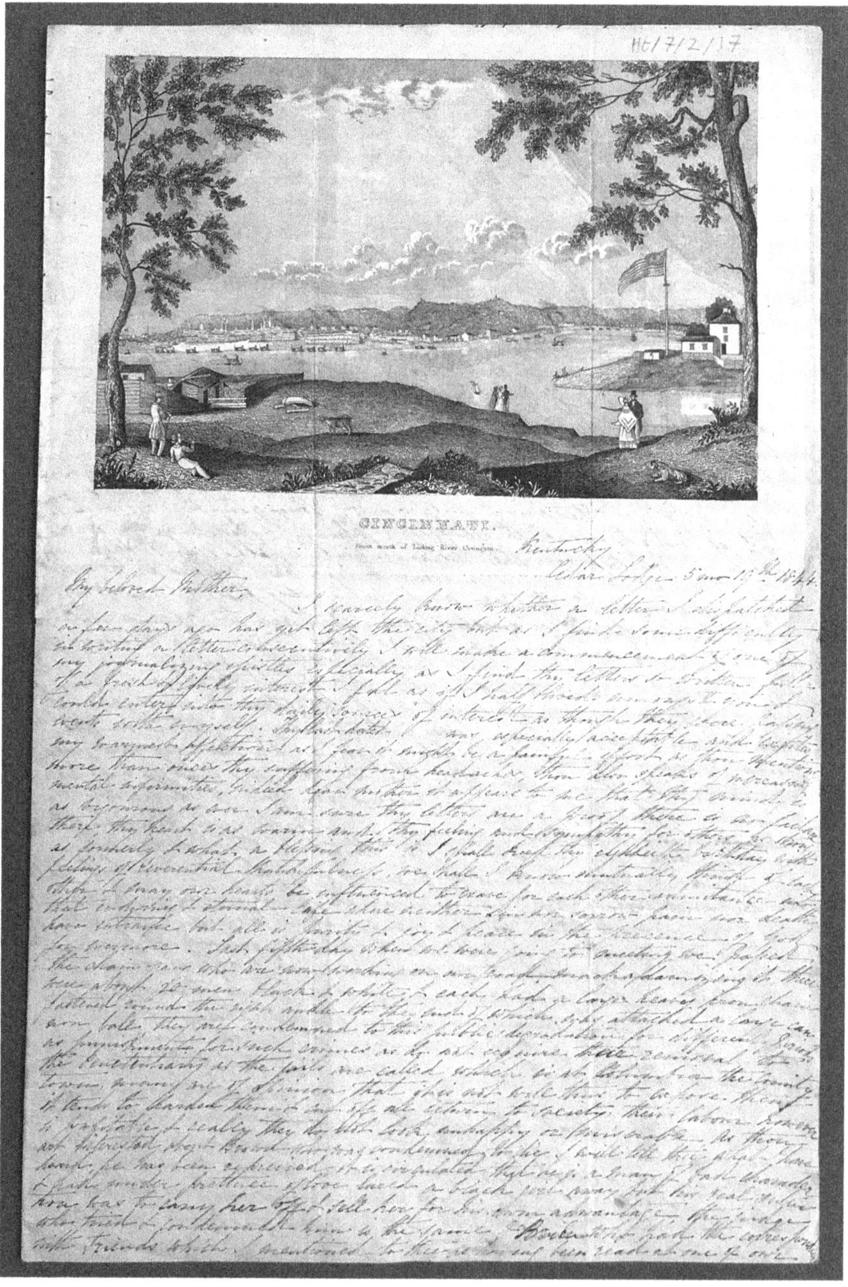

Ht/7/2/17

CINCINNATI.

Kentucky
Cedar Lodge 5 mo 17th 1844.

My beloved Mother,

Figure 9. Letter #19 to Ann Botham on stationery with an engraving of a pastoral scene overlooking the mouth of the Licking River. The Licking River enters the Ohio River in Covington, Kentucky, across from Cincinnati. Ht/7/2/17, Correspondence of Mary Howitt (1799–1888), Manuscripts and Special Collections, University of Nottingham.

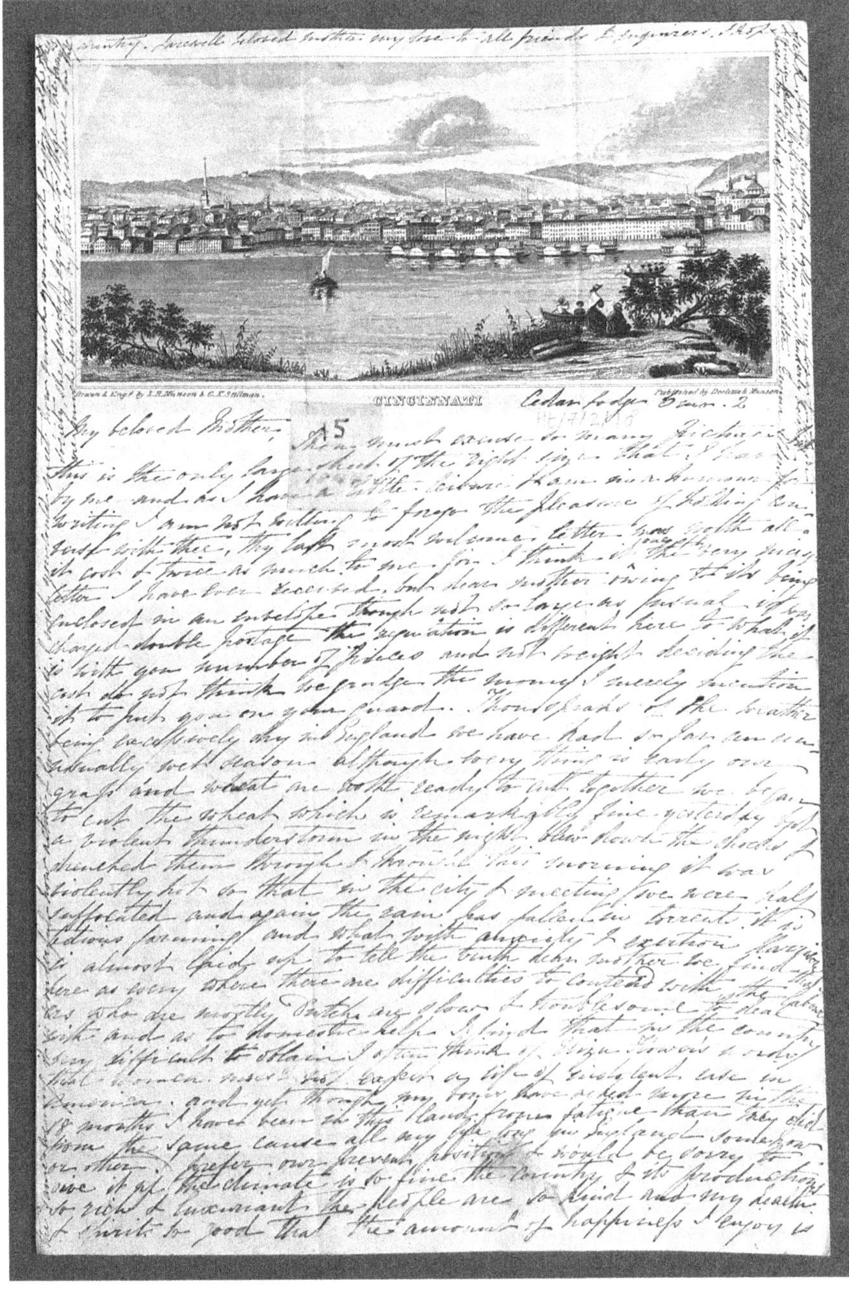

Figure 10. Letter #20 to Ann Botham on stationery with an engraving of Cincinnati, presumably from the Kentucky side of the river. Ht/7/2/18, Correspondence of Mary Howitt (1799–1888), Manuscripts and Special Collections, University of Nottingham.

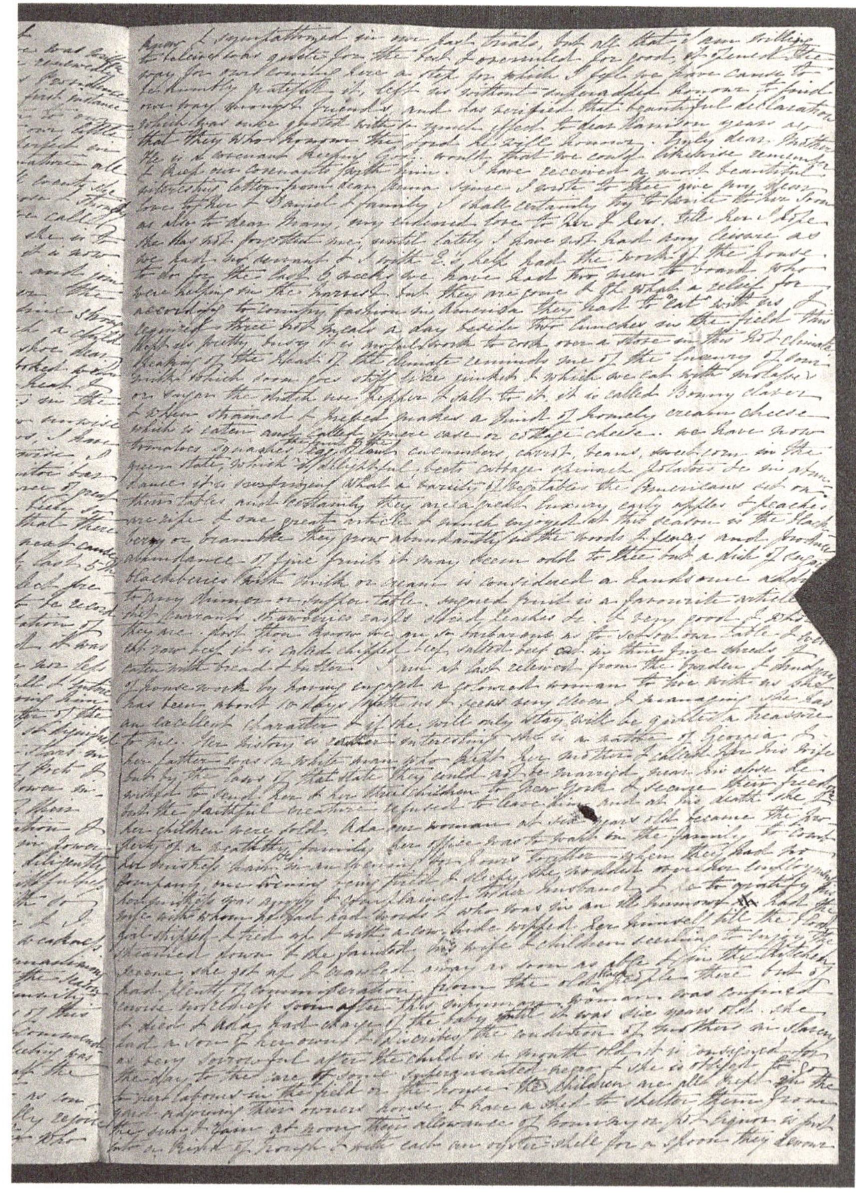

Figure 11. Letter #20 to Ann Botham. Note the vertical line in the left-hand margin, presumably Mary Howitt's marginalia from her preparation of *Our Cousins in Ohio*. Frequently they appear on letters, such as this one, written prior to the commencement of that project. Ht/7/2/18, Correspondence of Mary Howitt (1799–1888), Manuscripts and Special Collections, University of Nottingham.

Figure 12. Letter #28 to Ann Botham. The Penny Red stamp had recently been introduced along with the shift to pre-paid postage. These stamps would have been added by Anna or Daniel Harrison when she or he forwarded the letter on to Ann Botham. Ht/7/2/23, Correspondence of Mary Howitt (1799–1888), Manuscripts and Special Collections, University of Nottingham.

both sides: four different texts layered confusedly on top of each other. At one point, Alderson acknowledges a complaint from her mother about being unable to read the cross-writing and promises not to continue the practice.

The British postal system was emulated in other countries, and in the United States a two-tier rate system for domestic mail (based on distance) was introduced in 1845, followed by postage stamps two years later. Without the familiar mailbox of today, letter writers had to walk or ride to the nearest post office. International mail continued to create even greater problems, involving at least three separate charges, including carriage in the country of origin, shipping across the Atlantic, further transit in the destination country, and ground transit through additional countries if necessary. The year 1842 saw one of the greatest improvements in both speed and reliability of international mail as new biweekly steam packets reduced the time of travel between New York and Liverpool from six weeks to two. In 1843, transatlantic postage ranged from sixteen pence to two shillings per ounce (enough to buy 20 pounds of beef, 10 pounds of pork, or a bushel of cornmeal) depending on the shipping company.[90] Not surprisingly, Alderson's letters frequently mention the couriers (visiting friends and family) who would be carrying letters on all or some part of their route.

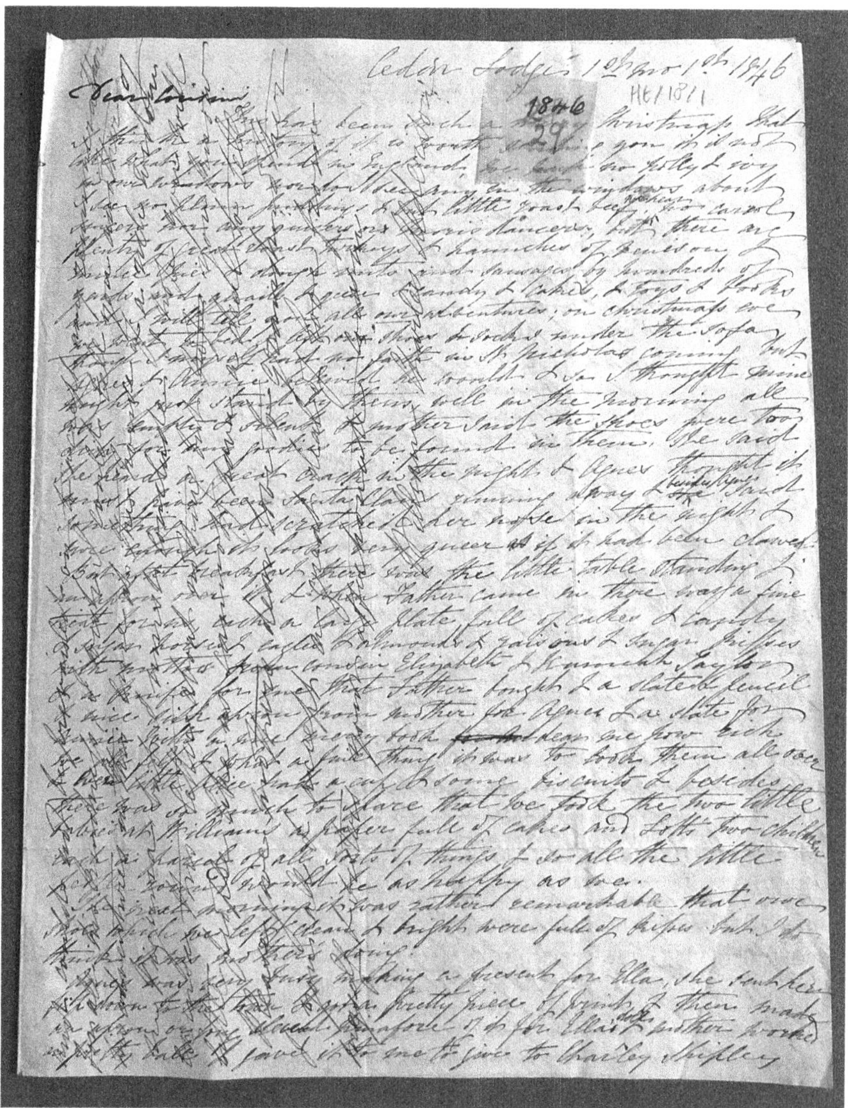

Figure 13. Letter #37 from William Charles Alderson to Margaret and Herbert Howitt. This is the first letter written in response to Mary Howitt's *The Children's Year* (1847; still in MS at the time) and possibly, even at this early date, with a view to publication in a companion volume. Ht/18/1, Correspondence of Mary Howitt (1799–1888), Manuscripts and Special Collections, University of Nottingham.

International mail now became the medium through which commercial and political activity could be carried on across far greater distances than had been possible before, fostering international alliances for women's rights, penal reform, abolition of slavery, and other causes. Pioneers in the use of global communication, William and Mary Howitt maintained a steady correspondence with literary and reform figures in America, including Ralph Waldo Emerson, William Lloyd Garrison, and Frederick Douglass. While the disembeddedness of rapid global communication might have obvious advantages for these global causes, Alderson's voluminous correspondence explores the less likely intersection between the possibilities of disembedded, global communication and the domestic desires for rootedness in a new land.

Editorial Practices and Principles

All of the texts included in this volume are held in Special Collections at the University of Nottingham as part of the Howitt Collection. They were transcribed onsite onto a laptop computer directly from the holographs in as close to a diplomatic transcription as possible, retaining all punctuation, line breaks, and other features of the texts, and making note of any non-textual features, including scribbles, lines, damage, etc. Later, information about paper size and the number of sheets, as well as information from the address panels, was recorded in a database. All of that information, along with the University of Nottingham reference numbers, is collected in appendix 1, "Physical and Postal Attributes." All of the letters were proofread soon after transcription, one person reading from the holographs and the other following along on the diplomatic transcription. Back in the United States, copies of the diplomatic transcriptions were edited according to the principles set forth below. Staff at the University of Nottingham graciously looked up passages that seemed likely to contain errors and sent corrections by e-mail. Prior to publication, the manuscript was again proofread, using the same procedures as before.

Recognizing that much of the material in this correspondence was published in a heavily edited form by the author's sister 170 years ago, my aim has been to protect the integrity of the original with as light an editorial hand as possible. To understand the experience of the immigrant writer and the nature of immigrant correspondence requires, if not a holographic text or even diplomatic transcription, at least an inclusive text or expanded transcription. At the same time, while conforming to the standards of modern scholarly editing, I have wanted to produce a readable text, one that would convey not just the material reality of the letters, but the struggle of an immigrant with relatively little in the way of formal education to reproduce in textual form, and possibly for subsequent publication, her hopes and fears, her joys and disappointment, her excitement, and sometimes her anger in response to all that she encountered in the New World.

Efforts at diplomatic transcription and highly inclusive representation have tended to focus on the writings of more elite writers, who are typically subject to much closer scrutiny by a larger body of scholars. Studies and compilations of immigrant letters and journals have focused on their instrumental value—as a means of generalizing about broader social and historical trends—and have been edited accordingly, with silent emendations, elisions, and normalizations.[91] Yet, as Mary-Jo Kline and Susan Holbrook Perdue point out, the need for fidelity in editing the texts of semiliterate writers is in some ways even greater insofar as one otherwise risks obscuring their distinctive writing practices and imposing "a false sense of authorial intentions."[92] Kline and Perdue's point is particularly germane to Alderson's situation in that she struggled with a sense of inadequacy as a result of comparing herself to her highly literate sisters and sought through the means of her correspondence to participate in her sister's literary success. In regularizing the spelling, punctuation, capitalization, and grammar, we risk eliding the struggle that makes her writing so important, just as Howitt did in editing the material for *Our Cousins*. For that reason, I have taken the principles of fidelity and transparency so scrupulously employed in any modern edition of the letters of Thomas Jefferson or Mark Twain to be of equal or greater importance in editing Alderson's immigrant letters.

Nevertheless, editing is always about choices, and in editing this volume, I have aimed at three goals: fidelity to the language and spirit of the author, accessibility to a modern reader, and transparency to the scholar seeking a more nuanced understanding of Alderson's strengths, limitations, and peculiarities as a writer. I have tried to retain that wonderful, sometimes impetuous, flow of ideas, suggestive of a mind fascinated by all of life, humble enough to be open to new experiences, but confident enough to pass judgment where judgment is called for. In doing so, I have left the text largely as I found it, making alterations only where a reader's experience of the sense and flow of the language would otherwise be impeded and doing so as transparently as possible.

Note on Source Texts

All of the letters are transcribed from their originals in Manuscripts and Special Collections at the University of Nottingham. In only one or two instances where I have been unable to decipher a word, I have relied on Mary Howitt's rendering in *Our Cousins in Ohio*. These instances are indicated in my notes. In my notes on published texts referred to by Alderson, I have generally referenced first editions and those she might have owned. As would be expected of a mid-nineteenth-century Quaker, Alderson's preferred Bible appears to have been the King James Version. In the frequent cases where a book was published simultaneously on both sides of the Atlantic, I have cited the edition corresponding to the author's nationality except where the distinction is of some relevance to my purpose.

Corrections and Emendations

One of the first problems faced by an editor of Alderson's correspondence is the absence of sentence or paragraph breaks. She rarely uses periods to end her sentences or capitals to begin new ones, preferring commas and sometimes dashes. In some respects, this punctuation is consistent with her fresh and impetuous flow of ideas, as phrases are piled one on top of another. Unlike her older sisters, however, Alderson had received little formal schooling; thus her writing frequently contains faulty parallel constructions, subject-verb disagreements, and other nonstandard grammar, spelling, and punctuation.

In place of Alderson's commas to separate sentences, I have generally introduced colons, semicolons, or full stops as I thought most consistent with the sense of the text. At the same time, I have generally introduced commas to separate some dependent clauses, prepositional phrases, and listed items. If my use of commas occasionally appears unorthodox or inconsistent, it is because I have tried in each case to use whatever punctuation (or none) most effectively captures the flow and sense of that particular passage without altering the sometimes unorthodox syntax. In keeping with Alderson's limited use of commas (except where we might put a full stop), I have not added a comma after the penultimate item in a list except where it is necessary to the sense of the sentence (as in her lament to Harrison that "Dear Mother, Mary, and thee are now almost my only correspondents"). I have also silently introduced apostrophes where appropriate and modernized instances of the long *s* ("mass" in place of "maſs"). I have silently capitalized the first word of a sentence where she has not done so, but I have not changed the capitalization of words that are or might be proper nouns. Other emendations are indicated with square brackets: most often the introduction of quotation marks, completion of names given only as initials, or an occasional letter where its absence would create confusion.

Sometimes what appears to be a nonstandard spelling could also be a function of orthography; in these cases, I have opted for the standard spelling. For example, the word "friend" sometimes appears to be spelled "freind." Although this error is not uncommon (as readers of Jane Austen's manuscripts will recognize), elsewhere in her letters, Alderson's *i* is open, like an *e*, and her *e* is closed like an *i*; thus I have chosen to give it consistently as "friend." Likewise, when what should be a pair of *m*'s (as in "accommodate") appears as a single squiggle, I have given her the benefit of the doubt and used the standard spelling.

Formatting

I have taken the liberty of adding paragraphs to the unbroken text, altering a feature of her writing that probably reflects a desire to save on paper and postage more than any orthographic intention. Leaving paragraphs unbroken would have presented the reader with long paragraphs of seven or eight pages in spite of radical shifts in the subject matter and even new dates. When a dash appears where we would expect a paragraph break, I have silently removed the dash and started a new paragraph. Other dashes are represented as em dashes regardless of their length in the original.

Following what I find a useful practice in J.A.V. Chapple and Arthur Pollard's *The Letters of Mrs. Gaskell*, I have used solidi (as in \insertion/) to indicate all authorial insertions.[93] Deletions are indicated with a line through the text as they are in the original. Where Alderson herself has stricken out the text with a line through it, but the text is still legible, I have reproduced the text along with the strike-out line. Single and double-underling have been rendered as such.

Frequently in the original texts, a pencil line has been added in the left margin. (See figures 6 and 11.) Given the correlation between those passages and contents of *Our Cousins*, it is likely that they were added by Howitt as she prepared her book. I have reproduced those lines in this text in as close to the same positions as possible.

Unrecoverable Gaps in the Source Text

Tears, smudges, and various kinds of damage, as well as some moments of exceptionally difficult handwriting, make some passages in this edition more or less a matter of conjecture. In these cases, I have given my best guess at the text in plain type and, where applicable, the cause of the obscurity in italics, all inside angle brackets, as in <*torn*> or <th-*torn*>, where a tear in the documents leaves only the first two letters visible. A word that is indecipherable due to handwriting is represented as <??>. Where I can make a reasonable guess at all or part of the word, I have given <word> or <??rd>.

Organization of Letters

The option of organizing letters by recipient was one I considered, because there are some interesting differences in the ways she writes to her various family members. In the end, however, I chose to organize the letters chronologically for two general reasons: first, some of the letters are addressed to multiple recipients, and second, immigrant writers recognized a secondary audience to whom their letters would circulate once the addressee had finished reading them. A third and more specific reason that makes it particularly difficult to define recipients in Alderson's correspondence is the fiction of a correspondence between Alderson's son, William Charles, and Howitt's youngest daughter, Margaret (or Maggie). The handwriting in every case is Alderson's; the voice, however, seems sometimes to belong to Alderson and at others to William Charles. Although much of this particular correspondence, especially that in William Charles's voice, seems addressed to his cousin, its purpose was quite explicitly to provide Howitt with material for her book.[94] Thus, although I have associated each letter with one or more recipients, to isolate individual recipients would be to risk misrepresenting the nature of immigrant correspondence and that of Alderson's correspondence most particularly. Readers who wish to follow Alderson's communication with a single recipient may consult the table of contents, which includes recipient names.

Much of the work of dating the letters was already done by the staff of the Special Collections department at the University of Nottingham; I have made only a few alterations to their ordering. In a few cases, I have placed a letter with an earlier date after one with a later date when the earlier date indicates only the commencement of a long letter composed over a period of time extending beyond the period of the other.

I have divided the correspondence into three unequal sections, each with its own introduction to the concerns in that portion of the material. The first and shortest section covers the Aldersons' journey across the Atlantic and through Pennsylvania, along with the year they spent in their first American home in Westland, Pennsylvania. The second section focuses on their first two years in Cincinnati from

June 1843 to December 1845. The final section covers the nearly two years from January 1846 to Alderson's death in December 1847, the period during which she was actively collaborating with her sister on what would become *Our Cousins in Ohio*. This section also includes a small group of letters written by William Charles Alderson, since much of their contents became material for Howitt's book. As a coda, I have included one letter from Harrison Alderson written to Ann Botham, describing the sad event. That letter seemed to me a fitting tribute to the woman whose pen left this outstanding record of a life lived on so many boundaries.

Note on Capitalization

Following standard practice, I have capitalized "Friend" when referring to a member of the Society of Friends. I have partially adopted Rufus Jones's practice, rather than that recommended by Friends General Conference, in capitalizing "Meeting" whenever it is combined with "Friends," "Monthly," or some other formal designation, but not when it is used more generally, as in "the first meeting to be established in Indiana" or "North American meetings." Likewise, I have chosen to use lowercase and a hyphen for "meeting-house" and, departing from Jones, lowercase for "minister," unless it is part of the title of a particular group, as in "Preparative Meeting of Ministers and Elders." I have capitalized "Orthodox" and "Conservative" where those terms are used not in their general sense but to designate particular movements in Quaker history. In the letters themselves, I have retained all of Alderson's sometimes inconsistent capitalization.

List of Editorial Symbols

\text/	Alderson's addition inserted as superscript
<??>	an entire word or phrase is illegible
<text??>	only a portion of a word is legible (in this case "text")
<text>	text at which I have had to guess with a reasonable degree of confidence
[2]	the beginning of the second page in the letter
[4a]	the first of multiple panels on a single page, typically the last page, on which the address panel appears
[1-*cross*]	text continues cross-written on page 1
[*cross*]	cross-writing continues on the same page
<text>	editor's note on the text (e.g., "*<letter broken off here>*")
<blank>	a space has been left, usually a date or name to be filled in later (e.g., "On the *<blank>* we came within sight of land")
<torn>	some text is obscured due to a tear in the manuscript

<***sealed***>	text is covered by the wax seal
<**text-*torn***>	part of a word is obscured due to a tear; the rest remains visible
[text]	editorial addition (used sparingly), usually of punctuation (a quotation mark or question mark), a name, or one or two letters, to assist with reading (e.g., "the[re] is a vine shading one end")

PART I

Leaving Home

THE *SHENANDOAH*, ACROSS THE ALLEGHENIES, THE FIRST WINTER

Six Weeks at Sea

The first set of nine letters documents a remarkable voyage, by sailing ship, railway, canal boat, and portage railroad across the Atlantic and over the Alleghenies, a period of discovery in which the Aldersons explored unfamiliar customs and practices in their new land. There is heartache and homesickness, but there is also rapid acculturation, testifying both to Emma's own strength of character and to the power of the support networks available to European immigrants. Although the Aldersons had not yet settled in a home of their own, we can already see the beginnings of Emma's exploration of what it means to be an immigrant and an Anglo-American. She never uses the term "Anglo-American" itself, but her letters explore that hyphenated identity of the immigrant, claiming not one nationality or the other but something entirely new, with only an uncertain kinship to either one.

In 1842, the year the Aldersons left Liverpool, steam packets had begun making the voyage in two weeks. The cost would have been prohibitive, however; so they opted for the more conventional, if more arduous, journey of six weeks under sail. The fact that they emigrated as a family indicates that they were better off than many immigrants who had to make the journey one at a time as resources allowed. Nevertheless, they traveled steerage, perhaps equivalent to economy class, not in cabins like the wealthier passengers. Published accounts from that time vary as to the quality of life on an immigrant ship, some minimizing the difficulties to promote emigration and others exaggerating those difficulties for the sake of a story. In 1835 the *Times* of London published the following account of steerage on an emigrant ship:

> In the steerage, two rows of double births are as many as should be allowed, but the agents and captains engage all these, and then another two rows of double births are built, the whole length of the steerage. Here the miserable passengers are obliged to place their luggage and provisions-boxes; . . . While the ship is in

> dock, with the hatches off, it is barely sufferable, but when at sea in a gale the misery is great. Sea-sickness drives the poor people to their births, slops are upset, chests, boxes, tins, and provisions breaking loose, and rolling to and fro. Perhaps the captain closes the main-hatch, and not unfrequently 200 human beings are pent up in that miserable hole.[1]

Thus most immigrants lived for six weeks at sea. Steerage passengers were usually required to bring their own food and cook for themselves in a common kitchen, sometimes with only a single grate and fire.

Judging from Emma's first full letter, the *Shenandoah*, commanded by Captain West, offered better conditions than those described in the *Times* article. Most of the family experienced terrible bouts of sea-sickness, but the tone of the letter is mostly upbeat as Emma rises to the challenges of life on a ship. Forming a miniature community of their own, passengers established friendships, visited with each other, and shared food. She found troublesome neighbors on one side and more congenial ones on the other. The *Shenandoah* was a temperance ship, which must have alleviated at least some of the difficulties common on shipboard in that day and suggests that Captain West's concern for the welfare of his passengers extended beyond the receipt of their fares at one end and the delivery of their persons at the other. Temperance ships had been growing in popularity since the late 1820s, when Captain Joseph Bates sailed out of New Bedford, Massachusetts, on the *Empress* with strict orders against swearing, drinking, and the use of nicknames among his crew.[2] A temperance ship such as this would obviously have appealed to the Quaker Aldersons.

Some of the steerage families hired ship hands to do their cooking, but Emma seems to have done most of their cooking herself and even reveled in the challenge of cooking at sea. "We have become very clever in sea cookery: our bread and rice puddings would be very passable on land; this morning I beat up the remainder with some rusks soaked in warm water, added a couple of eggs, some cinnamon and butter & sugar and a few currants which Ellen Friar gave me and when baked, a most excellent pudding, we all thought" (see pages 58–59). The sailors sang songs, two babies were born, a woman died, and the journey lasted a day shorter than six weeks. In just a few years, as steam packets became the norm, that time would be cut to two weeks, but the Aldersons were traveling at the end of one era and the beginning of a new one.

Across the Alleghenies

After a week with friends and family in Philadelphia, where they bought supplies and recovered their land legs, the Aldersons set out on the overland portion of their journey to Pittsburgh. Although it was only five days in length, Emma describes it as "the most formidable part of our travel, certainly much the most fatiguing" (see page 89). The full journey by the Pennsylvania Canal from Philadelphia to Pittsburgh was 395 miles, but the Aldersons made the first part of the journey by train to

Harrisburg, where they transferred to a packet boat on the Pennsylvania Canal. The boat would then be drawn out of the canal at Hollidaysburg and transported over the Alleghenies in one of the most extraordinary engineering feats of the century.

The Pennsylvania Canal had begun operation only about fifteen years earlier, in an effort to compete for access to the expanding west. The Erie Canal had been completed in 1825 to connect New York's ports to the Great Lakes; soon after that, work was begun on the Chesapeake and Ohio Canal and the Baltimore and Ohio Railroad, which would eventually connect Baltimore and Washington, D.C., to the Ohio River at Wheeling, Virginia (now West Virginia). If Philadelphia were to retain its vitality as a port city, some efficient means had to be found to transport people and goods west to Pittsburgh and the Ohio River.[3] The problem lay in the Allegheny Mountains, rising 2,500 feet above sea level. The idea of creating a series of locks to bring boats over the mountains was quickly discarded, and commissioners began to consider a canal tunnel 754 feet beneath the mountains' surface.[4] That, too, was deemed impractical, and Pennsylvania began looking for other means to retain access to its northern and southern neighbors.

The improbable solution was to pull the canal boats out of the water and onto specially designed railroad cars, to be hauled ten miles overland to the summit, an elevation gain of 1,400 feet.[5] A series of five inclines, each with two stationary steam engines at the top, would pull the railcars up the mountains. On level stretches between the inclines, the cars would be pulled by horses, mules, or locomotives. From the top (where travelers might enjoy some refreshment at the summit hotel), they would be lowered by rope along another series of inclines and level stretches to Johnstown and the western portion of the canal. On the western side, the elevation change would be 1,775 feet over a distance of twenty-six miles.[6] When the Aldersons made this journey, the Allegheny Portage Railroad had been in operation for eight years, having opened in 1834 following more than a decade of planning and three years of construction.

The Allegheny Portage Railroad was a brilliant but short-lived success. Humming with activity, the railroad drove innovations in boat construction, railway design, steam engines, wire cable, and more. Additional tracks were planned, and in the early 1850s, construction began on a new portage railway that would eliminate the sequence of planes and inclines in favor of a steady grade. What the designers had not counted on was the expansion of the rail industry throughout the country. With the completion of the Pennsylvania Railroad Company's first line across the Alleghenies in 1854, business on the portage lines dropped as precipitously as the mountains through which they passed. Three years later, the portage railroad ceased operation. Together the two portage railroad lines had cost nearly $4 million and produced roughly $3.5 million in revenues over their twenty-year lifespan.

Compared to the "miserably cramped" conditions on the train, Emma found the conditions on the canal boat quite comfortable and the food so sumptuous that afterward she could only say, "we are glad to return to plainer living." The boats were pulled by horses and included a spectacular crossing of the viaduct built above the Susquehanna River, where, according to Charles Dickens's report, "there is an

Figure 14. Head of Plane No. 6, Allegheny Portage Railroad, drawing by George Storm. Reproduced in Henry Wilson Storey, *History of Cambria County, Pennsylvania* (New York, 1907).

extraordinary wooden bridge with two galleries, one above the other, so that even there, two boat teams meeting, may pass without confusion—it was wild and grand."[7] Dickens had taken the Pennsylvania Canal along much the same route as the Aldersons just a few months earlier (he had begun on the canal in Philadelphia instead of Harrisburg). Not surprisingly, Dickens's fascination was with the characters among his fellow passengers, the engineering, and the general commotion of the day; in contrast, Emma's account deals more with the landscape and the vegetation.

From Johnstown, the Pennsylvania Canal descends to the Allegheny River, which it then follows into Pittsburgh. After two nights at the now historic Monongahela House hotel in Pittsburgh, the family continued south to Beallsville, where Harrison's brother Ralph lived, and then to Brownsville, where they stayed briefly with his sister Alice Mason and her family until they were able to rent a house west of Pittsburgh in Westland.

American Friends

As might be expected of any new immigrant, Emma Alderson missed her friends and family in England terribly at times during her first weeks in the New World.

"Oh, how continually you are the subject of my thoughts," she writes in one of her first letters:

> I may truly say my heart aches for love. What would I not now give for a sight of you, to enjoy again the dear privilege of your society? It seems to me now that all worldly things are worthless in comparison. The enjoyments and advantages of our present situation are outward: they satisfy not the heart. I may and probably shall feel differently in a while, but at present this seems to prevail over all. (see page 68)

Less than two months later, the heart still aches, but she has already begun to acclimate:

> I think of you & dearest mother incessantly and seldom can speak of you without tears; . . . the earth & its things have lost their shine in parting from you; yet I would not retrace our steps. I feel fully satisfied, as far as I can judge, that for ourselves & especially for our precious children, if we are spared to them, we have done wisely in coming. (see page 74)

The letters frequently begin with moments of longing, but they quickly move on to lively details of a land so full of promise that she wished only for her family to join her on that side of the Atlantic.

The Society of Friends was central to the Aldersons' lives during their first year and beyond. Beginning in the late 1760s and increasingly after the American Revolution, Quakers had moved to the area around Brownsville, Pennsylvania (located on the Monongahela River about 30 miles south of Pittsburgh). Many came from the South, especially from Virginia, as their consciences required a life apart from the institution of slavery. Their numbers grew quickly, and in 1782, Westland Preparative Meeting, four miles west of Brownsville and across the Monongahela, became the first organized body of Friends west of the Alleghenies.[8] Three years later, Westland was recognized as a Monthly Meeting, and Redstone Preparative Meeting was approved in Brownsville, near where Harrison's brother Ralph Alderson and sister Alice Mason would eventually settle with their families. In June 1797 the community laid out $20 for the purchase of four and a half acres of land on which to build a new meeting-house, which later that year became the home of Redstone Quarterly Meeting, established by Baltimore Yearly Meeting to meet alternately in Redstone and Westland. By the turn of the century, the Redstone area was home to eleven Quaker meetings.[9]

In 1812, Redstone Quarterly Meeting and its associated Monthly Meetings joined the newly formed Ohio Yearly Meeting, but the heyday of this hub of Quaker activity had passed as Friends moved west into Ohio, Indiana, and Iowa. Like many meetings at the time, Westland was deeply divided by the Society of Friends' first schism of the nineteenth century in 1827, between the followers of Elias Hicks (called Hicksites) and those who called themselves Orthodox. Although Hicks never published any systematic account of his beliefs, he preached a form of Quakerism that was more inward-seeking than many Friends felt comfortable with,

Figure 15. *A Map of the Meetings of Friends in Ohio Yearly Meeting, 1827.* Courtesy of Friends Historical Library of Swarthmore College.

urging Friends to recognize the authority of the "inner light" above that of scripture or church authorities. The formal separation began in Philadelphia but soon spread to most of the other Yearly Meetings in America. New York and Baltimore Yearly Meetings followed the Hicksites, while Indiana was mostly Orthodox, and Virginia and North Carolina were entirely Orthodox. Ohio Yearly Meeting was divided almost equally between the two.[10] By the time the Aldersons arrived in Pennsylvania, Redstone Quarterly Meeting as well as Westland Monthly Meeting had likewise been split into Hicksite and Orthodox factions for fourteen years.

In Westland, the Aldersons formed a close friendship with George and Ruth Smith that was to last throughout Emma's short life in America. George Smith was one of the leaders of the community, his father, Abraham, having been one of its founders.[11] The Aldersons shared the Smiths' Orthodox position in the controversy, as Emma makes plain in her denunciations of Elias Hicks and the Hicksites. Emma describes the Westland first-day meetings as crowded and the weekday meetings as drawing "a good muster," but the numbers were declining as members dropped away through waning interest, disownment, or westward migration.[12] Two other important Friends whom the Aldersons came to know were the Orthodox minister Edith Griffith and her husband, Amos, of Pike Run Meeting for Worship (subordinate to Westland Monthly Meeting).

Observations on a New Land

Emma's early observations of American customs and character are similar to those of many other Europeans, with emphases on Americans' resourcefulness, their brusque and unceremonious manners, and the prodigious amount of food on the table and in the markets. In Pennsylvania, where the Aldersons spent their first year, she learned about "flannel kicking," candle and soap making, maple sugaring, new methods of cooking, and more.[13] She learned about the "American (or Yankee) Jumper," a simple horse-drawn sled, built to carry either one or two people, which could be easily built or disassembled when no longer useful and, through *Our Cousins in Ohio*, first introduced that phrase to English readers. Suggesting a mind open to new experiences, Alderson's descriptions convey an enthusiasm for novelty and innovation rather than any sense of strangeness or alienation.

At times Alderson seems puzzled or even troubled by what she saw as Americans' tendency to embrace fringe social and religious movements. "It seems as if every absurdity could find adherents in America," she would later write to her niece Anna Mary Howitt in describing the Shakers. "I think climate has a great deal to do in the formation of national character, & certainly the Americans are a much more volatile & less reflective people than the English, . . . & their climate is one of violent changes of extremes of heat & cold, of fervency & frigidity" (see page 232).

In these early letters, Alderson describes one of the most fervent and interesting of those movements in the millennialist Millerite movement, led by the "prophet" William Miller. Based on careful calculations from the Old Testament, Miller had concluded that Christ would return sometime between March 21, 1843, and March 21, 1844 ("the prophetical Jewish year 1843").[14] Beginning with Miller's first lectures in 1831, the movement grew through the 1830s and the first years of the 1840s, drawing adherents from many different denominations. Because there was never any formal organization (individuals were encouraged to retain membership in their own churches), historians do not know how many people were involved, but modern estimates put the number somewhere between 25,000 and 50,000.[15] As Alderson notes, adherents gathered in their robes, prepared for the ascension; some froze to death waiting, while others forwent planting crops, convinced they would not be there to harvest them. Some of the actions attributed to the Millerites may have been exaggerated, but the enthusiasm was real.[16] The Great Comet of 1843 (one of the most spectacular comets in human history), which Alderson describes in a letter to her Harrison nieces on March 27, led the Millerites to a brief conviction that the end had indeed arrived.[17] When the second coming seemed not to have occurred (some argued that it had come in Heaven or in other less obvious ways), the date was revised to October 22. From there the movement died out, although one segment of its adherents became the Seventh-day Adventists.

Miller's conclusions have led him to be regarded as an extremist, while the enthusiasm of his followers suggests something like a collective insanity. Alderson seems to have shared that view of the Millerites, but her response also suggests a recognition of Millerism's consistency with the general tide of nineteenth-century American Christianity. Miller's methods and language followed those of mainstream evangelicalism, with revival meetings, exhortations to repentance, and so on. Some more mainstream preachers accepted his methods and worked with Miller, seeing his millenarian prophecies as only an incidental and effective method of gaining converts. Another element of Miller's appeal was his rationality. Using traditional methods of biblical interpretation coupled with "compelling historical evidence, . . . [Miller] explained how each person could discover the 'truth' he had found, thus making the secrets of revelation accessible to any believer."[18] Alderson may have been right to identify the movement as distinctively American ("surely you are not so foolish in England"), but as an evangelical adherent herself, to a denomination that had begun with a belief in the immanent return of Christ, she may have felt some sympathy with the excesses of her American contemporaries. The Millerites might have been "foolish" zealots, but many, she believed, were at least "sincerely zealous" (see page 92).

Not more than a week after her arrival in America, Alderson records her first encounter with racial discrimination, when a fellow passenger on the canal boat, a young black woman on her way to school in Pittsburgh, is allowed to eat only after the white passengers, and then only at the table with the servants. Throughout her life, Emma deplored the treatment of African Americans in not only the South but also the supposedly more enlightened North. On this occasion, she writes, "We spoke very freely on the subject & were marked in our attentions to the poor girl" (see page 71), demonstrating an open resistance to racism that would become a pattern in the Aldersons' lives, as when she writes later of the family's habit of inviting black tradesmen to dinner, contrary to the norms of Cincinnati society (see page 211).

Though adapting to a new world far from her old home was challenging on many fronts, the extended network of friends and family she found on the other side of the Atlantic eased the transition considerably. At least two of Harrison's siblings had already emigrated: Ralph Alderson, who had married an American widow, Ann, and Alice Alderson Mason with her husband, William. Already established in southwestern Pennsylvania, these connections were ready to help Emma and Harrison settle into their new home, and the Masons continued as close friends even after Emma and Harrison moved on to Cincinnati. Soon after their arrival, the Aldersons found themselves in a position to give as well as receive assistance. Throughout the letters, we follow the story of Daniel's brother Thompson Harrison and his family, who had fallen on hard times and by 1843 were planning a further emigration to Missouri. Finding him without the means of making that journey, Emma uses her correspondence to get help for him from friends in England, setting aside the belief she expresses elsewhere that poverty in America is inevitably linked to laziness, improvidence, or some other vice.[19]

If she missed seeing her sister in person, Emma took great pleasure in seeing her sister's books everywhere she went. In Philadelphia, she made one of her first American purchases: a copy of *Strive and Thrive* (1840), from Howitt's popular series Tales for the People and Their Children. In Brownsville, Pennsylvania, near where the Aldersons had spent the first winter, Emma found herself feted as the nearest thing possible to a celebrity when a shopkeeper discovered he was talking to the famous author's sister. Howitt's reputation was growing rapidly and would continue with her own books as well as her translations first of Swedish author Fredrika (or sometimes Frederika) Bremer's novels and then of the works of Danish author Hans Christian Andersen.[20]

Less pleasant family matters also emerge in this section that will run through the next few years of letters. Harrison's sister Elizabeth, who had come out with them from England, turned out to be an ongoing source of difficulty for Emma. During the first year, Elizabeth seemed to be spending as much or more time with her sister Alice Mason and brother Ralph Alderson as with Emma and Harrison, and in one letter, Emma describes her, perhaps with some annoyance, as being "but invalidish" (see page 76). By the end of that year, Emma is uncharacteristically direct in her criticism of Elizabeth for some unspecified slight: "We feel much hurt at Elizabeth's conduct . . . & can only say if she chooses to continue to do so after what has been said to her, she must take the consequences. I doubt not she will lose the respect of all her friends that think & judge aright" (see page 99).

The Botany of Home

Along with a copy of her sister's *Strive and Thrive*, one of Emma's first purchases upon arriving in Philadelphia was "a botanical work" (see page 67). She does not say what that work was, but its purchase marks a love of botany that was to help her connect with this new land while maintaining her ties to people and places back in England. Emma prided herself on a knowledge of plants picked up with her sisters in the fields and forests surrounding Uttoxeter when they were growing up. In the earliest letters, she sometimes disclaims any knowledge of the new landscape: "There was nothing English here. . . . The trees, of which I did not know the names, wore a foreign aspect, and the houses visible were log of a very mean description" (see page 69). But in the very next paragraph the sense of alienation disappears as she confidently gives names to a long list of familiar as well as unfamiliar plants: the Michaelmas daisy, the orange ranunculus, the perennial sunflower, the evening primrose, Virginia raspberry, sumac, arborvitae, rhododendron, "the Azalea, the locust, and many of our rare & beautiful exotics" (see page 70).

Lists like this, often with Latin names, appear throughout the correspondence, indicating a remarkable botanical literacy, but we also see Emma developing an emotional and aesthetic vocabulary appropriate to her new experiences. At this early stage of the correspondence, she reaches for stock phrases from the language of travel literature and picturesque description. If, as she wrote, "there was nothing English here," then it became "a scene that reminded me of some bright Italian or Indian river" (see page 69). Yet in her description of the Alleghenies from the same letter, a more original voice is already emerging:

> Our track lay on the side of the mountain; below us were deep valleys and frightful precipices all around, mountains over mountains, most sublimely beautiful, all covered with noble trees, some in the last stages of decay, bare & leafless, others glowing with the rich tints of autumn & others vividly green like the first fruits of spring. (see page 70)

If the beginning is the stock language of the Romantic sublime (something out of an Ann Radcliffe novel, perhaps), the weight of that sublimity is lifted unexpectedly by "rich tints of autumn" mixed with "vividly green" foliage. In England, Alderson had been a prolific reader, so it is not surprising that her descriptions frequently echo the books she had read, but as she puts names to the living things around her and language to the emotional experiences aroused in her by the landscapes of this new country, we sense that she is making the country her own. "Even [with] my small knowledge, it [botanizing] has given me an interest in the country from first setting foot upon its shore, that but for this and the love of the beautiful in whatever form it appears, I think I could never have felt" (see page 144).

If plants helped her connect to the new, they also helped her maintain connections to the old. In describing her plan for collecting plants and seeds for her relatives back in England, Emma tells her nieces, "it will be a delightful employment for me and the dear children and connect the idea of you with places & things the most agreeable" (see page 86). Botany was something she had shared with her sisters in England and something she could continue to share through the mail. Moreover, in this new context, Emma—long the pupil of her better-educated older sisters—would enjoy an authority of her own founded on observations of a world they had never seen. Sharing seeds across the Atlantic took the process a step further: living among the same plants grown from the same seed stock became another way of sharing a life together, as if the three of them, raised from the same seed stock but separated by 4,000 miles, could imagine themselves side by side, cultivating a common garden.

Letters, 1842 to 1843

1. [To Addressee unknown], July 8, 1842

We are lying off the Black Rock[1] probably till tomorrow, thinking mournfully of the dear, dear Friends we have left; may the Almighty bless you.
Farewell.
E.A.

2. To Ann Botham, August 17, 1842

On board the Shenandoah 8th Mo. 17th 1842

Literally, my beloved mother, this is the first opportunity I have had since our embarkation of writing even a few lines; how have I wished I could give thee a detail of all we have experienced, seen, and felt but that is impossible; our first week at sea was one of suffering, I began with sickness on third day and was very ill for three days, overpowered with the effect and exhaustion. During that time Harrison held up tolerably and poor Richard worked in spite of being quite unwell, Elizabeth took to her bed and, but for the exception of being up about two hours one day, has kept it ever since, this morning she has crept out again. But my great trial and real trouble has arisen from dear Harrison being so ill that I became quite alarmed for him. I do not wish to distress thee, but now that I trust it is passing over, I can look back and wonder how my spirits have kept up; I did indeed feel very forlorn. Poor Richard & I began to revive together and did our best amongst the children & for each other. I never saw Harrison so overwhelmed in body and mind; I once or twice thought he was going to sink.

To-day is a fine morning after two or three stormy days, during which we were obliged to have the deck lights closed and have been tossed about till we could scarcely stand. The children were cross and fretted with the confinement and inconvenience, and poor little Agnes seemed to want as much tending and nursing as the baby; she once said "if gramma was here, she would have her arms to spare for me." This is a dark picture now for the light, this fine morning, the windows are opened, the sun shines cheerily; you might almost expect to hear the birds sing, and every one is alive and good-humoured. The poor bed-ridden invalids have crept out; dear Harrison had his breakfast in bed and seemed to relish his food, which he has not done for many days.

Thou shalt have a detail of the events of the day, as they are amongst the best I can at present give. Richard and I got up early and, whilst I was washing and dressing the children, he loaded our kettle and fetched our daily supply of water, which is 11 qts. Tea and biscuit is our morning meal; out came one and another invisible till all the cabin was mustered; fat old Thomas Far shuffled to a corner of his sofa, & though groaning and, as his son John said,

1. The Black Rock is the site of Perch Rock Lighthouse, or New Brighton Lighthouse, built in 1827 at the mouth of the Mersey estuary just outside of Liverpool.

Figure 16. Black Rock Lighthouse, detail from an 1836 map of Liverpool, published by the Society for the Diffusion of Useful Knowledge, reproduced in Melville C. Branch, *An Atlas of Rare City Maps: Comparative Urban Design, 1830–1842* (New York, 1997). Courtesy of Princeton Architectural Press.

"dreadfully cross,["] was preparing to go on deck. Before we made ready to go out, we swept up our portion of the place, washed our breakfast things, & sent our ham & potatoes to be cooked for dinner, and left all in order against our return.

It was a delightful morning; although we are in such high latitudes that at night the thermometer has been at the freezing point, the air was pleasant, and the sunshine warm. I thought that if we were to have such days as these I should not care if our voyage lasted four weeks longer. Time went on quickly and with good apetites we heard that dinner was ready. After dispatching it we returned on deck for a time; Elizabeth ventured out, and we spent the time agreeably, conversing with one of the cabin passengers, a Scotch man, a medical man, who is going out to settle with his niece whom

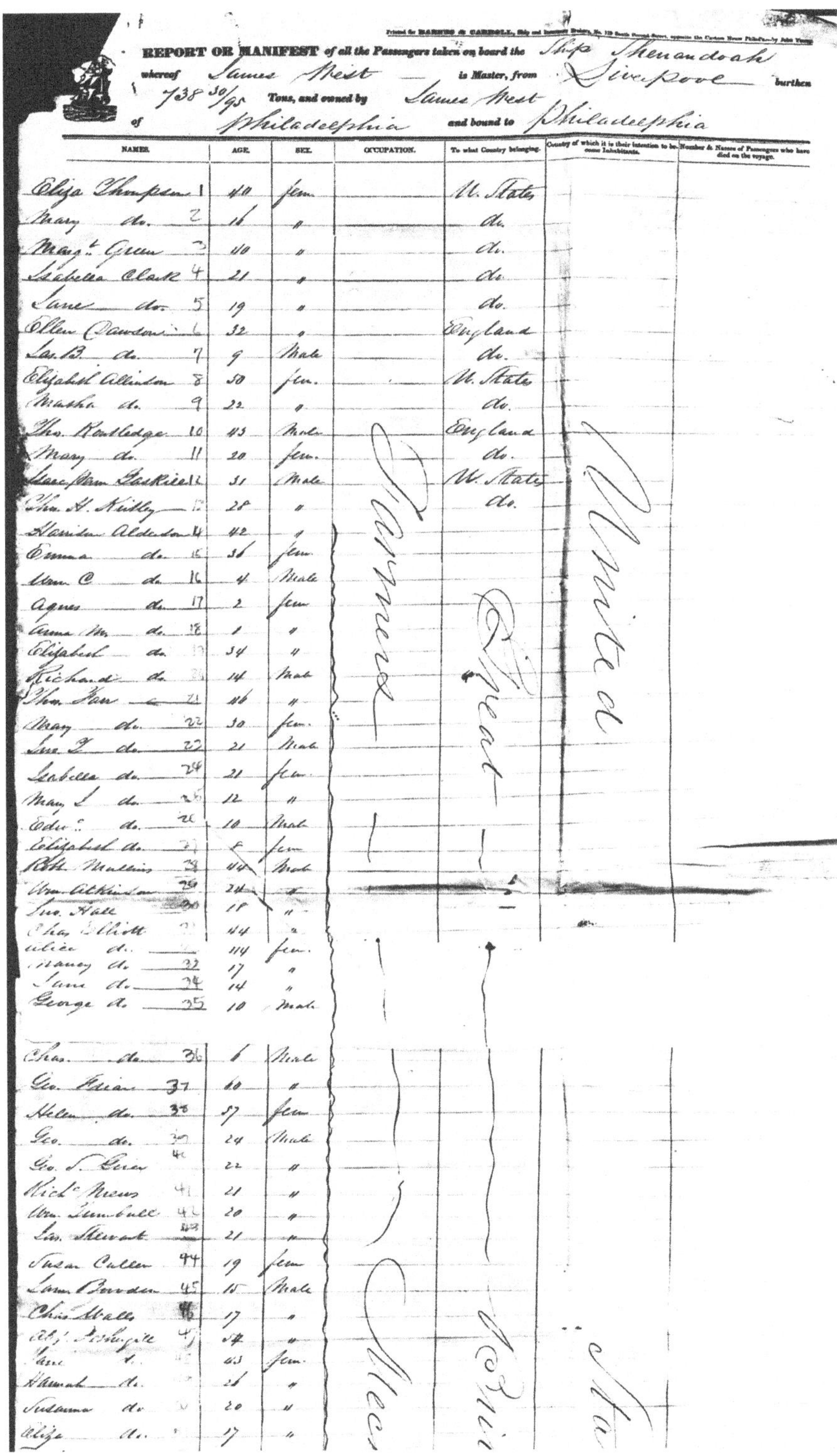

REPORT OR MANIFEST *of all the Passengers taken on board the* Ship Shenandoah *whereof* James West *is Master, from* Liverpool *burthen* 738 30/95 *Tons, and owned by* James West *of* Philadelphia *and bound to* Philadelphia

NAMES.		AGE.	SEX.	OCCUPATION.	To what Country belonging.	Country of which it is their intention to become Inhabitants.	Number & Names of Passengers who have died on the voyage.
Eliza Thompson	1	40	fem.		U. States		
Mary do.	2	16	"		do.		
Marg.t Green	3	40	"		do.		
Isabella Clark	4	21	"		do.		
Jane do.	5	19	"		do.		
Ellen Dawson	6	32	"		England		
Jas. B. do.	7	9	Male		do.		
Elizabeth Allinson	8	50	fem.		U. States		
Mashe do.	9	22	"		do.		
Thos. Routledge	10	43	Male		England		
Mary do.	11	20	fem.		do.		
Isaac Wm Gaskill	12	31	Male		U. States		
Chs. H. Neilley	13	28	"		do.		
Hariden Alderson	14	42	"				
Emma do.	15	36	fem.				
Wm C do.	16	4	Male				
Agnes do.	17	2	fem.				
Anna M. do.	18	1	"				
Elizabeth do.	[illegible]	34	"				
Richard do.	[illegible]	14	Male				
Thos. Farr	21	46	"				
Mary do.	22	30	fem.				
Jno. T. do.	23	21	Male				
Isabella do.	24	21	fem.				
Mary L do.	25	12	"				
Edw.d do.	26	10	Male				
Elizabeth do.	27	8	fem.				
Robt. Mullins	28	44	Male				
Wm. Atkinson	29	24	"				
Jno. Hall	30	18	"				
Chas. Elliott	[illegible]	44	"				
Alice do.	[illegible]	44	fem.				
Nancy do.	33	17	"				
Jane do.	34	14	"				
George do.	35	10	Male				
Chas. do.	36	6	Male				
Geo. Fenian	37	60	"				
Helen do.	38	57	fem.				
Geo. do.	39	24	Male				
Geo. T. Geer	40	22	"				
Nichl. Mews	41	21	"				
Wm. Trimbull	42	20	"				
Jas. Stewart	43	21	"				
Susan Cullen	44	19	fem.				
Jam. Bowden	45	15	Male				
Chris. Walls	46	17	"				
Abj. Ashugill	47	54	"				
Jane do.	[illegible]	43	fem.				
Hannah do.	[illegible]	26	"				
Susanna do.	[illegible]	20	"				
Eliza do.	[illegible]	17	"				

Figure 17. *Shenandoah* passenger list showing all the members of the Alderson family who emigrated with Emma Alderson.

he has brought up. There are 15 cabin passengers, all very quiet, genteel & agreeable looking but we have little to do with them as, though we meet on deck, their seats and part of the deck are as distinct as if they were railed off.

This evening a poor woman going out to her husband died. She had no relative on board, and having all to do for herself, fell twice down the gangway steps and hurt herself so seriously that she soon died, poor thing; she was sewed up in a blanket and lowered into the sea next morning;[2] the Captain read the funeral service very impressively, I was told. It was so cold & stormy and early, being only 9 oclock, that much as I wished it I could not go to see the ceremony.

We get our tea early and go to bed with the children, who get very much tired long before it is dark, but to sleep is impossible for our neighbours are the noisiest crew that surely ever crossed the Atlantic; there are a Father & Mother, oldest son and his bride, and 8 other children from 12 years & under. The son & his wife lay in bed for a week, and now that they come [2] forth occasionally only add to the universal confusion. The young woman talks incessantly, and the son scolds only secondarily to his Father: "I'll flog you, I'll knock your head off, I'll horse whip you, you monkey" are the usual expressions with which the children are hailed and hail each other. Then, for eating and drinking, it seems the business of their lives. I sometimes think what a paradise for such a family America will be; I expect they have eaten themselves out of house & harbour in England, and there they can gratify their craving propensities without let or stint. The din in an evening \from these people/ is inconceivable and only ceases as the extinguished lamps occasion darkness & prevent their seeing their way in search of meat & viands. Fortunately they have neither lamp nor candles, so that as soon as every light is out they are obliged to retire.

The Fothergil[l]s are in the second-cabin, which derives its light from ours. They have a quiet, comfortable corner, which, though comparatively dark, I have sometimes envied them. It looks so retired & orderly; how different would have been our situation had they been our neighbours. They come and see us frequently, & we lend & borrow like good friendly neighbours. We talk of going to A. F.'s house or Thomas Far's house as if we were living in the same street.

We have agreed with the cook, a black man, to dress our food & boil our kettle &c; the first week, R. did all himself at the general fire, but by this arrangement our comfort is greatly increased. We give him 15s for his trouble. Our neighbours have engaged the steward, a tall stout mulatto, to cook &c for them and give him 45s for his services, but I cannot say I should like

2. The lack of punctuation in the original leaves it ambiguous whether "next morning" goes with her being lowered into the sea or only with the captain's sermon, in which case she would have been lowered into the sea the night before.

his interference amongst our victuals.[3] It would be a fine subject for a painter when this said John Brown comes to take his orders from the good lady. His bow & his "what is your pleasure madam" are quite laughable. Our Mr. Black is a person of dignity—he ordered R[ichard] to take off his hat when he came into his kitchen. Dan, the under cook, who sleeps in a hammock swung in the centre of our cabin, is a perfect specimen of negro lightheartedness. I wish I could give thee an idea of the merriment & humour he threw into a story I heard him tell one night when he came to bed.

The Friars are very kind to us; Ellen F. comes to see us most days & brings the children little indulgences. I quite like to see her come; with her knitting in her hand, she looks so kind & motherly. Oh how often I, with what deep affection do I think of you all and especially thee, my beloved mother, & the dear people at Liverpool, and when one or other token of your kindness and affection meets my eye the feeling is often painful indeed. I love to dwell on the rememberance of the love & kindness which we experienced on all hands; it excites a feeling of lively gratitude towards our[4] dear friends whom we have left & also to him who is the source & fountain of every blessing.

Though we have experienced some trials & anxieties since our departure from England, I cannot say that one sentiment of distrust as to the step we have taken has been added to our cares. We have been preserved in much calmness and entire reliance on the protecting, supporting arm of our Heavenly Father. I have sometimes felt that that the quiet, trusting baby on my breast in the stillness of midnight was somewhat emblematic of that peaceful confiding frame of mind with which I was favoured, & dear Harrison's feelings have throughout been very accordant; I have often thought of dear Susanna Howarth's words: they seemed to rest on my mind for many days like a watchword "being careful for nothing—"[5] but it was the latter part of the injunction which appears so full of consolation, to make all our requests known unto God by prayer & supplication, and truly He, like a kind good Father, does hear & often—very often—condescends to answer his poor but unworthy dependent children.

3. *Wiley & Putnam's Emigrant Guide* notes that the larger ships often carried a second cook whom a passenger might hire for the duration of the voyage at a rate of four to eight shillings. *Wiley & Putnam's Emigrant's Guide: Comprising Advice and Instruction in Every Stage of the Voyage to America* (London: Wiley & Putnam, 1845), 55, https://books.google.com/books?id=qmsFAAAAQAAJ.

4. The word in the MS appears to be "four," but there is no likely group of four friends to whom she might be referring. I have therefore treated the first letter as an accident.

5. "Be careful for nothing; but in every thing by prayer and supplication with thanksgiving let your requests be made known unto God. And the peace of God, which passeth all understanding, shall keep your hearts and minds through Christ Jesus." Philippians 4:6–7 (King James Version).

22nd To day is a pleasant mild day with a soft south wind and tolerably quiet sea, but we are not making much progress, being again about to take a northerly direction. I believe we have not yet made half the voyage, yet considering that, with the exception of about 48 hours, we have had contrary winds, it is wonderful we get on as we do. The sea is interesting from its restless, never ceasing motion; every dash of the waves crested with foam is beautiful, and the tinge of the water [3] in the wake of the vessel is exquisite: it is the colour of the finest verdigris mingled with white foam. We now and then see a sea gull winging its way in the solitude of mid ocean or riding on the bosom of the waves, all & every-thing are objects of attention & interest to us where there is so little variety. The petrel is frequently seen; it is a beautiful bird of the swallow species but much more varied in colour than the land kinds; its back is white & light brown.

We find our dry toast very nice; indeed, it tastes quite land-like, and dear cousin Mr. Abbott's bread is delicious; it keeps admirably. Our kind friends in Charles Street little knew how valuable their apples and grapes would be; I have wished, when deriving comfort form them, they could know how great a kindness they had conferred upon us. The apples are an especial treat & doled out with great care. The Fothergil[l]s omitted bringing any, and now & then I spare Jane F. one. I have just taken her two & she said she had been thinking how gladly she would give a shilling for one. We sadly missed it in not bringing currants, raisins, figs, & plenty of apples. I make thick parkins and occasionally pasties & seed cakes which the cook bakes for us, & they form a nice change from biscuit & toast.[6] I should advise a family coming out to bring plenty of good flour & less biscuit. The treacle dear Daniel gave us is <u>most</u> excellent & now we are better; the children & we enjoy it with porridge. Some way or other we have lost our cheese, which we miss sadly & should do more so but for the little one sister Alice kindly gave to Harrison when he was in Dent; it is a sad loss, and we feel it every day.

Harrison, though much better, is still weak and poorly. I trust it may please Providence to bless this voyage so as to cause it to be the means of restoring and establishing his health & prolonging his life. Elizabeth keeps very close to her bed, though to day she has again ventured out & is on deck. Thou wouldst be pleased to see how greatly Agnes improves in her appearance; I believe the sea-air is exerting a beneficial influence over her constitution. Charley has never flagged but continues as stout and robust as ever. Baby is tolerable, but as she is cutting some upper teeth is sometimes, as may be expected, rather tedious. We have become very clever in sea cookery: our bread and rice puddings would be very passable on land; yesterday we had a boiled rice pudding with melted butter & preserves; this morning I beat up the remainder with some rusks soaked in warm water, added a couple of eggs,

6. Parkin is a ginger cake from Yorkshire, typically made with oats.

some cinnamon and butter & sugar and a few currants which Ellen Friar gave me and when baked a most excellent pudding, we all thought.

Indeed we begin to find things improve with us; we have a regular plan of procedure, and when we can get away for a few hours on deck, time passes quickly & pleasantly. Our noisy disagreeable neighbours still hold on, scolding, shouting, eating and drinking as though the opinion of others was worth nothing. Yesterday their epithets to each other were donkey, monkey, rascal &c. They are the talk and dislike of every one.

There are in our cabin next to the Fars, two young men & two young women, who are generally supposed to have run away. They came on board when the vessel was lying at the mouth of the river taking in salt, have little or no luggage, and the general suspicion is that they are not married, though one calls herself Mrs Robinson & the other Mrs Kay.

Scene at the present moment. The Fars having dispatched their dinner, Mrs. F drinking ale out of a silver tankard hands it over to one of the little brownies about the age of Agnes who drains it; a contention going one between John & his sister about an absent bottle, have now concluded it in order to eat pickles, which he met with in the search; the old man & the young wife still in bed (they only get up to eat & drink at supper time); Richard washing up our dinner things. The Robinson's, as they are called, sitting man & woman, eating a good dinner of eggs & ham from the same plate, one to each couple. Opposite us is a closet occupied by the sailors as a sleeping apartment; a fine bare-legged fellow is just gone to his four-hour rest; the stewardess in the farthest corner nursing her sickly baby; herring, ham, beef, tongues, tea-towels, tins, cans, & Dan's hammock in the centre constitute the ornaments of our abode. There is a poor fellow on board who is working his passage over & has charge of the cow, poney & poultry; the sailors have named him Jemmy Ducks. A quiet, inoffensive, obliging creature he is, but some of the sailors & passengers take a delight in teazing [4] him; they painted his face when he was asleep, tie his legs & annoy him in every way; they even threaten his life if he should complain to the Captain. I have felt so grieved that I requested a person to tell them that if they continued such conduct I will myself inform Captain West, & I quite hope he will be better treated. The Captain's eldest sone is one of the boys; he is a fine handsome youth of about 18 & in his sailor's dress reminds me much of dear brother Charles. I think he must have looked very like him. His handsome features, rich complexion & curling dark hair with a fine slim figure make him a perfect subject for a painter.

When on deck the day was damp & cold, we saw some grampus[7] sporting about; they rolled on the top of the waves and had every appearance of

7. *Grampus griseus*, Risso's dolphin. The name "grampus" has also been applied to other large fish and cetaceans, including the killer whale (*Orcinus orca*). *Encyclopaedia Britannica*, s.v. "Grampus," April 5, 2017, https://www.britannica.com/animal/grampus-mammal.

whales. I believe they are a small species: those we saw might be 4 or 5 yards long.

23rd. Almost a dead calm but so beautifully warm & bright that I feel willing to endure a little delay to enjoy such glorious weather. The sea birds are numerous & very interesting, skimming & swimming on the water beautifully. The sea is as still as a lake and tinged with purple in the distance as though it reflected \a/ crimson ~~cloud~~ sky, yet above it is clear blue with white clouds. I sometimes feel a sentiment of lively gratitude to the gracious Preserver of our lives, who thus from day to day protects and guides us through the perils & dangers of the stormy deep.

5th day was fine and deversified by the appearance of a ship which attracted every one on deck. It was a fine vessel in full sail as appeared for England, but though the Captain hoisted his colour & brought his trumpet to hail her, they passed without a single recognition or shew of civility. There was only one person visible on board.

Poor Harrison is again much indisposed and spent the day in his berth. Elizabeth lies almost continually in hers & were it not for Richard, I should be much perplexed how to get along. I have cause to be thankful that on the whole my health is excellent. I have headaches & sickness occasionally but still am fully capable to do all that is requisite. Many Whales made their appearance & manifested themselves by ~~throwing~~ \spouting/ up the water ~~upon the~~ before they appeared on the surface; gulls & petrels were also very numerous.

My faith in Mother Carey's chickens[8] is beginning to waver as they are constantly about the ship, and still we have fine calm weather. Indeed, calms are our prevailing complaints.

6th day. We had just dispatched our breakfast & were preparing dinner when six sailors made their appearance with the captain at their head to clean our cabin. Every box & package was removed and they proceeded to scrape & sweep the place & then "swab" it. It made a sad commotion; we had no place but a spot about a yard square at the foot of the stairs to eat our dinner, but as the day was fine we spent the time pleasantly on deck. All was \made/ very clean, but as the evening and next day proved very damp, all about continued wet & comfortless, and we got up with violent headaches & far from well.

1st day. A glorious day, our cabin again dry & healthy. All looks cheerful & gay on deck; most are better drest than usual. I could not help wishing we could assemble on deck to read the scriptures. This feeling I believe was general amongst the more respectable part of the passengers, yet no one seemed to like to propose it & thus it was omitted. Should another first-day be equally favourable \perhaps we may accomplish it./

8. A common term for the storm petrel, a pelagic bird thought to bring warnings of stormy weather.

It is quite amusing and delightful to see how much upon the whole the children enjoy themselves, The[re] is a little boy in the cabin. The two Fothergil[l]s and our two, they play at horses, shout & pull the ropes, performing as well as they can the manouvoures of the sailors and have a variety of resources for their own pleasure & to the amusement of us all. Agnes is quite a pet among the ladies & with the Captain; they bring her fruit & sweetmeats & do all they can to please & ingratiate themselves in her favour, but she is shy & dainty in bestowing her favours, especially toward the Captain, but the whole mystery was explained to me one evening when I was speaking to her & W. C. of the goodness of the Almighty, who had taken [5] care of us on the ocean. She said, ["]I love God, I should like to kiss him, but mama, has he hairs on his face.["] Captain has hairs on his face. In truth his wiskers are enormous & enough to frighten a child not accustomed to such a visage.

This is a temperance ship, and the crew are a body of fine active men, some of them really handsome. There are amongst them natives of seven different nations & it is interesting to observe the distinct national characteristics, from the short broad-set Dane to the the intelligent Swiss, the handsome Portuguese & the sentimental Italian. We all remark with pleasure the entire absence of bad language except in one or two instances. One day our neighbours wanted a job done; the carpenter was sent for, and a glass of grog offered as the remuneration. "I dont work for grog," he said & was walking off. They again asked him to do it. "I'll send you wood & nails, but do it yourself[,"] he said with contempt, & in truth he was highly offended & did not try to conceal it.

Captain West, like ourselves, begins to feel impatient to get to the end of the ~~yo~~ voyage. He says the cost of the ship is 25£ a day and the prospect is that we shall yet be some time as we have almost constant head winds.

3d & 4th days were very stormy and many of us were as much troubled with sickness as at first—I was obliged to go to bed at 4 oclock each day, but poor baby went with me & slept till 6 in the morning, she is a good little creature. 4th day night was awful and most like a storm of any weathers we have experienced. The ship rolled and creaked fearfully boxes and hampers were scattered in every direction, our chapter of accidents was a long one we had divers falls and upsets and broke much of our crockery which has been a great comfort so much pleasanter than this ware.

24th 8th mo. 5th day. At length we have reached the long talked of, long wished for Bank of Newfoundland. The sea has a most novel and beautiful appearance: it is of a light pea green, clear & bright when the sun shines upon it, like a sea of green glass. This light colour, which forms the body of the water, is interspersed with broad patches tinged so darkly that they look almost purple. This diversity of colours is, I believe, occasioned by the difference of depth, & the light parts, being shallow, reflect the sand & mud, which here is white. The soundings are about 45 fathoms. The Banks of

Newfoundland are about 600 miles long & 300 broad. It is a great cod fishery, & we saw many fishing smacks.[9] When favourable, ships passing over this part of the ocean frequently catch considerable quantities of fish, but as we had a strong, fair wind we were too anxious to avail ourselves of it to delay for any such purpose.

One day when the sea was rough we saw a contest between a whale and a sword-fish. They tossed & tumbled on the waters & continued the contest as long as we were in sight of them.

One night one of the spare berths in our cabin was curtained & prepared for the reception of one of the steerage passengers, and in the course of the night a baby was born. All was carried on so quietly that I believe I was the only one in the place that was aware all was over till morning; in the course of a few days we had another addition to our ship's company from the same cause.

We are much pleased to find the ship, as far as we are concerned, is perfectly free from bugs or the like annoyances. I am often rather nervous about our children mixing with the adjoining family, as the children must necessarily be very dirty; a weekly washing is all they generally get.—a ship is a sad place for morals, I would never willingly see any I love or am interested in exposed to such an influence & trained in such a school; were I by thy side I could tell thee sad things, of persons the would never suspect, but scandal is best not to put down in black & white, & in truth it is not very desirable to know such things.

Land birds begin to [6] appear soon; we passed the banks; two swallows were seen amongst the rigging, & a few days after a pretty little American bird and some pigeons were seen. All these symptoms are delightful, though our voyage is very long & somewhat tedious.

For the last two or three weeks, we found ourselves much more comfortable in consequence of forming acquaintance with some of the first cabin passengers, who are very nice people. The Captain's mother, who is a very nice old lady, almost always reserves her fruit after dinner for our children & is in other respects very kind & friendly. I have learnt a good deal from her of American life. There is a Mrs Green, the widow of Col. Green, & her two sisters, who are also very agreeable. The widow is a decidedly religious character & a most superior, intelligent woman. We feel now more in our element, for at first we had below no sympathy & above no admission.

On the <*blank*> we came within sight of land but the afternoon & evening were so foggy that we looked in vain for a pilot. Rockets were sent forth, blue lights burnt, a lanthorn hoisted on the mast head, but all in vain. The seamen prognosticated a storm, and as the wind was now fair, the land we

9. "Smack" was first used in 1611 to denote "a single-masted sailing-vessel, fore-and-aft rigged like a sloop or cutter, and usually of light burden" (OED online, s.v. "smack, n.3," accessed March 21, 2020, https://www-oed-com.pitt.idm.oclc.org/view/Entry/182375).

so much longed for was to be feared. Everybody was anxious, and as the evening advanced the feeling increased, but He who has protected us hitherto did not fail us at this juncture. The Captain & crew were up all night; it was moonlight, though cloudy, & by dint of great care they kept the ship out at sea, though so near the shore that the breakers were heard distinctly; the anticipated storm did not come till daylight, when the rain came down in torrents accompanied with vivid lightening but little wind.

About 9 oclock the pilot came on board; it was a moment of intense excitement, & to some of us deep thankfulness. All went on cheerfully; the sailors sang as they worked the ship and performed incessant labour with great cheerfulness, for our fair wind soon left us and they had to tack ship continually, but to see land, to enter the bay of Delaware, & to be relieved from the unstable motion of the sea was so delightful that we cheerfully bore the delay. The singing of the sailors is not the least amusing & interesting part of a voyage. Sometimes I have heard them in the night, their voices mingled with the dash of the water & the creaking of the vessel & thought it really fine. Now we are approaching the land they are in such high spirits that they sing continually; perhaps there will be fifteen or twenty men pulling at a rope & singing together, Pretty Sally or Billy Riley, but the one I like the best has no regular words except the chorus, which is "cheerily men." There was one man who always took the lead and sang what ever he liked, always keeping to the measure & time. One part was "We're bound for Philadelphia," ["]cheerily men cheerily men hi ho cheerily men; Farewell Shenandoah Cheerily men for we are homeward bound; Cheerily men cheerily men hi ho cheerily men.["][10]

It was on 4th day that we entered the bay, and not till first day morning did we arrive at the mouth of the Delaware. The scenery then became interesting and beautiful: trees, green fields, neat farm houses, villages, & towns rendered the sail most interesting. The wind was again fair for us, and we cut rapidly through the waters; the distance from the mouth of the river to

10. On a ship, "cheerily" meant quickly. "Cheerily Men" and "Billy Riley" were both "halyard songs," used for raising the sails, especially the topsails and topgallants, but "Cheerily Men" was also used for pulling in the anchor. Thus they would most likely have been heard at the beginning of a voyage, not at the end, which is when they appear in Alderson's narrative. Alderson might also have been familiar with "Cheerily Men" from Richard Henry Dana's immensely popular *Two Years Before the Mast* (1840), where it seems to have been one of the most frequent and popular chanteys. Stan Hugill describes "Cheerily Men" as "probably the most primitive and one of the oldest of all the heaving and hauling songs of the sea. It was obscene to a degree and most versions have had to be camouflaged, although . . . the very fact that it was sung in passenger-carrying ships . . . proves without doubt that it had clean words, since indecent shantying was tabu aboard passenger sailing vessels." Stan Hugill, *Shanties from the Seven Seas: Shipboard Work-Songs and Songs Used as Work-Songs from the Great Days of Sail*, 2nd ed. (London: Routledge & Kegan Paul, 1984), 233–234. I have found no published version of this song resembling what Alderson describes, but improvisation was common and a hallmark of a good chanteyman. "Pretty Sally" was not a work song but a "forebitter," a song reserved for social time.

Philadelphia is about 90 miles. We came within sight of the city about 4 oclock.

I forgot to tell thee dearest mother that about 6 miles below, the ship came to anchor ~~and a s~~ on what [7] is called the quarantine ground, & a surgeon came on board to examine the crew & passengers; every one, young & old, was summoned on deck & ready if need be to undergo personal inspection, but it appeared to us a mere form. As far as we went, we were counted to see that all were there and dismissed. As soon as the ship came along side the wharf, every passenger was required to leave, taking only their night clothes. The greater part of the crew left & the ship was locked up & only a watch retained.

Thomas Rutledge & his niece, the medical man I mentioned before as cabin passengers, had proposed to join us in our soujourn in Philadelphia, & that we shall travel forward as far as Pitsberg in company. They are going to Indiana. The Dr. & Harrison left us in the vessel & went in search of lodgings for us. In a short time they returned with a coach, & we were once again rejoiced & thankful to be under a roof on solid ground.

Now my dearly beloved mother I have tried to give the[e] something like a regular account of our adventures. I fear thou wilt have thought me trifling, but I have thought all was novel to you \as/ ~~&~~ well as myself & therefore would bear telling once at least. Besides, the ways & doings of an emigrant ship are really full of life & character, not the stately monotonous life of the first cabin, but the steerage & lower cabin, where people act independently & have to do for themselves; had we been out a week longer most in our quarters would have been without provisions excepting biscuits; many of the steerage were really wanting. I would another time bring an extra supply of comforts, cheese, ham, fruit, sugar & treacle. If you do not want them, there is sure to be somebody that does & will be thankful to buy. Our cream kept admirably & was the wonder of all; the steward often came to beg some for Capt West's coffee, & he himself requested to have the receipt. We were at sea 6 weeks except 1 day.

21st Yesterday Harrison brought me word there was a letter lying for me at Wm Evans'. H. was too much engaged to call that evening, but this morning he went & greatly to my joy brought dear Anna's most kind & welcome letter. I cannot express to you the pleasure it afforded me to see her hand writing & hear of & from you. I have felt since landing almost a heart sickness when I thought of you; perhaps I have had more leisure to think & feel, but a heavy sense of the reallity of having parted from you has made me often very sad. Indeed I seldom think of you without a feeling of such intense affection that it is painful. Every thing that reminds me of you appears almost sacred and too precious to be laid with and used as common things.

I long, my beloved mother, to receive a letter from thee and I hope, dearest Anna, thou wilt try to spare time from thy many engagements to write regularly & [8] tell me every thing about yourselves. You are the most interesting subjects upon which you can write. Give my endeared love to Daniel, Mary & Margaret Ann & the rest of the dear children, also to cousin Lucy Bayliff & her interesting family. The book Alice so kindly gave to W. C. has delighted us all. I have often remembered their great kindness & shall continue to do so.

Please, dearest mother, give our love to cousin Margaret Abbott; I intend to write to her as soon as I can find leisure, but you all know how little time I have for writing. This letter is all I can possibly prepare to go by the packet, but I intend to keep one constantly on hand to forward by such opportunities as occur.

The friends as far as we have seen are very kind & agreeable. W. Evans seems to be a very nice man; he came to our lodgings with Harrison & invited us most cordially to his house. If I can manage it we are to go & dine with them tomorrow. He said if he & his wife had not been leaving town, he would have had us all at his house. ~~he~~ Soon after leaving us a brother of Thos Hodgson called & a friend named Benjamin Warder & his wife, who invited us to tea.

We went after dinner to the exchange & took an omnibus to convey us to the Water Works, called Fair Mount. It is a beautiful place on the Sculkill [Schuylkill] & supplies the city with the finest water in abundance. The temples & statues which ornament the place are of white marble & look beautiful amongst the bright green foliage of the trees, some of which are quite new to me. Amongst the wild flowers we saw was a pretty little yellow snapdragon, the lesser michealmass daisy & in waste-places the stramoniums grows as nettles & thistles do with us. We passed up Chesnut Street & were at length satisfied we were in Philadelphia; the white marble steps, door ways & fronts of the houses are glitteringly pure & beautiful. The handles of the doors, which are all white, are silver or plate, as are all the metal about them. You, with me, would be pleased to see how green & fresh the trees & grass look; the scenery from Fair Mount reminded me of a gentleman's park in England.

We find provisions much lower even in Philadelphia than with us: beef is about 3^{d} a lb, \good brown/ sugar 3^{d}, butter 9^{d}, flour uncommonly cheap. We have the best bread & butter I ever eat in abundance, very good potatoes & other vegatables and 4 joints of meat to choose at at dinner, hot beef steaks at breakfast, cold meat & eggs at tea & pay for our board & lodging half a dollar a head a day.

But I must conclude as my time is very short. Harrison went last evening to B. Warder's to tea. He was delighted with their kindness and cordiality & describes their style of living as most beautiful for cleanliness & simplicity. They had amongst other good things stewed oysters & honey in the comb. I hope to get Sarah Perkins to take charge of this; dear Anna will read it & forward it to mother.

My endeared love is with you; Harrison sends his kindest love; give mine to the Ords, Edmondsons, Bensons & all enquirers. Farewell my beloved

Friends & believe me to be, in love which neither time nor distance can diminish, your warmly attached & affectionate daughter & sister,

Emma Alderson

Excuse all faults, I have written when & how I could, often on a box.

3. To Ann Botham and Mary Howitt, September 1842
Philadelphia 9th mo

My very dear Mother and Sister,
Since our arrival in this city we have been much surprised to find the weather really cold, so chilly that we should be glad to have a fire, but our inn room has no fireplace & it would be too much trouble to set up the stove. Therefore we have been obliged to unpack & get warmer clothing & be willing to shiver on.

The coal burnt here is very peculiar: it burns without flame or smoke & looks, when ignited, like a fireplace full of heated stones. What would you think of placing pies to bake & meat to roast uncovered on a shelf at the back of the fire, literaly in the chimney? Yet so our dinners are cooked & are most excellent. When a greater degree of heat for such purposes is required, a large plate of iron called the blower is drawn down over the front of the chimney & fire, & the heat becomes intense.

Washing here is a most extravagant price. I got a few things for the children washed yesterday, & for 18 articles actually paid a dollar: 75 cents a dozen is the usual charge.

Harrison has found the government officers most accomodating: we have not had to pay duty on a single article. They seemed afraid of giving trouble & in many instances took Harrison's word without any examination. Last evening we spent at B[essie] Warder's. I was much pleased with the appearance of all that we saw. <The> house was covered as far as we saw with Indian matting <??age>[11] stair-case, parlours, which opened one into the other <*torn*> with folding doors, there was a handsome mahogany <*torn*> <in each> room & chairs of some light wood beautifully <polished> with cane seats, the walls were papered <with> most delicate paper, almost white. There were no ornaments except a time piece on one chimney piece in a white marble case & a glass of flowers on the other. All was exquisitely neat & elegant but very plain.

We have purchased a piece of Indian matting. The piece consists of 40 yds at 40 cents a yard. Harrison has bought a stock of tea at 45 cents a pound and coffee at 11 cents. We find that, with the exception of clothing, everything we have purchased is as cheap & cheaper than in England: combs, buttons, brushes, german wool, netting <*torn*> &c we have bought considerably lower than we could with you. Books also—I went to a shop this afternoon

11. The manuscript is badly torn here, obscuring several words.

to purchase a botanical work, and saw Strive & Thrive, for which I paid 35 cents, about equal to 1/6.[12] They say all dear Mary's writings have been reprinted here.

The flowers in the glass at B. W.'s were white roses, the bigonia & scarlet Salvia, all of which were gathered in the open air. Fruit this season is considered scarce & not good; we have, however, bought fine peaches at about 1[ct] each & a small basket of apples for 2 ¼. There is a very great variety of productions, vegetables & fruits, some of which are entirely new to me. Tomatos are a very favourite article: you see them on every stand. They are stewed & eaten with meat & said to be very wholesome. There are water melons, pumpkins, melons, pepers, green Indian corn, sweet potatoes, grapes, nuts, peaches, apples, pears, plums & more than I can think of or name.

[2] The shops of Philadelphia are mostly wholesale shops where you can meet with the greatest choice in the articles kept & purchase at wholesale price. The retail shops are abundantly supplied, and we have been struck with the civility & in many instances kindness of the people. Different friends from time to time call upon us and appear very friendly & disposed to show us kindness. There is a heartiness in their manner that makes one feel they are sincere in their professions.

Farewell, my beloved Friends; I shall look anxiously for letters from you. You will be pleased to hear we are all, with the exception of colds, quite well. Our luggage went yesterday by the luggage trains to Pittsburgh. Richard & the young men of Thos. Rutledge's party left this morning with the remainder, & we ourselves propose to go on second day by the swift train, which reaches in 3 days.

I am hurried and must conclude. Harrison & Elizabeth desire their dear love to you all. W. C. and Agnes send their love to dear grandmother & aunt. I am, with very warm affection, your ardently attached daughter & sister,

Emma Alderson

4. To Ann Botham and Anna Harrison, October 7, 1842

Maple Grove near Brownsville 10th mo 7th 1842

My very dear Mother and Sister,

For to you both I shall address myself, knowing you are equally interested in our welfare, and as I have little time for writing I need not curtail my communication in order to write separate letters, knowing, dearest Anna, that as soon as thou hast read this thou wilt forward it to our beloved mother. Oh, how continually are you the subject of my thoughts, and the sense that we are so widely divided gives a melancholy cast to my feelings that otherwise I should not feel.

12. Mary Howitt, *Strive and Thrive: A Tale* (London: Thomas Tegg, 1840) was one of the first books in Howitt's series of Tales for the People and Their Children.

I may truly say my heart aches for love. What would I not now give for a sight of you, to enjoy again the dear privilege of your society? It seems to me now that all worldly things are worthless in comparison. The enjoyments and advantages of our present situation are outward: they satisfy not the heart. I may and probably shall feel differently in a while, but at present this seems to prevail over all, and yet how much have we to excite our warmest gratitude to our Heavenly Father, who has mercifully preserved us & permitted us to arrive in safety at our destination.

Last 7th day evening we reached Bealsville, where brother Ralph [Alderson] resides, & were kindly & cordially received, though not expected, as the letter H. wrote at Philadelphia had not reached [him] & therefore they were waiting in a state of daily suspense, not knowing what to think; our reception amongst our relatives has been most kind & affectionate. We are now at brother Wm Mason's where we are to remain till we take possession of a house Harrison has taken for 6 months. The family I am much pleased with. W. M. is a very kind, agreeable man. Sister Alice is one that I felt I could love as soon as I saw her; she is much like her mother and looks so kind and motherly that I have told her I should call her mother instead of sister.

The family at home consists of three grown up daughters & one younger one about 9 and two fine, intelligent looking sons. There is nothing vulgar or coarse about them; they have not the polish of educated people \but/ are nevertheless so neat & orderly in their appearance and house, so peaceful & kind, one to the other, that I quite rejoice in the knowledge of such relatives & look forward with pleasure to the prospect of living near them.

The country here is most beautiful, far surpassing anything I had imagined. It is, for America, highly cultivated, but wood still is the prevailing feature in the scenery. The country is hilly and presents most beautiful & varied landscapes; there is a noble line of forest marking the course of the river Monongahla; there are in the distance blue mountains & the whole face of the country as you look down upon it from an elevation is one continuation of farms, whose bright green fields & newly ploughed lands contrast well with the remains of wood which more or less are found on all. The farmhouses, many of them log & some stone & brick, have an air of comfort and a quiet home-stead look that reminds me forcibly of dear England. There only wants a spire or old grey tower to complete the picture & make it the loveliest sylvan scene that the eye could rest [2] upon, illumined with such bright sunshine and a \sky/ so clear & blue that there is nothing left to desire. The trees are just assuming their autumnal tints & much as I have heard of their briliancy of colour, it is far beyond my utmost expectation. We have seen them of the very brightest crimson, orange & yellow & green mingled in rich masses most exquisitely.

How often I have wished you could even for half an hour have beheld the fine scenery that we were continually beholding. Dear Daniel, weary with the bustle of business, what a refreshment it would be to his spirit to come here. We often say how much he would enjoy it & that this is truly a land to satisfy every hearty lover of nature who longs for escape from the turmoil of towns & town-life. I almost think dear mother might get very comfortably & safely across; I should fear nothing for her but the overland journey.

Though we were only five days in coming from Philadelphia, it seems to me the most formidable part of our travel, certainly much the most fatiguing. I shall try to give you some account of it but fear I cannot convey anything like a regular detail as I had no opportunity to write on the spot. We staid at P. a week & received on all hands the greatest kindness and the most marked attention. Amongst our friends was a brother of Thos. Hodgson, who was very kind. I should like you to tell him how much we felt his kindness. Our callers & invitations were numerous, but it would only occupy time to rehearse names of persons you do not know.

On second-day morning we left the city by railway to Harrisburgh, about 90 miles. The country was pleasant & some of the Dutch settlements beautiful specimens of neat & good husbandry, the houses in perfect order and, though stiff & devoid of ornament, admirable for their cleanliness & neatness. With all their capability, the American houses are externally as ugly and tasteless as it is possible—no creepers up the porch or verandah, no garden, often no tree near them. They look as bare & unsightly as may be. The people have a very good & worthy practice of sunning their bedding as they call it, so that you will often see a feather bed & sheets & blankets hanging out of the upper windows, which of course are very suitable but not very elegant accompaniments to a white or brick red frame house.

The railway cars, as they are called, are dreadful vehicles, great long carriages which will probably hold 40 or 50 with seats formed to hold two individuals, but then they must be two thin spare Yankeys, no good, well fed John Bull & his portly lady could possibly squeez into them. We were miserably cramped with our journey, & yet not over large any of us. As we approached the Susqueanah, the scenery became interesting & beautiful; the broad, bright but languid looking river was studded with wooded islands and reflected on its glassy surface the trees on their margin & oposite banks. It was a scene that reminded me of some bright Italian or Indian river. There was nothing English here: the maise was towering eight or ten feet in the fields by the road sides, crowned with [3] its graceful tufts of feathers. The trees, of which I did not know the names, wore a foreign aspect, and the houses visible were log of a very mean description.

At Harrisburgh we entered the Packet boat, our party about 50 persons. The fare was good & every one very agreeable. As a specimen of our entertainment I shall give you our bill of fare one morning at breakfast: at the top was a beef steak, next eels, then roast chicken, sausage, salt fish, stewed fowl & eels with bread, butter, cheese, \tomato, pickled beet,/ tea, coffee &c. The

Americans take only three meals a day—breakfast, dinner & supper, which are in fact three dinners. It did not suit us, and we are glad to return to plainer living.

Towards evening the canal approached the Susqueanah, and we were delighted with the beauty of the scene. The banks are, on the oposite side, steep & wooded to the water's edge, & the windings of the stream with its numerous islands present a constant succession of interesting objects.

After sunset we crossed the river; the bridge over which the horses went is a mile in extent. I wish I could convey to you an idea of this scene. The red light of the sky, on which the beams of the sun were reflected, tinged the waters, and the evening star, like a small bright moon, was visible on the surface. The woods, the river, the whole scene was exquisite, & we stood in silent admiration when one of the passengers—a thorough American—came up & said "now this is pretty ugly I guess." We stared, & he repeated his remark with gravity. In truth it was his way of saying it was more than commonly beautiful.

Our rout for the following day lay through similar scenery by the course of the Junietta, a lovely mountain river. Sometimes we sailed on the canal and sometimes on the river. The hills became more mountainous, but all covered to their summits with wood. Occasionally a turn in the stream would present an opening up [of] the mountains, some deep valley bounded by more distant wooded hills, or chains of distant mountains contrasting finely with the rich greenness of the nearer ones.

About ten o'clock on the third day of our journey we reached Holliday'sburg where we left the boats & again entered the railway cars in order to cross the Allaganhys. To describe the scenery is beyond my power. The first part of our journey we ascended by a succession of inclined planes and accomplished our descent in the same manner. Our track lay on the side of the mountain; below us were deep valleys and frightful precipices all around, mountains over mountains, most sublimely beautiful, all covered with noble trees, some in the last stages of decay, bare & leafless, others glowing with the rich tints of autumn & others vividly green like the first fruits of spring.

On the very summit of the Allagahny range is a tract of cleared land, a good hotel, & aparently every accomodation for the traveler. The time for flowers is over, but I observed on our route an elegant bright lilack michaelmass daisy which beautified the rocks and banks. There was also what I took to be an orange ranunculus, the perennial sunflower, the evening primrose, and as we crossed the mountains, I observed Virginian raspbery in flower & fruit, the Shumach, the arbor vita, the Rhododendron in great quantities, the Azalea, the locust, and many of our rare & beautiful exotics. We passed one beautiful mountain stream whose banks were fringed with the very luxuries of vegetation: tall stately Shumach, thickets of Azalea & Rhododendron, the Virginia & other creepers, the acacia, and many other very beautiful trees & plants. It was to me a most interesting and delightful journey, & I much wished [4] some of my dear friends in England had been there to enjoy it with us. We were much struck with the appearance of the uprooted trees; I do not think the circumference of the largest trees was above 6 yds & the earth & roots did not appear above an foot in thickness: I have seen many a little rose bush in England deeper rooted.

We again entered the boat at a place called John's town. Before it was light a young woman of colour came in; she was going to school at Pittsburgh; she was well-dressed & good looking and of agreeable manners, yet she sat apart &, unnoticed, was not invited to take breakfast until the first & second table had finished & then had to take her place with the servants. This was repeated at every meal. I asked some if this was intentional & was told none but the very meanest would condescended to eat with the blacks, that it was necessary to keep them at a distance, & such-like stuff. We spoke very freely on the subject & were marked in our attentions to the poor girl. It is deplorable how deeply & widely this feeling prevails. A friend told me that they did not encourage, I think the expression was ["]did not admit,["] any of this people into membership for fear of connexions being formed. It is a flimsy reason to screen a great injustice. Yet friends are decidedly amongst their best friends & have many benevolent institutions devoted to their interests.

We staid a day & two nights at Pittsburgh. I can scarcely suppose that the best hotels in London are more superbly fitted up, better served & appointed, than the Monongahela House where we staid. It contains 250 rooms & is a perfect specimen of order & good management; they all said the table was excellent. I was unwell & not able to leave my room, but do not be alarmed: I am now, I am thankful to say, in perfect health, and so are the children & highly delighted with every thing here. It is a complete farm, with all the abundant luxury of this fine country but none of the wasteful extravagance we have witnessed & deplored.

I am sorry I must conclude: my paper is exhausted, but I shall probably write again to leave at the same time with this, for I have yet a deal to tell you. I was delighted, my best beloved mother, to receive thy welcome letter on my arrival, as also the one from cousin Margaret & dear Mary. Give our dear love to all our endeared friends. Harrison is down at Pittsburgh; I expect him back tomorrow.

My dearest love to Danl & the dear children; accept a large share yourselves from your tenderly attached daughter & sister,

Emma Alderson

I am writing in our bedroom which is a little log-house adjoining brother's house. It has two windows & fronts the river, the banks of which are splendid in the tints of autumn. It is a lovely little spot & we sleep with the door unlocked: there is not a lock or bolt or window fastener on the premises.

5. To Daniel and Anna Harrison, November 30, 1842
nr. St. Clairsville Ohio 11th mo 30.

My very dear Brother & Sister,
Very much against our wish do I date this letter in Ohio. We came here about ten days ago to see our relations & friends in this part, accompanied by sister Alice Mason & bringing baby with us; the other two children we left under the care of two of our neices at Westland, our present home. Up to the time of leaving, the weather was mild & pleasant: the 1st of this month was warm and bright like a september day in England, and we continued to enjoy the Indian Summer for near two weeks. All assured us winter would not set in till near christmas, but to the disappointment of all it is set in with unusual severity, and we are weather bound at the house of our kind friends Wm Harrison & family, who have shown us every kindness during our week's stay with them.

In the first instance Harrison "took sick" as they say here. He caught a violent cold in going to Mount Pleasant last 7th day week and had a severe attack of sore throat. We had the doctor attending & I am thankful to say he is now convalescent. As far as he is concerned we might travel, but the intense frost is now followed by a heavy fall of snow. We are very anxious to get home, but the roads for a few days will be impassable for a wheeled carriage, and the Ohio with its masses of floating ice is between us and our children. So I try to be patient & think as well of our situation as I can, hoping all is going on well, & employing myself in working & writing to my beloved friends.

Our first visit was to thy aunt Sarah, dear Daniel. We found her quite an invalid in bed; her complaint is supposed to be an attack of water on the chest, but during our stay she became so much better as to be able to sit up most of the day. She is a fine old woman and gave us a kind welcome, but poor thing, she sadly wants a caretaker. Her comfort would be greatly increased by having some kind, attentive young person with her. She mentioned to me her wish for Alice to come: do you think it would do? She has a neice, a daughter of Mary Hustler, with her, but I do not think she makes, her very comfortable. Her daughter in law, when she can be with her, is kind & affectionate. Her home is with her own mother at Mount Pleasant. We saw her there and were much pleased with her. You were subjects of interest to them and to me. It was delightful to be with them as we could converse about you.

John Thompson is unmarried & living with his mother; he is a thorough old batchelor. Poor Sarah, she seems to have little to cheer her in her downward course. She frequently expressed a desire to hear from Daniel; she said she prized Anna's correspondence very much, but she should much like a letter from Danl himself. I hope he will write and that soon.

Hanna's son Thomas Harrison is living with Sara Thomasson; he is a nice lad about 12 I should think. When we were there, he had begun to go to school for the winter season.

Do you remember Wm Harrison & his family coming to this land? His sister Mary & married daughter joined them a few years after. They remember you & your kindness to them at Liverpool with affectionate gratitude. It would do you good to see them now and the abundance & comfort in [2] which they live. William has an estate (clear) of about 100 acres in the same valley as the Thomasson's. It is a wild spot; a small river called Little Mackmarrow Creek runs through it & the hills ascend almost immediately from its banks. There is very little bottom land, mostly wood near the water, but every cleared spot in the valley & on the hills is highly productive and William is a good manager. Their house is log cased with frame with a broad porch, or verandah, in front & looks & is very comfortable. There are good barns & sheds and close at hand a little log house which her father has built for Elizabeth, who is a widow, to reside in. Poor Betty is a helpless cripple but very cheerful & remembers Daniel well when he was a boy. They have plenty of every good thing, horses, cows, sheep, poultry, pigs; grow their own wool, spin & weave it both for their own use & for sale. When we were there they killed a cow mostly for their own use. That that was sold went for 2 cents per lb. Mary told us they had 13 hogs as big as jackasses ready to kill, all for themselves. It is astonishing the quantity of animal food the Americans consume: every farmer kills from ten to fifteen fat pigs besides a cow, and they have fowls without count to take whenever they fancy to have them. Turkeys are also abundant: we could buy a very fine one for 25 cents, a quarter of a dollar.

Indeed the cheapness & excellence of provisions is, I think, a snare to the people. Every meal is like a dinner, hot meat, pies & preserves being constantly on the table. We have sate down to supper, which is the evening meal, equivalent to our tea, at a farmer's table, when there a hot turkey & cold pork, apple pie, cheese, butter, bread, cakes, pickles, five different kinds of preserves, tea & coffee at table. When we are at home we adhere to our plain English style of living & very much prefer it.

Whilst Harrison was ill, Thompson came over twice to see him. He appeared very kind & wished us to call to see them on our return, which we did. He lives at Martinsville on the Ohio almost opposite Wheeling. He is out of a situation and thinks of going in the spring to Iowa, a vast tract beyond the Mississippi to which great numbers are going. It is probable he may do well but his means are limited; I fancy the loan or gift of 30 or 40 £ would be very acceptable & a real kindness. I thought perhaps cousin Smith would do as much for him.[13] Tell him this from me and, if done, the sooner the better as it would facilitate his plans greatly. Thompson said nothing to me nor I to him on the subject, but I felt interested for him and his family and thought I would mention it. His wife is a nice woman: they have but one child: the two oldest have died.

13. Probably Thompson and Daniel's brother Smith Harrison.

Thomson is an ingenious & intelligent man; he is a good cabinet maker & indeed seems to be able to employ himself in many ways. For 5 years he was clerk in two concerns in Wheeling, both of which failed & in each case his surplus wages were lost so that he seems to have been peculiarly unfortunate. I believe he has a good character for integrity & is now employed in winding up the concerns of a friend in Martinsville; he complains sadly of your silence.

I do hope, dear Daniel, thou wilt write [3] to him: it would do his heart good to hear from you. Oh, none can tell but those that have experienced it how the heart yearns & aches in a land of strangers towards those we have left behind; it is a feeling which returns again & again. It was hard to part, but the realization of it is not complete till we sit down in our distant home, & in the quietness of our solitary moments, the remembrance of those we most dearly love is continually with us. I can truly say I think of you & dearest mother incessantly and seldom can speak of you without tears; you are inexpressibly dear to me, and the earth & its things have lost their shine in parting from you; yet I would not retrace our steps. I feel fully satisfied, as far as I can judge, that for ourselves & especially for our precious children, if we are spared to them, we have done wisely in coming, and though, as Harrison & I have sometimes said when talking of you, all this heart anguish must be borne: it is a necessary consequence of leaving our native country & near & dear friends. Yet we have much to be thankful for, much to excite our love & gratitude to that kind good Providence, whose protecting care we have so eminently experienced. From first to last we have mercies to commemorate; things have fallen out wonderfully for us: here we are in a good comfortable house, the very one in all the country side most convenient for us, being only about a quarter of a mile from meeting & having much more of comfort & accommodation than is usual in this land. We keep a cow, & Harrison has a very fine horse, but at present we have neither carriage, carriole nor sleigh. We find the friends very kind; many of them are extremely so &, though somewhat uncouth & homely externally, I like them better the more I know of them. The men almost all wear clothing manufactured at home, and the winter clothing of the women is of the same description. I am now wearing a dark brown flannel dress of domestic manufacture, & our children are all clothed in the same article. Charlie's trousers are plaid.

One day we went to pay a visit to an old Friend who had often invited us. The house is one end log & the other an addition of stone; we found all in apple-pie order for a flannel kicking. The parlour, in which stands the old man's bed, had a large bright fire, the rag carpets looked well swept, & the tables were covered with clean white cloths. In the kitchen large vessels were standing full of soft water, like a preparation for a great wash. We were invited to stay the evening but on account of the children we could not, so R[ichard] alone remained. He said that about 8, ten or a dozen men came in, neighbours who had been invited. The flannel, which was a piece of 40 yds length of their own growing, spinning, dying & weaving, was soaked & well lathered with soap of their own make & thrown smoking hot upon the floor. The men arranged themselves with naked legs around it & began to kick it violently till it was in a foam. For near two \hours/ this was continued & after being rinsed it was stretched & rolled wet & left for the night. All was then cleared away & a good substantial supper provided.

The Americans make their own soap & candles and spin & weave both wool & flax. Their carpets are home made & some of them very comely; they are made of narrow strips of wollen rags cut & sewed together for the weft &, if they have plenty, of old red flannel peticoats to mingle with the more sober brown, which is commonly died with walnut husks. It make a very pretty clouded carpet [4] & lasts well.

Then they are most industrious bed quilt makers & most ingenious in patching & arranging them. It seems quite a science: there is the rising sun pattern, the pine tree, the fruit basket & an endless variety which I cannot name. The quilting of some of these is most beautiful; every young woman has a store of them. I heard of one woman who had 100 quilts & the same number of pairs of sheets.

They are very sociable: they have quiltings & corn huskings & apple parings; we had our apple paring & 4 young women came & staid two days with us to pare our apples & make the apple butter. This is excellent; I wish I could send you one of our large "crocks"—I think it must contain two gallons.

I have received two long & most interesting letters from dearest mother since our return. Oh, what delight does a letter afford. Do write often: I long to hear from you.

I am very anxious about dear mother: I fear she is not comfortable. Could you not, dear brother & sister, take a larger house & let her have a room in it where she could live & occasionally mingle with the family as might suit her? She can well afford to pay for any expence you might incur in this arangement. Oh, that she could come to us—how I should delight to make her comfortable & happy. It makes my heart ache to think of her latter days being embittered for want of a comfortable home.

Give my dearest love to Mary & Margaret Ann & the dear boys—I often think of them—and please give my love to cousin L Bayliffe & her family. Harrison unites in dear love to you all. He is now quite well; so are the children; baby walks; they often talk [1-*cross*] of you & their grandmother to whom they would like to send many things.

I think you might send this to mother: it perhaps would interest her. I often wish I had time to write oftener to her but as we are at present without a servant I have very little leisure.

My dearest dearest love to her & now, my dear brother & sister, farewell & in the war[m]est affection, believe me to be your tenderly attached sister,

Emma Alderson

[4] We are expecting Thompson over to see us shortly with his wife & child. H. had a letter from him in which he desired if we wrote we would give his love to you. Remember my message to Smith with my love. Do write soon. I <*torn*> once more farewell; I want to know how you are <go-*torn*> remember I am your [*cross*] deeply interested sister. Elizabeth is residing at present with brother Ralph; she is but invalidish.

6. To Ann Botham, January 16 to February 24, 1843

My dear & honoured parent,
Last week I dispatched a letter concluded by Harrison for thee, by our Friend William Evans of Philadelphia who has been paying a religious visit to this Yearly Meeting, Ohio, and was then on his return.[14] I was not myself able to attend the meeting he had with friends at Westland, but Harrison discribed it as a remarkable season; he bore a very decided & full testimony to the divinity of Christ and the precious doctrine of the atonement. His denunciations of the heresy of Hicksism were bold & faithful and his warnings to those who were congratulating themselves in an orthodox profession yet serving themselves & the world and seeking to add field to field & wealth to wealth were equally fearless & uncompromising. He is a fine man, spiritually & intellectually, and we had a great treat in the evening in spending about two hours in his society at Mildred Baleliffe's; he called upon us in the morning and really I felt sad when he left.

The greatest lack which we experience at present is intelligent society. The friends here are worthy kind people, but I feel as if I longed for intercourse with well read & polished people; we may probably find some such in the course of time or become reconciled to those about us. I feel we have great cause for thankfulness in the comfort of our own fireside; so long as we are spared to each other & have our children about us, we should be more than satisfied.

It would have amused thee could thou have seen us going to M. B.'s by moonlight; \two of/ our nieces hast come up to the meeting on single horse. One of them rode behind me on the quiet steed on which I have hitherto taken my lessons in horsemanship; Harrison mounted behind the other & thus we were spared traversing roads nearly shoe deep in mud. When we returned, they were some-what hardened by the frost. I do not know if I told thee that when I came from Wm Mason's to our present house, brother Wm brought me & our luggage in a cart drawn by oxen preceded by a horse. It looked rather strange to see the slow unwieldy creatures dragging us along and I wished thou couldst have seen us. The roads at this time of the year are very muddy; nobody thinks of walking & therefore it is of little consequence, but to us it is a privation. I must, however, except the turnpike which

14. This letter is missing.

is almost as good as or moderated roads in England. We traveled 60 miles in our journey to Ohio on good road that almost made me feel as if we were in our native land; the roads about us are bye and formed of limestone clay which in summer is hard & firm.

This is the 16th of 1st mo and a glorious day it is: the sun has shone without a cloud ever since we rose, the children are playing on the green, baby is trotting about in the porch, whilst I am sitting with the door open enjoying the pure fresh air. I have been sitting this morning reading out of doors; it is just like a warm April day in England. We took a stroll into the orchard & Agnes gathered a handful of seed vessels of different plants & some moss for "dear grandmother." She thought she would be 'pleased' with them. Harrison is gone to see a place on the other side of Brownsville which is offered for for sale.

[Jan] 17th Another bright delicious day; thermometer stood in the shade in the open air at 60; in the sun about noon, 100. We feel as if we could live out of doors.

2nd mo 2nd. The pleasant weather above alluded to continued about a week &, like the birds in the fable, we began to talk of spring & hoped that winter was quite gone, but wiser people told us otherwise & so it is. The cold has returned & rain, snow & frost, with the thermometer about 20 deg. below freezing which seems even more intolerable than before. One comfort is the existence of cold seldom lasts; a few days will probably bring another change. Whilst the weather was mild those who were intending to make maple sugar commenced their operations; a friend brought us a very beautiful specimen of sugar made in a camp about a mile distant the day before. It was a clean clear light brown resembling good 8° sugar in England.

On first-day George & Ruth Smith staid on their return from meeting & spent the evening with us. They were telling us about the process of making this sugar; they said they had sometimes made 600 cwt in a season, that one tree they tapped ran 22 gals of water in the course of the day; the sap does not flow at night.[15] The strength is greatest at the commencement of the season than later on, but on an average it requires about 7 gals to make a pound of sugar; only think of the amazing power of absorption in these trees.

The father of George Smith was one of the first settlers in this part; he showed us the step of the first meeting-house built so far west & called Westland as being the most outside station of Friends. It is about 55 years since they came; there were then 5 small clearings, all the rest was forest. At that time there were bears, wolves & panthers; he says they were obliged to make fires at night to preserve the sheep from the attacks of these creatures and

15. The British cwt, or hundredweight, is equal to 112 pounds. But one has to wonder if they really produced 67,200 pounds of sugar, requiring well over 500,000 gallons of sap. The letter of May 23, 1847, gives 20,000 pounds as the amount made in what "was considered a good season."

he remembers seeing the dogs driven over the fence near the house by a pack of wolves which durst not venture farther. The wild deer have disappeared with the Indians, but both were then not unfrequent visitors. The original house of the family was what is now our back kitchen: a small log house, in those days a very superior abode, as it has glazed windows & an upper story.

So George Smith is a worthy man; his habits & opinions are simple & primitive. He has a best bed [that] is reserved for all strangers from the travelling minister [2] to the poor black man who may ask food & a lodging in his way from place to place. They told us last week an Irish pedlar had requested & obtained their hospitality. It is not unusual to refuse such requests. Wm Harrison seemed to think their credit was almost at stake when obliged to decline taking \in/ a man with cattle when we were there. I have enquired from many and find it is a common practice though sometimes such kindness has been abused. Only a few evenings ago, about dusk, a man called and asked us to take him in; his appearance was anything but agreeable, so Harrison declined. He accepted of some food but appeared so angry that I was frightened & almost expected he would return and set the house on fire or some mischief, but there is a power to restrain even the wickedness of wicked men.

2nd mo 5th: Yesterday we attended Redstone Quarterly Meeting held this time at Brownsville, or Redstone, as the Meeting house is called. It was very cordial to see the kindness of the Friends, many of whom were to us strangers. They flocked about Harrison on the men's side & me on the women's and seemed anxious by kind enquiries & invitations to make us sensible of their good will.

I was much pleased with the countenances of some who I expect to find on closer acquaintance very agreeable & companionable, but that which pleased me most was the sermon of a woman Friend, a minister belonging to a small meeting called Pike Burn[16] a few miles distant and a member of Westland Mo Meeting. Her name is Edith Griffith \now in the prime of life, comparatively a young woman/; she is a woman of a fervent mind & her views are clear & scriptural. She preaches the <u>whole</u> gospel, such sermons as the holy women of old might have delivered, those who were co workers with the Apostles to whom Christ was every thing, the author & finisher of their faith, the only ground of hope in life & in death. My heart is thankful for such ministry; how would dear Anna have rejoiced in hearing her.

16. The actual name was "Pike Run." Land for the Pike Run meeting-house was purchased in 1797 by a group of Friends that included David Graves (the first Quaker settler to the area) and Jacob Griffith, perhaps the father or grandfather of the Aldersons' friend Amos Griffith. Pike Run Meeting split into Hicksite and Orthodox, but the Hicksites built their own meeting-house on the same property. The Orthodox group met until sometime in the 1850s, at which time Amos Griffith and his family were the only remaining members. See Boyd Crumrine, ed., *History of Washington County, Pennsylvania: With Biographical Sketches of Many of Its Pioneers and Prominent Men* (Philadelphia: L. H. Everts, 1882), 991–992.

But Edith is no traditional Quaker; she was \not/ a minister before the separation &, sorrowful to say, all her near connexions—Father, Mother, brothers & sisters—~~took~~ embraced the views of Elias Hicks. They valued her highly & used every means to draw her & her husband to their party. On one occasion they assembled at their house & brought what they considered the most powerful writings of their leader. She heard \their arguments, took/ their pamphlets & the Bible & retired into the orchard where she spent the day in reading & comparing & on rejoining them told them whatever they might think, she believed them to be in great error & could not unite with them. Her husband attributes his preservation to her instrumentality. We have had the pleasure of her company on two occasions & find her very agreeable by the fireside.

Great as was the devastation in the Society at the time of the separation, when ministers, elders & often the great majority of many meetings fell away, I am inclined to hope good has come of it. I believe that those that remain are more sound and decided in consequence, and the ministry is of a much more enlightened & heart searching character. It is also gratifying to know that the Hicksites are dwindling: the younger branches have generally fallen off to the Methodists & other bodies & the old people are becoming very careless. They were a large body here, but the muster now at meeting is very small. Awful to say many who began with Hicksism have ended in open & avowed infidelity, but it is a natural consequence.

To do the Friends of this meeting justice I must tell thee, dear mother, that before the autumnal quarterly meeting, there was a general repairing of the meeting house & premises, which I mentioned to thee as looking so forlorn. The Friends assembled and worked at it <u>themselves</u>, repaired the sheds, glazed the windows, put up new out buildings & horse block & made all very complete. At the two Autumn Quarterly Meetings we attended, one here and the other at Mount Pleasant, both in Ohio yearly meeting, the minutes of the preceding \men's/ Yearly Meeting were read; they were in the form of a small pamphlet, a copy of which I have tried to procure to send to thee, but as there is only a small number printed I do not know if I can succeed. To me it was very interesting & I thought must be so to all who had not the privilege of attending the yearly meeting. I think the plan might be adopted to advantage in England.

Friends here are very exemplary in attending meeting: first-days are often crowded & on week-days there is generally a good muster; they seem to think of nothing but going as a thing of course. The Monthly Meetings are held at this place the year round; it is small, being composed of two preparative meetings: Westland & Pike Burn. I am thus particular dear mother because I think thou wilt like to know all about our present location.

Harrison finds great difficulty in deciding where to settle; there \are/ places on every hand for sale but on some accounts we cannot quite conclude to prefer this neighbourhood, and yet we do not know which way to look for better things. Therefore, as we have a comfortable home which I expect we may occupy during the summer, we are inclined to wait patiently, trusting, I hope not presumptuously, that we shall be enabled to see what is best & receive superior direction in what is to us and may be to our children a very serious step and one involving very important consequences.

8th: The weather continues very severe; the thermometer stood this morning 2 degrees below zero, but as it is dry and quiet, it is tolerable. When there is a wind with such cold it is dreadful; I can give it no other name. We are all quite well \except myself a cold/; indeed, I think the dryness of the air makes it healthful.

People are all out with their sleighs; to day Harrison said one friend and his wife came to meeting in a Yankee Jumper. These are very characteristic picturesque affairs; they are sleighs of the simplest construction being a few planks nailed together on which is fixed a rude seat; the runners & shaft are one entire piece of Hickory wood which is very pliant & are just chopped away at the bend to increase their elasticity. In these things they will sometimes undertake a long journey with their saddle at the bottom of the sleigh that should a change come & the snow fail, which is very frequent, they may throw the jumper to the road side &, mounting the [3] horse, pursue their journey.

I do not know whether I told thee but the Indians foretold a severe winter from the multitudes of Grey Squirrels migrating southward; they were observed crossing the rivers in immense numbers and the poor little creature were so spent that as they landed those who were watching them killed them with sticks without difficulty. I think I have before mentioned that squirrels are a dainty dish here.

15th: Many, many thanks my beloved Mother and Sister for your most kind, most welcome letters which both arrived the same day and made me feel so rich & happy that I seemed to walk in another atmosphere for some days. To thee, my dearest mother, who art so dilligent & regular in thy correspondence, I am indeed deeply indebted; thy letters are a great treasure & in thy last I felt comforted, hoping I could gather that thou art more comfortable, but dear mother if things have not <u>quite</u> mended with thee do \ change thy quarters/.

Oh that I were near as to do something toward enlivening & soothing thy path. I often feel distressed in the sense of the great distance that is between us when I see many things about us which I think thou wouldst like, and the children when they hear me express a wish that dear mother had this or that say, ["L]et us send it dear grandmother, I am sure it would please her[."] Wm Charles said the other morning he thought if he was to go for her, grandmother would come; \however I do feel assured neither Anna nor Mary will let thee long remain where thou art not comfortable/.

I am sorry my dear mother that thou hadst such difficulty in making out our crossed letters & the more so as the last we sent which thou wilt be about receiving now, was even more crossed, but thou shalt not have the same to complain of again. All the letters thou mentions have arrived for which accept my warmest thanks. Thou mentions Alfred looking ill; dear boy, I hope he is better; give my love to him and Charles. Tell dear Anna that we intend to have a garden and have rejoiced over the flower seeds that Jane Edmondson & William Albright put up for us.

I shall love to celebrate here what have been familiar favourites at home; I feel disposed to retain our English habits, tastes & pursuits as much as possible and this is purely English. The Americans have no idea of a pleasure garden; their notions are confined to a square inclosure at the back of the house in which they very diligently raise tomatos, beets, lima beans & cabbages. But there are none of the beautiful trees & shrubs of the country tastefully arranged about the house & the instances are very rare of even a creeper trained over it or around the verandah; in fact they seem to abhor trees & hills & when I hear them talk of a "pretty country" or a very handsome section of country, I am sure it is level & not overdone with timber.

It would be a very great pleasure to see dear Wm & Mary's last works; it feels a privation not to be able to have them, as I do not suppose they will be to be procured here; so dear friends, if you can forward them sometime, do. Books are a real treasure here & I rejoice in having a tolerable supply; it was quite a refreshment to me to see a handsome bookcase with some nice books at a friend[']s house. They are rarely seen, but remember, should you kindly comply with my request, you must cut the leaves & inscribe them.[17] I wrote to dear Mary about six weeks ago & requested her to continue their bounty to us as usual so you can forward our copies.

19th: We have this day had a very pleasant friendly visit from the Brownsville friends Eli & Pheobe Haynes; they came in their sleigh to dinner & afterwards accompanied us to meeting. They are very nice intelligent people and we purpose paying them a visit, when I expect I shall be able to tell thee a good deal about the Friends of Redstone meeting. P. H. said she had sympathized much with us, for in leaving the state of Maine, she had parted from a dear aged mother & all her near friends. It felt comfortable to me to hear such kind expressions; indeed it is a cause of thankfulness to see kind friends raised up on every hand. I do think there is no other society in which such universal brotherhood is felt; you must come to a foreign land amongst entire strangers to know the extent & value of this badge of true discipleship.

We find the natives of the eastern states very superior in intelligence & they have an air of refinement about them, a personal neatness that distinguishes

17. At this time, books were printed on large sheets of paper, eight or more pages to a single sheet. The sheets were then folded and bound into a book. The pages had to be separated with a knife before they could be read. By cutting the pages and writing in the book, Emma's relatives could make the books appear used; thus no import duty would be collected.

them from the old settlers of the West. Of course they have had advantages which the latter did not possess.

Perhaps I may repeat things in my letters, but dear mother excuse me if that is the case & also if there may appear some inconsistencies; as for instance at Philadelphia we found most things cheap & on moving here very dear; we now know that those eastern cities are the depots from whence the West is supplied with merchandise so that in the stores here we have to pay the expense of carriage & the profits of the shopkeeper which often are very exorbitant. Besides, as new comers, we \sometimes/ may see & hear things eroneously which, however, I shall try to correct when I discover that to be the case.

It is a very bright idea of thine, dearest mother, to send our share of Pottery property in earthenware; it would be most valuable, but alas I fear that is lost to the family as will never realize us even a cent each.[18] It is amazing how much less we can do with when we try; our whole stock of crockery would soon be told & yet we seem to have quite enough & often have company besides. But, "there is a heap in the mind" as one of our American friends said.

There are no invited parties, [4] no formal visiting here; if your friends come to see you or you go to see them it is quite unexpected. At first I did not like this; people were poping in to spend the day on baking or cleaning day, often at the last time that one would have chosen to wish for them. But I do not care now; I do as other people: finish my work & then set myself to entertain them & we choose to claim the privilege of being English & treating them as we like & generally appear to give satisfaction.

Last fifth day as we had finished breakfast, a stranger well dressed walked or rather staggered in & without apology seated himself by our parlour fire. When he could articulate, for he was benumbed & almost stupefied with cold, he told us he had walked some miles that morning & was going to a little town about 2 miles farther to see a relation & was so cold he wished to rest & warm himself. We made him a good breakfast & he appeared very grateful. In the afternoon a neighbour brought his wife & child \in/ his Yankee Jumper to take "supper" with us; all this was quite American & required no apology. I mention it to give thee an idea of the free unceremonious manners of the people.

Tell John Thwaite, dearest mother, with our love to him & Lucy, that we do not live in the same Quarterly Meeting as James; we are about 50 miles distant from St[e]ubenville. We have not heard anything particular of him; we forwarded his parcel & letter from Mount Pleasant when there. Please give my dear love to Benson's Sen. & Jun. I love them because they are kind friends

18. The reference to "pottery property" is obscure. It is conceivable that, coming from Staffordshire, the family owned shares in pottery works, but there is no record of this in the biographies.

to thee as well as for their own sakes, but I do seem to love with grateful affection those who show thee kindness & attention.

I have written & shall forward by the same post with this a letter for dear Anne Edmondson; I am surprized I never told Anna she was one of my most valued friends, one whom I have long loved & whom I have often remembered with warm affection since we parted. I am glad Anna knows & admires her; she is a very superior woman, a Cornelia, I think. Do continue to write, dearest friends; the worst evils of distance are removed by a constant regular correspo\n/dence. We seem to live in each other's hearts in fresh & vigorous love by these means & I sometimes forget the mighty ocean when I am writing to you or receiving one of your precious epistles.

Elizabeth is still a[t] Wm Mason's. Harrison desires me to give his dear love to thee & our united love is to the dear Family at Woodside. Please give our love to S. Ord & all enquirers. We are very sorry to hear of Peter Little[']s distresses; please, dear mother, give our love to Betsy; I feel much for her. Brother Ralph has been in difficulty lately, but it was in consequence of the state of the times. He had much more owing \him/ than his debts, yet when pressed to make up a sum, found it impossible & the law took its course. It led to investigations which appeared honourable on his part & has excited the sympathy & kindness of his friends. He has an excellent practice & is much respected, is steady & industrious; I hope he will do well. Please give our love to Margaret when thou hast opportunity; both Harrison & Elizabeth have written to her; as also H. to brother John.

I long for thy next letter; let it be very circumstantial about thyself. I had a dream about thee the other night that made me very sad; I thought I was with thee &, in a long embrace, felt thy dear arms around me & the touch of thy soft warm cheek. Oh, in absence like ours we have many a heart ache; there are anxious thoughts & dreams and vague reports and longings of unutterable love but, dearest mother, we live in each other's hearts & in eternity, towards which we are all hastening. These things will be swallowed up in everlasting joy.

[1[19]] Tell M. A. with my love that I hope to conclude a letter to her to leave by the packet that will convey this. I hope I have forgotten nothing. If thou hast not see[n] "Old Humphreys Thoughts for the Thoughtful" get it & I am sure it will be a treat to thee. I thought of thee in reading "Aged Christians."[20]

19. The letter returns here to the top margin of the first page.

20. George Mogridge's *Thoughts for the Thoughtful, by Old Humphrey* (London: Religious Tract Society, 1841) was published in New York the following year. "Aged Christians" is one of the chapters, an exemplary tale concluding with the following moral: "It is a pleasant thing to converse with the youthful Christian, while he drinks of the 'brook by the way,' and ardently pursues his heavenly course; but it is more abundantly profitable to hear the heart-pourings of the aged, who are on the threshold of eternity, and to whom the everlasting gates are about to be lifted up, that they may have an abundant entrance into everlasting life" (168–169). Mogridge was not a Quaker, but Quakers placed great emphasis on the exemplary

Harrison's dear love; Wm Charles & Agnes say give our love to Grandmother; with feelings of very near & warm affection I am, beloved mother, thy attached daughter,

Emma Alderson 2nd mo 24t

7. To Mary and Margaret Ann Harrison, March 27, 1843
Westland 3rd mo 27th 1843

My dear Girls,
As your dear Grandmother mentioned in her last letter her intention of visiting Woodside, I think probably if I address this to you and she still be with you, it will be as agreeable to her to hear from me through a letter addressed to you as if I wrote immediately to herself. I feel that to her all my letters are due, in an especial manner, though by dint of close application I have written to others. Yet she is my chief correspondent & I seem to look at persons and things very much with reference to her.

Oh, dear Mary & Margaret Ann, assiduously employ the opportunity you now possess of pleasing and serving your kind, good Parents; make it the study of your lives to oblige and serve them. The time may come, and probably will, when with aching hearts you will recall the many obligations you have received from them, when \the memory of/ every act of unkindness or neglect will be like the sting of a scorpion in your bosom, when you would give all you possess to regain the departed ability of soothing and comforting those dear ones. Let your own plans, your own pleasures, give way if there is something that ever may be done for Father or Mother. Excuse me, my dear neices, in saying never let your dear mother do anything that you can do for her, and honor and cherish with respectful tenderness your beloved grandmother, who has the double claim of parent and the consideration of advanced age to excite the affection & sympathy of us her children, besides her unwearied kindness, her devoted attachment, to engage our gratitude and love.

I know the kindness of your hearts, and in saying these things only wish to direct the affection with which they appear to overflow into that course of conduct which will afford you true peace under whatsoever circumstance Providence may assign you. There are few virtues so lovely as filial affection; it is I believe acceptable in the sight of God, of angels and of Men.

Have you observed the wonderful comet which has of late made it[s] appearance \in the west/[?] At least we did not notice it before the 6th of this month; it then looked like a long clear ray of light rising immediately out of the horizon.[21] It has gradually risen in the heavens till we can see the whole

power of death-bed scenes, as evidenced by Anna Mary Howitt's fictionalized illustration of the Alderson children at the death bed of Dr. Jack (see figure 28).

21. "The Great March Comet" appeared in the sky from February through March 1843. This spectacular comet was visible in broad daylight next to the sun. Although Alderson makes no mention of the fact here, the followers of William Miller interpreted the comet as confir-

tail, but hitherto we cannot discern any star or bulb from whence it proceeds. It must be a splendid phenomenon to produce such a ray. We understand astronomers assert that the unusual continuance of cold is in consequence of its attracting the heat of the sun from the earth. However this may be, the severity of the season is exciting many fears, and the oldest men assert they never knew such a season. Commonly spring has made considerable progress during this month; at present there is not a vestige of it. The earth is bound \up/ with hard frost & covered with deep snow. Yesterday, the 23rd, the thermometer stood at 6 above zero: it was extremely cold & the light snow was lifted up by the wind like dust and had often the appearance of mist in the distance.

There has an opinion prevailed for some time that the end of the world was at hand. This is called Millerism & in some parts of this country the idea is gravely entertained. In some districts we understand the inhabitants have neither ploughed nor sowed, stating that it was unnecessary labour; some have even terminated their existence in the dreadful anticipation. One woman near us destroyed herself, and another a few miles distant died from excessive fear occasioned by a distant fire.

There is no doubt but these are awful times; I sometimes feel my mind solemnized under the sense with such feelings as I experience in a thunderstorm. However, I feel assured with the times and seasons we have nothing to do: it is our place to seek by divine grace to experience preparation for the great change, whether the end of times to us is in the dissolution of our mortal bodies or of \the/ world itself. If we are but sheltering beneath the rock of Ages, whatsoever storm may beat, we are secure, and though the heavens should be rolled together as a scrowl & the elements melt with fervent heat, yet the sheep and lambs of the blessed fold of which Jesus is the Shepherd are safe and need never fear, calmly relying on his compassionate goodness, on his enduring love & omnipotence, ~~they~~ knowing themselves to be his in life & in death: they can and do feel that all is and will be well. Let us then, one and all, with loving & obedient hearts, submit to the enlightening, transforming influences of that Spirit of grace which reproves for evil & leads us on to glory and to virtue. By the blessed effects of this we shall be doubly rewarded, experiencing the peaceable spirits of righteousness in this life &, in the world to come, eternal life through our Lord & Saviour.

I shall hope to hear from you or your dear mother soon & then you must tell me what kind of winter you have had & what is the state of mind & feeling in England about these things.

Last week your uncle Thompson and his wife with their infant, a little girl of about a year old, came over to see us and spent some days with us. They are looking forward to going in about a fortnight to Missouri. Their prospects

---

mation of their leader's predictions for the end of the world (Yeomans, *Comets*, 178–179). See pages 49–50 for more on the Millerite movement.

do not seem very bright, but I hope by industry and perseverance they will get forward. Your Aunt Hannah is an intelligent, sprightly American but very delicate; your uncle is welinformed & ingenious, but he has been unfortunate. He has promised to collect me seeds of the Prairie flowers which are said to be very beautiful & then I shall try to send you some. I have already laid up a few for my dear English friends.

We have in the orchard belonging to this house a fine Catalpa, which is hung with innumerable long pods that to me look very interesting and remind one of its beauty when in flower. I long for the [2] the coming of spring; everything we shall see and hear will be full of novelty and a deep interest, and whatever I observe worth noticing has a two fold charm to me as I look at it for myself and for my endeared Friends. I mean, if nothing unforeseen occurs, to make a collection as far as I am able of dried specimens for you and your dear mother. It will be a delightful employment for me and the dear children and connect the idea of you with places & things the most agreeable. In travelling I felt the advantage I possessed in having an interest and some knowledge of flowers & derived delight from observing them and recognizing old familiar favourites in their native haunts. Therefore I would encourage you to cultivate the taste you have for these or any other branch of natural history as so many chanels by which you can obtain information and derive pure pleasure.

There is one custom in this country which, though rather odd, I much admire. It is the practice of fixing upon the top of a pole, often over the signs of taverns, which generally stand apart from the house, little wooden houses, called bird boxes for the convenience of martins, blue-birds &c, and which they seem fully to understand and avail themselves of. I have seen them really very pretty models of the house itself, with first & second stories, doors, chimnies &c & neatly painted. There in the summer, the birds resort & build their nests and the people watch them feeding & tending their young. It is pleasant to me to see these little houses, as they are one of the few things in which the Americans show a little taste and feeling, something away from the weary drudgery of this getting along life.

We have observed some very beautiful birds this winter. One called the red bird is a splendid creature; it is about the size of a lark; the female is a bright flame color, the male a rich crimson with black topping and wings.[22] They sing prettily, something like a thrush. There is a little bird which seems in this season to occupy the place of our sparrow; it is called the Snow bird. It is dusky ash colour or brown on the back, has a white breast, which \white/ extends under the tail, & its bill is white; some of them have black toppings.[23] Then there are four or five different woodpeckers, some of them very finely varied. The Jay is a very common bird in this part, and the blue bird we occa-

22. Perhaps the scarlet tanager.
23. Perhaps the snow bunting.

sionally see; it has a blue back and wings & light cinnamon brown breast. The pretty black & yellow bird called the Baltimore Oriel is here called the hanging bird; it builds a curious hanging nest, and it was one of them that the little black girl held in her hand when she repeated dear aunt Mary's Sparrow's nest. Wrens are very common birds and their note is powerful and fine. I love the little creatures; they look like old friends & always remind me of our robin, but in this land of plenty the wild creatures do not seem so dependent on man as in England & seldom come for crumbs or picking about the house.

You have heard a deal about the peculiar mode of expression in this land. Some of their words, or at least the application of them, does strike a stranger very oddly; whether it is from a notion of delicacy or what else I cannot tell, but they usually call horses creaturs: "we drove the creatur steady for three days on the pike" is pure American; one woman, thinking I suppose to pay Anna Mary a grand compliment, called her a "smart little toad," and smart enough she is, imitating and trying to do all that she sees us or her brother & sister do.

We have \been/ cautioned by many kind friends to be on our guard against imposition, as the common tradesmen seem to think English strangers lawful prey. One blacksmith charged us 2 dollars for two heaters for our box iron, but I suppose he would be considered "a middling cunning business fellow," as I once heard one store keeper dissignate another.

The other day a kind neighbour sent us some Hominy. It is Indian corn beaten in a mill until the outer husk will come off; it is then boiled until it is quite soft and eaten in milk like firmity—or fried brown in butter or after bacon or salt meat; the children like it very much. It is the usual food of the poor slaves.

This winter time Wm Charles and Agnes have been much confined. Poor things, they long to be out, and this day the 27th there is a delightful change in the weather—it has been raining and is become quite warm so that the snow is beginning to melt rapidly. I hope it will be permanent; we shall all rejoice. The oldest men in the settlement do not remember such a long continuance of cold.

Tell dear grandmother that Wm C. can make himself very useful: he can husk & shell corn, gather up long grass & reeds from the orchard for kindling, bring me wood and tend upon his little sister when occasionally they have been able to play upon the green. It is very pleasant to see how kindly he leads her about and lifts her over the wet places, and acts the part of protector to her. The usual appelations for children \in/ this country are Tom, Sonny or little Son, and little girls are universally called Sis, or Sissie, [3] but the oddest is that you often hear great boys and even men calling their Father, Pap \or pappy/.

On coming to the country we were a good deal anoyed with the money but the principle is simple and soon understood. It is computed decimally:

there are small pieces called fips which are 6 1/4 cents; these are usually styled fip penny bits, levenpenny bits are levies, that is 12 1/2 cents; quarter dollars & onwards. We often receive in change notes of the value of five cents, a fip or a levie; these are commonly called shin plaisters.

Please give my kind love to Cousins E[dward]. & L[ucy]. Bayliffe and their family, I hope Alice is quite recovered. Tell Cousin Lucy we understand our relation Ann Shipley is still living at Cincinnati. Harrison intends going there as soon as the spring is so far advanced as to render travelling agreeable, and then he hopes to see them all so that I shall be able to tell her more about them when he returns.

A few weeks back your Uncle H. received a letter from Thos Albright stating that he & his family were intending coming this spring. We have thought that if your dear Father could ascertain whether they are coming our way and if so we should be obliged to your dear mother to choose for us a carpet to be sent by them. We want the best kidderminster that can be bought, what is called three ply if possible, a small pattern, two greens or green & drab 25yds in length & cut into 5yd lengths & slightly made up, also 65yds of stair carpeting of the same make and pattern as nearly as possible to be cut into 3 lengths & bound or hemmed, and a large Mackintosh cape, a dark drab very ample for riding in, and I want for myself a riding habit; if it is made to fit your mother it will not be far wrong for me. I am not particular as to colour and wish it to be made quite plain and not a very expensive cloth. All these things can be paid for out of funds in John Thwaite's hands. If he should have paid them into the bank he will before long be receiving more on your uncle's account when they can be settled for.

Tell dear grandmother I am surprized. We none of us mentioned Ralph Alderson's wife; she is a nice kind little woman, a thorough American, no scholar but a most excellent provider & keeps a liberal table. She was raised, to use her own expression, in the family of a rich German and married their nephew who died leaving her with one little girl; she has now another who is still a baby.

It is very common for people to take both boys and girls into their family for a term of years and bring them up to help on the farm or in the house. In some cases they turn out well and are a real comfort to those who took them. One friend in this meeting in this way brought up & instructed two sisters. One is well married; the other remains with her, now a helpless invalid, and attends upon her with the kindness & affection of a daughter. In this way orphans are raised & find comfortable homes and are felt to be no burden.

I fear this has been a very suffering season to the poor in England. I have often thought of them with an aching heart: without clothing, food & fire, what can they do? There seem to be no beggars here; at least we see none. I believe there is a deal of embarrassment & difficulty in trade & amongst farmers who have to make a living from their farms as money is very scarce

& produce exceedingly low, but wages are high & living cheap, so that the poor are well off. Formerly the wage of a labourer was ~~the~~ a bushel of wheat or the value of it a day. Now that it is 50 cents & under, many will not work for so little, which is not reasonable.

The common way of renting land here is "on the shares" as it is called, that is, to work the land, finding horses implements &c, & give the landlord a portion of the produce—some <times> half or more or less according to agreement. In this way people let out their orchards, sugar camps, hay fields &c, always giving to the person who will gather the fruit or work the land one half for their trouble.

Yesterday Elizabeth received a letter from Ellen Hanson of Blackburn in which she said dear mother was then in Liverpool. I am glad to hear this as it is a proof to me she is in tolerable health & able to commence her long journey; I have feared the severe winter would make her unwell. Should she have left, will you be so kind as forward this to her, for I shall not be able to write to her this month & fear she may be disappointed & though this is but a chit chat affair about things very trifling, yet I know she will excuse it.

Elizabeth is now come to live with us; her health is improved & I hope will continue so, but she still talks of returning.

[4] Give my endeared love to your Father, Mother, brothers & sisters and dearest Grandmother; we are hoping to hear from some of you. I hope Alfred is better, poor lad; my kindest love to him. Your Uncle wishes to add a few lines to your Father so I must conclude and remain your affectionately attached aunt,

Emma Alderson.

Elizabeth and your Uncle send their dear love to you all.
<A letter from Harrison Alderson to Daniel Harrison continues on the final page of this sheet, after which Emma has apparently written the following across the first page:>
[1-*cross*] 28th To give you some idea of the variations of temperature to which we are liable, the thaw I mentioned yesterday continued very steady, accompanied with much rain till about noon today. About eleven the Thermometer stood at 56 and it was very warm; since then we have had wind and snow storms, and this evening it is 28. Today I saw in the orchard a splendid redbird; it was about the size of a large blackbird, had a brilliant scarlet breast & body & the wings, head & tail jet black. The apples are generally done in this part, and people are now taking to their dried fruits as a substitute. They are stewed very soft with a little sugar and are used in pie and as preserves; in this way apples, peaches & plums are kept and when well managed are excellent. I wish I could send dear grandmother some dried peaches; we often say we think she would like them, but I fear I am spoiling this letter for her, so with dear love to all, farewell.

8. To Ann Botham, April 7 to 16, 1843
Westland 4th mo 7th 1843

My dearly beloved Mother,
By this time I hope thou hast received my two last letters: one sent in the 1st mo.[24] by a private opportunity to Philadelphia, the other to leave the 3rd mo.; post was addressed to Mary & Margaret Ann.[25] I thought probably thou wouldst be at Woodside and wouldst not object to hearing of us through them. A day or two after that letter left, we received thy kind letter dated 16th of 2nd month, one from dear Daniel, and one from B. Eastham, for all of which we felt truly grateful.

I hope, my beloved Mother, my last letters, if they have come to hand, will contain some information thou desired, & have removed any unpleasant impressions thou had received from Elizabeth's statements which, as they were understood, were very eroneous. She is dissatisfied and talks of returning, but what is the exact ground of her uneasiness I cannot tell; perhaps she thinks it is interesting to make complaints & excite the sympathy of her friends. She is now with us and, to do her justice, behaves very well, & we are much more comfortable together than ever expected to be.

I am afraid from an expression in B. Eastham's letter you may, some of you, think that we send flattering accounts to keep up thy spirits. Now dearest mother, do not let in such an idea; I speak of things & people just as I see them & they appear to me. Thou knows I usually look on the bright side, but then I live on that side & tell what I see & feel. I do not of course think it necessary to mention every little anoyance, for I have found anoyances in all places & situations, but they are such as come with the day & go generally with the day, & if the balance is on the agreeable side we have no room for complaints. Indeed, \here/ we have no ground for discontent: we came ~~as~~ strangers & have been received & are treated like old friends; we are blessed with health; feel ourselves in easy circumstances & enjoying many of the luxuries of the rich in England as horses & a carriage; are located in a beautiful & healthy part of the country in a home far superior to the usual lot of emigrants; have an abundance of very good things & what more can we desire[?] And as to scantiness of furniture, we have purposely avoided getting more than was absolutely necessary, not knowing where we might settle & knowing the inconvenience of carrying such things from place to place.

I expect some of you think there must be great hardship in not keeping a servant; to tell the truth, at first I felt it somewhat of a burden, but habit has already made it light & easy, and I have enjoyed such perfect health & such boyant spirits as the result of an active life that I feel quite repaid. I wish those

24. This letter is missing.
25. The second of the letters referred to here is letter #7. The other might be the same one referred to in letter #6 as being sent with William Evans to Philadelphia. If so, however, it would not have been one of the "two last letters."

in England who feel the pressure of bad times would try the experiment; it would be a blessing to many I do believe. But again I think of the poor; perhaps they might suffer. Here we have not that consideration to weigh. I think [2] I told thee we have a coloured woman to wash for us, and her sister comes the next day to iron for me, so thou sees I take things easily, and have so much leisure that I can often spend many hours on the green or in the woods with the children.

This is the 16th of the month and during the last week we have had delightful weather; it is now like warm 5th mo. weather in England. The trees are still bare but there are signs of spring on every hand: the green is as verdant as any grass plat thou ever saw; a fortnight ago it was covered with snow. In the woods I have found the Hepatica growing in abundance; it is our old favourite: the single blue, a lovely flower.[26] I shall dry some specimens for dear Anna.

I felt very much concerned to learn from thy letter the poor state of dear Alfred's health. I often think of him with much affection and do hope that the change of air & recreation may be beneficial to him. I think you have chosen wisely to go to Uttoxeter and am sure dear Anna and the children will enjoy themselves at Highwood. I sometimes wish the Frenches were in America; poor Hannah would be happy in the abundance of this land. She might deal out the good things of the earth with a profuse & liberal hand.

Sometimes, dear mother, my heart aches and the tears fill my eyes in the rememberance of many worthy good people who live scantily & eat the bread of carefulness in our native land whilst we live sumptuously every day. There are some who will miss thee in Lancashire; I often think of poor Betty Whalley & others who were needy; may He who regardeth the sparrows have compassion towards them and arise speedily for their releif. Possibly this may reach thee at Uttoxeter; if so give my kind love to all our relations & old friends: Betty Shipley, Sally Cope, J. & A. S., W. & L. S., Thos Salt, John & Hanna French, Ann Stubbs, poor old Sally, &c.

Harrison left us last 3rd day to go to Cincinnati; he wished to see that part of the country as we have heard it highly spoken of, and also to visit his own relations the Thistlethwaites & also Ann Shipley, who Ann Jones said is my father's nearest living relation. I should have much liked to accompany him but we concluded it best to remain with the children. I do not expect him back for a week or ten days.

Dear sister Alice [Mason] has been up twice to see us \since H. left/; she is an admirable woman, very pious & overflowing with pure benevolence. She feels to me more like a mother than anything else, but kind dear woman as she is, she always comes as a visitor, not to help me in the house as thou supposed. However, I delivered thy message to her with the affectionate fact of which she seemed pleased. In my letter to D[aniel] & A[nna] written on

26. Probably *Hepatica americana.*

our return from Ohio I sent a message to Smith [Harrison] on behalf of his brother Thompson, \unknown to him/. Danl does not refer to it in his letter, but as it was written in haste I am willing to hope it was merely an omission. Will you therefore not let it pass unattended to[?] We feel much interested for Thompson, poor fellow; owing to want of means he is not able to go to Missouri this spring as he had intended, but he thinks if he had the means he would purchase a little land in Iowa & commence farming. He would be glad if Smith would furnish 50 or 100₤ to buy a tract to work it for him. I expect it would be considered a good investment; the government price of land there is, I believe, 1 1/4 dollar an acre. I felt pleased to hear Richard [Harrison] [3] and his wife are coming; we think from what thou says they are just the people for this country. I hope they will find us out; I fear they will be disapointed in going first to St. Clairsville.

Some of our neighbours have been very busy dressing & spinning flax. They say times are bad & money scarce & so they must produce as much as possible at home. The men wear a deal of linen & linsey wolsey for summer clothing, (home made). For the same reason, great numbers have been making maple sugar this spring. The sugar camp belonging to this estate has been worked on "the shares." We went one day to see them at work; they had tapped 78 trees, some of them on both sides; the receivers were troughs made of hollow-cut logs. From three to four holes were bored \in the trees/ with a large augre & into them spouts made of branches of elder from \which/ the pith was extracted were inserted; through these it dripped into the trough. A boy went round from time to time to gather the sugar water whilst another attended to the boiling. A rude furnace and a small log hut were erected in the wood, & there three large pans were constantly kept boiling. It is a tedious process to reduce liquid with the very slightest sweet taste, as it is at first, to sugar or molasses.

Sister Alice tells me she is going this week to make a barrel of soap and we are to have fat from her to do the same for ourselves; I will send thee the history of the process. We are also "fixed" for making our own candles, having mould, wick, & tallow at hand to manufacture at our pleasure.

Half America is running mad about Millerism; surely you are not so foolish in England. The Methodists are making a great handle of it; people are flocking to the mourning bench to get religion, as they call it. Some are sincerely zealous; others are terrified out of their senses with apprehension. I heard of near a hundred individuals assembling on the evening of the 21st of March dressed in their ascension robes in the burying ground to meet their dead friends and with them \expecting/ to be caught up in the air. Some almost perished of cold. I send thee a copy of the 14th article of Miller creed to give thee a more clear idea of the grounds of this excitement.

["]14. I believe the time can be known by all who desire to understand and be ready for his coming. And I am fully convinced that sometime between March 21st 1843 and March 21st 1844, according to the Jewish mode of computation of time, Christ will come, and bring all his saints with him and that then he will reward every man as his work shall be."

Hast thou heard anything from dear Mary[?] I am hoping she will write to me; I long to hear from her. When we were last at Brownsville one of the store keepers, a very respectable man, began to talk of one Howitt whose book he was reading. It was the second Series of Visits, which his son had brought him as a present, he being originally from Northumberland.[27] When he heard I was "Mary Howitts" sister his delight was extreme; he called to the "good wife" to come and see and said it was a pleasure; he never hoped to have had to see anyone belonging to her. I felt a perfect love for the man when on parting he gave me a most cordial shake of the hand, all for love of dear Mary.

There is one thing my beloved mother that has been a cause of real sorrow to my mind ever since we landed, and that is [4] the part Friends have taken in the Abolition question. I expect thou wilt have heard that the Society discourages its members from taking any part with others in the promotion of this great & good work. Last yearly meeting its injunctions were strong & decided on the ground that it was charged with being a political movement, & moreover it was feared individual loss might be sustained by mixing so much with others in these things. It might have been & probably was necessary to strongly caution & advise on these heads, but to impose prohibitions & bind men's consciences in this way is, I believe, going too far, & the result has proved it.

A considerable body in Indiana, with Charles Osborn at their head, have established themselves into a separate Yearly Meeting, calling themselves Anti Slavery Friends; these hold correspondence & cooperate with the Anti Slavery Society, but only on this head dissent from their brethren. I am sorry for this movement: I wish they would have boldly & fearlessly acted as they conscienciously believed to be right & have awaited the consequences, I regret the separation on their own account & also for Friends. I am afraid it will make them even more decided in their opposition.

Oh, it is a sorrowful thing that Friends who have so conspicuously & so nobly sided in the good work should, now their struggle between good & evil, the kingdom \of light/ and that of darkness is at hand, fall away. They that were long experienced in the warfare might have been like leaders in the conflict; they would have been calm & collected when younger troops were giddy with excitement, a band of veterans in one of God's noble armies for the overthrow of a most crying & deadly evil; but so it is, at present they stand aloof.

27. William Howitt, *Visits to Remarkable Places: Old Halls, Battle Fields, and Scenes Illustrative of Striking Passages in English History and Poetry*, 2nd series (London: Longman Brown, Green, and Longmans, 1842).

I am thankful that thy health this winter is so good. The dear children are all well & very happy; they remember thee affectionately & never fail to crave a blessing for "dear grandmother" in their daily prayer. Farewell my beloved Parent; give my dearest love to D., A. & their family & with warm affection believe me thy tenderly attached daughter.

Emma Alderson

If it is not commonly known do not say any thing about what I have said respecting Friends & the Anti Slavery question. I do not wish to be the reporter of evil; it might do harm & could do no good.

9. To Ann Botham, May 16 to 28, 1843
Westland 5th mo 16th 1843

My dear and honoured Mother,
Thy letters have always been most welcome; I have felt them a blessing to be acknowledged with thankfulness, but none of them have given me such unqualified pleasure as thy last, dated Uttoxeter. In it I see that thou art contented and happy and oh what a load of anxiety has it seemed to remove from my mind on thy account.

I never thought of thee at Preston but with a heart-ache; could I have foreseen I would never have said one word to induce thee to fix there, but I did it for the best, though I have shed many tears in the apprehension that thou wast unhappy, and I do not wonder at it. The last first-day I spent with thee at M. A.'s filled me with misgivings; I thought possibly thou might not be comfortable there, and I am thankful thou hast fixed on quiet, happy Uttoxeter, where thou art known and respected and wilt, I trust, spend the remnant of thy honoured life in peace and comfort.

Oh how I love those kind hearted people; give my love to any that remember me and to whom thou knows the message would be acceptable, especially to those who show thee kindness and attention. I should like to know who and what the family are where thou lodges. I remember a man named Charles, a chair turner in Balance Street: is it he or any of his family[?] One thing, dear mother, let me just advise thee: if thou art not quite comfortable I would move till I found myself so. It is pleasant thou art in Balance Street, and the situation thou describes must be very agreeable.[28] I should think it must be George Alsop's surgery, and as I remember thy saying those old houses oposite were removed, the opening will be very pretty.

My mind often visits dear Anna at Doveridge, and I rejoice that this lovely season she will spend in a spot so congenial to her tastes.[29] I know how beau-

28. The Botham sisters grew up on Balance Street in Uttoxeter. The house is now identified by a plaque as "Howitt House," though no Howitts ever lived there.
29. Doveridge is just a little east of Uttoxeter. Perhaps she was taking an extended holiday there. This was a difficult time in her life as the Harrisons had nearly been ruined by a bad

tiful it will be & how much she and the dear children will enjoy the fresh pure country and what lovely flowers they will gather in the Dove meadows and Eaton Woods and by the way side. I shall never again see such lanes as those with their beautiful hawthorn hedges and green sloping banks beautified with primroses and violets and ficary, and as summer advances with stellaria and camphion and forgetmenots & those lovely ferns that have many a time filled my heart with gladness & gratitude for so much and such abounding beauty. There are no fox-gloves, no heaths, no golden furze buses here, so love them as your own peculiar wealth; but there is most splendid scenery and lovely glorious flowers. We ramble in the woods and are startled into delight with new and unknown plants and my first thought and wish is for dear Anna till the children sometimes wonder at me. Agnes generally says, ["L]et us send it to dear grandmother,["] but Charley usually corrects her by saying, ["]No, grandmother does not love flowers, we will send her something else[."]

Tell dear Anna we have found a most lovely elegant wood anemone, a very delicate little pale blue flower called Inocence (Houstonia cerulea) Arum triphyllum, a small arum with three parted leaves that for elegance of form excels any thing I ever saw; it looks to me like grecian sculpture.[30] The Trillium pendulum is a splendid flower. I found it the last time I was in the wood; it grows about a foot high, has three rich green diamond formed leaves about three inches below the nodding flower which is composed of a three leaved calyx and three rich ovate petals of a dazling white; in the centre are 6 bright yellow stamens. Altogether the flower when expanded is rather less than the palm of one's hand. We have found a very beautiful Phlox and many other plants, all of which, when rare, I have preserved specimens to send you when the opportunity offers. Excuse this botanical sentence but I am sure dear Anna will be interested in it; if I had time I would keep a botanical diary for her.

But I long to give you an idea of the surprising loveliness of the country now that spring has really come and the trees are in full leaf. The delicate tints have not yet passed away; the rich full green foliage of the sugar maple contrasts finely with the pale olive of the oak \and the yellow green of the walnuts/. The dogwood is in full flower and looks here and there like a fall of snow, so white & full in the blossom; it is said that the Indians planted their corn (maize) when this beautiful tree was ~~blossom~~ in bloom.

The country (at least in this part) is worthy of its name. It is still Pennsylvania, a land of woods, for although ploughed fields, and the greenest of

---

business speculation on the part of Daniel's partner and Anna was about to undergo a crisis in faith that would end with her conversion to the Church of England.

30. Punctuation makes it difficult to see that she is describing three flowers here: the "elegant wood anemone" could be any of several species; *Houstonia caerulea*, or innocence, is the flower also known as Quaker ladies or bluets; and *Arisaema triphyllum* is the jack-in-the-pulpit.

meadows are seen on every side and in fact predominate, yet from eminences which overlook the surrounding country for many miles, beautiful woods lie in the vallies and crown the hills or skirt their sides, some so extensive that they remind you of the times when the Indian and the wild deer inhabited these noble forests. There is a tree about 20 or 30 feet high said to be peculiar to the Monongahela that has been very conspicuous of late. It was covered with a profusion of small pea shaped deep red flowers so as to look at a distance quite red; the common name is red-bud.

About a fortnight ago the orchards were extremely beautiful and the air was full of the delicate scent of the apple-blossom and the cherry, pear & apple trees white with bloom. There is every prospect of an abundance of [2] fruit. Thou knows the peach with its pretty pink flowers; they <have grown> very full and there is fine promise in them. The weather hitherto is <delightful> & very like our pleasantest 6th mo weather—warm with a fine breeze—and every three or four days we have had a refreshing mild thunder shower. The thermometer ranges between 70 & 80 in the shade. The people here call it cool for the time of the year; to us it is deliciously warm & pleasant.

About 6 weeks ago our certificates arrived, and when I say they were all we could wish I say little; ~~to~~ in me they excited feelings of grateful affection and I esteem this last proof of your kindness & consideration very highly.[31] Harrison was away when they arrived & did not return against the Monthly Meeting. I offered them for presentation but George Smith, one of the overseers, declined receiving them, or rather the meeting through him, stating that when individuals of any importance came it was their custom to receive their certificates in their presence. Accordingly last 4th day ours was presented and it was gratifying to hear the hearty and unanimous satisfaction expressed. On reading them in our meeting, the heads of the meeting one after another arose & said "the certificates were very acceptable to them as had been the company of the friends whilst they had been amongst them." And to that purpose I mention this to give thee an idea of their way of proceeding. Of course there was no appointment made to inform us; thus we are installed members of this meeting, but how long we shall remain so is uncertain as we are at present looking to a removal to Cincinnati. It is, however, not quite decided; probably I shall know before concluding this.

The information thou mentions as being copied into the Irish Friend must have been contained in a letter to Anne Edmondson; had I been aware it would have been given to the public, I should have been more exact, though as far as I know I was correct.[32] I have felt much grieved at M[argaret] Abbott's

31. A "certificate of removal" was a document prepared by the Monthly Meeting from which an individual or family was departing and presented to the Monthly Meeting they intended to join.

32. The *Irish Friend*, published in Belfast by William Bell, had ceased publication the previous year. Alderson might be referring to one of the last issues, or she might be confusing it

conduct to thee &, had it not been in fulfilment of a promise often repeated, should not, I believe, have written to her at least at present.

I hope you have not in consequence of my request been at the expense of purchasing any of dear Mary & William's works for us. I find they are reprinted and sold here at a very low price; I saw Wm's Germany[33] advertised at 50 cents, rather more than 2/2. I have seen a most handsome notice of the Neighbours[34] in an American Review; indeed I think it bespeaks a healthy tone of feeling in this country that they are very favourite authors here.

We have attended the funeral of a neighbour lately; it took place the day after decease. There was a large company near, I should think 200, mostly in carriages & on horseback; none wore mourning. When we came to the house, the coffin was standing outside at the door uncovered & the corpse neatly dressed shown to any who wished to see it; it is not customary to provide refreshments for the visitors on such occasions. The burial was in Friends' grave yard and a very solemn season; dear Harrison spoke very impressively. The company on these occasions is often very promiscuous—Friends, methodists, Hicksites & professed unbelievers—so that they may be sometimes opportunities of sowing a little good seed; at least they may be improved so far as to exalt that dear name which I fear is by many lightly esteemed and which I trust is increasingly precious to us as we believe it is dishonoured by them.

[May] 28th: Richard Harrison has not yet arrived, nor have we had any tidings of him; I look anxiously for his coming. Thou rejoiced me by saying my request on behalf of Thompson had been attended to. I feel much for them; I do not know whether they will be able to make much out, still this assistance will give them a chance, & I much wished they should have it; he seems clever & ingenious & his wife is a lively well informed woman, but they are both feeble of body & of that class that are often objects of solicitude to their friends.

We have been at Poke run to visit our friends Amos and Edith Griffith and found them refined, agreeable people with a very interesting, intelligent family: the eldest girl studies botany & has all the appearance of being a superior young woman. They live in a very retired situation but have all the comforts and refinements that you would find in a Friend's house in the country

---

with one of its two successors, the *British Friend*, begun in January 1843 in Glasgow, or the London-based *Friend*, which began publication the following month.

33. Probably *The Rural and Domestic Life of Germany* (London: Longman, Brown, Green, and Longmans, 1842), which was published in America the following year, but possibly *The Student-Life of Germany* (London: Longman, Brown, Green, and Longmans,1841), published in America in 1842.

34. Probably Frederika [*sic*] Bremer, *The Neighbours: A Story of Every-Day Life*, trans. Mary Howitt, 2 vols. (London: Longman, Brown, Green, and Longmans, 1842). This very popular book was also published in 1843 in New York, Boston, and Philadelphia by other publishers.

in England: papered rooms, carpetted floors, great neatness & order in every part of their establishment.

Now, as I know all I can tell thee about ourselves is interesting to thy affectionate heart, I will describe to thee our carriage which Harrison purchased at Pittsburgh & brought on his return from Cincinnati. It is a handsome black pheaton with a cover or head that falls back in warm weather. It holds four grown persons & the children well, and we have lined it for the summer with some of that blue & buff gingham of which we had so much: it looks quite stylish & some of our friends joke us about our [3] <*torn*> new carriage. We have a most beautiful, powerful horse, the admiration of all who see him, full of spirit but very gentle. He is quite able to take us short journies now that the roads are good; when we have a place of our own I expect we shall keep a pair. I mean to have a horse of my own; at least I know dear Harrison will let me have one if I wish it. Sometimes it is more convenient to mount a horse than take out a carriage; besides they tell me I am fit for the backwoods as I can ride with a child on my knee & on occasion with Charley behind: no one cares for appearances here.

So now my beloved mother, if thou wast here we could take thee about in as easy & pleasant a carriage as is commonly used ~~at~~ in England and how rich & proud I should feel to have thee beside me. I never expected to be possessed of such an equipage; indeed dearest mother we daily feel that our blessings are varied & abundant. Thou will like to know what this said carriage cost. It had been used about 4 months & therefore was considered secondhand though as good & handsome as new and Harrison paid 90 dollars for it & a pole, & 35 for a double set of handsome new harness. I should think it could not be less in England.

You have often asked us if we would continue to take the Friend & we always have forgotten to mention it: we should much like to have it sent regularly and shall be obliged to thee or dear Daniel to order it for us; papers reach us from England for two or three cents.[35]

What has thou done with poor little Trim I hope he is with thee; we often wish we had him here: almost all the dogs here are great mastifs. Not that we grudge him thee, but I love the rememberance of all we left in England. We have a fine young shepherd dog & have called him Trim in honour of our old favourite.

Please dear mother tell me where I can address a letter to dear Mary; I long to hear from her & must write again soon when I know where she is. Thank you for the letters you have sent by R[ichard?].[36]

35. The *Friend* (London) had been in circulation for only three months. That she is already this familiar with it is a testimony to the effectiveness of transatlantic mails. It is also possible that she is referring to the *Irish Friend* and is unaware that it had ceased publication at the end of the previous year.
36. Possibly Richard Harrison, who is still expected from England as of an earlier point in this letter.

We feel much hurt at Elizabeth's conduct but really dear mother I find the less I think or say about it the best. All things considered I have hard work to keep wrong feelings down & can only say if she chooses to continue to do so after what has been said to her, she must take the consequences. I doubt not she will lose the respect of all her friends that can think & judge aright.

I find the Red bud is "The red-flowered Judas Tree." The children are all well & happy; they both desire their love to dear Grandmother, as does also Sister Alice who is spending a few days with us.

PART II

A Home of Their Own

FIRST YEARS AT CEDAR LODGE

Pittsburgh to Cincinnati by Steamboat

When the Aldersons left Pittsburgh for their new home in Cincinnati, they did so on a series of steamboats. Although steam power was relatively new in transatlantic travel, it had been used for inland navigation since about 1811. By the early 1850s, steamboat travel would begin falling away rapidly in the face of railway expansion, but it was near its peak in 1843 when the Aldersons boarded their first steamboat in Brownsville bound down the Monongahela for the 56-mile journey north to Pittsburgh.[1] In Pittsburgh, the Monongahela joins the Allegheny River to form the Ohio River, which winds for nearly a thousand miles until it joins the Mississippi in Illinois. The Aldersons traveled 480 miles from Pittsburgh to Cincinnati, a journey of several days that probably cost them about $5 per person for cabin-class tickets, down from $12 in 1825.[2] Alderson gives relatively little detail about this trip compared to the account she gives of the Atlantic crossing, but the "comfort and luxury" she refers to were legendary on the inland steamers. Traveling cabin class, as opposed to the less expensive deck class, the Aldersons would have enjoyed accommodations as elegant as the best hotels, with impressive staterooms and large, opulent saloons.

A steamboat offered other pleasures besides the luxury of its accommodations. Over a several days' journey, innumerable scenes unfolded along hundreds of miles of passing shoreline. The passengers themselves reflected virtually the whole social and economic diversity of America and much of the world besides. According to one historian, "it was traditional that despite wide differences in wealth and position all who traveled in the cabin should mingle on equal terms," although Alderson's own experience illustrates that the equality did not cross racial lines.[3] Other popular attractions of a steamboat would have been less attractive to a pious family such as the Aldersons. Music, drinking, and gambling abounded in spite of perfunctory gestures at curbing the third of these. Perhaps had she been traveling on the lower deck, she would have thought otherwise, but Alderson reports finding

Figure 18. *Map of Hamilton County, Ohio*, by William D. Emerson (1847), showing property owners. Courtesy of Library of Congress.

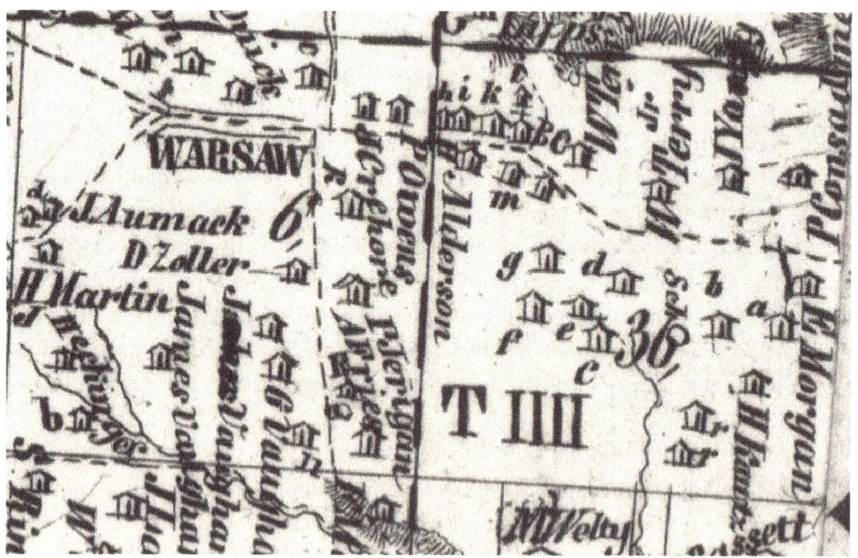

Figure 19. Detail of *Map of Hamilton County, Ohio*, by William D. Emerson (1847), showing "H. Alderson" and neighbors. Courtesy of Library of Congress.

nothing "offensive in the manners of the Americans. Spitting is quite discarded in good society" (see page 118).

The risks of steamboat travel were legendary. Contemporary newspapers abound with lurid descriptions of the latest explosions and sinkings on the river; Charles Dickens was hardly exaggerating when he wrote that "western steamboats usually blow up one or two a week in the season."[4] To a people on the move in a new and expanding country, these risks were to be borne: thus, the Aldersons packed their things and moved on toward their first, and Emma's only, American home of their own. The steamboat had slashed the travel time from the three weeks it would have taken by keelboat to only a few days; by the end of the decade, the age of inland steamboats would likewise come to an end as the railroad reduced the time from days to hours, cutting 470 miles of winding river travel to 316 miles by rail.[5]

Life in Ohio introduced Emma to a range of new American customs and ideas, many of which found their way into her letters home. There were rag carpets and quilts (or "comforts"), new plants and new foods, including the tomato, recently introduced to Ohio.[6] Then there were wood cooking fires, which she told her mother were "quite a science" (see page 132). There were irritants as well, such as mosquitoes and the American habit of kissing among friends: "At first I thought it was their especial love & kindness to my unworthy self, but I have found it is so general & universal that it ceases to be any thing more than an annoying ceremony" (see page 191). A source of greater concern and more ambivalence were the chain gangs, which she first saw in May 1844. "Many are of opinion," she writes, in reference perhaps to the prison reform work then being undertaken by Elizabeth Fry and other Quakers, "that it is not well thus to expose them; it tends to harden them & cut off all return to society" (see page 178). At the time, Emma was unconvinced that the prisoners were "unhappy or miserable," but later she would take a firmer position against chain gangs as she and Harrison came to know some of the prisoners.

Even before reaching Ohio, Emma came into contact with a more unequivocal evil in the form of slavery. After flowing south and then west along the Pennsylvania-Ohio border, the Ohio River goes on to separate Ohio, which was a free state at the time, from Kentucky, a slave state. To Emma, an inveterate opponent of slavery, the two sides of that river were like night and day. Whatever happiness or beauty she may find south of the Ohio, it is always covered by that dark cloud.

> The beautiful river is bounded on the Kentucky side by green wooded hills; here and there a gentleman's house peeps out from amongst them . . . , but I never look to these otherwise \lovely/ shores without a sadened feeling. I fancy every good house contains a slaveholder & every little cabin is an abode of misery. (see page 141)

For the rest of her life, Emma lived where a small hill or a clearing in the woods might open up a view of that darkened land.

Landscapes: Beauty and More Botany

The book on botany that Alderson purchased in Philadelphia must have been put to good use, because her knowledge and love of the natural world fill every letter. She found less variety in Ohio, noting "a greater sameness in the forest trees" there than in Pennsylvania. "We miss a certain oak which has dark rich purple and the scarlet Cornus florida, or dogwood, a specimen of which dear Anna will find amongst the plants I have sent. Here maple and beech predominate; they are considered as peculiarly indicative of good land" (see page 148). Nevertheless, she found much to admire, especially as autumn came on and "the remaining greens were intermingled with every variety of yellow, orange, red, brown and occasionally a purple oak with here and there the trunk & arms, \wreathed with the Virginia creeper/, of some dead tree starting up like great scarlet stiks in the very thickest of the forest" (see page 148).

Such descriptions indicate a remarkable combination of scientific and aesthetic sensibilities. Not only does she know the names (Latin as well as common) of most of the plants, but she also pays attention to forest types, the relationships between different species of tree and the soil they grow from. That ecological sense of how different plants work together has its aesthetic counterpart in her sense of the way shapes and colors work together to produce a visual effect greater than the sum of its parts. Terms such as "intermingled" and "luxuriance" appear frequently in her descriptions of the local flora, like the "fine prairie rose," which "grows in wild luxuriance &, when in bloom, looks literally like a garland of flowers" (see page 306).

Emma was writing some fifteen years before Charles Darwin published his theory of evolution by natural selection and, as an Orthodox Friend, she would have had great difficulty accepting any theory inconsistent with scripture. Nevertheless, she looks on the world around her with the same appreciation for the complexity of natural processes that led Darwin to "contemplate a tangled bank" with a sense of wonder that was more than scientific.[7] To the devout nineteenth-century Christian, the Bible was infallible, but the Quaker doctrine of continuing revelation meant that, at least theoretically, anyone might be blessed with insights leading to a more accurate interpretation of the Bible. Thus, she was comfortable drawing her own conclusion regarding the surprising appearance of marine fossils as far inland as Ohio. It was, she wrote to her sister Mary (the most progressive thinker among her correspondents), "remarkable and a contradiction in my opinion to the theory that the deluge was partial" (see page 142). Whatever we make of the conclusion itself, we should note the attention she pays not only to natural details but also to the historical context and the ongoing natural processes in which those details are embedded.

"Blunt, unceremonious manners": The Taste of a New Land

Alderson's exploration of the possibilities of a new identity in a new land leads her unsurprisingly to a concern for "taste," that aesthetic or cultural sensibility which, as Pierre Bourdieu has argued, "functions as a sort of social orientation, a 'sense of one's place', guiding the occupants of a given place in social space towards the social positions adjusted to their properties, and towards the practices or goods which befit the occupants of that position."[8] The word "taste" is used fifteen times in this section of the correspondence, frequently in association with ideas of refinement, elegance, and simplicity, all of which she identifies with an English taste. Outward signs of taste most often appear in gardening, familiarity with certain books, and interior decorating, but also in general behavior. More so even than religious or political views, taste figures as the principal measure of character.

Although initially, she is troubled by "the blunt, unceremonious manners of the people in West Pennsylvania" (see page 155), she later comes to accommodate those manners to her own Quaker distaste for ceremony and outward shows of piety, seeing in them a principled rejection of empty forms and a belief that "thanks were alone due to our maker & Preserver." However much she came to appreciate that bluntness, she finds Cinncinati more to her taste, with its "more English" "manners and style of living" due to its greater number of immigrants from the eastern cities. (Westland had been populated more by southern Friends moving north to get away from slavery.) In the Cincinnati Friends, she finds a blend of the "refinement & cultivation" she associated with England and the "warm hearted kindness" she had known in Westland (see page 133).

Like immigrants today, Emma finds much to love and admire in her new country—too much to consider returning to her old home—but she never wavers in her self-identification as an Englishwoman. She writes of England as "my country" five times throughout the letters and of herself as "too much of an Englishwoman to like American housemaids" (see page 151). Yet she has clearly become something other than the Englishwoman of England, making repatriation unthinkable. Many immigrants, including Elizabeth and even some of Emma's own children, did return to their native lands, but many more, for whom America had initially represented only a temporary sojourn, found themselves caught up in the new land. The degree to which the old and the new land contributed to the immigrant's identity varied widely, but in every case it was a hybrid identity and something to be forged anew by each family and individual according to his or her circumstances. The Aldersons left England with the full intention of making a permanent home in America, but Emma's letters make quite clear that adopting an American identity was not an option.

One of the characteristics that most troubled Emma about the American character was a rootlessness and lack of "local attachment," the result of which was a constant movement westward: "\one/ house can shelter them as well as another & a few more acres of land will tempt a man into the wilderness 500 or 1000 miles from the place of his birth" (see page 158). Yet if Americans showed a disregard for the conventional home as Alderson understood it, they were innovators in alternative forms of living, as evidenced by the nearly 100 utopian communities (based on Fourierist, Owenite, Shaker, Saint-Simonian, or other principles) established in the United States between 1825 and 1860.[9] Alderson had little personal interest in such "Owenism & infidelity & all the foreign efforts \by/ which men have sought to accomplish that which christianity can alone effect, social & moral reform," but they were part of that nation with which she had cast her lot (see page 436). Alderson's vicarious experience of such "efforts" came through her brother-in-law Thompson Harrison, whose involvement with the Fourierist movement's Ohio Phalanx for its short life, led her to be both more open to the movement's ideals and more critical of its failings.

Thompson had struggled through financial difficulties in spite of Alderson's efforts to help him, so his involvement with the Ohio Phalanx might have been one of desperation: in one letter, she describes his decision as "the last recourse of a hopeless man" (see page 202). Elsewhere, however, she acknowledges his enthusiasm for the idealism of the Fourierists: "his heart was warm & his hopes ardent that in a few years there would be an oasis of independent happiness in a wilderness world" (see pages 430–431). From their earliest days, Quakers had avowed a belief in the perfectibility of the individual and in the realization of God's kingdom on earth, two beliefs that might have helped Alderson to appreciate Thompson's enthusiasm, although she could not quite share his optimism. Unfortunately, his dreams were never realized, as the Ohio Phalanx, even more dramatically than most, collapsed under pressures endemic to the movement.

By the 1820s, Charles Fourier (1772–1837) of France had developed a complicated theory of human history based on the twelve passions that he believed drove human beings. Combining these passions in different ways, Fourier imagined 810 basic personality types, two of each being required for the formation of the communities he proposed. Within these communities, or "phalanxes" or "associations," as he called them, the passions would be given free rein; each member of the community would live and work according to his or her own "passional makeup"; resources would be shared according to need as well as skill and particular contribution to the community. The result would be an end to the competition and repression that characterized modern civilization and the start of a new era of freedom, cooperation, and social harmony.[10]

Although Fourier died before his plan could bear fruit, the American utopian socialist Albert Brisbane (1809–1890), who had studied with Fourier, combined forces with journalist and editor Horace Greeley (1811–1872) to bring Fourier's ideas to America. The first American phalanx was established at the Transcendentalist community of Brook Farm in West Roxbury, Massachusetts. At least 28 more followed in New York, Pennsylvania, and Ohio.[11] Many of the phalanxes were plagued with a lack of capital from the beginning as organizers rushed to establish the communities before they were financially prepared to do so. One of the most extreme examples of this situation was Thompson Harrison's Ohio Phalanx, organized by Elijah P. Grant, an Ohio lawyer, educated at Yale and a vice president of the American Union of Associationists, as those committed to Fourierist ideals were called. The community began in February 1844 on 2,200 acres, one of the largest properties of any phalanx, but they had purchased this land from James Shriver for $69,000 with no money down. (By contrast, two other phalanxes, Clermont and

Social Reform Unity, purchased land for, respectively, $20,000 with a $1,000 down payment and $2,500 with $100 down.) Within a year, the group was having trouble paying its debts, and Shriver repossessed the property, ruining the families and individuals who had invested their lives in the scheme.[12]

Poor financial planning was certainly one cause of the failure of these phalanxes, but no doubt many factors were involved, and success would have been difficult under any circumstances.[13] Rushing to organize their phalanxes and commence operation, leaders compromised not only financially but also in membership, accepting fewer and less suitable individuals than the Fourierist system required. In an 1845 letter to her mother, Emma suggests (based, no doubt, on Thompson Harrison's accounts) that corruption among the leadership may also have been a factor: the Ohio Phalanx, she writes, failed due to the "treachery" and betrayal of Elijah Grant (see page 259). In any case, relations between members and leaders may have been strained; in spite of the Fourierists' theoretical views on the goodness, or at least perfectibility, of the individual, Greeley wrote to Grant, regarding Grant's problems with the Ohio Phalanx, that he was up against the "faithlessness, selfishness, and baseness of Man."[14] According to Guarneri, the Fourierist communities were rife with contradictions because they sought to establish a utopian new order while appealing to the same selfish motives that governed the old society that they hoped to replace.[15] Certainly, for all the dedicated associationists, there must have been many more who were simply unable to provide for themselves and therefore would have been unsuited to the demands of communal living.

Family and Friends

This year was a time of change for Alderson's family in Ohio as well as for her sisters and mother back in England, with births, deaths, and other comings and goings. In the spring of 1843, William and Mary Howitt returned to England from Germany, where they had been since June 1840, learning German and collecting literary materials for their own work. Mary had also learned Danish and Swedish and had begun what was to prove an immensely popular series of translations of the Swedish novelist Fredrika Bremer.[16] Later she would also be the first to translate the works of Hans Christian Andersen from Danish into English. Surprisingly, Emma and Mary had had only one exchange of letters since the Aldersons left England. What seems to have moved Emma to break the silence was the death of Mary's son Claude in March 1844 following almost a year of intense suffering, the result of a knee injury sustained in Germany. It was a long and difficult year for the whole family, and Mary berated herself severely when Claude died. In one of several letters to Anna about Claude's death, she wrote,

> Poor dear Claude! at this very moment I see the unfinished translation lying before me, which was broken off by his death. Alas! I could have shed burning tears over this. How often did he beg and pray of me to put aside my translation just for that one day, that I might sit by him and talk or read to him! I, never

> thinking how near his end was, said "oh no, I must go on yet a page or two." How little did I think that in a short time I should have leisure enough and to spare![17]

If Linda H. Peterson is right, it was this moment that initiated Howitt's long engagement with collaborative writing, leading to and beyond her work with Alderson on *Our Cousins in Ohio*. The painful recognition of that conflict between professional and familial obligations, Peterson argues, led Howitt to "re-envision collaborative work and create a new kind of writing project that could encompass every family member."[18] It is doubtful that either sister had anything like *Our Cousins* in mind when they recommenced their correspondence, but as the sisters took up their pens to assuage a domestic grief, they bore out the claim I have been making that, for this family at least, public and private writing were inseparable. Mary's grief sprang in part from the perception of a conflict between her public writings and her private responsibilities as a mother. The more private mode of writing, renewed at that moment with her sister, led in turn to new forms of public authorship.

Howitt lost a child that year, while Alderson and Anna Harrison each gained one. Although both sisters delighted in the new additions to their families, Alderson's letters remind us of the fears and regrets that must so often have accompanied pregnancy in the days before reliable medical care and birth control. As Anna approached the birth of her eighth child, Emma wrote, "I am sure I sympathize with her in her prospect of an increase to her family. I feel what a trial such a thing would be to me and am strong & younger" (see page 154). When the child was born, she was named Emma Lucy, after her aunt in America. Soon Emma herself was faced with the frightening "prospect of again becoming a mother," as she told her own mother. "I had hoped to have been spared & for a time it was a great sorrow & humiliation to me. I felt as if, like Elizabeth of old, I would fain fly into the wilderness; I felt for dear Anna then, but now I am just reconciled" (see page 177). On July 15, 1844, the child was born two months early. Again, the name was chosen to reaffirm family ties across the Atlantic. Ann Alice, as she was called, owed her first name to her grandmother and her second to three of Harrison's relatives: a grandmother, a great-grandmother, and a sister.

Other changes were taking place in the Aldersons' Cincinnati household, changes that could make a big difference in the domestic economy of the frontier, where so much had to be done by hand. Elizabeth and Richard, who had accompanied the family on their voyage from England, followed them to Cincinnati, although Elizabeth seems to have been perpetually dissatisfied and talked regularly of returning to England. A few months after arriving in Cincinnati, she again left the Aldersons, this time to board in the city, where she taught at a Friends school. Having found her peevish sister-in-law more troublesome than helpful, Emma must have been relieved to see her go. More difficult was the loss at the same time of Dorothea, "one of the best helps in the country, a married woman who had been respectably brought up and could undertake & do every thing" (see page 131). She had gone to nurse a sick aunt, leaving in her place a nine-year-old daughter,

Mary, "the handiest little maiden in the union." At the end of July 1843, Harrison's brother Ralph Alderson died, leaving his wife, Ann, and two small children. Harrison and Emma offered to take them in, partly as an act of kindness, but also for the help they might give in running the household. They did not arrive until late November, at which time Emma reported, "I look forward to being greatly relieved" (see page 156). Unfortunately, Ann seems to have come and gone over the next few months, until, after a reference to her making candles with Harrison in February, there is no more mention of Ann or her children.

With the heavy seasonal workloads and the uncertainty of hired help, frontier children had to grow up quickly, assuming responsibilities we can hardly imagine today. Emma briefly considered adopting Dorothea's daughter, Mary, but then decided against it. Elsewhere in her letters, she describes this common practice as a practical, symbiotic relationship whereby the child received a home with parents, who in turn were assured of assistance then and in their old age. Although she sometimes complains in her letters about them, and especially about William Charles's innate selfishness, her own children appear thoroughly involved in running the home and farm. Perhaps there is some exaggeration when she tells Mary later that, by Anna Mary's fifth birthday, "she can chop wood & fetch in wood, milk Blackberry & even, when occasion requires, go up into the loft & give her hay" (see page 398), but clearly all hands were needed to maintain house and farm.

It was a common complaint among middle-class immigrants that domestic help was hard to find and unreliable and (at a dollar and a half a week) expensive when found. Sometimes Emma attributes the problem to the American spirit of independence and social restlessness. Servants in America, she writes,

> are too independent to be bound by ~~interest~~ honour: interest or any accident will prevent them fulfilling their engagements. I often think of the English hiring, of the earnest money & the sort of quiet confidence one felt that the servant would come at or near the time fixed. . . . All are, dispite their assertions, aiming at being higher: the middle class seek to be each as great & appear as well as the other & the poor are jealous & insolent towards their superiors, whom they feel such, though they will not acknowledge it. (see page 179)

Elsewhere she attributes the problem to "the hateful effects of" slavery, which she believed had made "labour & degradation synonymous" (see page 335). Either way, the lack of domestic help was a trial for the middle-class immigrant.

Throughout the spring of 1844, Emma was largely without paid help except for some with the washing, but in that time, she came to realize that servants could be a drain as well as a support, that an independence of mind and spirit did not always depend on freedom from work. "Work which at first was a heavy burden is become easy by habit; . . . I often feel that love & kindness enoble & dignify the meanest offices & make us happy in the midst of much personal exertion. I never had my health better nor moved with a lighter step & heart than I have done this spring & summer & were it not for the prospect I have before me, nothing should induce me to have a servant" (see pages 180–181). But that "prospect" of another child in July meant that she did need help, especially as that summer Harrison's laborers would be boarding with the household and would require "three hot meals a day beside two lunches in the field. This kept us pretty busy," she notes, for "it is awful work to cook over a stove in this hot climate" (see page 184). Fortunately, by June, Elizabeth had returned, having apparently improved in her attitude, and a month later, Emma was able to hire Adelle (or Ada), an escaped slave, who would stay with the family through the following summer. The story of Adelle's mistreatment and escape elicited not only Emma's compassion and indignation but also that of Mary Howitt, who added the material to Emma's later journal entries as part of *Our Cousins*.[19]

Friends and the Great Separations

Even as their family ties remained strong across such a great distance, by the early 1840s the three sisters were going separate ways in their religious faiths. Most of the American Yearly Meetings remained divided since the Hicksite-Orthodox split of 1827, and the Orthodox branch was only a couple of years away from its next split, between the followers of the evangelical Joseph John Gurney and those of the more conservative quietist John Wilbur. London Yearly Meeting, the closest thing to a final authority among Friends, had taken the side of the Orthodox and would take the side of the Gurneyites as well. In the midst of this turmoil, the Botham sisters were being pulled in three different directions.

The Aldersons embraced the so-called Orthodox model of Quakerism, with its adoption of more contemporary evangelical practices and a more open attitude about working with other Christian denominations for social causes. In her letters, Emma repeatedly condemns the Hicksites and Elias Hicks, whose ministry had catalyzed (if not actually caused) the great separation in 1827. The Aldersons had been received enthusiastically into the Friends Meeting in Westland and were similarly received by Cincinnati Monthly Meeting and its parent Indiana Yearly Meeting. By July 20, 1843, Westland Monthly Meeting had endorsed and forwarded the Aldersons' certificates to Cincinnati Monthly Meeting, and a group of Friends had been appointed to visit the Aldersons.[20] That their reputation had preceded them might be inferred from the prominence of the Friends in that group. One, William Crossman, had been appointed clerk for the Orthodox Meeting after the separation in 1827–1828, with another of the group, Ephraim Morgan (1790–1873), appointed to assist him. The other two, Harriet Steer (1795–1883), a recorded minister, and Phebe Shipley, were also among the more senior and influential members of the Meeting.[21] In any case, the Aldersons seem to have moved very quickly into the inner circle of Cincinnati Monthly Meeting: only a month after their endorsement, Harrison was given the responsibility of printing and distributing an important minute from London Yearly Meeting condemning the separation of the Anti-Slavery Friends from Indiana Yearly Meeting.[22] The following month he was appointed, along with Morgan and Crossman, to represent the Monthly Meeting at the upcoming meeting of Miami Quarter.

In July 1844 Harrison's stature in the Society of Friends was recognized again when Cincinnati Monthly Meeting "recorded" him as a minister. Although that recognition conferred no formal authority (or salary), it marked Harrison as a Friend of considerable stature and certified the legitimacy of his Orthodox (evangelical) views on Quaker doctrine and practice. Emma wrote joyfully to her mother that, "though by this act of man he is neither more nor less than he was before, yet it is a great satisfaction to have the full & entire unity of our friends and to see them so soon & so cordially receiving him as an honoured instrument in the good & great work of a minister of the gospel" (see page 183). Thus in October he joined the Preparative Meeting of Ministers and Elders prior to the annual gathering of Indiana Yearly Meeting.

With so many traveling Friends, word of mouth might do much to keep American Friends abreast of developments in the Society back in England, but the Aldersons also welcomed copies of the *British Friend* forwarded by friends and relatives. The *British Friend* began publication in January 1843 in Glasgow, taking over from the *Irish Friend*, whose publisher, William Bell, had fallen on financial difficulties and emigrated to America (eventually even to Cincinnati). The following month, publication of the more evangelical *Friend* began in London under the leadership of a group from London Yearly Meeting, including Josiah Forster and George Stacy, who visited the Aldersons, probably in January or February 1846. Although in the first few years, Emma makes no reference to the *Friend*, the visit of Forster and Stacy marks the beginning of her disenchantment with the *British Friend* for its "partizan spirit . . . prejudice and really incorrect statements" regarding John Wilbur (see page 299). The Aldersons' rejection of the Quaker peculiarities and their adherence to a more evangelical mode of Quakerism would have made them a more likely audience for the *Friend* from the beginning, but when the *British Friend* took the side of Wilbur and the *Friend* that of Gurney, the Aldersons apparently decided in favor of the latter. Stacy and Forster might also have used their time in America to promote the paper they had started, but Emma's letters do not indicate that she was aware of the role they had played in that regard.

Back in England, two major changes were taking place in the life of Emma's oldest sister, Anna Harrison. Following the collapse of Daniel Harrison's partnership with Octavius Waterhouse in 1840, the Harrisons had to forgo plans of early retirement and move to a smaller house near Birkenhead, while Daniel struggled to rebuild their financial situation and his standing in the tea and coffee trade. At the end of 1843, he entered into a new partnership with his youngest brother, Smith Harrison, and Joseph Crosfield, another member of the old firm, Harrison and Waterhouse.[23] The new business, Harrisons and Crosfield, was one of the many smaller companies looking for a share of the huge market that had opened up with the elimination in 1813 of the East India Company's 200-year-old monopoly on trade with Asia. The investment by Joseph's Wilburite father, George Crosfield, of £4,000 in the new venture helped make that possible and may also have helped the two families reconcile religious differences.[24] Harrisons and Crosfield was an immediate success: begun with £8,000, the company saw profits in the first three years rise £3,000 to £6,400, and within two decades the company had become London's third-largest tea trader, buying and selling nearly three million pounds of tea annually and a smaller quantity of coffee.[25]

The other change was in Anna's spiritual life. As the Aldersons were becoming more deeply involved in the Society of Friends, Anna was moving in the other direction, and by the end of 1843 she had left Quakerism to be baptized into the Church of England.[26] Anna may have been keeping that aspect of her life a secret from her sister; none of Emma's letters indicate any awareness of her change of heart. Although Emma could respect sincere Christians from other denominations, the respect she professes for her sister's religious life might have been more heavily qualified (as it was in letters to her other sister) had she known of Anna's conversion. "Thy letters," she writes, "breathe such a pure & heavenly spirit, do so evidence a mind redeemed & set on better things, that I rise from their perusal refreshed & strengthened and with an earnest desire to be thy humble companion in thy heavenward journey" (see page 387).

Emma was well aware of Mary and William Howitt's falling away from Quakerism, or at least from the kind of Quakerism to which she subscribed, as she chides them a few times for such infidelities as their "ancient partiality" for Unitarian doctrines (see page 196). Paradoxically, Howitt attributes that partiality to the force of her father's deeply traditional Quakerism: "So entirely was the fundamental doctrine of the Saviour being the Incarnate God hidden from us, that we grew up to the age when opinions assert themselves to find that our minds had instinctively shaped themselves into the Unitarian belief."[27]

William's progressive, liberal views had first disturbed Friends in 1824, when he published his elegy "A Poet's Thoughts at the Interment of Lord Byron," which was reprinted three years later in *The Desolation of Eyam*, a collection published jointly by William and Mary.[28] The Howitts' brand of Quakerism illustrates the complexity of the Quaker theological and political landscape. For them, the Hicksite conviction "that it is the [indwelling] Spirit, not the Scriptures, which is the ground and source of all truth" sanctioned a fuller engagement with "the world" than Hicks and many of his followers would have been comfortable with.[29] While the evangelical turn of Orthodox Friends helped facilitate a wider religious and political engagement with that world, the evangelical beliefs in the authority of scripture and sanctification through an avowed faith in the atonement through Christ's death were incompatible with the Howitts' staunchly liberal philosophy. When Mary criticizes Friends for their "contracted and sectarian feelings," she may have been referring as much to the evangelicals as to the quietists.[30] Shortly before leaving for Germany in 1840, Mary met with a group of American abolitionists, including William Lloyd Garrison and Lucretia Mott, and reported in disgust that "the English Friends will not receive her [Mott] because she is a Hicksite."[31]

Based on what Vanessa Morton describes as "a powerful and charismatic theological position, stressing individual inspiration and conscience as a bulwark against the tyrannical power of church authority,"[32] the activist Quakerism of Garrison and Mott offered the Howitts a more open and progressive alternative to the evangelical activism of the Orthodox British and Foreign Anti-Slavery Society. While liberal Friends in England adhered largely to the evangelical orthodoxy, a "self-consciously radical" movement of Hicksites was emerging in the late 1840s in the United States: the Progressive or Congregational Friends, who "repudiated practices that they believed hindered free expression" and "warmly endorsed virtually every reform."[33] Neither William nor Mary ever visited the United States, but their correspondence with Garrison, Mott, and others indicates that it is with this progressive Quakerism that the Howitts might be most closely associated.

Joseph John Gurney had visited the Howitts many years earlier, in 1824, soon after the initial publication of William's elegy on the death of Byron. In her *Autobiography*, Mary reports that although Gurney was troubled by William's praise for the notorious poet, he finally admitted that "'it was a beautiful, very beautiful thing,' and then almost complimented William on his poetic talent. . . . This was much from a Quaker minister, was it not? Bless the good man, and prosper his goings, is my farewell to Joseph John Gurney."[34] Howitt's muted appreciation for Gurney contrasts sharply with her sister's unqualified appreciation for a man she considered "a chosen instrument in diffusing gospel light & principles not only in our own society but through the christian world at large" (see page 409). And yet that appreciation seems not to have precluded some elements of resistance on Alderson's part to the Quaker orthodoxy that Gurney represented.

Another separation and the response from the main body of Friends illustrated the way in which Alderson's own moral commitments might clash with her sense of commitment to both family and Friends. For almost a decade, a group calling themselves Anti-slavery Friends, led by George Osborn and Levi Coffin, had pressed Indiana Yearly Meeting to take a more open stance against slavery. These Friends worked closely with non-Quaker groups, such as the American Free Produce Association, founded in 1838 to advocate boycotts of slave-produced goods and promote "free" alternatives, and the Liberty Party, founded in 1840. They publicly and unequivocally fought against Ohio's racist "black laws," which refused to allow African-Americans even so much as entry into the state, and against colonization as a solution to the nation's race problems, an idea supported by the leaders of Indiana Yearly Meeting. Although the Society of Friends had supported its members in the struggle to end Britain's involvement in the slave trade, leaders in the yearly meetings actively opposed the outspoken activism of these Anti-slavery Friends. As Ryan P. Jordan writes,

> The executive committee of the Indiana Yearly Meeting, beginning in 1841, closed all meetinghouses to "anti-slavery" societies because they were of a "hurtful tendency" to the Society. The meeting admonished Quakers to work "in unity" and "wait for direction in such important matters" as "anti-slavery" work.[35]

Believing themselves led by their Christian convictions, the Anti-slavery Friends refused to heed the admonitions of the Society's leaders and were expelled from Indiana Yearly Meeting in 1842. During the coming year, between 1,500 and 2,000 Friends established five Quarterly Meetings, thirteen Monthly Meetings, and a separate Indiana Yearly Meeting of Anti-Slavery Friends in Newport, Indiana, the home of Levi Coffin, "President" of the Underground Railroad.[36]

Having apparently failed to bring about a reconciliation with its minute to Indiana Yearly Meeting in 1843 (the minute Harrison had been charged with distributing), London Yearly Meeting deputed a delegation of leading Friends to Indiana in 1845. These included George Stacy and the brothers William and Josiah Forster, whom the Aldersons welcomed into their home the next spring. If the Anti-Slavery Friends were looking to the history of Friends' principled activism against the slave trade as reassurance that the delegation would take their side, they were sorely disappointed when the decision was made against them. Instead of addressing the issue of slavery, the report of the delegation appealed only to the "'preciousness and the safety of true gospel unity' and asked 'those who have recently separated' to return to the Indiana Yearly Meeting."[37]

Having been tasked, soon after arriving in Cincinnati, with printing and distributing a minute from London Yearly Meeting condemning the separation of the Anti-Slavery Friends from Indiana Yearly Meeting, Harrison Alderson would seem to have been on the side of the mainstream Orthodox in opposition to this movement of Progressive Friends. At times, Emma seems to share that opposition, as when she cites in letters to her mother and then again to Anna Harrison the "warlike spirit" of the Anti-Slavery Friends as the grounds for the separation (see pages 238 and 245). Yet, in a letter to her mother, she distances herself from that analysis and takes a more critical view of the Society of Friends for its reluctance to act more decisively against slavery or with more patience in its dealings with the Anti-Slavery Friends:

> Oh dear Friends you are very good for every thing but abolition. And yet we begin to understand a little better what are the reasons, whether sufficient or not I am not prepared to say, that influence Friends in their objection to the proceedings of the Anti Slavery Society. They say it is a political question, that the advocates breathe a warlike and offensive spirit, that they act intemperately and with imprudent zeal. I wish Friends had stood their ground (see page 133).

As the wife of a rising star in the Friends ministry, Emma would have to have been guarded about expressing any sympathy for the Anti-Slavery Friends or the sort of political action proscribed by the Society's leaders.

However, though she was unable to question more openly the ideas and practices of her meeting's Orthodox leaders, including those of her husband, we find more subtle suggestions of resistance elsewhere. As early as 1843, a comment to her mother that "those who court popularity in the Society must not be known as abolitionists" suggests a cynicism about the Society of Friends that we do not often find in her writing (see page 152). More private and domestic forms of resistance suggest some affiliation with the progressive Quakerism of her sister, to whom she writes regarding an "anti slavery sewing society" she attended "at the house of a lady in the country." "Of course," she writes with a note of personal triumph, "this is composed of the red hot stigmatized abolitionists & a thing little known amongst friends ~~but~~ and a very questionable affair altogether, but I am perverse enough to have rather a peculiar pleasure in their society & to give a decided preference in my own mind to their proceedings" (see page 425). Indeed, we might infer a quiet resistance from the mere fact that, despite her strong personal identification as a Quaker, she writes less about meeting business than we might expect, and from the frequency with which we find her at home while Harrison is attending meeting.[38]

In England, Alderson had chided William for his critical articles on Quakerism in *Tait's* written between 1835 and 1840, complaining to Mary that "he has not 'rightly represented' us by identifying us with Elias Hicks," adding that "I could go to the stake in maintenance of our being neither Hicksites nor Beaconites," referring to the ultra-evangelical schism led by Isaac Crewdson in Manchester in 1836.[39] In America, she retained that refusal to identify in a partisan way with either entity, seeking guidance instead from her own inner light.

Although geographical and theological separations between the sisters widened during these years, their correspondence marked a continuation and even a deepening of their relationships to one another. Sharing the births and deaths in each other's families, growing each other's plants in their gardens, and reliving the day-to-day incidents in each other's lives, they were exploring new ways of being together, ways made possible by the growth of the transatlantic mail system but still largely unexplored by the 1840s. Settling into her own home with her own family, including her first American-born child, Alderson seems to have experienced a growth in confidence from which to reach out on more equal terms to the older sisters who had often been more like parents than siblings to her as a child.

Letters, 1843 to 1845

10. To Daniel and Anna Harrison, June 1843
Cincinnati

My beloved Brother and Sister,
It was my intention before leaving Westland to have addressed a letter to you, but our engagements were so many and pressing that I was not able to accomplish it. So in a few days of leisure and rest after a long journey and much fatigue, I shall hope to be able to fill this sheet and dispatch it, when we must again buckle to and, if favoured with health, establish ourselves at last in a home of our own. Of course you will not be surprized to find us here; we told mother in our last that it was probable, and I have since regretted I did not retain that letter one day longer by which means I should have been able to tell her it was decided & consequently request all our future letters might be directed to us here. Harrison, however, made arrangements with the postmaster at E. Bethlehem to forward them so that I hope none will be lost.

It was not without feelings of regret that we left Pennsylvania and the beautiful rural district in which we have been located. The scenery was exceedingly rich and beautiful, such as for extent & variety of prospect & salubrity of air I never expect to see equalled, and we had become much attached to some of the friends, whose simple manners & kind heartedness endeared them to us, and they in their turn mourned over our departure as though some old & long tried friends were leaving them. It was an entirely rural neighbourhood, & habits and manners linger there that the onward progress of civilization and manufactures are fast sweeping away from the neighbourhood of cities & of the old settled states, and I rejoice that for a season at least we have had an opportunity of becoming acquainted with this chapter in the long & varied history of the human family. We felt it was not, as far as we could judge, the place & state of society that we would wish to bring up our children amongst, and whether we have acted wisely in removing them into the vicinity of this great & luxurious city remains to be proved. Certain it is there is an air of intelligence and refinement about all that we meet & see that makes one feel as though we had not the broad Atlantic between us and our own dear England.

But before I begin with Ohio I must tell you the few particulars I have noted as likely to interest you in Pennsylvania. We have had no time for botanizing of late, but one day we went down to pay a farewell visit at brother Wm Mason's. The Locust trees, which abound every where, were in full blossom, the trees in their richest & brightest green, the broad meadows & cornfields knee deep with their luxuriant produce; the cheerful notes of birds and pleasant voices of the grasshoppers & tree frogs were heard on every side. We rambled down to the river; the oposite bank rises boldly & precipitously, covered with a variety of beautiful \trees/. On our side, the hills recede & leave a broad tract of rich bottom land which principally constitutes the farm on the river's edge. We found the wild grape vine ascending to the tops of the highest trees & the elegant leaves just burst forth, amongst which the blossom was abundant. There grew the tulip tree (the blossom we have since seen), the mulberry, the Sassafras, the Locust, the spice-wood & various other trees. The Bergamot, the purple oxalis, the touch-me-not, & other rare plants grew beneath them.[1] It was a beautiful day, and our last visit to that kind, dear family is very pleasantly impressed upon my mind with many delightful associations.

Do you know the flowering locust[?][2] It is a most lovely & valuable tree: the wood is almost imperishable & it, unlike all other trees, enriches the land on which it grows. It is often of great size; the leaf is like the rose acacia, and the profusion of flowers are like the laburnum but white with a pale yellow middle; the scent~~ed~~ is that of the orange blossom. I have seen large trees perfectly white with flowers, & the air was full of their delicious odour. The prickley Locust or Honey Locust is quite another tree: its leaves are smaller & I have never seen it grow so high as the other, though it is a large tree. The thorns are enormous, many parted spines, sometimes 4 or 5 inches in length & branched like the antler of a deer.[3] It bears a large pod which we are told is filled with a rich honey like substance. The flower of the tulip tree is straw colour, each petal marked at the bottom with a broad patch of vermillion colour. When expanded it is about the size of the palm of the hand. These are meagre details, but I remember the time when my knowledge of these things extended little beyond their names \so/ that I should have rejoiced to hear more particularly of them, & I treat you as if you were as ignorant as myself. It will, however, be information to the dear children.

I think I have made you acquainted with George Smith. He and his wife were very kind friends of ours; he told me that in his land on the river bank there were some ancient tumuli and the remains of a fort, that in the centre of one of the large heaps of stones grew an old red oak tree which was uprooted in a storm. In its fall the root tore down a part of the mound & disclosed an immense quantity of human bones of larger dimensions than common men of the present day. Amongst the bones were remnants of pottery. The Indians, when questioned about these remains, said they belonged to a race that occupied the land before them.

6th mo 19th. Our journey to this city has been wholly by water. We embarked ~~in~~ on a steam-boat at Brownsville and, sailing down the Monongahela, arrived at Pittsburgh in the evening. The next morning we went on board one of the magnificent steamers that ply on the larger rivers &, in the enjoyment of every comfort & luxury which heart could wish, commenced

1. Spice-wood (*Lindera benzoin*) is a wild form of allspice. Bergamot is *Monarda fistulosa*, also called bee-balm; the "purple oxalis" is probably *Oxalis violacea*, or violet wood sorrel.
2. Probably black locust, or *Robinia pseudoacacia*.
3. Prickly locust (*Robinia hispida*, also called rose acacia or bristly locust) is a very different tree from the honey locust (*Gleditsia triacanthos*), which seems to be the tree described here.

the sail down the Ohio. The Monongahela & Allegahany unite at Pittsburgh and form the Ohio; it is a beautiful river, not broad but deep and full, and the banks are bold & richly wooded. The rich bottom land which is so valuable seems to al[2]ternate: when the hills recede on one side the oposite bank of the river will be bold bluff covered generally to the very water's edge with trees.

We passed some very pleasant looking little towns & cheerful farmhouses, mostly on the Ohio side of the river, for I observed myself what I have often heard remarked, that there was not that happy cheerful air on the shores of Virginia & Kentucky ~~than~~ as in the free states. There were mansions occasionally & miserably small huts on the one side, & farmhouses & towns and villages and pretty villas on the other. The small islands, mostly covered with trees, were beautiful objects, and many a fine bend of the river gave it the appearance of a small and beautiful lake.

The Packets are admirably fitted up and conducted: we had little state rooms where we could enjoy entire privacy or, entering into the long spacious cabin, enjoy at our ease the society of our friends. The whole is fitted up with the utmost elegance & is beautifully clean. The attendants were all coloured people. Our company was large and agreeable; I cannot say that I see anything offensive in the manners of the Americans. Spitting is quite discarded in good society, and though at meals all seem pretty much absorbed in themselves and leave the table as soon as satisfied, yet I think it is better to be left alone (which is usually our case) that [*sic*] have to hurry over your dinner with the uncomfortable knowledge that the eyes of half the company are upon you, thinking you are dreadfully long.

I am on the whole pleased with Cincinnati. It is very superior to any town I have seen since leaving Philladelphia & is built on the same regular & beautiful plan. Some of the streets are beautiful; the houses are built in a good style, are mostly painted white & have white doors with white metal handles & green venetian shutters, stand back & often elevated above the street, & are usually planted about with choice trees. The Alanthus[4] is a great & deservedly a favourite; it & the Catalpa are now in flower. The former bears a tuft of feathery pale green blossom which rise elegantly from amongst the palm-like leaves. Added to this, vines are trained over the doors or formed into alcoves and give the place a very elegant and pretty appearance.

I have not seen much of the city. The streets have many of them rows of trees on the edge of the pavement, which make them very pretty & form a delightful shade. The pigs are still at Cincinnati: great & little & middle-sized are prowling about in all directions and to my unpracticed eyes a great nuisance. We find a most agreeable set of friends here, very intelligent & refined & with all that warm-hearted kindness which I think is one very delightful characteristic of this people.

4. *Ailanthus altissima*, or tree of heaven, was introduced from China in the late eighteenth century.

Our relations the Shipleys I am delighted with; they are a most interesting family. Dear cousin Ann in her 83rd year has all the liveliness and cheerfulness of youth about her; she is a passionate lover of young children, is never weary of their company & noise, and is not only the grandmother of her family but of the meeting.[5] She remembers my father well, "dear cousin Samuel" as she calls him, & pleased me much by saying she sees a strong resemblance in me to him. She says he was her most intimate & dearest friend. The widow of her son William with her family resides with her. \She has/ 4 sons and three daughters, and two of these have families so that they are quite a patriarchal family &, though much afflicted with sickness & delicate health, yet the superintending care & sustaining hand of Divine goodness is so evidently with them that it is instructive to be in their house.

Ann Shipley was much pleased to hear of Cousin Lucy Bayliffe "the daughter of her dear sister" & wished me to give her dear love to her and to dearest mother & you all. Someway she reminds me most of our own beloved mother than any one I have seen since I parted from her. I love all old people for her sake & when I think I can discover a resemblance to her I am delighted.

There is a family here who showed Harrison much attention when here first. Their name is Taylor and their munificent benevolence rejoices and delights me. They are very wealthy, and their house is one of the most beautiful specimens of a well finished & well furnished house I ever saw. The two parlours communicate with each other by large folding doors of mahogany; indeed all the door are solid mahogany. The paper, the carpets, the furniture are of the very best & in delightful harmony; again we are amongst society who think books & works of art the best ornaments they can introduce into their dwellings, who have leisure to love & enjoy sweet flowers and the amenities of life, & I must say I feel more at home &, may I say it without presumption, more in our own sphere.

6 mo. 29th. Well now my best beloved Friends, brother, sister, and mother, let me introduce you to our new and beautiful home. Would that I could see your dear forms moving about in our house and that you could enjoy with us this delicious spot. How would dear Daniel love to join Harrison at this very moment in the hay-field and thou, my dearest mother, how delightfully could we accommodate thee with one of our parlours, which ever since coming into the house I have felt to be a supernumerary and thought with a sigh what a pleasant room for dear mother. Then how wouldst thou like to investigate all the accomodations: the parlours, the dining room, the kitchen, the summer kitchen, the various cupboards & closets, the wood-house & even barns, corn-cribs, waggon sheds, and appurtenances, all in most perfect order and, like the house, white. For dearest Anna, we have other objects of interest: in the front is a portico of two stories that goes from the ground to the roof & is adorned with roses; at the back is another \two storied/ porch,

5. See the Directory of Names for information on Ann Shipley (1760–1843) and her family.

broad & sunny, where we can dine or take tea & sit in very warm weather. At one end is a luxuriant vine, which has much promise for the autumn, & which this morning I have been training. The grass, which is now rather wild, we intend to plant & lay out in flower beds. [3] Then we have a large & very productive garden, & in it we hope to a raise abundance of vegetables & fruits & flowers, but all things in their season. The house is built about 300 yards from the road in a fine field ornamented with cedar, locust & other trees. There is an avenue of Locust trees, Catalpa & cedar from the gate to the house, all young flourishing trees. The orchard is large & the trees young; we have not much prospect of fruit this year. There is this house & 33 acres of the finest land, for which Harrison has given 4750 dollars, and we are within 3 miles of Cincinnati market, which for vegetables, dairy, produce, and fruit is very good. It is considered by all who can judge a most uncommonly cheap bargain: the house & buildings 7 years ago cost 7000 dollars in erection.

Our establishment consists of a woman servant, a Welsh girl, a stranger in the place, to whom we give 6 dollars a month; a man, \a German,/ who has 8 dollars per month & Richard. The latter, however, I expect will soon go to a situation to learn farming on a larger scale. We have at present only one horse & cow as the land is almost all uncleared with the exception of a few acres oats & corn.

We have to go to the city to meeting on 1st & 5th days. Cincinnati is built on one of those fine flats on the river's bank which the Americans prize so highly. The bluff receeds about 2 miles inland & leaves a broad fertile plain, which is moreover watered by a little creek. The number of inhabitants is calculated at about 70,000. It is a rich and increasing place. We ascend a moderate hill of about ¾ mile long in coming to our farm, so you may suppose we have greatly the advantage of those who live in the city, where all is so flat that the air is often stiffling, whilst with us we have always a fine breeze. In the city they drink the water from the Ohio, which is often very unclear; here we have a fine spring and a very large cistern of rain water.

The Catholics are a very large & influential body here; one of their cemetaries we see about a quarter of a mile distant. I one day saw five Sisters of charity conducting 24 little girls to the morning service; they were all dressed in light pink muslin frocks & bo\n/nets & white pinnafores. The sisters were dressed like widows in their deepest mourning; they have the charge of the orphan asylum and devote themselves to their education & attendance on the sick.

This may give you a very slight idea of the arrangement of our house.[6] I told you it is white with green venetian outside shutters & doors. There is no window tax in America and the people luxuriate in windows: we have 4 into our spare parlour & bed room. At Sarah Thomasson's they had six in their

6. See figures 20 and 21.

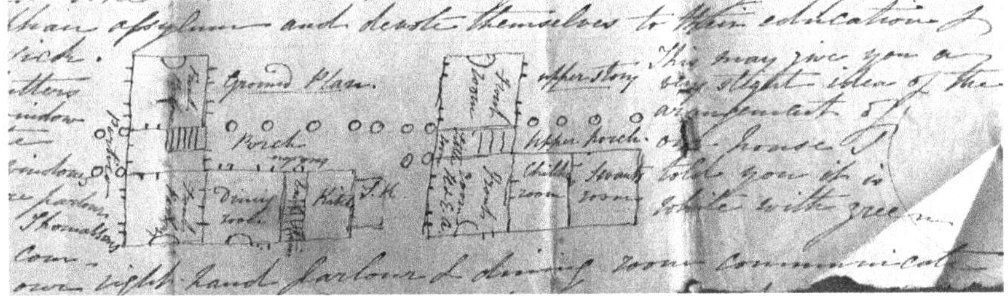

Figure 20. Floor plan of Cedar Lodge, embedded in letter #10. Ht/7/4/2, Correspondence of Mary Howitt (1799–1888), Manuscripts and Special Collections, University of Nottingham.

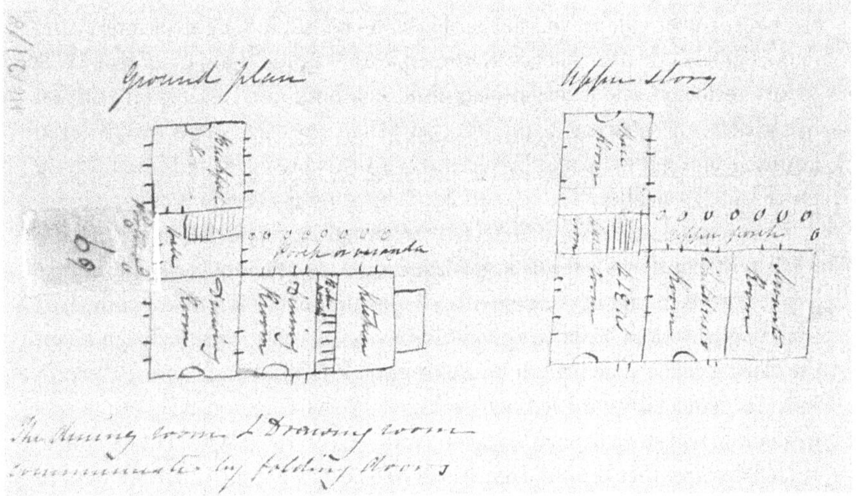

Figure 21. Floor plan of Cedar Lodge, drawn on a loose piece of paper. Ht/21/8, Correspondence of Mary Howitt (1799–1888), Manuscripts and Special Collections, University of Nottingham.

common living room. Our right-hand parlour & dining room communicate with folding doors, a very common & pleasant arrangement here.

This is a dreadfully egotistical letter all about ourselves & our house. Pray excuse me: I am not so wrapped up after all that I have not any thoughts & interests for you, my tenderly beloved friends, and for our dear native land. I fear from all we hear that there is sad agitation in Ireland. The Irish here are all excitement & we have seen some inflammatory addresses & songs in the papers that almost made me tremble for England.

We have heard of Richard [Harrison]'s arrival but have not seen him. I sometimes feel impatient for our parcel. Where are Wm & Mary? I long to hear from them. They are well known & much admired here. I found upon the centre table at the boarding house "The Home" published for 25 cents.[7] I partly read it & liked it much.

The people here are fond of the boarding system, it is so cheap, so little trouble, & gives so much leisure to lead a very idle life, but withall so comfortless that I wonder how any mother can give up the sweet privacy of home to lead such a dawdling insipid life.

Cousin Thos. Shipley, who is a very agreeable acquaintance of ours, told me yesterday at meeting that he and his sister were going East tomorrow. I shall therefore send this letter by him to Philadelphia, and therefore it must be necessarily shorter than it might have been had I not been obliged to conclude it. A kind friend has just brought us up two letters, one from dear faithful mother. My most affectionate gratitude flows towards her for it & in \a fresh/ rememberance of all her unwearied kindness. I shall never be a stranger from England so long as she sends me such delightful interesting details about our dear friends & connexions at <u>home</u>. I am glad dear W. & M. are returned: she has again her children about her, [4] dear creatures. I live in better hope of seeing them & theirs than any other of my own beloved family; I fancy they would be pleased with this busy spirited place. I have much to tell you about the schools &c. Education is abundant & good here.

Dear Daniel, \thou wanted details/: we bought a very fine quarter of lamb for 31 cents; butter is 8 cents, sugar from 5 to 6, soap about the same, cheese 4 to 8; flour is higher in consequence of speculation but is still low compared with English prices. Harrison gives his mowers 75 cents the acre; fuel is about the most expensive article in housekeeping: it is 1 dollar & quarter a cord. Wood is principally used & much preferred. We have not a grate in our house: we cook with a stove & burn wood on Andirons on the hearth. I like it much.

Tell dear mother the children are all well & very happy. When we went to see Cousin A. Shipley, Harrison said to Agnes, we are going to see Grandmother. She immediately replied, ["]Oh, then we are going home.["] She loves her grandmother dearly. I never saw a little child so steadfast in its affection.

We have been out this afternoon, working in the hay-field. There was a fine breeze & a blue sky with bright fleecy clouds. The clover smelt & looked like English hay & Oh, how do these things carry me back to the happy days of haymaking in the bank-close & town meadow, to the rememberance of dear Father & Charles [Botham] and many, many pleasant associations, & I live over again my childish joy in the experience of our own children, who delight as much in a ride in the empty hay cart as we used to do and are as full of merriment in jumping amongst the hay & all excitement if a mouse nest or a humble bees comb is found.

Tell all your dear children great & small that their Aunt Emma often thinks of them, & give my dear love to the whole household. Surely \sister/

7. Frederika [*sic*] Bremer, *The Home; or, Family Cares and Family Joys*, trans. Mary Howitt, 2 vols. (London: Longman, Brown, Green, and Longmans, 1843).

Mary will be writing to me soon: I long for a letter from her. Please give my dearest love to her & hers. Dear Harrison is wearied & gone to bed; he desired me to give his love to you & to tell D[aniel] he has just drawn upon him for 350 ₤. This he thinks is more than the sum in his hands, but John Thwaite will be able to settle with him, and should you not have sent those things I spoke of to Mary & Margaret Ann, we do not wish them, as we find we can get every thing heart can wish here & as low as in England. I asked a friend who was going to P.[8] a few days ago to purchase & send two little books which I thought would interest dear mother & possibly please you.

Farewell, my beloved brother & sister; excuse all imperfections; I write as I can & when I can, not as I would; a deal of this was written on my knee. May Heaven bless you.

Your sincerely affectionate sister,

Emma Alderson

11. To Ann Botham, July 25, 1843
Harlen Place nr. Cincinnati 7 mo 25

My tenderly beloved Mother,
I begin to feel as if the time was long since I addressed thee, and though I wrote to D[aniel] & A[nna] about a month back, which letter I expect would be forwarded to thee, still I fear thou mayst be ready to charge me with negligence, a fault of which I never felt less inclined to be guilty towards thee than at present time, for thou art continually in my most affectionate rememberance. Sometimes my feelings are very painful are very painful and there are times and circumstances that come with living freshness before me that make my heart ache. Oh dearest mother, in all—and I know it is much—that I have ever done to wound & grieve thee, forgive me; and could thou know the bitter tears that I have shed since we parted for these things, I think thou wouldst very freely indeed. I do not expect thou even remembers much that now troubles me; I look back on unimproved opportunities when I might have made thee more comfortable & happy, at times when through thoughtlessness or wilfulness I have caused thee sorrow and, Oh dearest mother, I think I have been the most ungrateful child to the best of mothers.

It does greatly comfort me to think thou art so well satisfied with thy residence at Uttoxeter; I can understand how much more at home thou feels there than at Preston and I think I was very stupid to oppose thy going but this I did for the best. Oh how often do I wish for thee in our new and delightful home; we often say we think thou wouldst enjoy our present country life and like the circle of friends amongst whom our lot is cast. The meeting, like most others in this country, suffered at the separation, but the Hicksites &

8. Probably Pittsburgh.

Friends are entirely divided here: they have separate meeting houses & need not, unless they choose, come in contact.

Friends are an increasing body; it is thought there are about 300 members. The younger part are very gay & have generally thrown off the appearance of the Friend; the elder in their appearance & manners a stranger might suppose belonged to the more respectable & intelligent part of the Society in England. We have been received amongst them with the utmost kindness and cordiality.

Our cousins the Shipleys are one of the most respected \families/ in the meeting; Ann Shipley is looked up to by young and old. It was the testimony of one who had known her long that in the whole course of his experience he had never known her to err in judgment. Her intellect is clear & affections strong and, though upwards of 80, sits at her work when able, and she strongly reminds me of thee. About her eye & forehead, there is a striking resemblance, though it is not so much in feature as her whole character that I see thee. There must be something in it, for Harrison remarked he felt as he used to do when conversing with thee; he could almost think he was sitting again beside thee, and Richard also said she was like my mother.

She lives with the widow [Phebe] of her son Wm, who died about 3 years ago & left 8 children, 7 of whom reside with their mother; 2 are married and have each a child.[9] Thomas [Shipley] lost his wife this spring; she was much beloved in the family. Cousin Pheobe is a humble minded christian; it is evident in her countenance & whole manner: one who has seen many trials and known much sorrow, one too that every one who knows must respect and love.[10] The young people are intelligent & interesting: the daughters have been engaged in teaching; they have now a small domestic boarding school & did we send our children to any school, theirs is the one I should choose. Thomas is a very fine man in every sense; John[11] has the Shipley face & somewhat of the reserve in his manner but [is] still very agreeable. Cousin Ann has been but poorly of late; we all feel anxious about her as well as many others. ["]Have you heard how grandmother Shipley is[?"] is a frequent enquiry amongst the Friends.

Next to this [2] dear family I must introduce thee to some very delightful Friends with whom Harrison became acquainted on his first visit to Cincinnati; their name is Taylor from New Jersey. They consist of three brothers & a sister, all unmarried; they are wealthy and of that happy number who seem to understand the true use of money. Liberal to themselves & others, their house is elegant & in the very best taste: their horses & carriages ~~eleg~~ beauti-

9. One of these grandchildren, Charles Shipley, was William Charles Alderson's closest childhood friend.

10. All historical documents give the name as Phebe, although Alderson almost always gives it as Pheobe.

11. Thomas's brother, born in 1813.

ful, they are themselves welinformed and most exceedingly, almost flatteringly, kind.

I heard it remarked by one, not a Friend, that they considered the Taylors some of the finest citizens in Cincinnati. Their benevolence is noble: I know one poor friend for whom they have fitted up a nice house & watch over her daily wants like brothers for an afflicted sister. Their sister, in company with another young woman friend, visited all the abodes of misery last winter & the family themselves relieved their necessities. Abraham, \the eldest,/ strongly reminds me of Daniel and in his manly bearing & kind courteous manners is more like him than any one I have seen since we left England. Perhaps I may tire thee with long details & descriptions of people thou hast never seen but I want thee to know some of those with whom we have now intercourse & from whose society we derive much pleasure.

I must just tell thee that here as elsewhere I find dear Wm and Mary are known & admired. Cousin A. Shipley is reading their works & likes them much. I was very glad to find they had arrived in England; I hope you are enjoying the rich treat of meeting together at Uttoxeter.[12] This is the 27th of 7th month; perhaps at this very time you are assembled, a loving happy family party.[13] Oh what a luxury to join you & hear & tell all that we have each seen & felt; I feel that delicious happiness of being face to face with those we so dearly love. I sometimes think if I have no more baby cares to engross my time & attention & thou, dearest mother, lives a few years, I <u>must</u> go and see thee. I could pay the a visit & return in three months; and this reminds me, Elizabeth talks of returning this autumn to England.

She seems very determined about the matter, & after telling her our opinion, we must of course leave her at liberty. She has made up her mind, I believe, to like nothing & admire nothing; whatever is her private opinion I cannot say, but she has never yet said she liked or admired our present home, one that every body else is delighted with. She is homesick & unhappy & to such nothing is beautiful or agreeable. She, however, behaves well & does what she can for me for which I feel obliged.

If she does go it will be a nice opportunity of sending thy buffalo robe which we have had by us for many months. I asked if I might trouble the friend who is taking this & our other letters to Philadelphia with it but the answer I received was, this hot weather it would be too bulky a parcel. It would please me much could thou receive it before winter; it is a great shaggy rough thing after all, dear mother, so don[']t expect anything very nice. I shall also try to send thee some dried fruits.

12. William and Mary Howitt had recently returned from an extended stay in Germany (June 1840 to April 1843), where they had learned the language and embarked on a series of translations.

13. The emphasis on this date, July 27, suggests that it carries some significance, perhaps someone's birthday. Of those living in the Howitt-Botham household, Margaret Anastasia Howitt's birthday (August 2, 1839) is the closest.

We are about 700 miles in the interior of America & surrounded by as much civilization & refinement in this immediate neighbourhood as the most luxurious taste could desire. The style of building & furnishing is very good & substantial. I have been in houses as elegantly fitted up and adorned as any private dwellings I ever saw in England; it is not uncommon to have a suite of rooms communicating by massive \polished/ mahogany or cherry tree folding doors, all the other doors to correspond, & paper and carpets and furniture of the most beautiful kind. The Indian matting used in this country in summer is very elegant and very cool & pleasant; we have it on two of our [3] rooms.

Our house in comparison with some of the city abodes is a plain dwelling; it is embosomed in trees and looks very picturesque from many situations. It is built of brick and coloured white with green \venetian/ shutters and, with its portico in front and its large double porch at the side, looks well and is very pleasant. Our view is pretty much confined to our own fields bounded with woods, beyond which rise the wooded hills of Kentucky on the opposite side of the Ohio. We have had a large hay harvest, about twenty two acres, but as the weather was fine, it was beautifully got, though dear Harrison was one half of the time so poorly as to be quite disabled from work or even much attention to it. He was overdone with exertion consequent on our coming & having \his/ hay to attend to and one of his old stomach attacks came on. He is, I am thankful to say, much better, and I think this situation will suit him nicely. The land is in a high state of cultivation; produce sell[s] well in the city, especially hay and dairy or garden produce, & the district is considered remarkably healthy.

Thou wilt be pleased to hear the children are all very well. Agnes is troubled with the hives as they are called in this land, an imption[14] something like dear Anna Mary Howitt used to be troubled with; this occasionally makes her fretful but on the whole she is very happy and very amusing. She sends her dear love to grandmother & wishes she could send her some cherries. She is a child that makes queer old-fashioned speeches & in her way loves to act the woman; she was very proud last week with a little black apron made out of some poplin that was part of dear grandmother's gown, & very much she thought her consequence increased by it. But the finest child we have is Anna Mary; happy and independent, she trots about from morning to night singing her own little songs and talking her own small talk & is the delight of the household. She is her brother's favourite and they play together and Wm Charles delights to amuse & please her. Charley is in many respects much improved; I think, dear mother, he is growing out of his childish foolishness. He is one you may reason with and convince & I do hope that as his judgement ripens and his understanding expands by the aid of divine grace,

14. I have not found "imption" in any dictionary, but that is clearly the word in the text.

his heart will improve & he may become a wise & good child. He is a dear boy and one that I trust, if he lives, may some time be an ornament & a blessing to his circle or in the sphere in which he may move.

Sometimes, dear mother, I look at our three children with their clear intellects, good health & high animal spirits & think, as a mother as well as a wife, I am more than commonly blessed. Oh that my heart was more fruitful in love and gratitude & good works. I often look round & wish dear Daniel & Anna were located as much to their taste as we are to ours. I think the society of Cincinnati would please them. Could not thou prevail upon them to come & come thyself also[?] We only want you to make me perfectly happy as regards earthly things.

Dost thou know, Joseph & Susanna Neville and three of their children are come to this city[?] Their intention is to settle here, and we understand that Joseph proposes being a commissioned agent. They are at present boarding but are looking out for a house. [4] I suppose Joseph's prospects are good, but what is very discouraging is that he arrived here suffering from a severe attack of inflamatory rheumatism & does not seem to improve so that he is obliged to stand still and wait patiently for improvement. He contrives to creep down to the sofa & there remains during the day. Susanna is just the same active energetic cheerful body she ever was; she seemed much rejoiced to find us here, and the pleasure of thus meeting so far from home was mutual. I have not yet had much opportunity of conversing with them but Susanna enquired very kindly after Anna when I saw her. The weather has during the last 6 weeks been very warm but seldom oppressive; there is generally on the hotest days a fine breeze and hitherto the appearance of the country is green & as little burnt as it is in a fine summer in England. We clothe very lightly and to me the summer has been so far delightful. Commonly we have a shower about every ten days; it has been now dry a fortnight & this evening is threatening rain, which often comes as quietly & mildly as our showers in England. We have had very few thunderstorms.

The fire flies are abundant & to us an interesting object, but very different to what I had imagined them; to look at them thy are very similar to those little black & red cockroaches we used to call coachhorses. In an evening they are visible rising up from the ground & flitting amongst the trees like bright sparks.

The people that possessed this place had a perfect passion for the Locust, Catalpa & Cedar trees; the field in which the house stands is laid out like a lawn with them. We propose calling the place Cedar Lodge from the great prevalance of this tree. The Catalpa has flowered; it bears a cluster of white blossoms marked inside with yellow & purple & is sweet. I regret that I missed drying a specimen as I was then very much occupied. We have a beautiful Althea now in bloom; it is white & looks at a distance like a large blush rose tree; it flowers most abundantly. In the pretty gardens in the city I have observed it of all colours: single & double, purple, white, pink, blush; and also the oleander: it grows to the height of 4 or 5 feet & is covered with a profusion of flowers.

The green-house plants of our country grow here in the open air; it is the native region of many. The trumpet creeper is a splendid thing; its large clusters of scarlet flowers often attract the humming bird, who buries itself in the long neck of the flower. The vine is cultivated moste abundantly & with great success here: there are very few houses in the retired streets of Cincinnati which have not an alcove or a porch covered with them and now hanging with rich clusters. We have them about the house & growing up hurdles in the field; there is a fine vinyard within sight of our house.

How is dear Alfred[?] I often think of him & fear that he will be a source of anxiety to his dear parents who have indeed much to try them and are often in my thoughts with much sympathy and affection.

Thou wilt be pleased to hear that the city manners and style of living are so much more simple & English than in west [5] Pennsylvania that the change is very pleasant to us; we sit down to an almost English tea when we visit: no hot meat, no pies, no great variety of hot cakes, but all plain & simple like home. The Americans always spread a white cloth at every meal; you see the clean white table cloth in the meanest log cabin and fruit is an indispensable article at every meal; they are raised on apples, to use their own phrase. There is one thing especially in the neighbourhood we have left that is quite a costume: the sun-bonnet; it is generally made of printed cotton, a straight piece about 3 qrs[15] long stretched over a straight piece of pasteboard & drawn behind with a large curtain a quarter of a yard deep to cover the neck so that they are bonnet & tippet in one. We find them very convenient for ourselves & children.

Our certificates were indorsed & forwarded to the last monthly meeting. It seemed a time of general welcome, and the expression of approval was warm & cordial. It seems strange how kindly & affectionately we have been received by all since the day of our arrival in this land; I do believe we ought to ascribe this to the goodness & favour which has attended us all, unworthy as we are, our life long.

I think, dear mother, thou wilt be pleased to hear that in his religious appearances Harrison has met with the most unequivocal proofs of unity & sympathy; and I may tell thee dearest mother in confidence that it is one evidence to my mind that our coming was right, that his appearances are so much freer and fuller and I think more powerful than when in England, where he often spoke as one bound and in fetters & seemed to labour often in great weakness. I am inclined to hope from his doctrine & the authority often attending that he may be instrumental for good: a faithful & effective

15. Probably three quarters (qrs) of a yard, or 27 inches. OED Online, s.v. "Quarter, n.," accessed May 3, 2020, https://www-oed-com.pitt.idm.oclc.org/view/Entry/156027.

labourer in the Lord's Vineyard. It is a high & honourable vocation & I trust nothing will ever turn him aside from a full discharge of his whole duty therein.

Give my endeared love to Danl & Anna & their family and also to dear Wm & Mary and theirs. We have heard our parcel is waiting for us at Martinsville but it is difficult to obtain it without some one of our acquaintance was going there; I long to receive it. Write, every one of you, as often as you can; we love to hear of & from you. Thy letters are very interesting indeed; thou canst not be too exact in thy details and tell me all about thy self: dost thou continue to suffer as much from headache as ever? I often wonder if thy dear head is aching as usual.

It seems from thy accounts as if trials & sorrows awaited our dear native country. There was a large Irish meeting on the fourth of July, the day of celebrating the national independence, when 2000 dollars were subscribed for the Repealers.[16] I am very jealous for my country in these movements; may the Almighty interpose his omnipotent arm for the sake of the righteous and save & protect England from ruin.

Please give my love to Ann Stubbs, the Friends and Mary Webb & her Father if thou hast an opportunity, also to the Blaggs, J. M. Rushton and any who remember me and are kind to thee. I hope this letter will be not be very expensive; I began on a half sheet without knowing, and as we had a private opportunity [6] of sending it I thought I would write on and tell thee so much more. Harrison has been writing to Ann Ecroyd; I love her dearly for being such a warm and true friend of thine. I believe I shall never write to Margaret Abbott again; I will try not to bear malice but I feel much hurt at her conduct to thee. Well dear mother, these are amongst our trials as christians: we are to receive & bear with wrong things in a right spirit.

I often often think of dear Father on these occasions, how much the meekness of the true disciple shone conspicuously in him. Oh I have thought more of dear Father's example & precepts since I came here than ever before: his frequent & strong appeals to us on behalf of holiness and virtue "to love virtue," and as my heart has yearned over my own children, I have felt how excellent were these exhortations.

When sister Alice was here she desired me to give her love to thee as also did Cousin Ann Shipley when we were conversing about thee.

I must now conclude as my time is spent. Harrison desires his dear love to thee and you all. Agnes said I must give her dear love to grandmother;

16. In 1840–1841, the Loyal National Repeal Association of Ireland established supporting bodies throughout the United States. However, between the date of the meeting described here and the composition of the letter itself, the movement was beset by conflict as the Cincinnati Repeal Association attacked Irish leader Daniel O'Connell for his firm abolitionist stance. Theodore W. Allen, *The Invention of the White Race* (London: Verso Books, 1994), 1:174; Bruce Nelson, *Irish Nationalists and the Making of the Irish Race* (Princeton, N.J.: Princeton University Press, 2012), 77–78.

W. Charles also said I must give his and tell we go out to gather blackberries & he should like to send thee some; he thought if he could find one as large as an egg it might be worth sending. Farewell my best beloved mother; I am most affectionately thy attached daughter,

Emma Alderson

12. To Ann Botham, September 6, 1843
Cedar Lodge nr Cincinnati State of Ohio 9th mo 6th 1843

My dearest Mother,
Only last first day did we receive your parcel sent by Richard Harrison; it had been detained from various causes but at length reached us safely, and very rich and happy did it make me feel.

I thought, dearest mother, when I saw the beautiful scarf thou sent me, of what Anna & Mary used to say: thou generally sent the very things that of all others were most acceptable. Last winter I lost my ruff & this will supply its place entirely & is much more to my taste. Besides, being thy work, [it] will ever afford me pleasure when wearing it, and I shall with pride exhibit it as thy work. Indeed I believe some of our friends consider thee a very extraordinary woman. I have so many beautiful specimens of thy industry & ingenuity to show and they seem to have as much pleasure in hearing of thee as I in telling; dear cousin Ann Shipley and I often talk about thee and she desired me to give her love to thee when I wrote.

Thy counterpane is a miracle even in this land of bedquilts and patchwork, but it is so novel & so admirable in its execution that all who have seen it are delighted; it is inexpressibly valuable to me when I consider that every loop was formed by thy dear fingers and it recalls delightful recollections when in that happiest part of my maiden days we lived together before aunt came to us[17] and thou used to knit & read & I to work or draw beside thee. It seems to me that there was a purity and simplicity of heart & life connected with that period that certainly, for a time at least, was lost. It seems all light & happiness when my mother's house was the very pleasantest spot on earth to me and she the sovereign blessing for whom my heart felt daily, hourly thankful.

Give my endeared love to my sweet dear sister Anna; I hope to answer her kind letter shortly but must here tell her how much obliged I felt to her for it & also for the many tokens of rememberance: the memoir, as far as I have read, is beautiful & does my heart good. The children were delighted with their presents; Charles hopes to be able to draw as well as his cousin Charles [Harrison] by the time he is as old but at present he is no scholar: as brown as a mulatto & laying in. I comfort myself [with] a fine stock of health

17. Dorothy Sylvester, Ann Botham's sister, who visited Ann and Emma from 1829 to 1830, enlivening what was for Emma an insufferably dull period in her life.

& country knowledge against the time when I shall have leisure to call him to books.

But Oh this American life! A month ago I was rejoicing in being possessed of one of the best helps in the country, a married woman who had been respectably brought up and could undertake & do every thing, and now the bubble is burst. She is gone to nurse a sick aunt & I am left with a little girl of 9 years old who, however, is the handiest little maiden in the union. I am going to say she is the daughter of the woman who has just left, and if we wish it, possibly I might have her to raise: that is bound to you till she is 18. But I do not quite like the responsibility, though many have found it answer[s] admirably, and in fact the only plan on which dependance can be placed. Some parents will give their children to another; one of our neighbours has a girl about 16 whom she is bringing up & educating, who was given to her on board a steam boat when she was two years old.

Give my endeared love to Daniel & Anna. This letter is written at so many intervals that I find I have some days ago penned a message to dear A.; still this may stand. My heart is full of deep affection to them & their dear family as also to beloved Wm & Mary and theirs. Oh I live in hope some day to meet again and that, too, in our native land. If thou, dearest mother, shouldst live, as I trust thou wilt, a few years & nothing unforeseen occurs, I shall certainly try to visit thee, and then I may see them all. I sometimes please myself with the joyful anticipation and yet dear mother I am very happy. I would like to go to England to visit you most joyfully, but to live \there again/ I have no wish; and could thou see our beautiful home and know all the varied blessings of this abounding country with its fertile soil & delightful climate, I think thou wouldst often unite with me in a frequent wish that those that I so dearly love at home were here too.

One great pleasure to me is the knowledge that here every poor industrious man or woman can partake of the good gifts of Providence as well as the more wealthy. The artizan can have his peaches, his beef steak, his melons, tomatos, chickens or turkey [and] almost anything his heart can wish, as all these are very cheap & wages high. It is true in Cincinnati, as in all cities where there is more or less distress; but all who are conversant with these things, and some amongst them the active benevolent, assure me that nine cases out of ten are notoriously the result of bad conduct & extravagance. The needy are mostly Irish \and colored/; the Dutch, who are \very numerous/, seldom or never so.[18]

Did I understand thee rightly when I read thy letter that something really was sent to Thompson [Harrison] by Richard [Harrison]. I certainly thought that was the case & longed for the parcel as much on his account [2] as my own and felt disappointed when as far as he was concerned there was a blank.

18. Alderson frequently uses the word "Dutch" to refer to people and things German.

I believe a trifle would be very acceptable every way & not the least so as evidencing an interest in him and his welfare.

As from T's letter to me I find R has not yet written to his brother [Daniel], I will copy what he says about him & \also/ his own situation: "To thy second enquiry as to how Richard is doing I may say that I think he may perhaps do well. He has got to work in Martinsville & does seem to take much better than I expected; I wish it may last but I am afraid it will not.[19] As to myself, we are barely getting along: I cannot get much to do that pays, and as for my trees, this drouth has killed about half of my grafts, but I am not quite discouraged. I still hope better times will come, yet sometimes almost lose my phylosophy amidst my manifold troubles. Just think & sympathize: only yesterday some hogs got into my lot and rooted up all my sweet potatoe hills; they were the only things that the dry weather seems not to hurt and they are gone, but so it is. None of my English relations write to me but Aunt Mary Thompson. With me English letters, like something else, are quite scarce." Poor fellow, he mentions his wife being delicate & the children sickly. I don't know what they are to do, & yet he thinks if he had a small portion of land in this neighbourhood he could get a good living as a nursery-man & gardener; probably he might, as it is a very profitable employment. I have heard it said that in good times the gardeners and farmers took home plenty of fippeny bits from market; the veriest trifles sell well in a large city. Thompson complained of drought with us.

The summer has been most delightfull: only a few days of hot oppressive weather. We were very seldom without a refreshing breeze and from time to time most beautiful rain that came so quietly and softly like a visible blessing from Heaven. We have be sorely annoyed with mosquitos; they were not very numerous with us but their bite is terrible. We are told strangers always suffer more at first than natives from them; to me they were a real distress. We got bars or mosquito curtains & then did very well, but the plague did not last ten days.

The weather has changed; the nights have become cold. We are glad of a blanket and a fire; I like our wood fires on the hearth wonderfully. We often say how dear mother would enjoy this pleasant cheerful warm hearth. I was taking lessons from Pheobe Shipley the last time I was there on the construction of wood fires. It is quite a science: first there is the back-log, the fore log, the middle sticks, & top sticks to make a complete convexity, concentration and continuity.

From what thou says I should think the thunder storms have been much more frequent and violent with you than us. We have here not experienced any of those violent and awful storms which I used to suppose inseparable from this climate.

19. Presumably Martinsville, Ohio, in Clinton County, about 35 miles northeast of Cincinnati.

The melons are now ripe and very delicious. The water melon is as large as a great pumpkin: green externally & red & white within; it tastes to me like sweet snow more than anything else. The musk melon is a delightful fruit. I am collecting seeds to send you when I have opportunity. The young green Indian corn, called here roasting ears, we like much; the husk is stripped off and the cob boiled & eaten with butter, pepper & salt. It is, I think, equal to green pease. We have had fine potatoes, pease, beans of various kinds, beets, tomatos and corn, but our garden is rather indifferently stocked this year. I wish I could get you to cultivate & <??> till you like them the beet & tomato. The latter we are all extremely fond of; it is allowed to ripen, and pared & sliced with vinegar & salt & pepper or stewed with butter, bread crumbs & seasoning; they are also pickled and preserved. It is considered a most wholesome vegetable but every body must have a seasoning. Few like them at first; it is only about ten years since they were introduced into this country & now no "vegetable patch" is complete without them.

I have often remarked almost with disgust and told you also of the eating propensities of the Americans; this is very much the case in the country, where people find themselves surrounded by so much variety & abundance, but we are pleased to see the manners of the city so free from this, at least amongst friends. We breakfasted at the house of some rich friends and our meal was almost bra[h]minical; we had plain brown & white bread cut in slices, \and butter/, fried potatoes, tomatos & egg plant, fried; no meat, no eggs, no preserves, all as plain and simple as an anchorite would provide.

I am much pleased with our Friends here; further acquaintance tends to increase our pleasure in their society & our esteem for their character. They are almost all from the East: Philadelphia, New York and New Jersey, and have brought their refinement & cultivation with them and at the same time have all the warm hearted kindness, I was going to say simplicity of character, that pleased us so much in the country districts.

I sometimes think, dear mother, of my grandfather and his neighbour when mingling with these dear people: Oh Mr. Wood you are very good for every thing but scour; [20] Oh dear Friends you are very good for every thing but abolition. And yet we begin to understand a little better what are the reasons, whether sufficient or not I am not prepared to say, that influence Friends in their objection to the proceedings of the Anti Slavery Society. They say it is a political question, that the advocates breathe a warlike and offensive spirit, that they act intemperately and with imprudent zeal. I wish Friends had stood their ground.

20. She could be using this word in the sense of rapid or hasty motion, though it is unclear what that might have to do with her grandfather and his neighbor, unless perhaps it is the slow pace at which these elderly men moved. Alderson's greatest annoyance with the Society of Friends was over their inability to move more decisively on abolition.

I believe, then, that much that now offends never would have been, but a circumstance occurred here within a few weeks that was pointed out to us as an instance to the unwise zeal of the antislavery. A Southern slave-holder came to Cincinnati [3] with his family and brought a little waiting girl with him, a child of 7 years old whose mother & relations were in the possession of this man. The anti slavery people heard of her & by some means got possession of her. The master demanded his slave; they said she was sent to Canada; he became furious, declared he would sell the whole family. A mob was gathered & some depredation & outrages committed but nothing like what was anticipated. The child was kept secure and the authorities declined to interfere and the man went away without his victim~~s~~.[21] I do myself rather doubt the policy in this instance of separating a little child from its mother, who must be sent thousands of miles amongst strangers to insure safety or be liable at any time to be seized & sold into slavery to suffer, perhaps, the penalty for the zeal of her Friends.

A few weeks ago a very respectable, good looking coloured man came to solicit assistance to enable him to redeem his wife & children. He was free himself, had purchased his own freedom & was renting a small farm in Kentucky on the estate of his former master & cultivating tobaco by which means he had already saved 100 dollars, when his master fell into difficulty & his wife & children were to be sold unless their estimated value, 1000 dollars, could be procured. He was trying to raise this sum but had only 300 & his on 100 towards it when he called at our house. He was respectably recommended & the truth of his statement affirmed by a very excellent man (an Englishman) in Cincinnati; I mean to call to know the result.[22]

Oh dear mother, with all her faults, England is the gem of the earth: I am proud of my country when I think of Canada, the refuge of the poor slave; when I read of the Anti Slavery convention held on British ground, of the noble & christian acts of our legislature respecting India; when I think of the noble sacrifice made to obtain freedom in the West & that the watchful

21. This incident is likely the one described in detail by Levi Coffin in which farmer D. P. Scanlan of New Orleans attempted to retrieve his nine-year-old slave Lavinia, who was concealed by Samuel Reynolds, Edward Harwood, and John and Elizabeth Coleman. Scanlan had brought Lavinia into Ohio, where abolitionists informed her that she was now, by law, a free person and helped her get away. Scanlan raised a vigilante mob in a nearby tavern, but the abolitionists rallied to repel them. Eventually Lavinia, dressed as a boy, was smuggled out of the city to Oberlin, where she later attended college before going on to missionary work in Africa. In retaliation, Scanlan ordered the rest of the girl's family, who were still in New Orleans, to be separated and sold. Levi Coffin, *Reminiscences of Levi Coffin, the Reputed President of the Underground Railroad* (Cincinnati, Ohio: Western Tract Society, 1876), 534–541. See also the contemporary newspaper accounts "The Press and the Mob," *Emancipator and Free American* (Boston), August 24, 1843; "Infamous," *Daily Atlas* (Boston), August 8, 1843.

22. Alderson also describes this incident and expresses these sentiments in letter #13 to Howitt (see page 140), though with some disparity in the details, including the value of the family, which is reported to Howitt as $2,000 rather than $1,000.

eye of Englishmen & the treasure of our land is spent in efforts to prevent other nations continuing the hateful traffic in men; and I rejoice to think that my children are English & I hope to bring them up with English hearts & sympathies & manners.

We attended our Quarterly Meeting, called Miami Quarter, held at Waynsville the 13th 8th mo. It is distant, about 40 miles, & our road, which was [a] fine turnpike, lay through the Valley of the Miami, which is a fine fertile tract lying between the big and Little Miami rivers that empty themselves into the Ohio above & below Cincinnati. We passed through Sharon, Palmyra & Lebanon, the latter a pretty town and standing in a very beautiful part of the country. We were much pleased in attending the African, Indian & School Committees; in the former we heard an interesting correspondence between the Clerk of the Committee & a judge O'Brien respecting the manumission of a coloured <family>. The Friend had been very plain & honest with him & the judge yielded to the "importunity of Friends & to gratify a whim of his sister." His letter was interesting to me as containing the explanations & sophistries of the slaveholders who endeavour to quiet their own consciences & satisfy others by various arguments & also showing the difficulties a right minded man has to contend with from the mad opposition of others. He desired Friends to be there ~~at~~ on a certain day to receive the objects of their interest.

The accounts from the Indian settlement were also interesting: there were about 40 children in the school & their progress in learning [was] very respectable. The tribe, which is called Shawnee, were holding nightly councils to consider upon the propriety of receiving another tribe, the <*blank*> who, having sold their lands in the Northern part of this state, were going westward & wished to settle amongst them.[23] These poor people, men, women & children, passed through Cincinnati, or rather came here to embark on the Ohio. They were, with their horses, two boat loads. It was thought there were in all about 500, some of them very old: one woman upward of 100. Harrison saw them; he thought they looked poor & somewhat degraded but they were on travel & some say they are the finest specimen of the Indian left & that every other tribe but the Shawnee would have received them with joy.

23. The Wyandot arrived in Cincinnati on July 19, 1843, and left on July 21 on two steamers, the *Nodaway* and the *Republic*, on their way to a new reservation in Kansas. In the wake of the 1830 Indian Removal Act, aimed at removing all Native American communities east of the Mississippi, the Wyandot were the last tribe to leave Ohio. They had sold their land near Sandusky to the federal government in exchange for a settlement of cash and other forms of assistance. The Wyandot hoped to purchase land in Kansas from the Shawnee who had relocated there earlier, but they were refused. Eventually another tribe, the Lenape (Delaware), sold them land in the fork of the Kansas and Missouri Rivers in what is now part of Wyandotte County. Carl G. Klopfenstein, "The Removal of the Wyandots from Ohio," *Ohio Historical Quarterly* 66, no. 2 (April 1957): 119–136; NaNations, "Wyandot Indian Tribe," accessed March 16, 2020, http://www.nanations.com/wyandot/history.htm.

We have gathered our apples and peaches; the crop is small, but it is pleasant to go into our own orchard & bring from thence our own fruit. I never see a fine peach without wishing I could send thee some, and the grapes: how I long that thou shouldst partake with us. Our vines, which are small & have been neglected because we did not know how to manage them, have yielded us about 20 lbs of grapes.

We have received thy last most welcome letter date 17th of 8 mo., & receive my warmest thanks for it. Oh how much do I feel rejoiced to hear of thy being so comfortable & to see such a good & happy spirit breathing through the letter, and the account thou gives of dear Wm & Mary excited my warmest sympathy. How often since have I thought of them & that dear suffering child.[24] Poor things, it will be a deep & heavy trial but from thy, or rather dear Mary's, account I trust it is sanctified to them. Please give my dearest love to them all; I shall write to dear Mary & wait no longer. True sympathy is not ceremonious; indeed I have not been exactly waiting for a letter from her but I made myself easy in my straightened circumstances as regards time, thinking I wrote last & hoping every post would bring me one from her.

Thou art right in thy conjecture respecting Anna Mary, or Nanny as she calls herself & I love to call her because thou wast so called when a child: she can both run & talk & is a child of funny tricks & merriment, the delight of the household. On seventh day when at breakfast she surprised us all by saying ["]meeting, meeting, Nanny meeting["] & nothing would suit her little ladyship but to go to meeting. So we took her with the other children in the carriage & left her at a relation's with one little maiden & she [4] supposes she has been a woman & at meeting.

Agnes is the same doll[-]loving child she ever was: she will play along & have all sorts of strange fancies about them. She is much less fretful than she used to be but the same affectionate clinging child & has moreover a lovely countenance. I often think of Wordsworth['s] expression, "her beauty made me glad.["][25]

At this Quarterly Meeting a Friend named Jeremiah Hubbard delivered a most powerful address to parents on the religious training of their children; the texts were from Lamentations 4th c. 3 & 4 v., and Job 39th c. 13 to 18 v. inclusive. He dwelt on the cruelty of the ostrich as being neglect and laid down the responsibilities and duties of parents most beautifully; he is rather eccentric but a most original & powerful speaker.[26] I like the ministry of ~~this~~

24. Claude Middleton Howitt (1833–1844). See appendix 2, "Directory of Names."

25. From Wordsworth's poem "We Are Seven." William Wordsworth and Samuel Taylor Coleridge, *Lyrical Ballads, with a Few Other Poems* (London: J. & A. Arch, 1798), 110–114.

26. "Gavest thou the goodly wings unto the peacocks? or wings and feathers unto the ostrich? Which leaveth her eggs in the earth, and warmeth them in dust, And forgetteth that the foot may crush them, or that the wild beast may break them. She is hardened against her young ones, as though they were not hers: her labour is in vain without fear; Because God hath

Friends in this country: it is full & scriptural, the whole gospel; they have profitted by their troubles.

Harrison desires his dear love to thee and is much obliged to thee for thy kind & encouraging message, also to Daniel & Anna, to whom he is obliged for her kind rememberance of him.

Poor Brother Ralph is gone; we found him in embarrassed circumstances & with a broken constitution. His ailments increased upon him & when we left Pennsylvania we thought probably a few weeks \or months/ might terminate his existence, which was the case; he died on the 27th of 7th month. From the letters Harrison received we have reason to hope he was in an humble, penitent frame of mind, regarding himself as a great sinner & seeking acceptance in the merits of a crucified & risen Lord who was his only ground of hope. Poor fellow, he had been sadly harassed & almost persecuted by hard & selfish creditors who showed the most reckless, heartless determination to strip him of every thing that I ever heard of. Harrison is likely to lose about 150 dollars by him; he lent him, besides money, a horse worth upwards of 60 dollars, & that has been seized contrary to all law & justice. To recover it H. would be involved in a law suit & rather than do this he will not push his claims.

His widow and child are left unprovided for; we have offered her a home and shall be glad to have her with us & bring up her little Mary with our children. She is a fine baby, about 15 months old. Elizabeth has engaged herself as teacher in a school under the care of friends \in Cincinnati/ and boards in the city, so that should Ann come to reside with us, it will be both convenient & pleasant, as she is a woman that both Harrison & I have always felt pleased with. She is a good managing little body & we would pay her for her services & get a woman to wash besides. But we have not yet had her answer.

Cousin Ann Shipley desired me yesterday to give her dear love to thee & tell thee thy kind message was very grateful to her. She is a dear woman & it is next to sitting by thee to talk with her about Uttoxeter; she knew the Bells & the Pipes & the Harts & the Loxley family personally & old Sammy Bentley &c., all her connexions & relations England over, for they were many.[27] Poor thing, hers has been an interesting and eventful life & she reminds me strongly of thee in one respect: her intellects are as bright, her memory as good & her industry as untiring as a person of half your age; you are shining examples to us younger women.

I am sorry my paper is nearly exhausted for I have much to tell thee, but I mean to begin a letter as soon as this is dispatched & take thee to live with

deprived her of wisdom, neither hath he imparted to her understanding." (Job 39:13–17, King James Version).

27. Perhaps Mary and Dorothy Bell, Humphrey Pipe and his family, Uttoxeter banker Thomas Hart (d. 1813) and his family, and the Loxley family, whose estate young Emma and her sisters passed each Sunday on their way to Meeting (Howitt, *Autobiography*, 1:55). The identity of Sammy Bentley is unknown.

us; that is, thou shalt have a daily detail of all that is worth telling. Cousin Ann S. told me to tell thee to get a work called the "New Home, who will Follow."[28] It is such a good discription of the backwoods life & is written by a young woman who was \a/ scholar of hers & with whom she is well acquainted. I am now reading Forest Life [1842] by the same person & can see that she knows what country life in America is.[29]

We have had 5 days of rain & clouds, a most unusual thing \in summer/. I am sorry to hear thy dear head has ached so much but hope [with] this cool weather it will improve. The children desire their dear love to grandmother; they were much pleased with thy message. Harrison also desires his once more, & accept, my much endeared Parent, the most affectionate love from thy tenderly attached daughter,

Emma.

I am very sorry I was so negligent about directions; I recollected the business as soon as I had dispatched the letter; thy last, however, reached safely. Farewell. May the blessings of the Most High be with thee & his soul sustaining presence <pour> to comfort & support thee by day & by night in health or in sickness.

Please give my love to Ann Stubbs & all thy & my friends at Uttoxeter and also to Aunts Wood & Sylvester & Ann Lyndon.[30]

13. To Mary Howitt, October 3, 1843

Cedar Lodge 10th mo. 3rd 1843

My dearly beloved sister,

How constantly of late thou hast been the subject of my thoughts, and with what strong and deep affections and sympathy I have daily dwelt upon the sense of you as I have pictured you watching with anxious love your dear suffering child it is vain for me to attempt to express.[31] Oh, how I long to know at this moment how you all are and if, as I sincerely hope, dear little Claude is better, but I have sorrowful misgivings that it will be a long and painful trial. God grant that beneath this seeming evil, good and a great blessing is concealed. Oh I do most firmly believe in the promise that all things shall work together for good to them that love God, and I trust, my dear brother and sister, you are of this number.

It is one of the most trying results of being so widely separated from those we love that the mind is distressed with anxious thoughts; tidings reach us but their date is so far back that we naturally anticipate or forebode addi-

28. Caroline M. Kirkland, *A New Home, Who'll Follow? Or, Glimpses of Western Life* (New York: C. S. Francis, 1839).
29. Kirkland, *Forest Life* (London: Longman, Brown, Green, and Longmans, 1842).
30. Dorothy Sylvester. No other aunt on the side of her mother (formerly Ann Wood) was still unmarried, so it is unclear who "Aunt Wood" might be.
31. Alderson's misgivings were prophetic: Claude Middleton Howitt died March 22, 1844.

tional sorrow, and yet we ought to be of a hopeful mind, seeing seeing that in our own persons and that of our friends we have witnessed so many mercies. It seems as if our life long had been one continued series of blessings. We have received good of the Lord's hand & shall we not receive evil?

And yet I do not like to call our trials evil, but how do we we shrink from suffering whether of mind or body. It makes my heart ache when I think of the severe pain, the long suffering days & wearisome nights poor dear Claude must have undergone since his accident. It makes me think of our beloved brother Charles,[32] and never could I enter so fully into all the misery he must have known as since I came here—the privations and distresses of the voyage the loneliness and desertion of his sick & dyying chamber surrounded by strangers in a foreign land. Oh I have dwelt on these things till the thought was too painful for endurance.

Excuse me dear sister reverting to this subject. I began my letter hoping to speak comfortable words & I fear the dismal strain I have fallen into will distress rather than cheer thee. I do not know how to ask a letter from thee, fearing thou art so much occupied that it might be adding to thy burdens, but once again to see thy dear hand-writing and hear from thyself what I so much long to know—how you are going on, what you are doing and feeling and hoping—would indeed be most gratifying.

I go into the book-stores and see piles of thy works and am filled with amazement and affection at the sight of these evidences of thy persevering industry and mental vigour. The translations of F. Bremer's works are, I may truly say, the rage at present; a bookseller told me a hundred copies of The Home was nothing: they were exhausted in a few days.[33] They lie the most conspicuously on every counter, and you are asked have you seen them almost as a thing of course. Thy Tales for the People are also very popular; they are written for the thinking working classes, and such the Americans truly are.[34] Thou says thou considers it a proof that the good & excellent is appreciated in England by the great success which has attended the publication of thy translations there; I think they cannot have been better received there than here.

There is beneath many peculiarities of manner & expression a simplicity & kind-heartedness in the American character which enables them to understand and enter into the spirit of these writings entirely. I am not prepared to join the hue and cry against the Americans. I have seen society under two extremes in this country, the entirely rural and highly polished, and I love and find much to admire in both, but I think I like them best in their unmixed

32. Charles Botham (1808–1825). See appendix 2, "Directory of Names."

33. Bremer, *The Home*.

34. Tales for the People and Their Children, Mary Howitt's series of exemplary tales published between 1840 and 1868 by various publishers in England and America.

& genuine character in the country in Pennsylvania, the land of woods and hills & bright, rushing rivers where the people live on their own wealth, making their own clothing and raising on their own land almost all that is necessary to the supply of their daily wants. They are a kind-hearted, hospitable people, and now that we have left them, we often look back with affectionate remembrance.

In the cities there is a deal of activity, a growing desire for intellectual improvement and that kindliness which exhibits itself in the country in the various forms of good neighbourhood, in visiting and attending to the sick and aiding the distressed in mutual presents and mutual aid, here prompts to various institutions for the amelioration and improvement of society.

The great drawback & national blot is slavery and the still more unchristian, irrational and universal prejudice against colour. There are few, very very few, who are prepared to give the black-man the sincere right hand of fellowship, to set him at their tables and talk with him by their fireside as an equal. I could have been glad had thou in thy "no sense like Common Sense" spoken more strongly, more indignantly, against these things.[35]

We now and then are strongly reminded that we are not in a land of universal freedom. A few weeks ago a very respectable coloured man came to request contributions to enable him to purchase his wife and children who were about to be sold from him. He had obtained his own freedom and was culti[2]vating tobacco on a little farm \in Virginia/ when the reverses of his former master required that his property should be sold & the man's family, being considered a part, were valued at 2000 dollars, & this sum the poor fellow was trying to raise. There was a camp-meeting holding in the neighbourhood & a woman at our house recommended him to go there. He said he durst not for probably he should there be mobbed & beaten & perhaps stripped of his money.

Canada is the place of safety & refuge to the poor escaped and runaway negro & I often feel proud of my country when I think even on this Western Continent she shelters and protects the oppressed of other lands. John Bull is a fine old fellow, yet I trust Heaven will bless him & grant him a green & hearty old age. Long life to him, dear man.

Cincinnati is a very flourishing & increasing city; it is supposed to contain about 70,000 inhabitants. There are many settlers in this neighbourhood who remember it without house or inhabitant or nearly so. An old neighbour of ours says when he came here 50 years ago there were only 5 houses. The hills which generally border the Ohio here reach about 3 miles inland and form a noble plain of about 5 miles long. On this is situated the city and the rich cultivated grounds that supply it with abundance of the finest vegetables. As a dear pious Friend remarked to me, she never ascended the hills

35. Mary Howitt, *No Sense Like Common Sense; or, Some Passages in the Life of Charles Middleton, Esq.* (London: Thomas Tegg, 1843).

& looked down upon the town but she thought of the beautiful passage "as the mountains are round about Jerusalem, so is the Lord round about them that fear him.["][36]

The beautiful river is bounded on the Kentucky side by green wooded hills; here and there a gentleman's house peeps out from amongst them and a pretty town lies in a corresponding plain or tract of bottom land forming a pretty object as we drive to & from, but I never look to these otherwise \lovely/ shores without a sadened feeling. I fancy every good house contains a slaveholder & every little cabin is an abode of misery.

Our home is situated about 3 miles and a half from the city on the high ground & is in what is called the Miami Country. The land is fine & slightly undulating and, what is a very unusual thing in this land, planted with ornamental trees: the Locust, cedar & catalpa are the principal. The house is a good brick building with a two storied porch in front &, at the back, a broad upper & lower piazza where in summer we used to take our meals under the shade of a vine. The doors & windows have all green venetian shutters which, as the house is white, give it a very neat appearance. There are three parlours, a good entrance hall, front & back staircase, and all the conveniences of a good house in England.

The outdwelling are excellent & all white so that they are really rather ornamental than otherwise. The fields have been as green and as full of grass through the summer as English meadows. The lawn in front of the house has yielded two fine crops of clover and, as it is never grazed on account of the trees, is now in beautiful verdure. There is a richness and fulness in the foliage & vegetation of this country which, with the bright transparent atmosphere, strikes us as very beautiful, & other English people remark it \also/. The trees never assume that tame sombre tint that is prevalent with us in 7th & 8th month; the greens are vivid till autumn changes them into yellow, orange, purple, brown, & scarlet, still mingled with remaining green, till all fades away like the passing of a fine rainbow.

We have met with some very kind & agreeable friends here, excellent & superior people whose acquaintance I feel to be a privilege. One family, the Shipleys, are near relations; Ann Shipley, the grandmother, is my dear father's first cousin & remembers him as her early & dearest friend. She sometimes tells me of her youthful days when she was left a young wife with 5 children & lived where Joseph West did & Father used to come in to spend his evenings with her. She sat at her work with the candle on a small stand & he would sketch her likeness from the shadow on the wall or tell her some of the odd adventures he met with in his daily rambles. Once he lodged at a

36. Alderson is conflating two different passages: "As the mountains are round about Jerusalem, so the Lord is round about his people from henceforth even for ever" (Psalms 125.2, King James Version) and "The angel of the Lord encampeth round about them that fear him, and delivereth them" (Psalms 34.7, King James Version).

farm-house where was a cupboard in the great chimney without a door. There was set a large apple pie with a knife in it where all the family helped themselves & supped the fruit all with one spoon. This outdoes America in the far West—these relations of ours are very pleasant people & I feel wonderfully at home with them and that it is very grateful to one's heart to meet with one's own kith & kin: I begin to think the ties of relationship have mysterious strength.

We went to the Quarterly Meeting in Waynesville up the Miami Valley about 40 miles & travelled through a very rich & highly prized part of the country. Indian corn is the principal growth of this district, and we saw whole tracts of many hundred acres in which it attained the height of ten feet at least. We lodged at the house of a friend who has turned his attention to the cultivation of the castor bean. He had one field from which he expected to gather 800 bushels of the bean; each bushel, it was computed, would produce 2 gallons of oil, so that here at least would be 16000 gallons of castor oil. One would wonder when it was to be consumed.

Through the whole, I believe, of this district fosil marble or limestone abounds; we find large blocks of it in a little run in our fields: marine shells, bones of fish, & some very fine specimens of coral are very perfect. It is to me a matter of much wonder and speculation from whence these things came. It did not seem so surprising to find them on an island of a few hundred miles in width like England, but here in the heart of this great continent to find them in such amazing abundance [3] is remarkable and a contradiction in my opinion to the theory that the deluge was partial. I shall send a few specimens with some other little things to dear Claude.

The fire-flies have been beautiful this summer, darting about like little shooting stars; the common people call them lightening bugs. Here every creeping thing that has not wings is called a bug & every trailing plant a vine; thus we have cucumber vines, water & mush melon vines, butter bean vines, & all the wild creepers are stigmatized as poison vines, even our poor innocent old friend the Virginian Creeper that throws its elegant leaves & tendrils over every old stump & fallen tree in the woods. It is delightful to see our old favourite garden flowers growing wild with a beauty & luxuriance of which we have no idea. The fences & woods have lately been very gay with the Solidago, many a head of which would have more than covered this paper. The asters, our michaelmass-daisys, are now most beautiful. We have a thicket in which the Impatiens fulva, or speckled jewel weed, has been most lovely; the Hepatica in spring with other very beautiful flowers delighted me exceedingly; perhaps you have seen them in Germany, but in England we have no idea of the great beauty of the major convolvulus, or morning glory as it is called here. They have a very pretty way of training it round the doors & windows or about the pillars of the veranda, which really is very elegant: when the bright parti-coloured blossoms are expanded the effect is brilliant.

In the woods we find all the various species of Uvularia, some quite new to me & very pretty. Then the balsam grows here in the gardens as I never saw it grow elsewhere: I believe it is a native.[37] The colours are so varied & so rich & the plants so large & well-flowered it will be a favourite with me when I get my flower garden "fixed." The Althea, the Shumach, Catalpa Locust, Alanthus, Oleander, & many other shrubs & trees make town and country beautiful in spring & early summer with their various blossoms. I say town because the streets of Cincinnati are many of them planted with rows of ornamental trees, & the houses stand back with verandas & porches, over which the vine & other climbing plants are trained.

The cultivation of the vine is much attended to here, and in the country there are many vineyards and the grapes are very fine; we have a few vines but hope to have more. The indigenous vine is often found in the woods but the fruit is small & flat & tasteless in comparison with the European. The apple, cherry, quince, peach, and various kinds of melons are very good & abundant, but in our opinion the peach is the great luxury of the season; it grows & bears well, & though our crop has been very small we have had some bushels. Oh how often have I wished I could send dear mother some of our fine juicy peaches; I know how much she liked them. They have been selling at about 50 cents a bushel in the market.

It is now about a year since we arrived in this country and as each <ami-*torn*> has come, our landing, our journeying till we reached our destination in Pennsylvania <*serious MS damage*> I have felt my heart, cold & insensate as it is, swell with gratitude under a sense of the mercies we have experienced during the past year, crowned with be<ing> possessed of a delightful home, whose capabilities are such that it may be made all that the most fastidious mind could desire, placed also amongst agreeable, kind, intelligent people, and though the separation from you, our blood relations, is often painfully felt, yet the kind and constant intercourse we have had with dearest mother and Anna has tended greatly to heighten it even at the same time that their most affectionate letters have endeared them greatly to my heart. I am quite comforted to receive such cheerful happy letters from mother since her residence at Uttoxeter. I had many an aching hour on her account, fearing she was not happy, but now I think she has found a home and is amongst those who love and respect her, where the crowd is not so great that she is lost in it, & I am relieved on her account.

It is a great favour that through the awful cold of winter, and it was extreme, and all the heat of summer, we are now arrived at the most agreeable & healthy season of the year, the long pleasant "fall," and have enjoyed excellent health. We have to be sure had occasional colds & little ailments but on the whole all are & have been healthy & the children have thriven & enjoyed themselves as any parent could wish.

37. Balsam, or *Impatiens balsamina*, is actually a non-native, originally from Southeast Asia.

I may as well be in the fashion and have a bear ~~as well as~~ \like/ other people. Well, my bear is a most excellent help to me in all & every thing that is to do.[38] Here he sits with one of his old shop aprons on paring quinces for drying, after having milked the cow & done all the dairy work, that I may have leisure to talk with thee.

We find servants hard to get & very uncertain; I have had two, each of which staid with us just one month, & we are now putting on with a little girl of 9 years old to do all the odd little rough jobs whilst all help a little, & thus none are distressed. Indeed this fine weather, I quite enjoy our freedom, for when we had a girl we were obliged to live like Americans; now we are alone, we can be as English as we like, and in an afternoon I have my school when the little girl & the children say their lessons; in an evening when all are quiet, Richard reads to us, and in this way we manage to pass our time very pleasantly.

We have been down to the little creek to gather a few fossils for Claude & what a lovely afternoon it was: the sun shone through the bright green beeches; the atmosphere was so transparent, the sky so blue & fleecy, clouds so white, and the pebbly course of the run so winding & picturesque with a sloping wood above us that I should have loved to have some of those dear ones who are absent with us to enjoy it.

Please, dear Mary, send mother word we have dispatched a parcel which I hope will reach in [4] safety. It does not contain much, but I do not want it lost; there are a few dried plants for thee, no correct specimen of the wild flowers but something for thee to look upon as having grown in America and been gathered by myself & the children. Thou mayst be sure I have not much time for botanizing, and at the very best season, in the month that the Indians called the month of flowers, we were moving from Penna & settling in our new home & lost the opportunity. I had looked forward to with so much pleasure of seeing & gathering many rare flowers, but what a blessing do I feel this task, & even [with] my small knowledge, it has given me an interest in the country from first setting foot upon its shore, that but for this and the love of the beautiful in whatever form it appears, I think I could never have felt & I hope to instill these tastes into the children, to teach them to walk on the face of the earth with their eyes open & hearts warm to acknowledge the wisdom & goodness of the Creator in all his works.

I am rejoiced to hear through dear mother that the Dr. & Pheobe are satisfied with their change.[39] I doubt not it is their superior knowledge & intelligence that reconciles them to endure privations that dishearten or disgust

38. "Bear" seems to be a term of endearment for Harrison. See page 145, where she uses it again in this way.
39. This reference is probably to William's brother Godfrey (1800–1873), who married Phoebe Bakewell (1806–1864), but as far as I know they did not "endure privations," as Emma says here. In letter #22, also to Mary Howitt, Alderson again asks after "Pheobe [*sic*] & the Dr" (see page 198).

other people: they have recourses & pleasures that others cannot understand and may be happy where they would be miserable. I believe it is often this very circumstance that occasions people to give such contradictory accounts in the very same situation. When thou writes give my dear love to Pheobe; I sometimes look at the drawing she gave me & remember her with interest & affection.

Have you ever been in company with the musquito? I have an idea they are common in the south of Europe. They are a dreadful scourge and must be intolerable where they abound. I have a theory that they and bugs & some other of their species never were in Paradise but either followed the tempter out of the bottomless pit or belong to an after creation, to the thorns & briars that formed part of the curse for sin. These musquitos have an impish look: their back is humped; they love darkness & dark impure places & sound their shrill fiendish note over their victim with all the malice of an infernal, but cold nights are come & they are becoming scarce. I impaled one & stuck it in a box of butterflies for Claude: it is the one fastened with a needle. These butterflies are very poor, but I am no ent~~y~~omologist: I bought them from a poor man & such as they are Claude must accept them.

Is Anna Mary returned? If she is, give my endeared love to her: I hope she will write to me. What an interesting group you must have around you: I should love to see them. Try to describe them & tell me some thing characteristic about each.

Give my dear love to William. I hope some day to welcome [1-*cross*] you to our transatlantic home. Thou must excuse this desultory letter: I fear it is very little worthy of its long journey, but I write when I can and at long & frequent intervals. The blots are an epistle from Anna Mary; Harrison—dear, I forgot, bear—sends his love to thee and thine; he is just now making long necklaces of the quartered quince which are tomorrow, when the sun shines forth, to festoon our upper piazza; in the absence of his majesty they will ornament or <loop> fine.

Oh I must tell thee what a unique carpet we have in our dining room: it is a shaker-rag carpet made at a Shaker establishment in the neighbourhood. There are the old ladies' red flannel & linsey-woolsey petticoats & yellow flannel waistcoats & the old gentlemen's grey coats & I think they must wear green, however—it is a prevailing colour—with here & there a strip from a dear brother's old shirt just for relief, all wove together in very pleasant confusion. It is a queer looking affair & I expect you would despise it, but they are common in the country & when we were choosing I was quite willing to have the carpet that would be worn without anxiety and \be/ in all respects, taste excepted, equal to the finest in the land.

Our adjoining room is very pretty. It has three windows and is laid with Indian matting & furnished with maple tables & awled oak chairs of a very beautiful make. Here we have our books & bestow all our elegancies. I have no time to be lady at present, but I love to go into that room: it has an English look.

The style of furnishing in the city is very costly & rich: a suit of rooms is the fashion & these are often fitted up with polished mahogany or cherry tree to imitate it & with the massive folding doors \of the same/ looking like the gates of Gaza, and the delicate paper & mirrors & other beautiful things make one forget we are in the Western parts or rather centre of America, for the West is now thousands of miles hence—the Americans, are like the great He goats that Daniel saw, they push north & south, east & west and know no boundary but the ocean.

Farewell my dearly beloved sister; I often think of the happy days I used to spend with you at Nottingham [2-*cross*] & of thy more than sisterly kindness to me when I was a young woman. Shall I ever kiss thy dear cheek again? The thought brings tears into my eyes. May Heaven bless thee, and thine be your trust & crown of rejoicing in prosperity and you[r] stay and support in the hour of trial and adversity. In near affection, I am thy attached sister,

Emma Alderson

Didst thou receive a letter I wrote to thee in the winter & address to Heidelberg?

[4] Just mention to dear Anna that I have dispatched a parcel & request her to excuse my giving her the trouble to forward the respective contents, but possibly it may be examined & therefore it is best to leave all loose. Thine as ever,

E. A.

14. To Ann Botham, October 29 to November 14, 1843

Cedar Lodge 29th of 10th month 1843

My dearest Mother,

When I concluded my last letter I promised to keep a regular journal for thee and much \do/ I wish I had done so, as often little things occur which, could I daily note them, would, I am sure, be ~~char~~ interesting to thee as characteristic of our life and the country in which we reside.

The last month has brought great changes and to the farmer been a very busy season; the last crops have to be gathered in, which are Indian corn, or as it always called here, corn, as a token of preeminence, I suppose, over all other grain, potatoes, beets, apples, quinces and all late fruits. The cider mills have been very busy for a month or more. We have some neighbours who have large orchards and have made a great deal of cider from them; it sells at *<blank>* per gal. We, and indeed all America, make & use cider vinegar which is very excellent and, in its purity & wholesomeness, very superior to the manufactured vinegars of England. In this neighbourhood land is too valuable to be employed in the culture of wheat, oats &c for market; the farmers generally grow enough for their own use.

Within a few miles of the city, gardens, orchards, vinyards and dairy produce occupy their attention and are usually very lucrative. Milk & butter selling are very profitable; milk sells at a fip—that is 6 1/4 cents—a quart & repays best of any thing, but it is a toilsome business. They take milk only once a day about 3 oclock in the afternoon, though I have heard of some who take the first milking, which is about 3 oclock in the morning; the milk sellers milk at 2 or 3 \in/ the morning & again at noon. We keep three cows and make butter which has a very good name and is as yellow and sweet as any butter I ever saw in England; it is all the result of Harrison's good management, but unfortunately, as I cannot announce this fact to the world, I get a great deal of credit & praise that does not belong to me. We get 20 cents a pound now; in the winter it is often much higher, but this is a family price, which is often given the year round if you contract to supply regularly.

It is often surprizing to me when I see the large fields of Maise, or Indian corn, which is so much cultivated in this rich district and consider the constant & unremitting labour which it requires to bring it to perfection. The earth has to be worked as fine as a garden to receive the seed, which is dropped by the hand into holes about a yard apart; it is, when about a foot high, to be ploughed & reploughed & keep with the utmost exactness from weeds, so that when you see the stately plant towering perhaps 10 feet high, crowned with its tassel and its broad leaves full & green, it is a very beautiful sight, the rows so straight & regular that they make one think how easy it would be to shoot an arrow through that tall corn from one end of the long field into the thick woods beyond. After it has been dressed so as to leave only three stalks at most to each root & thus ploughed & tended, it requires little more attention till the cob begins to ripen, when good economical farmers blade & top it, which consists in breaking off the now useless tassel or, as botanists would call it, the male flower, & stripping the leaves from the stem. These are carefully stored up for winter fodder and then the poor widowed stalks, looking miserable enough, are left to be brought home at leisure; or it is cut unbladed and bound up in sheaves and placed in large shocks in the field, there to remain through the winter or to be stripped of leaves & cobs as required. The husking and shelling of the corn are all tedious processes, and yet after all this labour, it is sold at 18 3/4 cents or at most 25 cents—a quarter of a dollar—a bushel. When it is sold unshelled, two bushels count as one, or rather a double bushel is given. We have bought good new cornmeal for 25 cents the bushel this season; it is excellent for feed, and we like the corn cakes & mush very much, though I do not think it equal to oatmeal; but only think if the poor in England could have bread & food at this cheap rate—what a blessing it would be.

Now all this long desertation \on corn/ seems to come as naturally to my mind as the ripening and gathering of it does to the season; corn is the great object of attention. Now shortly "butchering time" will come & then they tell us you will hear nothing spoken of in Cincinnati but pork; it is the absorbing, all important, overwhelming topic of the winter months. However that may be, we have cut and shocked part of our corn & bladed the rest & Richard and our man are now getting in winter potatoes. I remember the time when I thought there were no good potatoes in America; somebody said so. What a mistake it was: the early potatoes are excellent & the late ones appear equally good in their way; then there are the sweet potatoes for which this part of the country is famous; they are, I should think, a species of yam, and we begin to like them, for to all these novelties one requires a seasoning. To me they resemble roasted chestnuts.

Till within the last few days which have been cold & frosty, and during which we have had a fall of snow, the woods have been very beautiful with the glowing hints of autumn; but owing to a greater sameness in the forest trees, the hues are not so varied as they were in Pennsylvania. We miss a certain oak which has dark rich purple and the scarlet Cornus florida, [2] or dogwood, a specimen of which dear Anna will find amongst the plants I have sent. Here maple and beech predominate; they are considered as peculiarly indicative of good land.

The woods both in Ohio & Kentucky are, however, very beautiful; the remaining greens were intermingled with every variety of yellow, orange, red, brown and occasionally a purple oak with here and there the trunk & arms, \wreathed with the Virginia creeper/, of some dead tree starting up like great scarlet stiks in the very thickest of the forest. The hills, where divested of wood, are of the brightest emerald green, & the river, with its now full and rapid stream, forms a scene of such varied & glorious beauty that I often long you, our beloved friends, could witness it. The houses & villas that are built near the river both in Kentucky & Ohio are all white and enliven and increase the natural beauty of the scenery.

With the \autumn & the/ frost have returned the gorgeous sunsets & that peculiar appearance in the horizon which I think I must have mentioned to you before as reminding me of the poetical expression "rosy eve and morn."[40] It occurs immediately before and after sunset and is most remarkable opposite to them, yet sometimes extends round the horizon; in the bases it is deep blue or violet surmounted with a delicate rose tint fading off to pale yellow. I never observed it in summer and think it is the result of the frosty state of atmosphere.

Though the weather is so very cold and one might suppose winter was fairly come, all assure us we shall yet have a month or 6 weeks of delightful

40. In *Our Cousins in Ohio*, the phrase is reduced by Howitt to "rosy eve" (*OCO*, 239). It may refer to the Quaker poet John Greenleaf Whittier's *Moll Pitcher: A Poem* (Boston: Carter and Hendee, 1832):

> If the sick spirit might receive
> A blessing from the rosy eve,
> Or light from star—or balm from air—
> Or joy and gladness any where,
> Safe from itself,—how much of bliss
> Would mingle in a world like this! (208–213).

warm weather, that this cold is only Squaw-winter and usually preceeds Indian summer. If so it will be most welcome, for though the flowers and the beautiful foliage will have mostly passed away, yet warmth will be very delightful; I think I feel the cold more after the delicious long warm summer.

It is now a fortnight since the foregoing was penned & at that time I hoped to have finished and dispatched this long ago but really, dearest Mother, my time is at present so very fully occupied that I have not before today, when I am at home with the children whilst the others are gone to meeting, been able to take a pleasant hour's converse with thee. I have feared thou mightst be looking anxiously for a letter which, not coming as usual, would be a disappointment; and when I think of thee perhaps low & poorly, as I fear thou wast when thy last received letter was written dated *<blank>*, I am really grieved, but I have hopes thou wilt in the intermediate time receive a few small tokens of our love in a parcel which was to leave Philadelphia on the 25 of 10th mo by Tomas P. Cope and also the buffalo skin which was sent about the same time but I do not know by which ship. I am anxious to hear of the safe arrival of these things as I consider them an experiment. I shall try to gather up from time to time such things as I know will interest you and forward them as we have opportunity.

I thought from what thou says in thy last that perhaps Susan Alsop would cultivate some of the trees & shrubs of this country if I send the seeds; I have therefore laid up the Prickly & common Locust, the catalpa, the prickley Ash, the various kinds of Althea & some others for you, and I think thou wilt love to see these, to us familiar, objects growing near thee.

Oh dear mother, I do hope thou art comfortable & hast every want supplied. I think of thee continually, often with the vain wish that thou wast with me; I feel that to make thee happy & comfortable would be be the joy of my life. Art thou well waited on in sickness, my heart has often asked when I thought of thee low & unwell. Indeed dearest mother, I do rejoice that wine or anything else is beneficial to thee & I am so far from judging thee for taking it that I strongly recommend thee to continue the use, nay I beg thou wilt. I expect the stimulus is necessary; Cousin Ann Shipley says a sip of wine now & then in the course of the day does her much good. I was quite pleased to hear her say so; I thought I could tell thee & perhaps it would be a strength to my request.

I thought of thee, dearest mother, when I saw a friend one day who came to see us bring a small flat box covered with green baize; it contained a soap stone as they are called here, some kind of stone which is found in New England. This was heated & placed in the box & she set her feet upon it in the carriage or by the fire; now I thought a hot brick would be a good substitute for thee & perhaps the contrivance would relieve thee sometimes in thy head as well as keep thy feet warm. Bricks are now in great request at meeting; there is a goodly row of them on the stove for the women friends. It is a mark of civility to hand them to one another: if an elderly friend comes in, some younger one will fetch her a brick for her feet, and, to show how the city goes "a-head" of the country, there are a pair of small tongs of a peculiar construction provided for their use. I have often, even in meeting at Westland, been tempted to smile at the bang with which the poor burnt fingers threw the hot brick into its place.

Thou canst not think dearest Mother how delighted I was to receive a letter from dear, dear Mary after a long silence of, I should think, a year & a half; ~~for~~ there was much in it to make me very sorrowful and I have wept many tears on their account. I have thought of their affliction and that dear child's suffering with painful anxiety. I fear from what Mary says he will lose his limb if not his life as the consequence of this accident. May the Almighty sanctify and bless this trial to them and their children and, Oh, the love that may be that is underneath; we may ascribe this and that as the source of our sorrow, but the Lord, perhaps seeing our divided hearts, the unworthy objects that hold our affections and absorb our interest, calls us, draws us by these means to himself, that in him, the alone source of happiness and peace, we may indeed be blessed.

I have a hope that thou hast been able to accomplish thy intention and art spending the winter with them; if so this letter may reach thee under their roof; give my most affectionate & sympathizing love to Wm & Mary & their dear family & especially to dear Claude, and tell Mary a few days before the arrival of hers I had sent a longish letter for her by a friend from Philadelphia. She is so kind as to offer to send me her translations; most thankfully shall I receive them, for I have no great respect for the pamphlet editions of this country, though I am glad to avail myself of them in order to read the works. But Oh, I love a beautiful book—good [3] inside and out—and shall be proud to lay the handsome English edition on our table if she has the opportunity of sending and would direct to the care of Thomas Winn, Merchant, Second Street, Philadelphia for us; it will without doubt sooner or later reach us, probably free of cost in safety. Since we have been here I do not know with the exception of two letters if we have paid postage for those sent, there are such constant means of forwarding them by those going East. I have lately finished the Neighbours[41] & dear mother I laid down the book strengthened and animated in my course.

I was beginning to feel weary and somewhat oppressed by Sister Ann's long delay & my continuing in consequence to have so much to do as the cold weather came on, but I seemed to me that in the cheerful faithful performance of duty there was so much to sustain and comfort that all sense of burden banished.[42] Can we have a higher, purer source of happiness than in promoting the comfort & welfare of those we so dearly love in spending &

41. Frederika [*sic*] Bremer, *The Neighbours: A Story of Every-Day Life*, trans. Mary Howitt, 2 vols. (London: Longman, Brown, Green, and Longmans, 1842).

42. Upon the death of Harrison's brother Ralph in 1843, Alderson invited his widow, Ann, and their daughter, Mary, to reside with and work for her family. See letter #12 to Ann Botham (page 137).

being spent for them[?] Besides I find my health is so good & my spirits so light that I cannot complain if I would & the little snatches of time I do get for reading or writing make me enjoy it with all the zest of a hungry apetite. Besides, Ann surely will come; we look for her every day, and though she will bring another child to add to our little flock, she will also bring able hands & an experienced good householding talent, and then the children and all its never ending weariness I shall gladly delegate to her. I am too much of an English-woman to like American housemaids & therefore shall sweep & dust for myself.

In the parcel I have sent a head of broom corn; it is a handsome plant & of it all the true American brooms are made. I have often thought these brooms bore a striking analogy to American housewifery & illustrate pretty well the degree of neatness that prevails in this land, yet in Cincinnati I have been in houses that would not suffer by comparison with the neatest friend's house in England. Our friends the Taylor's look as if every thing was laid under french polish; all is so beautifully clean & bright, & at dear Ann Shipley's there is a quiet grave neatness despite of sickness & a large family that will tell you christians live here. As we burn nothing but wood, the having [of] a good supply for winter is a matter of great importance. We are just getting our in and have paid 2 dollars a cord for it; in the city it is 3 and a half but we are near the woods. We reckon that from 15 to 20 cord will serve us well through the winter.

I am going to tell thee some of our darker experiences; we find our neighbours sadly given to take or try to take advantage. One man who engaged to supply us with wood at a certain rate summer & winter told us now it was so dear in the city he could no longer let us have it at the fixed price; another asked 20 dollars for a cow & Harrison bought one quite as good with a calf for 13. We have occasionally bought salt, meat, apples, &c & have be usually charged above the market price. Harrison looks longingly back to his quiet honest neighbours at Westland; they were mostly friends & so kind & upright that the contrast is striking and <u>then</u> they say at New York a man's word is his word, but in Ohio & at Cincinnati do not trust them. However we must be on our guard; we shall soon know who are trustworthy & who not & then we shall do, but it sadly tries Harrison.

We went one day to get some iron work done. The smith's shop is by the road-side 1/2 mile beyond Warsaw, a small village near us. There he wrought a very civil young man, the son of a magistrate, a squire Williams who lived hard by in a great red frame house whose ten windows on each side & doors in lower & upper story looked unsightly enough. These upper doors are very characteristic & very mysterious to me; there they are without sill or landing, just as if they were for the accomodation of breaking the neck when agreeable without going far about <*torn*> or ladder.[43] I could not help thinking

43. Parts of the manuscript are badly torn here.

the people that live there have wings surely as well as feet, for common legs could not mount in and out.

The squires in America are very undignified sort of personages. One with whom Harrison had transactions in Pennsylvania, called Squire Passmoor, once paid us a visit; he had been a shoemaker but quited that occupation for the more honourable & lucrative calling of magistrate. It was winter & there walked very unceremoniously into our parlour a great fat pole faced man whose long dark hair hung in straight lines round his head, a weather beaten slouch hat, a larger home-spun & home made dark brown great coat & the usual riding attire of the country: pieces of green baize tied with white tape round his knees & legs. He looked rather ungainly, but after all, the man's voice and conversation were superior & I felt he had be chosen probably for his qualifications rather than a fine house & courtly exterior.

[November] 14th. This morning a friend called on us; his name is Francis Gillingham from Massachusets. He is on an errand of mercy, going to release 14 slaves, the joint property of his wife and some others. They are at St. Louis in circumstances; my heart blessed him in his good work. Now and then things of this kind are occurring to cheer & comfort one, though the thick mist of prejudice has spread like a gloomy heavy atmosphere over the land. I do believe those who court popularity in the Society must not be known as abolitionists. We are marked as such, but perhaps our privilege of English will allow us to pass; for my part I rather belong to this persecuted number, though I still regret some of their proceedings.

That great good man John Quincy Adams has been paying Cincinnati a visit; last fifth day when we went down to Meeting the city was all astir. The milatary & people were gone to meet him and accompany him to one of the hills that surround the city where he was to lay the foundation stone of an observatory which is to be erected there, the telescope for which is to come from Munich & cost 5000 dollars. It was very wet & therefore the dear old man, now 78, was prevented delivering an oration but in the evening he went to \a/ large temperance tea party. I shall get a young man who is now with us & witnessed the scene to sketch the town crier who, well mounted, gave notice of the event.[44] I expect thou wilt wonder why I have such a mighty love for this man whom I never saw. I know him best as the avowed advocate of antislavery principles in Congress & out of it, and being one of the very few public men of high & virtuous principles, he is especially enobled & endeared to my heart.

Our young friends are commencing the winter well; they have opened a first-day school, the chief object of which is to give instruction in the scriptures. They have also a sewing society which meets every week at Abraham Taylor's, his sister Hannah, [4] who is now returned from Philadelphia, being the principal mover in this & many other good works. Their object is to visit &

44. See figure 22.

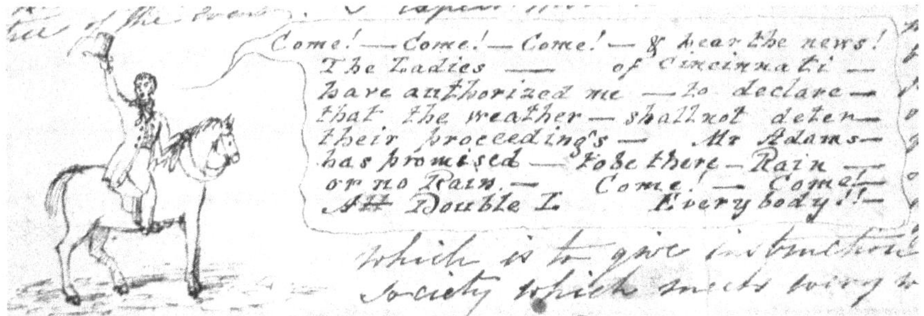

Figure 22. Town crier (artist unknown), embedded in letter #14. Ht/7/2/13, Correspondence of Mary Howitt (1799–1888), Manuscripts and Special Collections, University of Nottingham.

supply the poor with clothing during the winter. They are making shirts & other things for a poor coloured man who is almost in a state of utter destitution. He is confined in the town jail on charges of manslaughter & is to be removed to Columbia, there to endure imprisonment for life.

When we were on the point of coming here, some friends told us Cincinnati was no place for friends; the Society never flourished there; now some are saying Cincinnati is become a school of Prophets. Truly there are some choice spirits in the meeting, some staunch good plain ones & some others who, though not quite so conformed in hat & collar and gown & bonnet, are I believe of the number of those whom the Searcher of Hearts approves; at all events they are rich in love & good works.

I think, dearest Mother, thou wilt be pleased to hear that Elizabeth is engaged in a school taught in Friend's school house where she gives so far much satisfaction and has a good number of pupils. She boards in the city with a friend named Ann Townsend of whom I must have told thee before. The last time I saw E[lizabeth] she requested me to give her love to thee. Poor thing, I think she has profited by the past & is really improved; friends are very kind to her.

I know thou likes to hear every thing peculiar in this country so I will tell thee how we have been preserving our quinces & larger bell-pears. According to the most approved method, we boiled fresh sweet cider down to ~~½~~ \one half/ and then put in the fruit which, being well boiled, is excellent without any sugar & will in this way keep for years. I wish I could send the a jar; it would be so nice for thee to take at night when thy throat is dry.

There is a sister-in law of Hanna Carpenter residing near Cincinnati. I have made enquiries respecting her & find she is still living in the State of New York, <u>where</u> I do not remember. She keeps a store & is highly respected and doing well. Her husband is dead; he was a Hicksite but always treated her with the utmost kindness & respect. Her sister seemed much pleased to hear of thee; I think she said she had heard Hannah speak about thee.

I send thee a sketch of our house; it is a very correct resemblance & though somewhat rough to send so far & make a double postage, will I fancy be interesting to you as giving you an idea of our home. The young man who has drawn it for me is an Englishman \George Henry Knight/ who came with letters of recommendation from David <Dockray>. He has had a good education & been instructed in civil engineering, but not having his health, he is come to America to try what change of climate & farming will do for him. I am afraid his office habits will prevent his being a good farmer & fear he will not do for Harrison. We seem rather in a difficulty about him.

I often think of dearest Anna, from whom sometime back I received a very kind letter. I am sure I sympathize with her in her prospect of an increase to her family. I feel what a trial such a thing would be to me and am strong & younger; I have only three & she, dear creature, has seven. Give my dear, very dear love to her and tell her I hope this is her little Cecil to be the blessing of her declining years. I am afraid she will suspect me of joking when I really feel serious for her, but let her come to America & then I will answer she has no more of these troubles.

I have more to say but must <*obscured*> conclude with my heart overflowing with love to thee my dearest mother. I long for thy letters; they do me good and make me happy in the belief that thy heart is sustained & comforted by the blessed hope & faith of the christian. May the living presence of the dear Saviour be sensibly near thee at all times but more especially in times of sickness and depression when heart & flesh fail & when outward comforts lose their power to please. Oh that I could be with thee at these times.

Harrison's dear love; the children are well & Charley is learning to write; his first letter he says shall be to dear grandmother. Once more, my tenderly beloved mother, farewell.

Thy attached daughter,

Emma

I sent thee a very little dried peach with the books; thou must boil it in water till it is quite soft & pulpy, or eat it in its dried state as a candy.
Cousin Ann Shipley desires her dear love; she is always pleased with a message from thee.

15. To Anna Harrison, November 20 to December 1, 1843

Cedar Lodge 11th mo 20th 1843

My beloved Sister,
Thou hast been so much the subject of my thoughts of late that, having an opportunity of conveying letters by a friend as far as Philadelphia, I am determined to avail myself of it and write to thee, not that I have anything new or interesting to tell thee, for we seem to lead very quiet, monotonous, at this

season almost isolated, lives, but then I am confident thou wilt be pleased to hear from us, and writing seems to my mind the escape valve by which my feelings find comfort and relief.

I often think of you with a yearning heart and with an affection that borders on painfulness, and sometimes when I have filled my mind with the sense of you till I could almost think I had but to raise my eyes to behold you, I awake as from a pleasant dream to the startling reality that half a world seperates us.

I don't know how it is, but when I receive a letter from England, delightful as it is, it makes me also sad. I feel at such times how much we have lost, how dear, how increasingly dear, you all are to me. I am thankful for dear mother's sake that thou and Mary are still in England and comparatively near her, but Oh, if you could all be here, how happy should I, and I am inclined to think should we all, be.

It seems to me that in a worldly point of view we have been so greatly gainers by our removal to this land that I sometimes wish you could participate with us. I know you would admire & enjoy this country & the simple rural lives one can lead combined with a degree of refinement and elegance that sometimes makes me almost forget I am in America. Then the Friends are so kind & society so good, as Susanna Neville today remarked, the society is not only civilized but polished & as good as we should meet with in most parts of England [so] that the great drawback to which thou refers in thy letter is not felt here.

I remember how chilling, how icy, the blunt, unceremonious manners of the people in West Pennsylvania struck upon my feelings. I was weak enough to cry at the plainness of their speech and uncouthness of their appearances, the blunt "yes" and "no," until I learned to estimate their worth and to understand independent of national feelings they were many of them actuated by principle in these things, declining to give \the/ usual complimentary thanks for civility on the ground that thanks were alone due to our maker & Preserver.

My precious sister, the time is drawing on when thou art again likely to become a mother. I do indeed sympathize with thee in the prospect, especially as thou says thy health and spirits are bad; may the Almighty support & strengthen thee bodily & mentally. It may be for the best; I trust it is: all which calls for the exercise of resignation, faith & patience, is and will eventually be blest to us, and dear Anna, that which is a trial to thee may be the means of exciting virtuous exertion and tender love from the older children. Entrust the dear baby to the care of one of its sisters; let her feel that her happiness is increased by a sense of usefulness to thee, and as the faithful affectionate nurse of an infant brother or sister under thy eye, she may relieve thee of all the bodily toil and encourage them to be above the littleness of feeling mortified even by the public performance of their trust, not to be ashamed of being seen carrying the child, only ever of being known to be its sole nurse.[45]

I do not yet like quoting myself but I have nursed my four children in the face of the world & have had much peace and enjoyed additional good health as the consequence. Perhaps thou mayst not like to mention the subject before, but when the event is over, give my dear love to them & tell them I shall rejoice to hear they are performing this act of filial piety.

Oh what a heart-strengthening book the Neighbours is. I read it with much pleasure & profit too. It seems to me that philosophy & literature are taking the side of Christianity, that directly or indirectly the Kingdom of Heaven is progressing. How do I sometimes long for the increase of this Kingdom of Heaven within and around us, and what is it but submission to the regulating controlling influences of the blessed spirit of Christ upon us[?] The more I think and experience the more am I convinced of the sterling value of the spiritual views of Friends on this point. The work is an inward individual work \between God & our own souls/ and it is a comfort to me to find that all true christians, some more clearly and some dimly & almost unconsciously, are united on this head.

We have lately been reading Newton's Cardyphonia.[46] It delights me because he exalts the Saviour in all his atributes so highly; Christ was truly his life, his light, his hope, and can we love him too dearly whom the Father so often declared to be his wellbeloved? Can we exalt him too highly who is placed at the very right hand of God?

How sweet the name of Jesus sounds
To a believer's ear;
It soothes his sorrows, heals his wound[s],
And drives away his fear.

To me there is something peculiarly redeeming in the name. I feel, and in times of sorrow & trial have found, it falls on my heart like balm, like dew on the earth or a cooling breeze in the heat of summer.

[2] For some months back I have been doing without a girl. Indeed, since we came we have only had a servant two months and it is surprizing how comfortably we have got along although we have had company \often/ and Richard & a maid in the house besides the three children and ourselves. Yet despite of having unusually good health and getting through generally to my own admiration, I began to be sadly tried, especially as I was necessarily so much confined, but now I am glad to say sister Ann, poor Ralph's widow, is at last come, and I look forward to being greatly relieved. She is a plain little

45. Interestingly, Emma is advising Anna to do just as their mother had done when Emma was a baby. Ann Botham had given the care of Emma to Mary and the care of Charles to Anna (Howitt, *Autobiography*, 1:94).

46. John Newton, *Cardiphonia; or, The Utterance of the Heart; In the Course of a Real Correspondence* (London: J. Buckland and J. Johnson, 1781).

active woman, one of those happy mortals who, having been brought up to hard work, find it no hardship. She has two children who are both with us at present. The eldest, about 6 years old by a former husband, is going to live with her Father's parents; they are such Germans, whose style of living is a perfect specimen of the habits of their clan in this country. The other, called Mary, is a pretty little blackeyed, fair skinned child of 17 months old & seems to fall in amongst our children, who are much pleased with their little cousin, like one of the family. I love to see them, dear little things, playing together or sitting round the table; it makes me happy to see their sweet innocent faces & their queer merry tricks.

I have a hope that we shall be able to make Ann so comfortable that she will make her home with us. She is a trusty conscientious active woman whose preference is for cooking and scrubbing, the two departments that I dislike much. I am housemaid and shall, I hope, be able to instruct the children.

Wm Charles is beginning to write & I intend to give him some knowledge in geography & simple arithmetic; he learns with great facility & has an enquiring and comprehensive mind. I am amused sometimes at his habit of giving a reason for everything, and generally a very sensible one too.

Agnes is still in the ranks of ignorance: she can neither say her alphabet nor sew, but she is the best peeler of potatoes in the house. She is fat & rosy & her light bright hair & blue eyes and dimpling cheeks make her a very comely little damsel. She is here as elsewhere the pet of all our friends; the little children rejoice over her as an especial favourite and dance round her & lead her about as one whom they wish to honour.

Anna Mary is a perfect Johnny Bull with a great round red face, which would be very common but for her bright large intelligent eyes \and fine forehead/. She is full of humour & sings & shouts, climbs on chairs & tables & her father says [is] the most mischievous child that ever was born. She can say almost any thing and sings "cheery men" with her brother like a little sailor.[47]

We see few children of our acquaintance whom we approve as associates for ours. There is a forwardness, a want of simplicity about American children which I do not admire; their manners are blunt & there is a sad want of respect in their conduct towards superiors that grieves me. Besides, even amongst friends the children are dressed up so fine & the seeds of vanity so nurtured that I am afraid of its influence on ours who are human nature in these things. I want our children to be adorned with intellectual & moral graces, & until they have understanding and wisdom to prefer and seek these rather than the vulgar ornaments of dress, I should like to keep them as much as possible out of the influence of such as evidently place it in the very first rank.

47. See page 63*n*10 for this song, "Cheerily Men," which they learned from the sailors on the *Shenandoah*.

We have not had a very pleasant fall: it has been wet and cold. In the 10th mo we had severe frost, which killed the beans, tomatos, melons, cucumbers &c and changed the foliage so that when a few storms had passed over, the beauty of the landscape was early gone; the woods were certainly very fine for about a fortnight.

There is a fullness & vigour in the vegetation of this country which gives great richness to the appearance of the forest. I remarked the bright vivid green remained unchanged till autumnal tints appeared. The weather in this month has been much milder, sometimes even warm, occasionally a bright day in which the sun shone forth with the heat of a fine October day in England. It is still comparatively mild, but raw & foggy. If we were in England we perhaps should say there is no such weather as this in America, at least not \for a/ continuance.

I sent dear mother a sketch of our house in my last letter to her; it will give you some idea of our home. The little building to the left is the woodhouse with the bird box on the end; we front east and the large piazza is south. It is a delightful spot in summer; the[re] is a vine shading one end of it, which is not given in the drawing, under the screen of which we often get tea in warm weather. From this we look over our own fields on to the woods which form a boundary on that side.

We have been forming a large circular bed opposite the front door, in the centre of which are a cedar & some alanthus \trees/. Here we intend to collect a variety of the beautiful shrubs & flowering trees of the country, roses &c. Did I ever tell thee that the sweet briar is the wild rose of this country[?] Oh how I wish you could pay us a long visit & give us the advantage of your superior taste in laying out our garden & yet I feel we must not have a deal \in this way/. I pleaded, & indeed dear Harrison lets me do as I will in these matters, for this bed & a flower border on the other side, with a collection of evergreens near the piazza.

I feel very indifferent about fine furniture or any other costly thing, but I do rejoice myself in the idea of beautifying the grounds, of availing ourselves of the many advantages of this fine climate. I long that the children should love home & remember it as the happiest, sunniest spot upon earth to them. One reason we have thought [3] that the Americans have so little local attachment is that they very rarely embellish or adorn their homes: a bare house, a good barn & other conveniences of the kind are all they think worthy their attention. Thus the imagination & affections are no wise engaged on the side of home; ~~another~~ \one/ house can shelter them as well as another & a few more acres of land will tempt a man into the wilderness 500 or 1000 miles from the place of his birth.

There is more taste in & about Cincinnati than we have seen in any other part. During the summer season they have splendid flower & fruit shows, and Horticultural societies hold out encouragement & inducements to the cultivation of the useful & beautiful. The Dutch are great gardeners; between us & the city there is a fine rich tract cultivated by some Germans as market gardens. It is really a beautiful sight, the neatness & regularity of the beds, where every variety of fine & rare vegetable is cultivated. It often reminds me of a neat piece of patchwork.

I have told you of the vinyards; from some of these considerable quantities of wine is made. One of our neighbours made 1000 gallons; it sells at a dollar a gallon. We made grape jelly of some of ours; it is delicious & very beautiful. I intend to try to dry raisin[s] another season.

We went last first-day to see the Nevilles in their own house. Joseph has been again ill but was recovering. Poor man, he finds great difficulty in dragging himself along, & when I have looked at him & his poor distorted hands & thought that on him depended the <*torn*> of that large family, I have been ready to wonder how they are possibly to get on. Susanna is cheerful & very pleasant; she shows great energy & could it be practicable for her to transact business would, I doubt not, succeed admirably. They live in a distant part of the city or I should like to go to see them frequently. It seems to give them pleasure to see us. The house is a one-story building, five rooms in succession with a large piazza on one side; it is comfortable, though not very convenient. We invited them up to spend a few days with us in the autumn; they seemed to enjoy it much.

Poor John Thompson, I really feel for him under his heavy trial & great bereavement; please give my love to him. Is he at home & who has charge of the infant? We had a letter from your aunt Sarah a few weeks back. She seems to [be] in good health and says Richard is doing well, that he gets plenty to do.

1st of 12th mo. We are just returned from passing a visit to Cousin Ann Shipley. She is a most interesting woman and has been telling me of her visits to the Oneida & Stockbridge Indians. She was one of a committee appointed to visit them & once was at the house of one woman who kept the Pilgrims Tavern. She entertained them with strawberry pie & the finest wild strawberries gathered out of the adjoining meadow. She was highly delighted with a fine white Irish linen apron Cousin Ann wore, marked [in] the corner "A. S." The woman declared it was the most beautiful thing she ever saw & C<ousin Ann pre>sented it to her.[48] 9 years after, she again visited them & on opening the door saw this woman <*torn*> and her two daughters, the one \an/ adopted child which she called Charlotte, & Charlotte sitting together. The woman rose up & exclaimed, "why here is the very woman; here is A. S. We were talking about you.["]

Another most noble looking woman delivered an animated address; her tones & gestures were full of grace and dignity. She was a christian, & though they could not understand a word, the effect was powerful. One old man, a missionary, said he had been preaching for twenty years & did not know that he had done any good the whole of that time. Cousin thought he must have

48. Parts of this letter are torn here and had to be reconstructed.

been a "dry preacher." Friends do not seem to effect much in their settlements amongst the Shawnee tribe. They have been unfortunate in their selection of superintendents. When a suitable person has for a time lived amongst them, very beneficial results have ensued.

There is an impenetrability in the Indian character, a bias so strong & decided to their own modes of acting & thinking that it is very difficult to make much way amongst them. Occasionally a bright example of Christian character appears & then this original & poetical turn of mind shines forth with peculiar grace.

When sister Ann came down the river, there were on board the boat a cargo of slaves. It is honourable to Cincinnati to know that not one was permitted to land. They were immediately put into a boat & rowed to the oposite shores of Kentucky. It is not, I am sorry to say, a universal feeling, but there is a large & influential portion of the community who hate slavery & watch every opportunity of breaking the shackles of the slave & assisting him in his endeavours to obtain freedom. Some doubt the policy of this course; it has tended greatly to exasperate <the> Southern men, but it is the fruit of zeal in a good cause, though it may be overstretched.

The friend I mentioned in my last to mother is returned from St Louis & has succeeded in securing the emancipat[ion] of 14 poor miserable enslaved fellow creatures. Some of them accompanied him homeward. What a rich reward of peace must he enjoy on his return to the bosom of his family.

Sister Ann has described a very novel occurrence which took place near Brownsville: a camp-meeting of the blacks. She says there were about 700 coloured people assembled, and their appearance was most respectable. The preachers were all coloured & their discourses very superior & powerful: some thought they never witnessed a scene of the kind so orderly & impressive. There were upwards of 100 tents on the ground, which was in the midst of the woods & it lasted about a week.

I wonder how people can rail against the climate of America; it is to my feelings most pleasurable, at least in summer, the atmosphere so clear & bright, the warmth so delicious that except a very few days there was nothing oppressive; at least I never felt it so, and the winter hitherto is very mild. We are told here it seldom last[s] 3 months, and never so severe as nearer the mountains. The present dull season is said by all to be very unusual; the mornings & evenings in fine weather are delicious.

These scratches are a note from little Nanny: I expect there is a seal of love for you if you will receive it so. [*There are some random pen scratchings in the lower left-hand corner here.*]

Please tell dearest mother with my endeared love that we have received two British Friends. It is a very great pleasure to have now & then an English periodical or newspaper. We seem to live in great quietness, but I often think of you and the conflicted state of our dear country. It seems from what dear mother says & the reports of rumours that reach us, that religious & political struggles distract and destroy her peace.

[4] Oh what a distressing thing it is that military rule should be resorted to, that the poor, hungry wretches who are pleading for bread must be put down by the sword and that an army is needed in Scotland to protect the churches. I used to love the Queen, but there appears to me something heartless in her employing herself in paying what must be very expensive visits whilst the country is in discord & distress, but perhaps we are not able to judge of men & things from the very little we know.

I want dear Wm to send us his paper regularly when he commences it.[49] We shall then have full & enlightened accounts of what is going forward. I seldom look into an \American/ paper; I have but small respect for them: they are cheap & look mean & I never can fancy there is much principle or talent about them. I liked Mrs. Childs's Anti-slavery Standard but she has given up the editorship.[50] It was something rather approaching treason to read it, but I did not care; I rather, more than rather, liked to see it on our table.

I am waiting anxiously for a letter from dear Mary, and to receive intelligence of her dear suffering boy. My heart often aches for them; it is indeed a heavy trial; may it be overruled for good.

When thou writes, tell her with my very dear love I hope, if she has not already, she will as soon as possible let me hear from her. And dearest sister, surely I need not tell thee how much we should love to hear from thee or Daniel or the dear children. Could not you send a long joint letter, a perfect folio of correspondence?

I am almost envious when I see other people reading letters; I long for the delight of having one of my own, and yet I feel that you have all been most kind in this respect. We have had more letters than most, I believe. Thank you, dear dear creatures, for all your great kindness.

Oh what a balme do those parting presents possess in my heart; I feel when I look at them a sense of the dear affection that was in your hearts \at that time/. When I look back at the time of leaving England and you all, my tenderly beloved friends, I sometimes wonder how I bore it. I remember the heavy sorrow that pressed down my spirit, & yet I could not shed a tear at our parting. How we watched your beloved forms from the ship, and how dear the receding land, which was privileged with your presence, appeared. It seemed as if all that was pleasant & dear was given up & a wilderness was before us, and yet how many mercies, how many unmerited blessings, have

49. There may have been some proposed periodical that never came to fruition. William Howitt did not produce his own serial publication until 1846, when he joined John Saunders in publishing the *People's Journal*.
50. Lydia Maria Child edited the *National Anti-Slavery Standard*, a weekly newspaper published in New York and Philadelphia, from 1841 to 1843. The publication ran from 1840 to 1870 under several editors.

we to commemorate since that time. The goodness of the Lord, which knows not limit nor bound, which is equally felt to the remotest corners of the earth, has followed us, unworthy as we are, and all we have to desire is more thankful hearts & increased ability to serve & love him more faithfully.

I think I must tell you we enjoy perfect health. Harrison \is/ quite robust and the children look as ruddy as they did in England. In summer they looked rather pale, but the cool weather has brought back their fresh looks. But then we live still in the English style, have animal food only once a day and [1-*cross*] avoid many of the injurious habits of the Americans: pastry, preserves, hot bread continually & rooms overheated with stoves, besides tea & coffee three times a day. Each of these are well in moderation, but it is the constant use which is so objectionable.

There are many species of favourite cakes that are almost universal at this season, & unsuitable food they are. Buckwheat cakes in boiling curd and look pretty ~~brown~~ things but cause a plentiful supply of carbonate of soda to be very necessary. One cake here called hot biscuit I have often thought of telling thee of. It is so simple, so good & convenient, if you want something extra. In about 2 lbs of flour rub two oz of lard or butter, a little sugar & salt; then take a \tea/spoonful of Pearl Ash dissolved in a little water, & mix it with sour buttermilk. Immediately before the effervescence ceases, mix the cakes into a nice, light dough, roll them out about one third of an inch thick, cut them with a tumbler & bake directly in a quick oven; they are usually eaten warm.

Danl likes to know the prices of provisions. For fine flour we gave about a fortnight back 4 dollars a barrel; potatoes are 37 1/2 cents a bushel, \good/ butter 20 c. a pound, sugar 7 c. lb, beef 8 c. the best cuts, fowls 10 c. each (a cent, you know, is a trifle more than our halfpenny) molasses wholesale 25 c. gal. rice 5 c. \corn meal 25 & 37 1/2 bushel/ &c. Cloathing we think generally some little higher than in England but not much.

I fear thou wilt think this letter very trifling & insipid, but we do not live amongst the stirring scenes & here it seems to me that the neighbourhood is so highly cultivated that there are fewer objects of interest naturally than at Westland, where we lived amongst the woods.

The snow-birds are come. Dear little things, they seem to have a great penchant for the little white berries on the cedar trees. Do not elevate your thoughts to cedars of Lebanon, broad & spreading and offering shade to thirty horsemen. These said cedars appear to me ~~like~~ some species of arbor vite or juniper. They are young to be sure but grow conical from the ground.

I did not intend to cross this so will conclude; I could ramble on in this way half the night.

Farewell my dearly beloved Friends. My love to your whole household as also to Edward & Lucy Bayliffe & family. Cousin Ann Shipley desired me to give her love to her; I fancy she would be much pleased to hear from her & she is worth pleasing. Send my dearest love to mother & believe me to be thy tenderly attached sister, Emma Alderson

I hope you have received the parcels, the plants &c & Buffalo hide. I am sorry when I think of it that that parcel was no better worth receiving. It went by the Thomas P. Cope.

16. To Ann Botham, December 31, 1843

My dearest Mother,
Long and anxiously did I await the arrival of thy last, dispatched the 2nd of 12th mo & oh what a comfort have its pleasant contents and all the affection it expresses been to my mind. I had begun to fear the indisposition thou mentioned in thy preceeding letter was still weighing thee down and preventing thee complying with thy usual and most acceptable practice of \a/ monthly epistle, and my mind pictured thee in suffering and depression till I was really unhappy. Perhaps I am ungrateful to a merciful & gracious Providence so soon to give way to discouragement & fearful anticipations, but when so widely separated from those so inexpressibly dear to us, nature is apt to be unusually sensitive. Thy account of the kindness of our old friends and neighbour affected & delighted me. Dear people, give my love to them & heartily thank them from me for all these attentions to thee, my endeared mother.

There is an expression in the early part of thy letter that made me almost wild. I laid it down to talk with Harrison about the practicality of thy coming over & once more enriching & gladening our home with thy presence, but when I heard thy detail of those things & remembered how comfortable thou now art I felt that, much as I should myself rejoice to have thee, it would be giving thee too much trouble and be a breaking up of present happiness that I could not ask. I am sorry to hear thou art so much confined this winter but hope with care thou wilt not be so great a sufferer as thou hast sometimes been.

Thank thee, my beloved mother, for the valuable contents of the box thou mentions as having packed up, and most of all do I feel the kindness and love that prompted thee to prepare it, but dearest mother, it makes my heart ache to think that thou shouldst stint thyself of thy nice things. Use them still, dear mother, and the longer they have been in thy possession and use, the more I prize them. I never look [2] <*top line is cut off*> retained them and enhance their value to me by using them thyself. I fear thou must often feel the want of them now.

I am sadly afraid the box, when it reached you, would be so overhauled & perhaps changed as to render its poor contents worse than worthless. The books which thou says had arrived in the postbag & were charged 12/10 I cannot account for except they were two I requested a friend to forward from Phillade[lphia] early in the summer, but I hoped they would be sent by private opportunity. Although I should like thee to see them, I hope thou wouldst refuse them at that price.

I sent thee two small volumes, "Forest Life," which I thought would amuse thee and which I think contain a good discription of American manners. I durst not send any dried fruits, understanding the duty on them was very high. I enclosed thee, however, a very little of our dried peach marmalade; indeed this box was an experiment & only contained such trifles as we thought would go free. I hope thou hast received thy Buffalo skin; that was by far the most valuable & either as a lining in thy chair or as a hearth rug may contribute to thy comfort.

This is New Years eve and there has been a general firing round the neighbourhood & in the city. One of our neighbours came to give us a salute under our windows on christmas eve; it was kept up through the night & at day break, there seemed to be one universal volley. I think the Americans are fond of gunpowder; it is a practice here on New Years day for the young women to sit in state to receive the calls of their unmarried acquaintances (gentlemen) & it is said that, as they are always expected to take a sip of wine with them, this is an occasion on which many break their pledge & thus begin the New Year with intemperance. The children on Christmas eve hang up their stocking on going to bed for Santinick or St. Nicholas to fill it with sweetmeats. Our kind relations did not forget our children; they had [3] each their stocking hung up & filled with the rest with almonds, nuts, sweetmeats &c. It was a delightful surprise to them to receive them.

There was a few weeks ago a very sociable assembling of women Friends at the meeting-house to assist in making cushions for the seats; we were requested to come at an early hour & bring our dinners & very pleasant it was. I was only there the first day; it occupied four days to complete the work. On further acquaintance with the Friends we find many excellent, actively benevolent, intelligent individuals, but our dear Cousins and the Taylor family are our chief and most agreeable Friends. I love them dearly and am thankful to a kind Providence for casting our lot amongst such congenial society. Ever saving and excepting the endeared members of our own family, there are few that I have met with that I love and admire so thoroughly.

I expect thou wilt smile [&] perhaps be angry at me for being so much taken with strangers, but think, dear mother, how cordial it must feel, when separated from all we love, to meet in a strange land with intelligent, kind, excellent, refined people who seem to receive us into their circle with affection & pleasure, and are watching to promote our pleasure & interest. I will give thee one instance out of many: Harrison's last payment was due last month and, as his bills had not been drawn in \time,/ he would have found some difficulty in being as punctual as he wished had not Abraham Taylor, the elder brother, come voluntarily & paid the 1270 dollars without so much as taking an acknowledgement from Harrison.

The year began rather dismally with us; a fine cow which calved a few days before came ill and on the second of the year died. Harrison had given 12 dollars for her; she was an excellent cow. It <was a> disappointment as we were calculating on having an abundance of milk & butter with the addition of her milk. The other day Harrison & sister Ann were busy making candles from the tallow taken from her; we are preparing to make soap of the remaining fat. Oil is usually burnt here; they use the large bronze lamps with opaque covers and a very pretty lamp made all of glass. Of course thou hast heard of lard oil; it is obtained from lard by pressure & is a very nice oil to burn, having no smell & giving a clear good light. We bought a gallon for 50 cents yesterday, about 2/2. We understand it is exported from this city to England. The remainder of the lard is called stearine & is made into candles which some think little inferior to spermacite,[51] though I do not quite agree in that opinion.

This is the great pig-killing season at Cincinnati and heads, feet, & sausage meat are abundant & cheap: the usual price of a fine head is 10 cents; we bought sausage without a bone for 3 cents; spareribs are 1 cent. It is computed that about 200,000 pigs are killed and packed down as pork during the season. Great quantities of heads & other unprofitable parts are sent to the soap houses; I often wish the poor in England could partake of this overplus of good food.

We have been making a very good dish called scrapple from heads. They are boiled till the bones will quite leave; it is then chopped fine, the fat from the liquor with which we mix a quantity of corn-meal & then add the meat seasoned with pepper, salt, sage & cayenne & when cold it is cut in slices & fried. I thought when eating it, it was a dish which thou wouldst enjoy.

The winter is very open, and during the latter end of autumn & so far in winter we have had a deal of wet weather. The roads are dreadful, being formed of mud, which works into \a/ deep stiff mass like [4] \mortar/ and when it freezes is so hard & rough as, till a little worked down, to be almost impassable. We have gone to meeting lately on horseback; we have two fine horses & I much enjoy the exercise. We found that when bad weather came, one horse was not able to drag the carriage through the mud, so that we were obliged to get another; they are fine useful creatures & both together cost Harrison about 22£.

The Nevilles have lost their youngest child; he was just two years old. I was with them at the time of his death. Joseph contrives to attend to business; Wilson \Greenwood/ & his wife are here & Joseph has put him into a shop or something of the kind. It was very interesting to me in attending the funeral of this little child to see the burying ground belonging to Friends. It is about 2 miles from the meeting house & some of the graves are beautifully kept. The son of Cousin Ann Shipley, \William/, and her grandson Thomas's wife are buried there; there were small head-stones with their names upon them and cypresses growing at the head & foot of each grave;

51. Alderson has overwritten her own text, attempting to correct the spelling. The result is difficult to make out but appears to be "spermacite," a misspelling of "spermaceti."

the turf was beautifully kept. It did great credit to the heart of Cousin Thomas who frequently spent much time on first-days there. There were two Friends lying side by side, who a little less than a year ago were killed together at a fire. It was the first time their widows had visited the spot since their interment and it was most affecting to see them kneeling together at the graves of their husbands, weeping & probably praying for strength to support them under their great loss; they are both young & have families.

The children are well & getting on tolerably with their learning. Charles writes & reads a little & is acquiring some knowledge in geography; we are reading Mungo Parks' Travels[52] to him, with which he is much interested. Agnes sews & has learnt her alphabet; little Nanny talks of dear Grandmama, because mother & the others talk about her. Little Mary is a sweet, black eyed, rather palefaced child; her mother [Dorothea] is a great assistance to me but she only talks of staying with us till spring.

I cannot understand about the money sent to Thompson & I am confident he never received any.

I am sadly cramped for room and must conclude. Cousin Ann Shipley desired me to give her love to thee, Harrison sends his, and accept my endeared affection, my tenderly beloved mother. I hope there is a letter on the way.

That the God of all comfort & consolation may be ever sensibly near to bless & sustain thee is the prayer of thy attached daughter,

Emma Alderson

I hope I have omitted nothing. I hope to write again very soon.
Harrison feels very grateful to thee for thy kind intentions respecting the stockings. My very dear mother, it is on a piece with thy constant attention & kindness. The following are the proportions:

40 stitches & 41, welt 14 rounds
55 seams to raising 4 times 6 between
20 seams narrow 17 lines 22 seams to heel
Heel: 20 seams and 6 narrowed
Foot: 35 stitches 48 seams & narrowed to 20 stitches front & back

17. To Ann Botham, January 28 to March 9, 1844
Cedar Lodge 1st mo 28th 1844

My beloved Mother,
This is such a thoroughly winter day that we have been detained from meeting (for the first time by weather since we came here). We were ready to go and the horses in the carriage when there came such a violent storm of snow

52. Mungo Park, *Travels in the Interior Districts of Africa: Performed under the Direction and Patronage of the African Association, in the Years 1795, 1796, and 1797.* (London: W. Bulmer, 1799) https://catalog.hathitrust.org/Record/008697840. The book was a tremendous success and went through numerous printings.

& wind that the animals were terrified & the air so thick that driving would have been dangerous, so we were obliged to yield to the elements and stay quietly at home with the children. It has been a pleasant, quiet day.

Dearest mother, let me thank thee again for the Pictorial Bible; it is an invaluable treasure and a constant source of delight to Charles, who is allowed to look at it as a reward for good behaviour. I always think of thee with a renewed sense of thy unwearied affection and kindness when I look at it.

What a variable climate is this: last third-day we sat with the doors & windows open; the sun shone, the birds sang & I began to talk of spring & almost the impossibility of being again inconvenienced with cold, when on 4th day frost came, & since it has been extremely bitter, the Thermometer to day 20 below freezing and hurricanes of snow & wind.

Last week Harrison began a new trade; he was glazing our broken windows & he does it excellently. Glass is remarkably cheap here; we get panes of very good quality, 15 inches by 11, for 10 cents each. Harrison is going to purchase a box of 180 panes for a hot-bed frame for 2 1/4 dollars. Window tax is not known in America, so that there is no drawback to having as many windows as you choose. There are few rooms without 3 and often 4; we have none excepting the kitchen & one chamber with less than 3.

I am beginning to know something about our immediate neighbours. The road from the city into the country lies on one side of our land; about a field-breadth from the house on the other side of this, opposite our fields, are first a very neat Lutheran Chapel built of frame & whitened; next a neat little white frame occupied by a tailor [William Lotte], a native of Hanover; above, almost opposite our gate, lives his brother [Frederick Lotte], a cabinet maker & joiner. They have each a little lot of 4 acres for which they gave 400 dollars each. This latter lives in a log cabin; the neat white curtained little window had often struck me as giving an air of comfort to the place. Beyond is an ugly, new, uncoloured frame house which was building when we came. I have felt a prejudice against these people who worked both first-day & week day at their house ~~when we came.~~ There lives a professor of music who goes daily to the city to practice his art so that when we want a dance we have but to run across the orchard & call upon our neighbour's services.

About half a mile on the road is the little village of Warsaw; there are a tavern, a store, a blacksmith, a shoemaker &c so that thou sees, dear mother, we do not live in a wilderness. Indeed I should often be pleased were we farther from the haunts of man. The red bird, the blue jay, the owls with their wild mysterious call, the turtle-doves & many other things that delighted me at Westland are never seen here; at least we have neither heard nor seen them. But here are dear friends; here is polished & refined society and above all our own beautiful house, which as the spring advances I hope to see embel[l]ished with planting & adorned with flowers & creepers. Oh how I shall wish for you then!

[January] 29th. A bright cold day. We walked down to the city to see a man & his wife, whom we have some thoughts of engaging; they are from Hanover. The man is to work on the farm, the woman to help me; they have two children. As they talk English very imperfectly we hope little if any harm can come of our occasionally mixing with them; Cousin Pheobe Shipley says Dutch children are not like American. We propose to give up the kitchen & room above to their use and live ourselves in the parlours, of which there are three. We shall cook & the rough work will be done by the woman in the kitchen. Perhaps thou wilt think this is a hugger mugger scheme as dear Father used to say, but there seems no alternative: girls will not hire out so far from the city, and as these people are recommended for their honesty and many other good qualities, I am hopeful.

We observed the people very busy getting large blocks of ice out of the canal to store for \summer/. There has been great fear that, should the winter continue so wet & open as it has hitherto been, none could be procured; however, the present frost will enable them to obtain the sufficient supply. It struck me as something quite unEnglish in the summer to see the ice-cart driven about & the men with a large lump \of ice/, clear as crystal, suspended by an iron hook, calling as the respective houses they undertake daily to supply.

I have been told the workmen of the city lately struck for increase of wages & gained their point; from the 1st of March the joiners are to receive a dollar & a half a day, an enormous wage when we consider the price of provisions—equal, I should think, to 12£ in England when the difference of living is considered. Tailors are to have double the price formerly paid for making a coat &c.; some friends of Harrison were telling him that 30 dollars is the cost of a good coat, & yet every body is well drest. I often wonder how they manage; the ladies are superb, in the very height of French fashion and often, too, very ridiculous. We once saw two walking in the street; they had white bonets with plumes of white feather, bright green velvet coats very short, lined with white & gold & brown\coloured/ <scheine>[53] silks. It sounds simple enough, but the extreme of the fashion that was evident, the hoop-like bustle, amused me much.

[January] 31st. Harrison returned from the city with letters; the mail is come and it now arrives only once a month, and there are no letters from thee or any of our connexions. It is hard to reconcile the mind to be satisfied to wait a long, long month without a prospect of hearing from you. I think

53. This word appears in a more labored hand, as if Alderson were experimenting with something unfamiliar, but it does appear to be "scheine." The meaning and her intention are obscure, but she might be playing with the word "shiny," perhaps spelling it in such a way as to mock what she considers the pretensions of these German-American women. It also could be her spelling of "*chiné*," a fabric in which "the threads . . . are dyed or printed before weaving with resulting clouded or flame effects." Florence M. Montgomery, *Textiles in America, 1650–1870* (New York: W.W. Norton, 1984), 200.

dear Anna & Mary might write rather often. I will not murmur: I love you & know you love me & therefore will be content; I should be rejoiced beyond measure to hear from them.

Dearest mother, [thou] art [2] such a good faithful correspondent that my great fears when I do not hear, as I expect, from thee are for thy health. John Thwaite in a letter to Harrison says thou hast lately suffered much from head-ache. Dearest mother, that I could see and try to sooth thee in all thy seasons of trial & depression. I can but pray for thee, my beloved parent, that the rich and alsufficient consolations of the Gospel may be thine, that the sustaining arm of divine goodness may be around thee and the blessed presence of the dear Saviour so sensibly near that comfort & gladness may cheer thy solitude like visible lights. I have thought much of thee whilst reading a very precious book called The Life of Sarah Hawkes.[54] I would like thee, dear mother, to get it & read it; it beautifully exemplifies the blessedness of being a loving practical experimental christian. It is calculated to gladden the heart in the renewed assurance of the faithfulness of our God. We have also lately had an excellent work translated from the German, Elijah the Tishbite. The author is a clergyman amongst the persecuted portions of the Lutheran church in Prussia.[55]

One of the letters H. received was from Thos. Albright; he says they had a long voyage of 10 weeks, one succession of calms, that they did not experience a single squall. They are in good health and located at Hannibal, a town on the Mississippi above St Louis. Poor T. A. never can go quietly & prudently into anything: he jumps into every scheme that offers immediately on his arrival. At this place he made a purchase of an unfinished house & a lot of land on which he proposes to build others to make a large income, as rents are high there. From our knowledge of the river scenery of this country, I think his description of the place is good; he says "the plat of land is about 4 minutes walk from the throng of the main street here and, being half way up a cliff or bluff, there is a most commanding view of the Mississippi and the town of Hannibal, with high lands and Islands covered with wood bordering the town & rising out of the water, forming altogether one of the most agreeable prospects I ever before remember having witnessed elsewhere. ["] Dear Sarah Albright added a few lines to me in her usual cheerfulness & beautiful submission: she thinks she shall be very comfortable when they are settled; her greatest regret seems to be that there are no friends and that they are so widely seperated from us. It would have been a great pleasure to have had her near us.

2nd mo 2nd. We have engaged the people I mentioned before; the man is to have 136 dollars a year, house room & pasture for a cow, & we pay the

54. Edward Harrison, *The Extraordinary Case of Sarah Hawkes: One of Extreme Deformity, Cured by a Method Founded upon Simple Principles* (London: Joseph Robins, 1832).
55. F. W. Krummacher, *Elijah the Tishbite* (London: Religious Tract Society, 1836).

woman for washing, ironing & extra work. I shall tell the[e] hereafter how it answers.

[February] 25th. It is long, my dearest mother, since I wrote the above and we have been much engaged in the interval. We attended the Quarterly Meeting about the 10th of the month; it is always held at Wainsville about 40 miles distant. The weather was cold but fine &, enveloped in buffalo robes, we enjoyed our journey much. Our party was Abraham Taylor & his sister and Harrison & myself; we had their carriage & our horses & with these dear people had a most agreeable journey. The meeting is, as most Q[ly] meetings westward are, held on a seventh-day; we staid the first day meeting & on our return visited a very nice interesting family of the name of Stroud. They live in a \retired/ log house but have given it an air of neatness & even elegance by planting & whitewashing & throwing about the place an air of taste. They have 6 daughters, well educated handsome girls; they study botany, read and study together at the same time that they dye & spin & weave, make soap & sugar & molasses and all the various things that make American life so full of activity & independence. \One of them is an enthusiastic admirer of Mary's poetry/. In the neighbourhood of these friends is a large Shaker settlement called Union Village. The friends gave us an interesting description of a visit to them, but as I hope in the course of the summer to see the place myself I will leave describing till then.

Wainsville, I think I have told the, stands in the Miami Valley; it is a rich fertile district abounding in that part in sugar Maple, a certain proof of rich land. Great quantities of sugar are made there; some manufacture from 1 to 2000 lbs in the season. It has been fine sugar weather lately: frosty nights & bright warm days. I have been into the woods to look for flowers but found none. We went, however, to get some trees & shrubs to plant about the lawn; we got the dogwoods, Cornus florida [dogwood], a specimen of which I sent Anna, & the spice wood, a very aromatic shrub, the twigs & berries of which it is said the Indians chew to allay their hunger in traversing the Forest. Harrison has been glazing a hotbed frame; he is quite a clever workman. We are expecting this week to plant apples, peach & shrubery; it will now be a very busy season with us, forming the garden, planting & bringing all into the order we wish.

Sister Ann has left us for the present and the family I have previously mentioned are come. Hitherto they do well & all is very comfortable; we find ourselves very independent as they board themselves & are willing to help & do all the rough work. The dear Shipley family are still greatly tried with sickness & ill health; at the present time there are only two or three of the family well & yet they are so beautifully resigned, so uncomplaining & cheerfully submissive that it is quite instructive to be with them. Dear grandmother is very infirm but does, as they all do, what she can for the rest; she is an admirable woman. I love her for her own sake & think because she make me think of thee. She is always pleased to receive a message from thee & often desires me to give her love; it would be a great pleasure to her to hear from time to time any particulars thou cares to send of Cousin Ann Jones to whom, if thou hast an opportunity, give our united love.

Before <*torn*> Ann went, we set up a quilting frame and made two comforts <*torn*>. [3] I wish I could send thee one, but as I cannot do that I can tell thee how to make them. They are universally used here instead of a great load of blankets in cold weather & one of them with a blanket or two makes a bed warmer than half a dozen blankets without. The comfort is an under quilt made of dark print on both sides, between which is spread from 3 to 4 lbs of cotton wool & then it is quilted in largish diamonds. It is light & warm. I often thought of thee when making ours.

Our dutch people sleep between feather beds without either blankets or sheets. We see many ~~d~~Dutch habits in this neighbourhood such as wooden shoes, sour crout, vinyards on the declivities of the hills, and a disregard of the sabath. In summer it is not infrequent to see people work in their gardens and the brick yards or other avocations. Our Dorothea has been knitting this afternoon. I suppose she thinks there is no harm in it & as she cannot talk English nor I ~~d~~Dutch I cannot of course make her understand my sentiments on the subject.

3rd \mo 1st/. Thank thee, my beloved mother, for thy most welcome, long expected letter; thou art a fine faithful correspondent & thy letters are a great comfort to me as well as very interesting. I seem as if I lived again at Uttoxeter; give my love to the Friends and all thy kind friends. I did not, as thou supposed I might, hear from either Anna or Mary; it would have been a great pleasure had they favoured me with a letter but I must be patient. Thou never fails me my good kind mother.

I am tired of talking about the parcel: its contents were so trifling, but I am vexed at those cheating custom-house officers. The books I sent were American works published in America: Forest Life I believe at New York, & Mrs. Lincoln's Botany at ~~Boston~~ New York also.[56] I should never have thought of sending you English works, but let it pass; it is annoying & I am sorry thou shouldst have had so much thought & anxiety about them.

We have received very few British Friends: only three numbers I believe. I regret much if they are lost as it is a very interesting publication and especially so to us now. I like its liberal broad philanthropic character; it is consistent but not narrow & sectarian and makes me love the English Friends that dare to be good & great & to lend the right hand of fellowship to every cause which promotes the welfare of humanity. Here Friends have narrowed & are narrowing themselves in till they are alarmed at the expansive character of true christian benevolence. They are many of them groping in the

56. Almira Hart Lincoln Phelps, *Familiar Lectures on Botany* (Hartford, Conn.: H. and F. J. Huntington, 1829), https://books.google.com/books?id=9WYXAAAAYAAJ. This popular work was reprinted and revised many times over the next three decades.

dark mists of prejudice & party. I think it a favour that we live much out of the influence of these things as they exist & are felt in many portions of the society here, but we from time to time hear a little of what is going on.

The children are well & look as ruddy and stout as if they had run for the last six months on the fells of Westmorland. We have reason to feel thankful that this is considered & has so far proved to us a very healthy district. We have gusty winds in winter & fine cool breezes in summer when in the city they are almost suffocated with heat & gasping for air. The land around us is in a high state of cultivation; there is some wood remaining, but the great proportion are fine, well fenced fields & gardens.

We went lately to a nursery garden in the neighbourhood. It was interesting to see the great variety of ornamental forest trees & flowering shrubs there collected together, mostly native, but I was disappointed in finding that the Rododendrons, azaleas, kalmias & other evergreens which grow so profusely in West Pennsylvania will not vegetate here. The soil or climate do not suit them. I fancy it is too mild & hot.[57]

This letter has been a long time on hand & will I fear be somewhat out of season, but as our lives are very quiet & unmarked by incident I have not seemed to have much to record & I sometimes fear I tell thee things twice over. If so, excuse me: my leisure is small & often much interrupted & I forget what I have said at such long intervals.

Richard is going to leave us on second-day; he has had a great desire to be a joiner, which is an excellent business here and can be carried on in conjunction with farming. A farmer here, & many there are who is a good carpenter, has the advantage over his other neighbours if he practices his art only for himself. Harrison has obtained R[ichard] a good situation with a very respectable builder & house carpenter & we have got him good boarding at a Friend's house. The terms are dollar & a half a week for the first year; this just pays for his board. The next <year> he is to have 100 dollars, which we expect will board & clothe him. <*torn*> lad, I hope he will do well & prosper: it is his first beginning of the <*torn*>, but he has as good & fair a chance as most.

Tell me, dearest [4] mother, how it is that Daniel has again gone into partnership & what wonderful change of feeling & sentiment can have induced him to take George Crossfield's son of all others into his firm.[58] I had hoped thou would have told me all about it in thy last, but as thou dost not mention it I am fain to ask. This is a world of changes, some for the better & some for the worse, but \may/ all be overruled & work together ultimately for good;

57. The problem is in the soil, which is has too high a pH.
58. We know nothing of the earlier resentment Alderson refers to, but it might have had to do with Crosfield's friendship with and support for John Wilbur against Joseph John Gurney in the second great schism among nineteenth-century Quakers. The Aldersons (and perhaps the Harrisons) were ardent Gurneyites. In keeping with my policy of minimal alterations, I have retained Alderson's frequent misspelling, "Crossfield."

the end crowns all. Give our united love to Danl & Anna & their family & to Wm & Mary & theirs. I fear from what thou says poor dear Claude is not much better.

The blue birds are come, a certain signal of approaching spring. The weather is generally mild & like our fine 4th month; we have been gardening today. I never work in the fresh upturned soil without thinking of the happy days of my childhood & youth & that pleasant garden at Uttoxeter where I laboured & rejoiced often with thankful heart over the beautiful result. I would like that our children as they grow up should have similar tastes & associations in our present home. They do not feel the blank that is often so sensible to my mind; they do not miss those kind eyes whose pleasure & admiration would give a charm to me that I feel \so much/ the lack of & that would give an impetus to our efforts which one cannot feel \at present/. It seems as if in living thus in a foreign land we had to live abstractedly just in these things, at least for ourselves & our children. Friends we have, dear kind friends, but \it/ is expecting too much to suppose they can take more \than/ a passing interest in us & our concerns. To be thus uprooted & torn from all our nearest & dearest ties & connexions & placed amongst strangers, though the very kindest, is often a solitary isolated feeling. If we live & our children live, they will supply somewhat of that that is lost, & they will take root & grow freely in this \to us/ strange soil.

William Charles is hoping soon to be able to send a line or two to thee, but poor child, I fear he will have trouble with his eyes. Thou knows he always appeared near-sighted; he now complains of pain & dimness & often cannot say his lessons in consequence. He learns with rapidity & is a very intelligent child, but should his sight be affected, it will be a sad drawback. He & Agnes love thee & often talk of thee, & little Nanny takes up the word by imitation & says sometimes "who made this? did dear grandmother?["] It is a proof that dear grandmother made and did a deal for us. I am often amazed how many evidences of thy never ceasing kindness I me<et> at every turn. Thank thee my tenderly beloved mother for all, <counted> & uncounted. Harrison desires his dear love; he says he is thinking of writing to thee himself. With very near & dear affection I am thy attached daughter,

Emma Alderson

3rd mo 9th

18. To Ann Botham, April 22 to May 6, 1844 [59]

Cedar Lodge 4th mo 22nd 1844

My very dear Mother,

The spring with all its varied attractions and numerous occupations is upon us, and day after day, nay week after week, have slid along and found a long

59. See figure 8.

intended letter to thee uncommenced; but my tenderly beloved Parent, if I have seemed more tardy than usual in writing, do not suppose it is in consequence of abated affection or in any way a symptom of neglect. No, thou art as much the object of my tenderest affection as when we were constantly together or after the first pang of separation, when a painful sense of unuterable love made me miserable. Those feelings of anguish have subsided, but my heart fondly turns to thee \&/ my beloved sisters with a steadfast & unalterable & I think deepening attachment. It seemed as if on reading thy last letter the whole fountain of my affection was stirred towards you all: for our dear Anna & her dear little baby \with its beautiful name [Emma Lucy], many thanks/; for dear Mary, with her anxious cares over poor Claude & all \the/ kind & loving sympathies that they all display on his behalf, devoting themselves, as I know they do, to soothing his sorrows & aleviating his sufferings; and for thee, my dearest mother, who art the centre of our joys & sorrows, who weeps with those who weep & rejoices with those who can rejoice; and I longed to write to each & tell you all I then felt. I hope thou wilt be able to visit dear Mary this spring. It would, I am sure, be a comfort to her & I fancy the fine air of the neighbourhood of London would invigorate & cheer thee.

I often wish for you to enjoy with me the fine climate [2] and many pleasant accompaniments of our present situation; the spring has progressed with unparrelled rapidity, to me at least. Three weeks ago we had a return of winter, & the trees, which were then leafless, were encased in ice & hung with icicles, & when the sun shone upon them the effect was most beautiful, looking like branches of silver or glass sparkling in the sunbeams. Well, in the course of a week the peach trees were in full bloom & the forests began to assume the first tender tints of bursting foliage. The peach orchard is a beautiful sight: whole masses of bright pink blossoms as red as the rose, contrasting with the white bloom of plum & cherry trees & the fresh verdure of springing grass. That, like a pleasant vision, passed away & another week brought the apple trees into bloom, filling the air with a pleasant, delicate fragrance & looking most lovely. Remember orchards: orchards are every where where man has been for a few years, for fruit is a staple commodity of life, a part of our every-day sustenance & therefore the country abounds with this wealth of the earth. This is the third First day since the actual commencement of spring & the Forest trees are in full leaf. The buckeye, which is a species of horse chestnut, is in bloom & forms a fine shade in the heat of the day; the maple has rich masses of foliage; the dogwood is pearly white with its blossom in nooks of the forest; the red-bud or Judas tree has been splendid but its beauty is gone. We observed on the opposite shores of Kentucky one portion of the wooded hills assumed a bright pinkish purple tint from the quantity of these trees that were growing there.

5th mo 6th. Well my best beloved mother, after a long interval I again resume my pen, hoping this time I shall be able to finish my letter & dispatch it. We received a few days ago a token of thy kind rememberance in a British Friend in which the first intelligence of dear Claude's death reached us. Poor child, for him I trust it is a happy release from a state of much trial & suffering to one of rest & joy & peace, but Oh I feel much for Wm & Mary & the family. I know their keen sensibilities heightened by continued claims upon their sympathy & affection, and though their sorrow will be subdued, it must have been deep & they have known much heart anguish in consequence both before and after the event. May this & every trial both past & future only serve to wean their hearts from earth to heaven & direct them to seek their happiness & draw their comfort and fix their dependence on Him who changeth not amidst all the changes of time. I have thought a deal too of dear Anna lately; I fear I might in my last letter seem impatient & inconsiderate towards her & dear Mary about writing. I long to see a letter from them & yet I know how much they have each had to engross & absorb their whole thought & attention. Give my dear love to them \and theirs/. I sometimes in thinking of thee fancy thee at Upper Clapton; if so I think thou wilt be a source to comfort Mary & the family.

I have been much absorbed with the cares & labour of household concerns, but with the latter I hope soon to dispense as I have hired a girl & tomorrow the Dutch family I told thee in my last we were taking by way of experiment are removing into a little frame house Harrison has built for them. The man [3] suits Harrison & therefore he concluded to locate him on the farm; this house is a specimen of this universal species of dwelling, for as the new countries rise out of the wilderness state, the log cabin mostly gives way to frame houses. They are, as thou mayst be aware, moveable; we have often seen them travelling up & down the streets to our great annoyance mounted on a multitude of wheels & drawn by numerous oxen or horses. They are transported any distance. Ours is a dwelling of one room with a chamber above. The frame-work or skeleton of the house is first erected, all having been previously fitted together; it is only like putting up a child's toy. Then the weather-boarding is nailed on, one board wrapping over another to exclude the wet; afterwards the shingles for the roof & then the floors, which done, in go the family to enjoy themselves to their hearts' content, & greatly to my comfort the cost of this house which has a small milk cellar & a little leanto for the stove in summer is 80 dollars & the rent is to be 20 d. a year. I expect Harrison could get 30 from an indifferent person.

Oh that thou couldst see this glorious country now that the full beauty of spring is expanded. The locusts have bloomed, but their light elegant foliage is a constant admiration to my eyes, contrasted with the cedars & catalpas by which we are surrounded. The roses are in full bloom. I would fain send thee a nosegay which is beside me filling the room with rich perfume; it is composed of red & white roses, privite blossoms & a very elegant syringe called here Philadelphus \& sweet briar/.[60] Dost thou remember the trumpet honeysuckle[?] It is now in full bloom & grows to the tops of houses or over posts in the gardens like a very common thing, but its rich clustering scarlet flowers are very beautiful.[61] Last week we paid a visit to a friend in the country; their house was covered on two sides by this honeysuckle, the double red multiflora rose, & \other/ white & red roses.

I think it may interest thee to know the productions & seeds we have sown in our garden. We have asparagus & rhubarb beds, rasberies & currants, pease ready for table, beans of various kinds, Indian corn for roasting ears, sweet potatoes, which are a species of bulbous rooted convolvulus, spinach, beets, carrots, cabbage, squash, water & musk melons, cucumbers, tomatos, herbs, lettuce & radishes, pepper, parsnips, parsley &c., & yet ours is not a large garden nor particularly well stocked. Besides these we have large beds of pumpkins for our own use & fodder for the cattle. In the flower beds around the house we have planted many roses & other beautiful shrubs & set our flower seeds which our kind friends gave us on leaving England, J Edmondson & Wm Albright, & though many of them will of course fail from being kept so long, others will perpetuate our old favourites & serve to remind us of old friends & long past scenes. Dost thou remember an old rose tree which grew in our old garden under the apple & damson trees[?] It had a red stem & a single bright pink flower & was thornless. It is one of the common roses of this country & is here called the dogrose, but I call it as we used to do the rose without a thorn & prize it much; we have a fine one now in bloom under \one of/ our dining room windows.[62] I have been trimming our vines a la Dutch to day. It is quite a science but a kind neigh[4]bour, a New Englander, instructed me yesterday. We have fine promise of grapes; I wish thou couldst partake.

Harrison is gone to the Quarterly Meeting & I and the children are left at home to enjoy the beauty & quietness of the season. I told them this morning I was writing to thee & asked what I must say from them to dear grandmother. Agnes said tell her to get younger that she may come and live with us, and Annie says I want to go to grandmother; Charley sends his dear love. They are wild, sun loving little creatures, and as rosy & healthy as if they lived on a fell side. We quite think if people will only retain their simple habits & live in the country it is as healthy here as in England, some low swampy river situations excepted.

60. Sweet briar (*Rosa eglanteria*) was introduced by English colonists as early as the seventeenth century.
61. The trumpet honeysuckle, or coral honeysuckle (*Lonicera sempervirens*), is a native species, unlike the now more common Japanese honeysuckle (*L. japonica*).
62. What is usually called dog rose, *Rosa canina*, has thorns and is a native of Europe and common in Great Britain. Alderson may be thinking of smooth rose, *Rosa blanda*, which is practically thornless and is native to Ohio, although it is now listed as threatened.

Dear cousin Ann Shipley spent a week with us some time ago; Cousin Pheobe & her family & Cousin Ann of course have removed into the Country to a beautiful village called Mount Auburn of which thou mayst have heard. It is situated on one of the hills East of the city & is one succession of small & often very elegant villas, each standing in its own garden grounds & fields. It made me think of some of the villages near London; the houses are all white & have mostly verandahs & porches & are, as I said before, very pretty. Joseph Nevilles have also removed to a nice little place there; I shall miss our Cousins much from the city for I never went to town without going to see Cousin Ann & she seems to regret the removal as a privation, but I hope with the blessing of Providence it may be beneficial to them in point of health. They are an interesting lovely family & Thomas the elder son is a counterpart of Daniel: the same dry humour, the same quiet kindness, the friend of all & the Father of his family. I love him dearly for his own sake & for the constant resemblance I trace in him.

I suppose I ought to tell thee, dear Mother, that in the 8th month I have prospect of again becoming a mother. I had hoped to have been spared & for a time it was a great sorrow & humiliation to me. I felt as if, like Elizabeth of old, I would fain fly into the wilderness; I felt for dear Anna then, but now [1] I am just reconciled. It is a dreadful season to be laid up in, what with heat & mosquitos but so it must be & I hope all will go on well. Write often; I sometimes feel as if thy kind presence & sympathy as of old would be inexpressibly precious. Farewell my best beloved & most valued Parent; may every blessing & comfort be thine is the sincere prayer of thy attached daughter.

Emma Alderson

19. To Ann Botham, May 19 to June 14, 1844[63]
Kentucky
Cedar Lodge 5 mo 19th 1844

My beloved Mother,
I scarcely know whether a letter I dispatched a few days ago has yet left the city but as I find some difficulty in writing a letter consecutively I will make a commencement of one of my journalizing epistles, especially as I find thy letter so written full of a fresh & lively interest. I feel as if I half lived amongst you & could enter into thy daily sources of interest as though they were passing events with myself. Thy last, dated <*blank*>, was especially acceptable and excites my warmest affection as I fear it might be a painful effort as thou mentions more than once thy suffering from headaches. Thou also speaks of increasing mental infirmities; indeed dear mother, it appears to me that thy mind is as vigorous as ever. I am sure thy letters are a proof there is no

63. See figure 9.

failure there; thy heart is as warm and thy feeling and sympathy for others as strong as formerly & what a blessing this is. I shall keep thy eightieth birthday with feelings of reverential thankfulness.[64] We shall, I know, mutually think of each other & may our hearts be influenced to crave for each other admitance into that enduring & eternal life where neither sin nor sorrow, pain nor death have entrance but all is purity & joy & peace in the precence of God for evermore.

Last fifth-day when we were going to meeting we passed the chain-gang who are now working on our road mackadamizing it; there were about 20 men, black & white, & each had a large heavy iron chain fastened round the right ankle to the end of which was attached a large cannon ball. They are condemned to this public degradation for different periods as punishment for such crimes as do not require their removal to the Penitentiary, as the jails are called, which is at Columbia, the County town. Many are of opinion that it is not well thus to expose them; it tends to harden them & cut off all return to society. Their labour, however, is profitable & really they do not look unhappy or miserable.

As thou art interested about Brown who was condemned to die, I will tell thee what I have heard: he has been reprieved. It is circulated that he is a man of bad character & had, under pretence of love, lured a black girl away, but his real intention was to carry her off & sell her for his own advantage. The judge who tried & condemned him is the same O'Brien who had the correspondence with Friends which I mentioned to thee as having been read at one of our [2] Quarterly Meetings. They call him a "fine man" here but I have not much opinion of him. This is the American version of the story; it may be true but they are very unwilling to speak the whole truth where slavery is concerned.

I saw in the paper of this city, whose principles are decidedly anti-slavery, in an account of a dreadful steam-boat accident, mention of 7 servants of a Mrs. Somebody having perished. I knew they were probably with others, poor slaves chained & fastened, down in the hold \to/ whom death thus speedily gave freedom, but in the public paper no appeal was raised for the poor, who are thus liable to be exposed to sudden & inevitable horror & death. The opportunity of pointing out this as one awful consequence of this system of iniquity was omitted or left to the dispised & hated abolitionists. May the Lord bless & prosper them & give them grace & wisdom to carry forward their good work without blame in the face of a captious, cold & deriding world.

6th mo 14th. Now this was to have been a daily record and here at near a month's interval I resume my pen to finish. I hope this letter, as Harrison says, S. Neville has an opportunity of sending to England free of expence. I have been spending a few days with our kind cousins at Mount Auburn and

64. May 23 according to unverified sources on Ancestry.com.

whilst there received a most affectionate welcome letter from dear Anna full of interesting details & breathing that pure & pious sentiment which is so characteristic of her. When I remember my blessings, the privilege of hearing from you, my beloved relatives, is indeed one of the highest; I always valued your correspondence, but now at this distance, that which serves from time to time to bring us so near & dear and renews with fresh & lively feelings all the love and intimacy that I feel your letters to produce is inestimable. They are to me golden epistles and my warmest thanks flow to you for them. I often regret that my leisure is so very limited that I cannot, when I would, take up my pen and tell you all the thoughts & feelings & observations that pass before my mind & with which the idea of you is generally interwoven.

So far I have been without any assistance in the house except washing, & till lately ironing. We have engaged people from time to time, but they—that is, the class who go out—are lamentably faithless. They are too independent to be bound by ~~interest~~ honour: interest or any accident will prevent them fulfilling their engagements. I often think of the English hiring, of the earnest money & the sort of quiet confidence one felt that the servant would come at or near the time fixed. As far as our observation goes, this universal equality does not essentially promote happiness. All are, dispite their assertions, aiming at being higher: the middle class seek to be each as great & appear as well as the other & the poor are jealous & insolent towards their superiors, whom they feel such, though they will not acknowledge it. It is a great comfort to live in a country where abject poverty is unknown & where the destitute & distressed, who are such from circumstance or accident, are not so numerous but that the efforts of individual & united benevolence are adequate to their relief. We often say it would be almost intolerable now to us to witness the poverty & suffering of the poor in England. Here we see no half-starved ragged children, no signs of abject wretchedness on any hand, & yet that quiet contentment that is instilled [3] as a religious duty into all classes, that submitting & resigning themselves to the simple faithful discharge of their own peculiar duties is little known here; hence that restless ever moving spirit which drives the inhabitants of the eastern states westward & the residents of the west beyond the Mississippi into the wildernesses of Iowa & Oregon.

Elizabeth is come back to reside with us. Her school became so small that it did not seem worth while to continue it & \as/ she is inclined to be useful to us I really find her return an advantage & on many accounts prefer her being with us. I think she is much improved by her residence & experience in the city; besides, I believe she has some very good advisers here & in England I am sure she had some very bad ones; so I can make allowances & hope for the best.

I must tell thee, dear mother, of an association we have lately formed amongst the mothers of the meeting—& there are many young & older of this class—to aid us in the great work of training & educating our children as religious, moral, & intellectual beings & to bring them up as good consistent Friends. We are scarcely organized, but our last meeting was a very encouraging & interesting one & we had the company of a dear friend from Mount Pleasant, Rebecca Uptagraph, the daughter of Jonathan Taylor. She is a zealous anti-slavery woman & one who is ready to go heart & hand into every good word & work, a most able minister, too good for many in this land. Well, the subjects under discussion were religious instruction & the moral influence on the minds of children, of indulgence in dress & living, as also the desirableness of simplicity in these things in order that the precious time of mothers might not be unnecessarily consumed and occupied. We had a deal of good advice & much useful information from R. U. & in conclusion a most beautiful & pathetic prayer. I believe there were none there but felt it a privilege to be present.

For a month past, the market has been abundantly supplied with early vegetables & fruit; we had excellent green pease in the early part of 5th mo. Strawberries have been very plentiful; it was said in the season 300 bushels came to market every morning, mostly from Kentucky. They sold at a fip a quart, that is 6 1/4 cents. I had some sent to me which I preserved; they are a fine scarlet & more acid than ours and make a delicious preserve. Raspberries are now as plentiful & about the same price. We have a tolerable supply & a good many of the very finest red currants I ever saw. This is indeed a fine country, overflowing with every good gift of Providence. When I contrast the past, when the price of an extra tea-cake or bun was really an object & every little superfluity felt as almost a questionable encroachment on the rigid economy I used to think necessary, with the plentiful stores I can now command—milk, butter, cream, poultry, eggs, pork, vegetables, fruit of the best & rarest kinds, all our own produce, & other things so low that in England they would create astonishment: coffee at something under 5^{d}, sugar 3 1/2^{d}, loaf di[tt]o 6 1/2, a quarter of lamb 10^{d} &c.[65]—I often wish those I dearly love & to whom the painful virtue of economy is still so requisite could partake with us in our abounding blessings. Besides, the country is so beautiful, the people so kind, that except the separation from you, I feel in every thing we are gainers. Oh dearest mother, that I could introduce thee to some of our dear Friends here—kind warm-hearted refined, yet simple ~~peopl~~ in their habits & manners—I am sure thou wouldst love them & they thee. We often talk of thee together & they enquire after thee about thee like an old acquaintance.

Thou must not suppose because I have no woman, girl, or help, as they are called here, that I am oppressed. Thanks to a kind good Providence, work which at first was a heavy burden is become easy by habit; besides my own

65. It is unclear how many of these prices are per pound and how many might be per unit (a loaf of sugar or a quarter of a lamb).

kind dear husband [4] will do anything, however menial, to lighten my toil & assist me & ~~were~~ I often feel that love & kindness enoble & dignify the meanest offices & make us happy in the midst of much personal exertion. I never had my health better nor moved with a lighter step & heart than I have done this spring & summer & were it not for the prospect I have before me, nothing should induce me to have a servant.

The children are well & happy. Agnes & Charley send their love & W. C. says I must tell thee that when he is a man he will ~~come~~ \go/ and see thee & bring thee here to live with us. We have a parlour which we often say thou wouldst delight to call thy room if thou wast here.

Dost thou remember in the sketch of our home the front porch, which is two-storied[?] It is now garlanded with the most beautiful wild rose I ever saw; it is called the Prairie rose & grows so luxuriantly that it would, if trained, soon cover a house. The flowers are a deep rose pink & grow in clusters of from 10 to 12. It is, though single, a splendid plant. The roses in this neighbourhood are very various & very beautiful; many, I think, must have been brought from France, as I do not remember to have seen the same kinds in England, & the climate is so favourable to flowers that they bloom with a luxuriance & profusion that astonishes me.

The blossom of the Catalpa is just passing away but it has been most beautiful. Our trees were studded with large clusters of the fine, white flowers, which look noble amongst the broad, light green leaves & these in contrast with the dark junipers & feathery locust were to my taste a rich & continual feast of beauty. I shall venture to enclose one single flower of the catalpa; its snowy whiteness is gone but the figuring of purple & yellow remains. The flower is about the size of a common foxglove & I should think there are 50 of them clustered together in one spike & 500 of these on one tree.

I have not said one word about dear Mary. I often think of them & shall write as soon as possible. Dear Harrison sends his endeared love. I have not said half I want to tell thee but must conclude as my paper is full.

Thy warmly attached & most affectionate daughter,

Emma Alderson

20. To Ann Botham, June 2 to July 24, 1844[66]

Cedar Lodge 6 mo. 2

My beloved Mother,

Thou must excuse so many pictures but this is the only large sheet of the right size that I have by me, and as I have a little leisure & am in a humour for writing, I am not willing to forego the pleasure of holding converse with thee. Thy last, most welcome letter was worth all it cost & twice as much to me, for I think it \one of/ the very nicest letters I have ever received, but dear

66. See figures 10 and 11.

mother, owing to its being enclosed in an envelope, though not so large as usual, it was charged double postage. The regulation is different here to what it is with you, number of pieces and not weight deciding the cost. Do not think we grudge the money; I merely mention it to put you on your guard.

Thou speaks of the weather being excessively dry in England. We have had so far an unusually wet season although every thing is early: our grass and wheat are both ready to cut together. We began to cut the wheat, which is remarkably fine, yesterday, but a violent thunderstorm in the night blew down the shocks & drenched them through & through. This morning it was violently hot so that in the city & meeting we were half suffocated, and again the rain has fallen in torrents. It is tedious farming, and what with anxiety & exertion, Harrison is almost laid up.

To tell the truth, dear mother, we find that here as every where there are difficulties to contend with; the labourers, who are mostly Dutch, are slow & troublesome to deal with, and as to domestic help, I find that in the country very difficult to obtain. I often think of Eliza Flower's words that women must not expect a life of indolent ease in America, and yet though my bones have ached more in the 18 months I have been in this land from fatigue than they did from the same cause all my life long in England, some how or other I prefer our present position & would be sorry to give it up. The climate is so fine, the country & its productions so rich & luxuriant, the people are so kind, and my health & spirits so good, that the amount of happiness I enjoy is [2] as large, nay far, far larger, than I have any right to expect.

7th mo. 24. What a long interval has elapsed since the above was written, and it has been an eventful period to us in which we have renewedly to acknowledge the continued goodness and care of a gracious Providence, whose dealings with us are rich in bounteous blessings. In the first instance, though latest in order, thou must know that the expected addition to our family has arrived and another beloved child is added to our little flock. It is a dear girl, greatly to my joy and comfort, perfect in all respects, although very small, being two months premature. All—that is Harrison & Elizabeth—pronounce her like thee. At all events she is a very different looking child to the others, having \a/ large nose & strongly marked features; may she be like thee in all respects. We call her Ann B. or Botham; that is not quite decided; however she is to be thy namesake.

I have been unusually well this time. It is now 9 days since the event and I am going about the house and join the family at meals and am, I believe, as strong as ever. The baby takes the breast & seems likely soon to become a fine strong child. I think Anna Mary Howitt must have been such a child. I never look at her feed without thinking of the little shoe dear Mary made to fit her when she was six weeks old. I often looked with dread at the event coming on in the fearful dog-days, when heat & mosquitoes prevail in their strength & I have shed tears in the thought of the desolateness I should feel without thee. How unwise & evil thus to anticipate trials & make to ourselves sorrows: I have found the warm weather an advantage rather than otherwise, I am royally laid when in bed under a handsome mosquitoe bar, & though thy presence would be now, as at all times, a source of great pleasure & a highly prized privilege, yet my attendants have been so kind and the attention & sympathy of our friends so great that there has not been room to think a murmuring thought.

The next cause of thankfulness is what I am sure thou wilt rejoice at. Last 5th day was our monthly Meeting & a minute from the select preparative meeting was presented recommending Harrison to be recorded as an approved Minister [of] this meeting with the full approbation of both men & women's meeting to which it is separately offered. It was accordingly done &, though by this act of man he is neither more nor less than he was before, yet it is a great satisfaction to have the full & entire unity of our friends and to see them so soon & so cordially receiving him as an honoured instrument in the good & great work of a minister of the gospel, than which, in my estimation, there is no calling so noble & so dignified, seeing that they who turn many to righteousness shall shine as the stars in the firmament. How does the glory of statesmen, of Philosophers, of Poets & Painters grow dim in comparison except as they have used their power, influence, or talents to promote directly or indirectly the cause of their Redeemer.

Added to this I must tell thee that in my estimation & in the opinion of many others, dear Harrison's gift has increased in power & life so that I trust, not having hid his talent in a napkin, he is diligently employing it in his Lord's service, & the increase consequent on faithfulness, which is promised, has not been withheld. He speaks often with so much clearness, force & even eloquence as quite astonish me & I am thankful to see so much strength arising out of great weakness.

A Friend told me that she never knew a case receive such unanimous approbation as this did in the select Quarterly Meeting, and that the season was one not to be forgotten as being marked with unusual solemnity & favour, that seeing H. was a comparative stranger, the elders of this meeting had gone with the intention of stating the fact of the recommending minute which accompanied our certificate, but that the feeling was so strong & sufficient that when all was concluded a friend at the close of the meeting just mentioned the circumstance rather as confirmation than as argument.

I know thou wilt thankfully rejoice with us and therefore give thee these particulars as due to thee who [3] knew & sympathized in our past trials, but all that, I am willing to believe, was quite for the best & overruled for good. It opened the way for our coming here, a step for which I feel we have cause to be humbly grateful; it left us, without superadded honour, to find our way amongst friends and has verified that beautiful declaration which was once quoted with so much effect to dear Harrison years ago that they who honour the Lord he will honour. Truly dear Mother, He is a covenant keeping God. Would that we could likewise remember & keep our covenants with him.

I have received a most beautiful, interesting letter from dear Anna since I wrote to thee. Give my dear love to her & Daniel & family; I shall certainly try to write to her soon as also to dear Mary; my endeared love to her & hers. Tell her I hope she has not forgotten me.

Until lately I have not had any leisure as we had no servant & I, with E's help, had the work of the house to do for the last 6 weeks. We have had two men to board who were helping in the harvest, but they are gone & Oh, what a relief, for according to country fashion in America they had to "eat" with us & required three hot meals a day beside two lunches in the field. This kept us pretty busy; it is awful work to cook over a stove in this hot climate.

Speaking of the heat of the climate reminds me of the luxury of sour milk, which soon goes stiff like junket & which we eat with molasses or sugar. The dutch use pepper & salt to it; it is called Bonny claver & when strained & pressed makes a kind of homely cream cheese, which is eaten and called Smere case or cottage cheese.

We have now tomatoes, squashes, \the fruit of the/ egg plant, cucumbers, carrot, beans, sweet corn in the green state, which is delightful, beets, cabbage, spinach, potatoes, &c. in abundance. It is surprizing what a variety of vegetables the Americans set on their tables, and certainly they are a great luxury early. Apples & peaches are ripe & one great article, & much enjoyed at this season, is the blackberry or bramble; they grow abundantly in the woods & fences and produce abundance of fine fruit. It may seem odd to thee but a dish of sugared blackberries with milk or cream is considered a handsome addition to any dinner or supper table. Sugared fruit is a favourite article <in our> diet: currants, strawberries, rasps., sliced peaches, &c. & very good & whole<some> they are. Dost thou know we are so barbarous as to set on our table & even eat raw beef[?] It is called chipped beef: salted beef cut in thin fine shreds & eaten with bread & butter.

I am at last relieved from the burden & drudgery of housework by having engaged a coloured woman to live with us. She has been about 10 days with us & seems very clever & managing. She has an excellent character & if she will only stay will be quite a treasure to me.

Her history is rather interesting. She is a native of Georgia & her father was a white man who kept her mother & called her his wife, but by the laws of that state they could not be married. Near his close he wished to send her & her three children to New York & secure their freedom but the faithful creature refused to leave him and at his death she & her children were sold.

Ada, our woman, at six years old became the property of a wealthy family. Her office was to wait in the family to comb her mistress' hair \&c./ in an evening for hours together when they had no company. One evening, being tired & sleepy, she nodded over her employment. Her mistress was angry & complained to her husband, & he to gratify his wife, with whom he had had words & who was in an ill humour, ~~he~~ had the girl stripped & tied up & with a cow-hide whipped her himself till the blood streamed down & she fainted, his wife & children seeming to enjoy the scene. She got up & crawled away as soon as able & in the kitchen had plenty of commiseration from the old \black/ people there, but of course no redress. Soon after, this inhuman woman was confined & died & Ada had charge of the baby until it was six years old.

She had a son of her own & discribes the condition of mothers in slavery as very sorrowful; after the child is a month old it is consigned for the day to the care of some superannuated negro & she is obliged to go to her labours in the field or the house. The children are all kept in the yard adjoining their owner's house & have a shed to shelter them from the sun & rain. At noon their allowance of hominy or pot liquor is put into a kind of trough & with each an oyster-shell for a spoon they devour [4] their meal.

Does not one feel how near they are brought to the lower animals? The alowance of the slave is scanty both in food & clothing: two suits a year, coarse linen for summer & flannel for winter, is the supply of the field people, and \every week/ a peck of corn or potatoes or rice with occasionally a scrap of meat or a few salt fish is all that is given for food. Their garden & a little poultry supply any luxuries they may ever enjoy.

Their morals are in a fearful state & light & knowledge are forbidden. Marriage is not encouraged & the master & sons of the family have a large offspring rising around them who, to suit their convenience, are sold & transported into hopeless slavery.

About five years ago the family who possessed Ada removed to Madison in Indiana. There in a free state, not having the power to retain her as a slave, they offered her her freedom for 400 dollars. This by incessant labour, washing, & nursing & other means she paid to within 60 dollars when, growing weary, she, by the advice of her friends, disguised her boy as a girl & came to Cincinnati. Her intention was to go to Canada, but this she gave up. Yet the fear of seizure of her boy haunts her. She thinks they will not touch her, but the child, they tell her, should they go to Georgia or Kentucky, must go with them. A kind hearted landlord in the country has him under his protection & wished to send him to the public school, yet such is the prejudice against colour even in these free states that the neighbours rose in indignation at the presumption & even instituted proceedings in law against him. Imperfect, however, as the laws are for the coloured race, there was nothing that they could do \as punishment/ for such a crime, \yet/ as a peace offering the child was taken away.

There has been much excitement of late from disturbances in the Mormon settlement. They are a strange, wild people, both hated & feared in their neighbourhood; I send thee a few papers containing an account of the event, together with some other trifles I have collected, all unexizable. Cousin Thomas Shipley, who is going to New York, has promised to forward it by private hand; if it reach thee it will be well; if not it is no great loss.

We have not yet heard or seen the box; I hope it will get safe here. I cannot tell thee what a pleasure it was to me to hear of thy regaining thy sight, to think of thy again enjoying with renewed dearness this great blessing of life; to be able to read & write & look upon the beautiful fields & flowers without dimness must be delightful.

The children are all well. Agnes has been a week with our kind friends the Taylors. Dear Cousin Ann Shipley comes often to see us; last <week> she rode over & returned [1] the same evening. It is wonderful how active & lively she is. I wish you could meet; how much you would enjoy each other's society. She desired her love to thee. The family are much benefitted by their residence in the country.

Farewell beloved mother; my love to all friends & enquirers. I hope Joseph <Shipley's> daughter is better; my love to them & cousin Betty.

With much love, I am, my tenderly beloved parent, thy attached & affectionate daughter,

Emma Alderson

21. To Anna Harrison, September 2 to 13, 1844
Cedar Lodge 9th mo 2nd 1844

My beloved Sister,
When I received thy last most welcome and interesting letter it was my full intention to have replied to it very soon, but time has passed so rapidly away that months instead of days have intervened, and the duty is still unperformed. To you who live still amongst your old friends & associations, who have frequent opportunities of personal intercourse with dear mother & Mary & can, if it be needful, have daily knowledge of what is passing in the family, I think it is impossible to convey ~~the~~ an idea of the comfort your letters are to my mind. I am selfish enough to be delighted with the assurance that you still remember us with undiminished affection, though I could never, I believe, doubt that I am interested beyond what words can convey with the details of your doings and in knowing a little of what is passing amongst you, though they are but very hurried glimpses of the great whole, and I am thankful to a kind Providence who continues to preserve you in life & health to be a comfort & a blessing to each other.

I never see dear mother's hand writing without a very vivid sense of gratitude that she is still spared to us, dear creature. I often feel that her kind & constant correspondence is as a steady ray of sunshine in my path, and I often think what a blank it would be to me if ~~her~~ she was taken from us, for the idea of mother is associated in my mind with all I see & hear, & I think of things as I know they would interest her. How much more should I enjoy our good things if she could partake with us. We seldom gather fruit without wishing dear grandmother could have some, for the children have caught the feeling & often express it. If there was but a great railway & no custom house officers, you should all have partaken of our dainties: our melons, grapes & peaches and many rare & excellent vegetables.

This has been a most productive season in the garden and field. We have had very plentiful crops of hay & wheat & our barns and storehouses are ful of the fruits of the earth. We are eating of our own grown bread & most delicious it is. I have often felt thankful for plenty of good food, but it seems to me that what we produce ourselves is more excellent still. I think of the many genial showers, the glorious mornings & bright & glowing sunshine \the gorgeous sunsets/, the winds & most beneficent though awful thunderstorms which have all contributed to the growth & perfection of nature, & every slice of bread reminds me of that love & wisdom who appointed them & ordained such beautiful results.

The early part of the summer was wet, but for the last two months we have had delightful weather and lived almost altogether out of doors, that is on the ~~porti~~ piazza, where we take our meals & usually sit. I am now writing there, shaded by the vine, whose changing leaves & clusters of purple grapes remind us that summer is passing away, but at present all is green. I lift up my eyes and look upon green fields and woods in the foreground & over on to the green hills of Kentucky, which bound our view. On this side is a light blue haze that forms a fine contrast to the transparent brilliancy of the nearer scenery. Our views are none of them extensive nor very varied, but there is a quiet sylval beauty about us, an entire seclusion in our own little domain that is very much to my taste. On this side in summer we cannot see a house; on the other are dwellings peeping out amongst the trees, a little white chapple whose porticoed front makes it a picturesque object & a glimpse into the distant country which is always blue & <shad-*torn*> & makes me think of mountains, though I know in the gradual ascents of the country they are but very moderate hills.

Did I ever tell you what a noisy country this is? From one end of the land to the other during the summer months, day & night there is a continual chirping & humming & croaking. In the early part of the season the frogs begin & keep up an incessant whir like an old spinning wheel; then as the warm weather advances come the grass hoppers and Cata-dids & Cata did'nts & loud toned locusts that set up a cry like the rattle of fifty pebbles in a tin can. The earth & air seem full of them, especially in warm nights & yet so soon do we become accustomed to even uncommon things that now I seldom notice them. I do sometimes think of the still nights we used to have in England & how rare a thing a grasshopper was there, & here they fly before one in thousands & tens of thousands as we walk in the grass, but excepting the Cata-dids they are brown & ash coloured.

I have had little chance of rambling this summer & my botanical observations have been very limited—but I have seen some very beautiful [2] flowers brought from the woods by a friend of ours, and in passing along I have afresh remarked the luxuriant beauty of the garden flowers and creepers; our city is called the city of roses & truly I never saw that lovely flower in its full beauty till now. There is such a variety of climbers—dark & light red, blush

& shaded—that bloom in clusters as large as a child's head & these are trained round the piazzas & up the houses most beautifully.[67]

The balsam and morning-glory, the marvel of Peru and Prince's-feather are here splendid flowers because so large & luxuriant, and in fact every thing of this kind attains a perfection of which, under our chilly skies, you can form no idea. Even the privet has such rich clusters of blossom that I never before thought it capable of so much beauty.[68]

I will try to describe a place belonging to a Friend here whom we visited in the spring. The house is placed on one of those steep hills which border the Ohio and overlooks the river at a point where it forms a double bend, being lost on either side between its high banks so that it has the appearance of a lake. The opposite shores of Kentucky are wild & uncultivated, mostly covered with Forest trees. Between the house & the river is a broad tract of rich bottom land in the highest state of cultivation & right is the distant city & its populous suburbs, left the farms and villages that occupy the space until you reach the mouth of the little Miami. The house is \white &/ approached from a small lodge up an ascent so steep as to require the garden to be made into terraces. The walk was bordered by the Pyrne Japonica in full flower.[69] The house has a double Piazza, the upper one surrounding it and upon which the parlours & bedrooms open. These piazzas are covered with climbing roses & and other beautiful creepers, and from them we had a splendid view of the country in the bright sunshine of a fine spring afternoon & in the mild light of a glorious full moon, a yellow moon such as we read of in the Iliad but never see in England.

This Friend is an Irish-woman & has brought her old-country tastes, & being at leisure & moreover rich can gratify them. She has her greenhouse, an humble one to be sure, & a little bijou of a flower garden laid out with walks & little pet flower-beds & a basin & fountain in the centre & a summer-house at one end. Then she has roses covering every wall & white jesamine & our old friend the <lissium>, or as it is here honoured by the name of Wash-

67. This is the first of four instances in which Alderson uses a child's (or baby's) head as the basis for a size comparison (see also pages 191, 363, and 398). Whenever Howitt has incorporated the material into *OCO*, she has, perhaps out of a sense of delicacy, omitted that comparison.

68. The name "prince's feather" has historically referred to various species, mainly in the genus Amaranthus.

69. Possibly *Pieris japonica*, or lily-of-the-valley bush, an evergreen shrub native to East Asia. *P. Japonica* was introduced to the United States sometime in the nineteenth century (Walter S. Judd, e-mail with author, April 7, 2020), and a British publication in 1884 describes it as "little known" but "by no means new" ("Garden Gossip," *The Florist and Pomologist, and Suburban Gardener* [August 1884]: 128, https://www.biodiversitylibrary.org/item/272732). References in the American press do not appear until later in the century; so it is somewhat surprising that Alderson would have found it as far west as Cincinnati.

ington's bower,[70] & the dear old laburnum: Oh how I love to greet the pleasant faces of such old & worthy Friends.

Above is the Kitchen-garden in beautiful order & above that the hill, crowned with the primeval Forest. Then there are fruit tree[s] of every kind and a long covered walk covered with vines trained up trellises & every convenience that heart can wish for, comfort as well as ornament. I thought, could some of those who think there is nothing good in America only be brought here, they would be almost as much astonished as the wild Indian, who fifty years ago followed the buffalo & wild deer through the trackless forest on these very hills.

Speaking of the Indian reminds me of a Friend who belongs to our Quarterly-Meeting, who is lately returned from a two years sojourn amongst the Shawnee tribe, who are under the care of Friends of this and Ohio Yearly meeting. His name is Thomas Wells; he is an Englishman of a most energetic, ardent mind. I love to hear him preach: he shows so much of the missionary spirit & in his prayers beceaches so beautifully for men of every colour & clime that it does my heart good. He spent a night with us & gave us many interesting particulars about the Indians, their habits & character, but I cannot recollect anything particularly new to communicate.

We are very busy making a milk-house. There is a well near the back-door of extremely cold-water be with such a strong sulpherous taste as to be very disagreeable even for common use. From its smell these springs are very common in this part. Harrison is sinking a kind of cellar near the well which is to have an opening into it to admit the cold air & as it is to be arched over & only about a foot or two above the ground, we hope to have a first-rate milk house. The materials for forming it are principally got out of our own fields and are the fosil limestone of which I sent you some small specimens. It abounds in this district, but what is remarkable there are no boulder stones; at least I see none on these elevations. The earth they throw out is all a kind of light clay & soil without any pebbles.

What a delightful treat you must have had in dear Mary's visit to you. Mother mentions her being at Liverpool & that you were all gone a tour in North Wales. Thou must write, dearest Anna, & tell me all about her visit & how she looks after being so long abroad & every thing about her & yourselves. I won't give way to the thought, but I do sometimes think it almost unkind that I should only have received one letter from her in two long years, and yet perhaps I have myself to blame: I have never written to her since I heard of poor Claude's death & I am sure courtesy, if not sisterly kindness, [3] should have suggested that. But dear sisters, you with your many servants

70. Washington's bower is probably *Lycium barbarum* (also wolfberry or matrimony vine), which was originally from Eurasia but naturalized in Britain and later introduced to North America.

& lives of comparative leisure little know what a busy day ful life we lead in America. There is to make & mend for husband, children, Richard & myself & I am become a tailoress into the bargain. Then we have company to receive & entertain & to visit back again occasionally & baby to nurse & the children to instruct & the house to keep in order & sometimes we have help & sometimes & the far greater portion of time without.

We have a delightful home surrounded by our own unencumbered acres, which produce us every comfort & luxury we can desire; we have a choice society of friends, whose intercourse & many kindnesses are a constant source of pleasure and excite our grateful affection; we have a carriage & fine horses to take us wherever we wish to go, and yet the drawback to all these is that there is almost of necessity much bodily toil, especially in country life, and very little leisure to take our ease amongst all our comforts. Yet I often think it is far better to be wearied in body than worn with anxious cares & fearful anticipations for the future.

This reminds me, dearest sister, of the comfort, nay the great thankfulness, I have felt on your behalf that Daniel was so blessed and prospered in his business. It is many months since thou told me & often has my heart rejoiced & been grateful on your account in the rememberance.

Last 5th day the women Friends met after meeting to consult together about a package of clothing they are preparing for the Indians. They consist of every species of common clothes for children from 5 to 15. Some have given money, some a piece of linsey or calico or jean. Some articles [are] made up & now they contemplate meeting at each other's houses to make up what is still in the piece. Contributions are expected from Ohio Yearly meeting & other places & the whole are to be forwarded before winter. The number of children to be supplied is about 200.

The Indians are still an improvident race & consequently very dependent. Their generosity is so great that their only garment or last crust are divided with the yet more indigent. In the early settlement of this state, a boy named Spencer was stolen by the Indians & trained by them in the practice of all their habits and became in every respect one of them. He eventually returned to his friends & settled at Cincinnati where he amassed a large fortune & built a handsome house, but he retained his love & partiality for his old Friends & used to invite large parties of them to visit him & entertain them in the Indian fashion.

Poor things, how are they fa<llen>. A friend told me he had wished for me one day at his store. An Indian chief in full costume with large heavy earrings and a proud but melancholy countenance called to solicit assistance to enable him to prosecute his journey to Washington, where he was going to appeal to Congress. He was accompanied by an interpreter & when he arrived at the city was pennyless.

There is one custom which prevails here that sometimes troubles me: the women are the most determined kissers I ever saw. At meeting and at parting one must submit to the ceremony & though it is very pleasant in those we love, yet to receive a salute from everybody young & old, whether one cares for them or not, is somewhat trying. I have taken some pains to avoid it. At first I thought it was their especial love & kindness to my unworthy self, but I have found it is so general & universal that it ceases to be any thing more than an annoying ceremony.

Dost thou remember the plant I gave to Susanna Beakbane with its beautiful clusters of red flowers[?] I recognize it in many a garden as the Oleander. It grows here to a large size & blooms beautifully as also does the Pomegranate, double & single, & the Azaleas of many different colours. The trumpet creeper & the trumpet honeysuckle, red & yellow, are grand flowers here from their profusion of bloom. Our garden has produced us asparagus; rhubarb sallads; potatoes; beans & peas; cabbage; spinnach; beets; carrots; turnips; parsnips; water, musk & citron, cantelope melons;[71] squash; the purple egg plant or guinea squash; sweet corn; gourds; tomatos; and sweet potatoes, a species of yam I should think, though the plant is a convolvulus with large bulbous or rather tuberous roots like a long potatoes & which is cooked \like it/, sometimes boiled at others roasted. It is very sweet & good. The egg plant bears a large egg shaped seed of a dark purple colour; we have one ~~in~~ on a plant now as large as a child's head. It is sliced & fried & tastes like a rich animal substance.

The gourds we grow for ladles; they are this shape[72] and become very hard when quite ripe. Then when one side is cut away they make very good "dippers"; in primitive times when people lived in the woods and stores were rare, they used to grow their milk bowls & basins. They must be similar to the African calabash.

A short time ago when we were returning from the City, we met the Sisters of Charity with their little Orphan children returning from a country ramble. They had probably been spending the afternoon with someone. First came about 25 or 30 little girls in their pink frocks & sunbonnets & two sisters, then a carriage with the two others. On the knees [4] of one was a young baby in its long pink dress and, in the very folding of her arm around its little form, there was so much love & tenderness that I thought a mother sits there. After them followed a waggon load of other children. The dress of the sisters is a plain black stiff dress, a small black shawl & black close cottage bonnet; in winter they wear a scanty black cloth cloak. They are by no means recluces; we often see them in the streets & occasionally I have observed their casting a hasty side glance at some passer-by or other attractive object.

71. The citron melon (*Citrullus lanatus* var. *citroides* or *Citullus amarus*) is related to our watermelon but harder and lacking sweetness. It is cooked and sweetened for candied fruit or jams.

72. See figure 23.

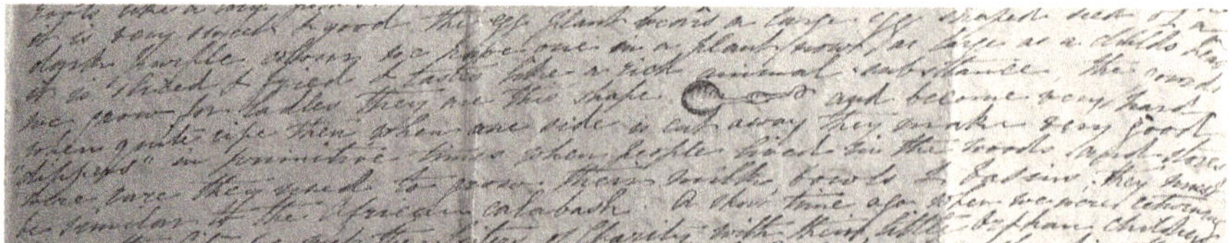

Figure 23. Drinking gourd, drawing inserted by Emma Alderson in letter #21. Ht/7/3/3, Correspondence of Mary Howitt (1799–1888), Manuscripts and Special Collections, University of Nottingham.

I have written thus far and have neither mentioned thy nor my children. I wish, dear sister, I could give thee as graphic & interesting particulars about our family as thou gives me of yours. How glad I am thou finds thy two grown daughters such a great assistance to thee: dear mother speaks very highly of them. If thou wast here thou wouldst feel rich & independent; indeed, I assure thee I look forward with much pleasure to the time when my three girls will be available, when we can go hand in hand in intellectual and moral culture & find even the very cares which make life so burdensome to the mother of a little family a means and source of happiness by exercising the affections and, in a cheerful, happy performance of duty and the practice of self-denial, \seeking/ to promote the comfort of each other.

I have spent a very happy morning with the children around me on the piazza. Charles is getting finely on with his reading & writing; he is reading Peter Parley's Geography, a very nice book & the source of much interesting information & conversation.[73] He is a fine, intelligent boy, overbearing & proud-spirited, but easily convinced & immediately prepared to give up & adopt the right course if left to himself.

Agnes is a lively interesting child and is beginning to help in her way, though she is volatile & somewhat spoiled. Yesterday she mended her sister's pinafore; today she has been doing the same for her nightgown. She is a great favourite with our friends the Taylors, whom she occasionally visits for a week. They are rich &, being five unmarried people, indulge her sadly, but she is so affectionate & withall so pretty that her waywardness is somewhat more tolerable.[74]

Anna Mary is a noble hearted, bold spirited original child who can climb fences & will run to the horses & into every species [1-*cross*] of danger with

73. Samuel Griswold Goodrich [Peter Parley, pseud.], *A Grammar of Modern Geography* (London: Thomas Tegg, 1838). Believing that children should be given facts packaged in an appealing form rather than the falsehoods of fiction, fairy tales, and imaginative literature, Goodrich published a popular series of books on various subjects. In a later letter, William Charles quotes from another of Goodrich's Peter Parley series, this time on the kangaroo mouse.

74. Only Joseph, James, Abraham, and Hannah are mentioned in the letters. No mention is made of the fourth brother, Nathan H. Taylor (1805–1893).

the air of a little hero. She is full of odd speeches & often makes me think that sister Mary would be such a child when she was little. Poor little Ann Alice, who is quietly asleep in her crib, where she mostly is from being one of the very least of living human beings, is growing a very fine hearty looking child. A very queer looking little maiden she is, as she has never worn caps & is dressed in short clothes.

Oh how I should love to see thy Emma Lucy; kiss her for me every day for a month to come. If I was nearer I would make her a frock or two.

I want thee to send this to dear mother as I fear I shall not get another letter written this post, so I must not go on with my crossing. This is a poor worthless scrawl, but what can I write about, shut up as I am except once a week to meeting? My world is very narrow.

Well it has been wide enough.

Farewell, my beloved Anna. Give my endeared love to Mother, Daniel & all your dear family & believe me thy attached sister,

Emma Alderson

9th mo 13th

[4] Please give my love to Cousin Lucy Bayliffe & to thy Aunt & Uncle R. & M. T.[75] as also to any of our friends who may enquire after us. Harrison desires his dear love to you all; Elizabeth also sends her love do <*five lines entirely and intentionally blotted out*>

22. *To Mary Howitt, October 13 to 21, 1844*[76]
Cedar Lodge 10 mo. 13th 1844

Well now my beloved sister I will break the long, long silence and commence a letter to thee, hoping to hear from thee in reply. It is now about a year since I received thy last very interesting and most welcome letter & if I remember right I had dispatched one to thee a few days before it arrived.

We have each of us seen important changes in our household since then. We have had another dear child added to our little circle & thou, my beloved sister, hast been called upon to relinquish one endeared to thee by a long season of suffering. Dear boy he was, whom I never saw, but I loved him as thy child and had formed a high idea of his brilliant talents & sweet & amiable disposition. Harrison has often spoken of him as a cheerful, openhearted boy whom he very much admired, and dearest Mary, my heart has often ached for you when I thought how much sorrow you must have known in witnessing his sufferings & in parting from him though it may be but for a season. I have hoped that either thou or dear Anna Mary would send me a few particulars

75. Possibly a very loose use of the word "aunt," since neither Daniel nor Anna had living aunts or uncles with these initials.
76. The concluding date for this letter is an estimate based on the reference to the wedding of James Taylor and Elizabeth Shipley (October 24, 1844), which would "take place in a few days" (see page 197).

of his illness & death; it is a painful subject for you but one of deep interest to me and I should love that our children should know all they can about their little cousin about whose accident they were so much interested.

We are far seperated, but I try to keep alive a warm affection and interest in the hearts of the children for their distant relations: they shall know you all as familiar realities, and thoughts of you shall be so mixed up with their earliest recollections & associations that they shall love you as those that they have seen & known in their brightest & happiest days, and their uncles & aunts & cousins are all so good & invested with so many excellencies that they are the models on which they have to form themselves.

I want that they should be English children in America, for the more I see & can compare in my own mind, the more do I love my own dear country. I often say to myself there is nobody like John Bull, so generous, so unselfish, so like the father & friend of the whole world. The Americans are very good to themselves; they make extraordinary efforts to improve their country and exalt themselves; they are very earnest & often ~~too~~ very successful, too, to promote measures to remove evils & improve society. But they work all at home & for home; they have little of the open heart & open hand that seeks the sorrowful & oppressed & rejoices to do them good. They can oppress & be easy; they can see suffering & feel very ~~easy~~ cold & well satisfied in their own exemptions. I speak nationally: there are, and let us rejoice with thankfulness over them, some fine exceptions, but on the whole they are a selfish people & their failings are such as mark ~~the~~ individual selfishness. I do not think thou wouldst admire them. You would enjoy the refined intellectual society in New England; you would be amused at the busy commercial well-to-do aspect of things at New York; you would admire the sober elegance of Philadelphia and see many novelties in these Western States; but to live in America I am sure you would never wish. There wants the polish, the grace, the warm heart & sterling integrity of Old England.

Now whilst I am writing this, comes a kind friend all the way from the city on a raw autumnal afternoon, when it looks as likely to pour down rain in the course of an hour as not, to bring me a letter from my husband, who is at the Yearly Meeting. Am not I ungrateful? No, I love many here very dearly & have cause to do so, for we have been treated with overwhelming kindness and moreover admire & love them for their own sakes. They are the salt of the earth and would be ornaments in any country.

This is a season of great excitement and politics run high. Wigs and Democrats are the two contending parties. The Wigs are, as I understand them, somewhat similar to our enlightened Wigs: from them are hoped all measures which tend to improve and ameliorate society. The anti-slavery men hope more from them than any other party because their principles are liberal. The Democrats are \our/ Tory and Chartists united: they uphold all old abuses and at the same time would overturn all law & government. [2] May we be preserved from their domination, for of all rule, mob rule is the worst.

The principal elections at present are governor of the State, members of Congress & Legislature, and various other subordinate officers; then comes the Presidential election: the candidate of the Wig part is Henry Cay; that of the Democrats Van Buren, and on the result of the former depends which of these two men are president. There are daily political meetings in the city and neighbourhood; a few nights since, they had each a torch-light procession. It was described as brilliant: the houses were illuminated and the ladies placed themselves on the steps to hail them with banners.

You will of course have heard of Charles Fourier and his system of association. There are two societies formed on his plan in this State; one near Wheeling is called the Ohio Phalanx, and Thompson Harrison, Daniel's brother, has joined them with his family; they have a fine farm of upwards of 2000 acres of land on the River, 1000 of which are cleared; the remainder is forest and the predominating timber sugar maple, & white oak, locust, poplar or Tulip tree, & black walnut. A vein of coal 4 ½ feet thick crops (as it is called) out of the hills, and the Wheeling vein, 7 feet thick, is found on the river bank. They have a large temporary frame building erected on the farm for the accomodation of those associated & there are various shantys & other buildings scattered about. They take their meals together at a public table, and each family has a separate room; each individual from 7 years old is expected to labour & the adults work, I think, 10 hours a day, and the overplus of their industry, when their maintenance is paid, is put down to their own account. This is, as I understand it, the outline of their plan. There are many in this country who from various causes are at their wits end for a living. Poor Thompson is one these & for such this is a tolerable recourse, but all domestic comfort seems sacrificed. It may do for the French with their limited ideas of home comforts, and it may do for Americans who can live in boarding houses & every species of tenement that has four walls with a roof & a capacious hearth to cook plenty of good things, but it would not do for Englishmen in England.

The children have the hooping cough, but so far it is very mild. I am sorry it has commenced so late in the season as probably it will linger with them through the winter. Poor little Ann Alice has it the worst, and I fear it will go hardly with her. She is a sweet placid little creature of a meek and quiet spirit and so far has been very little trouble—certainly in our family a good specimen of an American child.

You must know both the lights & shades of our experience. We are at present without help & have our own work to do except washing, \for/ which we can hire. It is very difficult to get girls to come into the country & stay with you, and wages are high when they do come, about 7/ of our English money, a dollar & half a week is the usual wage. In some things it is pleasanter to be without, for many of them expect to sit down to table with you & if they take it into their head to go out for a day or so you are simply informed of it & obliged to smile consent. After all, dear Mary, it is so well when our children are our wealth, when the more we can gather around our table are, instead of burdens, a revenue of comfort & happiness & riches.

I look hopefully toward the time when our three girls will, under my eye, render us independent of all these trifling annoyances & we shall experience that purest happiness derived from a cheerful fulfilment of duty & the promoting of mental comfort & enjoyment. I do not want them to be drudges: I believe women may be intelligent & have intellectual tastes & pursuits & yet be actively domestic.

I am sorry to say that absolute infidelity and various modifications of unbelief prevail to a frightful extent in this land; Universalism and Unitarian [3] doctrines are amongst the most predominating. Excuse me if your ancient partiality for the latter opinions still remain, which I hope they do not. I know that such men as Channing and Bentham and Bowering and Mrs. Barbauld & Lidia Maria Child & many others of the good & great have held those sentiments, but no man or set of men can recommend error nor overturn or set aside the simple and efficacious plan of redemption by Christ as set forth in the New Testament. Dear Mary, I am not going into any religious argument with thee, but I have been thinking much on this subject whilst attending a very interesting meeting held by a Friend with the children. Oh, how beautiful did it seem to invite them to the Saviour as their alsufficient Redeemer, to one who having paid the penalty for sin was by his spirit drawing & inviting them to become wholly his &, as of old, ready to lay his hands on them and bless them. How near does Divine goodness appear to the hearts of little children in the person of Christ, and how simply & fully may their hopes centre in him as the medium through which they are to deserve every good.

Please tell dear Mother that the box she sent has arrived, though we have not yet received it; I am glad it is safe, as I had many fears it was lost. Thou, my dear sister, wast so kind in thy letter as to offer to send me some of thy works; the English editions I have a great desire to see and, if thou couldst sometime do so and direct them to the care Thomas Winn, Merchant Second Street, Philadelphia, they would I doubt not arrive sometime. I expect it would be best to write in them so that they could not be considered new books.

Anna mentions that thou art writing a history of thy childhood: how I should love to see that.[77] Didst thou ever publish the illustrated edition of thy ballads[?] What is William working? I have seen none of his works since the Second Series of Visits.[78] The other day I was invited to a party to be exhibited as Mary Howitt's sister to a gentleman from New York; poor things,

77. Mary Howitt, *My Own Story; or, The Autobiography of a Child* (New York: D. Appleton, 1844). This was the final volume in Tales for the People and Their Children.
78. William Howitt, *Visits to Remarkable Places: Old Halls, Battle Fields, and Scenes Illustrative of Striking Passages in History and Poetry*, 2nd series (London: Longman, Brown, Green, and Longmans, 1842); published the same year in Philadelphia.

if they expected to see anything remarkable, they would be woefully disappointed: it would only instruct them what commonplace relations great people can have.

Perhaps thou wilt have heard of the glory of an American Autumn, or Fall as it is here called, till thou art weary, but surely dear Mary, nothing can exceed the splendour of the Forest trees this season. We have had a remarkably fine dry season for some months now. Previously we had a great deal of wet, & vegetation in consequence acquired a vigour & beauty that was unusual, so that now when the full rich foliage has changed to every shade of brown, yellow, orange, crimson & dark purple mingled with bright green, it is splendid indeed to see the river winding its course ~~through~~ between hills covered with these trees and watch the sunbeams glittering on its surface & illuminating the woods reflected on its bosom. The river is always an interesting object to me. We do not see it from our house, but we pass about a mile on the bank in going to & fro to meeting. There are the various craft plying up & down this great highway of a great continent, from the little fishing boat, the raft & flat bottomed trading boat to the gay steamer, all green & white & sending up only wreaths of light, feathery steam, for as they burn only wood, their track is not marked by a black ugly column of smoke.

There has been a great rage for weddings in this meeting: the third within a few weeks is to take place in a few days between one of our cousins, the Shipleys, & an intimate friend of ours.[79] The "passing" as it is called was very odd to me: the first monthly meeting they sent in a note expressive of their intentions; at the next, the upper seat in the meeting was left vacant, & after the opening of the business, the young woman was called upon to take her seat, which she did accompanied by her [4] mother. There, poor body, she remained till her intended husband, being apprized that all was ready, attended by his Friend, came & took his seat beside her. They then stood up & took each other by the hand & declared that they still continued their intention.

We were invited guests at the last marriage and the dinner was conducted in American Country fashion. The family all waited upon us: neither father, mother, grandmother, brother, nor sister sate down. There was roasted turkey, roasted pig, ham & beef \at a side table/ all put upon each plate, to which were added sweet potatoes, turnips, beets & common potatoe, so that we had each a perfect pile on our plate. We waited till all were served & then the master usually gives the word, please begin, & all is in active operation. When each has eaten their fill, & all leave some thing on their plate, it is removed & in comes, plate by plate out of the kitchen or some side place, ~~a plate~~ three

79. James Taylor and Elizabeth Shipley, October 24, 1844. Harrison and Elizabeth Alderson's names are recorded on the marriage certificate, but Emma's is not. Nevertheless, she may have been there and failed to sign the certificate (*Record of Marriage Certificates of Cincinnati Monthly Meeting*, Quaker Rare Collection, Watson Library, Wilmington College, Ohio).

or four pieces of pie. On these were apple, peach & preserve, accompanied by a cup of syllabub. It would distress some delicate stomachs to be so abundantly helped. I often wonder what becomes of all that is left; probably it is the pigs' portion, but after all, it is shameful waste & makes me sigh for the needy, hungry poor of dear old England. How many an old woman's & little child's heart would it make glad.[80]

Dear Harrison has been at the Yearly Meeting. There were upwards of three thousand friends there & on the first day it was supposed there were about five thousand assembled.

I wish I had been there that I might have told you all about it for it must have been a novel & interesting sight. We have had a great treat in the company of John Pease; he spent a night under our roof. What a dear man he is & how one loves ones' own countrymen. It is the most pleasant thing that has happened to us \since we came/, to see him & hear him preach. Whenever you can, go to hear him. He enquired very particularly after you & said he had seen you at Stoke Newington shortly before leaving England.

I do not want to be inquisitive but I want to know every thing about you, so tell me all thou can, all your concerns literary & unliterary: is Anna Mary married or likely to be? what is Alfred to be? how do the other children look & who are they like & what accounts have you from Pheobe & the Dr [Godfrey Howitt] Give my love to them when thou writes.

Please tell dear mother I shall begin a letter for her immediately. I hope she is well & just tell me how thou found her in her house at Uttoxeter. Oh, how I wish I could go and see her.

[1] Farewell, my beloved sister. Harrison unites me in dear love to you all, and in much affection, I am, dearest Mary, thy attached sister,

Emma Alderson

23. To Ann Botham, October 25, 1844
Cedar Lodge 10 mo. 25 1844

My beloved Mother,
Nothing but a succession of the most pressing engagements would have prevented me writing to thee many weeks ago and substituting letters to my sisters for others to thee. I have written to both Anna & Mary since I wrote to thee but hoped that those letters would be forwarded so that thou would have some idea how we are going on. Thy last interesting letter, written at Upper Clapton & containing thy likeness, I have received & thank thee, dearest mother, for them; they are very precious to me and the more I look at the picture the more I can trace a resemblance and recall thy dear form and countenance. Oh, it has often brought the tears to my eyes & made my heart

80. Emma's contrast here between the feasting Americans and England's hungry poor may reflect her awareness of her sister's social activism. In the next letter, to her mother, the wedding is described but without the strong social commentary

ache to look at it. I sometimes think what would I no[w] not give for the blessed privilege of kissing thy dear cheek & enjoying thy society for one day, nay, one hour. I think every body is happy that can have their mother with them and do something to promote their comfort & happiness; how would it enhance the value of every good & every blessing if thou couldst partake with me, but I do hope & trust dearest mother that thou wants for nothing.

I know thy generous heart & I fear thou mayst deprive thyself of comforts for the sake of those who are dear to thee. How many thanks do I owe thee for all the various tokens of thy affection contained in the box which has reached us in safety & overwhelmed me with its stores of nice things. But dearest mother, I fear thou has robbed thyself & am sure thou hast sent me thy best gown and all the nice stockings so valuable as thy work and the night caps & gowns and the beautiful rememberances for the children & the precious family relics; all these, dear mother, we do most sincerely thank thee for, but it made me sorrowful to take them for I could not help saying dearest mother has stripped herself of all her nice & choice things, & her room & drawers will look \so/ bare for lack of them. William Penn's grave is hung up in our best lodging room and is an interesting thing to many here. Harrison is quite set up with his spectacle case; he grows more & more in love for antiquity, so that this, as being somewhat oldfashioned & unlike the unsubstantial things of modern days, is exactly to his mind. He desires his dear love & thanks.

We have also much to acknowledge from the dear people at Liverpool, but I mean to write to them & thank them then. Only tell them with our dear love we are exceedingly obliged & that could they know how happy Agnes is made with her doll they would be repaid for all their trouble. It is indeed a beautiful gift for the poor child who is as fond of dolls as ever she was.

Our children have all the whooping cough, but so far they have had it very favourably; even Ann Alice bears it well & thrives & looks remarkably pretty under its influence. She is a dear little creature with a pair of very bright blue eyes & a sweet placid countenance. She is the best tempered child I ever nursed; I often wonder where she got all her good nature & easy, quiet temper: \not/ from her mother I am sure. I began from the first to lay her down awake. I find the advantage of it daily. She sleeps many hours in the morning and goes to rest in her little crib like the other children at 6 oclock \in the evening/ & there rests like a woman [2] till I take her to bed. I hope thou wilt like her name. Harrison had a worthy grandmother & great grandmother & has a kind good sister named Alice & we united it with thine for distinction from Anna Mary or Annie as she is \here/ called.

Some weeks back we had a very great treat in the company of John Pease, who came here on his way to the Yearly Meeting. He had two meetings in the city: one with friends alone & the other the next day on the occasion of a wedding. He spoke in both at considerable length & certainly most powerfully & beautifully. He spent a night under our roof. We greatly enjoyed his visit; I told him I hoped on his return he would sometime meet with thee & be able to tell thee how we looked in our transatlantic home. He remembered thee with affection & thought with me that cousin Ann Shipley & thou were remarkably alike. Dear woman, she desired her love to thee the last time I saw her.

Harrison went to Richmond, about 60 miles distant, to the yearly meeting from its commencement with the meeting of ministers and elders to its close. It occupied exactly a week & H. describes it as a very interesting occasion; there were many subjects of interest brought forward. The question of education was discussed more favourably than heretofore & it was agreed to endeavour to raise the sum of 4000 dollars to complete & bring into operation a Yearly Meeting school which was commenced some years ago & has been at a standstill for want of funds & support. In some of these remote districts there has been a strong prejudice against a liberal education. It was abhored as innovation but I should suppose this is lessening. Once a friend said to me very sarcastically, ["]I suppose thou can read & write & knows grammar & geography & an abundance of fine things besides," evidently not thinking I was any better for so much learning.

The season in the early part of the summer was so unusually wet that westward on the Ohio, Mississippi & Missouri there were dreadful inundations & the houses, cattle & crops were swept away, so that in many places they are likely to suffer greatly for want during the winter. Amongst others, the Indian settlements on these & other rivers are destroyed & injured & some very powerful & very touching appeals were made on their behalf in the Y Meeting, which were followed up by a subscription & application to other Yearly Meetings to follow their example.

There were supposed to be about 3000 friends in attendance, and on the first-day near 5000 were collected. Richmond is a small town & the number to entertain such a crowd few. Frequently friends have been eaten bare before the meeting was over, so to relieve them a farm of about 200 acres was purchased by the Yearly Meeting & two good houses erected for the entertainment gratis of such as would avail themselves of it. The meeting read & adopted a very spirited decided pamphlet issued by friends in London against slavery and 2000 copies ordered to be printed: 10000 to be circulated amongst friends & the other ten in the slave states.[81]

I heard a pleasing circumstance the other day: a gentleman in Kentucky whose chief property consists in slaves has decided to give them their freedom. He has thirty, and proposes to send them to Liberia; a few of the old ones have declined going & for these & some little helpless children he provides at home. He has given 1000 dollars towards the expence of transportation. I do not rejoice that they are sent to Liberia, for I think a great deal of

81. Presumably Emma has either omitted a zero in the first number or added one in the second.

cruelty is connected with the Colonization scheme, but the laws of the slave states require a master who manumits to provide for & be answerable for the conduct of his former slaves.

[3] Last 5th day one of our cousins the Shipley was married to a friend of this meeting, James Taylor, of whom & his brother & sister I have told thee.[82] It was a very gay wedding & we of course were amongst the invited. The bride, who is a tall elegant girl with a classical head & countenance, was dressed in rich white silk with white silk scarf & bonnet. She had three brides-maids in rich sage coloured silk & white scarfs. We were about 30, dined on a very handsome dinner, & in the evening about 60 guests were assembled. The folding doors were thrown open at 9 and a most elegant supper provided. The table was spread with large ornamented iced cakes, jellies, fruits, preserves, sandwiches, blancmanges &c. & tea & coffee and lemonade served from side tables. The company all standing round yesterday, we went down to pay the bride [a] visit, for here visiting usually commences the day after the marriage. I had provided a light dress for the occasion, but when thy handsome present arrived I preferred it & made it up, and very much it was admired. I have told thee these particulars, frivolous as they may appear, that thou mayst have an idea how things are done in this country.

What a sorrowful account thou gives of Thomas Kennersley's death; I feel very much for his family and when thou sees Harriet K. please give my kind rememberance and the expression of sincere sympathy with her under her severe trial. The inundations I mentioned before have occasioned almost universal sickness: fever & ague prevails almost every where in those parts. A young man named Mark Ison from Colebrook-dale has just returned from a trip up the Mississippi & tells us this. He saw the house where the Albrights reside & describes it as a fine situation & a pretty place, but I fear from his account, they will partake of the general sickness.

I never see pumpkin pies, which at this season are daily on our table, without thinking of thee, for I remember thy speaking of them at Milford-<*cut*>. The pumpkin is an abundant produce & grows to a very large size, sometimes a complete burden to carry. We stew the pumpkin &, when boiled to a pulp, run it through a cullender & add eggs, sugar, butter or cream, & spice & bake it in flat dishes lined with crust. They are very good & I frequently say I think thou wouldst enjoy them.

This has been a remarkably fine season and the woods have been splendid, glowing with every shade of crimson, yellow, orange, brown, & green. But it is all over now & the cold weather is, I fear, coming fast upon us. We have enjoyed the summer much; to me it is delightful & the weather is never too warm for me, for in our elevated situation we have a breeze in the hotest weather. In the city it is oppressively hot, but in winter I am almost congealed;

82. Elizabeth Shipley. See page 197 for more details about this wedding between two of the Aldersons' closest friends.

I feel as if my energies were frozen up & I could do nothing but sit by the fire, and yet I suppose I must stir and work too, for as usual, we are without help, & really I am so tired of the consideration which hired people require that in many respects I find a liberty & ease in being without. Elizabeth makes herself very useful and does far more than I ever expected she would. I don't know how she likes [it]; I fear not very much.

The children desire their dear love to grandmother and say I must tell [4] her they are very much obliged to her for all her kind presents. Indeed dear mother, I feel as if I had not half thanked thee, there seems so much to acknowledge. I am afraid thou will find this letter a worthless epistle, but I shall be obliged to conclude hastily as Mark Ison is waiting to take it down to the post office & I must send it this mail to let thee know the things have come to hand.

I have sent Mary an account of the situation where Thompson has settled himself; perhaps thou wilt see it. It is like the last recourse of a hopeless man, I think, but I may be prejudiced.

Farewell my tenderly beloved mother; whenever thou canst write to me, thy letters are always a source of great happiness to me. I shall be pleased to hear thou hast got safely settled for the winter; it was a long journey for thee but thou art an extraordinary woman.

I observe \with pleasure/ that thou art at work without thy spectacles in thy picture.

Give my love to dear Anna Mary & thank her very sincerely for it. Harrison desires his dear love. My heart overflows with affections to thee & you all. May every blessing be yours; thy attached daughter,

Emma Alderson

Harrison is paring apples for Apple butter. I wish I could send thee a jar; it is excellent & would do thy cough good. Excuse all mistakes I have no time to correct.

24. To Ann Botham, December 1 to 26, 1844

It seems my tenderly beloved Parent as though our correspondence was becoming less regular than it was some time since. The mails arrive and bring me no letter from thee, and now this winter season I know that I must wait a whole month before I can reasonably look again for a letter. I could be satisfied and would not task thy kindness if I was sure all was well and that thy silence is not the result of indisposition, but at this distance I have many anxieties, and the fear of thy being ill makes me very unhappy. I wish, dearest mother, when thou art unequal ~~to~~ or disinclined for the task, dear Anna or the girls at Liverpool would write in thy stead. Thy letters are always so welcome and so interesting that I feel the lack of one a great privation, and so would one from them be instead of absence & distance weakening my affection & diminishing my interest in them. I often feel that my beloved Sisters and their families are dearer than ever.

I love you all with an intensity that is positively painful and had I known what it was to be so far seperated from our own I think I never could have consented to leave England, especially during thy lifetime, and I sometimes say that had we been willing or understood the practicability of doing as we do here, we might have retired into the country & lived very comfortably in our native land—that is, done without a servant & possessing land, produced almost all we consume within ourselves. To be sure, here we have a very excellent house, a carriage & pair of fine horses, & when I wish to go out I have a man to drive me if Harrison is not inclined or at liberty to go out. We have fruits & flowers and vegetables about us such as only the rich in England can possess, but all these are small compensation for the seperation from you; the advantage is prospective for our children.

I still think it is a wise and desirable change: with the commonest industry and management, no one need know want or even difficulty in America. We are beginning to see that this is decidedly the country for the poor and working man. Wages are high, in some cases a dollar & 75 cents—that, in our English money, will amount to near 9/ a day. The commonest artizan can get a dollar & quarter, & a labourer 75 cents, which is about 3/6 so that taking the cheapness of provisions into account they are well off & their wives, by washing in the city, can get 75 cents a day. We in the country give 50 cents to our washer & when we have a servant we give her 7/ a week, but for people in the middle ranks such as we, who have to hire & live somewhat like our neighbours, having on our tables many luxuries which in England are quite dispensed with, the difference is not so great, especially near a city. The Americans, if they <?> were as frugal as the English, would all be rich, but they seem to extend their wants to the utmost limit of their means.

I love to hear the stories of the way in which the old settlers, now many of them wealthy people, first began their course of careful industry & accumulation \in the West/. They will often tell one that the fine, highly cultivated neighbourhood in which they reside, with its rich farms, was when they came a thick forest, that they cut down the trees from \the grounds on/ which the old log house stands to build it & cleared bit by bit, till the country opened into the beautiful state it now is, with fine pastures, noble corn-fields & the still untouched & highly ornamental remains of its wilderness state in the skirting woods & the noble river.

Last week a Friend of this meeting spent a few days with us. She is a little hard featured old woman, a strict disciplinarian and stickler for consistency, and I have often been struck with her clear-headed remarks in meetings for discipline. She has known much sorrow as all her children have gone off to the Hicksites & left her in her old age in a religious sense a solitary widow. She is a native of Carolina & interested me with her accounts of many persons &

things—the events of the American war & her own life. She was one of those who from nothing, by industry & care, became wealthy, at least in her own estimation. She said when she was married all her possessions were clothes of her own manufacture, a bed of her own making & a cow & calf with three sheep, which her father gave her. Her husband had a little land but was in debt 3£, her weding dress was all her own spinning & weaving except her cap & apron, which were of fine cambric manufactured by her sister.

The first horse they bought was from a stranger travelling from Kentucky. He had a wild breed in a part of the Forest & offered them a "crittur" wild from the woods & eight years [2] old for a saddle, "a great coat pattern" of her own making which she had by her, & 12 yards of shirting linen like some she had there in the loom. They [a]greed & in a fortnight the man brought the horse, as "fine & black & slick" as ever was seen, & the goods, which they had worked day & night to complete, the husband at the saddle & she at her spinning & weaving, were delivered, & for two yards more of the linen, the man broke the horse & made him available to them. Well, by persevering industry they got on so that on their removal from Carolina to this Western country they brought 2000 dollars with them.

Susanna Neville has also been to pay us a short visit & I have very much enjoyed her society. I fear they are not doing any great things in the way of business. Joseph is still lame, though much better than when they first came. They are very careful & patterns of economy, & I do so admire poor Susanna who in all their <trials> & reverses & difficulties still bears up with a cheerful countenance & hopeful spirit & never utters one complaining sentiment.[83] We have talked together about you & all her friends & our mutual acquaintances & enjoyed retracing the past. Many things endear her much to me & I am glad they are settled in this part as it is a mutual pleasure to be near each other.

Hast thou heard of the death of Poor Sarah Albright[?] I mentioned in my last letter to thee that that part of the country was then very unhealthy; she & many of her family had the fever & sorrowful to say she, the very prop & comfort of them all, was taken. Harrison had a few weeks ago a letter from Thomas Albright informing us of the event. I felt much shocked; I have always hoped to see Sarah in this land. She, like Susanna, was a pattern of cheerful submission & I had hoped we might, by sympathy & kindly feeling at least, have contributed to throw a little sunshine over her cloudy path, but I trust her trials have had their legitimate effect, & by weaning her affection & drawing her mind from this world, led her to seek the consolations of religion & fix her hopes on the blessed results of redeeming love & mercy.

Oh the horrors of slavery! A short time ago a poor man called to ask charity; he was pale & emaciated, and poorly though decently clad. He had been

83. See pages 159, 165, 239, and 456 for details of Susanna Neville's trials.

a mason but was crippled in the arm by a musket ball which had been shot into his shoulder. The particulars of the case were these. He lived at St Louis and there a neighbour, a slave-holder, had a black man, the property of another, entrusted to him. This poor creature gave him some offence & the inhuman brute actually flogged him to death. He was taken up for the crime & this man & some others appeared as witnesses against him. To use his own words, he did not believe in slaveholding, for his father, who was a Quaker, had always raised them to hate it. So he swore to the fact of having seen this man flog the slave till his flesh to the bone was like <??> & many pounds dropt out; one woman "allowed" (thought) it might be 14. The wretch was fined & left at large. He was so incenced that he tried to shoot those who had borne testimony against him. ~~and~~ One man he shot at in a garret but missed. This man, on returning from his work, went out to chop wood in his yard, when a bullet shot from a stable near struck him in the shoulder & passed through his chest. His arm has been useless ever since, & thus a quiet man, the father of a little family, was disabled for life & left to beg for his & their support. The villian was taken & again tried & sentenced to ten years solitary confinement in the State Prison, & as an evidence of the truth of the statement, the man showed us a manuscript copy of the trial with many respectable attestations of its correctness.

Last 5th day was what is called thanksgiving day.[84] This is ordered by Congress annually to return acknowledgement for the blessings of the past year and crave their continuance for the coming season. Each State is expected to comply, & that was the day chosen by this state for the occasion. It is a good thing to remember our many many favours & to acknowledge our obligations to the bounteous giver of all good, but Oh how much more acceptable than these formal ceremonies would acts of mercy & justice be in the sight of Heaven, to loose the bonds of iniquity & let the oppressed go free. I am proud of England when I think of the noble offering of twenty millions ~~to~~ as the purchase of freedom in the West Indies. All my politics hinge on slavery & no-slavery, & I have been sadly grieved at the result of the election, to think that that abominable man with his low <*illegible*> Lane name, should have been the choice of the country, not for the man, for I do not know if there is much to choose between them—Clay & Polk are both Slaveholder[s]—but the latter is the slaveholder's man, the upholder of the system & a promoter of the Annexation of Texas, which all think will rivet the chain & give the interest a preponderating influence. Harrison says they will rejoice in England on account of the tarrif question. My comfort is, & I think I may say only hope, that, though men toss & fume & strive & plan, a mightier Power controls the destinies of nations & over rules all ultimately to his own righteous purposes.

84. November 28, 1844. A November Thanksgiving had been celebrated by states and colonies for many years but was not formalized nationally until 1863 by Abraham Lincoln.

12 mo 26th. I began this letter with regrets and fears. Oh, how entirely all was stilled by the arrival of your precious letters. What a \treat/ had I; how much do I owe you, dear kind mother and sisters for these constant proofs of your thought & affection for us. You are so exact in your [3] accounts that I think it is next to living with you to receive such details. I know the house Wm & Mary have removed to from thy description: what a pleasant, convenient place it must be. I almost covet one of those nice cupboarded & closeted dressing-rooms: it is just what I want to make our house complete. And dearest Mary in her great kindness has told me how you all look so beautifully that I feel as if I had seen you this christmas. Dearest mother, mayst thou have a pleasant christmas and a happy new year abounding with the comforts & consolations that are to be found only in the path of the humble, trusting Christian.

Oh how my heart is filled with love and sympathy for dear Anna & Mary. They have had their trials, and some of them very heavy, but I trust they have know[n] them converted into blessings. I shed fresh tears over poor Mary's account of Claude: dear child, it would be a heart wringing sorrow to part with him, but for him what a blessed lot. Please give my endeared love to them and their interesting families.

Our children are very much pleased with the messages of love, & all desire me to give their love to thee. Thou shalt have a lock of Charley's hair, dear mother, when it is grown a little more unless he goes bodily himself, for he often talks of going to see thee: it seems to be a fixed purpose in his mind. He is a fine active boy with a great deal of thought and reflection about every thing. In reading his geography, which as it is written for Americans has a spice of their self-conceit, it says that the rulers of America \are/ all wise & good. When Charley read this, he said "mother I don't think they are wise & good when they have slaves & are so cruel to the Indians, does thou?["] He is a great hater of war, slavery & drunkenness.

Santa-claus has been very kind to him and his sisters this season. They have had a bag of sweetmeats & each a new book sent them by our kind friends the Taylors, whose generosity & affectionate kindness is constantly showing itself in acts of love. I wish thou couldst know them for they are a noble hearted family. Nor are the dear Shipleys less so, but their means are more limited, and yet how true kindness is plentiful in recourses: a bunch of flowers, a little fruit, plants, and many little niceties out of cousin Phebe's store closet show what a kind loving heart she has.

Dear Cousin Ann <will> be pleased with your messages. I always like to have one to deliver from thee, She now & then comes to spend a few days with us, and I love to see her by our fireside; it looks so like having thee, & she says it is like coming to see a dear daughter. She never brings any work, but her first request is "now Cousin has not thou got <a> stocking or some coarse work for the children for me?["]

I am pleased to hear Susanna Frith is gone to reside at Uttoxeter. I think it will be pleasant to thee to have her there: she will be one of those who will be at liberty to come often to see thee and will, I know, enjoy & appreciate the privilege of thy society.

Please give my dear love to her & Betty Shipley and Joseph & Anne & Ann Stubbs and all our old friends especially those who continue to show thee kindness. Is poor old Sally living[?] Give my love to her if she is and Richard & Sally Gee: they were kind to me when I was a little child.

I told thee in my last how safely the box arrived: thank thee again for all its valuable contents. If ever you have a chance, would you send me some seeds of our wild plants: primroses, cowslips, forget me not, ferns, crocuses & snowdrops. I see no flowers that please me as well, and I want some laburnum seeds and hawthorn and the bonny broom.

I am very sorry that last parcel was so worthless. The time of seeds was past & in despair I had thrown many I had collected for you. The shells I thought most valuable: they are gathered from the Ohio & other streams. One circumstance respecting them is remarkable, that those found in the large ~~stre~~ strong currents are thick, whilst those in still & feeble streams are thin & easily broken. I have a fine lot of seeds laid by for you this autumn and, as the custom house officers are so very obliging as to pass such trifles, I shall send them by the first opportunity.

We have been "butchering our hogs" this week. They shot them according to the fashion of this Western Country & heated stones red hot in a fire of logs out of doors to boil the water to dress them. We have been busy making sausages, which are to be smoked & put by for summer; pork pies; liver worst, a dutch dish, being heads & liver boiled together & chopped & seasoned & then put down in a dish & cut out & fried as it is wanted; scrapple I told thee of last year. I wish thou couldst partake with us; I would fain send thee some of our sausages. Do, dearest mother, get every comfort thou desires, & if thou ever feels straightened or lacks means, [4] draw on my share of principal. Now do this, I beg, if thou ever wants any thing that would contribute to thy happiness.

How kind of dear Anna to return with thee to Uttoxeter & how wonderful it is, my dear mother, that thou art able to travel as thou does. I am better satisfied than ever since I have Mary's description of thy lodgings & situation, and when it ceases to be quite agreeable go and live with her as she says she would like thee to do. Thou coudst have a room entirely to thyself &, when they had company or thou wished for quietness, retire to it.

I showed thy likeness to Susanna Neville: she says it is excellent. It is a great treasure to me, & often when they are all gone to meeting & I and little Annie & baby are alone in the house I bring it out to have a melancholy luxury in setting it on the chimney piece to look at through the long solitary day.

Ann Alice comes on nicely: she is a delicate looking child but very good. I have just taken her to bed &, though wide away, she laid her little head on the pillow, betook herself to her thumb very meekly, & without a murmur I left her in the dark, & this she does every night. I undress her with the other children & put her to bed awake without any disturbance.

Dear Harrison was much pleased with your kind messages. He is the kindest & best of men: I do think there is nothing he will not do for me. Oh how little do I deserve to be so blessed & how do my blessings abound. I sometimes think none surely have so many kind friends & such an accumulation of every good thing as I, and yet I am not grateful to a gracious Providence who has bestowed them as I ought to be.

Harrison desires his dear love; Elizabeth also sends hers, and in the most entire affection, I am, my beloved mother, thy tenderly attached daughter,

Emma Alderson

Give my love to Ann Lyndon, Aunt Wood & Aunt & Mercy Sylvester.

25. To Mary Howitt, January 20, 1845
Cedar Lodge ~~12~~ 1st mo. 20th 1845

It seems, my very dear Sister, as if a new and very delightful pleasure was opening upon me in the commencement of a correspondence with thee. How earnestly and anxiously I had looked for a letter from thee until I had at length almost relinquished the hope, I cannot tell thee, but when thy two arrived within a week of each other & two from dear mother & one from Anna with them, thou mayst faintly imagine my joy; I seemed to walk on stilts for some days and to dwell on the sense of my treasures as a miser over his wealth. I thought then, as I have often done, surely none had such dear kind friends as I, so considerate in their affection and unwearied in their kindness, and I think so still; would that I could return it sevenfold into your bosom. As it is, I can but sigh over my impotency and love you with all my heart.

Dear mother had given me a very good idea of your home & the family and I used to think I could see you all & understand how you looked & what you did, but now I seem as if I had been to pay you a visit & shall from time to time repeat it so that I forget the Atlantic rolls between us; perhaps it may not always. I feel as if you will come to America, and how I love to anticipate such a supreme pleasure; the hope makes me happy. To see one of my own dear relatives in this land & under our roof would be most joyful; I fear I should do some silly thing, perhaps go besides myself.

And then I am sure to you it might be a most interesting journey; you should study American life & manners, not on the stages & steamboats & in hotels, but in the remote country districts & in the domestic arrangements of the interior. You should visit the mountains of Virginia & the northern states, go over the Prairies when they are a wilderness of flowers, visit the new settlements & Indian tribes beyond the Mississippi, and then go into the glowing South "where all save the spirit of man is divine":[85] no, not all, for alegators bask on the river banks & deadly snakes infest the flowery wood. But there the yellow jesamine hangs in festoons in the forest; the palmeto grows thick & beautiful; the orange blooms & ripens its fruit; there are fields of rice & cotton & coffee, & there, too, is the slave with the host of accompanying horrors & deep interminable misery.

It has been a great comfort to my mind to hear from thee and dear Anna of dearest mother's house & situation. To be in lodgings, I have no doubt, she is as well circumstanced as she can be, and your accounts united with her appearances have tended greatly to satisfy my mind. Still, dear sister, if she could be under either your or Daniel's roof in times of sickness & to receive the continual attentions that genuine affection suggest, would seem to me still better. I think she might have her own room & fireside, in either case, to retire to & sit by when she prefered being alone. I know you have both offered her this and my heart has blessed you for it.

Dear, how I have wished she could get to us; could not you come in the summer or autumn & bring her? The voyage in a steamer is a trifle & the journey across the country is very easy & pleasant; about five days brings us from Philadelphia to Cincinnati, & two thirds of the journey are on board the steam boat, where you have every comfort & luxury that heart can wish.

This is a most mild and delightful winter; we seem to partake of a northern & southern climate. Some times we have a cold nip that makes me say nothing would so so soon send me home again as the intense cold. Once this winter the thermometer stood only 4 above zero, and then came bright, mild, dry, sunny weather like our warm April days, and I go out to see if there are no green leaves burst or flowers budding. Then again we have had awful thunder storms and torrents of rain. There is [2] seldom enough snow for sleighing; the people are passionately fond of this exercise &, when a chance does occur, avail themselves of it night & day: sleigh-riding as they call it. A fall of snow is a jubilee, but none had they here last winter, & none in all probability will they have this, for in a few weeks we shall have spring. Yesterday the sun shone so warm & bright that we rambled about without bonnets, & to sit on the Piazza in the open air was delightful.

Our children retain their worldly English looks & enjoy most perfect health. The people kill themselves & make their children puny palefaced things with good living; they give them animal food pies, preserves, pickles & hot bread three times a day, & as often tea or coffee, though in this latter instance there is a great reform: it is the fashion to drink cold water & nothing else, & many young people adopt it. Our children have their mush & milk in a morning & a plain English tea for supper & are in consequence, \under

85. Lord Byron, *The Bride of Abydos: A Turkish Tale* (1813), canto 1, line 15. Alderson might not have been reading Byron, as this line was quoted in numerous books and periodicals.

the blessing of Providence/, in better health than others. Thou tells me to write about them and therefore wilt excuse my motherly weakness in making them a topic in my letters; poor things, they have little to distinguish them but extraordinary wildness. I often wonder how other people manage to have such quiet orderly families & wish I could see them at home, for when one goes a visiting all is in "holiday fix." However, when the children will give up play & \we/ come to read & talk together, I find them very interesting.

Poor Charley has a weakness of vision which makes reading painful & sometimes impracticable, but his mind is thirsting for knowledge & his greatest treat just now is to hear me read a book of voyages & trace their course on the globe. His knowledge of geography is very good, I think, for his age & his ideas of countries & animals very correct. He sometimes sits down to tell me all he knows of different animals: the camel, for instance, of Asia or some country in Europe. He is a dear child and is outgrowing some of his childish ways; if you enter into contention with him or make him feel the rule he is the very spirit of perversity, but leave him to himself & he generally chooses to do right.

Agnes is a sweet little girl with a fair, bright face, a dear complection, blue eyes, light hair & two pretty dimples; she is the lady in our family, and even in her blue pinafore & cotton sun bonnet looks superior. She is easily guided & soon relents if she is naughty. Sometimes when we are sitting at work, I repeat a hymn to her; she will look up & say "Mother, I will try to be very good & then I shall go to Heaven.["] She is the most ardent lover of flowers I ever saw & will cherish a flower as fondly as ever little maiden did; she always had one about her as long as there were any to gather.

I often pay Anna Mary the compliment of thinking she must be like what thou wast when a child of three years old; she has a round fat common face but a pair of large intelligent brown eyes & a noble forehead & is as full of fun & queer ways and speeches as a little monkey. She said at breakfast, ["]poor Father.["] ["]No,["] said Agnes, ["]father is not poor.["] ["]Well he got a poor dinner any how.["] Then she came to me with a bright piece of tin & holding it up in my face said, ["]will you look at the great Persian King?["] Her heart is brimful of love & she will come & claps me round the neck & say, ["]I do love thou so dear["]; she has a queer jumble of thee, thou & you, and in trying to be the friend makes many funny mistakes.

Poor Adelle is come back to us; she left for a few weeks to nurse a sick friend in the city, and seemed as glad to get back to us as we to have her. Her son was with her \here/ for about a fortnight; now she has sent him to Columbus, the Capital of the State, \100 miles distant/, to learn a trade & be educated. Poor thing, I have felt much for her in this separation; it has been a great act of self-denial to part with him, the only living thing that she has to love & call her own. He is a fine, intelligent boy & she one of the most sensible women in her station that I ever met with, with the strictest sense of propriety & a most unselfish spirit.

It is quite touching to me to see her retiring ways; she will scarcely sit down in our presence & to sit down to table with us I could not prevail upon her on any terms. I dare say thou wilt think I would never try; neither would I if it was not the custom in the country for girls to do so, white I mean, [3] & hating these abominable distinctions I have occasionally invited the coloured people as a testimony against the unrighteous practices of the country. A respectable tradesman from the city came here one day; he was a mulatto & we invited him to join us at dinner which we were taking; he did so & has told far & near our unprecedented kindness.

They are making great efforts to establish a coloured orphan Asylum in the city, which is much needed, for though the blacks are required to pay taxes for schools & the support of the poor, they are excluded from the public schools & no provision is made for the aged, helpless & indigent but the Pest house as it is called, that is a portion of the fever hospital. These orphan Asylums are an honour to the country; they are common & well conducted. I once visited the one for white children; the number was about 80, but one thing I remarked in the midst of all their comforts, & much to rejoice over for them, I never saw such a set of grave melancholy little faces. It seemed as if the sense of their sorrowful condition pressed heavily on their little hearts & made them sad in their foreign home.

The coloured Asylum we saw in Philadelphia was the contrast of this: their faces beamed with intelligence & good humour, but then the blacks are naturally a light-hearted people. Did I tell thee that one of the little girls repeated thy sparrow's nest, adapting it to the hanging nest of the Baltimore Oriel & did it very well too.[86]

There was a ministering friend at meeting a week or so ago who was going into Kentucky to seek interviews with the ministers of congregations & other influential men on behalf of the poor slaves. Sarah Emlen who is now in England went on a religious visit to the south some years ago, & such was the effect of her pleading & labours that many slaves were manumitted in consequence.

Thou mentions Lindley M. Hoag. He is the youngest son of a family of 11 and all ministers; they are called the preaching family and I believe I have heard that old Joseph Hoag, who is himself a minister, as was his father, has 21 of his connections who are so. One daughter, Elizabeth, is married to a friend of the name of John Meader. They are both fine ministers & admirable people devoting themselves to their great work. The wife believed herself constrained to preach [at] first, but it was an inconceivable cross owing to so many of her family being so engaged. They removed to a distant part of the country & then, when unknown, she thought it would be easy to give up. Scarcely had she got her house "cleverly fixed" than a friend came to see her;

86. Mary Howitt, "The Sparrow's Nest," *Sketches of Natural History* (London: Effingham Wilson, 1834), 53–54.

she asked her such close questions about her name, present & past, that at last she was obliged to say it had been Hoag. "Oh, Hoag—one of the preaching family art thee," & she said she felt ready to drop. She gave up, however, & she and her husband sold their little farm & spent their living literally in going about to preach the gospel. When they returned to Rhode Island they took a room & employed themselves in carding wool for a subsistence, & Elizabeth said she should be happy to remain in her humble employment if she might be permitted to stay at home. Subsequently some kind friends have established them in a small store. John Meader has been out extensively amongst the Indians & is a truly enlightened man.

Thou must tell me every thing thou possibly can about yourselves & the family; I was much interested in dear Anna Mary's journey, and tell me what you are writing & just describe one of your evenings when the literati come out to visit you. It seems to me you live in entirely another world to us. Thou canst not think how oddly thy question, ["]What are your amusements,["] sounded in my ear; I could tell thee my occupations, but as for amusements it is obsolete, and yet we are very happy. Shall I tell thee what I read? Any of thy books when I can get them, and now & then the reports of some benevolent society. I am reading now the 19th report of the Prison Discipline Society of America[87] & find it very interesting & then I read the bible & books to the children. But talk to me of books: oh how often I rejoice now that I had the opportunity of reading when I was young & enjoying your intelligent society, which was better than books, & yet I was not half as industrious as I now would be if I had the chance, at least I think so. I long to see thy autobiography & read it to the children & if I knew the title would get it. I am sorely vexed at the conduct of the American publishers. They are [4] hateful things, those cheap publications, scarcely a page in which there are not two or more blunders, and paper & type are miserable.

Thank thee, dearest sister, for proposing to send us your works, English editions, and please give my love to Richard [Howitt] & tell him I should be very much obliged by a copy of his Australian Experience.[88] It would indeed be interesting if you could get a good private opportunity; it would be best & be sure to cut the leaves & write the names in each vol. & then they cannot be charged duty. Our other parcel from dear Mother & Anna came quite

87. The Prison Discipline Society operated from 1826 to 1854 to "promote the improvement of Public Prisons" (Constitution, article 2) in the form of better living conditions and attention to the special needs of juveniles, women, and the mentally ill. Prison Discipline Society, "Nineteenth Annual Report of the Board of Managers of the Prison Discipline Society, Boston, May, 1844," in *Reports of the Prison Discipline Society, Boston*, vol. 2, *1836–1845* (Boston: T. R. Marvin, 1855), 331–446, http://books.google.com/books?id=-b8JAAAAIAAJ.

88. In 1845, Richard Howitt (William's brother) published two books, identical but for their titles and a frontispiece in the first: *Impressions of Australia Felix, during Four Years' Residence in That Colony* (London: Longman, Brown, Green, and Longmans, 1845) and *Australia: Historical, Descriptive, and Statistic; with an Account of a Four Years' Residence in that Colony* (London: Longman, Brown, Green, and Longmans, 1845).

safe & the duty was only a little more than 20/, a trifle considering its contents. Dear creature, how I wish I could send you something in return; I will, however, collect plants & seeds most industriously. I wrote to thee about two months ago; did my letter reach thee? I have since that written to Mary & Margaret Ann[89] & dearest Mother; please send this to her. I shall not be able to write another letter before they must leave & I do not like to disappoint her, dear creature; it is all I can now do for her, and it is a very great pleasure to do even this.

I feel tempted to tell thee a little story I have often thought might be interesting to you; it is of a family at Westland who went to Iowa when we were there. Their name was Hilles; the Father had been clerk to the Quarterly Meeting at the time of the separation & went with the Hicksite party; his wife was a friend and suffered sad persecution from home for her attachment to the old cause & for her steady attendance of meeting. I have heard the friends say she would come in & hurry out like a culprit, always sure of abuse & insult when she got home. Her children loved her & clove to her, but the eldest son Wm was her darling child & he loved her as warmly in return. He & a brother, contrary to her will, went a journey into Indiana & whilst there the mother died suddenly & the sons on their return heard the melancholy tidings. They said that Wm as he approached the house cried aloud in the agony of his spirit. He daily visited & sate for hours over her grave & at last his reason became permanently affected. David Hilles was a fallen man; he drank & got into debt & yet there was a superior air about him, & his conversation was intelligent & interesting & his family were better educated than most there. Well, he sold his farm & went & purchased in Iowa. I should think it is not often that Americans go as reluctantly Westward as the young people did. I felt so much for them that it made me quite sad when the time of their departure arrived. The Father & a Friend rode over to Pittsburg the day previous; the sons took their heavy goods on a flatbottomed boat down the Monongahela to that place, & the daughters followed next day in the Steamer, all expecting to arrive about the same time. The horsemen got in first & in the night David was taken suddenly ill. When his children came he was speechless & died in a few hours; they had to delay their journey to inter him & then went on their melancholy way to their new home beyond the mountains.

[1-*cross*] I will not cross this far on dear mother's account, but I seem to have a deal to say yet. Harrison is from home or he would send his dear love, I am sure. Wm Charles & Agnes send their love to Aunt Mary; I hope you will soon come & see us. Little Ann Alice is well; give my dear love to Mother & the dear family at Holt Hill. The Shipleys were much pleased with thy message; dear Cousin Ann is a precious relative & her family are very kind & an interesting set of young people.

89. Presumably this letter to Mary and Margaret Ann is lost.

Farewell my beloved sister; my dear love to Wm, Anna Mary & the boys & kiss Miss Margaret for me. Thy tenderly attached sister,

Emma Alderson

26. To Ann Botham, February 8 to 27, 1845
Cedar Lodge 2nd mo 8th 1845

My tenderly beloved Mother,
As Harrison is from home at the Quarterly Meeting & I am prevented walking down to meeting as I intended by Anna Mary's being very unwell with a feverish cold and therefore I propose to commence a daily journal to be carried on till the time when it will be necessary to close this for posting. It seems to me that our lives are so quiet & unvaried that I often wonder when I begin a letter how I am to fill it with any thing that shall make it worth its cost at the end of its journey & yet, judging from myself, those letters are most interesting & most valued that speak most of those I love. So always write about thyself & dear Anna & Mary & their families, for every day makes you dearer & more increases my affection for you.

We have already begun to Anticipate Wm & Mary's visit &, dearest mother, to expect thee with them. Thy room in summer—the warmest place in the house—is fixed upon for thy bed in winter. Harrison says he will not get a new carriage till thou comes, though ours is far worn, because we must have one that will best suit mother. We want thee to bring thy own easy chair that thou mayst feel quite at home in this far distant land, & oh how I delight to think of introducing some of our dear friends here to thee: the Taylors, who are the very personification of affection & kindness, have begun to rejoice with me in the prospect of thy coming, & dear Cousin Ann Shipley, how thou wilt enjoy her society & she thine. How you will talk together of the past & feel like sisters in heart & mind.

The children are quite impatient to see thee and often ask me if I think grandmamma is packing up now; now, perhaps dear mother, this may altogether surprise thee, seeing thou hast not intimated thy own intention of coming thyself. The fact is dear Mary in her last letter told me there was a possibility of their coming to see us, and then she thought thou mightst be willing to accompany them. Oh, how that possibility has filled my heart with joy and I have dwelt upon the idea till it seems to me a reality & I was sure you were coming. We often often talk of it and think you must not delay but come this very summer. The voyage is by no means formidable in a steamer: they are seldom more than 14 days. John Pease was only 12 in crossing the Atlantic.

It is rather curious that a letter of mine which crossed dear Mary's proposed the very plan she herself laid down, so I think when we were both of one mind, ~~there~~ \it/ could not be altogether irrational.

I am very sorry to find, dearest mother, from Mary's letter that thou art likely to change thy lodgings: I do hope some as comfortable and as much to thy satisfaction will be found.

It begins to seem very long since I received one of thy dear letters but as the latterend of the month approaches, we begin to anticipate the great pleasure. Lately we have not received any of the British Friend's <??> we a great comfort in the absence of a letter because when directed by thee I feel tolerably sure all is well.

We have had the children all of them sickly with feverish colds. Baby seemed dangerously ill for many days so that this letter, which was to be a journal, is to be finished in haste to be ready for the mail. Ann Alice is better & the rest quite well.

Living almost out of doors for the last week has been most delightful spring weather. This is the 24th of 2nd month: the birds are singing, the grass is becoming green, and Harrison has already sown early pease & set potatoes. Today I have been helping him to trim the raspberries & currant bushes & I thought, suppose dear Mother & Wm & Mary partake with us of the coming fruit. I never plant a tree or flower but it seems to lead me into a train of pleasant anticipation: perhaps your eyes will rest upon those things and enjoy with me their beauty. I never loved the place so well as now I think you may see & enjoy it with us.

[2] Spring is a busy time here as elsewhere: nature is so luxuriant that it seems to us the trees want a wonderful deal of pruning; then the grape vines, as they call them, are all to be arranged & pruned. Harrison has been making soap & preparing to make candles, and then there will be a second soap-making from the refuse fat. There is a hot bed to be seeded, and "cleaning house" & making garden come as truly as the spring itself. Those bright warm days with cool frosty nights are called sugar days, & very busy I expect the farmers are in the country, though this season Orleans sugar is so cheap I should think they will scarcely give themselves the trouble. We have bought very good moist sugar for sweetening for 4 1/2 cents a pound, & by the hogshead it is only 3 cents. The very zealous Ab~~b~~olitionists, however, will not use slave produce & therefore give a higher price for maple sugar & molasses.

[March] 25th. We have today been out with the children to spend the day with a friend who lives about 8 miles from us. It is a fine elevated situation \overlooking woods & fields of pleasant country seats/ and at one time has had a deal of attention paid to its improvement. There is an assemblage of beautiful trees & shrubs; the evergreens are beautiful; there is a noble weeping willow whose elegant pendant branches have already assumed a tender green & contrast beautifully with two golden willows, the still leafless branches of which are now intensely yellow & look like a net work of gold. We have come home loaded with rose-bushes, "raspberry vines" & other trees & shrubs & tomorrow we shall be busy planting our treasures.

I wish I could send thee a variety of seeds that I have collected for you. When I think of the last parcel, it seems so poor & worthless that I am ashamed of it. I scarcely expected it would reach you & thought if it did not it would be no loss.

I have read lately Mary's Two Apprentices;[90] it is a good story & reminds me of many circumstances & persons that are very familiar: Parson Goodman is Jo~~h~~nathan Stubbs & the poor sick soldier's widow who died at the Talbot surely I have heard thee speak of visiting. I can remember in my earliest recollections seeing thee with a hamper of magnum bonum \plum/ preserves for her. What a wonderful talent Mary has of appropriating every thing, and yet, dear mother, I wish she would again write such volumes as birds & flowers & Fireside verses.[91] Truly they are fireside things with us: I feel it always a treat to read them to the children & they love them as much as I do. I have tried to get her own story which I long to see, but in vain. Indeed, from the questions of the booksellers, I should think it has not yet reached this country.

There has been a deal of public excitement respecting a Miss [Delia] Webster, a young lady from New England who was teaching a school ~~in~~ at Lexington in Kentucky. She was charged with aiding, in conjunction with some clergyman, in the escape of three slaves, taken up, tried, and sentenced to two years imprisonment, which includes hard labour. These are startling things, but they do good: the more prominent the evil & hatefulness of slavery ~~is felt the~~ are the better. Awful as it would be, I could rejoice that the sins & abominations of the system should be known & proclaimed with a voice of thunder from east to west, & then the voice of smited humanity would pronounce its downfall. The mischief is they are hid & covered in darkness & men are too fearful & selfish to undertake their removal. I often wonder at the apathy & coldness of many who will acknowledge the desirableness of change but take little pains to effect it.

[March] \26./ In one of thy letters thou mentioned Thomas Robson asking thee if we had mentioned the [Ephraim] Morgan's. They live at a very handsome house in the country about a mile from us and are very pleasant people. Harrison & I have just been walking over to call upon them. One of their daughters married a few weeks since & is going to her husband's home in Virginia, so we have been to take leave of her. As usual he is not a friend; I say as usual for it is a remarkable exception if a young man or woman are united to one of their own society, and yet they are [3] retained members. They send in "an offering" or acknowledgement to the monthly meeting, which is commonly accepted & so one is made up, but they are poor members & their children are neither one thing nor another.

90. Mary Howitt, *The Two Apprentices: A Tale for Youth* (London: Thomas Tegg, 1844).
91. Mary Howitt, *Birds and Flowers and Other Country Things* (London: J. Green, 1837); Mary Howitt, *Hymns and Fire-Side Verses* (London: Darton and Clark, 1839).

The loss society is sustaining is becoming so obvious that Friends are beginning to look about & consider what can be the cause. Some have attributed it to the influence & associations formed at the district schools to which Friends have been in the habit of sending their children & a committee has been appointed to endeavour to form a monthly meeting school of a superior kind & conducted in accordance with the principles of Friends. Harrison is one, and they have had several meetings & been canvassing amongst those that have children & he has found it very interesting, but so far nothing decided is arrived at.

The accounts from the Indian settlement were very interesting at the last Quarterly Meeting. Thomas Wells is again with them, and I think things will prosper under his superintendence, for he has more of a missionary spirit than most. They have endured great privations this winter, having to live on Indian corn bread & a little animal food once a day, which to an American sounds very like great distress. Poor things, no doubt they have much to endure. I often think I should like to visit them.

Little Ann Alice gets on a little, but she is a remarkably weak child yet. She begins to take a deal of notice & ~~k~~ has a smile for every kind face that greets her. She is a most gentle, meek little creature & I sometimes think, if she lives, will be a lovely character. Poor child she seems to have been born under an unlucky star if such things there <*MS badly torn here*> came prematurely had the hooping cough when <*torn*> months old has had sickness & is deprived of <her> natural food, for she has weaned herself, & yet we never had a baby that required less nursing & was so quiet & every way good as she.

I used to think it never would be my lot to have as good children as other people; dear little things, they are as wild as gipseys but I do believe are very innocent \&/ unsophisticated, and that I feel to be a great blessing. Faults that lie on the surface are comparatively trifles.

Agnes & Charley have each bespoke the pleasure of sleeping in a little bed beside grandmother and waiting upon her. They all call out to me to send their dear love in this letter and say they hope soon to see thee. Charley is nursing baby & says tell grandmother little sis sends her love too.

I had a very nice letter from dear Mary Harrison, a nice intelligent affectionate letter that does her heart & intellect great credit. I was very much pleased with Sister Mary's discription of her & I think this letter very characteristic; dear Anna, I hope, will have comfort in her children. There is no earthly joy for a parent comparable to that of seeing those we so dearly love & who have been the subjects of years of anxious solicitude and constant care & watching becoming that which we have desired & prayed for.

Please give my love to all our old Friends & especially to those who are kindly attentive to thee. I shall long to hear how thou art fixed in thy change of lodgings: I do hope thou wilt be comfortable. How I wish I could peep at thee & yet more be with thee to do all in my power to contribute to thy happiness.

I fear I must come to a hasty conclusion of this letter as it is time for us to leave for meeting & it must be posted to day. Poor Joseph Neville has been & still is confined to the house; he has been again afflicted with his old attack of inflamatory [4] rheumatism. I feel very much for them, for all seems to depend upon Joseph's health, & their trials & anxieties in their situation & family must be great indeed. I often wonder if Anna ever goes to see Eliza; poor thing, she seems to have all the burden of supporting the family herself & I think must be making very praiseworthy exertions & I think is deserving of every encouragement from her former friends who knew her in such different circumstances.

Harrison desires his dear love. Give our united love to D[aniel] & A[nna] & theirs & W[illiam] & M[ary] & their family, and with the warmest & truest affection, beleive me to be thy tenderly attached daughter,

Emma Alderson

2nd 27 1845

<two inches left blank>
Cousin Ann Shipley & her family are much as usual. I have seen less than common of them this winter as we now live much more distant. Cousin Ann desired her love to thee when I wrote.

27. To Ann Botham, April 4, 1845
Cedar Lodge 4th mo 4th 1845

How many thanks do I owe thee, my tenderly beloved mother, for thy unnumbered kindnesses & for thy steadfast continuance of them in writing so constantly such dear, long, interesting letters. Thy last, dated 2nd mo 11, together with one from dearest Anna, which I hope to answer by this mail, arrived three days since & filled me with gratitude & love. I have many, many blessings all unworthy as I am & your kind consideration & affectionate rememberances often excite in my heart fervent acknowledgements to the great source of good and ardent love to you my dear, dear friends.

It is an unspeakable comfort, widely separated as we are, to feel and know that time and distance rather increase than diminish our affections. Oh, to meet again! What happiness! My heart sometimes aches to see thee, my dearest mother, and yet the hope that this may be in this life is faint, but if we are counted worthy through mercy to be of the innumerable company of those who assemble round the Throne of God & the Lamb, how joyful will our meeting then be. This separation which now feels so long & painful will have passed away as a dream, only of consequence as it & every other trial which awaits us, as it has tended to wean our hearts from earth & fix them on higher & holier things. I often wish, dearest mother, that we could look at this life more constantly & abidingly as a state of probation & preparation for a better; then each event as it overtakes us would assume a new character. We should rejoice in suffering as that which sends us immediately to God for comfort & strength; we should endure temptation with firmness as the test and confirmation of virtue; the cross would be pleasant to us as the wisely appointed means whereby the kingdom of Christ should be established & the dominion of evil subdued within us. The trifles which now occupy our minds, fill us with pleasure, & excite our anxieties would scarcely claim a passing thought.

I have been much occupied this spring both in body & mind in planting & beautifying & arranging our garden & it has sometimes seemed in my reflective moments as though a voice answered: the kingdom of Heaven for which we are taught to pray & for the coming of which the gift of live is given & mercifully continued from year to year consists not in roses & vines & flowers & shrubs & pleasant trellises & arbours but in the devotion of the soul to God in submitting to the convicting regulating influences of the spirit of grace, which would draw us from every evil thing & take away the sting of sin which is rankling in our heart & fill us with love & peace & joy & cause us to bring forth abundant good fruit to his glory. And yet I do feel that the good gifts of a gracious Providence are not to be despised or enjoyed with indifference. All, I fear, is being too much occupied & engrossed by them till there is no room for better things in the heart. It seems to me it is well to remember our blessings in order to kindle again in our cold hearts the flame of love & gratitude, & yet the riches of redeeming love so exceed all outward earthly blessing, & if cherished shall endure to us when all these fail us, that it would be best for our minds to dwell & abide & move & more in this anchor of the soul.

Dearest mother, I often think of thee in thy solitude & the prayer of my heart is that thou richly enjoy those consolations & that support which are inexpressibly beyond all that the nearest & dearest earthly friends could bestow inasmuch as they proceed from one who is nearer to us than Friend or child or brother, who knoweth our frame & remembering we are [2] dust, deals very mercifully & tenderly with us & has manifested his unutterable love by laying down his precious life to purchase for us redemption & eternal life. Oh dearest mother, cling to him in all thy trials & conflicts. I have often harrassed & distressed myself with anxieties & fears & vain wishings to be with thee & then the comfortable thought has come to my relief: how much better to commend my precious mother to the care & keeping of Him who is the only source of all true comfort & strength.

I am very sorry to hear thou hast suffered so much this winter & been so closely confined to thy room. I fear the time must have often seemed long & wearisome, especially when thou hast been in pain, but now the pleasant spring is coming, I hope thou wilt experience relief & be able to go out & enjoy thyself as usual. Thou does not say anything about changing thy lodgings, so I hope thou has not had occasion to do so; however let me know exactly all thy movements & where thou art & all thou feel & does. I love to think I know all about thee almost as well as if I had seen thee within a few months.

The winter as been unusually mild <here> & spring has seemed to be coming for six weeks, but occasionally cold has kept things back. Now, however, flowers are very abundant in the woods; the peach orchards are in full bloom & exceed all we have hitherto seen for richness & beauty, contrasting so finely with the bright green grass & the snowy whiteness of cherry, pear & plum blossoms which is now out. Our orchard & grounds begin to show the good effects of dear Harrison's care & industry: he has pruned & scraped & tended them like a professed nursery-man & they are vigourous & thrifty in consequence.

Wm Charles has often said when looking at the bright red blossoms on the peach trees ["]Oh how I wish dear grandmother & aunts in England could see these. Does not thou think, mother, they would be delighted?["] Dear child, he has an ardent love of nature & goes daily with his two little sisters to a small wood near to gather wild flowers, or he will ramble down to a little creek to hunt for fossils; notwithstanding his shortsightedness nothing escapes him. He is becoming very useful to his father & is an excellent nurse: he carries baby about & gives her flowers & keeps her quiet when I am busy.

Agnes, too, can sew very neatly & has a notion of trying to be useful, but she is very volatile. Anna Mary, we say, is to be the worker in the family: she is the most persevering child to dabble in mud & water & help in her small way when we are busy that I ever saw. She is so original, a few days ago she sate by me when there was a storm & the lightening flashed vividly; she said "perhaps they are making a fire in heaven, perhaps so, mother." Surely none but the child that called the moon a great mushroom & the stars little ones would have thought of such a thing. I know thou likes to hear about the children & so wilt excuse such trifling particulars.

Ann Alice is still a small child but is coming on nicely. She takes a deal of notice, but I fear will be very backward at walking. We intend to try the effect of cold bathing in a few days.

Thou wishes to know how it is that we belong to Indiana Yearly Meeting. Though in Ohio, we are bordering on Indiana & only withing 60 miles of Richmond, where that yearly meeting is held. Mount Pleasant, where Ohio \YM/ is held, is 250 miles I expect from this place, so that we naturally fall into the boundaries of Indiana. We are not amongst the separatists on the Anti slavery question, though I have much sympathy with them, but in separating I think they did harm both to themselves & the cause they so warmly espoused.

This week I have dispatched a package of seeds, literally nothing else, for Anna; I hope she will send thee some. They are to go by Hannah Taylor [3] to Philadelphia &, if he is not gone, be given to the care of John Pease, but possibly they may be too late or the parcel too large, & there seem so many iffs about it that you must not expect them till you get them. I have had much pleasure in collecting them & there is a considerable variety—tell dear Anna most of them in our climate will require sheltering in warm situations & the Ceprifedimium, or balsam, & Ipomea are house plants. The Dodecatheum Media, or Pride of Ohio, I find is very rare; there are only about 4 seeds, but if one grows it may be a treasure. It is said to be undescribed by botanists & is called Ohioensus.[92]

Dear John Pease has left a pleasant memory behind him. I never knew any one move amongst contending parties with so much of the meekness of the dove & the wisdom of the serpent: he held on his course in the calm dignity of his high calling & when asked for an opinion on conflicting points replied "if he had any thing to do in this land it was to preach the gospel & not to enter into controversy." His visit to us was like the coming of a brother: so kind, so free, as if one's very heart was open to him & he to us.

We have many & dear friends here, but there are thoughts & feelings that we cannot open to them. It might give offense; they could not understand us; in fact they are not English & in England alone the spirit of true individual \liberty/ is understood & acted upon.

About three weeks ago, a little vessel built about 100 miles up the river at a place called Marietta sailed from Cincinnati for England & many took their passage in her for Liverpool. She was a small ship of only 150 tons burden & very light, only for summer seas; the route was down the Ohio & Mississippi to New Orleans & from there to Liverpool. I feel interested in their fate; it seems to bring you nearer if ships sail from England into the very heart of the continent.

I am glad thou hast reade "Life Amongst the Spindles."[93] I have not myself seen it but have often heard of it & wished I could send it thee. The is a large factory just completed in the city. It is not yet working but has a particularly neat appearance outside. We heard that a deputation of 9 young women from Lowel arrived to conduct it, but I fear a large city like Cincinnati will not be so favourable to the maintenance of order & morality as in a small town in New England.

It is long since I heard from dear Mary & I begin to feel anxious to have another of her interesting letters. I love to think I know exactly how you are all going on, and it was so pleasant to begin a regular correspondence with dear Mary that I feel jealous of its ceasing. Dear creature, I hope she is well & that the family are all in good health.

How thou must have enjoyed dear Anna Mary's visit; she must be a sweet, good girl. Give my dearest love to her; how I should like to hear from her.

92. *Dodecatheon meadia* is in the primrose family.
93. Charles Knight, ed., *Mind amongst the Spindles: A Selection from the Lowell Offering; A Miscellany Wholly Composed by the Factory Girls of an American City* (London: Charles Knight, 1844). Both the English and the American (1845) editions included a letter from Harriet Martineau.

Also, dear mother, give my most affectionate love to Wm & Mary, & Danl & Anna & their families.

I find I have not time to write more than this at present. We have a good servant but my time nevertheless is constantly occupied. I often think my days of leisure are in the unseen future when my girls grow up & I have no young children. As it is I will always try to write to thee or Anna or Mary each month so that thou canst hear of us regularly, for I feel in writing to one I write to all. We are anticipating a change in the postage, which will render the cost of correspondence considerably less & yet there is no money we so cheerfully pay as postage & none that procures us such pure pleasure.

I think, dearest mother, there is not a day passes but I feel the loss of thy kind assistance; every thing I see reminds me of thy unremitting help: all my great work, all the children's things are of thy making & I often wonder as they wear out how they are to be renewed. I mend & patch as I never did before to make them last and often wonder how I thought myself busy. The Americans are a very social people & expect us to visit & of course come again, so that is a great drawback upon my time &, as Harrison is a sort of public character in the meeting, we try to be as general as we can in our acquaintance to avoid giving offence. However, we get on wonderfully, so do not think I am complaining, only as I said before, I miss thee in every thing, but above all the sweet privilege of thy dear society.

[4] Agnes says "Give my dear love to Grandmother & tell her if she will come I will wait upon her & do all her errands.["] Annie calls out ["]Give my love & tell her I can bring chips & wood for her fire.["] Wm Charles also sends his, & Harrison, who has a tooth-ache & is gone early to bed, desired me to give his dear love & say he hopes to write to thee very soon.

We were pleased to hear a little Blackburn & Preston news, as we have not heard from any lately there, nor can I expect it. I owe Jas. Benson, S. Ord Junr, Mary Abbott & Lucy Thwaite all letters; when thou writes, give our love to them & say we often think of them. Poor F. Blagg, I am sorry to here his health is so declining; please remember me to them and the Shipleys, especially Betty, whom Anna says is sinking fast. Also my kind love to Susanna Frith & Ann Stubbs. Where are Joseph Burgess' family?[94] Dear Hannah, I was looking at some of her fair hair & a funny little note she wrote to me when we were children & I thought with much affection of her and our childish intimacy.

Thank thee for the account of Joseph Cloud. I was speaking of him to a friend a short time ago & then wished I knew more particularly the circumstances.[95] Sometime I should like that remarkable narrative of Thomas War-

94. The Botham sisters' paternal grandmother, Rebecca Shipley, had two sons, John and Joseph Summerland, from a previous marriage. John's daughter Rebecca married the Quaker Joseph Burgess of Grooby Lodge near Leicester. Although of the same generation as Emma, the Burgesses would be a good deal older, making it likely that Hannah was their daughter.
95. For more on Joseph Cloud, see appendix 2, "Directory of Names."

ing the Stay-Maker if thou wilt send it me.[96] Poor Aunt Wood is gone; she was a worthy woman, I do believe, & I loved her, little as I knew her. I am glad the Lyndons are doing so well; if Ann is comfortably married it is a nice thing: I do believe she deserves a good husband. She gave one very substantial evidence of true piety in her dutiful conduct to her father. Thou asks after H[arrison]'s sister Mary: we have not heard from her since she came & though I do not like near connexions to be indifferent one of another, yet from all I have heard, I do not much desire to be intimate with them: they are genteel needy people. Thou remembers how craving she used to be in her letters & that, I find, is her character. But not a word of this; I don't think H. or E. knows \any thing about/.

Farewell my tenderly beloved Mother; may every blessing & comfort from above be thine is the sincere prayer of thy attached & affectionate daughter. Dear love to them at Woodside, Upper Clapton. Elizabeth <desires her> love.

Emma Alderson

28. To Ann Botham, May 21, 1845

My Tenderly Beloved Mother,

I am afraid thou wilt not receive letters from me so regularly as I once was able to write as my engagements of late have greatly increased & leave me little time for that pleasantest of all employments, converse with my dear absent friends. Your constant rememberances of me warm & comfort my heart; surrounded by ten thousand blessings, I sometimes feel low & oppressed, & how like balm to the aching heart is affection so deep & fine as thine.

With thy last most welcome letter, one arrived from dear Anna Mary, a most interesting and pleasant epistle full of delightful details & giving me a most affectionate interest in the dear girl~~s,~~ who must be a sweet amiable creature. Her account of her visit to Uttoxeter delighted me because it told me so much about thee. I read her letter to Cousin Ann Shipley & she said, "what a sweet dear girl she must be"; so I had thought myself & so I was proud to hear *her* remark also. I want to write to her very soon but fear this post may leave before I accomplish a letter; one thing she said which I must notice even in thine: that they began to fear I did not think their letters worth postage.

96. The story of Thomas Waring the stay-maker was published in *Howitt's Journal* in 1848 as a story "communicated to us by a beloved octogenarian relative." "*Remarkable Dreams: Warnings and Providences*," *Howitt's Journal*, 3, no. 62 (1848):157. The relative might well be Ann Botham, who was living with the Howitts at the time and who, according to Mary Howitt, was an avid storyteller (Howitt, *Autobiography*, 1:61). On the other hand, this letter suggests that Alderson associates the story with an "Aunt Wood," possibly a sister of Ann Botham (née Wood). Either way, Emma might have been familiar with the story before its first published appearance. The story is about a Quaker who, for no reason that he can discern, is called to travel to a nearby town and then led to a particular house. When he knocks on the door and tells the occupant of his unknown mission, he finds that she had been about to commit suicide and is saved by his arrival.

Dear creatures, did they know how I mourned over their long silence as a real trouble & what joy it now is to hear from dear Mary or her; the thought of postage would never occur to them as it never did to me. Besides, was it a consideration with us, set your minds at ease, dearest friends, for the Americans, who with all their pretentions to independence & superiority do not like to be behind the English, have altered the postage regulations & our letters will now not cost us more than 10 cents when under half an ounce, that is, about 5 1/4^{d}, so we shall get letters cheaper than you.

It is a great comfort to me, dear mother, that thou hast concluded to locate thyself near dear Anna, who will I am sure be a solace to thee and look over all thy wants as only kind, good daughters can & be thy nurse & comfort in sickness or sorrow. My heart has often ached & I have shed many tears over the thought of thy solitude. I have looked at Ann Shipley surrounded by her children & grandchildren & thought of thee so far from any of thine with reproaches for ever leaving thee, but if thou has lodgings near D. & Anna, I think thou wilt find them all we can desire for thee.

I do hope this will reach thee at Woodside instead of Uttoxeter. I owe Anna a letter & shall devote one half of this sheet to her, hoping you are so near each other that you will read them together. We have had for the last three weeks Thomas Albright & daughters \visiting us/. They came quite unexpectedly and as they have be quite separated from friends, & the society of Hannibal is far from congenial, they have lived very solitary; they have never been at meeting since leaving their own country & seem to enjoy the privileges of our situation <*torn*>. They are two very fine girls: the eldest, who is about 19, is considered very <handsome>; she is a very nice girl. She was to have been married this spring to a <young> man settled in Iowa, but their certificates did not arrive & of course <*torn*> <could> not be married as friends, so they are now waiting till they receive <them>. Agnes, the youngest, is about 15. She is not so good looking as her sister, but I <*torn*> I like her better; she is rather reserved but very kind & a girl I should <*torn*> of very good abilities, one that will make a plain useful woman, they <seem> industrious & clever & have been well brought up by their mother. Poor thing, I often wish she had lived to accompany them; there are few besides our own dear relations that I should have had as much pleasure in welcoming to our house as Sarah Albright. I think there is no doubt she fell a victim to the unhealthiness of the climate.

We have lately been up to the Quarterly Meeting. Ours is called Miami Quarter; it is held at Waynesville near the Big Miami river. ~~one of~~ The most interesting part the business to me are the committees which meet to transact the affairs relating to the people of Colour, the Indians & Education. In the African Committee, friends were strongly urged to establish schools for Coloured children in every monthly meeting and, when possible, in each particular meeting, and the reason assigned was that the State has passed laws prohibiting the coloured people being educated in the public & district schools, & some have actually been prosecuted. This was thought to be a strong argument against our children being sent to these schools & our own members teaching in them, so that the necessity to have seperate schools was again felt to be additionally strong.

The is a coloured school at a place called Harveysburgh which has been established about 6 years & in which the number taught has usually been about 12 besides adults.[97] The place belongs to a family of the name of Harvey, and some member of the family is usually employed in instructing. The mother told me this summer she was going to undertake it & that besides this she has three children in her family whom she has taken from time to time to <u>raise</u>; one is yet an infant. She said that many, even friends, thought she made quite to free with the blacks, but for her part she had great comfort in what they were able to do for them.

The committee were requested [2] to procure situations for a number of coloured people, about 40, who were fleeing from oppression in North Carolina. By recent laws the free people of colour are forbid to remain in the state except under the most grevious restrictions, & these people were seeking an asylum in this neighbourhood.

The Indian settlement is going on much as usual. They have endured many privations this winter but are looking forward with hope to better things. Thomas Wells & his wife are gone again to reside amongst them and to help the few friends there in their various duties. They are endeavouring to introduce sheep & the spinning-wheel & loom amongst them. Hannah Wells told me one woman came to her & asked her many questions about her dress; she showed her her own flannel gown & told her she spun & wove it herself. The woman was wealthy for an Indian: she had fine horses & went home to sell some that she might buy sheep & now has a fine flock & manufactures herself. The great boys help on the farm &, under the direction of a friend, have flourished & planted forty acres in corn this spring.

The Quarterly Meeting was large, I should think as great as any held at Liverpool or Manchester, and as the day was warm & dry, there was a large attendance of babies & young children, who kept up a "pretty considerable" din ~~&~~ notwithstanding their mothers were provided with large bags of cakes <*illegible*> to amuse & comfort them.

We returned by way of Springburrough & spent the night with those pleasant, hospitable friends I once told thee of who live in a log cabin.[98] It looked beautiful, with fine sugar maple trees scattered about the field in front of the house, in the openings of which we looked upon a rich extent of

97. The Harveysburg Free Black School was opened in 1831 by Quakers Elizabeth Burgess Harvey and Jesse Harvey. See appendix 2, "Directory of Names," for more information.

98. Springborough, now called Springboro, was home to a large Quaker community and an important point on the Underground Railroad. Ron Rollins, "Living with History: Letter from Springboro," *Ohio Magazine* (August 2006): 15–16. See page 242 for Emma's earlier reference to this family.

distant country. The house itself is a long, rather low building, whitewashed & having sweetbrier & roses growing about \it/ & its little rustic porch up to the very eves. In the back ground is a fine orchard on one hand & a maple grove on the other. The walls of the chamber we occupied were bare logs whitewashed, & the woodwork throughout the house was unpainted, unvarnished black walnut, but the whole was so beautifully neat & clean, the linen so fine & white & the marks of education & refinement so conspicuous, that I thought it really elegant in its simplicity.

Our ride home after meeting was through a most beautiful country. Now we passed through the pleasant shade of the green, green woods; then there was an opening that showed the distant country, richly cultivated, bounded by woods or the bright blue sky. Again we saw a cheerful looking farm house or a noble grove of maple trees, or sugar camp as it is called, with it rude <log> hut & boiling aparatus & ceased to wonder that the farmers in this <neighb>ourhood make hundreds, nay thousands, weight of sugar in the <*torn*>.

We passed through Union Village, the Shaker Settlement, & it was <with> feelings of more than common interest I looked upon its neat and <beautifully> clean dwellings & observed the order & quietness that reigned <all about> the place. As it was first-day, of course no business was going <forward>. All was as still as a friends meeting in this great modern monastary. <*torn*-re> were some moderately sized houses, some painted green, others yellow or white or red but all as neat as if late on seventh-day evening the painters had just finished refreshing the whole. There was one large building where upwards of 100 brothers & sisters were accommodated; the meeting house was close at hand, and as we passed, a troop of boys looking like little old men in grey pantaloons, large dark waistcoats with laps & broad straw hats came two & two out of the school. Then a company of girls, each the facsimile of the others, walked across the green; they had brown frocks, small white \book/ muslin[99] handkerchiefs pinned very three corneredly upon the waist & straw bonnets with a strawcoloured curtain; they looked like a company of nuns. Joseph Taylor says everything seems to flourish here but the women.

There was a splendid orchard & fine, well kept gardens & lands & cattle of the very finest. This was the lower village; from it to the upper is about half a mile, & a plank path is formed by the road side for these neat & cleanly people to walk to & fro upon, but not in pairs: no, that is \not/ Shaker fashion. In their dining rooms they was seperate breadths of carpet, one for the brethren, the other for the sisters to walk upon.

99. Possibly the muslin used in bookbinding, but more likely "a fine kind of muslin owing its name to the book-like manner in which it is folded when sold in the piece" OED Online, s.v. "Book, n.," accessed March 29, 2020, https://www-oed-com.pitt.idm.oclc.org/view/Entry/21412.

When we came to the upper village, Agnes, who was with us, begged so hard for a glass of water that we stopped at a large pea-green house & requested a little. A ruddy, well fed, elderly man in the grey pantaloons, long lapped waistcoat & a red brown, large, loose open gown met us & very politely invited us in with "walk in strangers, take the left hand rooms.["] The[re] sate a tall, stately, very thin, very pale lady Abbess looking woman reading the [3] the bible. I said I feared we were intruding; she very politely assured us not & requested us to be seated. She told us there were 8 living in that house & that there had been a funeral that morning of an aged brother who died the night before. She said it was a good way to live as they did so retired & away from the temptations & vanities that were in the world, that they made almost all their own clothing & had a room in each house set aside for devotion beside the chappel. She made me try on her bonnet & said she liked my cap very much. *<drawing of a bonnet appears here>* This is the shape of the bonnet made of wove straw pasted on pasteboard & varnished. Her dress was a brown calamanca[100] petticoat, grey cloth slippers. Her shemisse sleeves came half way to the wrist & there was a narrow piece of black ribbon tied round each arm as mourning, I suppose, for the dead brother. She had a very neat habit-shirt fastened up the throat with three buttons & a small turned down collar, a buff muslin handkerchief pinned tight down like the others & a hood-like muslin cap just set on her head & having two loose tabs hanging down. Her hair was all combed back; her muslin hood made us think of the French Prophetesses from whom mother Ann, their spiritual mother, is derived, or rather on whose model she formed herself.

This woman lent us a book called the Testimony of the Shakers containing their history & principles.[101] Their religious opinions are monstrous: they are gross Unitarians & practice all mortifications in order that they may crucify sin in the flesh & win heaven by austerities. Their mode of worship shocks our common sense & makes one pity & mourn over such frightful delusion. I fear I shall have tried thee with this long history, but as Harrison has promised to write something in the remainder of the sheet, I know he will make it more worthy of thy acceptance.

Agnes, who is beside me, desires her dear love to thee; mine flows most affectionately to you all.

Harrison has not found time to write as he intended & our time is so very limited that I must conclude this as it is, hoping thou wilt excuse it[s] utter

100. Also "calamance" or "calamanco," "a woollen stuff of Flanders, glossy on the surface, and woven with a satin twill and chequered in the warp, so that the checks are seen on one side only; much used in the 18th c." OED Online, s.v. "Calamanco, n.," accessed March 29, 2020, https://www-oed-com.pitt.idm.oclc.org/view/Entry/26141.

101. Benjamin Seth Youngs, *The Testimony of Christ's Second Appearing: Containing a General Statement of All Things Pertaining to the Faith and Practice of the Church of God in this Latter Day*, 3rd ed. (Union Village, Ohio: B. Fisher and A. Burnett, 1823). First and second editions were published in 1808 and 1810.

worthlessness; it is to go to Liverpool by a gentleman who is going from this place to England.

We are all in usual health. The children are looking well & enjoying the fine weather; the spring has been a very unfavourable one so far. For weeks, nay months, we have had little or no rain & the vegetation is almost at a standstill. Seeds <cannot> come up for want of moisture, <??> & sometimes it is warm, sometimes very cold, & from time to time frost, which has cut off all the fruit, of which there was abundant prospect, & in many parts the Indian corn & potatoes & even the grape vines, which to the poor farmer is very discouraging.

However, I trust a kind good Providence will still remember the wants of his creatures & visit us with showers & blessed rain, which is such a beautiful emblem of his gracious visitations of Heavenly love to the languishing & thirsty soul, which without him is all barren & incapable of bringing forth any good fruit. May this Dew of Israel be abundantly shed abroad on this heart, my beloved mother.

I sometimes think perhaps an awful visitation is at hand to chastize & correct if possible this guilty land. Mildred Ratcliff used to say a heavy day of reckoning awaited the country for their oppressions of the Indians & Negroes.[102]

Harrison desires his dear love to thee, mine to Danl & Anna & their dear family & to dear Wm & Mary & theirs & in much love, I am as ever thy warmly attached daughter, Emma Alderson

5th mo 21st 1845

29. To Anna Mary Howitt, June 10, 1845
Cedar Lodge 6 mo 10 1845

My beloved Neice,
I feel that I cannot thank thee sufficiently for thy most kind and acceptable letter. I have often wished I could hear from thee & have one of thy warm hearted letters, which breath so much the spirit of youth and take me back to those happy years when I used to spend weeks & months of happiness with thy dear parents at Nottingham amongst books & with leisure to enjoy at ease the luxury of reading & all those delightful walks. Our deep enjoyment of nature, our gathering of flowers in those beautiful fields & lanes such as are not known in all America, for our fields are not flowery; we have no hedgerows & no flower covered hedge banks, nor ferny glens \no blue mountain tops nor village-spires & bells/, and alas our children will never know of these pleasant things but from books or description.

102. See the entry on Mildred Ratcliff in appendix 2, "Directory of Names," for a possible explanation for this comment.

Thou wilt wonder, then, what there is to admire & love in the scenery of this country. To me, it has its own great beauty: the woods in spring, summer and autumn have a continual & peculiar charm. Such masses of rich foliage are not seen in England, where the climate is so much less favourable to vegetation. Beautiful flowers such as we cultivate in our gardens grow in these noble forests & the rolling character of the land, though it never assumes a bold mountainous aspect, still produces a rich variety of landscape: fields & woods & cornfields, houses & villas make a pleasant scene.

There are also the bright & beautiful rivers, giving life & bringing to the wildest deserts the luxuries & comforts of the farthest earth. They are like mighty railways on which the busy craft of steam and other boats are constantly plying from the shores of the Atlantic to the great Pacific, from the Canadian lakes to the Gulf of Mexico.

We have also delicious fruits & the brightest skies to ripen them & give a glow & depth of colouring to every familiar flower & bring in perfection, many that are known to us only as the denizens of hot & green houses, that if we will, we may have our fill of these gems of the earth. I never saw roses so varied & so beautiful as they are in the gardens here. They seem to me like the aristocracy of their species, as though their petals were more ethereal, their leaves more delicate & the clusters of their richly tinted flowers were not the product of common earth—the yellow, the the blush, the pink & deep crimson or purple, the white & blush moss & varieties of which I know not the name, but their great beauty delights me.

Perhaps I have told you often of these things, but as each season brings them round I feel as if I longed for you to enjoy them with me.[103] I have sent a package of seeds to dear Anna by John Pease. I hope they will reach & bring you some specimens of the flowers that grow about us, but the collection is very limited & there are many things that I could wish you to have that I was not able to procure.

Thou asks me to tell thee all I can about the Shakers. Our knowledge of them is very limited, but fortunately a few weeks ago, in returning from the Quarterly Meeting, we passed through one of their settlements and called at one of the houses. The place is called Union Village & is altogether inhabited by them. It lies a a rich fertile tract of country abounding with that surest indication of a good soil, the beautiful sugar maple, whole groves of which containing many hundred, nay thousand, trees are left & are the sugar camps where in a good season the farmers will manufacture two or three thousand weight of sugar.

The whole appearance of Union Village is that of thriving and attentive industry; their gardens, orchards, fields & even woods have an air of neatness & prosperous care that is quite relieving. There were no great half decaying trees & logs lying beneath the trees & giving even to the pleasantest

103. This comment suggests that other letters to Anna Mary may have been lost.

forest glades an air of waste[2]ful negligence that annoys & grieves me. The houses stand irregularly & are of various sizes & for various purposes. They are very neat & clean externally but exhibit no marks of taste such as vine covered verandahs, roses & honeysuckles up their sides. Perhaps these things are too pleasing to the corrupt nature which they love to cross & vex.

Some of these buildings are very large, containing from 80 or 100 inmates. The men & women live under the same roof, but all the ties of nature are dissolved. A husband told a friend that his wife was no more to him than any other sister, though she was residing under the same roof—parents & children, husband & wife all annihilated in the "Shaker." The village is divided into upper & lower & they are about half a mile apart. A foot path formed of single plank connects the two; it is not seemly for brother & sister to walk side by side. They have even seperate breadths of carpet in the dining rooms to walk upon.

As we passed, the boys & girls came out of school, walking two & two across the green to a neat, low building very like a Friends Meeting house, which was the chappel. The boys looked very like little old men, having grey pantaloons & long backed black waistcoats with laps & broad straw hats. The girls had brown stuff gowns, small clear muslin handkerchiefs pinned down in front & a very peculiar straw bonnet, called shaker bonnets here, with a buff cotton curtain & no ribbon except strings upon it.

~~In passing~~ We called at [a] pea-green building to ask for a glass of water & were very politely requested to enter with "Come in strangers" & desired to take the left hand door. When we entered a tall, thin, somewhat elderly woman who was sitting at an open window reading a bible rose & handed us chairs; she was very communicative & told us much about the schools & their way of living, which she said was certainly the best that could be thought of, for they lived peacefully there away from the temptations & trials to be met with in the world. She said their friends sometimes came to see them, but they soon ceased to wish for much intercourse. She lent me a book called the "Testimony of the Shakers," for she said they were not ashamed of their principles & from that I might learn them & somewhat of their history.[104]

Beside the chapel for public worship, they have a room in each house appropriated to purposes of private devotion.

How well all this sounds & yet the~~ir~~ childish mimicry & absurdities in their worship destroy all the beauty & even rationality of the system. But to return to our good sister, she was really a dignified specimen of the community & her tall figure & thin spiritualized countenance looked admirable & would have been a good study for a painter. She had grey cloth slippers, a brown calamanca petticoat, a very beautiful habit shirt, button[ed] tight up the throat with three buttons & having a small turn-down collar, a buff muslin handkerchief pinned strait down over it & her chimise sleeves hung way

104. Seth Youngs, *The Testimony of Christ's Second Appearing.*

down to the wrist, round the upper part of which a narrow black ribbon was tied as an emblem of mourning for a "departed brother" who had passed away the evening before & was interred that morning. Her cap was a sort of hood made of clear muslin \being stiff/ with small tabs & set loose on her head. Her grey hair, turned back off her fine forehead, just appeared under it. She admired my cap & made me try her bonnet & on the whole seemed as well pleased with us as we were with her.

A man belonging to the establishment came in with our gentlemen & we soon after left. This man was a fine ruddy faced fellow & proved to have been formerly a friend. One of our party had known him well in former years & gave us his history, but his dress was somewhat remarkable & so I must describe it, as it was the \sabath/ costume of the men this summer season. He had grey pantaloons, the long lapped black waistcoat, & a \short/ loose surplice like gown made of a kind of puce coloured stuff \with wide sleeves/ hung loosely over his shoulders. His hat was a broadbrimmed straw. He looked well & so did all the men.

We were told every thing thrives here but the women & no wonder; they pine for the sweet charities of home. This man is called Gideon Hughes; he was a thriftless scheming man & brought himself into difficulty, so he determined like many another drone to join the Shakers. He took his wife & children with him, but she, poor woman, could not fall into their ways & practices. In truth she was a good Friend &, though a meek spirited creature, left [3] the establishment & located herself in a cottage as near as she could get to those she loved yet could not be with. Here she lived a few years very melancholy & at last died heart broken.

The shakers are said to be very rich. They are industrious & their neat waggons covered with a white sheet are often seen in the city bringing goods & manufactures to be disposed of & they have such a name for integrity that whatever comes from the Shakers brings its own recommendation with it. Thus Shaker seeds, Shaker herbs, carpets &c are all better thought of than common articles.

Almost the whole of their clothing is made in the village. It must be an interesting sight to see them engaged in their various branches of industry on a week-day. When you come we will go & spend a few days amongst them.

I have been looking over the Introduction to the Testimony which contains a history of the rise of this singular people & find it so curious that I cannot make extracts of it without spoiling the whole. Thou knows they acknowledge a woman named Ann Lee as their spiritual mother & receive by the hands of angels messages & letters from her. They trace their origin from the Quakers & French Prophets but the whole revelation of light was perfected in Ann Lee who came to America with some followers in 1774.

"The ship in which Mother came over while on her passage sprang a leak, in an uncommon manner so that the <p-*words obscured by a tear*> crew to keep her above water. The seamen being greatly discouraged and the vessel near sinking, Mother and the Elders with her, believing in Him that sent them and confiding in his protection, put their hands to the pumps and encouraged the seamen so that they arrived safe at New York on the 6th of August 1774."

The account concludes with the following verses: <*There follow about 16 verses of "A Memorial of Mother Ann."*>

Now if I have wearied thee with this long history of folly and delusion thou must excuse me. It seems as if every absurdity could find adherents in America. Witness the Mormons—a wilder species of delusion surely never led captive a weak multitude than that. I think climate has a great deal to do in the formation of national character, & certainly the Americans are a much more volatile & less reflective people than the English, liable to strong excitements, & have much less of benevolence & genuine milk of human kindness, & their climate is one of violent changes of extremes of heat & cold, of fervency & frigidity.

I was delighted with thy account of thy visit to Uttoxeter and of thy dear grandmother. If she conclude to settle near you I think thou wilt be a great comfort to her, & the climate of the south would suit her better than even Woodside, but whichever she decides upon I shall be comforted when I know she is near you.

How kind of you to send us the books! What a treasure they will be, for though at present I have little leisure for reading, I love books & to accumulate them as some of our best wealth. They will just arrive in time to be placed in a new book-case that Lotte is making for us of bird['s-]eye maple.

Please give my love to thy Uncle Richard [Howitt] & thank him very cordially for his kind rememberance of us; I shall be much interested in the account of his adventures & experience. I wish he would sometime pay us a visit. How I shall rejoice when you can fix a time for your visit. I calculate upon it as a certainty if we are spared.

Give my dearest love to thy Father & Mother & brothers & kiss little Margaret for me. I cannot tell you what a great pleasure it is to hear from you. Write as often as you can. Ask thy dear Father if he will sometime favour me with a letter, & tell thy mother she must not forget the packets sail once a month. Tell me if I can do any thing for you, send you any particular papers or periodicals, or obtain any information for you. I have but limited means of knowing things but I would do any thing in my power to please you & feel that it was increasing my own happiness.

When thou writes to grandmother & aunt Anna give my dear love to them. The children & Harrison are well. Thy uncle loves thee so well that I know he would send a very kind message if he were at home.

Please tell us when thou or thy mother writes next to whom the packet of books is consigned, that if it does not arrive we may write & enquire for it. I cannot bear the thought of losing it.

Farewell

[1] I wrote to grandmother about a fortnight since; I sent the letter by a gentleman going to Liverpool. Farewell my beloved neice. May all thy good designs be blessed & strengthened & thy days be bright & peaceful under a sense of duty well performed both to God & man is the sincere desire of thy attached aunt Emma Alderson.

30. To Anna Harrison, July 19, 1845
Cedar Lodge 7th mo. 19th 1845

How often, my beloved sister have I fixed to write to thee and as each opportunity has been allowed to pass by I have thought of thee with feelings of peculiar affection & regret, as thy last most welcome & most excellent letter seemed one which called for the expression of more than ordinary interest and love which it excited in my mind towards thee. Thoughts of you are so constantly the companion of my mind and the rememberance is so strong & vivid that I often forget the immense distance that separates us and think our absence from each other cannot be great, that we shall meet & talk of all those things which are nearest & dearest to us, and my beloved sister, I know thou wilt cordially unite with me in the desire that our union of heart may be in the best things, that truly as we advance on our journey of life we may draw towards that one blessed point & haven of rest which is the bourne of every traveller heavenward, even the dear son of God, the Saviour & hope of the whole world.

Oh, what comfort is there in sheltering under this Rock of Ages; there is no nook or corner of the world so remote but we feel we can realize & rejoice in him; the firmament is not ~~more~~ so universal as the sensible canopy of love which is to be experienced by every true believer in Christ & perhaps, when measurably seperated from the outward enjoyments & wonted comforts in which we are accustomed to \take/ comfort & rejoice in, our knowledge of this truth is increased. Unworthy as I am, and so great often is this sense of unworthiness on my mind under the knowledge of infinite unfaithfulness, rebellion & shortcoming, that I am ready to fear I have no right to speak of or lay claim to the name of a believer. Still, this blessed hope & assurance has refreshed & strengthened me on the wide ocean \&/ in a foreign land when I have looked at my husband & children & thought in all the vast continent, this little family, this handful, are all the living I care for or that care for me. Yet the thought that a prayer hearing, prayer answering God was everywhere, that his presence was as truly to be known & felt in the farthest solitude in the wildest desert as in our own favoured land was solace & joy inexpressible. May we go on hoping & trusting & above all obeying & fulfilling the whole manifested will of God until in his wisdom he shall bid us exchange time for eternity, the joys & sorrows of earth for the brightness & perfect righteousness of Heaven.

I sometimes fear, dearest Anna, that I take too much pleasure in the things of sense, in the many comforts & enjoyments by which we are surrounded.

I look on the brightness of the summer sky & breathe the balmy air of morning or the softened luxury of evening, on the tender moonlight through vine leaves or beneath forest trees on the bright green earth with its rich luxuriance of fruits & flowers & feel as if my heart had almost its fill of happiness & was amongst those who have received their consolation & are full.

I often think if you could be here you would see much to enjoy as well as myself. There is something in country life which is so near the realization of our ideas of earthly happiness that those who are contented with simple pleasures find little left to wish for beyond such a lot as is assigned them.

This year Harrison has his farm worked on shares & he has nothing to do with it but receive half the money obtained from the sale of the produce. There is one large field of ten acres cultivated in corn (Indian corn) & potatoes; then there are cabbages, beans, melons & other vegetables for market. The first crop of hay is got in & the meadow is beginning to look \again/ rich & deep in clover & to smell delightfully with its sweet blossoms.

Vegetables sell high, very little less in this market than in England & there seems to be demand for any quantity. Harrison occupies himself with attending to our own garden, pruning his fruit-trees, chopping wood &c & leads what I call a very pleasant country life. We have abundance of chickens & ham & bacon of our own raising & curing so that we never think of going to market, [2] for our garden & orchard supply us with vegetables & fruit in abundance.

I often think it is a mark of the benevolent wisdom of Providence that in this warm climate these things are so various & abundant. We seem to have little relish for animal food in summer except it be salt beef or hams, & it is generally considered unwholesome, but then we have potatoes, cabbages, pease, beans, beets, squashes, sweet green corn, tomatoes, sweet potatoes &c &c. and usually have two or three different kinds at dinner with fruit & milk.

The late frosts cut off most of the apples, pears & peaches in the district, which people lament as a great loss, such things either fresh or dried being an article of daily food. We have had an abundance of the finest raspberries, some currants, a fine crop of grapes & a great quantity of black-berries in the fences. Thou wilt smile at the mention of the latter, but they are so fine & so abundant as to be quite a consideration in their season. They are brought to market in great quantities & are eaten with milk & sugar or boiled; they make an excellent preserve & are quite medicinal in their properties, being considered almost a specific for diareea. We go out in the cool of the evening with the children to gather them, & very pleasant rambles they have proved. Dear children, when our heads are laid low, the thought of our blackberry gatherings & the bright summer evenings when we stood & watched the broad green leaves of the tall corn in relief against the glowing golden west will be pleasant landmarks in their childhood and seem like visitations into fairy land.

I think a field of Indian corn in the full luxuriance of its growth a very splendid sight. It often attains 8 or 10 feet in height & its broad leaves have are \of a/ deep rich green. The summit of the plant is crowned with the feathery male blossom, which is called the tassel, & at the sides amongst the leaves grows the ear, sheathed in many folds & terminated by a long thick tuft of silken threads of a pale green colour. There are hundreds of acres on the rich Miami bottoms in which it is cultivated in the very perfection of agriculture: not a weed is to be seen & the crop is planted in the straightest lines & at exact distances as the horse & plough have to pass through it at various times to keep the soil light & free from weed & it is often hoed besides. One old friend from Carolina said speaking of her youth, I was raised in the cornfield.

The humming birds have begun to frequent us. We have now flowers growing around the house & these fairy things flit about drinking the dew & honey from their cups. Never did I feel the beauty of any poetry more than when I read Mary's piece "The Humming Bird" in the Sketches of Nat. History: its truthfulness & poetic beauty threw even a charm over the bird itself.[105] Dear Mary, how I love & admire her writings; it always does my heart good and refreshes my spirit to read her poetry; I hope she has not become altogether prosy. I sometimes feel impatient for the time when she will visit us. I feel assured if we live we shall meet in this land & I often think when I see anything that interests & pleases me, how much dear Mary will enjoy this.

I expect thou wilt see Francis Thompson who is the bearer of this. He paid us a visit a few weeks ago & we were much [3] pleased with his company. He will tell you all about our home & the appearance of things about us, of the city & our friends there, with whom he became acquainted. They are admirable specimens of human nature & an honour to the country and the name of American.

The same week that F. T. was here a friend from Leeds came to Cincinnati, also on business. He brought a letter from Thomas Shipley's daughter Caroline.[106] It was delightful to see kind faces fresh from England, for, though strangers to both, we could converse of persons & things mutually interesting & familiar & the pleasure was such as only an emigrant can realize.

B. B. tooke letters & a paper for Danl from Wm Charles which he promised to deliver himself: I hope he will. He spent a night with us & can tell you much about us. I only wish some of our own near & dear friends could come & see us as we are.

105. Mary Howitt, *Sketches of Natural History* (London: Effingham Wilson, 1834), 133–136. This popular book was reprinted inj 1834, 1836 1839, 1842, and 1848 in both Boston and London.

106. The relationship of these individuals to the Shipley family is unclear. The Aldersons' Cincinnati friend, Thomas C. Shipley, had only one child, Charles Shipley. Presumably the two mentioned here lived in England.

The children enjoy excellent health &, though they do not make much progress in book knowledge, their characters are daily developing & on the whole I feel we have cause to be thankful on their account. They have each their failings & infirmities, but they are points that promise better things. Anna Mary is our finest child with an open intelligent countenance. She has a constant fount of good humour & has so much originality that she has a name of her own for every thing. She is a persevering, industrious little thing that will take her can to gather fruit & not stop till it is filled. She often says, mother, when I am a woman I mean to milk the cows & wash for thee.

Agnes has a little fretfulness in her disposition but there is an air of refinement, a gentleness & polish about her that gain her general love & cause her to be preferred & noticed more than the others. The 17th was dear baby's birth-day. She is the jewel in the family; a perfect doll in size, she has a most innocently sweet face with her hair curling round it and is the best & quietest child I ever saw. She does not attempt to sit alone nor walk, but she rolls about on the floor until she is sleepy & then takes to her finger & sucks it till she is asleep.

Wm Charles has so much difficulty in reading from his imperfect sight that we have been obliged to suspend his lessons for months, which is a great drawback at his age. He has a mind to enjoy & improve rapidly with instruction, but I find little leisure to give him that undivided attention that he requires. He can assist Harrison in many things & is very useful in his small way.

How I should like to take a peep at you & see thy children & the changes three years have made in them. The baby \of that day/ is now a chattering little girl with her own character & exercising her prerogative of free will, & dear little Emma Lucy, her beautiful name will be a good certificate for her through life. Kiss the sweet child for me and give my dear love to all the young ladies & gentlemen.

Does it not seem strange to see them growing up into actual men & women & feel that they have the serious realities of life to contend with[?] We have many toils & cares for them in childhood, but the anxieties for their welfare when they have to act an independent part, when they are exposed to the trials & temptations of life, must be many indeed, and I do not think they are fewer in this country than in England. Perhaps the chances of obtaining a livelihood are better, but it seems to me that sin and folly are as rife here as in England [4] & that spirit of independence & rejection of restraint which characterizes even the children in this land prevent a Parent exerting that salutary influence over them which under the blessing of Providence is a great safeguard to them in youth.

I fear dear mother is becoming increasingly infirm. If I could hear of her being comfortably fixed by thee or dear Mary it would be a great relief to my mind. I do not think it will do to let her remain at Uttoxeter another winter:

it is too far from you & too solitary for her, dear, dear creature, when she is confined for months to the house & possibly to her room. Do, dearest Anna, try to get her to leave before the summer is over. I shall feel as if a great care was removed from my heart. Her letters are as interesting as ever, but I am sure from what she says she often feels very much alone.

Give my endeared love to her. I have sent her a book which, as containing the history of the settlement of this neighbourhood & the rise & progress of Cincinnati, will I think interest her.

Write often, dearest Anna. Would Danl sometimes favour us with a letter, we should feel it a great treat, & I have great pleasure in the correspondence of the dear girls. Mary's last letter was a very nice one indeed.I trust thou wilt have comfort in thy daughters, that they will feel it their privilege to \aim at/ being thy companions in every good word & work & make their happiness consist in a dutiful attention to the will & wishes of their dear parents. Oh, what a beautiful character is a kind & dutiful child, & what a warrant for future welfare and excellence in all the relations of life. Dear children.

Give my most affectionate love to one & all. As M. & M. A. are thy helpers at home, so I trust Charles will be to his Father in his toils & anxieties in business.

The poor Nevilles are I fear again to be greatly tried in the loss of their eldest daughter, a fine promising girl who is in very delicate health, far gone we all think in consumption. Poor T. Albright is also struggling with many difficulties & above all with the contentious spirits of obstinate & undutiful sons.

Farewell, beloved sister. I could write much more but lack of time & space forbid.

That thou mayst feed in the green pastures of life & drink largely of the living waters that descend from God for the refreshment of the faithful ones & shelter in the blessed fold of which Christ is the good shepherd is the prayer of my soul for thee, my beloved sister.

[1] Harrison's dear love to thyself, Daniel & the family. W. C. & Agnes beg me to send their dear love; mine to Cousin L[ucy] Bayliffe & most affectionately to you all. Farewell, my endeared sister,

Thine,

Emma Alderson.

[1-*cross*] excuse all blots & blemishes I write amongst many interruptions.

31. To Ann Botham, September 13, 1845

My very dear Mother,

I have rejoiced for thee since receiving a letter from dear Anna Mary describing thy rooms & giving such a graphic account of its furniture & general appearance that I have felt as if I could see thee at work or reading, enjoying the quiet luxury of their pleasant home &, what is most delightful, with the happy consciousness that thou art surrounded by those thou loved & who love thee & find deep pleasure in endeavouring to make thee happy. It has often made my heart ache to think of thee when at Uttoxeter, far from thy children & receiving from strangers or mere friends those attentions which to us it would have felt a high privilege to bestow & when I have seen Cousin Ann Shipley in the midst of her children & grandchildren, the loved & honoured head of all, I have felt a pain of bitterness to think we ever left thee to live alone. But now I am comforted: I know that Mary & Anna Mary will be like loving daughters to thee, & dear William will cheer many an hour with pleasant converse & reading.

Dearest Anna, in a letter I received from her, regrets thy decision in favour of Clapton as a great disappointment. I do not wonder at her feeling it as a loss, for we all know the value of thy precious society, & yet dear mother, as thou could not have been accommodated in their house, & their family is so much larger, I think it is better thou shouldst be with Mary & I do expect thou wilt meet with choice friends in the meting who will find thee out & help to keep up thy connexion with the society.

I quite hope thou wilt see John Pease in some of his visits south; he paid us a delightful visit, the memory of which is very sweet, & I want thee to hear from his mouth about us and about the state of society in this land. He has left a very beautiful & very appropriate address to the friends here written just before embarkation, which I should much like thee to see as it is very expressive of the state of things here.

There is, as thou wilt I expect be aware, much division in the society. It seems as if the spirit of disunion was amongst friends. In Indiana the seperation on account of abolition has become a settled thing. It was sorrowful to see the society split for a testimony [2] that was dear to every good friend, & yet so much excitement had been given way to & such a warlike spirit was professed by some leading abolitionists that possibly there was some ground for the fears of weak minds, & the lukewarm & indifferent joined in with their cry of danger. But I always thought that if instead of withdrawing their hand from the good work, friends had sought to stand their ground & been faithful & consistent, much that they found cause to object to never would have existed. There is a disposition in those friends who left the society in their zeal for abolition to return. Some have done so & others are wishful so to do, & I trust friends will receive them with open arms. The five friends who are on their way from England & are expected to be at the coming Yearly Meeting are on a mission of christian love & their chief object in this visit is to restore peace & bring back the wanderers.[107] We look forward with much pleasure to their coming. Harrison has written to meet Wm or Josiah For-

107. There were only four: William and Josiah Forster (brothers), George Stacey (clerk of London Yearly Meeting), and John Allen.

ster at New York, inviting them to our house & we shall in a few days be looking for their arrival. I hope to hear from thee by then.

There is another devision of a much less reasonable character headed by John Wilbur in New England on account of J. J. Gurney & his writings. It is extending to the Yearly Meetings of Philadelphia & Ohio & is likely, if not checked by divine interposition, to produce most direful consequences. It has been characterized as a most senseless thing & such we think it from beginning to end. John Wilbur has set himself & his opinions against the advice of his best friends & the discipline of the society. His objections against Joseph John are personal & frivolous, & his adherents in his own Yearly Meeting are only about 120, but when these things begin there is no knowing where they will end: pamphlets are written & circulated, party spirit gains ground & spreads, & tens become hundreds & hundreds thousands. I intend to keep a very detailed journal of the Yearly Meeting & send thee all the particulars of it externally & internally.

In this Western Country, all is so primitive & unique, so original & peculiar, that even to the more polished people of the Eastern States they are subjects of remark & amusement. Last week we had two visitors of this discription, the one a minister, a blacksmith who has a minute to hold public meetings with those not friends & in a settlement of coloured people. The ministers here pay their own [3] expenses when traveling & he, being in very low circumstances, came to see if the rich friends of Cincinnati would assist him.

The other came into the thick woods without half a dollar in his pocket & a wife & family to support & is now a thriving nursery-man. He told us of an old Friend in his neighbourhood who came out in the ministry when he was 80 years of age and was both large & eminent in his gift & was instrumental in greatly increasing the meeting where he resided. This man was convinced in a garrison when he was quite a youth. There was a friend of the name of Thomas Bales who traveled in Ohio & the then far west, visiting the Indians & the scattered settlers in the woods. He was the first friend who crossed the Ohio. He & his companion were, on one of these journeys, taken by a party of soldiers on the frontier & carried to the fort as spies. When they understood their errand, the rough soldiers ordered the Friend, if he was really a preacher, to preach for them. He asked time and after a period of silence spoke so effectively as to satisfy them & convince the youth, who afterwards became a good & valuable member of the society. Thomas Bales fell sick & died on one of these journeys & as there were then no sawn planks of which a coffin could be made, they hollowed out the trunk of a white walnut tree & laid him in that & interred him in the forest.

Thou wilt be sorry to hear that the Nevilles has lost their eldest daughter. She was a fine, tall girl of about 17 years of age & has died of very rapid consumption. It seems as if their trials were many & various & yet, poor things, they seem cheerful & submissive through all.

A son of Thomas Langley of Litchfield has been at this place seeking employment yet unwilling to work. Poor fellow, he has evidently been brought up with idle habits & has little inclination for industry, & such make poorly out in this land. He told me his mother & two other brothers were in Nova Scotia & well satisfied with their situation. They are far separated from friends, but excepting it may be to the mother, I expect this is no hardship to them.

In Anna Mary's last letter but one, she mentioned having sent a box of books consigned to some American Publisher or bookseller. We have not heard of it & I fear shall lose them if we cannot find out who the person is to whose care they were intrusted. If we knew, we would write & request them to be forwarded & pay all demands upon them, for books pay duty & they may be lying at the Custom house, & if they lie there twelve months unclaimed, they will be sold.

If Wm & Mary are in Italy please, dearest mother, attend to it as soon as thou canst on their return. I hope they will have a pleasant journey. I wish they would write to me ~~fro~~ [4] on their journey How I should love to have a letter dated Rome or Venice or Genoa: the very names are full of romance. Hast thou read D'Aubigney's History of the Reformation?[108] We are reading it, & I thought of thee: how much thou wouldst admire it. Luther was a noble instrument in the hand of the Almighty for effecting his great purposes.

The children are all well, as are we. Is it not a cause for thankfulness that since we came we have had no sickness of any account &, excepting when Ann Alice was born, have never had to call in a doctor[?] As far as our experience goes, the country is healthy, and the climate is delightful. We have now had five months of summer & look forward to two & perhaps three months of bright, warm, pleasant weather, what many people consider the very prime of the year, the Fall & Indian Summer.

We were walking in our garden \this afternoon/, & I thought how I could like thee to see it. There are pumpkins as large as little barrels and squashes like huge bottles and tomoatos by bushels & red peppers & our fine beds of sweet potatoes, all so little known in England and all so excellent. I love to see those large succulent plants such as the squash, which runs over a great extent of ground & has large broad leaves & great yellow flowers & produces green & white fruit something like a bottle in form. We use them as a vegetable, but our great preference for them is in pies: they boil to a pulp which is rubbed through a collander & with eggs, sugar & spice makes a delicious custard. I shall send you some seed of the various kinds.

Harrison & the children desire their love; Anna Mary says I must send as much as a horse can carry. My endeared love to the good people at Wood-

108. J. H. Merle d'Aubigné, *History of the Reformation of the Sixteenth Century* (New York: The American Tract Society, 1835), a history of the Reformation with a strong Protestant bias, originally published in French.

side & all your household. I am, my beloved mother, thy warmly attached daughter,

Emma Alderson

32. To Ann Botham, October 1845

It was a very fine morning the 28th of ninth mo when we left Cincinnati in company with our Friends Abraham & Joseph Taylor for Richmond, a distance of 60 miles. The first tints of autumn upon the forest trees made a beautiful variety amongst the rich green foliage and caused us often to exclaim at the beauty of some noble maple that towered above the rest with a crown of rich orange or another that looked like fretted gold amongst the bright surrounding green.

The fields of Indian corn have lost their palmy vigour & look brown & sered and ready to be stripped of their precious produce. The Miama valley is remarkably rich & productive & its fine bottoms especially favorable for the groth of corn, which often attains here the height of 10 feet. Brown corn is also much cultivated; we saw many fine fields of it; its elegant tufts look not unlike rice, & the effect of the plant is prettier, I think, than the Indian corn.[109] They cut the top off & lay it in tiers to dry; we saw large barns full of it. Probably now you sweep your parlour with brooms made from corn grown in this neighbourhood, as it is becoming an article of extensive exportation.

We dined at Hamilton, the county town; at the public table there were upwards of thirty, and I was amused to see the people leave the table in an incredibly short time & others take their place. A private room & table no one thinks of asking for.

The country here is varied & beautiful. We crossed the Great Miama by one of the covered wood bridges so universal in this country & pursued our journey to Fair-haven a small village in a low valley where we proposed to rest for the night, but the aspect of the great brick tavern was so comfortless & uninviting that we concluded to go 6 miles farther to a private house where we had been informed there was good entertainment. It began to rain & was quite dark when we arrived there, & on our applying for lodging, the master of the house, whose name is Jacob Lybrook, a moravian, & this place is called the Lybrook Settlement, said it was very inconvenient to take in strangers.[110]

109. "Improved King Philip" corn, also called Brown corn, after its originator, John Brown of New Hampshire. "This new variety of corn, as figured in the Patent Office Report for 1853, is uncommonly attractive, both for its size and beauty, and seems to possess a rare combination of excellencies; for its stalk only grows about five feet high, and hence it will bear closer planting, and do better in shady places, such as orchards, than most other varieties." "Varieties of Yellow Indian Corns," *California Culturist: A Journal of Agriculture, Horticulture, Mechanism and Mining* (April 1859): 462, https://books.google.com/books?id=exQLAAAAIAAJ. Given the date of this letter, Brown corn must have been available well before the date of its registration in the patent office.
110. See the Directory of Names for more information about Jacob Lybrook.

Their house was full of boarders & moreover his wife was ill in the fever, but, however, such a night as this he could not turn us away, & we must take up with such accomodation as they had. The place had a well to do look: there was a bright, blazing fire of logs on the hearth; the floor was covered with a handsome home made carpet wove in stripes of green & red & yellow; every table & shelf was covered with a clean white cover bordered with a deep netted fringe of a quarter of a yard in width; the windows had white dimity curtains, & altogether it was a neat country house & displayed marks of ingenuity & industry very creditable to the poor sick mother & only daughter & the "raised" girl whom they had brought up from an infant. After supper, which, as is always the case in the country, we "eat" in the kitchen, we were shown up into our bed room.

Our party was increased by [2] another carriage load of Friends, & we were two two married couples, two single women, & our Friends the Taylors. There were three beds in the room here, as the old man said the girls & the men who had women might sleep, & there was another bed in an adjoining room for the young men. We astonished the people by our amusement at the arrangement. The people who have lived in a log cabin or are surrounded by others living in such, with their one room, cannot understand our fastidiousness in these things. The beds were beautifully clean & there were piles of handsome homemade quilts & blankets in the room that that testified of good management & industry. \We, however, arranged things more to our mind & had a good night's rest./

We were now in Indiana & the level country & thick woods, the deep black loam & thinly scattered log houses made us feel that the characteristics of another & more recently settled State were around us. There is a wild solitude in many of these locations, sometimes on the banks of a little stream surrounded by the yet uncleared forest, with patches of corn & potatoe ground contiguous to the house; the cattle graze \in/ the woods. Then you come to a tolerably good house with its ample barns & large orchard & a wide extent of clearing, fenced & cultivated with plenty of stumps & old logs telling of by gone days when the deer bounded through the forest glade & the Indian pursued the buffalo in solitudes seldom had by the white man.

Often in travelling we encounter a company of "movers"—people going westward in search of more land & prosperity. One company we saw this morning; there were two waggons filled with beds & household furniture & the women & children. The men drove the horses & four cows that looked poor & weary, possibly from long travel. These people never go to the taverns: they camp in the woods or by the way side, make a good fire against an old tree or stump, cook their provisions, & lie down to rest on the ground or in their waggons if it is cold & wet. Men travel hundreds of miles in this way to market from remote districts. But the return of these poor people is most sorrowful, as return they often do after a residence of a few years. The man usually falls a victim to the unwholesome atmosphere of the new countries,

& then the widow & family gather up the wreck of their little property & go back, sickly & disheartened, to their former home.[111]

Richmond is a pretty little town on the banks of the Whitewater River. It spreads over a deal of ground & there are gardens & orchards attached to the houses generally, which, being mostly white, have a very pretty appearance amongst the trees & shrubs. Our party is very agreeable, between twenty & thirty, principally Cincinnati friends, & our accommodations are excellent.

~~Third-day~~. The Select Meeting met at 10 oclock on second-day morning [September 30] & the meeting for Sufferings at 3 in the afternoon, but as I am not of the privileged number who attend these I cannot relate any of their proceedings.

[October 1] Third day. [3] I should say in the evening we went to the Indian Committee; the information given in the reports & the letters read were very interesting; it was stated that four years ago the Indians said, ["]the Quakers used to talk to us about planting corn, sowing & ploughing, and we were glad to hear them, but now you come like the other Missionaries and ask us to go to your meetings & talk to us about your religion & we do not wish to change so we will not go to hear you." Now a great change has taken place; the present superintendent is a truly pious man & his labours are eminently blessed; he combines religions with the literary instructions at the School.

One meeting was described; it was attended by many Indians. One of them said ["]we are come to sit with you and worship God, we want to love him and we want that our young men should be sober & not drink the Devil's drink, but they will do it so long as their white brothers will bring it & give it to them.["] Another said ["]I am come to worship God with you & love him & talk to my children & family around our fire about him. I know that he is every where doing us good & I know too that there is a Devil who tries to do us harm, for there are so many wicked people in the world who drink the fire water & do wrong.["] In this way the[y] conversed with Thomas Wells, who, having given up all to go with his wife to live amongst them, must feel amply repaid by such results for all his sacrifices. Josiah Forster spoke most beautifully & impressively, urging friends to turn their attention to the religious instruction of these poor people, & I trust now that it is becoming more the concern of the Society to Christianize as well as civilize them. The number of children now in the School is 56 and they are now erecting new buildings for the better accomodation of the family and for the introduction of spinning and weaving.

[October 4] Fourth-day morning the Meeting commenced with a meeting for worship, which was large. A friend from New England, John Meader,

111. Neither the original punctuation nor the sense of the sentence makes clear whether the phrase "after a residence of a few years" belongs with the preceding sentence here, as I have given it, or with the following sentence.

brother in law of L[indley] M[urray] Hoag, spoke from the heart. His address was striking; he spoke of the precious fellowship which those enjoyed who walked & dwelt in the light of the great work of sanctification & justification by the Spirit & blood of Jesus and urged to dedication & faithfulness.

The Indian committee met this evening instead [of], as I said before, on third day. (I had got a little confused in the order of things.) Fifth day morning the meeting for business commenced at 11. But I will first describe the meeting house & grounds. They stand about a quarter of a mile out of town; a beautiful sugar grove surrounds the house, & the fine turf is delightful to walk upon. Here amongst the tall trees are tied hundreds of horses & carriages, and parties of friends are walking about. The house is a large, very red brick building of two stories; the windows have lead coloured venetian shutters, & altogether it has a neat, plain appearance. Within, the walls are white-washed & the wood work unpainted. Adjoining is a large school house, where a friend's school is taught under the care of the committee of the monthly meeting. The doors are kept shut until meeting time, ~~when~~ & friends are assembled around <them> in a dense crowd until the time arrives, for of course all are are anxious to secure a good seat.

The business commenced with calling over the names of representatives. Then the minutes & certificates of ministering friends & elders, members of other Yearly Meetings, were read, one for Sybill Jones from New England who, with her husband Eli Jones, has been paying family [4] visits at Cincinnati. They are very interesting young friends who have devoted themselves to the service of their Lord & who are diligent in doing good. They have travelled in remote districts, visited prisons and seamen on solitary shores & islands & left much to fulfil what they believe to be the will of their Master.

John Meader, who has travelled on a religious visit amongst the Indians, Cornelius Douglas, & many others are with us, but above all our dear English Friends on their mission of love and peace: may the Prince of Peace direct & bless their labours. The reading of an epistle from London Y[early] Meeting expressing the objects of their coming & a minute accompanying were read at this time, & deep feeling & sympathy for them in their great undertaking expressed. Friends were exhorted to give them their prayers that their coming might not be in vain and to receive the wanderers, should they be willing to return with open hearts and arms. The Epistles from the Women's Yearly Meetings of London, Dublin, New York, New England, Philadelpha, Baltimoore & North Carolina were read & names proposed for a committee to prepare Essays of answers to return. Then a committee of young people was appointed to take copies of each to be sent to the several Quarterly Meetings of which there are 13. These send copies to each Monthly Meeting so that these epistles circulate through the whole Yearly Meeting & supply reading for the whole year. The London general epistle was read, & a sealed paper laid on the desk from the seperating body ~~of~~ in New England, that is to say, John Wilbur's party, the propriety of reading which was submitted to the consideration of four friends. The Meeting concluded with some very beautiful & appropriate remarks from Sybil Jones.

Four O'clock the African Committee met; the reports read were interesting as showing an increasing desire to promote education & circulate the scriptures amongst them, & friends have assisted in the liberation & removal of individuals. It was satisfactory to hear that these things were claiming the attention of the Society & possibly with increased concern, but I could wish that more could have been told as having been done. It is a good work & I want that they should be zealous in it with a zeal that brings forth abundant fruit.

After the African Committee the one on Education met. This is a subject of deep & increasing interest in the Yearly Meeting. The effects of sending children to the public schools of the country are apparent in an evident departure & undervaluing of all that is peculiar in practice & doctrine amongst Friends, and it is now a matter of desire, & indeed adopted as a rule, that each monthly meeting should establish a good school to be taught by a member & conducted in a manner consistent with the views of Friends. This has led to much attention on the part of some, & the lack of suitable school books was brought before the committee. There is a great variety of these, but many of them are highly objectionable. The histories inculcate a warlike [5] spirit & hold up the character of the warrior as an object of admiration to the youthful mind, and there are many indirect as well as direct way in which the lessons of children might tend to train their minds to the adoption of our views, & a hatred of oppression might lead to an abhorence of slavery; poverty of heart & life might be made so attractive that the very child might desire to experience the great work of regeneration to be going on by submission to the sensible influence of the Spirit of Christ in his heart & the intellectual improvement lead the way to religious advancement. These considerations are the results of what passed \in/ the committee. At present the number of children to be instructed is very large; in one Quarterly meeting I think from 900 to 1000 were reported as being of a suitable age to receive instruction & the means but very limited at present. I shall add when the report is laid before the meeting at large the number of such children.

[October 6] 6th day morning. The State of Society as laid before us in the reading of the answers to the Queries from the several Quarterly meetings led to much feeling & the expression of great interest of behalf of many who had many difficulties to struggle with, separated widely as they are from each other in low circumstances & pressed under the weight of worldly cares, to encourage such as these to confidence in the good Providence of the Lord whose is the earth & the fulness thereof.[112] The cattle upon a thousand hills are his and he can bless the little or blast the much, so that we must be faithful

112. Psalm 24:1 (King James Version): "The earth is the LORD's, and the fulness thereof; the world, and they that dwell therein."

in his service and willing to sacrifice in faith to Him who will not let us go without our reward.

~~The~~ encouragement to a daily reading of the scriptures & the observance of a pause for thanksgiving before meals was strong, and the young people were solemnly invited to come and join themselves to the God of their fathers in an everlasting covenant, to remember the prayers & tears of their parents and conform to their wish by unreserved obedience to every manifested duty.

Dear mother, this is a very meagre sketch of an address we had from Sybil Jones. She is a woman of a very fervent spirit and a beautiful mind; her speaking is to me liking hearing fine poetry & this, in connexion with her devoted character & the great sacrifices I know she has made in the performance of apprehended duty, make her services particularly touching to my mind.

The sealed letter from the Seperatists in New England was pronounced unfit to be brought before the meeting.[113] A document or declaration of faith from the body there was read; it consists of extracts from the writings of our early friends principally & was, as they thought, required from them because \of/ the charge of unsoundness from the opposing party. What a pity that members of the same religious society should accuse & criminate their brethren. Surely if christian charity prevailed, we should not strive about words, & let rents & divisions prevail for the sake of any man.

[6] A minute was issued by the men's meeting & signed in ours condemning the conduct of the seperatists. In the evening the youth's association for the promotion of the interests of the boarding-school met.[114] We walked over to a friends house to see our old friends George & Ruth Smith from Westland; it was like meeting near relatives. George Smith said they had not had a greater treat since crossing the Ohio. His rigid Oliver Cromwel face beamed with kindness & affection. I have told thee what a good creature Ruth is, her going from house to house to nurse the sick & comfort the afflicted. Thou mayst be sure it was as great a pleasure to us to meet them as they expressed it to see us. There was a large company & 10 or 12 carriages stood in the yard.

113. In 1845, New England Yearly Meeting was the first to split between the more inward-seeking, quietist "Wilburites" (followers of John Wilbur) and the more evangelical "Gurneyites" (followers of Joseph John Gurney). Rufus M. Jones, *The Later Periods of Quakerism*, 2 vols., (London: Macmillan, 1921), 1:521–534. Other Meetings would split along the same lines, though Alderson's own Indiana Yearly Meeting remained Gurneyite.

114. Indiana Yearly Meeting was at this time raising money for the establishment of what would be called simply Friends Boarding School when it opened on June 6, 1847, in Richmond, Indiana. Originally a "select" school, open only to Friends, admission was opened to other denominations by 1865. Later it opened a college department and subsequently became Earlham College (Thomas D. Hamm, "History," Earlham College, 2010, http://earlham.edu/about/campus-history/history/). For a full account of the rise of Friends Boarding School and its evolution into Earlham College, see Thomas D. Hamm, *Earlham College: A History, 1847–1997* (Bloomington: Indiana University Press, 1997), 1–34.

[October 7] Seventh day morning. This was a very solemn meeting. We had a visit from two Friends from the men's meeting, and I trust their labours of love will not be forgotten.

[October 8] First day. Meeting for worship commenced at 10. I wish I could give the faintest idea of the scene without: it looked to me more like a great fair than anything else. Hundreds of carriages & horses were on the ground & tied round the fences; thousands of people were assembled & yet the quietness & order made one feel it was no fair but a great gathering like the coming of the children of Israel of old to celebrate some solemn feast and sacrifice. It is said the meeting house holds from three to four thousand persons—some say five thousand—& yet many could not be accommodated.

John Meader spoke \on Peter denying his Lord/ and now & then a feeble voice in the body of the meeting broke the solemn silence. One woman said we might have the form to a hair's breadth & yet be no better than a dry twig. We see, she continued, in a great storm great limbs torn from the forest tree; they are covered with green leaves & look very fair, but examine them and you find a speck at heart which caused weakness & occasioned their destruction. So it is with the christian: unless he is so fixed to the true vine that the sap of life can freely circulate, he falls away in time of storm & trial & becomes dead to spiritual things. She stood near me as she spoke these words with great earnestness, & her whole frame agitated with emotion, & she was evidently a woman in the humblest walks of life.

In the afternoon we again met for worship; the meeting was as large as the morning and surely never was a more powerful address delivered. We were urged by the death and sufferings of Christ, by the long suffering mercy of God, by his goodness & Fatherly care, by the eternal welfare of our never dying souls, to obedience & dedication. Oh, I thought, if our hearts are not of adamant we must be broken under such an appeal.

Sybil Jones had an appointed meeting with the coloured people in their little meeting house. There were about 100 men & women, very still & attentive, and a few friends present. It was kept a profound secret for fear of a press & only a few invited amongst the rest. I esteemed it a great favour to be of that select number; it was to me one of the most [7] interesting & impressive meetings I ever attended. I thought indeed that the evidence of Divine regard was visible; it seemed as if one spirit, that of love of God & man, animated and warmed every heart.

Sybil & her husband were both engaged in testimony & she in solemn supplication on behalf of the oppressed, of the sorrowful & the ignorant, and for their oppressors also, that He, in whose hand are the hearts of all men, might lead them to the practice of mercy & justice and induce them for the love of Christ to give up this & every other evil thing. I never heard preaching more tender, more fervent, more ful of the knowledge of the human heart, of its sorrows, temptations & hopes than theirs. How beautiful was the love of God dwelt upon in his Providential care, in his compassion to poor fallen man in sending his welbeloved Son to die for us & redeem us from all iniquity of the worthlessness of all earthly goods & the glorious blessedness of eternal life. It seemed as if their Heavenly Father had sent abundant comfort \to this poor people/ to sustain & strengthen them in their varied trials. One poor woman said to me after the meeting, ["]Oh what a strength & comfort this has been to me.["]

Our dear English Friends except Wm Forster, whose health is feeble, were present & seemed to enjoy the opportunity as much as we did. We have reading in the Scriptures morning & evening in the family, about thirty, which is very pleasant.

Second-day morning, The meeting for business commenced at 10 with reading the answering Epistles. If thou attends the next Yearly Meeting \in London/ note the Indiana Epistle. I was on the Committee appointed to prepare it & the work eventually fell to my lot. It appeared to me a very serious & important thing to undertake & I felt very much humbled under it, but, however, the meeting seemed satisfied & Friends may, I believe, receive it as a faint expression of the state of things & the feeling of the meeting.

Ohio Yearly Meeting is in such a divided state owing to this Wilburite question that they could not agree to send epistles as usual. Indiana, however, addressed them in a very appropriate manner. It was striking to me to observe how excellent & as far as I could judge \many of/ these epistles were very imitable to the time & for the place addressed.

Sybil Jones went into the men's meeting & was, Harrison said, very remarkably engaged. John Meader appointed a meeting for the young, which we did not attend. Afterwards he came to our boarding house to take tea with us, and a large company we had, amongst the rest Elisha Bates, who is here holding meetings as a methodist minister.

John Meader gave us some very interesting details of his visit to the different tribes of Indians, especially the Cherokees. Young Wolf, a chief who had embraced christianity with his whole family, was a man of remarkable mind & very deep piety.[115] He was a preacher amongst his people & had induced the \chief[s] of the/ several tribes beyond the Mississippi to assemble once a year for holding a great council to promote the moral & political welfare of their nations. He had induced them to decide their quarrels by arbitration, to give up the use of ardent spirits, & many other things.

John Meader described the meeting he held with them. They arrived on the day of their usual ~~time~~ assembling for worship & offered to give place to them, but this the Friends declined and sate down amongst them. When their service was over, Young Wolf, turning to the Indians, said, ["]brothers, these men have come from a great distance to see us; their hearts are burning with

115. By the late 1820s, the Methodists were ordaining ministers among the Cherokees; Young Wolf was one such minister.

the love of God & for his sake they have left their homes and wives & children to come to preach the gospel to us.["] They remained a while in silence, when John Meader spoke at some length. At the close, Young Wolf said ["]let us conclude this solemn opportunity with prayer & if our Heavenly Father supplies words, well; if not we will seperate under the influence of good.["] They then knelt down & remained in solemn silence about ten minutes, when the younger daughter of the chief broke forth in a fervent impressive prayer & on its conclusion the company withdrew.

The sister of Young Wolf was the first of her nation who embraced christianity. She said to the Friends "mine was the first stony heart that was broken by the almighty power of the gospel & now,["] pointing to the people, ["]behold the children that God has given me.["]

After this conversation, there was a little pause, when Elisha Bates addressed us. Poor man, his voice was choked with emotion & he said ["]Friends I love you I love [8] you; I love all on whose hearts I believe the name of Jesus is written." He spoke at some length & it was affecting to hear him, but I thought it was not like Elisha Bates of old; it seemed as though a man he was shorn of his strength. He regrets, I believe, the bitter spirit he gave way to and the cruel things he said of the society & wishes to convince us that now he feels only charity & love to us and all men. The evening closed with a very beautiful address from John Meader.

Third-day morning. The minutes of the Meeting for suffering were read by a friend from the men's meeting. They are very interesting, being a detail of the proceedings of the yearly meeting during the past year. They have published & circulated many thousand copies of an address from London Y. M. on the subject of Slavery, maintained a correspondence with New England Yearly Meeting & issued a cautionary epistle to their own members on the subject, petitioned the legislatures of Indiana & Ohio on the disabilities of the people of colour & capital punishment, have provided that the expences of ministers from distant yearly meetings shall be paid out of the Yearly Meeting stock &c &c.

The School, African & Indian reports were also read. The meeting closed with a very beautiful sermon from our friend Sybil Jones, and after a most solemn silence the concluding minute was read & we seperated.

Our dear English friends dined with us, and in the evening there was a public meeting.

This, dearest mother, is a very fair account of our Yearly Meeting. It was to me a very interesting & instructive season, & I was pleased to see the dignity with which the business was conducted by the clerk & prepared to subscribe to George Stacy's remark that, combined with much simplicity, there was much talent.

This is a large Y. M., about 24 thousand friends, and it is computed that 8000 of these are children, so that education is necessarily a subject of great importance & yet it may be said to be only beginning. The boarding-school is in an unfinished state. We went to see it; it was commenced on a large scale & would have been a fine building, but only one wing is erected & that has only bare walls & roof. The windows are not put in, the floors are unlaid, & it will be a year before it can be completed.

Last Yearly Meeting, friends were directed to raise 4000 dollars for that purpose. Only 3800 were obtained & as a last recourse the meeting this year raised a subscription during one of the sittings. Many who, though wealthy, had not contributed a cent gave their 5 dollars then in the face of their friends & 500 were raised. Truly, as John Pease once remarked, friends here have yet to learn how to give, that is country friends.

The school is built upon the Farm belonging to the Y. M. It consists of about 350 acres, & has two small farm houses upon it. Here all who choose to avail themselves of the privilege may have provisions & lodging gratis, but they are expected to cook \for/ & wait upon themselves. The fields were full of horses, & one day we were told 130 had dined there. The consumption for three days was, I think, 260 gals. of coffee, 450 loaves of bread, 400 pies & 1200 lbs of beef, besides fruit, potatoes & other vegetables. People usually bring beds & bedding.

I have not time to say anything more than that. I long to hear from thee: it seems a very long time since I had a letter.

Joseph Crossfield & James Tuke have been here.[116] They are two nice young men & it was a great treat to have their company for a short time, especially as J. C. could tell us about the dear family at Woodside.

I wish those stockings thou so kindly hast provided for Harrison would come. I thought the other day, if dear mother were here poor H. would not have such cobbled heels.

Harrison desires his dear love. E. also sends love. In very much affection, thy tenderly attached daughter,

Emma Alderson

33. To Ann Botham, October 25, 1845
Cedar Lodge 10th mo 25

My best beloved mother,
I have a hope of getting this ready for the coming mail, but should I fail in doing so, you will receive a letter addressed to the youngsters from Charley which, uninteresting as it is, will give you some idea of our daily course, for the children of the house seem so mixed up in all that is going forward that to give a diary of their sayings & doings speaks for the household.

And yet, dearest mother, I want to let thee feel something of what is in my heart towards thee. Oh, what an almost anguish of love have I felt for

116. See appendix 2, "Directory of Names," for more information on James Tuke, Joseph Crosfield, and William Forster.

thee since the arrival of thy parcel; it is not the things which it contains, beautiful & valuable as they are, but the sense of thy untiring affection that fills me with gratitude & love inexpressible. I feel as if the whole lifelong debt of kindness so often undeserved had been brought to my remembrance & oh, my mother, how can I thank thee. I have looked back to the days, the happiest of my life, when we lived together at Uttoxeter & every hour seems marked by thy kindness, and this continued to the very hour of our separation: how hast thou suffered my wants, enriched me, toiled for me, and still, though the wide ocean & half a continent separates us, still that ~~liberal hand dispenses still that~~ thoughtful loving heart projects, still that liberal hand dispenses.

It seems as if every thing was sanctified by thy touch; the very stitches on the wrappers are endeared to us & could thou have witnessed the delights of the children, thou wouldst have been rejoiced. They all thought grandmother had sent them the things of all others the nicest & most imitable. Agnes held her box & its pretty contents on her knee all the next day & said, "my beauty I cannot bear to have thee out of my sight. Dear, dear grandmother." Indeed it seems to me as if the whole world contrived to make us happy; within a few days we have received both the parcels from England. That rich treat of books that dear William and Mary sent us have come safe to hand, & would that I could thank you as I feel for them also. I mean to write to dearest Mary in answer to her most welcome letter; I have a deal to tell her, but in the mean time they must accept our most affectionate thanks for this great treasure. The package had been lying at a book store in the city some months & it is almost marvelous to think that this & thy parcel came quite safe & uninjured & not an article missing.

Harrison is very much obliged to thee for the stockings & purse. They are beautiful & are not to be worn till spring, when in his low shoes he can exhibit his mother's handsome present; such are my orders & so I have laid them by till warmer weather which we begin to anticipate in a few weeks after a very severe winter unbroken as yet with the pleasant intervals [2] of mild bright weather which we have had other winters. I do hope it has been a milder season with you. I often think of the scarcity of food & the consequent inconvenience to all classes & misery to the poor.

It is rumoured here that there is a change in the ministry & if so I hope it may lead to the repeal of the corn-laws & also do away with the possibility of war with America.[117] If so, shall we not thank a gracious Providence who so overrules & disposes events & whose eye of mercy & pity yet watches over nations & individuals. How beautiful is the idea that "as the salt preserveth the sea so the prayer of the saints sustaineth the earth." God himself inspires the prayers he is prepared to answer, and we may believe that many are the

117. If my dating of this letter is correct, then the rumor is false. The change in ministry did not occur until July 1846.

righteous who have pleaded with their Heavenly Father that in his own way & by his own means he \would/ work out a great deliverance. Also in the advancement of his kingdom in the earth, in the progress of his glorious cause, \is/ ~~does~~ prayer often the pioneer in the wilderness, the messenger of coming mercy.

I thought so when I read a letter from those devoted servants of the Lord, Eli & Sybil Jones, of whom I told thee in my letter from the Yearly Meeting. They have been since leaving Cincinnati in Maryland & North Carolina & have had wonderful & crowded meetings with slaveholders, who received them most kindly & with the utmost openness, though with an unsparing voice they denounced the iniquity of their evil systems. I thought of that little meeting at Richmond with the coloured people & how she pleaded for the oppressors as well as the oppressed; I have no doubt by those & similar exercises she was preparing for the work before her. Poor thing, in her letter she said, often in the evening "I seem to hear my children calling me home, but a voice seems to answer not yet: go onward and tell the poor wandering sinner of Jesus, tell him all that he has done for him & thee & win his soul to Christ." She is a singularly interesting woman, tall & slender with a countenance that glows with animation & an eye that beams with the energy of inspiration.

Dear mother, how beautiful it is when we see the rich & strong watching over others for good like older brethren of one great family, noting the lack & need, not of the very poor, but of the struggling, careful, & yet hard pressed tradesman with his large family & their many wants. Our friends the Taylors are essentially of this class; if I see a poor friend come into meeting in a new gown or bonnet I suspect they are at the bottom of it. Yesterday Harrison went down to negotiate for Abraham; you must know Abraham is a prototype of [3] Mr. Latimer,[118] & I pay him no especial compliment by saying so, for he is one of the most sterling, noble hearted men I ever met with. Well, he had noticed a family who make a good appearance but we know to be straightened in thinner clothing than he thought good this cold season & asked Harrison as a favour to contrive without hurting their feelings to get them to accept a handsome great coat, but when he got there, instead of one thing, there was a pile. Thou knows what a many excuses rich men can make to lay aside anything: this they don't like & that does not fit & so on.

He drove H. to the gate & then went on to make a call & it did my heart good to hear with what a grace & with what thankful heart the mother received all for her sons who had indeed suffered, she said, & they could not afford to buy new. Surely he that feeds the young ravens puts these thoughts of love & sympathy into the heart of \a good/ man for his fellow & makes him his \own/ right hand to dispense his mercy.

118. A character from Mary Howitt's novel *The Author's Daughter: A Tale* (Boston: Waite, Peirce, 1845).

Poor cousin Ann Shipley is at present very weak; she was overturned in their carriage &, though not much hurt at the time, has not been out since & continues poorly. Dear old woman, I should miss her sadly if any thing was to happen to her.

Give my dearest love to Danl & Anna & theirs; I have thought a deal about them lately & intend to write very soon to dear Anna. In one of thy letters thou enquires after John Whitlark. Things I fear have gone but gloomily with him; he married some years ago his housekeeper, who has proved a termagant & with whom he is very unhappy. I am very sorry for the poor children; he was doing but poorly in worldly things & talked of removing to Iowa or Missouri.

Thos. Albright's eldest daughter is married & gone to reside in Iowa but, poor old man, he and Agnes are still at Hannibal & I fear in but poor circumstances. He is at the end of his means & his schemes but half completed, tied to the place by his property, wishing to get away, & harressed by his untoward children. I fear they must be very unhappy. If he could be persuaded to remove with Agnes to Iowa, it would be best, but then his property would be as good as sacrifised. We have been spending a few very pleasant days in the city with our friends the Taylors & very much did I enjoy the little holiday from daily cares. It is indeed a blessing to have a home for the heart as well as the foot. I think indeed that our cup runs over; would that overflowing gratitude might be the small [4] return.

I often think if thou wast only here how thou would love some that are dear to me & how they would honour & love thee, but I am thankful, dearest mother, that thou hast found a home; I bless them in my heart for their kindness to thee and feel a quiet peaceful assurance that in an atmosphere of love thou must be happy. I wish you were more amongst friends for thy sake and also for William & Mary's too, but, dearest mother, with thy own about thee & the enriching consolations of the gospel, the sustaining comforting presence of thy Saviour, and a glorious eternity before thee, thou wilt, I trust, be enabled to feel very independent of human helps & human support. When this is denied us, it is often wisely overruled in love to lead us more entirely to the fountain of strength & peace & joy.

Thou asks me to describe the tomato. It is a fruit of various sizes: some are not much larger than a small walnut, & others produce fruit as large as a great man's hand; some are red, some yellow, but all taste alike, slightly acid & very cool & juicy in the heat of summer. We stew them when peeled, with bread crumbs, butter, pepper, salt, & a little sugar & I think them excellent. I like them also sliced raw with pepper & salt, & I think they make a nice preserve. We have some boiled in sugar & dried which are called American figs &, if any chance offers, there are some laid by to send to thee; they are Harrison's doing & he talks of preserving as many next year & you are to have a box.

I wish you would petition Parliament to let kind people send their little boxes to others duty free. Oh how this custom house fetters one. I shall also try to send Anna Mary seeds for her garden; I hope Wm Forster Sen. may return in time to convey them.

[1] Farewell my tenderly beloved mother. Give my most affectionate love to the household; accept my endeared love.

Thy attached daughter.

Emma

The children desire their dear love & thanks; those beautiful engravings delight me. Our scrap-books are a rare pleasure to our friends['] pictures.

34. To Anna Harrison, November 5, 1845

11th mo 5, 1845

Thou has often, my beloved Sister, been in my most affectionate rememberance of late, and I have thought of thee with feelings of deep interest & sympathy, fearing from all we hear that thy health is at present very delicate. Thou sayst little of it thyself, but I am sure from dear Daniel's letter and also from what Margaret Ann says, thou art a continued, though patient, uncomplaining, sufferer.

Oh, with what painfully intense feelings do we think of you when we know you are in sorrow or suffering. It seems as if then and only then I could realize the distance which seperates us, and the aching certainty that the opportunity of comforting and aleviating is gone perhaps forever makes us take refuge in the only hope left, that of commending our beloved Friends to Him by whose good & gracious Providence we have been preserved & sustained through the past & whose rich consolations are abundantly bestowed upon His faithful, dependent creatures amid the trials & afflictions of life. Nay all these, as means of drawing our heart & thoughts from earth to Heaven, may be designed as our best blessings, for these light afflictions, which are but for a moment, work for us a far more \exceeding and/ eternal weight of glory because we look not at the things that are seen but at those that \are/ unseen.

Dearest Anna, I know thy sincerity and the devotedness of thy spirit, and I think of thee as one whom the Lord loveth and believe thou art of that happy number who experience the fulfilment of his gracious promises of love & mercy in the dear Saviour, and what a happy security is there in our minds for our dear, dear friends when we know their refuge and hope there. In life and in death these are safe: they may be tried, for many are the afflictions of the righteous, but the Lord delivereth them out of them all; nay, they are but as the steps by which they ascend higher & higher toward the gate of the celestial city. And beloved sister, though we go often mournfully on our way because of manifold temptations, yet how animating is the thought that He who has taught us to pray that his kingdom come is ~~at~~ near by, the blessed influences of his own holy spirit to carry forward his own work in us, even the great work of regeneration whereby we may experience redemption from the power, as well as a certain hope from the penalty, of sin.

How beautiful & excellent is the word holiness. [2] It sometimes seems to me to be worth a life of sorrow & suffering to possess, and yet how does nature shrink from the smallest cross, how inert in action, how cold & dead in feeling. "The greatest wonder in redemption is the frozen indifference with which man contemplates his redeemer's work."[119] Oh yes how often do we realize the truth of the declaration "no man can come to me except the Father which sent me draw him."[120]

We were very much pleased with the short visit of Joseph Crossfield & James Tuke; J. C. took my fancy exceedingly. There is something so amiable & unpretending about him that I felt I could love him from the first moment, and then he could talk so pleasantly of you & spoke of Daniel's kindness in such grateful terms that I talked to him more as a relation than a stranger.

Thank dear Margaret Ann for her letter & thee for the book. Also I wish I could send you something ~~also~~ in return that would interest you. To tell the truth, though books are abundant here as well as with you, I seldom see anything purely American that I think excellent. All the best literature as far as I know is imported. I am reading one of this class "Principalities & Powers" and really feel benefited & instructed by it. If thou art not familiar with it, read it for my sake; it seems to me to throw light on many dark places in my own experience, to urge to greater watchfulness & prayer & to excite to gratitude & love. I think Mary & Margaret Ann would enjoy it.

We have attended our Yearly Meeting this autumn and much enjoyed it. I sent a few weeks ago a sort of journal of its proceedings to dear mother which you will probably see. It was written in great haste & sent in a hurry so that I scarcely know whether it had beginning or end but hope she would excuse all imperfections. Indeed, I often think you must think I am growing quite illiterate. I seem to forget how to spell; it never was a thing in which I excelled & really I am losing all faculty to do it at all with correctness. Fortunately my children do not all inherit my deficiency: Wm Charles seems to have a natural talent for this accomplishment.

I am [3] much pleased Smith [Harrison] has so kindly remembered his brother Thompson. I have often felt very sorry for him and wished he could have the means he thought sufficient to give him a good chance. Whether he ever will be a prospering man is to be seen now, as what Smith has given is five times more than he himself proposed as a sufficiency to begin the world again. We have not heard from or of him lately, but of course shall now give my kind love to Smith & thank him from me for this.

Tell dear Margaret Ann I shall rejoice to welcome her to America, but does not thou think you could all come & bring dearest mother with you? Joseph

119. Charlotte Elizabeth Tonna, *Principalities and Powers in Heavenly Places* (London: R. B. Seeley and W. Burnside, 1842).
120. "No man can come to me, except the Father which hath sent me draw him: and I will raise him up at the last day" John 6:44 (King James Version).

Crossfield says Daniel's health is not good & I am persuaded this fine climate & country-life would be most beneficial to him & to thee too, dear sister. J. C. can tell you also that in coming here privation is an imaginary thing: we have good society, kind friends, a fine country, delicious climate, and all the comforts &, I think I may add, all the luxuries of life.

I am very glad, dearest Anna, that thou canst have the privilege of having all thy children around thee. It must be very pleasant to Daniel to have the boys with him in the office. I hope the confinement is not too much for dear Charles; I fancy him growing a fine, tall young man.

Do you remember Wm Bell, the editor of the Irish Friend[?] He & his family are come to settle at Cincinnati. He has been residing at New York & had a "dry goods store" which answered well & he & his wife were much respected, but on account of the delicate health of one of the daughters, he has removed here. Two of them have been to spend a few days with us; they are very Irish, though I dare say very nice people.

Please give my dear love to cousin Lucy Bayliffe.

We have had a delightful autumn, with some weeks of genuine Indian Summer weather: bright, warm, hazy days & cool, sometimes frosty nights, and the forests as usual have been my admiration & delight.

The children & I had a little pic nic to enjoy the woods one fine day. We took our dinner and, with baby in my arms, off we set on an [4] an exploratory expidition. The first wood we came to we sate down amongst the dry leaves by a little rocky stream to eat our dinner in order not to have any longer the trouble of carrying it. We followed the bed of this creek and amused ourselves with gathering fossils whilst whilst Wm Charles & his cousin Charles Shipley waded in the ~~stream~~ water. Thus we went on; we came to what I thought very beautiful scenery: the hills rose from a little green plain on which sheep were grazing & along which the stream flowed over its rocky bed; the woods were glowing in the bright sunshine in brown & yellow & orange intermingled with green, and above \was/ a sky intensely blue, over which skimmed the most silvery white clouds. It was a lovely woodland valley, shut in, as it seemed, from the noise & turmoil of the life by hills on every side. I thought it quite a discovery & must take you there when you come.

It seems as if good consistent friends' lives were half made up of going to meetings. I believe I usually have to tell you Harrison is gone to a Quarterly or some other meeting. Well he is now attending our own and a neighbouring ~~meet~~ Quarter as they are called here & so I [1] cannot send a message from him, but Wm Charles & Agnes desire their dear love & Elizabeth sends hers.

I have sent the dear girls a few flower-seeds, all of my own gathering, though nothing rare, and thee a few dried tomatoes. I dare not send many for I do not know how this is to get [4] to Philadelphia to meet J. C.

My dear love to all. This is a miserably dull affair but let me enliven it up with a most affectionate farewell from thy tenderly attached sister Emma.

My dear love to mother. I shall send her a little parcel by the London Friends.

35. To Ann Botham, November to December 24, 1845

My beloved Mother,

Thy letter dated 26th of 9th month I received a few days ago, and accept my most hearty thanks for these delightful proofs of thy affectionate rememberance. What a happy thrill does the announcement of a letter from thee send through my heart; it is like greeting the countenance of a dear friend, and when I look at the characters thy dear hand has so lately traced and read the tender sentiments of interest and love dictated by thy affectionate heart I feel as though I was holding pleasant converse with thee, my beloved parent, and arise refreshed & comforted and often strengthened to endeavour more faithfully to fulfill my duty in the Sight of Him who has so blessed me.

But Oh how unworthy do I also feel of thy love and of the varied blessings which have been and are heaped upon me. It is very sorrowful to hear such distressing accounts of scarcity in dear England. I often think that we, in this abounding country where all has been produced in so much plenty and perfection during the past summer, have cause for more than common gratitude to a kind, good Providence, who has made such a difference in our favour. Fruit is scarce, but it is the only lack we know; the crops of wheat & corn are abundant & unusually good & yet the prices are high, which, as this is decidedly an agricultural country, makes it prosperous. Flour is from 5 to 6 dollars a barrel, cornmeal 50 cents a bushel, pork 5 c. a lb, beef 2 ½ or 3 cents, & other things in proportion.

I often wish the poor in England could obtain & understand the use & value of Indian meal. It is spoken of as an article of exportation & could you once receive it good & get to use it commonly I am sure you would all like it. I intend to write a short article upon its uses & preparations and send it to William for insertion in some popular periodical.[121]

In this land of plenty there is something peculiarly trying in the idea of want of food or clothing. I doubt not there are many that endure all the evils of poverty, but they are so few comparatively that they are by no means conspicuous & scarcely visible, & when I think of the toiling, ill paid, half famished poor of England, of the misery & wretchedness of the aged and of little children, my heart is very sad, and I think I love my country more as my sympathies are drawn out in the rememberance of her misery. May the Lord overrule this for good. It may be that the iron screw of necessity will bring out justice and mercy from the aristocracy and oblige them to grant that the blessings & good of the earth should freely flow into the land.

121. See letter #36.

And yet you must not suppose there no distress in America. In the cities, the unfortunate and improvident are always to be found & this winter fuel and provisions are so unusually dear that many are in want of these necessaries of life. 2000 dollars have however been subscribed and soup houses & donations of coal & wood are dispensed & will contribute much to mitigate the sufferings of the poor.

Until about the middle of the 11th month we had a beautiful mild autumn, many weeks of delightful weather, what is called Indian summer but from that time the winter has set in unusually early & most intense the cold is. The thermometer often is many degrees below zero; the river has been nearly frozen over & navigation stopped. To me the cold is very distressing; it affects my whole frame & especially my eyes, but I keep hoping for a change as this degree of cold in this neighbourhood does not often continue long. I never am so well satisfied that thou art best in England as in winter; [2] it seems to me that thou couldst not have endured so much cold or at least must have suffered exceedingly. I sometimes say if thou wast here thou wouldst have to be in bed to keep thyself warm; and yet I am ashamed of my complainings when I consider our many comforts & the privations of others in this country & England & the long summers so delightful & so productive of blessing.

Our children are all well, which is a great favour. Agnes is becoming an intelligent clever little girl; she sews nicely & feels very proud when she can do something which looks womanly & useful. She will soon be able to read, which will be a great help & comfort to me. I often tell her she is to be eyes to me and Charley, whose eyesight is still very defective, which is a great drawback to his prospects in improvement. We have lately been reading Pilgrims Progress to him & it was a perfect treat to me to witness his intense interest in the story at the storming of Giant Despair's castle. He said, ["]Oh, I feel that I tremble all over.["] It is certainly a wonderful production. To me it was as interesting as to Wm Charles, only in another way: its quaintness, its originality, its deep instruction are excellent & I would advise you who must sometimes be wearied by the excesses of modern literature to refresh yourselves by a deep draught of John Bunyan.

Charley is naturally selfish, and what a comfort it is, dearest mother, to see a better spirit evincing itself. I could have wept tears of gratitude on a little incident that occurred lately. Thompson Harrison was here & when he was going Charles came with a countenance glowing with generous feelings & said to me, ["M]other, I wish that English shilling that Joseph Taylor gave me would go here, I should so much like to give it to Cousin Thompson because thou knows he lost all his money in kentucky, but however he might get it changed & so please give it me.["] I would not check him in his generous purpose, but avoided being present, yet I heard little Annie say when Thompson declined the kindness, ["]Oh do take it; Charley has plenty of money, lots upstairs in his purse, so do take it[."]

Anna Mary is to be the original of our family; she will get a book & take a picture for a subject & tell long tales about lions & deserts & wild forests. She is a merry child & sings little songs like a ballad singer, one about Dandy Jem of Caroline is at present the prime favourite.[122] Poor little Ann Alice is, like myself, sadly pinched with the cold; she is still a meek, peaceful baby in arms for she is too feeble to walk at present. Agnes & Anna Mary who are sitting by me send their dear love to thee; they are always much pleased with thy kind messages to them.

We have not yet received the parcel you have so kindly sent, but on obtaining the publisher's address Harrison wrote to one of our friends at Philadelphia & we hope to hear by him that they are safe. Thomas Winn has failed some months ago & therefore the direction to him could not avail anything, as he has left the city & probably Pennington did not know how to dispose of them. I trust they are safe. It will be a sad disappointment to lose them. Thank you most heartily for all your great kindness before they come to hand & even if they never should I wish I had some means of returning it, but it really seems as if the little we could send was not worth the trouble & expence before it reaches.

I am very glad, my beloved mother, to hear thou art so comfortable with dear Wm & Mary. I know how much they will rejoice to contribute to thy happiness, and to me the idea of thy being with those that love thee & feel it a duty & pleasure to promote thy comfort and enjoyment is so much more agreeable than to think of thy being with strangers. Give my most affectionate love to them all. I long to have a letter from dear Mary. I believe I am indebted to dear Anna Mary for a very interesting one which is yet unanswered. Dear girl, I hope [3] some day to see her a welcome guest under our roof. We have had frequent visitors from England this summer & none can tell but those who have left their own land how pleasant it is to see even a stranger from England, how much more to see once again our own dear friends.

Poor Thompson Harrison has been to see us. He joined, I think I told thee, a company of associationists located at a place called the Ohio Phalanx. He put into the undertaking his whole property, about 800 dollars, and was so enthusiastic that he joyfully endured great privations. At one time he said he sat down to the public table when the bread was so far from him that he could not reach it & often had only one meal a day, but by perseverance things began to mend. The association consisting of about 200 men, women, & children produced their own provisions & adopting the graham phylosophy, which is to live on a vegetable diet, got on very well, but the President betrayed them & in a few days the whole was broken up by the treachery of him &

122. A blackface minstrel ballad. Later, Alderson sharply criticizes her German neighbors for staging what sounded like amateur minstrel shows (see page 303).

some whom he gained over, & Thompson left the place with a buggy & an old horse as his portion. His tools also he took, & that was all he had left of his whole property; his wife was wiser than he &, claiming their beds & bedding as her own, never let them go to the place, and these they have to begin the world again. Smith['s] donation has come opportunely, but I fear it will do them little good. The kindest & best plan would be to purchase a farm, ~~for them &~~ retaining the possession & paying the taxes for them; let Richard & his family, Thompson & his & Alice live upon it, by which they might get an abundance of the necessaries of life. We both think no other help will be availing.

These associations on Charles Fourier's system are very numerous in America & combined with Grahamerism are very popular among a certain class. To me they are interesting and if men were all virtuous & honest might be very happy, but alas, the materials of which society & especially such societies as these are formed are the desperate & ill-doing in worldly things. I do not mean the vicious, for they wish and require good characters as an essential for admissions. I shall send you some interesting papers published by them.

This is the day preceding Christmass, & this letter has been many weeks on hand. I have many interruptions from my eyes at present to working & of course other things. Oh how I miss thy kind assistance, but somehow I manage to get along & hope for better times; my great desire is to be spared to watch over our dear children, that is that both of us pray to be permitted to remain with them in a strange land & that I may have the use of my hands & eyes to supply their wants, intellectual & physical.

[4] Dear Harrison is well and desires his dear love to thee & the dear Family at Clapton. Give our dear love to Daniel & Anna & theirs. I wrote to Anna & sent a small parcel for her by Joseph Crossfield which I hope would be in time to meet him in Phila.

Harrison is kept very busy attending to our live stock, chopping wood &c. We have three cows & 7 hogs, 4 of which we shall kill for our year's consumption; this is the great hog time in the city & the number killed is almost incredible: a hog a minute is the calculation in the great establishments. Thou enquires in one of thy letters after Richard [Alderson]; he is still in his situation with a builder in the city & according to the plan of this country receives wages 2 1/4 dollars a week. He is a fine looking boy & bears a good character. He was pleased to be remembered by thee & desired his love, and so did Cousin Ann Shipley when I saw her last.

And now my beloved mother, I must bid the farewell. May every blessing be thy portion & the joys & comforts of our blessed faith sustain & strengthen the[e] daily, nay hourly, throughout thy whole earthly pilgrimage. In the most endeared affections, I am thy attached daughter,

Emma Alderson

Excuse blunders, I am in haste. Please give our kind love to Ann <??> & all our dear old friends. A merry Christmas & a very happy new year to you all; Charley's dear love; Agnes desires her dear love to cousin Margaret.

36. To William Howitt, December 28, 1845
Cedar Lodge 12 mo 28th 1845

My dear Brother,
Yesterday I received a most welcome letter from dear Mary, which I am impatient to answer, but as I have set myself a task which I cannot feel satisfied to delay, and time is a somewhat scarce article with me, I think I will not allow myself to do even the pleasantest things until I have at least tried to accomplish what I have proposed, which is to say a few words to thee on the excellence & value of corn meal, that is Indian corn or maise.

We have felt intense interest on behalf of the suffering poor of England who, when we left our country, were enduring great hardship & privation from depression in trade, & when I saw the cheapness, abundance & excellence of every necessary and comfort of life in this favoured land my heart used to ache for those who I knew would have received with thankfulness the very husks with which the swine were filled. But how much worse must their condition be, present & prospective, when the direful effects of the last unfavorable summer are felt in all their dreadful consequences, when deteriorated & unwholesome food is sold at an exorbitant price.

Since we have become accustomed to the use of corn in its various preparations which we found so good as very soon the like exceeding, we have often remarked what a blessing it would be to the poor of England & Ireland if it could be introduced and might be allowed to enter the country at a low duty or, what would be still better, free. It is now considered very high but the best quality dressed & ready for bread is retailed in the stores at from 40 to 50 cents a bushel which weighs 56 lb, & this thou knows is not \one/ 1/2 \d/ a lb, reckoning 22 cents to the shilling.

It is always considered best when fresh ground, but it is the opinion of men who are well acquainted with the subject that when kilndried it would not suffer by being kept any length of time & would not injure by transportation. Or if you wished to enjoy it in ~~its~~ perfection the grain could be sent & manufactured in the mills in England.

[2] In this Western Country in the rich vallies & river bottoms the Indian corn attains a height and beauty which is very striking, and this last season was peculiarly favourable to its growth, being very hot & dry [&,] after much rain, realized to my mind more than ever before the idea I had always formed of it. It not unfrequently rises ten feet and is crowned with the fine feathery tuft of male blossom of a pale sickly yellowish green which contrasts beautifully with the broad, deep, rich green leaves of the plant.

It is in ful vigour in the early part of the 8th month & from the time of planting which the Indians used to commence when the ~~beautiful white~~ \in the woods the/ Cornus Florida has expanded its beautiful white involucre & the red bud is crimson with its innumerable pretty little blossoms. From that time till it begins to tassel, as it is called, it requires constant attention & frequent working, but its abundant produce & great usefulness repays all this labour.

Thou hast heard me often speak of the green corn or roasting ears used as a vegetable in summer & a great luxury & universal favourite it is. We are told it is preserved for winter use in New England by being put into cases hermetically sealed which perhaps may find its way to you, but these are luxuries. It is in its ground state that it becomes so valuable as food for man. Of course you know what excellent provision it is for animals: the horses, cows and pigs all eat it greedily, and it is most fattening, and the flesh is considered superior which is corn fed ~~to any~~; the stalk & dried leaves make good fodder for cattle.

Hominy, which is painfully associated in my mind with slavery, being a principal article of food with the slave, is the grain devested of the outer husk by pounding in a mill or by machinery. The Hominy mill of the south is a stump or block of hard wood hollowed out, to which a heavy pestel worked by a lever is attached. The corn is usually given to the slave unprepared, a peck for the weeks supply, & so great is the press round the mill that often the short space allowed for meals is not sufficient to enable all to prepare enough for use.

The grains when freed from the husk are of a pure white & look very pretty like the finest tapioca. They are simply boiled \till soft/ in water & with the addition of a little salt & butter ~~are~~ \it is/ liked by many as a vegetable on the table. It is very good, I think, eaten in milk & when sweetened & spiced is not unlike or English firmity. Sluts Hominy is made by steeping the grains in weak ley, which loosens the outer coat so that it is easily removed without labor.

But now I must tell thee of its various preparations as bread &c. It makes excellent gruel prepared in the same way as you make oatmeal gruel and mush is the porridge of the North of England & Ireland, but it is best when very well boiled. In summer we eat it cold with milk for supper, & the children and we are very fond of it.

[3] It is considered a great improvement to brown or white bread to have a certain proportion of corn meal in it; we put about one third in our common bread, but being of a dry nature & our wheat flour also very dry, potatoes are a great improvement, but when the wheat flour is, as it frequently is in England, too moist, it would be an invaluable corrective. We put it in dry; some make it into mush, but I think it makes the bread clotty & unpleasant.

Warm Indian Bread we seem to consider an essential part of our breakfast. In winter it seems to have taken the place of buttered toast with us & is excellent & very cheap. It is made in this way: to a quart of sour milk or butter-milk add as much meal as will make it into a thick batter, a little salt & about a teaspoonful of saleratus, which is nothing but potash dissolved in a little water; this acts upon the acid of the buttermilk, corrects it & the effervescence causes the bread to be light. A spoonful of coarse sugar & about a table-spoonful of melted butter or lard is a great improvement. Pour it into a well buttered tin about an inch thick & bake it in a quick oven. It is best eaten hot but very good cold. Of course we eat butter & sometimes butter & molasses to it.

When sour milk cannot be procured, mix it with sweet milk & add a table-spoonful of vinegar. The potash should not be stirred in till just before putting in the oven. Another way to make this kind of bread is to pour boiling sweet milk on the meal & when cool add three eggs well beaten & a little salt.

Indian Slap Jacks, somewhat like our English crumpets or pikelets, are made by scalding a quart of Indian meal. When lukewarm, add a few spoonfulls of flour, half a tea cup of yeast & a little salt. \When light/ pour them on a well buttered bake stone \in small cakes/ & pat them hot with butter. A more common way & perhaps the best is to mix the meal into boiling milk & water. When cool, stir in the remainder of the meal so as to make it a thick batter, two table spoonful of flour to a quart of the liquid, three eggs & two tea spoonfuls of salt.

Johnny Cakes. Scald a quart of sifted Indian meal with sufficient water to make it a very thick batter. Stir in two or three tea spoonfuls of salt—mould it with the hand into small cakes. In order to mould them up, rub a good deal of flour on the hands to prevent their sticking. Fry them in \plenty of / boiling fat or lard. When brown on one side they must be turned. It takes about twenty minutes to cook them—when done, split & butter them.

Hoe Cakes. Scald a quart of Indian meal with just water enough to make a thick batter. Stir in a couple of tea-spoonful of salt & two table-spoonful of butter. Turn it into a buttered bake tin & bake it half an hour.

If you want some thing very rich & good, you can make Bannock or Indian cakes in this way. Stir to a cream a lb of butter & 1 1/4 lb of brown sugar, beat six eggs & mix them with the above ingredients. Add a tea spoonful of cinnamon, the same of ginger—stir in a pound & three quarters of I[ndian] meal & a quarter of a pound of wheat flour. The meal [4] must be sifted. Bake it in cups or \small/ tin moulds & eat it cold.

I shall long ago have wearied thee with this long desertation on cookery, but I have felt stimulated to persevere, hoping it might furnish thee with means of saying a few words to the public. I could find in my heart to write to the Premier if it might open the way for its introduction into England at this sorrowful juncture. There might much more be said on its behalf, but I think this perhaps enough at present.

Now perhaps you will think all this earnestness fuss & nonsense, & that I need not have given you the trouble & put you to the expence of a letter for such a cause. Well be charitable; I seem impelled to make the attempt to do some good by the constant thought of the misery of the poor & the inconveniences of all classes.

Tell dearest mother with my most affection rememberance that we have heard of her parcel being safe at Philadelphia. I hope soon to hear the same of the books you sent, for which receive our warmest thanks. I <u>long</u> to see them.

My dear love to you all. It has been dismally cold but is now somewhat moderated. You cannot conceive the painful effects of the cold when the thermometer is below Zero.

Don't be surprised if Miss Margaret receives a letter from Charley: the mention of Mary's Children's Year has made me think of writing a diary for our children in the person of Wm Charles addressed to his cousin. It may prove somewhat novel & interesting being a detail of a country life in America.

What do our letters cost? I am shocked to think mother had to pay 4./ for my last, but I remember it was double & perhaps over weight. Farewell dear brother. Harrison's dear love to all, Thy ever attached & obliged sister,

Emma Alderson
excuse all blunders

PART III

The Final Years

The last two years of Emma Alderson's life saw a growing engagement with the affairs of both the world and the Society of Friends, though the balance between the two was not always easy. It may be that her confidence in herself as an observer and interpreter of her new country was continuing to grow, or perhaps it was an awareness of the possibility that, through the agency of her famous sister, her own writing might find a wider audience than she had previously imagined. In any event, the final period of her correspondence is marked by a greater awareness and more candid critique of the issues confronting her various communities. Most important in this period was the evolution of the collaboration with Mary Howitt, through which Alderson came to imagine herself as something of an author.

Alderson's response to the arrival in 1846 of Thomas and Sarah Frankland from England indicates a new phase in her identity, if not as an American, then as something of a native in her new land. Alderson had no doubt known the Franklands sometime between about 1831, when she and her mother moved to Everton (now part of Liverpool) to be near her sister Anna Harrison, and May 1833, when she married Harrison Alderson in the nearby Hardshaw West Monthly Meeting and moved north to Blackburn. The Franklands had also been members of Hardshaw West and were married there. Alderson's enthusiasm in her letters beginning September 1846 about the arrival of these old friends is understandable, but her interest in their well-being and their settlement in America also illustrates Alderson's transition from new immigrant aided by others to established Anglo-American coming to the aid of the next generation. The Franklands brought, perhaps among other letters and gifts, a letter from Anna Harrison referring to some other letters she had sent that had apparently never arrived, which evidences the continuing value of family and friends moving between the two countries.

The Franklands' credentials as Quakers might not have met Alderson's full approval. Thomas, a linen dealer, had been disowned for insolvency: the Hardshaw West minutes of 1840 reported that he and his business partner "acknowledge that they extended their business in 1838 and 1839 much beyond what their means warranted and seem aware of the reproach they brought on the Society by their improper conduct."[1] Presumably unrelated to that incident, but of potentially greater concern to Alderson, might have been the difference between the views held by Thomas Frankland as a Quaker minister and those held by Alderson's husband. In openly criticizing "those who esteemed the Holy Scriptures more highly than the society did," Frankland was speaking out against the growing evangelicalism of the Society of Friends and against Joseph John Gurney, the Orthodox leader whom Emma Alderson so much admired.[2] Nevertheless, from November 1846 on, her letters are filled with expressions of concern for the Franklands' well-being and pride in their success, as they open a school in Cincinnati and Thomas secures "a situation with our good friends the Taylors" with a "comfortable living," for which "they seem very gratified" (see page 397). Six months later Alderson writes, again with great pleasure, that Sarah Frankland has taken the lead in organizing a group of women to make clothing for famine relief in Ireland.

Race and Racism in America

Alderson, who opposed slavery and abhorred racism in general, found herself well situated to observe and comment on this aspect of American life. Cincinnati had been home to a robust and vibrant African American community since early in the nineteenth century, and that community persisted in spite of some of the most pervasive racism in the North. Cincinnati's strong economic ties to Kentucky on the other side of the river led white Cincinnatians to side more often with Southern interests than might be expected of Northerners. One historian has called it "the northernmost southern city": situated at the crossroads of three different cultures, Cincinnati's African Americans had to contend simultaneously with "a southern racial code, northern segregation and discrimination, and western frontier mob violence."[3]

The "Black Laws" enshrined in the Ohio constitution from 1806 barred African Americans from military service, jury duty in trials of white individuals, and poor relief. In addition, as a disincentive to settlement in Ohio, they were required to register with the government and post a $500 bond. Registration and bond payment were enforced sporadically and punitively in the wake of race riots that flared periodically during the first half of the century. The first such riot—perhaps the first race riot in America—erupted in 1829 and resulted in the departure of more than half of Cincinnati's African American population, many of them to what was then the British colony of Upper Canada. A second occurred in 1836 and a third in 1841, only two years before the Aldersons' arrival. By 1841, the black community had rebuilt itself with schools, churches, newspapers, mutual aid societies, Masonic lodges, and more.[4] Thus, when racial hostility, fueled in part by an economic depression, broke out once again, African Americans were less willing to leave than they had been twelve years earlier. Instead, they armed themselves and stood their ground, though in the end they were outnumbered by hundreds of armed white vigilantes, whose arsenal even included a cannon. When the militia intervened, the black community was placed under martial law and forced to give up the weapons they had used to protect themselves. Leaders were made to promise to "conduct ourselves as [an] orderly, industrious, and peaceable people," to comply with the Black Laws, and to "suppress any imprudent conduct among our population, and ferret out all violators of order and law."[5] Although justice had not been done in response to the attack on their community, African Americans had fought successfully for their dignity, their freedom, and their right to claim Cincinnati as their home, gaining a new self-awareness and instilling in their community a sense of purpose and belonging they had not had before.[6]

Less than two years later, the Aldersons arrived in Cincinnati. Though she makes no mention of the 1841 riots in her letters, Emma was keenly aware of the issues. In early 1845, Emma described the Black Laws in a letter to Mary, explaining that, "though the blacks are required to pay taxes for schools & the support of the poor, they are excluded from the public schools & no provision is made for the aged, helpless & indigent but the Pest house as it is called, that is a portion of the fever hospital" (see page 211). Indeed, the Aldersons had been in Cincinnati only a few months when a smaller riot erupted over the rescue of Lavinia, a nine-year-old slave, from her master, Mr. Scanlan, who had been visiting the city from his home in New Orleans. The rioters were suppressed, and the girl was sent to Canada. Although Emma was pleased with the rescue, she lamented to her mother, in words that may have expressed her own sense of separation, "the policy in this instance of separating a little child from its mother, who must be sent thousands of miles amongst strangers" (see page 134).

Another incident that greatly interested Emma was the settlement of some 300 former slaves in Ohio who had been manumitted by John Randolph (1773–1833) of Charlotte County, Virginia. Randolph's will had provided for their manumission after his death and had also given them $30,000 to buy land and settle in the North. Randolph had served in the United States Congress and (briefly) Senate from 1800 to 1829 and as ambassador to Russia in 1830. An unstinting opponent of federalism and a fierce defender of the property rights of slaveholders, Randolph was also among the founders of the American Colonization Society, which was aimed at deporting freed slaves back to Africa.[7] Later, he rejected the Colonization Society's scheme, calling it "bad and mischievous" and motivated by "a spirit of morbid sensibility, religious fanaticism, vanity, and the love of display."[8] However, Randolph's will was contested for many years, and it was not until 1846 that the former slaves arrived in Mercer County, Ohio, to take possession of land they had purchased.

Mercer County had been chosen due to the recent establishment of another community of African Americans in connection with a school started by white abolitionist Augustus Wattles. Even before their arrival, Mercer County residents had begun organizing to deny these freed men and women access to their land. The angry residents met them at the canal port and demanded that they leave: "denied the homes of free men," Emma wrote, they "remain outcasts & wanderers in a land calling itself Free" (see page 343). Not content with expelling that group, the white residents met again to pass resolutions expelling the rest of the country's African American population as well, and only intervention by the governor brought peace to the situation. Eventually the "Randolph negroes," as they came to be known, dispersed through western Ohio, settling as individuals and families. Years later, their descendants would bring lawsuits (unsuccessfully) in an attempt to reclaim the land that had been taken from them before they had even seen it.

Such incidents made it difficult for Emma to embrace her new country. In her estimation, they were too much a part of the American identity: "there is a spirit of intolerance here which is constantly manifesting itself & causes a thraldom of mind that is anything but freedom," she wrote to her mother, adding, "there is no despotism like that of the mob" (see page 368). "Is it not a sin that the whole nation does not raise its voice against such wicked proceedings[?]" she asked her sister Anna (see page 368). Thinking of British Canada as "the place of safety & refuge to the poor escaped and runaway negro" had made Emma proud of her Englishness (see page 160). She would no doubt have been disturbed to learn that even in Canada, where many of those refugees settled, they faced racial intolerance, intimidation, and even arson.[9]

Closer to home was the Aldersons' relationship to Dr. Jack Kett, the "Negro doctor," and his wife, Jane, who lived nearby. Practicing African American physicians were unusual but not unheard of, as the 1850 census lists two in Cincinnati.[10] In 1839, another African American doctor had been run out of town on charges of quackery, though, as an article in the *Philanthropist* noted, "it is well known, that there are several *white* quacks in this city, whose practices have been as injurious to the community, in all probability, as those of the Black Doctor."[11] The Ketts kept "two very fierce dogs chained up to defend them," Emma explains, "because rude people & boys are very fond of playing them rather more than rude jokes" (see page 304).

Yet the Aldersons' relationship to the Ketts appears in the letters to be more paternalistic than truly fraternal, insofar as it is usually characterized by acts of charity. When Dr. Jack dies, the Aldersons learn about it only by chance but are reassured that they will be invited to the funeral: "He told me there was to be a 'funeral' preached at the grave side that day month & we should know. They marvelled how they could have forgotten to send us word of his death, but Mr. Hudson the coloured preacher would be here then & they hoped we should also be present" (see pages 314–315). Later they learn that "the 'funeral' had been preached this morning and a 'right smart company were there,' but to our regret we missed it as they forgot to tell us or rather send us word in time" (see page 346). Emma's use of quotation marks around both instances of the word "funeral" is curious in its suggestion of irony, though Mr. Hudson was, for all we know, a legitimate preacher. One wonders whether the repeated omission of any invitation to the Aldersons was entirely accidental or really an indication of the tension that persisted between even relatively open-minded black and white Cincinnatians.

Most likely, Emma's belief in a true friendship between her family and the Ketts helped reaffirm her personal and public identity as English and therefore as a representative of the truest form of liberty, unlike her German and Irish neighbors, who figure consistently in her letters as crudely racist. Another time, Emma proudly tells Mary about the "respectable" "mulatto" tradesman whom they invited to dinner and who "has told far & near our unprecedented kindness"(see page 211).

The Aldersons were regular visitors to the Colored Orphan Asylum, which operated on Ninth Street between Elm and Plum from its founding in 1845 to 1866, when it was moved to Avondale on the north side of the city. The Colored Orphan Asylum was founded largely through the efforts of the African American community with the help of Quaker Lydia Mott (1807–1875)[12] and others, which may explain some of Emma Alderson's intense interest in the institution. As she notes, the Colored Orphan Asylum struggled financially in comparison with its white counterparts, St. Joseph's Catholic Orphan Asylum, run by the Sisters of Charity, and the German Protestant Orphan Asylum on Highland Avenue (the largest of the city's orphanages, though Alderson never mentions it by name).[13]

The interest Emma took in Native Americans likewise reflected her identification with the Society of Friends, a group that had taken a strong, if often paternalistic and assimilationist, interest in Native American affairs. "While [Quakers] condemned U.S. policies of conquest and removal and tried to hold the federal government to the terms of treaties, the Quaker vision for the Indian future involved assimilation and adoption of Christianity."[14] Emma attended the Indian Committee meetings at Quarterly and Yearly Meeting, and she writes in detail about the work of Thomas and Hannah Wells and others at the Shawnee Mission School just south of Kansas City. The Wellses had recently taken over the superintendence of the school from Thomas and Esther French, a change that Emma declares "has given that establishment a character it never before possessed—that of a religious institution" (see page 421). She admired the educational and political work that Quakers were doing on the Native Americans' behalf, but the paternalism is often evident, as when she describes to her mother one failure of Thomas Wells:

> He had a while back great hopes of some who had become regular attenders at meeting and seemed so far broken off from their customs that at the approach of the spring dances which, like all their dances, is a religious ceremony, he ventured to advise & exhort them not to join their people on the occasion. He appealed to their convictions & understandings, but this interference was so unpalatable that they went away, joined the *<blank>* & returned to their nation—that is, fell back into its wild practice & corrupt habits & superstition.

Such was the "unconquerable tenacity in the Indian character" (see page 433), and yet, paradoxical as it may seem to us today, these missionaries persisted in their efforts at Christianizing and assimilating the Native Americans even as they fought for their legal rights.

Alderson had anticipated the Mexican-American War (1846–1848) with trepidation in her early letters; with its commencement in 1846, that trepidation turns to fierce and unequivocal denunciations. The Quaker peace testimony made war of any kind and for any reason unacceptable, but the imperialist motivations behind this war, and its likely effect in extending the dominion of slavery, made it more so. "The annexation of Texas," she tells her mother, "was an evil thing because it was intended thereby to strengthen & perpetuate slavery & these are its early bad fruits: war & bloodshed" (see page 341). Humanitarian and moral objections bolster her political objections, as she mourns the suffering and loss of life on both sides, among soldiers as well as civilians. Even news of American victories, she writes, caused the family to sigh "more deeply at the thought of the dead & dying, and a shudder of horror passed through the little company when they remembered the sufferings of the wounded under that burning sun & in the unwholesome dews & reflected on the unprepared soul hurried into eternity" (see page 328). Accounts of drunken debauchery in the military camps might have been enough to turn the retiring, teetotal Quaker against the war, but these and excesses of violence against Mexican citizens are, in Alderson's account, the consequence of "the brutalizing effects" of war on otherwise decent human beings (see page 395). Her outrage is always against the war itself and the policies that brought it on, never against the individuals on either side of the conflict.

Although the war with Mexico continued through the remainder of Alderson's life, we find less mention of it during her last year, when her attention seems to have been drawn to the famine in Ireland. If slavery and the "unrighteous war" with Mexico gave occasion for an identification with Britain and its slave-free colonies in Canada, the famine helped her to appreciate and identify with the generosity of the American people. Although her letters convey some sense of guilt about living so comfortably while so many starved on the other side of the Atlantic, the predominant feelings she expresses are sympathy for the Irish and pride in the efforts of Americans to raise food, clothing, and money in their aid. Just as her sister's domestic sphere became a site of literary production, the Irish famine seems to have made the Aldersons' a site of charitable industry in support of relief efforts, as the children donated money and initiated small business ventures to raise more: "The dismal accounts of scarcity in Ireland excite deep interest in the minds of the children. They often ask 'would not the little children there be glad of this good dinner[?'] & one undertakes to lecture the other on any occasion of dissatisfaction with the sinfulness of ingratitude when so many would be thankful for such good porridge or nice bread" (see page 404). Here, to a degree impossible with more political and contentious issues such as slavery and the Mexican war, the domestic sympathies of the private sphere can be directed outward toward action in the public sphere.

Domestic life offered another opportunity for civic action, insofar as the Aldersons recognized the impact of consumer choices on the various modes of production. Long before today's marketing of "Fair Trade" goods, they bought only maple sugar to avoid supporting the slave economy of the Southern sugar plantations, "a sort of market testimony which most understand of our feelings on the subject" (see page 420). Likewise, although there were practical reasons for burning wood rather than coal in America, a chapter from William Howitt's *The Boy's Country-*

Book about the conditions in English coal mines led the Aldersons to rejoice that their wood fire owed nothing to such suffering (see page 309).

Alderson's involvement and identification with the Society of Friends continued to deepen during these final years of her life. Her account to her mother of the 1845 Yearly Meeting in Richmond, Indiana, is one of the most enthusiastic letters in the collection, evincing especially her passion for humanitarian issues, including the rights and conditions of African American and Native American people, education, and prison reform. Although she laments her absence from Yearly Meetings in 1846 and 1847, she does not explain why she failed to go. Perhaps pregnancies kept her at home; in any event, those years included three pregnancies, two of which ended with stillbirth or miscarriage and the final one with her own death as well as that of the child.

Nevertheless, letters from this period record the involvement of her family with many of the leading Quakers of her day from England as well as the United States, who carried news, eyewitness reports of family members, and parcels back and forth across the Atlantic between the Aldersons and their family in England. It is a testimony to their own rising position in the Society of Friends that the Aldersons often hosted these visitors in their home. One source of Emma's pleasure in these visits was no doubt the news from home, but she also enjoyed the intellectual conversation she otherwise missed in America. "Except in a few rare instances," she writes, "English friends are very superior to those of this country; . . . they as Englishmen have a heart for all the world, & that few of the Americans possess" (see page 292). Years earlier, she had written about her love for the "liberal broad philanthropic character" of English Friends, in contrast to American Friends, who have "have narrowed & are narrowing themselves in till they are alarmed at the expansive character of true christian benevolence. They are many of them groping in the dark mists of prejudice & party" (see pages 171–172). When she sides vehemently with the British evangelical Friend Joseph John Gurney against the quietist American John Wilbur in the "Second Separation" of Friends in 1845, one detects, perhaps more than her own purely doctrinal position, an enthusiasm for the opportunity to identify herself with the English party in a matter of such importance.

Becoming an Author

The most dramatic development during this period in Alderson's life was the commencement of the journals intended for publication by Mary Howitt in England. At this point, perhaps, we feel most keenly the one-sidedness of the correspondence; we can only wonder what words of encouragement, caution, or instruction Howitt offered to her admiring sister. Howitt's side of the correspondence would no doubt help us understand the workings of this transatlantic domestic collaboration. As it is, we must make what we can out of one side of that conversation.

Alderson's letters to Howitt had been a great deal less frequent than those to Anna Harrison and their mother. The fact that Howitt resided in Germany during the first part of Alderson's new life in America may partly explain that difference, but we also know that Alderson struggled with feelings of inadequacy in comparison with Howitt, who had become a successful author (see pages 13–14). Alderson had written only three times to her sister by December 1845, when she wrote a long letter to William Howitt on the virtues of "Indian corn," which she hoped he would publish in the interest of alleviating hunger in the British Isles. This letter to William marks a new stage in the growth of Alderson's self-confidence as a writer, attributable in part, perhaps, to her having been tasked earlier that year with writing an epistle on behalf of Indiana Yearly Meeting, to be read at the next London Yearly Meeting. She described the job proudly to her mother as "a very serious & important thing to undertake" (see page 248). In her December 1845 letter to William, she also mentions for the first time the project that will culminate in *Our Cousins in Ohio*: "Don't be surprised if Miss Margaret [Howitt] receives a letter from Charley: the mention of Mary's Children's Year has made me think of writing a diary for our children in the person of Wm Charles addressed to his cousin. It may prove somewhat novel & interesting being a detail of a country life in America" (see page 264). Although there is no definite suggestion here of publication, Alderson is at least modeling her own writing practice on the publication work of her sister.

Early in this period, a series of five letters (37, 38, 40, 42, 43) in journal form seem to have been composed not "in the person of" William Charles but largely by the boy himself to his cousin Margaret Howitt. Although the handwriting is his mother's, the language is not, suggesting either that he was dictating to his mother or that she was recopying his letters. After May 1846, letters in journal form continue intermittently, but the language and selection of material are now more clearly Emma's. In these letters, there is no first-person narrator as in William Charles's earlier letters; now he is referred to by name. Alderson figures in the third person, usually as "their mother" or "his mother," as opposed to the more intimate proper noun, "mother," used by her son in his letters. Thus, it seems that, for whatever reason, the boy lost interest after a few months and his mother took over the project she had conceived back in December.

Howitt describes her sister's correspondence as "a faithful narrative of her children's life for a year" and her own efforts as amounting merely to "compilation" of those letters.[15] So thoroughly accepted was this romantic fiction of *Our Cousins in Ohio* as an eyewitness account of a year in the life of an artless immigrant, that an 1871 obituary of Harrison Alderson described the book as the "simple account of a year of home-life of the three elder children at 'Cedar Lodge,' . . . written by Emma Alderson during the last year of her life."[16] What is excluded in such a fiction is both the transformation of the narrative under Howitt's professional editorial hand and the incipient professionalism of Alderson as an observer, commentator, writer, and shaper of her own narrative.

From both the content of *Our Cousins* and the pencil lines in the margins of Alderson's letters (presumably Howitt's), we know that when Howitt began that process of compilation, she pored over all of the correspondence, not just those

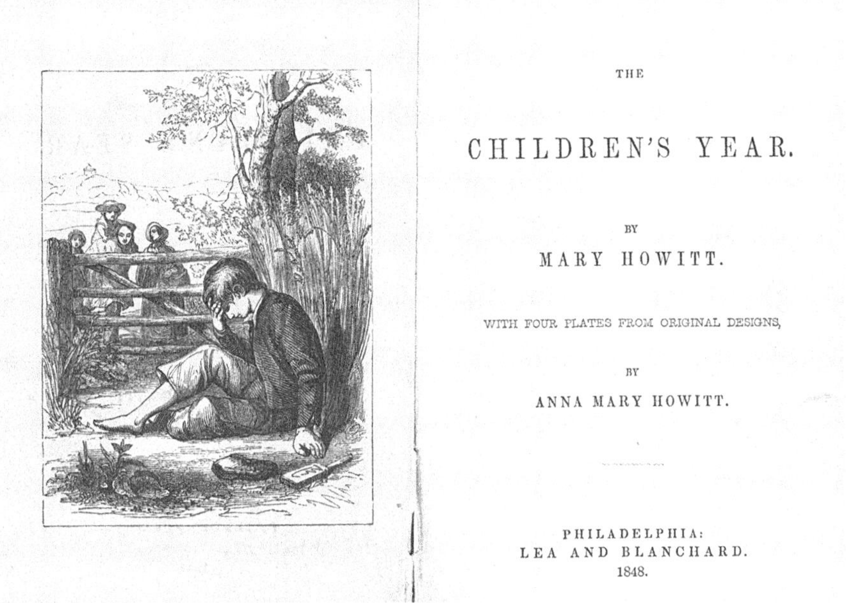
THE

CHILDREN'S YEAR.

BY

MARY HOWITT.

WITH FOUR PLATES FROM ORIGINAL DESIGNS,

BY

ANNA MARY HOWITT.

PHILADELPHIA:
LEA AND BLANCHARD.
1848.

Figure 24. Title page and frontispiece from an 1848 American edition of Mary Howitt's *The Children's Year.* English and American editions were illustrated with engravings from the drawings of Anna Mary Howitt. The frontispiece in the English edition depicted the children engaged in a tea party with their dolls.

letters intended as part of the account. The final result was a neatly rounded year drawn from more than four years of material, reproducing the conventional pastoral structure of Edmund Spenser's *Shepheardes Calender* or James Thomson's *The Seasons.* The cyclical, seasonal narrative might be consistent with the narrative of a woman's everyday life, everyday life being marked, as Jennifer Sinor has argued, "by cycles and repetition. The cyclical nature of women's bodies—menstrual and birth cycles—replicates the cyclical nature of the day and repetition of the mundane."[17] In this case, however, the violence done to Alderson's writing obscures the growth that takes place over this four-year period.

The selection of content, too, while drawn almost entirely from Alderson's writing, represents only a narrow slice of Alderson's real experience in America, reflecting Howitt's own literary and political goals. *Our Cousins* was marketed quite explicitly as a "companion volume to *The Children's Year,*" an overseas extension of the earlier book's domestic ideology.[18] Moreover, as Linda H. Peterson has noted, *Our Cousins* represented an exercise in "nation-building" and in the transplantation not only of "English domestic values onto American soil" but also of "certain British social, cultural, and political values, including the Howitts' Radical abolitionist views."[19] In *Our Cousins*, domestic values and activities drive, but also paradoxically dehistoricize, a reformist, humanitarian agenda. Alderson's critiques of slavery, racism, chain gangs, militarism, and other political issues are

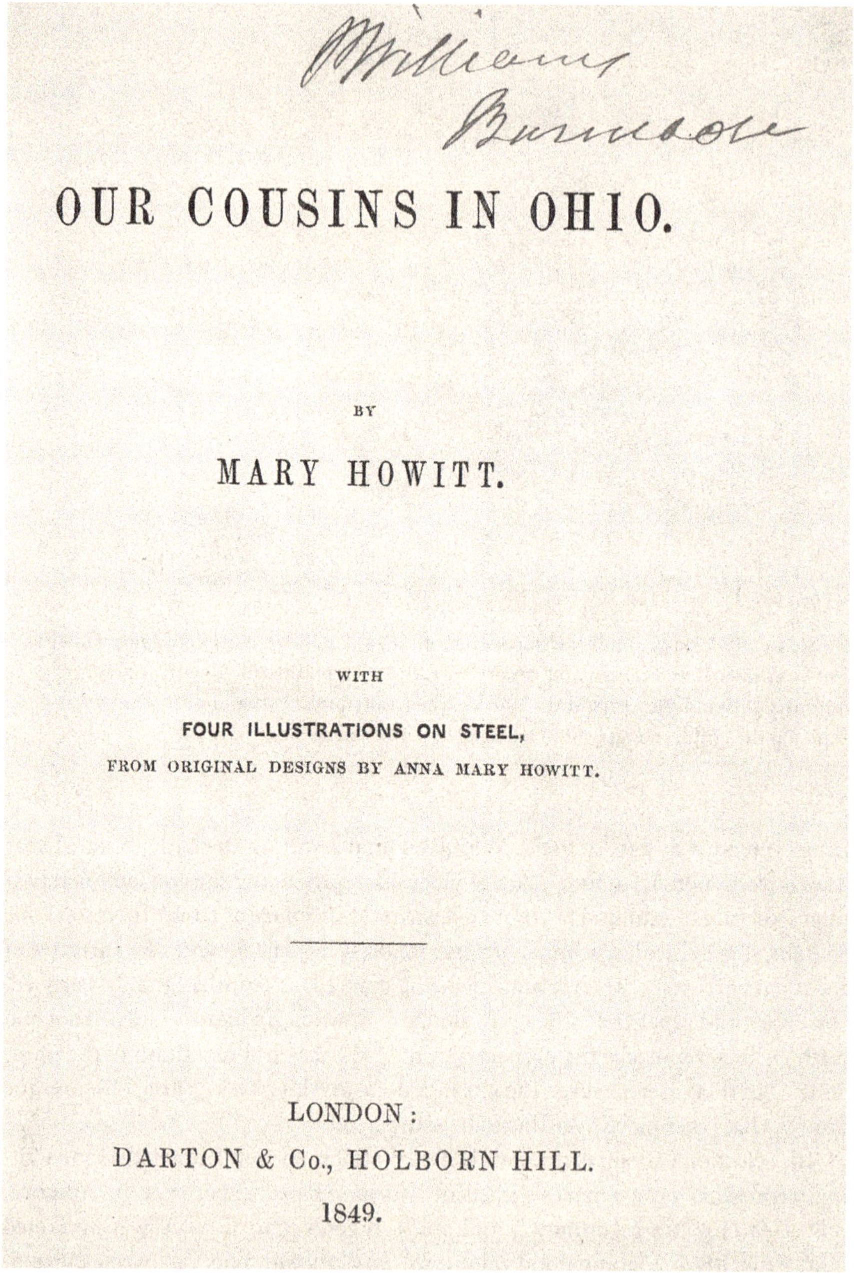

OUR COUSINS IN OHIO.

BY

MARY HOWITT.

WITH

FOUR ILLUSTRATIONS ON STEEL,

FROM ORIGINAL DESIGNS BY ANNA MARY HOWITT.

LONDON:

DARTON & Co., HOLBORN HILL.

1849.

Figure 25. Title page from *Our Cousins in Ohio* (London, 1849). Only the English editions included the four engravings from drawings by Anna Mary Howitt. Courtesy of Louisiana State University.

Figure 26. *Willie & Nanny Carry Home the Black Snake*, engraving from a drawing by Anna Mary Howitt, in *Our Cousins in Ohio* (London, 1849), opposite frontispiece. Alderson's and Howitt's fascination with this big snake may be connected to their having read and written about Charles Waterton's *Wanderings in South America* (London, 1825), in which large snakes feature prominently. See p. 326 for Alderson's description of this scene. Courtesy of Louisiana State University.

Figure 27. *Arrival of the American Jumper*, engraving from a drawing by Anna Mary Howitt, from *Our Cousins in Ohio* (London, 1849), opposite p. 42. See p. 301 for Alderson's description of this scene. Courtesy of Louisiana State University.

Figure 28. *Dr. Jack's Death Bed*, engraving from a drawing by Anna Mary Howitt, from *Our Cousins in Ohio* (London, 1849), opposite p. 89. Oddly, neither Alderson's actual children nor their counterparts in *Our Cousins* attended Dr. Jack at his deathbed. Courtesy of Louisiana State University.

Figure 29. *Willie Finds the Lost Cows*, engraving from a drawing by Anna Mary Howitt, from *Our Cousins in Ohio* (London, 1849), opposite p. 213. Interestingly, this incident seems to have been invented by Howitt for *Our Cousins* to explain a peculiar change of heart in favor of the children on the part of a formerly irritable neighbor. Courtesy of Louisiana State University.

retained in *Our Cousins*, but they are largely isolated in the frame of the pastoral year from any particular historical events.

Although there is no reason to think that Alderson would have objected to her sister's work, the letters give us a much more complex picture of an immigrant woman in antebellum Ohio: a mother and a housewife, but also a sister, a naturalist, an abolitionist, a Quaker, and a writer negotiating the intersections of these identities through her writing. When she tells William Howitt in December 1845 that her account "may prove somewhat novel & interesting being a detail of *a country life in America*" (see page 264; emphasis added), it is clear from her use of the indefinite article that Alderson is thinking, like a writer, of a readership and its general interests. By the middle of 1846, the possibility of professional authorship begins to appear very real, if still remote: "I have had some visions of a sofa & dinner service &c. if this should really ever prove worth thy trouble of arranging & publishing, but am not very sanguine on this head" (see page 336). The following year, Alderson is making her own editorial suggestions and requests, including that her sister not "give the real names of the grown persons at least. It would do as well to alter them & might be like telling tales," adding that "I intend to continue it: two years thrown into one will be fuller of incident" (see page 405). Generously, perhaps, Howitt represents *Our Cousins* as being largely the work of her sister, but as the letters make evident, that work as it appeared in print obscures much of Alderson's *real* work and a good deal of her identity.

The End

Our Cousins begins and ends with Christmas tableaux of domestic cheer, reproducing what Jude Piesse has called "the recurring trope of the emigrant's nostalgic vision of England on Christmas day."[20] Sadly, Alderson's life in America did not end as happily as her sister's narrative. Since the difficult and premature birth of Ann Alice in 1844, two more pregnancies had ended in either stillbirth or miscarriage. In 1847, she was expecting another child, though this time she seems to have made no mention of the fact to her mother or sisters, perhaps wishing to avoid again having to send sad news, should that be necessary. All we know of the birth and death comes from Harrison's letter to Ann Botham a few days after her death (but before the subsequent death of the child). As a memorial, I have chosen to end the collection with this letter, the only one in whose composition Emma took no part.

The last few years of her life had seen a deepening of the friendship between the Alderson family and the Taylor family, consisting of brothers Abraham, James, and Joseph and sister Hannah. She had called them "the very personification of affection & kindness" (see page 214). Emma preferred the more serious Abraham, but the "gay young" Joseph, a practicing physician, was the favorite of Harrison, under whose influence Joseph grew, Emma noted, "much more thoughtful & serious & to me far more interesting" (see page 347). Emma always admired the Taylors for the unostentatious generosity with which they shared their wealth, and years later Joseph Taylor would endow Bryn Mawr College, the first institution for women in America to offer postgraduate degrees.[21] Perhaps at the time he had in mind his old friend Emma Alderson, who had been such an advocate for education, though she herself had been deprived of any formal education. She would certainly have appreciated this generous act.

On Friday, December 3, Emma went into premature labor as she had before, and at 3:00 the next afternoon she gave birth to a boy who seemed likely to survive. It was her most difficult birth yet, and for several days afterward her condition vacillated as she was treated by an unnamed doctor, who gave repeated assurances that she was likely to pull through. After two weeks of suffering, Emma took a turn for the worse, and the Aldersons called for their friend Joseph Taylor.

On Wednesday, December 15, Taylor "made his way" via a circuitous route from Cincinnati to their home, heavy rains having caused the Ohio River to flood and cut off the usual roads.[22] Taylor's prognosis was less optimistic than that of the first doctor, but Emma was well enough to share with Harrison "some serious & deeply interesting conversation." She told him that she had anticipated these difficulties and that she had found herself dwelling on a passage from Psalm 61, "lead me to the Rock that is higher than I" (see page 452). The night passed reasonably well, but the next day she became worse, and that afternoon she passed away. In her journal for that day, on the other side of the Atlantic, Anna Harrison reported that she had had a prophetic dream (the fourth of its kind), in which some "dear spiritual friend" appeared to her among a crowd of people in "lands beyond the great waters of an ocean immeasurable." She awoke with a sensation of "peaceful trust" and, in her mind, the same Psalms passage that had formed her sister's last recorded words.[23]

Letters, 1846 to 1847

37. To Margaret and Herbert Howitt [from William Charles Alderson], January 1 to 8, 1846

Cedar Lodge 1st mo 1st 1846

Dear Cousins,

This has been such a Merry Christmas that I think a history of it is worth sending you. It is not like what you spend in England: we have no holly & ivy in our windows, nor do I see any in the windows about; I see no plum puddings & but little roast beef; \we hear/ no carol singers nor any guisers or Moris dancers, but there are plenty of great roast turkeys & haunches of vension & mince pies & dough nuts and sausages by hundreds of yards and quails & geese & candy & cakes & toys & books and I will tell you all <u>our</u> adventures.

On christmas eve we went to bed & left our shoes & socks under the sofa, though I myself had no faith in St Nicholas coming, but Agnes & Annie believed he would, & so I thought mine might just stand by theirs. Well, in the morning all was empty & silent, & mother said the shoes were too dirty for any goodies to be found in them. She said she heard a great crack in the night & Agnes thought it must have been Santa Claus running away & ~~she~~ \besides Agnes/ said something had scratched her nose in the night, & sure enough it looks very queer, as if it had been clawed.

But after breakfast there was the little table standing & an apron over it & when Father came in there was a fine treat for us each: a large plate full of cakes & candy & sugar horses & eagles & almonds & raisins & sugar kisses with mottoes from cousin Elizabeth & Hannah Taylor & a knife for me that Father bought & a slate & pencil & nice silk apron from mother for Agnes & a slate for Annie with a nice merry book ~~for An.~~ Dear me, how rich we all felt & what a fine thing it was to look them all over & even little Alice had a cap & some biscuits & besides there was so much to spare that we took the two little babies at William's a paper full of cakes and Lott's two children each a parcel of all sorts of things, & so all the little people round would be as happy as we.

The next morning it was rather remarkable that our shoes, which we left clean & bright, were full of kisses, but I do think it was mother's doing. Agnes was very busy making a present for Ella; she sent her fip down to the town & got a pretty piece of print & then made an apron or long sleeved pinafore of it for Ella's \doll/ & mother worked a pretty ball & gave it to me to give to Charley Shipley [2] & Annie sent Marshall some cakes & so we packed them all up & sent them on New Year's day directed to Charles Shipley & Co. \These three children have each lost their mother poor things./

Agnes went down with Father & mother to meeting & they went to dine at a house where there was a party of 18 little children & they had a grand table set out with apples & cakes & figs & almonds & raisin & candies &

kisses, & there was a large iced cake more than half a yard across with two pretty sugar birds upon it in the centre & lemonade to drink; she said it looked so grand.

The kind Friend sent Annie & me a great heap & mother set them on the supper table & we had a very fine treat, but what was better, Ella sent Agnes such a pretty book: I should think there are hundreds of pictures in it, & Annie had a new book too. I drew on the slate a carriage & horse & man. Father says it is very good. I am trying to draw very naturally, & mother thinks I improve. Father read to us in dear Aunt Mary's Birds & Flowers. I like it very much.

I fed the little pigs & the great hogs when Father was away. Father brought home two haunches of venison that some kind friends in the city gave him and this reminds me that in the cold weather William told us that one morning he saw a wild beast at the spring, and it leapt over the fence with its long thin legs, so we thought it must be a deer, perhaps pressed by hunger to come in search of food, & our oats in the orchard tempted it.

[January] 2nd. We were to have killed our hogs but it was so wet & stormy the butcher did not come, but Father discovered the pillars of the corn cribs had given way & it was in danger of coming down, so Frederic Lotte came, & Father & he were very busy fixing it.

I read & did accounts & my geography, played at ball with Agnes & Annie. Mother gave us each an apple; I was so silly as to grumble because mine was least & so mother took it from me. Dear little Annie was sadly troubled & cut hers in two & gave me one half & I lent her my knife & kissed her for being so kind. I certainly will try not to be so foolish again.

Father read to us this evening in Robinson Crusoe about his shipwreck & being cast on the island.

Frederic Lotte said two little girls were burnt to death at Warsaw last week, & one was burried at the chappel on first day. How shocking.

[3] [January] 3rd. This afternoon Father rode down to the city, & just as we were quietly getting our tea he returned, bringing Joseph [Evans]'s Father & Mother & Sister. Now of course you do not know that Josey and his brothers are three little boys near Waynesville & I got very intimate with them when I went there with Father & Mother last summer.[1] Poor George had broke his arm in falling out of a pear tree three days before, but for all that we were very merry. We went down to the Miami and watched the men fishing & then we ran ~~down~~ on to their mill & saw the Castor Oil press & the place where they crushed linseed & afterwards we made caves in the dry gravel bank & little Josey worked better with his hands than we could with spades & you must know that they have two very large orchards with plenty of fruit & they have forty hogs to kill this winter: they are the largest & fattest I ever saw.

1. See pages 445–447 for a lengthy description of this visit and the Evans family.

It is a beautiful place where they live, overlooking the valley of the little Miami, and beyond are pleasant hills with pretty woods. In the valley the railway to Lima ~~comes~~ is laid, & we saw the engines & trains.

[January] 4th. We went down to Meeting. In the evening, Father read to us in the bible & I said all the pieces of poetry I know. I took little Annie on my knee & tried to teach her about Gen. Ad<??> but she is a poor scholar & will not sit still long enough to learn anything. I put on my new pantaloon & it was so bright & warm that I did not need my cloak. The ice is mostly gone from the Ohio & we saw a steam-boat once again coming to the city, but there were men & boys skating on the canal &, first day as it was, men were packing up ice for summer on the river bank.

[January] 5th. This has been a very fine day: the sun shone out as warm and bright almost as summer \use/ & the country looked so beautiful with a thin blue haze in the distance. I was very busy: first I husked corn & then I threw the load of wood that W[illiam] hauled last week into the woodhouse & at 12 o'clock Father & I went down to the city with the waggon & horses for a barrel of flour & there I met Charles Carpenter. He is about my age & we had a fine romp in his father's warehouse & watched a man mending a canal boat. He was thrusting hemp into the seams & then tarring it over.

[January] 6 7 8th. The weather has been so wet & dull that we are obliged to stay in the house almost entirely. I have been cutting out little boats with my new knife & find them swim well, but alas I have broken both blades, not, however, so much as that I cannot use them.

We made up a parcel for our little Friends the Warders; I sent Reuben a marble bag, Annie sent a ball to Jane, & Agnes made a doll's pinafore & sun bonnet for Bessie & there was a needle-book for Hannah.

The roads are very deep & muddy & the river is covered with masses of floating ice. Agnes & Annie went to meeting [4] & Cousin Elizabeth gave them each a pretty picture. Father has read a deal to me in Robinson Crusoe; I often wish I had been with him in his island.

Now, these dull days when nothing happens,[2] I will tell you a piece of poetry we have been learning. It is the lament of a Virginian slave for her daughters sold into Southern bondage[3]

Gone, gone, sold and gone
To the rice swamp, dark and lone,
Where the slave-whip ceaseless swings,

2. The punctuation leaves it ambiguous whether the phrase "now these dull days when nothing happens" modifies this sentence or the previous one. I find the former more consistent with what I understand of William Charles's usual manner, but neither would be inappropriate.

3. What follows is a selection of lines (perhaps transcribed from memory) from John Greenleaf Whittier's "The Farewell of a Virginia Slave Mother to Her Daughters Sold into Southern Bondage."

Where the noisome insect stings
Where the Fever Demon strews
Poison with the falling dews
Where the sickly sunbeams glare
Through the hot and misty air,
There no mother's eye is near them
There no mother's ear can hear them
Never when the torturing lash
Seams their back with many a gash
Shall a mother's kindness bless them
Nor a mother's arms caress them
x x x
By the holy love He beareth
By the bruised reed He spareth
Oh! may He to whom alone
All our countless wrongs are known [original is "cruel wrongs"]
Still their hope & refuge prove
With a more than mother's love

It is a fearful thing to the poor slaves of the middle states to be sent South & is often the punishment inflicted by their masters for absconding or for any other \great/ offence. We had a poor woman once living with us who had been a slave in Georgia & she gave a dismal account of their sufferings.[4] She paid 260 dollars for her freedom and at last ran away with her little son whom her old mistress used to threaten to send back into Georgia. She used to tell us how she took him one night & hid herself & him in a stable. It was very dark & rainy & there they \lay/ through the following day & heard the people in search of them & when all was quiet at night again, she dressed the boy in girl's clothes & through heavy rain away they went & got on board a boat in the river. Then they traveled through the country till, very weary & cold, they called at a little country tavern. The man was a kind abolitionist & took them & kept them a long time.

Paul she left there to assist in the stables & \she/ came to the city to get work. Paul was once with us for three weeks; he is a fine little fellow & is now gone a hundred miles off to Columbus to learn to be a shoemaker. His mother loves him better than anything in the world & he loves her dearly; one day he set out to come and see his mother for he said he could not live any longer without her, but fortunately someone that knew him met him & persuaded him to go back [1-*cross*] and could not be prevailed on to accept any remuneration for all his kindness. I wish I could tell you another of his adventures in this line at the house of a rich widow in Virginia, but I must conclude.

4. See pages 184–185 for a more detailed account of Adelle, or Ada.

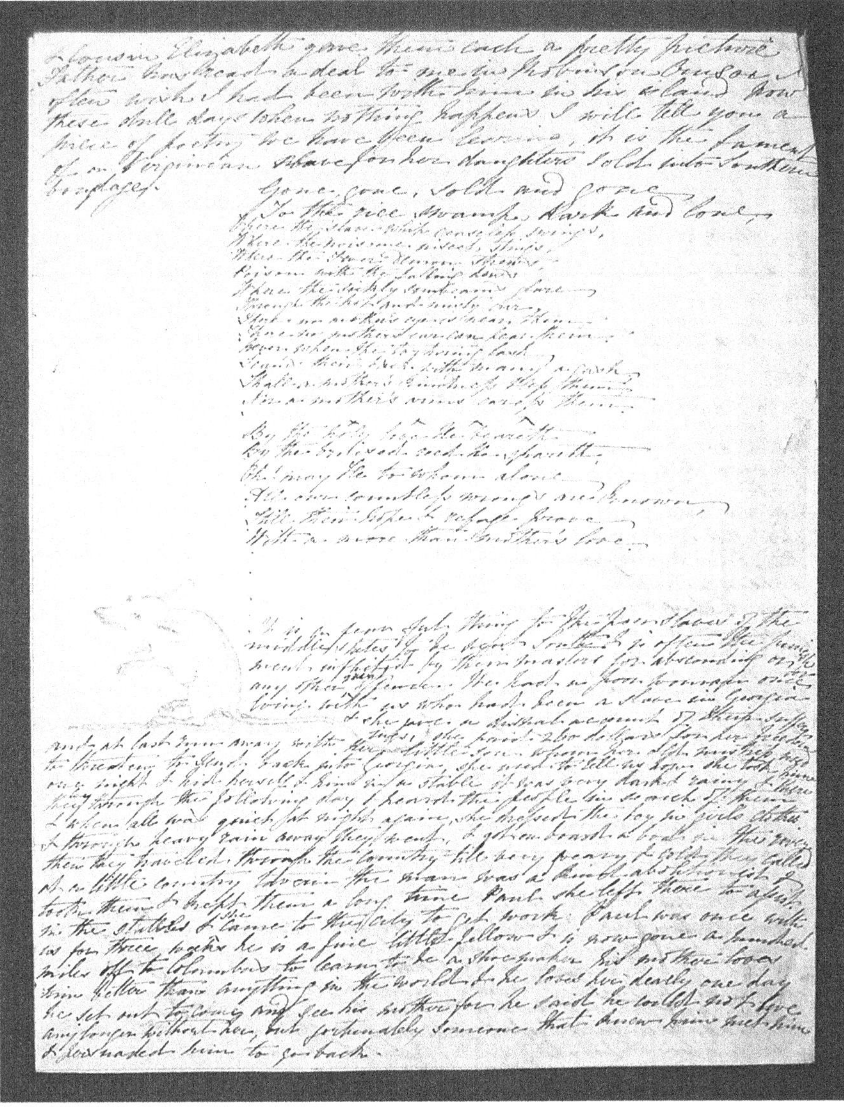

Cousin Elizabeth gave them each a pretty picture
Father has read a deal to me in Robinson Crusoe I
often wish I had been with him in his island now
these dull days when nothing happens I will tell you a
piece of poetry we have been learning, it is the lament
of a Virginian Slave for her daughters sold into Southern
bondage.

Gone, gone, sold and gone
To the rice swamp dank and lone,

[illegible]

Figure 30. Emma Alderson's drawing of a mouse appears in the first of the letters from William Charles (#37). For some reason the description of the mouse appears in the second of his letters (#38), in an entry dated January 9, 1846. Ht/18/1, Correspondence of Mary Howitt (1799–1888), Manuscripts and Special Collections, University of Nottingham.

I hope you will excuse this letter about nothing but ~~hope~~ you know little people like us cannot have a deal to tell. Please give mother's dear love to grandmother & you all & accept a great deal of love from myself & sisters. Your affectionate cousin,

William Charles Alderson

38. To Margaret and Herbert Howitt [from William Charles Alderson], January 9 to 20, 1846

[January] 9th. This morning as I was standing in the kitchen just before we sate down to breakfast, something came plump into a bowl of water that was standing on the table, & what should it be but a little mouse, one of the prettiest things you ever saw. They call them jumping mice, and jumping they are, for they leap yards at a bound. They might be called the kangaroo mouse as they are formed like them with short fore ~~legs~~ & very long hind legs. I will tell you what Peter Parley says about them soon. We have a [great] many in the house & barns; sometimes they run across my bed, & now & then we catch a glimpse of them in the day time. We have tried to draw the little fellow that was so clever this morning, but he looks in our picture as if he has hurt his paw & was asking you to pity him.[5]

Peter Parley's account is <?> "This little animal is very remarkable for the great length of its hind legs & its mode of progression, in both of which it bears some resemblance to the kangaroo of Australia & the jerboa of the old continent.

"It is found in America from Canada to Pennsylvania & no doubt still farther south, it is in size nearly the same as the common mouse. The head, back & upper parts of the body generally are of a reddish brown colour, somewhat resembling yellow. There is a similar species of mouse in Labrador and the Hudson's Bay country."[6]

A friend of father's rode up to see us this afternoon; he has been in the East Indies & seen Elephants & rode upon them & seen the tiger hunts, & he told me he saw a great shark caught at sea & that it lay three hours flapping its great strong tail upon the ship's deck. ~~but~~ It was not strong enough to beark it in but it made a terrible noise. He told us that last week a live Buffalo was brought to the city from the Yellow Fork on the Missouri river. It was a very large one & was killed & its flesh sold as a great rarity.

[January] 10th. To day we have had a sad slaughtering; our three fat pigs were killed; the butcher shot them. I believe they did not suffer at all as they each fell immediately & did not even squeak. They made a large fire in the barn yard & heated great stones red hot to put into the water to scald them. Now we have only three little pigs left, but we have a beautiful little red & white calf & two cows & a great calf & two horses & about 25 hens & Agnes' guinea fowl, and Milo, a great buff & white mastif, who looks like a sweet, gentle swan, always clean & neat, & my own little pet Fanny, the prettiest little

5. The drawing appears in the previous letter. See figure 30.
6. Samuel L. Goodrich [Peter Parley, pseud.], *Tales about Animals* 3rd ed. (London: T.T. and J. Tegg, 1837), 169, https://books.google.com/books?id=VRlMAQAAMAAJ. This popular book went through numerous editions through the nineteenth century. None that I have consulted matches the language here exactly, so there is no way of knowing which edition they were reading. See note to letter # 21.

yellow rat dog you ever saw. Joseph Taylor gave it me last summer; she was a funny little puppy then, but she has grown very handsome & we all love her. She is so cunning that when she sees the chickens about the house she chases them to the barn yard gate but never offers to touch them. We have also a cat & that sums up our live stock at present.

The two last days have been very busy making sausages and <such> like, but we children, being more in the way than of use, found it somewhat dull. I shelled about half a bushel of corn, but what is that compared with the work of some boys. Icles' boy told me when I went an errand there he had a waggon load of corn to shell & wood to chop beside before he went to bed & [2a] yet he took time to string my bow, which David Solo, the butcher, gave me, which I thought very kind.

[January] 14th. To day Anna Mary went down with Father & mother to ~~play~~ pay a visit to the city. Agnes & I staid at home & amused ourselves as well as we could. William put us \up/ a swing in the wood house, a thing that we have long wanted & which we shall find a source of much enjoyment I expect.

[January] 16th. This afternoon Father & Mother came home & very glad we were to see them & to hear Annie's account of their journey, but first I must tell you they brought the long looked [3a] for package of books and Oh, what delight we had in opening it. They brought us oranges & cake from Hannah Taylor, but to see those beautiful new books was far better to me. The little table was brought, that dear little table on which our christmas gifts were laid out & on which stands the candle when we read pleasant stories in an evening, & while mother was untying the string little Annie danced round them ~~same table~~ for joy like a savage round his fire. I laughed & we all laughed to see her.

Now I cannot [2b][7] tell you how happy ~~thy~~ your dear Father & mother have made us. Anna Mary, whose heart is full of love to all in her long catalogue of those she knows with especial affection, always sums up with ["]and I love dear Aunt Mary as much as all the world["] & we have good reason to love her. How many a time have we listened by the hour with delight to her stories & now we have a fresh supply, all so charming & pleasant, both outside & inside. I wish we could send you something that would please you as much and make you understand how grateful we all are.

What would you think of making a dinner of grey squirrils? Perhaps, like me, you would think it such a pity to see their slender little limbs cut up & fried in [3b] a pan that you would not enjoy them at all to eat. I remember the bright sunshine & the pleasant woods where in summer we see them bounding from tree to tree, & how active & full of business they are in the

7. This sheet has been filled differently from that of the other letters, with the address on the third page instead of the fourth. It also fills the pages in a different sequence, sometimes jumping back and forth between pages. My notation for this letter is intended to suggest the different portions of the page on which each portion of the letter is written.

Fall when acorns & hickory nuts & beech nuts are ripe. You must be very clever to find a sound one left under the trees, because the grey squirrils & chitty monks, or ground squirrils, are always on the spot & nothing escapes their vigilant little eyes, but all are carried off to their storehouses, a fine and ample store against the dreary winter time. When all this comes to my mind I have little comfort in what many think a great luxury, & so because people will buy them & eat them, they are shot & brought to market, [4] and Anna Mary says they had some one day to dinner when she was in the city.

They went to call upon a friend at whose house was a lady with a little boy; he was a fine handsome little fellow that the lady had taken out of the Orphan Asylum and adopted him as her own. There were himself & two little sisters &, as their father & mother were both dead \and they were poor & had no friends,/ they were sent to the Orphan asylum, but, however, they have all been adopted into families, and \may be/ happy I hope, but I think what the old miller said to Jack is very true "there's nothing like a father and mother in all this world."[8] However, these people must be very kind to this little boy, for when they found he felt lonely & wanted a companion, they went to the asylum & fetched a little girl to bring up with him. What a pity it was they did not take one of his own sisters at the first & then they might have grown up together as if they had still been in their father's house. Oh how much we should love our little sisters; what a miserable thing it would be to be seperated like these poor children & never meet \again/ perhaps, or only as strangers one to the other.

In passing along Fifth street Father says they saw at a foundry a great iron cage; it is 12 feet long, 11 wide & 8 high and looks like an enclosure for a grizzly bear and his family or may be for a generation of hyenas; but no it is for an appendage to a jail in Louisiana, and it makes one's blood curdle to think what an instrument of cruelty it may become in those horrible southern States, where slavery has hardened men's hearts \so/ that compassion is an alien to their nature, and human suffering & human life ~~a~~ things unheeded.

[January] 18. Whilst we were at meeting the fire-bells rung & Oh what a noise & riot there is in the streets when the engines go rattling past. Men & boys shouting fire, the bells ringing, hailing through trumpets, and making such a discord that one might fancy an army of Indians was at hand with their terrible war whoop, and this is occurring night & day. When they were in the city, there were two alarms: one night it was a gambling house which had been burnt down a while ago, was rebuilt & again destroyed intentionally & so they go on. Sometimes the fires are accidental but as often intentional. There are fire companies & engine houses in every part of the city & some think it is ~~sometimes~~ done by bad people to give them an opportunity

8. William Howitt, *The Life and Adventures of Jack of the Mill* (London: Longman, Orme, Brown, Green, and Longmans, 1844), 11. William Charles may be quoting from memory since the word "all" does not appear in the original.

to steal. But if you could see the fire companies parade the streets as they do one day in summer in beautiful uniform, thousands of them with music & garlands & their engines glittering with polished brass & rich colors of scarlet & green or blue, you would think as I did it was a very animating & splendid sight, and yet people say the more fire companies there are the more fires, and so I suppose it is.

[January] 19. It has been a bright cold day, the snow is upon the ground & sisters & I played with our new sled that Richard made for us. I dragged them down the little hill towards the vines. We call our sled the Swallow's wing. I have often seen the boys with pretty painted ones: one was called the Wasp, another the Belle of the West.

Father has read a deal to us in Jack of the Mill & very much I like it.

[January] 20th. Father's dear friend Joseph Taylor has been spending two days with us. It has been dismal weather; yesterday it rained & froze until the trees were cased with ice & looked as [2c] though they were transformed into glass. When the sun or moon shines upon them in this state, they have a very brilliant & fairyland appearance, but last night was dark & gloomy & as we sate by the wood fire burning brightly upon the hearth \& heard the storm without/ we thought of benighted travellers & houseless wanderers & Joseph Taylor told us some things that I think will interest you.

He said he was on the Ohio & wished to land on the Scioto river.[9] It was midnight when the steam boat passed & he was landed from a little skiff. It was exceedingly dark & rained hard, but with his carpet bag in his hand he made his way through the mud till stopped by the high bluff. Here he could find no way of ascending, but rambling one, he managed to get up the slippery bank &, coming at a fence, followed it till he came to a log cabin. He roused the people & begged for shelter, but they told him they were all sick in the fever & neither could nor would admit him. They told him the direction of the next house, towards which he made his way. The man of the house, in answer to his request, which had assumed almost command for entrance, [said] that indeed his case was so sad, though his wife & children were sick, he would do the best he could for him. So he took him in, built up his fire, & spreading some clothes on the floor, took his children out of the bed & told him to lie down on it. There was but one room, so that the ~~husband &~~ \poor/ wife was in the other corner. However, they had a comfortable night's rest & in the morning the man set out the breakfast table & invited Joseph to partake. The fare was so coarse & poor that he said an involuntary feeling of discontent & almost disgust arose in his mind, but the father's fervent thanksgiving for all so reproved him that he felt humbled & instructed. The man lent him his horse to go about the country.[10]

9. A tributary joining the Ohio River at what is now Portsmouth, Ohio.
10. No continuation of this letter exists.

39. To Mary Howitt, February 15 to 21, 1846

I feel, my beloved Sister, as though I might almost justly stand charged with ingratitude in not sooner answering thy most welcome, and I may say long looked for, letter, but dear sister, I find at present so much difficulty in writing or reading on account of my eyes that I know thou wilt excuse me entirely when I tell thee the cause. This is one of the few times I allowed the last Packet to sail without conveying a letter to some or other of you, but as I find myself somewhat better I will avail myself of the opportunity & prepare early for the next chance.

How greatly, my beloved sister, are we indebted to you for the noble present of books which came after some delay safe to hand & what a treat I have had in reading them, till one afternoon whilst reading the President's Daughters I was seized with a dimness & have been unable to read any more since.[11] Yet do not be alarmed; my sight on the whole is good though rather weak. The complaint is solely in the eyelids & I am going to put myself under medical care for it & hope soon to be quite relieved.

Those books are to me a great enjoyment; I trace in some of the characters ~~the~~ a resemblance to some or other of our dear friends & acquaintance & I have thought it will be a delightful way of making thee acquainted with them to introduce them under their names.

The Author's daughter I read with intense interest & am glad to find it is a universal favourite. Everybody tells me they are delighted with it & could not lay it down till finished. To me it was peculiarly interesting because in Frank Lawford & his home I thought I could see a sketch of William & your abode & style of living, & then Mr. [2] Latimer is the most finished model of our own, I may say my, friend Abraham Taylor, because I never felt such an admiration & friendship for any one as I do for him out of our own family & connexions, the same inaccessible dignity, the same condescending kindness & nobleness of heart & mind, combined with the utmost simplicity, so that henceforward he is Mr. Latimer & as such thou must feel an interest in him for me.[12]

Then I have a dear friend Elise, \one of/ the loveliest women I ever saw. She has her weaknesses as well as perfections and is altogether a sweet creature whose beautiful, delicate countenance I love to look upon & who is with a refinement that sometimes renders the small trials of every-day life the means of accute suffering, yet in the beautiful order of her well aranged home & in the superior bearing & management of her children, shows a mind of no common order.[13] She & her husband are the only decidedly literary

11. Frederika [*sic*] Bremer, *The President's Daughters: Including Nina*, trans. Mary Howitt, 3 vols. (London: Longman, Brown, Green, and Longmans, 1843), https://books.google.com/books?id=QFhVAAAAYAAJ.
12. Mary Howitt, *The Author's Daughter: A Tale* (Boston: Waite, Peirce, 1845).
13. No other mention is made of Elise, her family, or her cousin, "Sophia."

people I am acquainted with, and at their house I see all the modern literature of the day & hear subjects discussed and meet with specimens of scientific research that others do not trouble themselves with; there is always in the depth of winter a basket of sweet hot house flowers, a rare plant, or a beautiful cluster of evergreens on the parlour table.

They have a cousin residing with them whom I must introduce to thee as "Sophia," an enthusiast in nature & botany & one whose whole life seems to be spent in being useful to others & promoting the happiness of those around her; she is rather past the bloom of youth yet like Sarah of old "a very fair woman." When she heard I was sending a parcel to you by Josiah Forster, she set to & made a couple of acorn pincushions for Anna Mary & Margaret. So they must accept them as a small remember- [3] ances of the ready kindness of my friend "Sophia" than as anything very worthy in themselves. The cups were gathered in the woods of Ceasar's Creek, a wild & picturesque spot. I have sent thee a packet of seeds, various in kind as thou wilt see, most of which I gathered in our own garden. I hope they will grow; Anna Mary's packet was given to me by Elise's husband. Dear Mother will find a few specimens of Ohio shells & a parcel of dried tomatoes from Harrison. I hope, if you like these, to send you a large quantity & also, if practicable, a keg of tomato ketchup; I think it the best sauce for fish, hashes &c. I ever tasted. I have an idea both these might be made a profitable article of exportation.

Thank God, for to Him alone can I ascribe the praise for the proposed measures of government.[14] Oh I sometimes fear it is too good ever to be accomplished, that some fatal accident may interpose between you & us & the proposed good. I am rejoiced that corn-meal is already introduced & that by this means an immediate supply of good wholesome food is provided for the poor. Did Wm receive a hasty letter on its domestic use which I sent perhaps six weeks ago[?] Little did I think at that time its introduc was so near at hand. I think I shall regard with tenfold gratitude the bright sun & genial shower & abundant productiveness of this favoured country because I shall know that my own dear native land will profit by the great good; I have sometimes looked round on our rich fruits & many, many blessings & thought, Oh they only give me ~~only~~ half pleasure because those I love best cannot partake.

We have had a very severe winter, most intense & continued frost & an unusual quantity of ice & snow, yet it may be that our spring and summer may be even more beautiful & abundant in consequence. We hope this year to be spared the late frosts which cut off the two last seasons our [4] peaches & great part of the apples. I have sent thee two kinds of squash, or sweet pumpkin, of which we make cheesecakes, and very superior we think them, both for pies and as a vegetable. We cut them when ripe in slices, take out

14. In January 1846, responding to the famine in Ireland, Prime Minister Robert Peel had proposed modifying the Corn Laws. His own Conservative Party was furious, but he persisted, and on May 15, 1846, they were repealed.

the seeds & pare off the rind & boil them till they will mash to a fine pulp; when eaten as vegetable a little butter, pepper & salt are added. They are tender when young & even here require to be protected from the late frosts by hand glasses. I think you might raise the water- & other melons so far as to make them, when green, into preserves; they are equal, I think, to preserved ginger when well done. I shall send thee a good authentic receipt before it is too late in the season, but gave away my American receipt book the other day & have not yet replaced it. If I can, I will send thee a copy; it would be useful in many things.

I do hope, dearest Mary, thou wilt see Josiah Forster & George Stacy, who are both your neighbours; they have promised to call upon dear mother, and I think thou canst not fail to be pleased with them for their kindness & intelligence. It is now a week since they left Cincinnati & their visit to us, though short, was a great treat. Someway I alway fancy that, except in a few rare instances, English friends are very superior to those of this country; there is a refinement and polish, a cultivation of mind & enlargement of views & feelings that is not characteristic of men here; they as Englishmen have a heart for all the world, & that few of the Americans possess; & yet I love them & feel grateful for unnumbered personal kindnesses, but it would please me better to see them making a few steps outward in overcoming the unreasonable prejudice against colour than to receive a cart load of favour in my own person.

[5] You will, I fear, think the letters of Wm Charles to his cousins silly, and yet the idea possessed me so much from hearing thee mention the Children's Year, that I thought I would risk it. I have found it to myself very interesting to watch the children—their little adventures & ways of doing & thinking—besides, if you want to be acquainted with them, I think it will be the most likely way of making you know their characters. I find, as our out of door life increases, more to interest & relate & perhaps in the end, dear Mary, it will be somewhat original to thee & them to know how children in America spend their days & what they think & say amidst such a new life.

Tell dearest mother I often think of her when I am writing for them & fancy, childish as it is, she will like to know how her grandchildren behave in their far distant home; I must write to her how my heart turns with love inexpressible at the thought of you. We often talk of you & Oh sometimes I feel as if I should take wing & fly across the Atlantic; if ever I have the means & am able, I will certainly pay you a visit. Give my dearest love to Danl & Anna & their family; I begin to think I must write thitherward & so I will soon, for I seem to have a deal to say to them.

Dear little Ann Alice is still a baby in arms; she was one of \the/ least children I ever saw, except perhaps thy Anna Mary, but now she is growing a fine rosy cheeked girl who rolls about amongst her playthings the day through & is as little trouble as ever child was that did not walk. Every body told me I should never raise her & I had many a grave hint not to set my heart upon her, [6] but after all I believe she is going to deceive the wise ones & prove a fine child as she is a sweet, dear one.

[February] 21st. I write from Mount Auburn where I am very pleasantly spending a little time with our dear kind relations the Shipleys. Cousin Ann is well & it is delightful to me to be with her; she reminds me so much of dear mother; she supplies her place to me as much as it is possible any one can do it, though there is no one like her to me. Cousin Phebe is a sweet woman, devoted to her family & friends; Poor Caroline [Shipley] is still the suffering invalid but patient, as lovely as ever.

Write to me, dearest sister, and tell Anna Mary I should love to have a letter from her; dear girl, how does she get on with her painting? I feel very much interested in her progress & often look at that likeness of dear mother she so kindly sent me. My endeared love to Mother, Wm & every member of thy family. I am most affectionately thy warmly attached sister,

Emma.

40. To Margaret and Herbert Howitt [from William Charles Alderson], January 28 to March 2, 1846

Dear Cousins,
It is now a week since we closed the last letter and not much of consequence has occurred. The weather has become very mild & pleasant & we have enjoyed it once again; to run on the turf & feel the bright warm sun and the soft vernal air is a great happiness. To be sure, we do not expect winter is quite gone, but these are the first visitations of spring, and delightful they are.

To day we were helping mother transplant some rosebushes; father is busy pruning the fruit trees, & sisters & I have had a great piece of work in dragging the branches to one place to store for peasticks. Yesterday when Agnes & I were at the gate a little short-legged white dog with black-ears & queer bluish spots upon its back joined us & when we drove it away it would not leave us, so we fed it & all to day it stays & looks as if it intended to make its home with us. It makes us think of the little badger hound, with the crookedest legs that ever were made,[15] & if it does stay we must give it a name. I think it shall be Timothy, so as our farm horse is Ben & we shall have a dog Timothy, we shall be something like Jack whose history has pleased us much. Father is reading Captain Fremont's journeys to the Rocky Mountains & Oregon. I mean to tell you some of their adventures.

2 mo. 1st. I have been chopping a pile of kindling wood to-day & sisters & I have fine romps in the hay loft. It is a very large place & we can jump & roll

15. A reference to the moralistic poem about the "Greyhound and Badger-hound," who "each in his different arts and ways / Deserved the master's love and praise." Otto Speckter, *The Child's Picture and Verse Book*, trans. Mary Howitt (London: Longman, Brown, Green, and Longmans, 1844), 157, https://books.google.com/books?id=nA5mAAAAcAAJ.

about famously. We go now & then to look for eggs there & sometimes we find nests hid in snug corners with eggs in them & very nice they look. To day we went into the hen house & saw a horrible sight: a poor hen torn to pieces mangled & bloody on the floor. We think some wild animal or perhaps a hawk found their way in & murdered her.

Little Timothy still stays with us. I love to play with him; poor fellow, he looks so meek & submissive & seems to say ["]please let me stop with you & I will be very good; I will not come into the house to dirty it nor do any think to displease you.["] Milo & Fanny walk in and out quite bold & careless as if they thought ["]we have a right & no body shall prevent us, we are the dogs of the house,["] whilst poor little Tim just peeps in at an open door, wags his tail & walks away. I beat fanny to-day for quarrelling with him.

Father was away to day & I had to feed the pigs, that is give them some cobs of corn; let the cows out to water; give the little calf hay & feed the chickens.

I forgot to tell you that on fifth-day when we came from meeting, we stuck fast in the mud twice & poor Farmer had hard work to drag us out, even when father went & pushed with all his might at the wheels, and now the bridge over Mill Creek is broken down & we cannot get with the carriage except on the most vilanous roads & by going a long way round even by them, so we shall have to stop at home, which after all is no great hardship: the days are delightful & we play out & help Father & Mother in gardening. Yesterday Father pruned his vines & dug about them & the young apple trees, & we are going to have a large piece of ground ploughed & prepared for planting many hundred vines.

Little Alice rolls from one end of the floor to the other & calls ["]dad dad["] & plays with playthings & is very amusing; we all think her a very pretty little girl. She has rosy cheeks & such pretty curling hair & her little eyes are as bright as two diamonds and yet look so soft & meek that we call her dove's eyes.

This evening Richard came up to see us. He brought mother a very nice mahogany Knife-box, his own work. He stayed all night, and the next morning we amused ourselves with looking over the beautiful engravings dear grandmother sent.

[February] 9th. Agnes had a great wash to-day, all her doll clothes, & I was very busy planting a little vinyard. We all went in the afternoon to Warsaw to take Annie's shoes to be mended. I daresay you think Warsaw must be a grand place: no, it is a small collection of houses [2] about half a mile from us, where there is a tavern, a store, a shoemaker's & a blacksmith's shop. We now & then go over & then we pass our kind Friend Mary Creole's [Crehoe's] house. We like to go & see her; she has a fine garden & orchard & sends us vegetables & flowers & we take others in return. She has a cat bird in one cage & a red bird in another & three or four canaries, and her horse she calls Barney & her cow Dolly & she raises turkeys & grafts trees & is as happy in her country occupations as can be; ~~but~~ she has no children, yet she is very good to us. Hers is a pretty house, white with a large broad piazza before the parlour, & the \green/ venetian shutters open upon it. Above, a fine large pear tree forms a fine screen from the sun; the kitchen end is lower & has roses growing round the windows & doors & at one end she has a fine young fig tree. It bore figs last summer.

[February] 10th. Joseph Taylor came up this afternoon to see Father, who has not been well. He brought me & Agnes each a guinea fowl. Another kind friend sent us some apple; we have many friends who are very good to us, and I think, as Annie sometimes says, we ought to be very thankful.

Before I leave Mary Creole I must tell you that her cow Dolly is of the Shaker persuasion. She was raised at the settlement of Union Village & has imbibed some of their prejudices: she has a great dislike to women & children, especially the latter and sometimes makes towards the fence at us as if she would like to give us a hook with her great horns. She is a fine creature; they gave 40 dollars for her, but Father says she is no better nor handsomer than our Pink who cost only 16.

[February] 12th. As Father is gone to the Quarterly Meeting, mother and I walked down to meeting. The road was dry and good & we had a pleasant walk. We saw on the river bank a sight that interested us much: they were hauling a steam boat on land to repair it & had 40 horses, 4 abreast to drag it out. Between each team the axle-tree & wheels of a waggon was fastened & when the boat left the water it was heaved upon huge rolers. It was a fine sight when at the signal "go ahead" the horses gave one mighty simultaneous pull & as though their limbs sinues & vertebrae were knit into a great leviathan, drew the ponderous weight a few yards onward. We often see a frame house or barn taking a journey in this manner.

The temporary bridge over Mill Creek is repaired. The stone-bridge was swept away last summer in a thunderstorm. When we first came there was an old covered wood bridge, but that was one night burnt down by a man whose horse's foot got fast in a hole & he was determined never again to be stopped by the same cause so he set fire to it before he rode home.

Mill Creek is a small tributary of the Ohio; it is said to be very beautiful in its course. As we see it, it is a very serpentine but rather dull stream as only a few solitary trees of button wood rear their white trunks & branches by its side. The forest with which the valley was once covered is gone & brick yards are in their place. I will copy you a song about this little river & the Indians that once hunted on the shores.[16] Mahketewa is the Indian name of the creek.

16. William D. Gallagher's "Spotted Fawn" (1845) was an immediate success when it was sung by S. B. Duffield in Cincinnati and sold as sheet music by Peters & Co. of Cincinnati. William T. Coggeshall, *The Poets and Poetry of the West* (Columbus, Ohio: Follett, Foster and Col, 1860) 144, https://books.google.com/books?id=QotDhcgByroC.

On Mahketewa's flowery marge
    The red chief's wigwam stood
When first the white man['s] rifle rang
    Loud through the echoing wood
The tomahawk and scalping knife
    Together lay at rest
for peace was in the forest shades
    And in the red-man's breast
        Oh, the Spotted Fawn!
        Oh the Spotted Fawn!
The light & life of the Forest shades
With the red-chief's child is gone.

By Mahketewa's flowery marge
    The Spotted Fawn had birth
And grew as fair an Indian girl
    As ever blest the earth
She was the red-chief's only child
    And sought by many a Brave
But to the gallant young White-Cloud
    Her plighted troth she gave
        Oh the Spotted Fawn &c.
From Mahketewa's flowery marge
    Her bridal song arose
[3] None dreaming in that festal night
    Of near encircling foes
But through the forest stealthily
    The white men came in wrath
And fiery deaths before them sped
    And blood was in their path
        Oh the Spotted Fawn &c.

On Mahketewa's flowery marge
    Next morn, no strife was seen
But a wail went up where the
        young Fawn's blood
    With White Cloud's dyed the green
And burial in their own rude way
    The Indians gave them there
While a low & sweet-toned requiem
    The brooks sang and the air
    Oh, the Spotted Fawn
        Oh the Spotted Fawn
The light & life of the Forest shades
With the red-chief's child is gone.

In walking down to the city I got very footsore & as mother had to come next day to attend a funeral I stayed at cousin Elizabeth Taylor's. The next day Abraham Taylor took me to a store & bought some oranges & ground nuts for sisters. These ground nuts are brought from the south; they are like two cornels enclosed in a thin shell. They are roasted before they are eaten & taste something like cocoa nibs. Abraham Taylor drove us home in the evening.

For the last fortnight we have had such dismal weather, such constant storms of snow & sleet, such biting cold winds & intense frost, that we have kept very close to the house.

The English friends have been to see us and we have been collecting seeds & shells for them and have sent you some by them.

One day sisters & I went over to Mary Creole's to fetch some pop corn. I wish we could send you & dear little cousins at Liverpool a bushel: it is the prettiest sight to see it pop on a hot fire-shovel & look like the loveliest little white lilies. It is very good to eat in this state or made into pop-corn candy that is made into cakes ~~with~~ by pouring boiling toffee upon it when popped.

It is milder to-day & I have been round the fields with my sled. I thought if I had but Milo I might have caught a fine rabit. I see their tracks all over the snow. The birds are so tame that they come & pick up the crumbs close to the dining-room window. I saw a most beautiful pair of blue birds. I think you would admire them: they are so blue with bright cinnamon coloured breasts. We have a pair that build in a bird-box at the end of the carriage shed.

The catalpa trees look very beautiful to-day; their long pods are covered with a coating of ice & I thought as I looked at them they had the appearance of hundreds of little glass swords.

I wish you and I could read Capt Fremont's Narratives of his journeys to the Rocky Mountains & Oregon.[17] I know you would like them as much as I do. I seemed to live amongst buffalos & Indians for many day after reading it, but I must copy a few incidents to give you an idea of the work. They are travelling in Missouri 29th of June "A few miles brought us into the midst of the buffalo swarming in immense numbers over the plains, where they had left scarcely a blade of grass standing. Mr Preuss, who was sketching at a little distance in the rear, had at first noted them as large groves of timber. In the sight of such a mass of life the traveller feels a strange emotion of grandeur. We had heard from a distance a dull & confused murmuring & when we came in view of their dark masses there was not one among us who did not feel his heart beat quicker. It was the early part of the day when the herds are feeding and everywhere they were in motion. Here and there a huge old

17. John Charles Frémont, *Narrative of the Exploring Expedition to the Rocky Mountains in the Year 1842* (Washington, D.C.: Taylor, Wilde, 1840), https://books.google.com/books?id=AyoUAAAAYAAJ.

bull was rolling in the grass and clouds of dust rose in the air from various parts of the bands, each the scene of some obstinate fight.

Indians & buffalo~~s~~ make the poetry and life of the prairie, and our camp was full of their exhilaration. In place of the quiet monotony of the march, relieved by the crackin of the whip, and an avance donc, shouts and songs resounded from every part of the line, and our evening camp was always the commencement of a feast which terminated only with our departure on the following morning. At any time of the night, might be seen pieces of the most delicate and choicest meat roasting en appolas, on sticks around the fire, and the guard were never without company. With pleasant weather & no enemy to fear, an~~d~~ abundance of the most excellent meat, and no scarcity of bread or tobacco, they were enjoying the oasis of a voyageur's life. Three cows were killed today."

[4] 2nd of 3rd mo. This is a bright morning & the warm sun is melting the snow & making it run in torrents from the house tops & down every little ravine. We begin to look at the snow with something of the affection with which we regard autumn flowers. I have been digging & piling it with a feeling that perhaps it is our last chance this season.

I am going to send this by our Friend John Allen from Liskard in Cornwall, who has staid behind his company on account of ill health. I hope you will see these dear Friends: they can tell you a deal about us. How would you like a little more Buffalo hunting[?]

"July 1. As we were riding quietly along the bank of the river (the Nebraska or Platte River[)] a grand herd of buffalo, some seven or eight hundred in number came crowding [. . .]" *<The rest of the page, over 80 percent of it, is filled with quotation and summary of this great buffalo hunt.>*

I must now say farewell. Sister's dear love with mine to you & Uncle, Aunt, grandmother & the rest of our cousins. If you do not like my long letters send me word.

Your affectionate cousin, Wm Charles.

41. To Ann Botham, March 23, 1846

3rd mo. 23rd 1846

My beloved Mother,

I begin to look forward with impatience to the coming Packets, hoping to receive one of thy ever welcome letters. The last only brought us a British Friend~~s~~, but as it was directed by thy dear hand I took it as an assurance that all was well. It was cause of regret to me that I could not write to thee last month, but we were just preparing for the English Friends & my eyes were so weak that I could not write without much suffering; but now I am thankful to say they are better & by avoiding working in an evening I get on very well.

It was a real pleasure to us to see those dear friends; their home in the city was with our Friends the Taylors, but they came up and spent part of two days & a night with us. That is, Wm & Josiah Forster & George Stacy, & very rich did I feel whilst they were under our roof. They all enquired very particularly after thee, & Josiah Forster & George Stacy promised to call upon thee; they both attend your meeting. They kindly undertook to convey a small box containing a few trifles for you. I had intended to have sent thee a daguereotyped group consisting of our two selves & the children, but my eyes being so bad I did not think I was fit to present to you, but I hope to get one executed & sent by an early opportunity.

John Allen, the other Friend, was detained in Cincinnati a week after the others by indisposition & came up to see us afterwards. He is a nice man from Liskard in Cornwall & mentioned many Friends whose names were familiar to me from hearing thee speak of them. He also took a few seeds & a letter to the children, which were omitted before.

This has been a most severe winter & I think [2] our Friends must have suffered very much, travelling as they did in Illinois, Indiana & Iowa in the depth of winter when the Thermometer was often below zero, & none can imagine how cold it is when that is the case. But Spring is come & the weeping willows are in leaf & other trees begin to bud; the grass is become very green & we gather the early spring flowers in the woods. But the melting snows, of which there was an unusual quantity in the mountains, & heavy rains have swelled the rivers & covered them with drift wood, of which amazing quantities come down every time the waters are high.

Dearest Mother, I am quite distressed at the partizan spirit of the British Friend; I hope thou wilt not take their prejudice and really incorrect statements as any thing to be relied upon. We who are on the spot & know the facts of the case know that their representations respecting John Wilbur ~~to be~~ \are/ very far from correct & that instead of being the injured suffering man they would represent, he has been borne ~~with~~ & laboured with for upwards of 12 years. He was a troublesome, contentious, obstinate man, & Friends could do no other than disown him at last. The best & wisest part of the Yearly Meeting of New England were unanimous in this opinion, & only about 300 individuals, many his own family & connexions, adhered to him. But he has his partizans in other Yearly Meetings & to such as these those incendiary papers in the B. Friend are life. They are quoted & trumpetted about & after all I should not be surprized if they proceed from Caleb Haworth or John Harrison. I hope they are not the voice of the Society.

[3] I think Joseph John Gurney one of the bright ornaments of our society & if his writings are not orthodox Christianity I do not understand it. Never again could Hicksism shed its withering blight amongst us if his beautiful & lucid definitions of Truth may circulate & diffuse light & knowledge into the minds of our children. I believe we scarcely know how much we owe him for dissipating that twilight gloom that hung over us & under which Elias Hicks in this country walked warily about, sowing his poison seeds which resulted in such a great & woeful harvest. I heard Cousin Ann Shipley

say only the other day she often could not understand how it was that for years he preached his insidious doctrines & no one suspected; but when the charm vanished & light did break they were astonished. But what awful devastation was accomplished! Let such a man come now & none with the bible in their hand & the daylight of well understood christian principles to assist them could be so deluded, & who has written so understanding & well as J. J. Gurney[?] Do not think us ungrateful, dearest mother, but we begin to wish not to have the British Friend. Josiah Forster says the "London Friend" is far superior; if thou inclines to take any, as I hope thou wilt, & shouldst send us those, we shall be very much obliged.[18]

I have lately written so many letters for the children that I think I need say nothing about them except that they are well as usual.

Hast thou seen a small account of Elizabeth Fry published in the Annual Monitor?[19] It is reprinted here in the form of a small pamphlet & is, I think, a most beautiful & interesting thing. I should like thee to see it if thou hast not; it is written by Susanna Corder. I am glad thou art interested in Frederic Douglass. I was intending to send thee his book if thou hadst not said thou hadst it.

I heard lately of two coloured women who are at present in the city trying to obtain subscriptions. They are a mother & daughter: the girl about 18, said to be one of the comeliest of her race. They are natives of Kentucky & have purchased their own & family's freedom for 1800 dollars, \the proceeds of their industry/. All are free but 2 children; the master is lately dead & these are in danger of being sold into bondage. The price set upon them is 800 dollars & they are trying to raise it in this great emergency by begging. I feel much interested for their success.

I sent a few days ago a most miserably shabby letter to [4] dearest Mary. Give my dear love to her & beg she will excuse me: I was badly circumstanced for ink & pens (a sloven's excuse) but as I was visiting had no alternative.

Dear Cousin Ann Shipley is well & desires her love, as also Cousin Phebe. They are a great blessing to me. I always feel at home with them.

I forget if I told you Harrison has been planting a vineyard. It contains about 700 vines & will be a very great pleasure to us if we live to enjoy it, but how much more could I only hope that you would partake. Richard is well & desired his love to thee; he is a fine lad & seems to be getting on well in his business.

18. In 1843, *The Friend* was established in London by George Stacey, Josiah Forster, and John Hodgkin as a more evangelical alternative to the more traditionalist *British Friend*, published in Glasgow by William and Robert Smeal. In another year, Alderson would be requesting *The British Friend* again, but now she seems to have been swayed by Forster's advice.
19. Established in 1813 by William Alexander, the *Annual Monitor, or Obituary of the Members of the Society of Friends* published brief death notices of all Friends deceased during the previous year, along with longer articles of more prominent Friends.

We have heard very distressing accounts of poor Thomas Albright. I hope they are not correct; one thing is certain, that except in his daughter Agnes, who I hope will prove a comfort to him, his children are, as they were in England, thorns in his side.

We are making a collection in the meeting to send the three female Friends at the Indian Settlement a present. Poor things, their situation is one to excite our deepest sympathy; the sacrifices they make in the path of duty are great indeed. It is an unhealthy situation, and they have suffered much from sickness this winter, & their privations in other respects are very great. I received a letter from the wife of the superintendent which excited my interest much on their behalf. I wish I had it by me to give thee some extracts.

Harrison desires [1] his love to thee & up jump the children with "send my dear love to grandmother[."] Mine most affectionately to thee, my beloved Parent.

Thy attached & ever obliged & grateful daughter,

Emma

42. To Margaret and Herbert Howitt [from William Charles Alderson] March 7 to 26, 1846[20]

Now my dear cousins, though the snow is quite gone and we talk of nothing but spring, it is not a week since I saw one of the most primitive of Yank~~ey~~ee Jumpers. It was made of two long branches of hickory, which is a very supple & pliant wood. These were bent upward to form the shafts, & on the body of the sleigh was a great smooth log. Fixed behind stood up a long pole, on the top of which a horse's tail waved as a pennon. Two men were riding bravely along on this old affair & seemed well pleased with the merriment of beholders.[21]

One evening the merry sleigh bells anounced an arrival at our door & our kind friends the Taylors, with whom I think you must by this time feel well acquainted, came in to make a call.

We have been very busy this week in having a smoke-house put up. Our neighbour the joiner had prepared it all ready and there was nothing to do but dig a foundation when the weather permitted & bring the frame & put it up just as you would build a play house, every part of which fits together. The weatherboarding and shingles are nailed on after, & in a few hours we have a clever little house where no house before stood.

Today father has hung up our hams & other salt meat & the first fire is set of green hickory logs, the smoke of which ~~are~~ \is/ considered best.

20. The date of March 7 is an estimate based on two factors: on March 2 in his previous letter, William Charles had said that the snow, which by the time of this letter was "quite gone" or just starting to melt, and sometime after starting this letter, he introduces a new date of March 8.

21. See figure 27.

[March] 8th. This has been such a warm bright day that we sate out on the grass & little Alice rolled upon a carpet & pulled the dry bents with great delight. We staid out on the Piazza talking & repeating hymns in the moonlight & last week, only 8 days ago, the icy wind & sleet made us feel so cold that we did not know how to keep ourselves warm even by a good fire. The ground was a foot deep in snow, & behold what a change a week has made.

[March] 9. To day Father & Mother were busy gardening, William is ploughing our new vinyard & I have been very busy chopping down young locust trees with my hatchet.[22] Sister & I played at driving a drove of 3000 hogs to Clafornia, Agnes sold them to me & I had to hunt them up out of the woods; Annie was the settler to whom I took them. The first drove I lost by straying & the \ravages of the/ wolves on the Rocky Mountains, so on my second journey I took Fanny & Timothy & found them of great use. That time we arrived safe & the Settler paid me 6000 dollars.

This last week has been a very busy one. On second day they began to plough the vinyard. Father planted out some trees: a weeping willow & a shumach. The weeping willow here grows to an immense size & is one of the most beautiful trees we have seen; its long pendant branches droop many yards [2] and wave most gracefully in the breeze. Besides, it is the first tree that is green & one of the last to lose its leaves, so you may be sure we admire it & no wonder it is a general favourite.

[March 10] Third-day. Mother & sisters & I went an errand about two miles in the country. The sun shone warm & bright & the birds filled the air with their joyful notes, but we often miss the sweet song of the lark on such mornings as these. Oh how sweetly would it be singing in England now beneath such a bright sky & warm sun; however it was very delightful without the lark. We went through a wood but found no flowers, but the trees are some of them in bloom as the elm &c. We had a fine view of the wooded hills by the river & down into the deep glen where we spent a pleasant day last fall.

At the house to which we went grew some very fine golden willows. They looked beautiful now like a net work of golden wires & rods. Here is the first vinyard that was planted at Cincinnati. It is 5 acres in extent & they often make some thousand gallons of wine from it. They reckon a bushel of catauba grapes will make 4 galls of wine.

[March 11] Fourth day. We had 5 men at work, and they planted vines today in good earnest. They made deep long holes like little graves & put a plant into each, which is to be trained to a \pole &/ frame. The vines are 6 feet \apart/ one way & five the other; I helped to fill up. There are 400 plants and 300 cuttings to plant.

[March 12] Fifth day. Still busy planting. Sisters & I went to Mary Crehoe's; she told us she had a young cow come to keep Dolly company because

22. Used for trellises or fence posts.

she pined at being alone; the young one she calls Bonnet maker & the old one red Shaker. She says she will give mother some seed of a calabash that holds 2 quarts.

[March 13] 6th day. We went another errand with mother to Johnathan Basset's, who lives on the edge of a great wood. We passed a new brick schoolhouse which was built last fall & by another little frame one that was put up by an old lady for her niece to teach school in. This old woman once scolded Father very much because Milo ran on to her Piazza when it was clean.

In we went through the thick woods, which grow on each side of the hills that rise very abruptly from a little creek that ran wending its way towards <*blank*> which flows into the Ohio. Oh, how beautiful do the woods look even though there are no leaves on the trees & the dry brown leaves crush so pleasantly under our feet that we forgot every thing in our gladness once again to be in the Forest. Here were huge grape vines growing up the tall trees \with stems/ as thick as a man's leg and looking like monstrous serpents ready to descend & devour us. So we called this wild vine wood & hope to spend a long pleasant summer's day in it.

I was pilot & led the way the best I could. Agnes had her plants which we gathered & herself to take care of, but dear little Annie stoped at every mudy or difficult place & holding out her little hand said "let me help dear mother over[."] We came home just before a great thunder-storm broke in torrents of rain.

[3] To day we went to Jack's Wood just across our meadow for sweet-briar & wild clamatis plants. It is a sweet little spot; we find many beautiful trees & flowers there: the dog tooth violet, the red bud, solomon seal, phlox & many others. It belongs to a blind old negro who is called Dr Jack in the neighbourhood. One day Father & Mother went to see him; the poor old creature was lying on a bed in a very weak enfeebled state. His old lame wife is his only attendant & as they can get no one to work their land, they told Father it must lie waste, for they can do nothing. The lower class of Dutch, who are the chief settlers in this neighbourhood, have a violent prejudice against the blacks & treat them with indignity. A set of them this winter fitted up an old barn for a theater & there represented rude vulgar plays in ridicule of these poor oppressed people. Father promised Jack to try to do something for him.

We begin to find the early spring flowers.

We have a dear little Friend named Jane Bonsal whom we love much; she is a gentle girl that all love & we amongst the rest. She has been up to spend some days with us & many a pleasant ramble had we whilst she was with us.

[March] 23rd. Last week there was a deal of rain & it, with the melting snows on the mountains, have swelled Mill Creek & the Ohio till they look magnificent. The river is covered with drift wood, great logs & trees sweept down by the violence of the streams, & large pieces of wood, the remains of barns & houses carried away by the waters. We see men out in little boats fishing it up & great quantities they collect in this way. It is said a small frame house with its inmates came sailing down a few days ago; there was a man, woman & two children & they made signals of distress when they came opposite the city & were at length landed in safety at Covington, a small town in Kentucky ~~oppos~~ on the other side of the Ohio. A gentleman told us he once saw a hay stack with about a dozen chickens \upon it/ (all fowls though venerable with age are "chickens" here): the rooster was perched, crowing loudly, but wether from joy or fear nobody could tell; on they floated & probably sailed many a mile in this novel journey. Once a warehouse filled with Whiskey & flour left the shore at Wheeling & sailed gallantly down the river till the current brought it to shore & the people busied themselves in landing its contents when, somewhat lightened, away it floated again & continued its adventurous journey for many a mile.

Whilst Jane was with us we went to a large \Catholic/ Cemetery that we can see from our lawn. We crossed our far meadow & by old Dr Jack's house; he keeps two very fierce dogs chained up to defend them, because rude people & boys are very fond of playing them rather more than rude jokes—\perhaps the old people are more alarmed than is necessary/. There is a deep wooded dell beyond his orchard which we crossed & on through the fields till we reached the cemetery. Half of it belongs to the Dutch & half to the Irish; the latter is very neat with nice gravestones & crosses [4] & pretty monuments like what we see in England; the Dutch graves are mostly marked by rude red wooden crosses.[23] Occasionally there is an enclosure with flowers & shrubs planted about the graves, but on the whole it has a very forlorn appearance. There are two dead houses for depositing the dead in winter, which is the case universally here. The coffins are ranged side by side ~~here~~ \in these places/ from the commencement of frost & when it breaks up the Friends go privately & inter the dead in graves.

As we came home we stood admiring the great tripple thorns on the stems of the prickly or horney locust. They look very curious \5 or 6 inches long/ hanging over the trunk in a pendant position suspended by a strong filament. Then, as we were crossing our field, we saw a great old frog come out of its winter habitation. He was taking his first sniff of the sweet spring air & hopped staggeringly along like something that was intoxicated. His eyes were dazzled by the strong light & he seemed as though he had not full use of his senses. Poor thing, we left him to recover himself & enjoy his renewed existence.

We have some kind neighbours [Shipleys] who live about a mile nearer the city on the brow of the hill that descends to the river. One morning Jane

23. The shared cemetery is an indication of the harmonious relationship between German ("Dutch") and Irish Catholics in Cincinnati, even though they remained largely separate, with their own churches, schools, and even languages for much of the nineteenth century. Such harmony was not characteristic of Irish and German Catholics in many large cities (Joseph M. White, "Cincinnati's German Catholic Life: A Heritage of Lay Participation," *U.S. Catholic Historian* 12, no. 3 [1994]: 15, https://www.jstor.org/stable/25154030).

& we had a pleasant ramble there to take some trumpet creepers. They live is a beautiful white house surrounded by Sugar maples. Elizabeth, the daughter, is one of our chief favourites amongst our grown up friends. She is a young lady that makes herself so pleasant & is so kind that to go and see her is one of our great treats. She lets Annie, their coloured girl, swing us in the swing & gives us cakes & apples and sends mother flowers & plants. Agnes was delighted to hear she wanted a trumpet flower to run up one of the maples, for she had one of her own that flowered last summer & nothing pleased her better than to take it as a small present.

We met a drunken man on the road as we came back & were sadly frightened. Janey said he was crazy: he talked to the pigs and it was wonderful how he should know my name for he called me Charley. It was quite a happy time whilst Jane was with us.

Dear Hannah Taylor came up to see Father & Mother; we love to see her: her presence is like sunshine in the house.*

26th Agnes is gone to spend some days with our little friends Hannah & Jane Warder. It is Jane's birthday & they are to have a little party. They went down in the market waggon & a merry shaking ride they had. Annie & I were on the look out for Father & Mother returning. When they came, a head popped out; Annie thought it was dear little Agnes; no; then we guessed it, one & then another & at last Isabella's merry laugh discovered it was our little cousin. We were rejoiced to see her; she reads to us & tells us merry stories & loves to ramble in the woods as well as we.

We have been into John's wood & brought home the first Spring Beauty we have gathered this spring, but the weather has been so cold & wet lately that the flowers make but poor progress. We saw a strange dog; Isabella thought it might be mad so we came home in a great hurry, but not before we armed ourselves with great sticks & putting Annie in the rear prepared for the defensive if the enemy approached. [5] There came also a woman to us & in her broken English told us not to bring our dogs there—Fanny & Tim were with us—or her ~~dog~~ cow would hook us; she had a great stick in her hand & at first we thought she was going to beat us, but when she was so civil Isabella thought it was best to be so too, & said ["]yes mam,["] & ["]no mam,["] & then I ventured to ask if we might come into the wood if we left the dogs at home, & she said ["]O yah, O yah.["] There are new tennants come to John's house & so we were glad to have her leave to go there.

About 4 miles from Cincinnati on a road that leads to no particular place but stretches on through little clumps of houses called towns & villes and by farms & through woods, no body knows where—at least I cannot tell you—is situated our house. It is a rather commanding looking place on one of the highest points of land about, & yet so little of an elevation, after ascending the mile long hill which lies between us and the Ohio, that only by seeing it & the Locust & Cedar trees by which it is surrounded from all places in the neighbourhood, do you find out that it is so high. This makes it bleak in winter but breezy & pleasant in the fervid heat of summer. The house is white with green venetian shutters; in front there is a two storied porch around which a fine prairie rose grows in wild luxuriance &, when in bloom, looks literally like a garland of flowers. At the back a broad Piazza which has also an upper story, is our favourite play place in winter & like a sweet summer parlour in warm weather; it is shaded by a vine and a scarlet flowering trumpet creeper. Here we breakfast, dine & sup in summer & sit often on the delicious moonlight evenings till bed time.

The house stands away from the road in the centre of a field which we call the lawn; the road leading to it is an avenue of Locust trees & on each side are planted alternately Cedar & Catalpa which look very beautiful; flower beds \are studded about/ & a sweet little arbour beside some flowering trees & shrubs are uninclosed by any fence, for as cattle are never admitted into this field, all remain safe & uninjured. The wood house is near the kitchen door & at the end of this a little bird house is fixed in which blue birds build every summer; in the farm-yard there is a waggon shed, a corn crib, a hen house & large barn, & down a little lane beyond we go to the spring, round which six locust trees are planted & near there is a fine button wood. We have two horses: Farmer & Benjamin Franklin, but we call him Ben; two cows: Owen & Pink; & two calves: one, \that is mother's calf/, a year old & another only a few months. We have hens & guinea fows; & Milo & Fanny, a great & a little one, are our dogs.

Oposite our gate are two houses near together; in one, a little log cabin, lives Frederic Lottee the joiner, a very respectable & nice man; \they are Germans/. He has two children; the oldest, Frederic, is a great favourite of ours; he is [a] pretty, blue eyed, fair complectioned Saxon. The Old Father & Mother came last summer from Germany & live with them. They bow to us as we pass but cannot speak a word of English; little Frederic speaks \it/ as well as we can. In the other house live Ritenbars; the father is a musician. They have two children, a boy & a girl, but Father & Mother will not let us play with them. They are naughty, rude children & say very bad words, so between us there is a great feud. Charley Ritenbar even throws stones at us and calls us names; Frederic Lotte says he will not play with him if he does so. Besides, he ~~saw him~~ comes into [6] into our fields & shoots the little birds with his bow & arrow, & Father says they do so much good he will not have one killed. I pull up his traps whenever I can find them; we love to hear the sweet little things sing & we have more than any one else because we do not disturb them.

We have some acquaintances in the city: Cousin Charles Shipley and Marshal Mulgrew & Ella Stewart are three little motherless children that live at Cousin Shipley's at Mount Auburn and are educated there; we love them all. Then there are Hannah & Jane & Bessie Warder, three sweet little girls; & Cousin Isabella Rogers, a merry creature as light & active as a fairy; & dear little Jane Bonsal, one of those that all love because she is so good & so kind;

and our old Friend Cousin Richard who came over from England with us & sometimes spends his first days with us. We all think it jubilee when he comes, & Isabella is gone & has taken Timothy with her; he was so mischiefous & scratched such great holes in the flower beds that Father said we must part with him. Isabella promised to be very good to him & so we let him lick our hands at parting & bade him farewell; I do think he knew something about it for he licked Fanny face & looked very lovingly at her. Last night Isabella read in the \Boys/ Country Book the History of Rover; I think no one could ill use a dog after reading that, & then we had the story of the Sheffield Cutler.[24] Oh how we all laughed at the old man's fright & rejoiced in the success of the poor aprentices.

I ought to tell you that at the north west extremity of our land, at the bottom of the orchard, Father built a small frame house two years ago & there lives Wm, our Farmer, & his brother in law, Joseph, \with their wives & babies/ & the grandmother of the household.

My dearest sister I have sent thee a very poor attempt to comply with thy request. Thou over rates this poor performance; however, I leave it to thy better judgment & gladly go on. The seeds are those of one of our sweetest wildflowers. My dearest love to mother & you all; thy affectionate sister,

Emma Alderson

* <*written across text on final page*> Jane & we were playing at having a party & Agnes went to the spring for some water when her foot slipped & pop she went in. Jane ran & pulled her out & a terrible fright she had but was no worse except a good wetting. We all laughed & Father thinks it may do her good & make her more careful.

43. *To Margaret and Herbert Howitt [from William Charles Alderson], April 1 to 16, 1846*

1st of 4th month

We have had a sweet walk today; we went into Jack's wood. Mother & baby were with us & we gathered a handful of beautiful flowers. The spring beauty is a lovely thing; it has five petals veined with pink & the anthers of its five stamina are pink; the leaf is long & grasslike & the flowers grow in a cluster.[25] We found also the first flowers of the bloodroot; we looked for dogtooth violets but it is rather early for them.

We sate down on the dry grass amongst flowers & the brown leaves of autumn & looked with delight on woods & hills & hollows & the shadows of the trees around us; the warm sunshine & song of birds filled us all with gladness. Alice clapped her hands & shouted for joy & then fell into a low warble

24. William Howitt, *The Boy's Country-Book: Being the Real Life of a Country Boy, Written by Himself* (London: Longman, Orme, Brown, Green, and Longmans, 1839).
25. *Claytonia virginica*, a member of the portulaca family.

of de-light; mother said, "Oh how good God is to make the earth so beautiful" & little Annie answered, "yes indeed we ought to be thankful." We came home by the woodpecker's column, a tall, bare, barkless, branchless trunk of a great buttonwood tree in the far meadow where the red-headed woodpeckers build in summer & where also numbers of the lesser species congregate.

In the afternoon we went on an errand to our Friends the Morgans. Washington, their coloured man, brought us home in a cart as he was coming to fetch some apple trees. Whilst he was opening the gate, we were playing & Agnes pushed Annie rather too far & out she went. It might have been a sad accident but as it happened she was not hurt. Frederic Lotte has made me a nice hickory bow; it will shoot many yards; he is a kind boy. I would have paid him, but he will never take money from us; mother says we must buy him a book. We found under some locust trees at the lower end of the meadow two poor kittens about half grown, lying dead; they were covered with shavings & their necks were twisted. We were sadly troubled & shocked & showed them to Frederic; he said he saw Charley Ritenbar drag them there & he believed he killed them himself.

[April] 2nd. A day of trouble. Sisters & I got to jumping & turning summersets on Louisa's bed—she is our girl or servant, as you call them. We knew it was wrong & had often been prohibited, & we even tore the cover almost to pieces, so mother said we must eat dry bread after we had had our mush at breakfast. For my part I thought I would as soon go without my breakfast as do without butter & molasses, so I went out to play whilst they were getting theirs; however, whether it was the sharp morning air or that I really was hungry, [2] going without breakfast did not suite me & I was obliged to them when they gave me a can of mush & milk.

Then Father & Mother went down to the city & I went with them and they took me to the Dentist & he drew out two of my teeth. It was a terrible pull; I was ashamed but I could not help crying out & my other teeth ached all evening so you may think I had not much comfort; however I went with a playfellow to his father's printing office & saw the men setting type & even printing papers.

[April] 3rd. To day a man with a cap covered with small bells, a porcelain pipe in his breast & a guitar in his hand came to the door & played us some tunes. I asked him where he came from & he said Frenchéman Frenchéman.

I have been farming Annie's new garden & getting a fence ready for my own. My eyes are so painful I could not do my lessons; I think \the extracting of/ those teeth have affected them & at the best they ache so much I cannot read much at a time & that is a great loss, but Father & Auntie are very kind & often read to me. We are now reading *The History of England*.[26]

26. Without additional information, it is impossible to know what "history of England" she is referring to. William Howitt's *History of England* was not published until the 1850s.

[April] 4th. Frederic Lotte came this morning to set up a frame in front of the back porch for the grape vines; the posts are red cedar & smell delightfully. It will extend <*blank*> yards & will in summer look beautiful with the vines & Trumpet flower trained over it. I went with Father in the waggon to a lumber yard for some boards. William's mare has a pretty little foal; it is ten days old & it squealed like a little baby when its mother is away when they took her to plough.

To day they are ploughing up the orchard & going to sow it with clover & oats so we shall have what we have long wanted: a grassy orchard. Hitherto they have grown corn & potatoes in it & we never had any comfort gathering the fruit. We have such enormous bonfires with the great weeds & corn stalks & all the rubbish of this luxuriant soil; often the horizon at night is illuminated by them. I have had to husk & shell a bushel of corn & am so tired; I wish the cows were at grass & would not want so much boiled corn, but since Owen had a little calf they have wanted twice as much, and really it is hard work when the sun is shining warm & bright & I think how pleasant it is in Jack's wood or by the little creek where we gather fosils. We have called the old calf which is black & white Blackberry, & the little one, Pink's daughter, Rose. Owen's calf the butcher fetched a few days ago.

We have Hyacinths, Primroses & Periwinkles in the garden & there will soon be plenty of daffodils. We had a deal of fun following William at plough & walking bare footed along the new turned up furrow. Little Frederic came in the evening & brought his little sister, Sophia. She cannot speak a word of English but we pleased her so well that she would not go home ~~but~~ [&] so we played on the lawn till dark.

[April] 5th. To day I have done all my lessons, read in the Guide to Knowledge & in Geography, & then Mother read the reign of Edward the Third to us. We have been playing at bringing timber on rafts down the Ohio; I had a [3] cargo of Cedar logs & Annie pine, and I have been fixing little garden seats out of the blocks Frederic Lotte gave us yesterday. It was pouring down rain & Father read to us in the Boy's Country Book, the chapter about Collieries & all the perils & hardships connected with getting coals; we were much interested & pleased, and as we looked upon our wood fire blazing cheerfully upon the hearth, thought what a comfort it was to think that no thought of suffering was connected with it: nothing but pleasing & joyful associations. To be sure we were burning up noble trees, but their branches had shadowed the green flowery earth & yielded shelter & sustenance to the gay innocent little creatures that inhabit the Forest, & by their removal way was made for fruitful pastures & joyful harvest fields for the cheerful homes of men & women & little children, for orchards & vineyards & pleasant gardens.

[April] 6. We were down at the lower end of the lawn getting the large bursting buds of the Buckeye, a species of hose-chesnut, and as I clambered up the stem of a wild poison vine that has hung itself over a locust tree &

killed it, I was just going to set my foot in descending on what I thought was a la[r]ge stone lying in a hollow stump, when what should it be but a buff hen crouching down on her nest,the strangest that ever was seen. We went quietly away & after a while mother went with us to look at it & there in a sort of tower lay on the ground 6 pretty white eggs; the lady of the ~~house~~ castle was gone & we left her nest undisturbed as Father did not think she belonged to us.

[April] 7. We are in a great bustle of white-washing & there are three men busy at the outside of the house and very bright and pretty they have made it; when the leaves are on the trees it will be nice indeed. We went down to see the hen's castle & found 7 eggs in it today; they look as snug and clever as ever.

[April] 8th. This is Good Friday & Mother said as all the little children in England were having a holiday we should too.[27] So she went a long ramble with us into the woods; Father was too busy to go with us. First of all we called at old Jack's to see how he was & leave him a pie; all the way there Annie's little heart was full of trepidation at the thought of the great dogs but she kept saying, ["]I will tell them, here doggie I have brought you a pie a good pie, please take it in doggie." She carried the basket; the four dogs did make a terrible barking but we saw the old woman's black face peeping from the porch & she called them off when she saw us. The poor old man is much worse & lay still on the bed & took no notice of us. His wife says they cannot get any one to work the land so it must lie; the fences are bad & no one will cultivate it; she cannot leave the house for half an hour & she has eggs and butter to take to market which would buy her meal & meat, but she said, ["]I think my old man's going and you know all men must die.["] ["]Yes,["] said mother, ["]& if they are prepared it is a happy change." "Ay, that is the end that is alone worth living for & He's been in that service 16 years."

When we left we went down the creek that ran dashing & murmuring over its stony bed; it flows into Bold-face Creek, the receptacle of all the little streams in our neighbourhood. We found abundance of flowers: anemones, violets, blood root & spring beauty & great beds of the leaves of the dog-tooth violet, but no flowers yet. At the tree roots which we called [4] hot beds were assembled the prettiest little group you ever saw; we brought our basket full. The root of the Blood root deserves its name: it is intensely red & the juice is a fine orange dye.

We thought we had had as pleasant a holiday ramble as anyone could desire, & yet we were pleased to see the white-chimney of the white house as we came homeward. Father thought when we told him our adventures we had better go & buy the old woman's eggs, so Louisa & we went & brought home 13 dozen at 6 cents a dozen; she seemed delighted to get rid of them so

27. Easter Sunday in 1846 fell on April 12; either Emma or William Charles must be making some mistake.

easily & they will do for us for store for next winter. She asked after the young lady that lived with us last summer, meaning Adelle, & when we told her she was married she was very merry. For you must know a few weeks ago Adelle walked up to tell mother she was going to be married in two days & going to live 20 miles in the country; she would scarcely sit down but kissed our hands at parting & invited us to go & see her.

The Friend that is whitewashing gave us two apples to divide; apples are very scarce & very dear &, of course, a great rarity. Jack's wife said he wanted one very much, so we were very glad to have these & set off to take them. We felt afraid of the dogs & seeing a black man near the house asked him to take them in; he had Jack's old horse fastened to a sled & was loading it with wood so he said, "You see I'm busy loading my cattle & cannot go." Presently the old woman poped out her head & silenced the dogs; she seemed pleased with our little present & sent mother a few fresh laid eggs. We brought home a beautiful nosegay of wild flowers & sent them to a sick girl in the city.

When we were at the gates in the evening we saw a great many people running to Lotte's—Rittenbars on one side & the Tailors on the other—& out came little Frederic & we asked him what was the matter; he said his little baby brother was dying, & he cried & looked sadly distressed, poor thing. It died at one oclock in the night.

I wish I could tell you a story Wm <Rambow> the whitewasher related last evening; I will try. He said he was at Galena in Illinois and he & about 8 others set out to go into the wild government lands in Wisconsin to cut lathes; some went for fence wood. In crossing a small river, the Muskegon, I think, the ferry man told them to jump upon three logs bound together with wild vines. This craft, to use his own words, sunk midleg deep in the water with their weight, & in this condition they were paddled over for a levey which is 12 1/2 cents. They went some miles into the woods, built themselves a shanty & had their bacon & corn ~~bannock~~ doggers, which are cakes made of Indian meal & water baked in the embers of a wood fire. Here they lived & cut wood to their fill & then hired a yoke of oxen & a sled & conveyed it to the river; they then cut down large trees, hewed off the limbs & made a raft on which they and their cargo embarked. Sometimes they paddled, sometimes "bush-savaged," that is, fixed a rope attached to the raft to a tree & drew it forward then to another tree & so on.[28]

At length their provisions failed & for two days they endured the misery of hunger; on the evening of the second day the captain of the party said he knew of a cabin on shore, so they secured the craft & landed but the cabin was two miles within land, through the forest. When they reached it the people were gone to bed, but they persuaded the woman [5] to get up, & telling her their troubles she took them in & prepared to bake biscuits, which is

28. Howitt gives "bush-swagged" (*OCO*, 79). I have been unable to find that phrase or "bush-savaged" in the *OED* or anywhere else.

a kind of small light cake, & fry some ham. The hungry men sat watching & would gladly have eaten her unbaked dough & raw meat; never did any one seem so slow as she. At last it was ready & joyfully they sate down; after eating heartily they threw themselves on the floor & slept sweetly & soundly. Next morning they commenced their journey & fortunately from another cabin purchased some flour & ham; the captain baked the cakes & Wm fried the meat next evening by their fire in the woods.

To day Joseph is sowing oats & William let me ride on Ben whilst he harrowed; we were husking knobbings, which are the small refuse ears of corn for the cows. Our corn crib is a fine place; on two sides there is lattice work & it is as warm & pleasant as a bed room. We rolled in the husks & jumped from the oats that lie in one quarter. Milo had been shut up to catch the rats; he is famous at that; he caught two great ones last night when Father & I went into the Cow house. But I was going to tell you that in his hurry to get away when the door was opened he knocked Agnes down the steps & she bruised her leg sadly. Poor fellow, he did not mean to do any harm, & when Father was angry with him Agnes stopped her crying to tell him it was quite an accident.

Annie was slave-driver to night & kept us very hard at work in the coffee & rice grounds; sometimes she whipped, sometimes she was kind & let us have a dance. Then she turned herself into a hornets' nest & we went to take her with fire & sword but she was so very fierce that she drove us away every time we approached.

[April] 16th. The guinea fowl has laid an egg; she has adopted one of the hens' nests in the stable & we have been to see the hen at the bottom of the lawn. No one has disturbed her & she is sitting. Fanny is very lame & looks out of spirits & sick.

The peach trees are in full bloom & look beautiful covered with their pretty pink flowers; a single tree is beautiful contrasted with the bright green grass, but an orchard of peaches is splendid; the various kinds have differently shaded blossoms. Some is pure white, some plale pink & other bright, whilst others again are of a dull deep rose colour. The trees are also beginning to be very beautiful in the woods; the sugar maple is a pale yellow green & looks like specks of sunshine in the brown & still leafless maples that surround it; then the buckeyes are a deep full green from the first & soon look quite shadowed; here & there the purple pink of the red-bud spines out along the borders of the forest or on the sides of the hills. The red-bud is the name given by the Indians; it is also called the Judas Tree from the circumstance that the bees are said to fall down dead under its shade from the poisonous quality of the honey. The frogs have begun their everlasting ["]chir, chir["] like the turning of a great spinning wheel and at night we hear a shrill monotonous whistle which some say is the note of the tortoise, but of this I am not sure.

Isabella told us that they have a girl (servant) named Sarah; she has been a slave \in the South/ & worked most of her life in the fields, but about 18 months ago she fell sick & her master, not liking the trouble & expense of supporting her when she was unable to work, brought her here & left her alone & without a friend in the city. [6] The cessation from labour & change of air wrought so beneficially that she is in good health & able to go into service; her inhuman master is dead & even were he not she is free by the Laws of Ohio which give freedom to every slave \voluntarily/ brought by their possessors & allowed to remain in it a certain length of time. She is a good tractable creature & very grateful for the least kindness, an article which probably she has known little of before.

There was an Indian youth at meeting a few first-days ago; he belongs to the Shawnee tribe & has been four years away from the settlement for education amongst the whites. He has a brother & sister living amongst their tribe & is going to see them but intends to return.

With dear love, your affectionate cousin,

Wm Charles

My beloved sister, As I have an opportunity of sending this to New York I hastily finish it; write & tell me if thou really thinks these foolish trifling details are worth troubling thee with. There is a long letter (the second) in the hands of John Allen which you will get by your yearly meeting. Thou asks me what games our children play at; they mix so little with others that they have adopted very few of those common amongst children; as thou wilt see, they make their own amusements and invent their own plays. Give my dearest love to dear Mother and to Wm, Anna Mary and all thy dear children. Farewell beloved sister. Send me a book whenever thou canst; I am so glad to have good English books and I think we shall not again have so much trouble nor give you as much; tell me what I can do for thee. Thy most tenderly attached sister,

Emma

Give my endeared love to Anna.

44. To Mary Howitt, April 18 to May 18, 1846
4th mo 18th

The first batch of little chickens, but alas there are but 3: something has frightened the hen, or she has been weary of sitting, and the remaining nine eggs are just left in a bursting state. In the evening Charles was in the cowshed and saw a great rat sitting amongst them. This was the deciding point & his father fetched a tin dish, laid an old silk handkerchief under them, & placed the little foundlings in the oven of the stove. Unfortunately they were forgotten, & when Charles came from meeting, a fire had been kindled. The oven was hot, & the eggs & consequently the chicks, who had managed to make very considerable holes & pop their heads through them, were all baked. We hoped the poor things were too young to feel much.

We have a cousin called Elizabeth [Mason] come from Westland to see us. As we sat at breakfast with the window open, a fine large bird came hopping & flying about an arbor vitae. It was a robin, a bird about as large as an English black bird but with a dark brown back & wings & orange red breast. Cousin E. said she was once sitting with her brother William keeping the cows from passing through the open bars when a robin alighted on his head &, robbing him of a few hairs, flew away to its nest in a distant fence. To day Richard came up and Charles & he went a ride, a great event for him as it was the first time he had been alowed to prowl & ride so far alone.

Whilst he was gone his Father & Mother & sisters went to see old Jack. They walked through the long, green, grassy pasture &, climbing the fence, entered the little wood; here ~~flow~~ phlox ~~&~~ uvularia & spring beauties abounded. They got large branches from the red bud, covered with innumerable purple-pink flowers; the blue, yellow & white violets were out & they gathered handfuls of flowers. In the road leading to Jack's house lay a large black snake about a yard & a quarter long, long dead; they are ugly looking creatures but said to be perfectly harmless. The dogs came barking towards them & drove little Fanny whining home.

In answer to the question how is the old man? the wife said, ["]oh sir, he's gone home, gone and paid the debt we must all sooner or later pay,["] & sure enough there stood the \vacant/ chairs in the house & on the porch, lately occupied by the funeral company. They had that morning buried him in his own woods by the side of another grave surrounded by a rude wooden paling, at the head & foot of which two trees are planted. Here a poor stranger who had come sick from his home down the river to put himself under Doctor Jack's care & had died at his house, had been interred, & here the old man himself was laid in his long quiet home.

His history is one of which a thousand parallels might be told. He had been a slave most part of his long life, during which time his wife & three children were taken from him & sold to go south, a dreaded doom! Afterwards he married his last & surviving wife & about 25 years ago purchased his own & her freedom. For himself he paid 250 dollars, for his wife 350 as she was much younger. They came into this part; he practised as a Negro doctor, saved money, bought his little farm, & as the old woman said, they have never known what it was to want since.*

[1-*cross*] * She was dressed in true negro costume; her blue gown was made to be sure of two different patterns, but it was whole & decent, & her head was bound up with a handkerchief, below which her short curling grey hairs appeared, what is rather uncommon enough among her people. She has lost her teeth but on the whole is a stout, good looking black woman. [*end cross*]

There sate the old coloured man who has waited upon him during his last sickness; of course you know Jack was blind. He told me there was to be a "funeral" preached at the grave side that day month & we should know. They marvelled [2] how they could have forgotten to send us word of his death, but Mr. Hudson the coloured preacher would be here then & they hoped we should also be present. After that the man said, ["]I will put up a railing round the old man's grave & what's to become of \the/ poor old lady I do not know; she's lame & desolate & I hate to leave her. To be sure I've a family in the city but they're grown up & my wife is dead.["]

"Oh["] thought I, ["]we shall see how it turns.["] Jack used to say when he was gone some "old nigger would come & marry his old woman["] for the sake of what he should leave. We came home by the grave & stood a few minutes to reflect on the "debt we all have sooner or later to pay."

[April] 23. The children and their mother went to tell an old German who works for their Father to come the next day. They went by the chappel & down a long lane which runs in a valley between steep hills; five years ago all was covered with woods; now log cabins inhabited by the Dutch are numerous & the hillsides are laid out in vinyards & gardens for raising vegetables. At the bottom of the lane is a run, or creek, which in winter dashes over its rocky bed. In summer a little half stagnant water trickles amongst the larger stones which compose it. Hills, some wooded & others partially bare, lock in the ravine here & make a very picturesque and pretty view.

The woods have burst into perfect greenness during the last five warm days & the children exclaimed with delight at their beauty. They gathered the pretty blue scentless violet, the tooth wort & robin-run-in-the-hedge, & seeing the poke-weed springing in the fence sides, congratulated themselves on taking home their handkerchiefs full for a dish of greens for tomorrow's dinner. It is \boiled &/ eaten when young but if allowed to be above 5 inches long is said to be poisonous & of course dangerous.

They followed the run perhaps a quarter of a mile, skipping amongst the stones, and at last the tops of peach & plum trees with their pink & white blossoms revealed the ~~house~~ situation of the house under the wood; here a dog met them & attempted to bite little Annie on the arm. Charles wished he had had a large stick to beat it, but a good natured old woman came out & silenced them, and they tried in vain to make her understand their errand; ["]no furstanden, no furstanden["] was her only answer. Charles was sure this was John's wife, but she could not comprehend. At last they asked for a drink of water. With a smile she brought a glass and, as if light had come to her mind, pointed to a steep hill beyond the house & said ["]worker fur uns. ["][29] So they went towards the place, & there was John & his daughter & son in law howing the ground for planting corn. The place was too steep & too full of stumps to be ploughed. He told them of a shorter way, but then there was the poke on the road, & Annie thought it was a pitty to miss it; however,

29. Howitt changes the woman's words to "*Ich verstehe nicht*" ("I don't understand anything") and "*Da sind mein Mann, und meine Tochter; sie werken fur uns*" ("That is my husband and my daughter; they work for us"). Mary Howitt, *Our Cousins in Ohio* (London: Darton, 1849), 92 (hereafter cited as *OCO*).

as they were tired they went over the fields & through a little wood & here they found a fine dog-wood there, with its large white flower-like involucres, & Charles climbed the tree & pulled some branches. Then there was the paw-paw, or custard-apple, in bloom. It is a singular looking, dark brown flower: the bush never grows very large, but it looks handsome with its bright shining leaves about the size & form of the common laurel. The fruit is about the size of a large kidney potato & has a rich, luscious flavour like custard & fruit mingled.

[April] 24. John came this morning and according to the universal custom in the country \had his breakfast with the family/. The hands take their meals with the family. The "hired girl" \here/ has some of the city manners & waits her turn when the rest have done. John is a worthy old man who speaks a little broken English & answers with an abrupt, peculiar loud yes & now when offered anything at table, which often tempts the children to smile, but all like John, [3] and John says he likes or, to use the American phrase, loves to be with them. To show you he is not devoid of politeness, though he never says mam nor sir, please nor thank you, he threw down his hoe last night & went across the field to take down the fence that they might not have to climb, but they thanked him & would not let him give himself so much trouble.

Wm. Charles was planting sweet corn today in the garden. For the table it is called sugar corn & is very nice \boiled &/ eaten green ~~like green pease~~ \or, as it is called, in the milk./ His father made the holes about 3 feet apart each way, & Charles dropped 4 grains into each; then Agnes & he weeded strawberries & afterwards made a sod seat in Agnes' garden & sowed their flower seeds.

[April] 25. Mary Crehoe came this morning to call & Charles went with her to carry a basket of plants. Of course Agnes & Annie would not be left behind, but Annie as usual was very dirty & untidy, for in half an hour she always manages to look as if she had not been cleaned for a day, whilst Agnes is always neat. Nevertheless she is a dear child & Wm Charles begged his mother to let him dress her; so he washed & combed & changed her, tied on her clean sun-bonnet, & brought her in quite neat.

On their way they made a great discovery that a tree which had always been called a paper mulberry was a fine large balm of Gilead, a species of poplar whose buds have a peculiar strong aromatic smell & are said to possess great medicinal qualities. The children picked up handfuls of the gummy coats of the leaf buds which had fallen off & Annie came home with her nose end finely japanned with them, which at first their mother thought must be a permanent dye as it neither gave way to soap nor water. Their kind neighbours sent home a fine variety of slips of chrysanthemums, for amongst her other nice things in the fall, she has always a frame filled with the finest kinds of these beautiful flowers.

After the children had said their lessons, their mother & they went a ramble in the wood. It was a sweet warm afternoon, but in going down a pretty little green valley they had a little dash to their pleasure by seeing a bull standing on a hill above the shade of the trees. So they steered up a steep bank in an opposite direction & to their joy found the purple spikes of the wild larkspur in full bloom &, amongst other things, the lovely blue & white collinsia & the sweet flowering hawthorn—not as pretty as the English hawthorn but still so much of an hawthorn as to make us all love it.

The first humming-bird we have seen this season was flying about this afternoon & actually came into the piazza. On returning from their walk, they passed the woodpecker's column &, hearing a loud knocking, looked up & near the summit saw a red headed woodpecker beating with his great black beak for insects. He was very secure in his elevated position & they watched him for long. He is a singularly beautiful bird with a white body, white under the wings & tail, & black above & on his back; his throat is a flaming crimson; the male bird has a fine topping.

5 mo 3rd The last week has been mostly wet, & of course the children have been much confined. Once, they went alone to John's; on their way they passed the dog-wood tree and broke off large branches. Here they met Charley Rittenbar, who told him it was poison & would make their faces swell half-a-yard across. He was very naughty & with a little switch tried to spoil their bouquets of wild flowers.

Farther on some little dutch boys asked them why they went so fast & could they not stop a bit. Charley said it was growing late & father said he must be back soon; they then asked them the time & Charles answered it was three when he left home. Oh, said the boy, your clock is too hurry. They brought back handfuls of wild larkspurs.

One morning Agnes & Charley got up very early & went before breakfast to tell the butcher to call; he lives at Warsaw & goes the round of the neighbourhood \twice a week/ with meat in his waggon. Then they hoed up plantains for the pigs & Annie carried these to them. Their Father was very busy nailing on the lathes on the summer house, or arbour; all the creepers are growing, the wild clematis, the prairie rose, the trumpet honey [4] suckle, & woodbine, the trumpet flower, Corcorus &c. It will soon be very beautiful: Wm. Charles' tulip is up & in bud. The seeds are beginning to spring in his & Agnes' gardens, but Annie has dug up & fixed hers again twice since it was planted & sown, so it is free both of flowers & weeds.

There is a pair of cat-birds building in one of the cedar trees, & the robins have built in a cherry-tree in the orchard. A beautiful pair of yellow birds have also somewhere a nest but they are so small & so shy that we cannot find them out; they are almost as bright a yellow as a canary but much smaller. One day we saw two sporting together & took them at first for large yellow butterflies. Then there are blue-birds, martins, pee-wees, & wrens in abundance besides, so that the air is full of their sweet notes & the bushes all seem alive with them. The trumpet honey suckle is covered with its clusters of bright red flowers & the humming birds come to drink the dew & honey out of their cups.

[May 9] On seventh-day after noon, the children had a pleasant ramble in the woods & brought home the may apple in flower. Its large white blossom looks very beautiful growing close to the stem under the shade of the broad polished palmated leaves of the flower stalk & amongst the large umbrella like leaves of the plant. The leaf is said to be poisonous; the root is used in medicine & the fruit is eaten & liked by some. It is about the size & has somewhat the flavour of a large gooseberry. They saw two woodpeckers very busy eating the ants or eggs on a great ant hill; they were so busy that they let them come within a yard of them.

[May 10] First-day. Charley & Agnes went to meeting with their Father & cousin in the carriage. When they came home some friends came to spend the evening & the boys & Charles rambled in the woods & brought home the beautiful white Trillium.[30]

[May 11] 2nd day. After breakfast Charley took a large basket & went to gather Lamb quarter, a species of wild spinach which is a favorite green at this season. Then he & Annie carried a barrow load of beets which had been hilled through the winter into the cellar. Agnes peeled the potatoes, it being washing day, & then they said their lessons & went out to play, which consisted in cutting grass for Farmer & little Rose, who is now allowed to have the run of the barn yard. Their Father was busy planting water, ~~melon~~ musk & cantilaupe melon seed, squashes of various kinds, all of which the children thought they must have in their gardens.

In the afternoon they went with their mother and cousin to see Mary Crehoe; her garden & orchard looked beautiful. They were busy hoeing their grape-vines & putting down stakes at each plant, but what struck Charles as most remarkable was the amazing quantities of caterpillars creeping over every thing—on the fences, roads, & trees. In the latter their great webs were full of the great black loathesome creatures. If once they become strong in an orchard, it is next to impossible to destroy them, & in time \from year to year/ they ruin the trees; whole orchards from being flourishing & green, in a few days are brown, as if a great fire had passed over them. But what is much more dreaded than even these caterpillars is the scourge of locusts which is said to visit whole districts every 17 years, and this is the terrible season with a portion of the country adjoining us. It is said the hogs have a wonderful instinct for discovering the larva, which is buried in the earth, & are rooting with their snouts very busily at present. Nevertheless, thousands & mil-

30. Howitt gives this as "frillium" in the English edition of *OCO* (101) and as "fullim" in the American edition, suggesting that she was unfamiliar with this common American perennial (Mary Howitt, *Our Cousins in Ohio* [New York: Collins & Brother, 1849]), 82.

lions escape their vigilance, rise, burst their shells, & mount [5] a great "hollowing" noise into the trees, so an old gentleman told us the other day, & as far as their hollowing goes we can bear testimony as a few stray ones every summer perched in the trees make a most loud & discordant noise; at first we thought it must be a bird but were assured it was the locust, & once Father laid his hand on one & it set up a cry that actually frightened him with its noise & suddenness & he saw it take wing to a distant tree.

After lessons Charley & his sisters went down the field to fetch a barrowful of logs to burn on the kitchen hearth; then Charley, having an industrious fit upon him, took a hoe & went with his Father into the vinyard. Here he worked hard till dinner & actually hoed 2 1/4 rows; so his Father told him he would give him a vine for himself.

It had been a very hot morning & at noon the clouds gathered & a terrible thunder-storm came on. Charles called his mother to look [at] a fine large locust tree in full bloom reflected against the black clouds; it did indeed look beautiful in relief against the dark sky; never have we seen these lovely trees bloom so richly before. The young green leaves are mingled with the pendant clusters of white blossom, of which there is the utmost profusion & the air is rich with their scent [&] ~~of which~~ that of the orange blossom.

In the afternoon his Father read the country boy's book, that never ending source of delight to the children. The hen in the stump has brought out a fine brood of young chickens; when we went last to look, she & her family were gone but a great heap of shells lay at the castle gate.

Rain, Rain, rain all this week, so that there was no going out & the confinement of the house was more than commonly welcome[31] from having been able to play so much before. The children were Kings, Queens & generals,[32] had a great dolly fit & Agnes dressed up her own & Annie's very nicely; then they fitted up a house in a corner of the parlour & a poor old wooden doll was Betty the maid. Charles had to attend to the Calf, give it water & grass, hunt up the eggs & watch that the chickens did not get into the garden as his father was from home at the Quarterly Meeting.

[May 17] On First-day the weather cleared & Charley, not being quite well, staid at home with his two little sisters and the girl; Agnes is gone to spend a few days at Mount Auburn. In the garden today the children saw a snake; they thought it must be a copper-head & went to fetch Fanny to kill it, but whilst Charles was finding her & providing himself with a great stick the snake marched off & they could not find it again.

Frederic Lotte told them he knows of five bird's nests in the cedar trees; he promises not to take them, nor to tell Charles Rittenbar of them. It is a pity, after all, that any boy has discovered them. The cat-birds have been very

31. Oddly, Howitt reverses the meaning by substituting "irksome" for Alderson's "welcome" (*OCO*, 105).
32. For some reason, Howitt adds "slave-drivers and squatters" to this list (*OCO*, 105).

busy building their nest but now it is completed & the male bird only is visible; he is a fine fellow & sings delightfully, but in the wet weather he made a dismal voice like the mewing of a kitten in deep distress. The Cat-bird is a species of mocking bird & the finest songster we have in this part. The mocking bird is brought from the Southern states & kept here in cages; cousin Isabella has one that her father bought her. Poor thing, it looks sad in its fine handsome cage, very different to our merry little catbirds.

[May 18] 2nd day. Frederic gave Charley a very noble sap whistle made from a black-walnut stick, more than 18 inches long; the notes are very sweet & made us think of the Shepherd's pipe. William Charles went to gather some locust blossoms for his mother when a tree [6] frog jumped from a bough on to his hat & then upon the fence. He caught it & he & Annie came running in with their treasure when lo! the white frog was become quite black. It was a pretty little thing, about the size of half a dollar, & on being put into one of the Quince trees it gradually returned to its natural colour of a pale ash-colour bordered with brown; it hopped & crept about & delighted the children with its activity.

In the afternoon father came home with our good friend Joseph Taylor; he staid all night & they all went a ramble into the woods & gathered flowers & killed a snake with an old rail, called on the old Black woman & found to the comfort of all that at last she has got some one to work her land: a \coloured/ man who has been a sailor 18 years & can probably plough the ocean better than he can plough land. William says the ground looks as if twenty hogs had been rooting in it, but a Dutch man never gives a coloured man a good word & at all events it will be better half done than not done at all. The sexton's art is not to be despised &, like all other things, is best done by those that understand it. Poor old Jack's grave has sunk half a yard & looks very miserable; surely before the "funeral" it will be put into decent order.

The Locust trees have been most beautiful, white with their lovely blossoms & so sweet that in the calm moon-light evening you might have thought an orange grove was at hand; day & night the air is rich with perfume but the trees looked most beautiful & the odour was sweetest when the yellow beams of the full moon fell upon them. They are also very fine in the woods; some parts of the Kentucky hills have been white with them.

We have a pair of red-birds built in one of the cedar trees; Father saw a beautiful one in the orchard yesterday. Farewell, beloved sister; my ~~thy~~ affectionate love to you all. I am writing to dearest mother & want to hear from thee. Thy attached sister,

Emma.

45. To Ann Botham, May 3 to 18, 1846
5 mo. 3rd

Now my beloved Mother, I will begin a letter to thee, though I do not purpose finishing it, but I find it so much easier to let a letter grow by frequent additions that I will adopt the plan for thee this time.

I received a few days ago thy letter dated 2nd mo & finished sometime in the 3rd, I think. Thank thee, my beloved mother, for it; the pleasure of receiving a letter from thee is greater than I can express & I often feel very unworthy of such marks of thy continued kindness & affection. Could I by any strange oversight so far forget myself as not tell thee how grateful we all feel for the proofs of this love contained in the box thou sent[?] It came quite safe & the things were all very beautiful & most acceptable. Harrison is delighted with his stockings, which, now shoe weather is come, he has begun to wear, as also with his purse. The children think grandmother has chosen them the very nicest presents she could & very often are the boxes brought out of the drawer where they are deposited to look at or show to their friends, and my engravings are peculiar pleasures; I always loved such things & here there is not much opportunity of indulging our taste. They are at present sent as a great favour to Mount Auburn for Caroline Shipley to look at. Dear girl, she is confined to her room & often to her bed & I was glad to have an opportunity of pleasing her so much. She has requested me to let her knit thee a purse, for sick as she is, she is the most industrious creature, & knits & sews continually.

One thing, dear mother, Harrison wished me to tell thee with his love & thanks that if, as thou mentions, thou knits any more for him, he wears socks here much more than stockings & as they are easier to do he thought I ought to save thee trouble by telling thee. But dearest mother, I think thou hast done enough for us, & ten thousand thanks for all thy kindness.

I hope, dearest mother, there is no need for alarm on the ground of war between England & America. It is now confidently reported that the Oregon question is settled by partition of the territory. I hope it is, but I do believe there is great disinclination to war in the body of the people here. All know & acknowledge the impolicy of it, & as far as we can judge, it is little worth contending for, with immense tracts of excellent land still uncultivated. What have the Americans to do in seeking to add to their already over large country by the seizing of such distant & unremarkable lands, & England, I am sure, has more dominions than have done her good long ago, but war with this country & Mexico is said to be inevitable. The annexation of Texas was an evil thing because it was intended thereby to strengthen & perpetuate slavery & these are its early bad fruits: war & bloodshed.

[2] We have had most beautiful weather of late, though the usual spring rains have been frequent & violent, occasioning floods & doing considerable damage to the farmers by washing their corn (Indian) out of the ground &

requiring them to plant a second time, but as it is not late in the season, the inconvenience is trifling. I never saw a more luxuriant season for flowers; the bloom of every kind has been extraordinary, that of the locust-tree beyond everything we ever before witnessed. The trees have been white & the air filled with a luxurious fragrance. I have often thought of thee during the past week & said I did not know how thy poor head would bear so much perfume.[33] However, to those who are not distressed by sweet smells, it is delightful, especially in an evening & whilst they were in their ~~full~~ beauty we had a full moon. Oh how I enjoyed looking at the trees in the yellow moonlight & inhaling the breath of sweet flowers, sweeter still on those calm delicious evenings.

There is also much show for fruit; the peach trees are literally loaded & pears & apples will be plentiful; I shall dry & send you some of all our luxuries. We dried the squash or sweet pumpkin, & fried, it makes excellent pies, quite equal to the fresh, so you can have some of these if you are not able to raise them by this time.

I hope you have received the seeds &, should the summer prove a warm one, may be able to produce them yourselves. The bunch squash[34] is eaten green, boiled entire, crushed up with butter, pepper & salt; the others ought to be near ripe, either as vegetable or for cheesecakes.

Dost thou know, dear mother, Joe Smith, the chief of the Mormons is dead[?] He was murdered & the settlement is broken up. There was a kind of civil war in that part against them; some say they have been hardly dealt with; others rejoice at their removal at any cost. They are gone into Oregon or California & it was said the train of emigration would extend 20 miles, that the first wagons would contain a printing press, print a paper & deposit it for the succeeding companies. ~~They~~ One half proposed making a great halt, building a village, planting corn & vegetables to be reaped & gathered by another company, who would follow in a few months. I once sent thee some paper containing the history of this people & the particulars of Joe Smith's death. He was a bad man & it is marvelous so many were induced to settle under his sway & to adopt his wild & wicked views and imposture.

We have some thought of going to pay our friends at Westland a visit in a few days. If we get off we shall take Charles with us & leave the three little girls under the care of Elizabeth[35] & a niece, Elizabeth, a daughter of Wm Mason who is come to pay us a visit. She [3] is a nice girl & has so far been very useful to me in assisting in sewing, of which thou mayst be sure I have

33. Mary Howitt notes that her mother had experienced headaches and difficulties with her vision owing to the herbs that her father-in-law collected, dried, and sold out of the family home when he was living with them (*Mary Howitt: An Autobiography*, ed. Margaret Howitt [London: W. Isbister, 1889], 1:31).
34. The bunch squash, a variety of summer squash, is more commonly called "pattypan."
35. Probably Elizabeth Shipley Taylor, or Elizabeth Alderson.

a great deal since I have not now thy kind assistance & my family is increased; besides my eyes do not allow me to work at night.

I often wish I could afford to keep this young woman; I could well do with her assistance continually, but we have one very good household servant who is living her second year with us & wages to her are so high that it is beyond our circumstances to keep two: a few pence short of 7/ a week is the wage we give; it would hire two good girls in England.

Ann Alice is a lovely child, by far the sweetest looking of our little flock, but though near two years old, she does not walk yet. Still, she roles about & amuses herself so well on the floor that she is little, very little, trouble. There is a look in her bright, intelligent eye when she is glad that makes me think of thee. May she be like her dear grandmother in other respects.

I have been tailoring a good deal lately; last night I nearly completed a plain coat for Harrison & I am not a little pleased with my performance. Harrison ripped an old coat to pieces: so we got a good pattern & for a summer coat I thought I have succeeded admirably & probably saved 10/ by my week's work, besides gaining the knowledge that I can do it. I have all along made Charley's clothes.

People dress very expensively & very fashionably here. We cannot nor do we attempt to compete with them, and I feel no inclination to do so. Would thou believe I have got an American \friend's/ bonnet? My own that I brought with me are so dirty & shabby they are not fit to wear & yet I cannot persuade myself to put on my smart new one: it looks like foresaking one's country & turning renegade. If I continue to feel as I do, I shall wear my old dirty ones on or try to make one as near like them as possible.

[May] \14th/. Did I tell thee of the removal of Wm Bell, the early editor of the Irish Friend, & his family to Cincinnati? They have recently lost their eldest daughter, on whose account they removed here. We heard in a letter from John Thwaite of the death of Ann Jones. I saw a letter written to Cousin Ann Shipley from Hannah Neave mentioning her sickness & declining health.

There has been a very interesting deputation of Friends to the Indian settlement. Two of them ~~were~~ \are/ very intimate friends of ours and we hope to be able to get some interesting particulars respecting the Shawnee tribe and also of the surrounding Indians under \the care of/ other denominations. A young Indian of the Seminole tribe, who maintained such a long struggle in Florida for their homes and the graves of their fathers, has also been in the city exciting much interest & sympathy [4] on behalf of his people. He is a youth of about 21, who has been educated at Philadelphia & converted to Christianity. His heart is warm with love to God & man & at the risk of his life he ventured to return to his people, who during his absence had suffered many, many wrongs which were summed up in driving them beyond the Mississippi into the farther parts of Arkansas. It happened to be the day of celebrating, the eating up the old corn when, according to Indian custom, all feuds & animosities are buried & forgotten, when he approached their habitations not without repeated warnings from friendly Indians \on account of his <excursion> with the Whites/ & fears of his own, but something within him seemed to say go on, & instead of scowling faces, he \was/ met \with/ kindness & shook hands with 4000 seminoles, [“]& let me advise you,[”] said he in relating this circumstance, [“]never to shake hands with 4000 of your friends at one time especially if they be Indians.[”]

The old chief Kenoba (I think that is the name) was fond of him; John Bemoe[36] used to go out with the people to shoot game, but on first day always staid at home with the chief, who was too corpulent to pursue the chase. One day Kenoba asked him why he did not go as on other days. John now felt that the time was come to avow his new faith & declare himself a Christian. He accordingly told the chief of the institution of the sabbath, of the creation, the fall of man & the grand Scheme of Redemption through Christ. Kenoba listened to him for three hours but said nothing. The next 7th day, however, he told the young men they must prepare for the morrow & not hunt the next day. They obeyed & in the morning he had them assemble & requested John to tell them all he had told to him. He complied, the sabbath was appointed to be observed, & from that time he has regularly preached the gospel to them, their missionary & adopted chief, for Kenoba has appointed him to be his successor. I had these few particulars from a friend who heard him relate them. We were disappointed in not seeing him, for on two evenings on which we were invited to be present at his lectures, we were prevented.

I am sure, dear mother, thou will be pleased to hear of Richard’s well doing; he is clever & steady at his trade & the wages he gets board & clothe him handsomely. He has been spending the day with [5] us and looks really a fine handsome lad. He is a great favourite with our children; of course I need say nothing about them as I send you such minute particulars in Charley’s letters; I think you must think them very childish \things/.

Tell me all thou canst about dear Anna & her family; I never hear from them now. Tell them I do hope they have not given up writing to me. My dearest love to them all, as also to Wm & Mary, dear Anna Mary and the boys.

Do these three leaved letters reach you for single postage? It is not worth paying anything extra as I can, I expect, if I try, get larger sheets. Be sure to tell me, for I do not feel offended at your objecting to pay double postage when it is so entirely unnecessary.

Our dear Cousins at Mount Auburn continue to endure many trials; it seems as if afflictions were their portion. Elizabeth, the married daughter whose marriage seemed a bright ray in the dark clouds that surrounded them, is now in a low depressed state, unable to see her friends & suffering severely

36. The text is unclear, but I have given “Bemoe,” following *OCO* (85) The American edition omits the last name altogether (71).

<from> a nervous affection. She has a baby a few weeks old, but at present this only adds to their cares & anxieties as its mother is entirely unable to pay any attention to it.

We rode up yesterday to see them. They were as usual cheerful & even spoke of the happiness of making each other comfortable. Cousin Ann desired her love to thee; she is always pleased to receive a kind message. The children all beg me to put their dear love in my letter. Harrison all sends his to thee & the dear family. Mine most affectionately to you all; I am they tenderly attached daughter,

Emma

5 mo. 18

46. To Mary Howitt, May 14 to June 14, 1846

5 mo. 14.

Charles went with his Father & Mother to the city & met Agnes on her return from Mount Auburn, where she had staid on a very pleasant visit. She went to dine with her little friends the Warders, & Charles accompanied his parents. A friend, whilst they were gone to make some calls, gave him a Dime, or ten cent piece; he went therefore & laid it out in a little wooden cannon. All exclaimed at his choice, but it is characteristic, as he has a peculiar predilection for warlike accoutrements; at the mention of sword or gun he is more than commonly attracted & usually asks his mother to read that over again, and yet he knows that war is wrong.

In the evening it became very wet, & in returning it was so dark that they could not see the horse's head, & it was with difficulty they got home. Anna Warder came with them.

Next morning the ground was so soaked & muddy that the children could not play out, so they went into the woodhouse & built a fortress & planted Charles' cannon & laid sieges & repulsed the enemy.

[May 16] Seventh day was bright & warm. After lessons they all went into the vinyard & pulled up the weeds from 9 rows of vines. Then they came home & asked leave to go into the woods, and as they had been good & had a visitor, it was to be an especial ramble. So their mother gave them some sandwiches & pie in a little basket which Charles carried; Annie took a tin can for drinking out of & Anna promised to be mama at dinner & distribute the provisions. They rambled in the woods & by the side of a little creek, where in a shady place with three little streams of water near to drink from, they got their dinner. Then, in crossing the stream to go on Anna Mary got her shoes full of mud & water, so she took them off to wade with Charles, & in her joy threw them down & lost them. Anna was so kind as to go back to seek them, & at last they were found.

In a few hours they returned, having had a delightful ramble & soon felt so refreshed as to set out to go with Cousin Elizabeth to the Cemetery. They said there were many beautiful flowers in bloom on & around the graves, & whilst they staid there were three funerals.

There are not a great many chippy monks or ground squirrils to be seen, but now & then we catch a glimpse of them under the fences or on the hill sides. One day Milo killed a poor little ground squirrel: he chased it into an out house under an old stove & Richard tried to rescue it & took hold of its tail, when, poor thing, its tail came off into his hand & it died instantly; so they thought Milo might as well eat it. The ground squirrel is brown with a stripe of black bordered with white down its back; its tail is darker than its body & long & bushy.

[May 17] 1st day. As Charles returned from meeting they saw a great concourse assembled on the river bank and going to perform the rite of baptism on some individuals. An old man with a long stick went cautiously into the water to ascertain its depth & some of the people rudely pushed a boy into the river between the minister & the person baptizing. It was a man who seemed rather confounded by his ducking but, after all, came out very decently.

After dinner they all went over to see Jack's widow. She as usual was on the porch & her four dogs barked most outrageously. The old lady had a new black dress on; her usual handkerchief \wound/ over her head and, as Agnes thought, looked very nice. The farmer was there, a handsome black man, very well dressed, & with great glee the old lady said she expected after all to make a good living that year. [2] The "funeral" had been preached this morning and a "right smart company were there," but to our regret we missed it as they forgot to tell us or rather send us word in time.

[May 18] Second day. Father came from the city with two friends & the children were, as is usually the case, at a loose end when company is in the house. There was the body of a large black snake thrown upon one of the Catalpa trees near the road, & Charles & Agnes went to fetch it a la Waterton.[37] It measured near two yards long & when they had done examining it, Charles went into the barnyard & dug a grave & his sisters & he buried it.

Next day he went with his father into the vinyard to hoe. There is a little bird that has built its nest on the summit of a raspberry bush; it has now has 4 pretty little downy ones in it, & now & then the children go to peep at them. \The old one is so tame as only to fly away to a short distance./ The cat birds have also young ones & are very busy feeding them; when we go too near,

37. Probably a reference to Charles Waterton, *Wanderings in South America, the North-West of the United States, and the Antilles: In the Years 1812, 1816, 1820, and 1824* (London: J. Mawman, 1825), which Emma read in England (Ht/7/1/40, Correspondence of Mary Howitt [1799–1888], Manuscripts and Special Collections, University of Nottingham). His narrative deals at length with the snakes of South America and impresses upon the reader his own fearlessness in dealing with them. She was a great reader of such voyages of exploration. See figure 26 for Anna Mary Howitt's illustration of "Willie" and "Nanny" carrying home the black snake, an incident much embellished by Howitt in *OCO*.

the old one sets up its pitiful mewing cry, but when undisturbed, the father perches on one of the adjoining locusts & sings morning & evening some of his sweetest notes.

The roses are in full bloom: there are blush & dark crimson & damask & sweet briar & large double pink & white roses & eglantine & little Burgundy. The children have each a large bush that bears pretty double pink roses, & their reward now after they have behaved well at lessons is to have one of mother's best flowers: \there are 23 different kinds/. The gardens are going on well: Charley's Mexican vine is twineing round a pole, his currant bush has currants upon it, the raspberry is in bloom, the pop corn up, & to day he transplanted balsams, marvel of peru, mexican oleander, & some golden willows. Agnes has larkspurs & ragged robin in addition, & her cedar is looking very flush and promises to grow finely.

[May 22] 6th day. The morning was so bright & warm that mother said to day we will breakfast on the piazza. So all was set out in the sweet morning air under the shade of the grape vine & a cry of delight escaped from the children as they came down at the sight. Never does food taste so pleasant \as out of doors/ nor so keek[38] a sense of enjoyment come over one as when seated round the cheerful breakfast table. Our eyes dwell on beloved faces, & around us are so many pleasant sights & sounds. This morning was one of deep enjoyment. Near were bushes of red & white roses, woodbine on the walls & a noble syringa, covered with its starlike flowers, side by side with a fine sweet briar in full bloom. The scarlet trumpet honey suckle contrasted with them & a little bijou of a flower bed surrounded with rude basket work was filled with blush & dark, crimson & pink roses \among which sported a humming bird/. Beyond was the clover field in bloom, the farmer ploughing in a more distant part & the beautiful boundary of the distant wood, the song of birds, the sound of the cow bells & lowing of far off cows, whilst now & then a breakfast horn told that some other household were going to partake of the bounties of Providence. It was a time to feel delighted & grateful.

Whilst at breakfast father looked up & said what is that on the trellis? Is it a mouse or a bird[?] [3] No, then is it a bat? No, it was a little tree frog so nearly the color of the leaves that had it been amongst them we could not have distinguished it. Its back was rough & warty, but it was a pretty agile creature & lept away very nimbly after allowing itself to be well examined.

On going down to the city the children were much amused by seeing a recruiting party with their "star-spangled banner," their fifes & drums, their uniforms of dark green & white & white waving feathers tipped with green. But their father thought it was a sad sight & sighed when he saw the poor foolish volunteers following in their train & thought of the unrighteous war, of the carnage & oppression, of the heat & misery they must endure in Texas.

38. Howitt renders this as "keen," which makes sense, but that is clearly not the word in the manuscript (*OCO*, 117).

As they sate on the green grass under the pleasant shade of the trees in the calm evening & heard the distant firing of cannon in Kentucky on account of the news of victory obtained by general Jackson, he sighed more deeply at the thought of the dead & dying, and a shudder of horror passed through the little company when they remembered the sufferings of the wounded under that burning sun & in the unwholesome dews & reflected on the unprepared soul hurried into eternity.

[May] 25. Charles & Agnes had each 2 cents, so they requested leave to go to the store at Warsaw for marbles, twine, & candy. When they came home, Charles thought his twine would make an excellent fishing line. Therefore, after lessons Anna Mary & he went to the little creek in John's Wood. He had a long corn stalk for a rod, his twine for a line, a crooked pin for a hook & a piece of dried venison for a bait. When they got to the flood gates where they proposed catching their dish of fish, the water was reduced by the dry weather to a little mud, & the prospect seemed somewhat unpromising; however, they met with consolation in John Solo, the butcher's boy, who gave Charley a piece of lead to weight his line & a real fish hook for a cent & took them to the road side & showed them a garter snake & a black snake which he had just killed.

Agnes was all this while busy making doll clothes & dressing her doll. She had a beautiful blush rose & bud for reading a good lesson. When Charles came home his mother read to him some remarkable accounts of toads & worms found alive in stone, & his Father read the history of the civil wars in Charles 1st time. After tea they went into the orchard; Charles fetched the step-ladder & Agnes a basket, & their kind Father got up into the Cherry trees & gathered a quantity of cherries. Charles was much amused with a bees' nest suspended to one of the branches; the bee was a black & white insect & seemed anoyed with their presence but did not attempt to injure them.

[May] 27. This afternoon the family adjourned to the front of the house away from their favorite piazza at the side. The grass had been mown away that morning & upon it they enjoyed a delightful afternoon. Father read history to Charles; Agnes sate on the grass, writing upon her slate her copy of <run-*written in childish letters*>; little Alice, placed upon a little comfort, her winter bed covering, played with rose-leaves & grass that Charles gathered for her, & Annie pulled every flower from her bush, a most [4] congenial occupation to the little maiden & with great glee showed her pinafore full of leaves she was going to dry.

Tea was set in this place under the shade of two Locust & the catalpa trees. The cedar gave out a sweet refreshing scent & the air was filled with the perfume of roses & honey suckle mingled with clover. Agnes brought with great mystery the secret dish which her mother had covered with vine leaves & exclaimed as she approached the table "no one must know what is here," when off came the frail cover & disclosed a plate of cherries. Bread, cottage cheese (the drained curds from sour milk) apple-butter, lettuces, raddishes

& butter with milk & tea formed this evening meal, which taken in this beautiful salon with the accompaniment of the song of birds & an occasional visit of their friend the cat bird, who perched over their heads & flew in and out of the cedar to carry his flies & insects to his young ones, was as may be supposed a delightful one. Agnes said ["]Oh, I never enjoyed my tea so much; all is so sweet so peaceful & happy.["]

The children found some golden Lady-birds upon a young vine & Cousin Elizabeth [Mason], who is their oracle in all such things, was called to look at them & tell their name, but she had never seen the like, not even in Pennsylvania. They were indeed beautiful, as bright & metalic as if they had been made of polished gold, & when they spread their wings, these were silvery. However, she could solve another marvel, which was a round ball that Anna Mary brought out of the barn-yard about the size and as perfectly round as a marble. This is formed by the "tumble bug," & soon after they had the pleasure of seeing this curious insect pushing a little world before it six times its own size. It moved it with real dexterity about a yard up a steep rugged little hill & then seemed satisfied when it was deposited in a nook under some grass. Some say this ball contains the eggs or grub of the insect, some that [it] is it[s] store of winter food. If we can ascertain the opinion of naturalists we will tell you.

[May] 28. To day a little visitor arrived whose mother being absent from home she is come to spend a week with us. William has again put up the swing, which has been down some time; the children find it very pleasant amusement. They played at going to meeting in their carriage: the Wheelbarrow was the carriage, Charles & Agnes the horses, & Mary [Dorothea's daughter] & Anna Mary the two friends. Then they played at fire engines: there was the shout of fire, the yelling & hurrying of the fire men, the rattle of the engine, the fuss & hurry of extinguish[ing] [5] the fire and a universal commotion. This was exchanged for cherry gathering. Charles climbed into the tree after his Father & gathered a quantity into his hat & then they had a fruit store in the carriage house & in the course of selling all were eaten up.

We have sad news to tell of our little birds in the raspberry bush. On going to it this morning Father discovered that the nest was torn down & the young birds all gone. Afterwards, when in the lower barn yard, he heard a chattering & noise &, looking up, saw a large brown bird pursued by two little ones who seemed very vehement & angry. Father thinks perhaps it was one of the smaller kind of hawks that had robbed the nest & was thus followed by the parent birds.

Father gave Agnes a very pretty purple & white striped parasol which will also answer for a sun shade.

[May 30] 7th day. Yesterday Louisa's sister's little girl died. She had been sick some time. She was a nice little thing & used, when she was well, to come trotting to meet the children when she saw them in the orchard, for they live at William's. To day they buried her, & cousin Elizabeth and Charles went to the funeral. The little body was dressed in a white muslin gown & had a cap with a lace border & bunches of blue ribbons on, and a frill round its neck tied with blue ribbon. They had covered her with boquets of flowers & placed in her hands a cluster of artificial flowers and, poor things, had done their utmost to beautify, as they thought, the dead & show their affection & sorrow. It is a severe loss &, as this is their second child that has died & there are none left but the baby, there were two lighted candles placed by this coffin. The minister came & preached to them in German & then they took the body in Father['s] carriage to the Lutheran chapel near, & the company followed; after the interment in silence they went into the chapel & sang a hymn & then dispersed.[39] Our dear little Alice is not well: she has been sick for two days.

[May] 30th.[40] Mother & Charley staid at home while the rest went down to meeting. Agnes has been impatient for first-day that she might use her parasol. Mary took the feather-fan because she could not take care of both & was to fan herself & hand it over to Agnes.[41] the weather is become very warm, the thermometer often above 85 in the shade; flies are very troublesome, especially at meals, & some musquitos have made their appearance.

Richard came up this afternoon &, as he and Charles were going through the barn yard, they espied that the mulberries were black & ripe; so Richard got up the tree & shook it for the children, and a great treat it was to gather them up. At supper they had such a nice saucer full with sugar & cream. Mother read to Charles an account of some missionaries in India, which interested him much.

[June 1] 1st of 6. mo. This evening a great event occurred. Little Fanny had a bed made in the woodhouse, & when Charles went in a few hours after, his delight was very great to see two beautiful little puppies, one a pale buff with a white stripe down its back & forehead, the other black & yellow intermingled. Father gave her some new milk & they left her very happy in her snug corner on her bed of straw.

[June] 2nd. Yesterday was showery, and to day all the gardening part of the family were out busy hoeing & weeding, and transplanting, Father with his tomatoes & cabbage plants, mother with her balsalms, cocks comb, portulacas, geraniums, &c. & the children, after weeding their [6] <*word missing*>, found their plants so diminished that they had many contributions from her beds, especially one treasure of a cock's comb to Charles & a fine scarlet Zinnia to Agnes. Charles has larkspur in bloom & was very proud to have sweet scabious for mother & some fine marigolds for Mary Crehoe.

39. This sentence would read a little more smoothly with the break after "silence" instead of "followed," but the trip to the chapel clearly takes place *before* the interment.
40. Alderson might be mistaken about the date here, because May 30, 1846, was a Saturday.
41. Emma's apparent approval of her daughters taking their parasol and feather-fan to Meeting is indicative of a certain open-mindedness; among the Quakers with whom she grew up, these would have been considered unacceptable marks of vanity.

Cousin Elizabeth discovered that the bee in the cherry tree was a dangerous ~~orchard~~ hornet, & at supper its destruction was decreed. So when it became dark the summons to bed was deferred, & about 1/2 past 8 Charles fetched a wisp of straw; Anna Mary carried the box of matches, Father a shovel of \hot/ embers; & Mary & Agnes ran before to witness the incendiary attack, which, though it was on a hornet, we could not make without thinking of the poor unsuspecting inhabitant who had quietly gone to bed little dreaming of such deadly foes at hand. The leaves were so thick that Charles was sent for a lantern, but at length the nest was discovered. The children ran to a distance with a shout of mingled fear & joy, & then the burning wisp was thrust up, & the poor thing & its house burned up in a few moments.

All the ploughing & planting is done on the farm. William has corn and potatoes up; & his oats & clover in the orchard are high. Poor Fanny keeps so close in the woodhouse, in her nest as Annie calls it, that Charles is sadly afraid she will suffer. He takes her bones & mush & milk & now & then water and watches over her very tenderly.

[June] 8th. To day Father caught Anna Mary's guinea fowl, the one we raised, & declared at last he should die, for he has become such a dreadful tyrant pursuing the fowls & frightening the rooster & domineering over all the yard, that there was no peace near him. He bit & struggled hard for life, but at last his head was chopped off & he was suspended by his legs in the cellar. He was a cunning bird & would scratch up the flower beds & hide behind the cedars, running round & round. In short, he was an incorrigible pest & moreover very noisy. We have had much quietness since he is gone, for the other pair are very busy sitting on twenty eggs in the weeds below the vinyard. One thing we must mention about the poor dead bird before we let him pass into oblivion: from a chicken, he formed the most remarkable friendship with a black & white rooster; they were, during the winter & spring, inseparable & often rambled together for days alone, but of late this amity has been broken & he has been very fierce even with his old friend.

[June] 9th. Today the poor guinea fowl was cooked & proved very good eating. He was stuffed & boiled & eat very like turkey; the children after dinner took a plate with a part of the breast & some nice green peas & other things to Louisa, who has been ill for some days & is gone down to William's to rest & be nursed. Agnes carried \some/ flowers, W. C. the plates, & Anna Mary ran before to drive away [7] Tulk[42] & Maltman, Wm's dogs, if they came out to bark.

Charles hoed in the garden with his Father & cleared one walk between the raspberries & currant bushes himself in the afternoon. His mother read

42. The manuscript appears to say "Tulk," but *OCO* gives "Turk," which is a more likely name (135, 260).

an account of the American Locust to him which is as follows. We have not time now to transcribe so must pass on to events.

The remainder of the week was spent somewhat desultory. Company came & with them playfellows for the children; they rambled about & went to the woods. Once over an errand to Warsaw to bring eggs & sugar from the store, they had each a cent to spend & the woman was very kind, taking down her porcelain figures to show them, which they all thought very beautiful. Then she asked the name of the little girl with them & they told her it was Bessie Warder & she said her name was Bessie & was kinder than ever.

They called at Mary Crehoe's on their return & she gave them a can of fine ripe mulberries & a basket of sage for their mother. The fire-flies, or lightening bugs as the common people call them, have made their appearance. The Catalpa trees are covered with their beautiful large spikes of flowers, which look splendid amongst their broad green leaves. We often say the Queen of England would be proud of one of these noble trees in her garden, & here they grow amongst the locusts & cedar trees like common things. The flower is milky white, about the size of a large foxglove; the lower lip is marked with orange & purple spots, & upon each spike there are perhaps fifty \or 100/ of these beautiful flowers, some expanded & others bursting the rich brown calyx or enfolded in it.

The puppies have opened their eyes, & the children think there never were a pair of handsomer \or/ fatter puppies seen. Charley takes Fanny her meals to the "nest" &, though she is very quiet & good, she will not allow them to take liberties, as she bit Annie's bare foot when she poked it rather too near her darlings.[43] The guinea fowl has also to be fed when she comes off the nest, & Charles mixes some Indian meal & water for her as also for the young chickens, of which there are three broods requiring care.

[June 14] In coming home from meeting today, Charles & his Father walked up the hill, & there they saw two tumble bugs very busy pushing up one of their curious round balls, one on one side & the other on the other, & up they pushed the monstrous mass as adroitly & steadily as two men could have done it. Once or twice it seemed inclined to roll back & then one sprang on the opposite side to stay it. It appeared to be composed of cow-dung (must I say the word), as was one which we found & examined, & is probably intended for food. A little farther on they observed another alone with a similar but smaller ball, and all were pushing up hill.

Charles has been very busy making water wheels for himself & sisters, & a very wet day yesterday gave him fine opportunity to set them in the dripping spouts & under the pouring water.

Your English ears [8] will be shocked at the word bug but you must know that it is indiscriminately applied to creeping & often to flying insects, & no

43. Howitt softens this passage by having Fanny give Annie only "a very decided warning" with a snap and a growl (*OCO*, 137).

one thinks it vulgar or disgraceful to talk of such things. The lightning bug is far below our idea of fireflies, which are used as gems and carried about as flambeaux: they are a small winged chaffer, which as it rises emits a bright light from its tail that as quickly passes away, so that in the evening they look like innumerable bright sparks rising out of the ground or floating in the air. It is said as the night advances they ascend & towards ten or eleven are seen amongst the branches & tops of the trees.

The trumpet flowers have opened their bright scarlet corollas to the sun & look as every flower does at its first appearing, more beautiful than ever. The humming birds dart about amongst them & sip the honey out of their elegant cups. The prairie rose has also begun to bloom, & its long pendant branches drooping for yards from the trees & portico are adorned with clusters of their deep, rose coloured flowers. Richard is come to spend a week, & he & Charles have been husking corn in the corn-crib. Richard made each of them a very clever husking peg, and altogether they did 25 bushels. Then they went a walk into the fields & watched the woodpeckers flying to & from the great mulberry tree in the pasture with the fruit in their bills for their young ones.

Whilst they were gone, Agnes & Annie went with their mother into the garden to gather raspberries, & when they returned they had all a saucer of \the/ fruit & milk for supper. Charles went with Richard to curry & dress Farmer, & he gathered a handful of hair out of his long black tail, & now Agnes & he are all excitement making fishing lines. Charles got two fine elder rods, & with a hook & a piece of lead which he bought from John Solo for a cent he has made a very decent equipment.

Richard [Alderson] has been very busy in his joinering, putting up a coffee mill, finishing the summer house with slate, putting on box-lids, & doing all the multiplicity of repairs & improvements which every house from time to time requires & which a practiced hand can perform. He has journeyed to & fro to Lotte's bench & back again, & Charles in his way has been his assistant.

William & Joseph began to mow the meadow, or lawn, as we call it. The rich scent of the clover has long perfumed the air, & the frequent showers & warm sun have made the crop unusually heavy. The raspberries are yielding an abundant crop & afford about an hour's work daily to gather them; the children each take a tin can & are very serviceable in the employment. We have found two more nests in the bushes, each with 4 eggs in. To-day we discovered that one brood are hatched.

As we sate at breakfast on the Piazza, enjoying the warm yet fresh morning air, we heard a distant rumble of thunder. Before our meal was over it became louder, & ominous dark clouds rose slowly in the west. "Richard run and help Joseph to put up that hay" said father, "I will go too & the rest must try if they can gather those rasp[berrie]s you left last evening." All hurried away, for the storm came fast. Agnes & Annie went with mother to the garden

& picked as long as the rain would let them; Annie is a most industrious persevering child, [9] and soon gathers her can full. Agnes said, "I don't know how it is but I can always work better when grown people are with me"; that is true, but her butterfly spirit loves to swing itself from pleasure to pleasure & has no preference for application to anything except amusing & dressing her doll.

The storm seemed to pass away but at noon returned after some very hot gleaming sunshine & soon blew a complete hurricane. It was grand to watch its coming. An icy wind preceded it & brought some hail & torrents of rain which obscured the light like a thick mist; then the wind drove furiously from the north-west & tore off branches from the trees hurling them forward in the tempest of rain; & last of all the loftiest & most beautiful locust tree snapped off in the middle & its great top was whirled to a ~~great~~ distance. Everything that an hour before had seemed to be rejoicing in conscious beauty, when the storm passed away, had a forlorn & battered look. The Catalpa blossom was all gone, the trumpet creeper was torn & injured, the hop poles prostrated, & great fears were entertained for the vines & the \early/ corn, which now begins to tower upwards & show its beautiful tassels.

Father went round to investigate &, after a while, to repair the damage by tying & propping; he found the raspberry bushes almost bowed to the earth, the nest where the young birds were just falling & one of the poor little things hanging head foremost out of it; the old ones were making a doleful cry in an adjoining plum tree. He set all to rights & no doubt left them happy & grateful.

In an hour or two Richard & Charley sallied with their axes to cut up the poor locust & drag its limbs into the barn-yard; here was an end to hay-making for one day, but the cool night gave promise of fine weather again <&> the next day realized it. Towards noon the grass had been spread & was so dry that William brought out the horse & waggon & all young and old were ready to help. The children all got on to the hay to tread it down & then rode to the barn on the loaded waggon; oh how grand did it feel to be moving in the birds' air & sunshine many yards above the every day earth.

In the evening, whilst at the farthest spring, the children were joined by John & David Solo, who had come into the next field to cut grass for their horse. John was quarrelsome & threw stones at Charley; he returned the insult with clods and at last got a severe blow on the head. David interfered but Charles drove them away with a club-like stick. John used bad words & this, it is to be hoped, will be the end of an intimacy of which neither Father nor Mother approves & which is carried on in the woods & lanes when the children are away from home.

Richard stormed another wasps' nest in the grape vines & took the Queen, a great black & yellow insect. Louisa is still sick and unable to do her work; the children now & then venture to see her but the poor girl has requested them not to go as the old woman is very cross & once sent them away in a very ill humour, railing & scolding in German. She was sleepy & wanted to take a nap & their presence disturbed her.

The children & their mother went out one evening to seek for a woman to come to wash &, as the result was very characteristic of American notions, you shall have it. They went to the log-house on the next farm formerly occupied by John, the owner of John's wood. It seemed as if there was a little fair in the field, so many white people & things together; there was a man in his shirt sleeves with a white horse ploughing, two other men & two boys hoeing, and a young woman to whom was their errand hoeing also. She was so busy she could not come, for they [10] had to hire hands themselves & every body was the same, "except your mother could go to oblige the lady." ["]My mother,["] said the boy, who was John Solo, ~~she~~ ["]she cannot go and if she could she would not." Then they went to one and another; all were too busy or too proud, till one poor woman, as a great favour which was to be a secret from her husband, came a day or two after, & in her heart I believe was thankful for the 60 cents, though she exhausted all her little stock of reasoning & phylosophy in proving it was no degration to go out & do a day's washing for a neighbour. Oh, the hateful effects of slavery which are felt in these things, making labour & degradation synonymous.

The hay making goes on bravely; the clover is all housed, most of it without a drop of rain. Now they are cutting the Timothy, & the poor Partridges, or quails, or Bob Whites, as they are called by all children, are in great trepedation & utter most loud & mournfully their loud note of Bob White in token of their distress in having their nests disturbed.

Cousin William [Mason] from Westland has come & gone, & with him yesterday went Cousin Elizabeth, of whom we were all very fond. William gave a curious account of the locusts & their devastation, \for/ their visit extended even there; they have stung the fruit trees & in many cases quite injured them, the branches hanging withered & dead. They were very numerous & their "hollowing" was inconceivable as they burst the shell which inclosed them in the nympha state. The people interpretted it to "Pharoh" & some said they cried "Egypt," also that on their wings was a clear, well defined W, for war; last time P was as distinct for Peace. The pigs, chickens, turkeys & all living things that would eat them are become very fat upon them.

Now I must conclude with very dear love to you all. I fear these letters will become very wearisome & the details to insignificant to interest you any longer; say so if you think so. Farewell, beloved sister & dear friends,

E. A

47. To Mary Howitt, June 30 to July 11, 1846
6 mo. 30

I was beginning, my beloved sister, to feel a little weary or rather discouraged in the continuance of our journal & but that thy letter has revived me,

I should almost have given it up fearing it was become wearisome to thee & not worth the trouble or expense it must be to receive so many sheets, & I fear they have been \very/ expensive as I have transmitted a sheet & a half, but I will do so no more unless thou assures me it has not been the case. Here we now pay for all letters foreign or otherwise by weight; anything under 1/2 an oz comes 500 miles for ten cents & I begin to fear you are rather more restrictive with regard to foreign letters. If so, pray dear sister, excuse my thoughtless[ness].

I am pleased to think that these minute details bring us more intimately into acquaintance & that thou thinks our country life so interesting &, so common as it is in events, interesting to thee and dearest mother. We live so retired and have so little time for reading and the occupations that engage your attention that I think to thee it must seem a very unprofitable sort of existence; sewing for the family & instructing the children with the occasional interruptions of visiting & receiving company leave me no leisure to indulge in the luxury of books; I sometimes hope it may be otherwise, but at present see no prospect. I have had some visions of a sofa & dinner service &c. if this should really ever prove worth thy trouble of arranging & publishing, but am not very sanguine on this head. Of course my share must be very small, but I will not deny that 20€ would make me feel very rich & I should be thankful to call as much my own.

The last day or two Charles and Agnes have been much concerned on behalf of a poor sick chicken. Charles carried it about in his bosom & gave it cold water in abundance (the best possible remedy for invalid chickens); they built it a little log-house on the grass & in the course of a few hours it is so far revived as to be able to peck & before night joined the brood under its mother's wing. Next morning to their great joy it came to peck the cornmeal food with the others & is now strong & healthy; it was, whilst sick, fed out of cups formed of the trumpet flowers & eat in the course of the day two of these full of soaked bread.

[June] 31.[44] Poor Blackberry has been unwell for some days and this evening came in so ill from the pasture that Joseph declared she would not live till morning if she was not bled immediately; he said a colt just by had died a day or two ago with a lump no larger than <??> \one/ in her throat, so Charles was sent in a great hurry to Icles to ask him to come & see her. It was a fine night, the sun was setting and the week old moon gave a pleasant light as they came towards home. Icle started; Charles thought he saw a snake & asked what was the matter. ["]Look there,["] said the man, ["]& come on as fast you can least it bites you;" and what should it be but a quiet tortoise walking across the road towards a pond on the other side. Charles just ventured to look long enough to see its four short legs, it[s] little head & tail \and

44. Again, Alderson may be confused about the dates, since there is no 31st of June.

poke its hard shell with a stalk of wild camomile/ to wish he could take it home.

In the meantime father had made an ointment of Gympson-weed, or stramonium, & lard & when they came they went & rubbed the throat of the poor creature, put her in a shed & left the bleeding till morning, as Icle said it was his son, who was gone to market, & not he who could do this. The next morning she was better & in a day or two quite well with frequent rubbing down with the ointment.

[July 1] 1st of 7th mo. Charles and Annie went down with their parents to the city; they saw a steam boat, the Caroline, leave the shore & steer its course westward down the Ohio for New Orleans filled with 400 soldiers, poor things. The cannon were fired, guns on the shore saluted them with land reports; as they passed, people waved their handkerchiefs & hats, & the men on board answered with a faint cheering, [2] but it was a melancholy sight to see the poor deluded fellows going to inevitable destruction to many; pestilence & death in various forms awaits them, & so had the sense of these things pressed upon their minds that upwards of one hundred deserted on the point of embarkation, and what is worse a whole waggon load were driven down to the boat in a state of helpless intoxication.

Richard said he went to the encampment where they have been lying for some weeks & where many scenes of riot & disorder have daily taken place. His visit was to two lads of acquaintance & in answer to his laconic remark "I'll tell you what boys; soldiering is not the fine thing it ~~has been~~ \is/ cracked as being" "no["], said they, "we have wished hundreds of times we had never left our work to come here."

This was an eventful day: they heard of the landing of 395 emancipated slaves, & I give you the account related to them by a friend who witnessed the scene.[45] It was about 8 oclock in the morning when the steam boat which brought them arrived. They were a motley group, men, women & children, old & young all decently clad & bringing along with them their waggons & household stuff & considerable property, some say near 50,000 dollars. The history of their emancipation is interesting, and the 9 years struggle since they obtained it between power and justice has nobly for the honor of the south terminated in their favour, and they are on their way to Mercer County in this State, which is chiefly settled by coloured people & where a large tract of land has been purchased for them. They were the property of John Randolph, a wealthy planter of Roanoke in North Carolina;[46] he was in his life-time a strenuous & violent ~~supp~~ upholder of slavery; yet even then his conscience witnessed against him & in one of these visitations

45. Howitt identifies this "friend" as "Uncle Cornelius," though there is no suggestion here that it was Joseph Taylor (Uncle Cornelius's model) who gave them this information.

46. Emma is mistaken in saying that he was from Roanoke, North Carolina; Roanoke was the name of his home near the Roanoke River in Charlotte County, Virginia.

of light & repentance he made his will liberating his slaves and providing handsomely for their transportation & maintenance in a free State. It is said that on his death bed, when unable to speak, he obtained a pencil & card & in an agony of mind wrote the word "Remorse." It was all he could accomplish, but how much does that one word convey. He felt that the redeeming act of his will did not satisfy an accusing conscience nor attone in the sight of Almighty God for a life spent in oppression & injustice.

I copy from a daily paper another version of this interesting scene because I want it to be as graphic & full of life to you as possible; I wish we ourselves had witnessed it.[47] "Main Street this morning presented a singular scene, one which never before occurred here & may never again;—just in front of our office & occupying the centre of the street for half a square was a crowd of negroes—men, women and children. They were dressed in coarse cottons apparently comfortable in bodily circumstances. They walked along from the river to the canal. They were in his lifetime the ~~proper~~ slaves of the celebrated John Randolph of Roanoke.

["]They are of all ages and conditions, from the infant upon the breast to the old man tottering under the weight of time & infirmities. They numbered, we believe, 395 in all. Whether they were all present, we are not informed. They had their baggage waggons along,—and all in all had a more comfortable appearance by much than have North Carolina Emigrants, who have been immortalized in the picture of our townsman Beard.[48] The last one was a stout but old and bent over man, who walked with a cane. The thought of him as one who perhaps had been reared with and played with the orator of Charlotte, and who when [3] [']Remorse['] wrung his heart had been remembered by John Randolph in his will & at his dying hour.["]

The children had a delightful visit at Mount Auburn: they played with their cousin; Charles & Ella climbed up into cherry trees to gather the fruit, eat till they could eat no more, stained all their clothes with the deep red juice of the morello cherries & came home ti[r]ed & Annie fast asleep on the carriage seat at 10 oclock at night.

[July] 4th. This is a day of universal jubilee in America; on it the declaration of Independence was signed and the anniversary is kept with a feeling of national triumph and rejoicing. Would that one more glorious 4th might come when the nation (then wholly great) should break the chains of slavery & declare every man & woman free free free. As all such times are ushered, so was this with the firing of guns & cannon, and even we in our remote

47. Much of what follows first appeared in the *Cincinnati Chronicle* on July 1 and was soon reprinted in other publications under various headlines, including "John Randolph's Slaves," *Emancipator* 48, no. 12 (July 15, 1846), 48 and "John Randolph's Emancipated Slaves," *Friend* 19, no. 43 (July 7, 1846) 343. The latter article cites the original article from the *Cincinnati Chronicle.*

48. James Henry Beard, *North Carolina Emigrants, Poor White Folk* (1845), oil on canvas, Cincinnati Art Museum.

home passed a disturbed night from their distant report & the loud & incessant barking of all the dogs in the neighbourhood & they are not a few; Milo & Fanny did their part in the general uproar.

The day brought company who left the crowded noisy city to enjoy the quiet beauty of the country, rendered even more sweet by contrast with the heat & dust & jostle of a gala day in a large town. One of our friends brought Charles a packet of shooting crackers, not the little feble things that he has been accustomed to buy at Warsaw but 75 large red rolls which are enclosed in a paper covered with Chinese characters & making a report as loud as a pistol. Frap, frap they went all evening, greatly to the delight of the children, especially Wm Charles & Anna Mary who, though they are always very litigious one with the other, are so similar in their tastes & pursuits that they make you think of the Swan on Sweet St. Mary's lake sails double, Swan & Shadow.[49]

[July] 5th. Cousin Charles [Shipley] came up with the family from meeting; during his stay the children have had a <??d> of joyous holiday. They swing and play till they are tired & swing again for rest & then go to fulfill some merry fancy till the heat & weariness bring them again into the wood house to the unfailing comforter, the swing.

One day they went to a neighbouring farmhouse to buy cherries; the man told them to fill their basket & come again after dinner when, if they chose, they might have half a bushel for nothing. Accordingly they went, but a revolution had taken place; the wife, finding her neighbours valued them, had changed her mind & thought she might as well dry some for herself & therefore when about a quart had been gathered the husband told them he was tired of their company & wished them to "clear out." It was rather an ignominious retreat & the children came home somewhat crest fallen especially as Father & mother strongly suspected they must have been rude or troublesome to have met with such a reverse.

[July] 9th. Charles and his cousin walked down to the city. It was a great pleasure to anticipate far before riding, and the two boys were up early and all impatience to be off on the road. They saw the "chain gang" at work mending it. They are men of both colours, black & white, who for several offences are condemned to labour thus exposed to public view. They have each a long iron chain, to which is attached a heavy iron ball, fastened round their right ancle. They work in silence and are not permitted to hold converse with any; an overseer with a loaded musket attends them and follows the waggon [4] which conveys them to & from their work in a buggy with this musket on his shoulder. It is a barbarous custom & one which many feel to be a disgrace to the country.

49. "The swan on still Saint Mary's Lake / Float double, swan and shadow!" from William Wordsworth's "Yarrow Unvisited" (43–44).

After this they came to the great steam-saw-mill & watched the saws at work "ripping" the boards. Next was the rolling mill with its huge iron rollers pressing the metal from the rough pig to the thinnest bars. Then they went down to Cousin Charles' father's store & got their pockets full of almonds & spent 5 cents in a glass of soda water each & afterwards refreshed themselves with a shower-bath & were amused with the multitude of things in the stores & streets: a dray running away, troops of soldiers, toys & pictures, and an endless variety of people & things.

[July] 11th. John Randolph once offered to a friend to manumit every slave in his possession if he could prove that they would be happier free than under his care and mild protection, for he was a good master. No argument this for slavery, but he knew the injustice of his country to the poor downtrodden African & doubtless felt he could secure him more comfort than the proud white men were willing he should enjoy. And now they began to feel the truth of this judgment based on the knowledge of injustice. When they arrived at the landing place near their destination, a mob met them & refused to let them proceed to take possession of their land, nor to enter the country, & they were obliged to turn off & form an encampment at a distance, there to wait the result & they now are, & possibly if allowed even to be quiet, here must remain many months.

With dear love to all ours, most affectionately,

Emma A. in great haste

48. To Anna Harrison, June 26 to July 15, 1846
6 mo. 26, 1846

Now my tenderly beloved Sister, though the chances are much against me, I will try if I cannot finish and dispatch this in time for the coming packet. Time goes on so rapidly that I was taken by surprize last evening on referring to the day of the month to find I had barely time to do what I have calculated upon for some days with great pleasure, writing to thee by this mail. Thy last, most welcome letter, received two days ago bearing date of 6 mo 25th[50] is a fresh call upon me to obey the dictates of my heart & tell thee how near & dear you all are to me and how greatly I feel the debt of gratitude I owe you for your kindness not to be understood by words in so constantly remembering us & writing to me.

I begin to think I act & feel like a spoiled child: when the time arrives for letters I am disappointed & unhappy if there are none for me, and yet thanks to your affectionate attention this is not often the case. Dear mother, Mary, and thee are now \almost/ my only correspondents & in time I expect all

50. It cannot be true that Anna Harrison dated her letter 6 mo. 25, since Alderson has dated this letter only one day later. It is possible that Alderson is mistaken about one of these two dates, or perhaps the date she is referring to on Harrison's letter was the Cincinnati postmark showing its arrival.

others will drop off, but I care little so that you remain faithful. I do not mean this should apply to any member of our family.

Tell the dear girls I begin to wish to hear from them; I shall write to them I hope soon. Thank thee my beloved sister for thy interesting history of your journey. To me it is peculiarly so & yet to every one I think it would be delightful & I mean to treat Cousin Ann Shipley & my dear friend Hannah Taylor with the journal. I am proud of my Friends in England & love that those whom I think worthy here should admire & love them too. But dearest Anna, there is one particular which thou hast omitted which has made me very anxious, and that is thou dost not say that thy health was benefited by the journey. May a kind Providence grant that this has been the case & that thou art enjoying improved health in the bosom of thy beloved family.

But dear Sister, should thou still feel the pressure of bodily weakness, I want to induce thee to try the effect of a longer travel: come this Autumn & pay us a visit; I can confidently promise thee much to please & admire. Oh, I can think with what glowing admiration thou wilt gaze upon our noble rivers, our forests & mountains & then with what quiet joy thou wilt behold us in our pleasant rural home. This is all I want, that those I love so tenderly could participate in our blessings, could be benefitted by what to us in outward things has been so desirable a change. Yet great as the pleasure would be to myself, I would not ask thee did I not believe all the sacrifises it would involve would be compensated by the advantages. I believe the voyage & the one of our beautiful [2] Falls would do thee great good, perhaps establish thee in robust health, and what a field of experience, what a fund of knowledge gathered in a few months. It seems to me that in a short time so much may be gained that do, dear Sister, think of it not as a wild scheme but as something reasonable & practicable (if thou canst feel it right). Do not hesitate; come and bring Daniel or one of the boys with thee; nay bring half a dozen: we have a house large enough to hold you all & to say you would be welcome is to say very coldly all I feel in the bare mention of such a thing. I would not try to tell thee how glad I should be: words are weak & powerless to express the earnest feelings of our hearts, and mine I often think are feebleness itself.

I am very glad that Smith [Harrison] has sent Thompson's money: poor fellow, he has been very anxious about it & began to look somewhat sceptical when I assured him it <u>would</u> come. He was in the city a few weeks ago on his way to the Gulf of Mexico with a boat load of goods consigned to his care. He looked very respectable & we were glad he was to all appearance in the way of doing something for himself & family. The flat boat navigation is a life of hardship & privation but full of interest to a mind like Thompson's. He has taken these trips before & used to interest me with the relation of his adventures. These boats are constructed somewhat like a \large/ long \covered/ box upon which is erected a shed or tent for the men on board. They work the boat with enormous paddles and are impelled by the force of the current alone, so that in summer when the rivers are low their progress is extremely slow. These and the ponderous rafts of lumber are often a very interesting & picturesque sight to me in our rides by the river.

I am sorry, dear Anna, I did not acknowledge your kindness in sending "Perfect Peace." I received it & admired it much & felt very much obliged to you for it.[51] I lent it to a young woman then lying on her death bed & understand it was a great comfort to her. She requested me to allow her to lend it to a friend of hers, a Unitarian in whose welfare she was much interested & who was in declining health. Of course I rejoiced in its being an instrument of good to any & consented but have not yet had it returned & begin to be uneasy & think of asking for it, for I shall not willingly lose it.

I am glad the flower seeds have come up. We have at present some spotted balsalms, the most beautiful flowers I ever saw; I shall save the seeds very carefully for you, as also the Cypress Vine. I hope you have that: it is a lovely flower. Tell me if you have the Portulacca? These are all Greenhouse plants but grow & bloom beautifully here in the open air. We have a few new wild flowers for you which I think will do well in the garden.

I am at present much interested on behalf of a number of manumitted slaves lately come from [3] Virginia. I shall send some papers to Daniel & Mother containing particulars, but lest they should not reach will just relate a little of their history. A few weeks \ago/ about 300 of them, men women & children, passed through the city towards their destination—land purchased for them in Mercer County & for which it is said 30,000 dollars were paid. On their arrival there, however, they were met by a mob who insisted on their proceeding or returning & refused to receive them amongst them on any terms. Respectable men interceded for them, appealed to their humanity and justice, but in vain: not a day might they stay & at the point of the musket were hurried into boats & obliged to take refuge in the woods on lands belonging to a Col. Johnson, a man of known benevolence to the coloured people & Indians.

These poor people were the slaves of a John Randolph, a wealthy planter in Virginia. He was a violent supporter of slavery but on the whole had the character of being a good master. Secretly he had convictions which induced him to give his negroes freedom at his death & he even provided liberaly for their maintenance & provision in a free state. It is said that on his death-bed, his distress was excessive, & on obtaining a pencil & card he wrote the word "Remorse." It was all, but it was a enough from such a man at such a time. His will has been contested for many years and at last decided in favour of

51. Probably David Pitcairn's *Perfect Peace: Letters-Memorial of the Late John Warren Howell, Esq., of Bath, M.R.C.S.* (London: J. H. Jackson, 1844), first published in London in 1844 and New York in 1845. With its emphasis on atonement by the historical Christ, this book would appeal to an Orthodox Quaker; its denunciation of "Unitarian heresy" along with the "errors of Popery" (47) might not have been appreciated by the Unitarian to whom Alderson's friend passed on this copy of the book.

the slaves. Yet now they are denied the homes of free men & remain outcasts & wanderers in a land calling itself Free.

John Randolph once said to Dr. Parish, his physician (a friend), if you will convince me that my negroes will be as happy in freedom as in slavery I will liberate them tomorrow. This tells nothing for slavery, but Oh what a comment on the ways & practices of America. He was with all his eccentricities a clever & discerning man & knew well what hardships & trials awaited them.

There is another subject that I think will interest you as well as myself. It is the fate of the Mormons, a large body who located themselves in Illinois under a worthless man named Joe Smith. He pretended to have found a new gospel & it is surprizing what influence he gained over the people who yielded themselves up to the darkness & delusion with entire faith. I know nothing of their religious opinions except that they were wild & false. However, about two years ago Joe Smith was murdered; his adherents, about 15,000, were assailed by the people of the neighbouring counties & a war of extermination commenced. They then concluded to remove & this spring set forward to cross the Rocky Mountains [4] in order to find a quiet settlement in Oregon. They are moving forward in large bodies, a thousand waggons in a train & from 3 to 4 thousand individuals in each company. It is said they suffer from scarcity; they plant & sow for the coming troop at each main halting place: 2,000 acres were planted with corn at one station, but it is a dreary region & those that travel through it encounter great difficulties.

What a deal of my sheet I have occupied & have not said half my say.

Our dear little American is a lovely child; she has passed her 2nd birthday [July 15] & cannot walk, but she plays constantly on the floor & is full of activity. She is a picture child, so our friends call her, a perfect St. John style of face: may she have his sweet spirit.[52] How full of benign charity was that favoured apostle & beloved friend of the blessed Saviour.

We have begun to make cheese & I succeed admirably, another step towards entire independence. It seems as if in this land most that is consumed at home may be made at home. I often wish I could enlighten you on the great value of pearl-ash or saleratus as it is called here.[53] We make delicious biscuits without any trouble: just take a basin of flour & rub a piece of butter about the size of a walnut & ~~with~~ \into/ a little sour milk or butter milk,

52. Of the four gospels, Quakers historically found most to admire in that of St. John, finding evidence for the "inner light" in his emphasis on the "Word." One explanation for the name "Society of Friends" is that it derives from John 15:15: "Henceforth I call you not servants; . . . but I have called you friends" (King James Version).

53. The term "saleratus," now obsolete, is first recorded in *A Treatise on Bread and Bread-Making* (Boston: Light & Stearns, 1837) by the dietary reformer and vegetarian activist Sylvester Graham (1794–1851). Pearl-ash and saleratus are not, as both Graham and Alderson suggest, quite the same thing, although they are both leavenings and similar to modern baking soda. The possibility that Alderson learned about saleratus from this source is intriguing, since elsewhere she is dismissive of "Grahamerism" for its association with the Fourierists (see page 260).

enough to wet it, put about a small teaspoonful of dissolved pearl ash; mix it into a dough, immediately roll it & cut it in small cakes & bake directly in a quick oven. They are brought hot or cold unbuttered to tea & split & buttered as eaten. They are excellent, cheap & convenient: perhaps you may in learning to use it get too much saleratus & then the cakes will be yellow & taste unpleasantly, but practice will soon make you proficient.

I make common pie crust in this way & roll a little butter or lard in to make it pastry. But here ripe uncooked fruit is preferred to pies, with sugar & cream or without the latter. It is a nice substitute for pies & with biscuit or bread & butter quite as good & much less trouble: we seldom take supper without it. Our supper is tea: in America no one takes more than 3 meals, an excellent <practice . . . *sealed*>

I shall say nothing of the children: you hear enough of them to grow weary of the subject. Harrison is well and very busy as usual; if it were not so, he often says, he thinks the state of things, the spiritual thrawldom & corruption, would kill him. I have my home & children & household & these things do no[t] come quite [1-*cross*] so near me, but believe me dear Anna, England is the land of liberty, religious & political. May God prosper & bless her, for she is the heart of the world, its blessing & its praise.

My dearest love to you all, as if named individuals. Give my love, my dear love, to Mother & Mary. Oh how thankful do I feel that dearest mother has such a happy home. Farewell beloved sister; remember next month's packet—thine, most affectionately,

Emma.

Dear love to Danl from both of us; Harrison's to thyself & the children—We have a good Dutch girl (woman) [Louisa] that has lived with us a year & a half. I find with good treatment I can keep girls here as well as in England & if they leave us it is always in kindness & good will: so one bugbear vanishes. Agnes & Anna Mary importune me to send their dear love.
Harrison says he intends to draw for Thompson's money immediately, but a friend having applied to him to pay 100 dollars for him in England, it is possible to accomodate him. Harrison will draw for two sums instead of the whole in one bill—so you will understand it if they come drawn in favour of two different persons.

49. To Ann Botham, July 12, 1846

Cedar Lodge 7th mo. 12th

It is now some weeks since I received thy last most welcome letter containing an account of the Yearly Meeting. I am glad thou wast able to be in London at the time, though prevented attending the sitting, which I never expected thou wouldst be able to do regularly. Yet thou wouldst enjoy meeting with so many of our old friends, and I doubt not to them it would be \a/ very great pleasure to see thee. I don't know any one whom thou mentions that I was better pleased to hear of than dear Ellen Masters. She was one of those that we knew & loved in our youth, and to me she always was a very kind friend. I often think of those pleasant visits I used to pay to her & William at Hawood, when I was treated as an honoured guest and also as a sister. What delightful rambles I took \alone/ on Cannock Chase & pleasant rides with William when he went to survey the roads.[54] Then we used to read in an evening & talk on useful & improving subjects; it was certainly very pleasant. I loved them & felt grateful then & the feeling remains strong in my mind. Please, dearest mother, if thou hast an opportunity, give my love to Ellen & tell her the rememberance of their kindness is a sweet memorial even in this far distant land.

There has been much anxiety here respecting the result of the Yearly Meeting, but as far as we are concerned, we have had little intelligence. I am rejoiced & I may say proud to find that England has so nobly contributed to the boarding-school & the Indian cause; that is one good result of the deputation of last year.[55] Friends here, there is little doubt, are capable of sustaining these things handsomely themselves, & some give munificently, but the body in dollars & cents are penurious. They have, as John Pease said, [“]to learn to give.” If corn, pork & apples were all that is wanted, there might be Egyptian store-houses filled with such things, but such contributions in this land are burdensome and unavoidable, & so the good cause languishes for want of means to carry it forward. However, England, the nursing-mother of the whole world, stretches forth her hand, and \all is well/. May she receive a tenfold blessing in Heaven’s best gifts as her reward.

Oh dear mother, how thankful did I feel when I read \in/ thy last that the Corn Laws are repealed; now I trust the free gifts of a bountiful Providence will pour freely into the country & it may again be truly called Happy England. It has been very sorrowful to think of any suffering for want. The miseries of the poor have often made my heart ache & I feel also for the difficulties & trial of the middle classes in [2] such circumstances. They have to endure many privations & to practise much secret self denial, and yet what a fruitful school for the virtues is this, and for the growth, too, of a dependent, thankful sprit. I often think that in the midst of the abundance & fullness here there is much forgetfulness of the kindness & bounties of Providence & a less grateful sense manifested, at least, than ought to be of his continued & unfailing goodness.

54. Little and Great Haywood are two adjacent villages on the northern edge of Cannock Chase in Staffordshire, southwest of Uttoxeter. The surveyor may have been William Howitt, who surveyed professionally in this area during Alderson’s childhood. The context, however, suggests that it was a different William, the husband of Ellen Masters, about whom no more is known.

55. She is no doubt referring to the visit to Indiana Yearly Meeting by London Friends Josiah Forster, William Forster, John Allen, George Stacey. See pages 113–114 for more details.

We have have had so far a most beautiful & fruitful summer. The weather is very warm, the thermometer frequently above 90 in the shade, and yet ten days have not often elapsed with[out] one of those refreshing thunder showers which cool the air & give a fresh impetus to vegetation. One of these is just occurring at present & I am sitting in the piazza enjoying its cooling effects & listening with pleasure to the pleasant sound of rain drops upon the leaves of the vine, which is covered with clusters of grapes, not ripe yet of course, but promising a fine harvest in the Fall.

This is now the wheat & hay harvest; we have got in our hay beautifully & have a very fine crop of both clover & timothy grass. The former is fodder for cows & we get two crops in the course of the summer; the latter is horse hay. Owing to the wild folly of the nation in prosecuting the war with Mexico, men are so scarce in the country that it is almost impossible to get labourers. In some cases the farmers have to give 2 dollars a day, and wheat is only 25 cents a bushel. Think of that—8 bushels of wheat for a day's work; 1 1/2 dollars is no uncommon price. The artizans in the city get it regularly.

Last 6th day, the last company of soldiers, or volunteers, went from Cincinnati for New Orleans. There have been about <*blank*> raised in the neighbourhood & state. Poor fellows, miserable hardships await them in that hot country & unhealthy climate. The heat, the mosquitos & fever, independent of the accidents of war, will cause much suffering & thin their ranks, and this is not the worst. It is shocking to hear of the disorders & depravity that prevailed at the encampment whilst they were lying a few miles from the city awaiting their embarkation; sober, quiet men & boys became complete drunkards; whiskey they would have & did get, despite of all the [3] efforts of the officers, who were themselves as raw in enforcing discipline as the solders were in observing it.

Cousin Ann Shipley lent me a paper containing a "pen & ink sketch["] of a visit to Clapton, a most interesting & gratifying account to me, & not the least so is that part in which the author speaks of my dear honoured mother, so charming & full of interest in her old age.[56] Much as I loved to hear the praises of Wm & Mary, that sentence respecting thee pleased me best.

Thank thee, my beloved mother, for thy ready compliance of my request respecting the "Friend." I was rather sorry I was so severe upon the British F. but they displeased me by their unfairness at that time. However, we shall

56. Beginning in April 1845, the *Boston Daily Atlas* published a series of "Pen and Ink Sketches of Popular Persons and Places, by a Cosmopolitan." A September issue featured "rural writers" William and Mary Howitt along with John Clare and Robert Mudie. It is a chatty society piece, with a great deal on the Howitts' appearances (her "calm, smiling, intellectual face," his "grave and sedate deportment," and the "two sparkling eyes, merry hearted children") and very little about their writing. John Ross Dix [A Cosmopolitan, pseud.], "Pen and Ink Sketches of Popular Persons and Places," *Boston Daily Atlas* 64 (September 13, 1845), Nineteenth-Century U.S. Newspapers.

be very grateful for the London Friend in its stead. I have a great desire to see that paper.

Tell dearest Mary our controversy is not with John Wilbur for the publication of those first letters, but with his contentious & uncharitable conduct since, which has continued for many years & was become intolerable. However, I will not quarrel with any one I love so well for thinking differently to me: she shall have her opinion & we will have ours & love each other very dearly through it all. I do not like the subject & hope I shall never write much upon it. There are more interesting & far worthier things between dear friends like us.

I am glad you like the children's diary but fear it may become wearisome. However, if able, I will continue it till you say so. I think such a thing might be made the medium of instilling good feelings & noble principles & shall leave it in dear Mary's hands to use it as she thinks best. I wish I had time to write to her but am preparing this to go to Philadelphia by our good friend Joseph Taylor, who is going to pay his friends East a visit.

I wish he would extend his journey across the Atlantic. I think you would then have a good specimen of an American, though in my opinion not equal to his brother Abraham, who is a noble man in every sense of the word. Joseph is Harrison's dear friend & their friendship is sometimes similar to that of David & Jonathan. An old Friend once said to me, ["]I often compare Harrison & Joseph to twins: they never seem easy separated," & so it is. There is a bond of union between them that binds them to each other like the tenderest sentiment \of/ existing between brothers. Joseph was a gay young man when we came & yet Harrison loved him as if he had been wholly one in practice with himself. He thought not of his collared coat, nor his cheerful [4] merriment, but felt the sweetness of his spirit & adopted him into his heart. Since he is become much more thoughtful & serious & to me far more interesting & has changed his appearance, a hard thing to do where so few are like him. He is a good man, I believe, & one who, with a full purse, has a large heart & liberal hand & for that I love him.

I hope Mary will not think me greedy & selfish, but I want to know if she will send me the People's Journal.[57] I feel much interested in it; I should be more obliged than I can express if she will let us have it. I expect I could get it in this country but I do not know. One thing I know, that with every want supplied I am rather short of cash, & three dollars, which it would probably cost me, would be a great sum out of my small allowance for clothes. However, if she cannot do it without inconvenience or if it costs her money, I will have one gown less in the year rather than miss it.

I will dry you tomatos & fruits in return for all your kindness & send them when I have opportunity. It is small return, I know, but it comforts me to think I can do something for you.

57. See Saunders, John, in appendix 2, "Directory of Names."

Figure 31. Portrait of Joseph Taylor, from Cornelia Meigs, *What Makes a College? A History of Bryn Mawr* (New York: Macmillan, 1956).

I have to acknowledge a very kind & interesting letter from dear Anna, which I have not yet answered but shall do so as soon as possible.

Give my dear love to her & hers & to dear Mary & William & the youngsters. We are all well. I need say nothing of [1] the children as I have sent 3 letters within the last three weeks telling of all things relating to them.

With dearest love in which Harrison & the children unite. I am, beloved mother, thy attached daughter.

Emma

50. To Mary Howitt, July 13 to 27, 1846
7 mo. 13

[July 13] Second-day. The Guinea-hen brought out her brood and a fine one it is; we cannot yet count them, they seem so numerous. William says there are 30 but we think not so many. The guinea hen sits a month and the male bird is very attentive to her; Father thinks he sometimes takes her place on the nest & that he shelters the young like their mother. We have seen little of either for some time except when they came to be fed; of course you know that the common hen sits 3 weeks. Our chickens of that sort are innumerable but they are all condemned to die before the grapes ripen, they make such destruction with them.

In the afternoon the children went to pick Catnip, a species of herb very useful for colds &c.; it grows every where, but Charles thought finest by the road side. Whilst there they met Charley Rittenbar & his sister coming from school; Charley as usual threatened to beat them. His sister interposed & at last they got home without much trouble, only Charles had a scuffle about some string that Rittenbar said he once promised him. Next morning at breakfast the history of his bad conduct was discussed & all were very angry at his naughty behaviour when mother chanced to go to the back of the house & heard one of those loud cries, half terror, half agony, which proceed from a child when suffering; the angry tones of Old Rittenbar & the crack of a whip were mingled with the cries. Oh what a revolution; from dislike to this bad boy we all changed to sympathy & almost love. ["]Why mother,["] said little Annie, "his father whips him for the smallest kind of thing, & so he gets whipped every day." Here was a solution of the mystery; all these desperately bad boys are such as have been brought up under the lash. The worst children we know—& there are some very, very sad ones in the country—are dreadfully whipped. An ignorant, passionate & often careless parent makes up his deficiencies in moral training by the cow-hide & violent words which harden & inflame the poor neglected child to hatred & desperation. Oh how we long now to devise some means to reclaim this poor lad & to establish a better & more efficient discipline in the family.

[July 15] 4th day 15th. Charles had a bad sore-throat & lay long in bed & even drank a basin of coffee before he got up; then he was so much better that he got up & went with Agnes & Annie to weed a pumpkin bed. He hurt his forehead against a quince tree with turning over heels to "skin the cat" as he called it; then he came in & said his lesson & in the afternoon his sisters & he went out with their Father to gather ripe blackberries. It is astonishing

Figure 32. Emma Alderson's drawing of birdhouses in letter #71. Ht/7/1/79, Correspondence of Mary Howitt (1799–1888), Manuscripts and Special Collections, University of Nottingham.

how abundant & excellent this wild fruit is; we do not go farther than our own fences & yet we gather many quarts each day. They are eaten \fresh/ with sugar & cream & are an excellent addition to dinner or supper. We boil them as jam & make a medicine of them, which is most useful & efficacious.

This is Ann Alice's birth-day & the dear little child is 2 years old, she is a sweet baby with a face beautiful with innocence & good humour & a deal covered with curling light-brown hair; she claps her hands in token of joy & gives the back of her right hand to be kissed when she wishes to show affection or be very gracious. Of course she is a great pet, and at tea, the table was set out with especially care to honour her Father's grandmother; cups & saucers were used, a bowl of sugared blackberries & a jug of cream were added besides curds, new biscuits & tomatos. The little one seemed to enjoy it as much as any body & received her presents [2] from brother & sisters with a sweet smile; Charles gave her his English teetoken (see figure 33), Agnes her new cup & saucer & Anna Mary her little dollie that cousin Elizabeth dressed for her.[58]

[July] 16. Annie & Charley staid at home with Louisa whilst Agnes went with Father & Mother to meeting and afterwards they went to drive with

58. Tea tokens were used on colonial tea plantations as a form of payment, which could then be exchanged for real currency. Other tea tokens may also have been used domestically as promotional items by tea companies. Harrison Alderson had worked in the tea trade for a few years before emigrating; his cousin (and brother-in-law) Daniel Harrison had recently established the successful firm of Harrisons and Crosfield. To the immigrant boy, this tea token may have been more than a bauble if it signified his familial connection to England and its colonial (tea-growing) outposts.

Figure 33. Tea token from Harrison & Co. Courtesy of Rare Coins and Tokens (https://rarecoinsandtokens.co.uk/).

their friends the Taylors. \Agnes brought Annie home a fan that cost 5 cents & Father brought Charley a nice new hoe hoe/; in the evening we all went to gather blackberries.

[July] 17. Gathered the first ripe peaches; apples & pears also abundant. This week we have had our first green-corn, bunch squash & tomatos out of the garden.

[July] 18th. In the afternoon their kind Father took the children & their mother a ride into the country to call on a friend; their road lay by the river bank for some miles westward, a route which the children had never before gone. The opposite shore on the Kentucky side was bordered by hills covered with woods which were very beautiful & reflected finely in the clear still water. Beneath them were only a few mean farm-houses & here & there a log cabin looking wild & solitary, possibly, we thought, the abode of some poor slaves. On our side the land is much cleared & cultivated, studded as far as we went with neat white cottages & handsome villas surrounded by beautiful gardens filled with shrubs & bright flowers & encircled with fruit trees & orchards, the hill sides covered with vinyards, some of them bordered by the forest & others extending to the very summits, \the bottoms with cornfields & melon grounds/. The road was enlivened with carriages, omnibuses & empty market waggons which afforded much amusement to the children, as did the little fishing boats here & there upon the river or an occasional flatboat, proceeding on its weary progress, impelled only by the current, which in such low water & on so still a day was slow indeed.

The family were not at home, so we returned by another road for variety, up the banks of Bold-face Creek; here the scenery was wild & often beautiful. We came to the foot of a long, steep hill & Father thought it too much to expect Farmer to draw us up in the carriage. Annie was soon tired & wished she had staid in, so Charley took her on his back & carried her to her great comfort & refreshment. When at the top, we had a fine view of wooded hills, little cornfields in the valley, the rocky bed of Bold-face & the remains of a half burnt log house with a vinyard on the right hand. It was a varied & picturesque scene & repaid us for the weary ascent.

We got home in time to enjoy a good supper on the piazza, enlivened by the bright beams of the setting sun. Agnes had the pleasure of gathering very pretty nosegays for mother out of her own garden; she has fine balsams, larkspurs, marigolds, marvel of Peru, blue bottle & many other flowers. Charles finds that his garden at the back of the smoke-house has a ~~bad aspect~~ \bad situation;/ the plants will not bloom with their western aspect.

This morning our first cheese was put into the press, a great event to the household. What drinking of whey by young & old, & what delicious curds on the supper table, & what a watching of the whole process, from the putting of the milk into the kettle, its coagulation & removing into the vat, & then the whole tribe of children ran before into the wood-house to see it placed in Frederic's Lotts new press. It is an event in the neighbourhood, for I do not suppose cheese is made within 40 miles of Cincinnati. The famous Western Reserve, \the Cheshire of America/, though in the State, is probably 200 miles distant.

The Indian Corn \in the fields/—or, as it is called here in preeminence, Corn—has now attained its full height of 8 or 10 feet & is in its utmost beauty; the broad green leaves are fresh & vigorous & amongst them the light green spath filled with the rich ear is conspicuous, whilst the plant is crowned with its elegant light brown tassel.

[July] 18th. William has begun to mow his oats &, in preparation for them, they have been clearing out the corn-crib, & what a busy morning have Charles & Milo had after the rats young & old. Waltman, William's dog, was there & the cat also after the little ones; Waltman caught hold of the rats & held them fast till Milo came to kill them with his iron gripe. We have found the guinea fowls which have been missing for many day; Father, Mother & all the numerous brood have been living in clover amongst the oats & kept wonderfully quiet amidst their abundant & luxurious feast.

One day a man came to know if we had any spirits of turpentine; he had a horse sick in the road & thought it would die if he did not get relief. We supplied his wants & Charles & Father went to see if they could render assistance. They found at the gate two waggons with their clean white covers drawn up & the horses out, the sick one rolling in agony on the green grass. [3] The men were farmers from Indiana who had come 80 miles with each a load of wheat to sell in Cincinnati; they had their provisions for man & horse with them, & after administering the medicine to the horse & seeing it somewhat better, prepared to light a fire, boil their kettle, & fry their meal; but we invited them in & they came & partook of a supper we had prepared. One man said as he walked towards the house "well, if temporalities would secure happiness you have it in this place." They left us with many thanks & even blessings.

This mode of travelling in covered waggons with provisions & utensils for cooking is very common, & we often see a group of such travellers around their fire on the edge of some pleasant wood. People travel \thus/ to market & often hundreds of miles in their migrations from one part of the country to another. These "movers" are very picturesque & a very interesting feature in society in this western country; taverns they avoid because, gaining nothing by them, their keepers often deny them the commonest civilities. The waggon is laden with beds, bedding, & household furniture, amongst which the women & children are stuffed; the baby's \wooden/ cradle often swings behind. The men walk, driving the team & ~~often~~ some half-dozen cows. It is a toilsome & weary journey, full of hardship & privation, but the golden west is before them, & they are hoping for great doings at the end, where land is so cheap & people so few. Alas for those that have to retrace their steps with expended means, broken health, & frequently lacking the Father, who from greater exposure has fallen a victim to the fever & ague in the unwholesome climate.

After writing the above I met with the following graphic description of such a returning company. Some three miles below the city the other evening we encountered a camp of travellers, eighteen in all. The sight was a novel one, but the appearance of the group made it peculiarly so. All bore signs of exposure and sickness: young & old were shaking with the ague, and they seemed more fitting for the hospital than the fatigues of a journey. "Where are you bound to?" we inquired. "Back to Kentucky." "Back from where?" "Oh! from Des Moines Iowa—we lived there two years—we have been sick all the time—ague,—ague, ague—we were worn out—and now we are going back to our old homes, to live and die there"—Cin. Paper.

The weather has been extremely hot—Ther 98 \in the shade/. Afterwards we had thunder & rain, & the temperature was little more than 50. We were all shivering; the children took bad colds & were creeping to the fire for three days. Now it is as warm as ever, the Thermometer mounting up to 90 in the shade. And amidst all these vicissitudes of weather, in the drenching rain & under a burning sun, in heat & cold, those poor unfortunate negroes are encamped in the woods bordering the canal, denied the homes & lands & provisions for which they have paid 30,000 dollars. The people are resolute in determination not to receive them, and these 350 men, women & children are living on ~~the~~ without other shelter than their waggons & tents & know not where to go. In a Slave State they may not be and a free State says "here they shall not be." Where are justice and humanity, and why is not the country loud in declaiming such barbarity?

[July] 25. Charles & Agnes have commenced blackberry gathering as a trade; they sell their blackberries for a cent a pint to mother. They gathered 6 pints yesterday & 8 today; they intend to do great things with their wealth.

They do not go beyond our own fields. Yesterday we found a most beautiful little tree frog; it was not larger altogether than half a dollar, of a bright green colour, white underneath & yellow, spotted with black on the under-side of the hind legs; its eyes were bright & sparkling & stood prominently from its head, making its profile very singular & intelligent. After examining it fully we let it go amongst some [4] shrubs. It did not change colour like the other when in our hands.

[July] 26. One morning the children were awoke with a strange sound in their room; Agnes thought it was a robber rolling a basket up & down the floor & hid her head under the bed clothes, but Anna Mary, who is much more courageous, got up to examine the cause & there to their great amazement, between the shutters & the window, were five bats flying & fluttering & trying to get out. Fortunately it was a cool night or the window would have been up & then they would have had them all in the room; father came &, opening the shutter, let them go. Last evening one was flying about the kitchen; Charles caught it in the morning & examined it, greatly to his admiration & pleasure. We have a little bee chamber in the attic, where they build and live in great abundance & unmolested but, we fear, are becoming too numerous.

After hoeing 5 rows in the vinyard & doing \sundry/ other things of the useful kind, Charles & his sisters went out to gather blackberries; his eyes were so weak & painful he could not attend to his lessons. He was very kind to the little girls, leaving them the low easy branches & pushing into the thicket or mounting the fence to get the high ones; this Agnes was very careful to tell as soon as they returned. They gathered 7 pints this afternoon & the firm have now 22 cents due to them.

Charles is divided in his mind between a gun and a belt for his hunting frock. He would like a belt to be sure, but then a gun such as Cousin Charles had, which only cost a levy & with which, however, they shot a bird, would be so grand & desirable. Agnes thinks she will buy a new fan when she has got 10 cents. Annie is all for candy; she thinks there is nothing so good in the world as candy.

[July] 27th. What a deal an active boy of 8 years old can do, was the thought of my mind many times this day; a catalogue of Wm Charles' work from 5 oclock to 8 in the evening will prove this. First mother called him early, & before breakfast he went to tell a woman to come to sew; then he went to Warsaw for some groceries, came back, said his lessons & went to collect the weeds Father had pulled up in the garden, got up potatoes for dinner, after dinner went to gather blackberries with Agnes, brought home 5 quarts, helped little Frederic Lotte to carry boards for flooring the new portico; then Annie and he hauled away the rubbish; nailed two sides to a box to make a little house for [1-*cross*] the puppies, of which, in gratitude after Annie had laid some hay for a bed, they took possession, having been dispossessed of their nest by the Cheese press; got supper, went to play, came to see them near the second floor of the portico, fetched up the cows, salted them, went to bed.

Farewell beloved Sister; love to all from your attached,

Emma.

51. To Mary Howitt, August 2 to 15, 1846
2nd of 8th mo 1846

[August 2] This very pleasant summer is rapidly passing on and each week seems to bring some new token of the approaching Fall; the fire-flies still continue to enliven & beautify the evenings, starting up & darting about like brilliant sparks, sometimes from the grass & shrubs, sometimes soaring in the air, & at others lingering amongst the branches of the tallest trees. The grasshoppers & common locusts are come & fill the air night & day with their music, making a ceaseless chirping which is loudest in the stillness of night; the tree frog mingles its cry in the general chorus, and evenings & mornings the birds still sing very sweetly. They usually bring up two broods during the long summer; our cat birds have built another nest \in the Cedar tree/ & are very busy feeding & tending their young.

William Charles & his sisters paid a visit to the coloured Orphan Asylum. It is in a pleasant, airy part of the city & though the number of children were few, only 8, we felt much interested in them: the eldest, a great girl of 14, is a cripple, having had her back broken in infancy; the youngest, a little girl of 4 years old, is called Elizabeth, a delicate, interesting looking child. Annie thought it would be very nice to come again & bring her an apple. There is something melancholy in visiting these institutions; excellent as they are, each little creature seems to have a solitary & peculiar interest; they lack the sweet endearments of home, the little indulgences & soothing tenderness which are interwoven in the rememberances of childhood & which flowed so sweetly & freely upon us from the inexhausted fountain of a mother's love. The Father, with his watchful eye, his heart, whose tendencies all tend \to/ one point, the welfare of his children, is not there. The nurturing hand of the mother is missed; they are fed & clothed, taught in the school & taken to chappel, but this is a threadbare life, & in the present instance all had too much the look of pauperism. The institution is now & has been struggling onward through many difficulties, chiefly that, because begun & carried on by the coloured people themselves \aided by a few benevolent persons/, the whites are cold & shy in its support, & we could only wish that all would, like ourselves, visit it in order that their hearts might grow warm in so good a cause.

Wm Charles was very naughty to Louisa last evening & was sent to bed without supper. He rose humbled &, we hope, convinced & promised both mother & Louisa not to do so again; his fault was picking fleas off Fanny's back & throwing them at the girl; it was a very naughty trick & not to be overlooked.

The oats are carried and the guinea fowls begin to make their appearance; the thirty have dwindled down to 12, but they are active, beautiful little things, very shy, & the old ones very fierce. One of the puppies is gone to a good home; the other looks very quiet & sad, like a child who has lost its companion.

Agnes has been staying some days in the city; she bought her new fan & Wm Charles spent a part of his money in suspenders, for which he paid 10 cents.

[August] 3rd. Little Mary is again with us, and Agnes & she have commenced making [2] some clothing for the little coloured orphan, Elizabeth. Anna Mary plucked some quinces for which Father reprimanded her & said she must not have either apple, peach or pear during the day. Agnes, who had told of her, was so sorry that she said she would be joined in the punishment, & both Mary & Charles ~~both~~ agreed to abstain also. The children went with Louisa to old John's; they found his wife & daughter very busy paring apples for drying; they cut them in quarters, core them & lay them on boards to dry in the sun. Charles went to John Solo's to buy a fishing pole, but he found it so old & shabby that he would not pay his remaining 10 cents for it and therefore took it back.

[August] 4th. Before 5 this morning Charles awoke & prepared to accompany Joseph with a waggon load of potatoes to market; the waggon was loaded the evening before and he had only time to dress himself & take a biscuit in his hand. It was a bright, pleasant morning & they were at a Friend's house in the city before breakfast; here Charles spent the day & Joseph called for him when he had sold his cargo. Charles went to see the hull of a fine steam boat which had be burnt the evening before and to examine the foundations of Mill-Creek bridge which they have begun at last to build again. Father is gone from home & Charles has charge of Farmer & the salting of the cows, his task of weeding, and to watch the peaches which are now ripening in abundance.

[August] 5th. According to Father's directions, Farmer was to be rode out; Charles was very impatient & asked Joseph to saddle & bridle him, but he was so fussy that he refused & he had to wait till old John came to his dinner out of the garden; then in great triumph he mounted. But alas, for his horsemanship, we all laughed heartily to see how willful Farmer was; he stood still or only went his own way, Agnes cried, "Give Charley the fishing pole; Farmer is idle & wants a whip." Mother, ~~&~~ Louisa & John laughed, & Charley called out in a kind of desperate dismay; Annie, who thinks it the grandest thing in the world to ride, took all gravely and said, "Dost not Charley ride good? I wish I might ride too."

Now Mary is here we have a very good school; Agnes & she read together and the three children spell & say the multiplication table in class. Mary has gone a deal to school & can lead Agnes & Charley admirably, who have no knowledge of school discipline & routine. Whilst Wm Charles attends to cyphering & geography, the little girls work at Elizabeth's pinafore and think how pleased the little child will be. Then they adjourn to the box of rags & make doll clothes during the heat of the day. Even Charles condescends to join and help them; he makes little bags for purses and larger ones for seeds, and they are very happy. When this wearies they go to the swing and gather blackberries or play in the shade of the cedar trees upon the grass.

One day Richard came up on a little pieballed poney called Johnny; he came to beg Fanny, & after much persuasion & many promises to treat her well, he got Father's & Charles' consent. She is to be instructed in this art of rat catching by a famous & accomplished dog, the best rat dog in the city, & is to return after a visit of a few months. Now we have only the little black mouthed puppy called [3] Wasp, and Milo.

[August] 9th. We had an unexpected pleasure in a visit from our cousins at Mount Auburn; Charles S[hipley] and Marshall came, and a most delightful treat it was to all. They romped & played and picked peaches and rejoiced in each other with great joy, and when they were weary sate down altogether on the piazza to talk like sensible men & women, to look at books & pictures and be quite rational.

[August] 10. We found this morning, to our great delight, a true locust adhering to the wall of the piazza; it has long been an invisible mystery to us, sending forth its loud cry in tree & bush but never to be seen: here it was in full daylight sitting still as if it came to be looked at. It had a large black & green body, plump & round like a great beetle; its eyes were black & prominent & its wings, which extended considerably beyond its body, were transparent, horny & strongly veined; \it was about 2 inches long/. We put it under a tumbler & after having satisfied our curiosity let if fly, & all afternoon it has been chirring in an apple tree as if rejoicing over its freedom. We are not quite sure it is the same as the 17 years locust but doubtless one of the species. A handsome Cata-did also paid us a visit; this is a low, slender insect of a bright green colour, much more elegant than the locust and not so great a rarity by any means; the Cata-did'nt is a roundish green insect about half an inch long. The gentleman is from 1 1/2 to 2 inches in length; they utter their loud cry in calm, stilly evenings and seem to rejoice in moonlight.

It was a fine afternoon & William had a cord of wood to fetch for Father, so Charles was very diligent in doing his lessons and got leave to go with him. Farmer & Ben trotted lightly along with the empty woodwaggon & William & Charles sate in front; they went down into the deep <ho>llows & loaded the waggon, which was nearly upset in the ascent; the wood looked very green & pleasant, the grasshoppers chirped, the birds flew about, a little squirril now & then ran amongst the grass or jumped from tree to tree. All was pleasant as it always is in the green woods & they returned home just as Father, mother & sisters sate at supper on the grass under the walnut-tree near the piazza.

In the evening Charles was busy making Agnes a Quilting frame, for as quilting is going on in the house, Agnes thinks she must have a petitcoat & comfort for her doll to be ready for winter.

[August] 13. This evening all went out to gather peaches to send next morning by William to market; then Charles helped Father to pack them in the baskets with nice clean hay. Little Alice was with the party gathering & seemed very glad when Charles or Agnes brought her a fine ripe juicy slice from some especially good peach.

[August] 14. All busy paring peaches for drying; we please ourselves with the thought that perhaps \grand/ mother & aunts may eat of these things & we love to do them. The thought of the possibility is cheering.

[August] 15. The morning was cloudy & some rain fell, but afterwards the clouds dispersed & the sun shone out delightfully, so Father & mother & Charles set out to pay a visit in Kentucky. They drove up Mill Creek Valley in order to make a call; the scenery was extremely pretty: hills partially covered with woods skirt this beautiful stream, leaving a broad fertile bottom cultivated to the highest degree as gardens, nursery grounds & studded with pleasant houses. The Miami canal is carried through it & gives an air of commercial prosperity with [4] its boats & trafic, its warehouses & bridges.

We arrived in the city in time to dine with our good friends the Taylors[59] & then walked down to the river to take the ferry boat; this is constantly plying every 10 minutes & is worked by steam. There were ~~horses~~ two \empty/ market waggons & their horses besides many people crossing at the same time. The town of Newport was our destination; it lies on the opposite bank of the Ohio; here is the garrison where a number of regular soldiers are continually stationed on a green. Outside the inclosure were the tents of about 300 volunteers; they were arranged in lines & looking very white & picturesque; amongst them men in uniforms were walking & sitting. We pept into one or two as we passed & saw the poor accomodations with which a soldier has to suffice himself: a little clean straw seemed to be all its furniture.

From this tented field we walked on to the Licking, a river which here empties itself into the Ohio & whose steep banks bordered with old buttonwood trees prove its claim to the character of beauty which it possesses. Here lay steam boats at anchor & the half finished butments of a fine bridge which was once begun but never completed. With the careless, untidy look of most of the houses, a partially finished chapel & other signs of neglect made us fancy at least we could discover the characteristics of a slave state: indolence & unthrift. It felt strange to tread on the soil of a slave-state & to see little

59. Howitt specifies only "Uncle Cornelius."

curly headed negro children running familiarly in & out of a handsome house whose proprietor, a member of congress, is a great slave-holder.

Steam boats were plying up & down the Ohio & looked cheerful & pretty in the setting sun as we recrossed the river & Charles was much delighted with the skeletons of two very fine boats on the shore in progress of erection. Charles purchased 3 clay pipes, a present for his sisters to blow bubbles with, as a small compensation for their having to pass the day at home, which to him had been so pleasant & full of interest.

On our arrival at our Friend's we were invited out into the piazza & there a feast of beautiful melons, water & musk, with lemonade were provided for our refreshment; after our hot walk to & from the river they were very cooling & delicious.

Excuse this abominably blotted sheet, I have not time to copy it. Farewell, my best beloved Friends,

E. A.

52. *To Mary Howitt, late August to September 21, 1846*
~~7~~ 8 mo.[60]

It is very seldom we see a beggar at our doors, not oftener on an average than once a month & being so rare we treat them with great consideration, seldom not unfrequently giving them silver & always a part of the meal that is going. Last week, just as we rose from dinner, a very decent looking German came & asked for some work & something to eat; he could not speak English, & Louisa interpreted. She gave him some dinner, & father set him to chop wood. In about an hour Charles pept into the woodhouse & & saw the man sitting on the sawhorse pulling horrible faces. He went again shortly & found him fast asleep on the ground. From this time his "wood saw" as Louisa calls it was at an end; he slept and slept till the sun began to get low & then we had to awake him and desire him to go away as we found he was so drunk that he could do nothing & we did not want him on the place all night.

Another \piece/ of our experience was little better. One morning a poor fellow came and begged some breakfast; he was Dutch also & asked for work. Father was not at home, but we set him to "graben"[61] the rhubarb bed & the ground under the Quince trees. He dug like a young gentleman who had never handled a spade before & managed to dig very tolerably a few yards square. Anna Mary recognized him & running to mother in the kitchen said "do you know who you have got at work there—it is the drunken man that last first-day, when Milo barked at him, knocked off the top of the spinnach with his great stick." She was right: there stood the great cudgel against one of the locust trees & we all remembered the old greasy black hat & coat when

60. This date has been added in pencil with the "8" written over the "7," suggesting a correction from July to August, perhaps by Mary Howitt.
61. The word "*graben*" is German for "dig."

reminded. However, he worked till evening & received his 30 cents, but has never come since to trouble us.

One first-day morning two old looking men, one with a long grey beard, the other aparently blind, came & begged. They were in wretched rags \~~& a bag on their backs~~/, a very unusual circumstance in this country \& a bag on their backs/. Father gave them a 10 cent piece & some of us even questioned if that was enough. In an hour or two we set off to go to meeting & what should we see in a shady nook on the grass by the road side but these sturdy rogues. The blind man was stitching at some clothes; the other, well dressed in good blue cloth clothes, was stuffing the old raged ones into his bag. Thus equipped, they were going to make their appearance in the city & spend the money good charitable people had given them. We begin now to think worthy industrious men need not & do not beg in this country.

For many days past we have been busy paring peaches for making peach leather and also for drying. The children are very fond of the employment. The peaches when pared are cut up & either laid on tins to dry in the oven or hot sunshine, or previously well boiled & \then/ spread to dry. This \pulp/ becomes very tough & so is called peach leather. It will keep any length of time & when used is soaked in water, boiled till quite pulpy & when sweetened makes excellent pies or preserves for winter use.

[September 1] 9th mo. 1st. For the last fortnight peaches, peaches, peaches have been the only object. It seems as if every thing came in spring tides here, and for the time are all absorbing. We have made peach leather, dried them, preserved them, boiled them in cider, made pies of them till we are tired & still they are not done. Last week a large bag of maple sugar came from the country; it was made by a person who makes many hundred weights every spring &, this year being very plentiful, father bought it for 7 cents a lb. We have one comfort in using it: the thought that no overseer's whip, no toiling weary negro have been employed in its manufacturer, that under a bright sun and amidst pleasant woodland scenes with many a merry laugh & joke, has it been made, for sugar making is always more or less a festival; parties of young people go to the "drawing [2] off," when it forms into cakes of most excellent candy & is a great & well deserved favorite.

Mary Crehoe brought us some of her fresh ripe figs from her fig tree; we eat them as a rarity, but all agreed we liked dried figs better. Next day the children set off to carry a basket of plums to a neighbour. The injunction they received was neither to eat themselves nor give to any one, but on their way they met Charley Rittenbar who asked them what they had in their basket & then rudely pulled away the cover. When he saw the plums he asked for some. Charles refused to give them as they belonged to Father & mother; he then said if they would not give he would take & offered to strike Charles in the face. To quiet him they gave him a handful & passed on, but he met them on their return &, finding his tyranny was so successful, would have some of their beautiful dahlias they were taking home to mother & got these also from them, more to the children's sorrow than even the loss of the plums.

In the evenings the musquitos were so troublesome that a bar was wanted for Agnes & Annie's bed, but the post was broken & the curtain could not be found.[62] So Charles & his mother walked over in the moonlight to Lotte's to borrow an auger. It was beautiful to see the tall palmy Ailanthus or Tree of Heaven reflected against the moonlit sky & contrasting their long waving branches against the feathery network of the locust & the broad expanses of the Catalpa leaves or the dark dense foliage of the cedars. They admired and rejoiced in a sense of the beauty & enjoyment of such a scene & were no less pleased with the friendly greeting of their worthy neighbour who was frying potatoe cakes over a small wood fire in her husband's shop, showed them the whole process, invited them to partake & then exhibited her store of dried apples, helped the grandfather to find the auger & proposed to him to go across & help to put up the post. Whether from rich or poor, in a log cabin or a marble palace, that genuine kindness, which is rich in deeds of love, is like found gold or odours of sweet flowers, a treasure to be rejoiced over, a blessing which nurses the heart in thankfulness to God, the author & source of all good.

The plays of children often exhibit a lively pantomime of the mummers & customs of those around them. This morning a large empty blanket box was standing upon the piazza. Charles & Annie placed a barrel across it & a couple of chairs in front which, duly bridled, served the purpose to two horses. Then mounting the board, they drove away with a loaded wagon containing casks of sweet cider. "Sweet cider, sweet cider" shouted Annie in the most technical tone, & now and then they had to stop to sell a few gallons, which was dealt out at the marked price of 8 cents a gal. Then they came home & went again with a load of water & musk melons: "water melons, musk melons, nutmeg, citron, cantiloupes," and the people came again to buy, the price from 1 to 5 cents. Then the ice cart came to the door & "ice ice ice" rang through the street; it was surprizing that, so occasional as their visits are, they had gathered so many city scenes & could throw so much life into them.

[September] 9th At sunrise Charley went down stairs. It was a lovely morning; white lines of mist amongst the distant wood showed the course of creeks & more especially of the Ohio, but with us on the more elevated ground, [3] the air was dry & warm & the yellow rays of the sun gilded the foliage of tree & shrub & shone brightly on the feathery crowns of Indian Corn in the meadows & on the hills. Charles wandered round enjoying the pleasant morning & watched William mowing the second crop of clover on the lawn, when suddenly he heard a rushing of wings & beheld a large flock of quails on their migration course; they flew onward with so little attention

62. The curtain is mosquito netting.

to surrounding objects that some of them struck against the trees & even upon the house, & Charles picked up three who were killed by the violence of the blow. Their bodies were warm & their little hearts had scarcely ceased to beat when he brought them in to his mother. Then, when Agnes & Annie had examined & admired them fully, they began to pluck them & prepare them for roasting. It was a great piece of business; the feathers were put by for a bed for Agnes' doll; they were plucked & singed & opened, & their hearts & liver & gizzard all prepared for the great roast & when laid on a plate ready for the fire looked very respectable & were indeed a dainty dinner for the three children, who previously went into John's Wood to gather a quantity of fuller's earth which we find of the best quality for cleaning a carpet. There they gathered up buck eye nuts, hickory nuts & walnuts, a proof of the near aproach of autumn & the progress of the rapidly passing year.

[September] 10. Father & Charles went to Rittenbars for "sweet cider" which they are making in a little press of their own. The wife took them into her parlour to show them her "crocks["] of apple butter & sent a dish as a present to his mother by Charles. Then Father & Charles sat down on the grass to peel peaches which are to be boiled in the cider to make peach butter.

A great hawk pounced upon a small flock of chickens; the hen set up a loud cry & flew boldly at him chasing him away half the length of the lawn; she came back in a while with her feathers standing on end & looking very consequential & important but rejoicing no doubt that her pretty flock was unhurt.

Last week we had great apple gatherings & many a basket of fine belle-flowers & fall pippins, of Newtown pippins, and many very good but name-less kinds are housed and put down in barrels in the cellar for winter use. One of the Fall Pippins measured 14 ½ inches one way & 13 the other & weighed 23 ounces; another weighted a pound. There they lie upon the din-ing room chimney-piece a beautiful specimen of fine fruit.

By the orchard fence below the quince trees is a plant of the mammoth pumpkin which \has one pumpkin on it/ measuring 14 ½ feet one way & 13 the other.[63] It is a very perfect specimen & yet nothing compared with some grown in the neighbourhood. One was the size of a large cask & weighed 130 lbs. Owen & Miss Rose with the hogs get fine treats of apples but neither Pink nor Blackberry fancy them.[64] We go these pleasant evenings after supper to fetch up the cows for milking; Owen always looks round for her bucket of apple parings & slop, & Alice, in her father's arms, watches her eating & says "poor poor"; she even dreams of her & says "poor poor" in her sleep.[65]

63. Alderson has clearly made a mistake, as a pumpkin 14.5 feet by 13 feet would be much bigger than any cask and weigh far more than 130 pounds. Likewise, an apple of the dimensions described would weigh far more than 23 ounces.

64. Owen, Miss Rose, Blackberry, and Pink are their cows.

65. Although the meaning is still not entirely clear, Howitt, in the American edition but not the British, gives the child's comment as "poor, poor moo!" to indicate that she is speaking of

[4] There is an autumnal character in the weather which reminds us that summer is gone; the air is light & transparent, though the heat is still very great. The clouds look brilliantly white on an intensely blue sky; yellow leaves come down from the locust trees when shaken by the breeze, though the mass are still green; the vine is ~~looking~~/losing its leaves & has ceased to be a shade at noon day, but its rich dark clusters of ripe grapes look beautiful amongst the remaining yellow leaves; the Altheas have long been in bloom, yet still are beautiful; the second flowering of the balsam is now very rich; the cox's combs have splendid heads of rich crimson velvet which might vie with the handsomest robe queen Victoria ever wore on her highest state days. Some of these flowers are as large as a baby's head. We have phlox, hibiscus of various kinds, Marvel of Peru, portulacas, geraniums, petunias, marigolds & dahlias in great beauty and perfection \we must not omit the cypress vine, ~~&~~convolvulus and wild clematis/; all look gay, yet we cannot forget it is the last floral assemblage we shall have. Nothing but the sunflowers and Michaelmass daisys have yet to bloom & they beautify not only our gardens but the woods & fences &, with the golden rod and touch-me-nots, make these very splendid.

Charles has taken his little checked bag & is gone into John's Wood to collect hickory nuts & buckeyes. There he saw a squirril, & Milo tried to catch it, but happily the little fellow was too nimble for him & ran up a tree. The woman at the log house came to look after her cows & asked Charles what he was doing; he showed her the buckeyes, & she said "those are no good, no good," but you may have them or anything else or swing if you like the swing.[66] It was very good natured of her & Charles thanked her & brought his buckeyes for Alice to play with.

There is one of our hogs which has got a sad trick of rambling; Charles has had many journeys after it into these people's potatoe field & "cabbage patch." At last they grew out of patience & turned it into the lane. Yesterday he went round the neighbourhood to seek for it, but it was no where to be seen and, as it was our finest and best pig, we do not want to lose it.

Cousin Thompson came last week; he has been a long journey down the Ohio & Mississippi to the Gulf of Mexico. He gave Charles a cane which he had cut himself from a "cane brake" on the Mississippi. He has seen alligators and groves of palmetos, fields of cotton & coffee & sugar with gangs of poor negro slaves working in them followed by a driver carrying a large whip. He has eaten oranges and pineapples, figs & other dainties which belong to warm climates, & yet he says he would not live in the South for the grandest plantation in Louisiana because of slavery. Each man there seems to live in

---

the cow or cows, *Our Cousins in Ohio* (New York: Collins and Brothers Publishers, 1849) 170–171.

66. Presumably the woman's words continue to the end of this sentence, but I have given the quotation marks as in the original.

his house as in a citadel, with a sense of danger & insecurity, constantly exciting vigilance & anxiety: how different to the free north where in country districts few lock their doors, the windows have no fastenings & every place is left open without fear or thought of ill.

Mother has promised the children a weekly allowance—2 cents each if they are good—but should they be quarrelsome, one cent is to be deducted and should they grumble or fail to do cheerfully as they are bid, the other is to be forfeited; thus they will have a little pocket money which they often think they want & be set on the watch against their too great & besetting faults. Seventh-day closed the first week of trial; Agnes and Annie each got a cent: Annie had been quarrelsome, Agnes fretful & unwilling to say her lessons & sometimes to do as she was bid. Poor Charles felt he could not lay claim to anything, so he quietly turned away with "well I know mother has nothing for me, but I will try next week to deserve both my cents.["]

When Charles went to water the horse & give him some hay, he heard a great chirping of little chickens in the loft & a hen which he disturbed flew down followed by two or three [5] of her brood, but the others were not to be lost & Charles & Annie searched about & found in all ten wee things just come out of the shell; some were in the hay, but four had taken refuge in a rat-hole & they were obliged to tear away a plank before they could get at them. They had had a terrible fright but seemed very happy when they got under their mother's wing, who we hope will take better care of them.

9/21st: This morning we rose early intending, should the weather be favourable, to go to visit a friend a few miles on the other side the city; the morning was still but cloudy, yet as the sun rose & the day advanced it gave promise of a fine day. Charles was eager for the journey & cheerfully blacked Anna Mary's shoes & took Farmer down to the spring before breakfast. In a ~~few~~ short time, all were ready & Father, Mother & the three older children set out on this long talked of visit; as they passed on the river-bank they were much excited by the sight of a fine black bear tied to a tree adjoining a butcher's shop. The animal walked to & fro with that uneasy air which characterizes wild creatures in confinement, yet it was perfectly tame & took gladly some bread given to it by a boy who was a pleased as the rest with watching its movements.

The sun shone by this time bright & warm & all nature wore that air of calm repose so beautiful & peculiar to autumn. The corn is becoming sere & ripe; the fruit is gathered or \still/ beautifying with its gold & crimson orchards & gardens; the woods & fields are as green as ever; the sky is richly blue and there is a freshness in the air which makes it especially delightful to inhale the passing breeze after the late fervid heat of summer. Another great wonder, beyond the city on a hill over which some few remnants of the old forest yet remain scattered, were two more bears tied as the other to trees; they are bought & fed by the butchers for the winter market, and their flesh is eaten as a great dainty.

Our friends were at home & greeted us very kindly; the house was an old country dwelling built of wood but comfortable & beautified with flowering shrubs & rose bushes up to the very eves. Round the rustic porch, a noble trumpet honeysuckle intermingled with woodbine is a perfect mass of flowers in spring. On the other side of the house the piazza is shaded by a luxuriant passion flower in full bloom & with its egg shaped fruit depending from beneath the dark leaves. Dahlias, hibiscus, petunias, roses, but above all, balsams like small trees covered with rich double blossoms of every shade & colour, spotted & streaked like so many roses, made the garden & the whole circumference of the house gay as flowers could make it. There was an abundance of grapes & other fruits in the orchard, & a fine old peacock \strutting about/. Our friend delighted the children much by giving each a bunch of its beautiful feathers which, in all their rich variety, are a mystery of delight to their young minds.

After a day of much pleasure we rode home enlivened by the mild warm [6] beams of the setting sun. Our only alloy was the sight of the poor chain-gang, who, on our return, were preparing to enter the waggon which in the morning conveyed them to their work; the overseer, who personifies to us a slave driver, was priming his musket & following the disgraceful procession in his own cart.

When we got home good news awaited us: Blackberry had a nice little calf, a beautiful little creature, milk white with brown tipped ears; we shall, if we keep it, call it the White Rose, as the other is the Red Rose.

With dearest love, your attached,

E. A.

The children desire their love to Anna & Uncles & Cousins. My dearest sister I want to hear from thee; do spare an hour out of thy many engagements for me. If thou couldst comprehend the thrill of joy the sight of a letter from thee occasions, & with what pleasure I hear of all your engagements & the subjects that interest you—it is like a glance into another sphere—thou wouldst think it worth thy while. Mine is a busy life, made up of domestic cares, & the intercourse I hold with you & writing & receiving letters is a great source of pleasure; I have little time for reading books, but I feel as if I learnt much from your correspondence of the literary world, & it refreshes & amuses me. Farewell; excuse all the egotism. My dear love to Anna Mary; I want her to write to me & tell me all about her studies.

53. To Ann Botham, September 21, 1846

9 mo 21st

As the time of posting letters draws near, I feel as though I could not let the opportunity pass of writing to thee, my tenderly beloved Mother, though I seem to have little to write about & nothing of any interest to tell thee. Yet if it is but as a memento of my continued love & the constant affectionate rememberance with which we all, & I more especially, feel for thee, it must go. Not a day passes but thou art the frequent subject of my thoughts & thou art mentioned by us with the warmest affections. I sometimes hope that the reverential love with which thou art regarded by us may be as a model for our children should we live to be old. I say it not in self commendation; I often look with an aching heart & with burning tears upon the past & wish those precious but lost opportunities of being a blessing to the best of mothers were still mine, but still I am thankful that thou art spared to our warm & tender love & that we can assure each other of these things & draw comfort & happiness in their expressions, and though denied the privilege of contributing to thy daily comfort, can we not commend thee to the care & keeping of Him who is the rich source of every blessing, who can sustain & strengthen thee in all <trials> & fill thy cup to overflowing from the eternal fountain of perfect happiness. May His blessing rest upon thy honoured head & upon every one who contributes to the enjoyment of thy life.

How does the knowledge of their love & kindness endear dearest Mary & her family to me! I feel as if their home, where thou art happy, was a bright spot on which my thoughts love to rest & my fancy to visit. I read with delight the description of thee & them in one of the "Pen & Ink Sketches." It warmed my very heart that a stranger saw you so beautiful & so happy. It was not that you were held up to the world as a bright picture for its admiration, but it brought such sweet & vivid assurance to my \own/ mind. I have seen you; I have sate with you at that pleasant tea table & heard your voices & dwelt upon your cheerful smiles till they are a reality, a truth, and have broken the long weary blank which four years separation had made.

We have just met with J. G. Whittier's volume "Lays of My Home," which from what dear Mary said of him I felt very impatient to see, and I am delighted with it.[67] What a freshness & vigour, what an enlightened mind & complete adoption of all the great & good & stirring questions of the day. I have made much enquiry about him, but can hear nothing more of him than that he is a plain New England friend, but the jealousy which is felt by many against active exertions in the cause of humanity causes him to be regarded by some with distrust. However, I do hope his works will spread far & wide. I think they are such as will find their way into every generous heart.

I am much interested in Wm & Marys undertaking; I hope the paper will become [2] an organ of good to the nation.[68] We occasionally see it highly commended & extracts from it in the Blackburn Mercury & other papers that John Thwaite sends us, but I want to have the whole. I mean when Harrison writes next to J. T. to desire him to take our names as subscribers, that is, pay the advance money & then it will reach us regularly.

67. John Greenleaf Whittier, *Lays of My Home* (Boston: W. D. Ticknor, 1843).
68. *Howitt's Journal* began publication in January 1847 but only lasted until 1848, when it was taken over by Willoughby & Co. and merged to form *People's and Howitt's Journal.*

I never like American reprints of English works. I suspect them, & besides I know in execution they are always inferior. I fear you have not received some papers I sent about 6 weeks ago. They contained some very interesting accounts I wanted you to see. Since I have sent some numbers of a paper published by the coloured people of Cincinnati, not for any particular merit but as a curiousity.

Are not you interested in the Randolph negroes[?] Poor things, since I wrote last, some of them have been received into employment & probably the minds of the people will soften towards them, but meetings have been held & resolutions agreed to expel every coloured person from the county within a year & that after the last of December they will neither deal \with/ nor use them, neither sell \to/ nor buy from any of the race. Is it not diabolical? Is it not a sin that the whole nation does not raise its voice against such wicked proceedings[?]

Last evening as we sate at tea on the grass a stranger presented himself. We invited him to the table & after some conversation he told us he was from Illiricum [in Bosnia], that he sailed for America 8 years ago from the harbour of Trieste. He was once a monk of the Benedictine order, then ordained a priest & had studied & read much, especially the scriptures in the original Hebrew & Greek, by which means he saw into the errors & superstition of Popery, renounced its doctrines & left the Austrian dominions for a wider \& freer/ field of usefulness. He consideres himself a commissioned messenger of a new era, one of those chosen to announce the Millenium. He thinks Friends were visited with a clear light, that they were sons of the morning, but the day is advancing, a great event is at hand, & new agents are called to carry forward the work they so well began.

He is an advocate of peace & temperance, a denouncer of all oppressions & a desperate foe to the Papacy. I like to hear him talk; there was in these things a correctness in his views that pleased me, though in some other things it seemed to us his mind is clouded; but his apparent earnestness & sincerity pleased me much. His blue eye kindled with enthusiasm & his priestly face lighted up with intelligence when he spoke. He was short & thick built, with his brown hair drawn upon his high forehead & their spread & tied in a knot to hide, I suppose, his shaven crown. His dress was truly German: a broad straw hat, \light/ blue linen coat & pantaloons & black vest. He preaches or, as he terms it, delivers his message in meeting houses [3] & school houses or wherever he can & his errand to us was to ask leave of Harrison to speak in our meeting house. Of course Harrison did not feel authorised to give it, but referred him to some of the influential friends.

Dost thou remember hearing of Rebecca Martindale's brother Thos Bragg & his family coming to this country? His wife is a sister of Wm Boodle, a very, very nice woman. They are come to reside here and are a pleasant addition to our acquaintance, I feel much pleased with Ann Bragg: she reminds me very much of her brother Wm: she has the same kind eyes & is a very sweet woman. Her family are a very superior & interesting set of young people.

We have had a very warm summer, as has been the case with you. How didst thou bear the unusual season[?] We begin to be naturalized to these things & to me it is pleasant, but of course it is more trying in England. However, I am glad to see the prospects of the country are so prosperous—we hear excellent accounts of the wheat crops & the harvest in general. I trust the rumour of the potatoe blight is false; you have not a substitute & where could it be found for the potatoe?

Our Yearly Meeting is at hand, but I do not think either Harrison or I shall get [there]. Of myself I am certain. One Yearly Meeting after another goes by & Friends at each have talked strongly of separation.[69] Ohio is just over & no separation; Philadelphia passed by without it & now I hope the excitement & messiness will subside & that peace & love may again prevail. But there is a spirit of intolerance here which is constantly manifesting itself & causes a thraldom of mind that is anything but freedom. There is no despotism like that of the mob: witness the doings of Mercer County & towards the Mormons. But dear mother the latter were and are a strange deluded company, but as citizens they were peaceable & ought not to have been outraged. It seems to me that the soil of America is like a volcanic region liable to spout up fire & open earthquake rents at times unlooked for & unbidden. I know you think differently of this country; you think of the Democracy as it is in the West & South at least, and as it is ever liable to be where the people are behind their institutions.

Tell dear Mary to write to me; I shall try to send her one of the children's journals. I fear she will grow weary of them: how can they fail to be monotonous when the scene is laid within the narrow precincts of 33 acres[?] [4] For except in our journeyings to & fro to meeting, we seldom go from home, so you cannot expect much variety. Say, however, when you grow tired & I will desist sending,

I must get thee to give my dearest love to Anna. I received a delightful letter from her giving an account of their Welsh journey. I have been very glad to hear in thy last of her improved health; dear creature, may she long be spared, a blessing to her husband & children & an ornament to society,

69. Alderson is probably referring to tensions between the more evangelical Gurneyites and the more traditional Friends (Wilburites) associated with the ministry of John Wilbur. Indiana Yearly Meeting and Cincinnati Monthly Meeting remained firmly in the Gurneyite camp. Of course, she was well aware of several separations that had occurred in Indiana Yearly Meeting, beginning with the Hicksite-Orthodox split in 1828 and followed by the separation of the Anti-Slavery Friends from the Orthodox in the early 1840s (Sabrina Darnowsky, *Friends Past and Present: The Bicentennial History of Cincinnati Friends Meeting [1815–2015]* [self-pub., CreateSpace, 2015], 96.

I am hoping when Thos & Sarah Frankland arrive to hear again from her, perhaps from you all. I wrote to Anna last month; again, give my endeared love to them all.

Last week Thompson was here on his way from the South, where he has been for some months. He looks well & seemed in good spirits; I never felt him so like Danl's brother before; of course I loved him better than at any previous time. He gives a sad account of society in the southern States: the insecurity & comfortless distrust, every man is in his house as in a fortified castle. His arms may be said to be always in his hand; human life is little valued & the people groan under the curse of slavery & yet are so helpless & dependent on their slaves that they will not give up the darling misery. When will the blind eyes see, the deaf ears hear, the bondsmen of Satan break his goading shackles?

Harrison has had two letters from the Friends who were here last year. Josiah Forster in his kindly mentioned you; I hope thou often sees him & George Stacy. Please give our love to them.

Harrison's dear love to thee & Wm & Mary; [1] mine to the whole household; endeared affection, thy attached daughter,

Emma

54. To Ann Botham, September 1846

Copy of a letter sent by an Indian Girl at the Shawnee School to a friend at Cincinnati[70]

6 mo 21, 1846

Respected Friend,
Agreeable to promise I take my pen to inform thee that we are all well at present. Several of the children have had the chicken pox, but they have got well. When Ann (~~the teacher~~) came up to read to us last night, she brought Thomas Wells' letter which thee wrote. The children all remembered thee and were glad to hear from thee and were glad that thee had not forgotten them.

Thomas Wells brought 17 sheep, and we washed the wool and picked it last week. Zeri and Eli painted the house while we had four carpenters at work last week. One Indian is making laths, and a white man is nailing them on. Angeline and I are studying Arithematic, Geography and Grammar.

Thomas and Hannah Wells went to Westport last fourth-day and took two of the little boys with them.

70. Mary Howitt reproduces this letter in its entirely, largely verbatim, but indicates that it was sent to "Mrs David Hutchinson," an entirely fictional individual. Abraham Taylor (1795–1873), the model for David Hutchinson, was still single when Alderson died. He married Elizabth Robeson Shoemaker (1809–1855) on August 20, 1848.

We have 12 cows that give milk—their calves are killed—and 6 that have calves. We have a very good garden this year. They expect to commence harvesting next week. Six new scholars came since thee was here. I got a letter from Virginia two weeks ago. I got it on fourth day; I wrote to her the next seventh day. Peter Cornstalk is dead; he was at the council when you were here.

Zeri and Miriam are gone to the Methodist mission today. Ann and I are down in their house writing. (These friends are the teachers; Ann is an assistant in the house.) Eli has the charge of the school to day; Miriam has the charge of the chickens; she says there are about a hundred little chickens. We had good many swarms of bees this year; several have went off. James has his face swelled almost all the time, the bees sting him so much. We went to John Wolf's about a week ago. Ann went with us. They have a very good garden. Ann looked so tired and pale. Sally Wolf lent her a horse to ride home. Two of the little girls rode with her.

The school is broke and I have to quit till after dinner. There are two women; they have their babies tied on boards; they say that it will make them straight.

There have been good many strawberries this year. Thomas Wells & Ann Staunton went to Independence. Big Blue was so high that the water ran over the little waggon bed. Ann got us some very pretty new bonnets. They are the same shape as Virginia's bonnet. They are very cheap; they cost only a dollar a piece. She got three: one for Susan Fish, one for Angeline, and one for me. That Indian woman is well. Thee knows that woman that had a hen sitting on goose eggs on the bed in a little basket; she has a very good garden; she has some tame cherries ripe. Ann and us girls went there the other day; we went to get some tansy.

[2] Ann is gone to take a walk with the little girls on the Prairie to pick flowers. We heard from you twice before you got home. There were some Indian men came from hunting saw you at Lexington.

Ann and Susan and Angeline and I went down to the creek to wash bed quilts. Alfred took us down in the little waggon. After we had done washing we sat down on a log waiting for Alfred to come after us. We looked behind us and there stood a bold looking Kaw. He stood there looking at us; we were nearly scared out of our wits. Afterwards came along a whole tribe of drunken kaws and we were scared worse, and we hid ourselves behind the log. We were afraid to leave the quilts because he might took them.

The little girls want me to tell thee they know how to pick wool. Ann says they were very smart to help. Angeline sends her love to thee. Miriam says she wishes to be remembered to thee. All the little girls say 'I like her': I put it down just as they expressed it. Susan Fish sends her love. I still look towards coming in the Fall if my Father is willing for me to come.

I conclude & remain thy Friend,

Lucia B. King

I should be glad to receive a letter from thee if thee thinks worth while to answer this. Give our love to Maryann Donaldson.

My dearest Mother,
I requested to be allowed to copy the above, feeling assured you would all be pleased with such a specimen of Indian thought & feeling. It is from a girl of 15 at the school to a member of the committee who visited the institution last spring. She describes her as a beautiful, intelligent creature.

One little incident she mentioned as indicative of her character: last Fall her Father came to take her away in order to betroth her to some one but she refused to accompany him. She was not going, she said, to marry cheap, to be sold for a bushel of corn and a horse to any one that would buy her. She has a great desire to spend some years amongst the whites & ~~I~~ ours has been selected as her future home, but I am fearful of engaging in such a responsible undertaking & think I shall decline, though on some accounts I should like it much and feel such an interest in her that I should rejoice in the opportunity of endeavouring to promote her welfare & happiness. If we were alone, dear mother, I would joyfully engage to do my best, but someway I always find a counter influence at work, which makes the addition of others very trying & to them I believe very baneful. It is underneath & therefore I cannot meet it, but it is to be seen & felt in its effects & makes me avoid all occasions of manifestation. Thou wilt understand me & I need say no more; it is the cloud in my sky, the thorn in my path, and I must bear it.

I am very busy at present quilting. That nice black poplin skirt thou sent me I have now in the frame; I want to make it last & look handsome & nothing sets things off so much as quilting. Besides everybody here wears them, winter & summer, in the former for comfort, in the latter for pride. Besides my petticoat, I have a comfort in hand made of that nice dark brown wrapping gown thou gave me. It was becoming old in its first, [3] but is now beautiful & renovated & I intend it for our own bed. I wish to preserve every relic of thy kindness & this is the way I can best return that; besides, every day I shall see it &, did I want things to remind me of thee, it & ~~a thousand thing~~ countless other proofs of thy love continually fill my mind with grateful affectionate rememberances.

I would gladly make & send thee a comfort for thy own bed; they are the most delightful winter coverings, so warm & so light. I believe I have described them, or I would do it in hopes thou wilt get one before the next cold weather.

Dear Anna says you have a very hot summer. The heat must have felt excessive. Here the thermometer has been between 90 & 100 in the shade. It is very regular & to me very pleasant; I like to feel in a glow of warmth & there is so often a pleasant breeze with is that it is seldom to me oppressive. Besides, we all enjoy excellent health, which is an inexpressible favour.

Of course you know the government here have met the abolition of the corn laws with a removal of the Tariff. I am rejoiced; I hope it will be to the benefit of the countries, but there are many that think otherwise as regards America. Well, they can bear a little abatement of prosperity; they do not need to dread starvation, though trade is a little checked, and in my heart the interests of England are dearer to me than that of any other country.

I shall never be a blind American. I cannot sympathize with them in many things; this war I abominate & hope they may be humbled in their proud boast; then there is a lawlessness in the country that makes me tremble sometimes. A gentleman said to me a few days ago "if popular opinion wills a thing <the> law is a nulity": that is, if the mob is determined to destroy individuals or communities, the executive stands by & does not interfere. Countless acts of violence and aggression prove this; I have sent you some papers which I hope will reach you full of such details. Indeed they are of daily occurrence.

I want thee to see the account of the Mormon migration & Randolph negroes: I think them especially interesting events. I should think since the wanderings of the Children of Israel there was never a paralel to the Mormon mobs: upwards of 10,000 people with their goods & cattle, making their way across the barren plains of Missouri & \through/ the passes of the Rocky Mountains, planting & sowing for coming bodies. Each party contains from 1000 to 1500 individuals. It is said they are enduring much privation & suffering from hunger. The mad rage of the people is so desperate that those who have ventured to remain in or near their old settlements have often experienced lynch law. The very harvest labourers do not escape.

And yet with all my sweeping prejudices against the nation, there are many whom I love & esteem \it/ a blessing to be associated with, as beautiful specimens of human nature as it has been my lot to meet with: intelligent, kind, refined & yet with a simplicity of heart & manner, a genuine piety & noble elevation of soul that hates all meanness & what is dishonourable that it is refreshing & strengthening to be with. I am glad Mary is acquainted with some of these excellent of the earth from this land. [4] I hear the Hutchinson family spoken of with the highest admiration by all who know them.

What can have made George Stacy so lenient to the slaveholders of Maryland[?] I can entirely subscribe to dear Mary's indignation against all slavery however mild. Good Thomas Shilitoe never paliates, no, nor John Woolman nor Anthony Benezet. It is the slang of some parties here & I have often been told that the slaves in Kentucky are better off than the poor in England. In that which constitutes the convenience of meat & drink for the support of the animal I grant, but in all that gives dignity to man as a rational & immortal being, give me a ~~poor but~~ free, though poor, man. Freedom is the crown ~~of his~~ and seal of his nobility.

Write soon, my precious mother. I have been alone this last week; Harrison is gone to the Quarterly meeting. According to the etiquette of this country I am going to be invisible for the next three months. No body goes out after a certain time that is desirous not to transgress the bounds of strict delicacy, and as home is a pleasant prison, I gladly submit to the general law. Do not make thyself anxious: I always do well at such times & trust to do so \on/ this occasion. I should have been glad to have been spared, but when such thoughts come, that beautiful verse of Mackay's answers,

~~He who shirks from daily work~~
Who lags for lack of daily work
And his appointed task would shirk
a soulless slave &c.[71]

& I dare think no more such thoughts.

My kind Friends the Taylors have been twice up to visit me during Harrison's absence. They are amongst those that I should be proud to make you acquainted with.

I want to put in the receipt for drying tomatoes for dear Mary, so with a heart full of the warmest affection, must conclude, my beloved mother,

Thy attached daughter,

Emma.

55. To Mary Howitt, September 27 to October 20, 1846
9 mo. 2[72]

[27 Sept 1846] Here are Charles & I alone on a bright autumnal first-day, and the dear lad is sitting in the shade on the piazza looking at his pictorial Robinson Crusoe; we have read in the Bible till he is tired & now he wants the relaxation of pictures. I have just given him a piece of maple-sugar candy because he has been so kind & good in doing a many little "chores" to use a favourite American phrase. The whole family besides himself, Alice & me are gone to the city to meeting, so he has fetched me tomatoes from the garden, brought in some fine ripe musk melons, tended his little sister, raised water, lighted the fire & gone into the stable to see how White Rose is & into the pasture to look at her mother, Mrs. Blackberry. So I think you will all allow he deserves a kind word & a child's reward.

To go back to the last week; we have had a great event. Father set out one day with Farmer & the old carriage & brought home a nice new one with

71. Charles Mackay, "Daily Work" (1846):
Who lags for dread of daily work,
And his appointed task would shirk,
Commits a folly and a crime;
A soulless slave—a paltry knave—
A clog upon the wheels of Time.

72. Perhaps, uncertain of the date, Alderson intended to add a second digit following the "2." The previous journalistic letter to Howitt ends on September 21, and the first date in this letter is October 6. I have therefore given the commencement of this letter as Sunday (as evident in the first sentence), September 27.

handsome stuffed sides & cushions as soft as a bed with lamps, & shafts \for Farmer/ and a pole also for him & Ben when the roads are bad; what delight was it to the children to meet him at the gate & have the first ride. Then as it stood in the barn yard, what rejoicing was there over its appearance; Annie walked round it & made a kind of speech: "What a fine horse & what a fine carriage & what a length from the end of Farmer's nose to the back behind, Oh how grand." Charles was quiet and pleased. And Agnes calculated on all the pleasant rides she should have with Father & mother & \that/ perhaps little Alice would ride in this carriage, for she has an unaccountable dread of all vehicles & trembles & cries when taken near them, ~~only~~ one only excepted which is a~~n old~~ box nailed to the wheels of an old play waggon in which her brother & sisters have lately drawn her about & which has been their favourite amusement. There sate she on a piece of buffalo skin with a long whip made of a branch of weeping willow, peering from under her little sun bonnet & now & then getting a cry of pleasure. Charles was harnessed as horses, Anna Mary was driver & Agnes pushed behind.

This waggon has also been of ~~great~~ use in "hauling" great loads of Squashes from the garden to the cellar, large \yellow/ crook-necks, one of which is a load for Charles, and marrow squashes & Kushaws which are green & white, all of which make excellent pies, or more properly cheese cakes, & are besides delightful vegetables; they keep well till the middle of winter & some kinds even longer.

But all this pleasure has had one great drawback: the lost hog is not found, & what is worse, our neighbour appears inclined to be very litigious. Yesterday he set his dogs on another which happened to be in his pasture, for he keeps bad fences & they will get through & when remonstrated with, told Father he would tear them to pieces if they did come into his fields. The children who were present came home in an excitement of indignation; they concluded that if the man really was that bad it would be necessary to shoot his dogs. And Charles very gravely asked me this morning to give him a dollar that he might buy a gun to be in readiness. Of course it was hard to convince them of the evil of revenge & that these schemes spring from this wicked spirit. They had heard Lennitt in his broken English insulting Father & threatening the lives of the hogs, & they could not help being angry.

Agnes has been trying very hard to learn to read well that she may have a new straw bonnet for her doll which Mother has promised to make for her as soon as she can do without spelling the words of one syllable, & now having arrived at this desirable consummation, the platt[73] was brought out, & and under Agnes' direction a very tastely little "gipsy" was constructed & trimmed, with [2] some pretty purple & green gause ribbon that has been long hoarded up for the occasion; then there were the lappets & the small strings & such a variety of things to \be/ added that it took her the whole

73. Probably a misspelling of "plait."

afternoon to fit it up; & how proud & happy did this well earned & long talked of bonnet make her. Even Father admired her taste & wondered how she had caught all the little niceties of the mode. Annie was offered a bonnet too but she has no lurking vanity, no regard for dress in her own person nor even in her dolly, so she begged to have her share of straw worked up into a little basket, & now all were pleased & glad. It is worthwhile to break off from the sterner duties, the press of daily life, to play with \a child/ or even make a play thing for it; half an hour spent in this way has something of the freshness of spring flowers & sunshine, of little running brooks & the songs of joyous, careless birds in it, & we return to our daily path of wise gravity with refreshed & softened hearts.

Whilst the little girls were thus amusing themselves, Charley was gone with Father & William to fetch a waggon load of wood; they had to go about 2 miles & the wood in the coming evening began to look very sombre before they left. Neighbour Lennitt had told Charley yesterday that early in the morning he had seen a large wolf come out of his wood & run across the pasture & someway Charles could not help thinking of the wolf and looking fearfully into the dark nooks & behind the old fallen decaying trunks that here & there lay scattered on the ground. He had amused himself whilst the sunshine enlivened the wood with gathering his hat full of ripe pawpaws from the bushes. These are called the American custard apple; they form the principle undergrowth in these western woods; \it does not grow east of the Alleganies/ & are a very beautiful ornament. The plant has somewhat the appearance of a loose growing laurel; its leaves, though not evergreen, are larger & polished & the blossom which comes in the early spring is a curious dark brown mysterious looking flower. The pawpaws Charles brought were about the size & shape of a middling kidney potatoe: green, but when pared the pulp is the colour of boiled custards & the flavour that of custards & fruit mixed, but somewhat sickley.

Yesterday Father was riding out & espied our lost hog in a neighbour's yard; he came back for Charles who, with the assistance of a boy on the road, brought it safely home, & now he is penned up to prevent his rambling &, if possible, to prevent contention with our neighbour. To day who should present himself but Paul, Adelle's boy, as the children call him. He looks very smart & is just come to make us a call before he leaves the city; he has a large patterned purple & white roundabout nankin pantaloons & a handsome black leather cap & his bright intelligent face looks really handsome. He would make a fine picture [3] of a goodlooking & lighthearted coloured lad. He has been to pay his mother a visit in her new home & is now going back to his trade. After Paul had exhausted his nice speeches & said what he seemed to think very pretty things, he asked Charles to go out & let them look round for he had had been telling Joe as they came up all about the place & the adventures he and Charley had had together. Joe was a little coloured boy who came as his friend & companion. Off the three went, & in their rambles came into Jack's Wood, where they found so many hickory nuts on the trees that Paul climbed up some of them & shook them down in showers. The boys gathered them together, & in all there were more than a bushel & a half enclosed in their green husk which envelopes the nut & which expands in four equal parts by the action of the frost.

At dinner they all enjoyed the pot-pies made of boiled chicken, potatoes & pieces of pastry all boiled together, and the pumpkin pies after. Paul is certainly, for an American child, wonderfully well behaved: he never forgets to say "thank you & yes Sir & no I am obliged," & when they left the dinner table he took his friend Joe to task for not saying ["]no thank you["] when asked to have another piece of pie. He had in whispers been prompting him to good manners all dinner time. "Well,["] said Joe in exclamation, ["]I ain't used to eat at white people's tables." When they went away the children & accompanied them to the gate & a carter passing called out, "well nigger where do you come from,["] & a boy a little farther on threw clods of dirt at them. Thus it is, repelled from society, insulted at every turn, no wonder the poor coloured man feels himself degraded & every desire for improvement repressed because the reward of intellectual elevation is denied him. He is treated with contumely from the cradle to the grave; the colour of his skin brings upon him insult, even should there lurk beneath the dark exterior a mind illuminated with the brightest rays of virtue & genius.

10th mo. 6th: Winter, we hope, is still far distant, but we are preparing for it by laying in a store of wood & other fuel. Yesterday Charles accompanied his father \went/ in the waggon to fetch some charcoal which is burnt in a small stove with coke or wood on cold mornings & evenings just to warm the rooms. They went four miles farther in the country, up the course of Muddy Creek. The scenery was wild & pleasant through the woods, & often the road crossed the rocky bed of the stream. When they reached Tobias Miller's, the charcoal burner's, they found him busy at his trade; he had a pit filled with wood undergoing the process; it was tightly covered up with ashes & so nearly charred that he offered to fill the waggon with that, but Father feared it might be so hot as to endanger the whole taking fire, & so they went up to his house & got 20 bushels from the shed there. Muddy Creek is famous for lime burning & charcoal making; it is a rude but beautiful valley, little cleared & the houses mostly—log cabins—inhabited by Germans.

Since writing the above we have been a drive up Muddy Creek & a beautiful valley it is: wild & uncultivated in many parts, it presents delightful specimens of forest scenery. When we turned from the main road, the half cultivated land so characteristic of Americanism presented themselves; cornfields & pastures studded over with the tall trunks of trees which have been girdled & [4] left to rot themselves away, or the blackened stumps of such as have been destroyed by fire. But a belt of thick woods was before us & we soon entered it; here & there a log cabin on the borders of still less cleared lands showed that man had taken possession, but as we descended to the creek the woods hemed us in on every side, glowing in the waning sunshine with the first rich tints of autumn. The beech mingled its gold & green with the first red tinges of the sugar maples; the oak, though scarce, showed now & then its rich purple masses; and here & there on the borders of the wood the beautiful dog-wood intermingled its bright scarlet foliage with the deep greens by which it was surrounded & reminded us of its beauty when, \in/ spring, it is covered with its showy white flowers, & we projected a pleasant pic nic to enjoy these solitudes in the season of birds & flowers.[74]

In passing a deep, wooded hollow the fine apple scents of pawpaw came so strong & rich that we stopped the carriage & Charles & Father went down into the hollow to gather them from the bushes which grew there remarkably large. They soon returned with their handkerchiefs full of large ripe pawpaws, so rich & good that we had a great treat indeed; they taste, when in perfection, like a very lu[s]cious pineapple, and as these were as large as ~~a~~ great potatoes, were very full of pulp; we have saved you some of the seeds.

One place we were struck with as an unusual specimen of order & neatness: it was a log house of larger dimensions than common, surrounded by a low porch of plain boards. But very neat & orderly on it were the beds of the family sunning, as it is called; in another part lay a quantity of dried apples. The house within & without had been recently whitewashed to the very wood ~~house~~ shed & the saw horse & chopping-block; the windows were whole & bright. A somewhat unusual circumstance: behind the house on the steep hill side was a terraced vinyard, perfectly free from weeds; in the lower part, the garden sloped down to the road & contained some splendid balsams so fine and large that they looked like flowering shrubs, & at first we questioned what they were. The valley was so narrow as only to contain the road & the creek so that the opposite side rose steep, & high on it were clustered a number of neat log barns & outhouses, all in good order & free from the usual untidiness of Farm buildings. Here, said we, lives some worthy German, perhaps a David Lybrook, that good old-fashioned Moravian we visited last year; he was a gentleman even in his red flannel warmers and his homespun clothes.

It is Charles' work to fetch up the cows to milk in an evening; Anna Mary mostly accompanies him & afterwards they both practice their hand in milking Charles' cow, Pink. Anna Mary has adopted Blackberry who, for a young cow, is exceedingly quiet. They milk into their tin cans & bring Alice a nice treat; she is delighted to be carried down & often in the course of the day brings a bonnet if she can pick one up & takes it to the nearest person present & says "cow, cow" very imploringly. Besides fetching the cows, Charles also waters Farmer night & morning. Ben—or, to give him his full honour, Ben Franklin—is too fractious & father dares not trust him with so

74. Possibly an oblique reference to Mary Howitt's *Birds and Flowers and Other Country Things*, of which Alderson was especially fond.

small a boy. Farmer, however, to day behaved very ill & when he had drank threw up his heels, reared & threw Charles off; fortunately he was not hurt & as Farmer was chastised for his bad conduct, we hope he will not do so again.

The morning was spent by the children in the corn-crib husking corn, for as the pastures are getting bare we begin to need feed for the "critturs". Then in the afternoon, Father went to [5] dig up sweet potatoes; these are a favourite vegetable & with right good will did the children gather them & lay them in the sun to dry, & when a fine one presented, rejoiced over it as if it was a piece of sweet cake. Then Charles riddled[75] sand & they were safely stowed away in barrels next day, & put, as we hope, out of the reach of frost which entirely destroys them; they are a Southern production, the root of a large bulbous rooted convolvulus which we have often coveted to see blooming, but it does not flower \so/ far~~ther~~ north.

10 mo. 20: Housing roots is now the great object as the nights have become frosty; Agnes came in this morning and told of the havoc the frost had made: the balsams & the four-oclocks, the Mexican & Cypress vines, the dahlias, gourds, melons, beans and pumpkins are alas black as if they had been boiled. But the days are bright & warm; there is a blue haze in the air which makes us think of Indian summer and Father again was busy digging up parsnips, carrots & beets, which the children drew up to the house in their little wagon. The gourds or dippers, some like great ladles, others the shape of large long-necked bottles, were gathered & laid aside in the ganet for use.

Then, not too wearied to play, they set off to the woods to see if the boys & squirrils had left any hickory nuts. It was one of those sweet autumnal afternoons which fills the heart with quiet sadness; the earth glowed with green & gold & crimson, intermingled with hues of brown & yellow; the tall corn looked rich like fretted gold; the distance was blue as the sky with the fine haziness of the season, and yet the air around had a crysta[l]line brilliancy, warmed by the bright sun that made one think of midsummer. The children bounded into the woods amongst the rustling leaves with the activity of young squirrils; they gathered the pretty michaelmass daisy and the few remaining golden rods &, thanks to \the/ abundant season, in spite of bold hogs & the wild creatures of the wood, soon filled their <baskets> with nuts gathered on the ground. Some were very fine & John Solo, whom they met in their rambles, told them those he got a dollar a bushel for in the city.

This lad is a thorough Yankee. He gathers blackberries & pawpaws & nuts for sale; catches young red birds and sells them to Mary Crehoe \& her friends/, but alas they never live; barters all sorts of things to such fortunate children as chance to have cents; & now is tempting Charley with a fishing pole, line & two hooks, all fitted off with lead & cork for ten cents, & poor Charles thinks he could not better dispose of his hard earned ten cents than

75. Alderson is using the word "riddle" to mean "sift," an uncommon usage today.

in making this purchase, though there are no fish to our knowledge within miles of us & certainly no place where he may go to find them, for the runs & creeks are all so nearly dry this summer that fish in them are quite rare ~~in them~~. In the Ohio of course there are plenty, but to go there is quite out of the question.

On their way home the children met "Old Jack" as Annie calls her hobbling along; she spoke very kindly & asked if Mamma was well & if Father had any grapes or quinces to sell. A comfortable assurance this; if she can even think of buying luxuries she must have \a/ sufficiency of the necessaries of life.

My dear and honoured mother, I had hoped & intended to write thee a long letter, but when I tell thee that this is but the sixth morning from my confinement, I think thou wilt be willing to accept it as my apology, especially as I intend to commence & dispatch a longer epistle in a few days. So far I have been unusually well, Thank God, and am nursed & waited on with the utmost kindness & tenderest care. Dear Harrison is my nurse & even brings my food prepared with his own hand, is my doctor too, administers all remedies & sleeps in my room to attend on me at night; the rest of the household are also very kind & the dear children are emulous who shall wait most & least on mother. Agnes is a sweet little attendant on my room, helps me to wash & dress & goes hither & thither with much good will. So thou sees I am well off; the willing service of loving hearts is very acceptable in such times.

It was a vain wish, but like the yearnings of nature I could not suppress it too long: with almost childish longing for thy sweet precious company & sympathy during the few past weeks, I felt more than ordinarily the uncertainty of life & the termination of this event, & my mother was the constant companion of my thoughts. Dear mother, perhaps thou thought of & prayed for me too, & God has mercifully answered our prayers & brought me in safety through a season of some danger, I believe. The dear baby is gone; it was stillborn, [6] poor child. I anticipated it with more than common hope and affections but felt a trial to see it taken; it was a sweet & uncommonly fine boy, I think. I never told thee that last year we had a similar loss, so that this is the second time since Ann Alice's birth we have cause to be thankful that our little flock are in perfect health & improving morally & intellectually I hope. They often talk of "dear grandmother.["]

Thank thee and dear Mary for your last most welcome letter; my dearest love to you all & to dearest Anna & her family. Thou kindly asks to whom you should consign a parcel; I think it came through John Pennington to the care of a friend whose address I will get Harrison to add; it would be quite safe; or sent by any private individual to him, we shall be sure to get it. You are very, very kind: how can I repay you, and what can I do for you? But you must not suppose we have ever grudged any expence attending your parcels; they are always so valuable that whatever they have cost has seemed a trifle in comparison.

I am glad the seeds did well; the crimson twining plant is the Ipomea Quamoclit or Cypress vine, a species of Morning glory or major convolvolus. I have some nice seeds for you which I hope to send in time. Harrison sends his dear love to thee and all your dear family; Charles and Agnes also desire theirs. A kind friend has sent for Anna Mary to stay with her during my confinement.

The slate answers admirably; its honest details lead to conviction and are a stimulus to endeavour to conquer evil habits. "How how will thou like to hear of that from the slate," says Agnes; ["]The slate, the slate,["] cries Charley with a warning voice. It is read on a second-day morning with much solemnity in the presence of Father only, who thus has a review of the past week & comments or reproves as the occasion demands; the first was a black slate enough, the second so manifestly better that I subjoin it as a specimen.

1st day: all good till evening when Charles & Annie jarred a little <som?> oven. 2nd day: a day of pleasure; went to J Mackinellins; all good. 3rd day: very obedient, very peaceable. 4[th day]: Agnes fretful at her reading, Charles perverse about his arithmetic, some quarreling between him & Annie. 5th day: good. 6th day: began very well; interrupted by Paul's coming; very loving & kind to each other. 7th day: Charles grumbled at every thing, was selfish & perverse with his sisters about the hickory nuts, thumped Annie, scolded Alice & was cross to mother, even. Agnes slow in obedience; all improved before evening.

Thomas & Sarah Frankland and their family are expected daily; I am hoping to have letters by them from dear Anna & the girls at least. Thank thee for the London Friend; are they as hearty in the cause of humanity as the British? We shall <*sealed*> with the tenderest emotions of affection, thy attached daughter,

Emma.

Cousin Ann Shipley, who is always pleased to receive thy <*sealed*> messages, sent her love to thee the last time I saw her. My dearest love to Wm & Mary & all the family.

56. To Mary Howitt, October 24 to November 20, 1846
10th mo 25

[October 24][76] "A day of hard work." "Now mother," said Charles "what are we to do? There is our heap of butter nuts & hickory nuts & the Buckeyes for Alice to play with, all lying in the wood, & Father said at breakfast we must

76. I give the date as October 24 in spite of the dateline above because October 25, 1846, was a Sunday.

do all our work before we went for them, lessons & all." Poor children, they have rambled & played until it seems necessary to come to an end, and therefore the appointed task is to be fulfilled, so after a little encouragement & assurance that if they would work well there would be a fine long afternoon to play, Charley went to husk the corn & feed the horses. Agnes sate down to her small task of sewing, read her lesson & then sate down to help her brother to brush their shoes for the morrow, which was first day; we teach them as much as possible to wait upon themselves & others, hoping to render ourselves & them independent of hired help, which is so difficult to obtain in this land. Then they had to watch Alice in the warm sunshine on the grass & afterwards had to pick the green tomatoes from the frosted & withered plants for the pigs; poor things, they worked hard & before dinner time had gathered five basketful. Then Agnes had to go to the shoemaker at Warsaw to get her shoe sewed, but ~~there~~ \now/ all was done & away they went for their treasures. All was safe: the butter nuts quite dry & good, the hickory nuts just bursting out of their outer coats, the buckeye, with its light brown pupil bright & hard as if they had been varnished, & with pinafores & basket ful they returned rejoicing home, weary but happy. Charley sate down by the fire to rest & fell asleep before supper; he did not ask his aunt as usual to read to him after tea. Agnes also fell asleep; she did not nurse here dolly to night; even its new cravat, which she fringed so nicely yesterday, & the "gipsy" staid on unchanged.

[October 25] 1st day. Charles & Agnes went down with Father & Aunt to meeting. As Father had an engagement, Richard drove them home. After dinner, R[ichard] gathered some grapes from the vine round the piazza & then they all came & heard mother read about Willie Ellis & his good christian conduct to Capt. Stout.[77] Afterwards the children went with Lousia to the graveyard to see her niece's grave; when there they met the grave digger who told them he should starve with his bad pay, for said he ["]I only get 25 cents for digging \such/ a hole \as that/ & there is my neighbour the Irish man gets 2 dollars for every hole he digs." The graves he called ["]holes["] & coffins ["]boxes.["]

When Father came home he told us that the occasion of his staying was to go with some other good christian friends to hold a meeting in the prison with the chain gang & others confined there. When they got in they were all locked up with about 50 men, some ironed & dragging their long chains, others free; there was one man confined for murder. At first some of the prisoners laughed & looked careless, but they soon solemnized down & they had a very good meeting with them & the poor fellows crowded round them

77. "The Widow Ellis and Her Son Willie: Overcome Evil with Good," by Catherine Maria Sedgwick, was published in various periodicals beginning with Catharine Maria Sedgwick's *Love Token for Children: Designed for Sunday-School Libraries* (New York: Harper & Brothers, 1838), 9–33, which Alderson mentions by name elsewhere (see page 400).

at parting to shake hands & looked very serious & very thankful \and begged they would come again/. Father gave them some tracts.

[October 26] 2nd day. Charles fitted up his waggon with some new linch pins & with 4 more in his pocket to renew if those should break. They put Alice in the waggon & went to the shoe-makers to fetch Father's boot which had been left when Agnes got her shoe sewed. They got safely on their way home. As they passed [2] Mary Crehoe's gate, our kind neighbour invited them in to rest. In turning through the gate, the pins gave way & down came the waggon on the ground, but James Crehoe soon cut some strong, good peggs & fixed it up better than ever. Whilst this was doing, Mary C. gave them each an apple & showed them her fine crysanthemums of every shade & color, and then they set out to return home. ~~3rd day~~ In the evening they went with Father to Icles to ask him to come & kill the little calf.

[October 27] 3rd day. Yes, the poor little calf is to be killed, beautiful little white Rose, which we have, in our love and admiration, called lilly & snow-drift & fed & visited till we all loved it, for delicate beauty & innocence \is to be killed/. The butcher came & looked at it & said he would give a dollar for it, but no, Father said he would have it killed at home rather than sell it for such a trifle: it would be a great convenience & save the trouble of going to market.

So this afternoon we saw our neighbour Icle & his son coming across the field & the children ran in, for they did not want to be near when the calf was brought out & killed, and we got the history of the United States which we are reading & began to read with more than common attention one of its most interesting passages, the progress of Hernando Soto from the shores of the Mexican Gulf to the Upper Mississippi. We read of his wanderings through the unbroken wilderness, of his contests with the Indians, of his desasterous retreat & death on the shores of the mighty river he discovered & in whose waters he was buried; we traced his course on the map & by that time the dismal deed was done: White Rose was killed & skinned & Charles went out in time just to see the men hang up the carcase in the woodhouse.

There is a renewed intimacy sprung up between little Frederic & the children. He has come of late to join ~~in~~ Charles in his rides to & fro on the avenue upon Farmer; the quiet good creature lets them get off & on at pleasure & even Agnes & Annie now & then venture to ride behind one of the boys, but commonly they perform the part of running footmen, following with great glee the riders.

There has been great assuring that Frederic did not use bad words, that he does not quarrel nor behave ill, & because his Father lives in a little log house & they in a large brick one can never be a reason why they shall not play together. It is in this land—with thankfulness we may say it—merit, not rank or show, that make[s] way for a man. Many a squire \or "magistrate"/ lives in a log house or a little \mean/ frame one; many a judge follows his plough, and the very governors & senators are often little more than husbandmen.

Frederic has undertaken to make Charles a new cart; it is to be large enough for Alice to ride in, and Charles is to pay 15 cents for it if it should prove worth anything.

This afternoon, being seventh day, when all was done in preparation for the sabath, Father proposed as it was only 3 oclock that Charles should walk down to the foot of the hill and take the calf's skin to the tanners. To a child who has gone so little from home alone, this first setting out to walk two miles and return and transact business appeared somewhat formidable, but Charles thought he could do it. The skin was tied up in a cloth, a strong stick was found to hang it upon over his shoulder & with an apple in his hand he started. He met no one on the way to trouble him; a horseman as he passed asked [3] him if he was not cold, and two boys said "here's a lad: let us knock him down,["] but the other answered ["]no, he's a little boy, let him alone." So the better counsel prevailed, and he reached the tan yard in safety, had his skin weighed & set off back again.

As he came up the hill, a man in an empty wood-waggon said "Bob, will you ride[?"] Charles thanked him & joyfully got up by his side. (Bob \or Bud/ is the cant name for every boy in America, as Sis and Sissie are for the girls[)] This was a nice lift & they came on chatting till they reached the gate. It was getting dark & many an anxious look had mother & sister given for his return. Agnes had toasted him a slice of bread to his milk. There was a piece of cake on his plate & all was waiting his arrival when he came & amused us with the account of his journey.

[November 2] 2nd day. We were all very busy making apple butter. The children helped to ~~peel~~ pare the apples & quinces & when all was done they were boiled in Molasses & water until reduced to a strong thick pulp. \Sweet/ cider, much boiled down, is commonly used for the purpose, but we could not meet with any & found the molasses a good substitute. The making of apple butter is always a formidable undertaking; it has to be stirred for hours after all the paring, which is no small thing: when you think of a great coffer pan that will hold ten gallons over a great wood fire, you may form some idea of the seriousness of the engagement.

Our first apple butter making was quite American; four young women came to help & instruct us at the same time. We were a whole evening paring & then as it is not to be left when once begun till finished, they sate up till one oclock to boil it. When it is done, it rewards one well for the trouble, its rich spicy flavour, for I forgot to say a bag of spices ~~to boil~~ in the pan is an indispensable ingredient, is always grateful & it is a general favorite & very wholesome for the youngsters. This week has been very eventful in bringing us parcels & letters from dear England. One parcel contained nice presents for the Children from dear Cousin at Woodside, another a most beautiful little letter to Wm Charles from his old friend & playmate at Preston, George William. So delighted were the children with this that they have begun in great earnest to resume their writing lessons, which were suspended during the hot weather. Agnes was so anxious to have letters of her own that she wrote a whole slateful that afternoon & we go on now with great zest & no small promise of success in both.

Anna Mary has had an accident: the children had playmates & ran carelessly into the stable when Farmer was frightened by the noise & kicked. He struck A. M. under the knee & Wm brought her in screaming with pain & terror. Her leg was rubbed with Father's grand specific hot vinegar & saltpetre & she was put to bed; next day it was stiff & painful, & she crept & hobbled about miserably, but the morning after, she came bouncing down stairs, delighted to find she could walk well & even run. Charles was very kind to her during [4] the time of her lameness. He felt in some degree to blame & did all in his power to comfort & amuse her, often asking how her poor knee felt.

We have a man now named Henry, a Dutchman & a great favourite with Charles. He spends all his leisure helping him in his work and even saw Father & mother and Anna Mary set out to go to the Orphan Asylum without regret as he had Henry to stay with.

There were only three of the youngest children at home; the others were gone to the coloured school. Little Elizabeth was amongst those we saw. We took them some clothes & a bag of apples; poor little things, they were highly pleased with having each a fine large apple to eat.

Charles & Agnes have had many a journey after their cart, but though in progress, it is not yet done, and now Frederic's grandfather is dead & he is so busy he can do nothing at it.

Mother & the children went to the poor old man's funeral. When they got to the house, the company were all gone to the little Lutheran chapel \below, whither they went/. The coffin stood under the pulpit uncovered; the minister in a plain black dress without either gown or surplice delivered an energetic & apparently an affecting address in German. Many were in tears & the countenances of strong men were indicative of deep emotions. The preacher concluded with an earnest prayer offered with clasped hands & upturned eyes; whilst he stood, they then sung a german hymn. All the time the company remained sitting & only rose to receive the benediction, & then the coffin was carried to the grave. The minister threw in a spadeful of soil when it was lowered & said something; he then prayed again, standing, & the company ~~was~~ dispersed. Anna Mary thought the singing was "very delightful." Agnes said old Mr. Rittenbar (our musical neighbour) put on his spectacles & pulled such dreadful faces all \the time he was singing/. She tried to imitate him, but her pretty little face would not look ugly, so she effected no more than to make us all laugh.

One morning Henry reached a ham down out of the smoke house. It was laid on a table outside the summer kitchen till it could be wiped & hung up.

When Louisa went to look for it, it was gone, all was still & silent: nobody had seen anyone about. Milo's honesty is so well established that we could not suspect him & yet Charles & his sisters ran into the potatoe field from whence he came when called to ask William if he had seen him with a ham. Of course it was vain: we all thought it too large for him, had he been so disposed to convey it away & began to feel uncomfortable as the suspicion seized us that a two legged thief must have been about. At last on returning from the gate, mother spied Bull, William's great white dog in a hollow in the orchard. He ran off home when discovered & truly in the place where we first saw him was the unfortunate ham, almost devoured. It was wonderful how the dog had managed to eat so much in so short a time. He is now under ban & to be driven off whenever he comes about as a good for nothing thief.

[5] Next ~~evening~~ afternoon the children went with Louisa to the graveyard to plant some rose trees at her niece's grave. They found the grave looking very neglected & miserable, so they sodded it again & then planted a white rose at the head & a dark one at the foot. They found a weeping willow already planted at the head of grandfather Lott's grave.

The second & fifth of 11 mo. were Agnes & Wm Charles' birth days; they have been anticipated for the last 6 months by Agnes especially; she is now 7 years old. At first all was very quiet; the children all did lessons in the afternoon, but after dinner mother said now all must be dressed as for company. The parlour had a holiday look; there was a bouquet collected by Charles, which consisted of boughs of cedar interspersed with the scarlet berries of the burning bush & the beautiful \white/ clusters of the snow berry, zinnia, petunia, chrysanthemums, asters, catchfly & such other flowers as still remain in the garden. Dear little Agnes looked very pretty & very conscious of the honour of which she was the object. She was dressed in a green & brown gingham frock & black apron—white panties as they are called here—& her nice flaxen hair was combed with great neatness.

Father ordered the \little/ green & gold china cups to be set for all, and mother placed a cake covered with sugar on which A. A. was traced. The lamps burned brightly & Agnes blushed & smiled as the first cup was handed to her & she felt herself the object of especial attention, but she had the pleasure of handing her cake round herself so that this time her share came last. Then, when all was over & Alice gone to rest, we sate down & Father read us some beautiful poetry about Marian & the little Fisher Children: you know it.

Charles' birthday was a repetition of this except that he had two cakes on his table, one that mother made & one his aunt brought him from the city[78] & on his suppertable we had a splendid nosegay sent by a kind friend from her garden, consisting of roses & a variety of beautiful flowers.

78. According to Howitt, the second cake was a gift from Uncle Cornelius, "and like all Uncle Cornelius's presents, it was quite magnificent" (*OCO*, 260).

[November] 20th. Last week the children had a fine treat, one that they will not forget if they live to be old men & women. Our good friend Joseph Taylor invited them to go down to his house & he would take them to see a very fine collection of wild beasts. So on third-day Father & Henry were going down to the city with the waggon for a load of gravel & they were got ready, but just as they went out to see if the horses were in the waggon it began to rain, and they came in very disconsolate. It was one of those warm mucky mornings, which, had it not been Indian Summer, we should have said would certainly bring a drenching wet day, but after a slight shower & a sudden gust of wind, the sky began to brighten. Charles said he saw blue between the clouds & soon a bright sunshine followed & then cloud & then established sunshine. So there was a second dressing & after a deal of fixing, for poor Louisa left us today & she & her great heavy box which has followed her in all her wanderings from Germany hither, were to be of the party. She left us with many tears & many kisses for Alice & assurances of coming often to see us & then Charles gathered her a great bunch of chrysanthemums [6] and Agnes gave her a keepsake, a little bag she has been making for her & for which she bought nice green silk cord with her own money, & with the flowers in her hair & the bag on her arm, she set off to seek another home in the city.

It was rather late when they arrived at our kind friends who were expecting them. They dined & immediately set out to the "Mammoth Pavilion" to see "The Grand Zoological Exhibition," which employs 60 men & 90 horses, and in which above all the wonderful Herr Driesbach, the great lion tamer, performed his amazing feats. There were two mighty old elephants \Hannibal & Columbus/; on the back of ~~one of which~~ \Columbus/ Charles had a ride.

There were zebra's, monkeys, ostrichs, lions, tigers & all the animals commonly exhibited on such occasions, but all at once a drum beat, & the cry was sounded, ["]take your seats, take your seats,["] and all went at the word of command. When the wonderful Herr came forth, riding in a car to which the lion was harnessed, he brought out his "Tiger pets" & played with them, wrapped the boa constrictor round his arms & neck and jumped upon the elephants tusks as into an arm chair, turned summersets on his head & did innumerable feats of courage & dexterity; it was a perfect delight to the children. They were not troubled with the thoughts of the cruelty which must have been employed to reduce their savage natures to such a degree of submission. I forgot to tell of the monkey which rode on the back of a wee pony with two ensigns in his hands, standing whilst his steed galloped & capered, reared & pranced enough to dismount any man, woman or child.

Time went on and, as it was evening, our good friends requested the children might stay all night. What a winding up to so much pleasure; it was almost too good & yet it was a reality, & when they came home next day the wonders of the show & dear Hannah Taylor's kindness were equally the subject of expatiation. They had a large parcel of candy, cream candy & rock candy & lemon candy, pea nuts & almonds to bring home to enjoy with poor little Alice for she was not forgotten, though absent.

57. To Anna Harrison, November 1846
I have felt very much concerned, my dearly beloved sister, since receiving thy letter sent by Sarah Frankland, in which thou mentions having written twice previously to me & not having received an answer. Dearest sister, how does the idea of thy even thinking me negligent distress me; to be so is so entirely contrary to my will and feelings that it would be impossible and never, dearest sister, however appearances are against me, do thou think it of me.

Thy letters I received and most sincerely do I thank thee for them. They always awaken in my heart the warmest sensations of love and a grateful sense of thy kindness; nay dear sister, thy letters always seem to breathe such a pure & heavenly spirit, do so evidence a mind redeemed & set on better things, that I rise from their perusal refreshed & strengthened and with an earnest desire to be thy humble companion in thy heavenward journey.[79] I have sometimes read parts of them to dear Cousin Ann Shipley, knowing that she could enjoy & apreciate the beautiful sentiments, and so completely has she become acquainted with thy character that she often says "what a sweet dear creature thy sister Anna must be."

Dearest Anna, I can ill express the depth of affection which seems to increase in my heart towards thee & thine, and could it be possible I would neglect thee? I have been intending for many weeks to write and hope by this time thou hast received a letter written in reply to the one thou sent in the summer containing thy interesting account of your journey into North Wales. It was written some months ago & but \I still/ felt that I was thy debtor, I was looking forward to the pleasure of writing, which I hoped to have accomplished before my confinement, but my time was so fully occupied preparing the children for winter and putting the house as much in order as I was able that it remained unperformed.

Never do I remember so deeply feeling the uncertainty of time as in this prospect: it seemed to me as if death was continually before my eyes and very awful did it appear. My past life seemed so like a dream, so vain & unprofitable, and I could take no comfort but in the unutterable mercy of God, in the dear Saviour. I longed more & more to feel his preciousness, to build entirely and alone on Him, the rock of Ages, and to know my manifold sins & transgressions blotted out in his blood & forgiven [2] for his sake. It was a time of deep mental suffering & a heart searching season, and I never told to any one before what were then my conflicts. I have clasped my children in an agony of affection & wept tears over them which they little understood, not knowing if I might be permitted again to embrace them and call them

79. Either Alderson is expressing remarkably universalist sentiments for an Orthodox Quaker in the 1840s or she is unaware of Anna's baptism into the Church of England.

mine & thought the dark grave would soon hide their mother from them. But God has been very merciful to me: he has restored me in health & strength & my heart is often bowed in gratitude to Him for this unmerited favour. Oh, that the sense thereof may stimulate to increased devotedness & greater faithfulness and that the impression may be permanent.

The dear little baby was still-born. I had looked with more than ordinary affection & hope, should life be spared me, to this child & it felt a trial at first, but there was no room for mourning in the midst of so many mercies & I who am so weak & unfit to have the training of immortal beings whose home is in Heaven, whose destiny is eternity, might rather humbly rejoice than repine at being spared this added responsibility.[80]

The children were much pleased & obliged to their cousins for their kind rememberances. They have begun their writing lessons in good earnest again. During the hot weather it was difficult to get them to apply themselves & writing was suspended; they now have resumed them of their own accord as they have become very ambitious of correspondence with their little cousins, who will perhaps write to them in return. I should like them to begin this letter intercourse as soon as they are able: it will keep alive an interest in each other & out of it may grow warm & deep affection & the longer I live the more I prize our English origin, connections & friends and wish the children to grow up more English than American.

I have also to thank dear Mary for her pretty pin cushion cover. You are very, very kind and we have many beautiful & valuable mementos of your affection, which I hoard as a miser hoards his treasures. They are all locked up & now & then the children & I go & look at them & it is an occasion of speaking of you and recalling a grateful sense of your love. I never valued presents as I do \these/ now that they are memorials of the affection of those from whom we are so widely seperated and who are so tenderly beloved. I wish it was in my power to send you more than thanks.

The Franklands [3] arrived safe after a stormy & perilous passage. They have been to spend two days with us; we found it very pleasant to renew our acquaintance, especially as they could talk about thee and tell us a deal of English news: that is always interesting. Poor things, I feel very anxious for them to get on; they have taken a house & propose opening a school; I wish it may answer. They said Alice came with them, and Sarah has heard since from her. She was then at Richard [Harrison]'s at Martinsville.

Thompson was here some weeks ago; he has been sick since his return home from the south and the children had the measles, but I expect they are all better now.

I am glad, dearest Anna, that thou hast a nice garden and that the seeds we sent you have afforded thee pleasure. I have a great store of Ipomea Quano-

80. In letter #55, Alderson gives the same news to Mary Howitt but also tells her for the first time that she had had another stillbirth the previous summer.

clit seed for thee: we never had it so luxuriant and beautiful as this last summer. I shall try the experiment of enclosing a small parcel of seed in each of my letters as they are now charged by weight. Those I shall send this time are a wild flower called Miami Mist, a lovely thing & I like its name too. I wish I knew its botanical name but will get it, & perhaps I can add some Portulacca. This requires a green-house, though it grows beautifully here in the open air. It is singular that all these fine, rare flowers sow themselves \here/: Petunias, Balsams, Portulaccas, Ipomeas &c.

I have seen little of the beauties of the Fall this year. We took some delightful drives as the trees were beginning to change colour, one to a wild valley through which runs a stream called Muddy Creek, a sequestered, solitary place where now & then we seemed buried in the ancient forest. Old button wood trees with their white ~~stem~~ trunks bordered the stream, whilst the steep rocky banks were covered with noble beech & maple intersper[s]ed with the crimson dog wood, the pawpaw & other smaller trees. The very houses looked as if they belonged to the period of the Pioneers: little log cabins so small & rude that we, in these days of extended frame & brick, wondered how a family could be accomodated within their narrow limits.

Here we gathered the fruit of the pawpaw or American custard apple. It is about the size and shape of a large kidney potatoe, covered with a thin green skin which becomes nearly black when ripe. The pulp is the color of custard & very rich & luscious like pineapple & cream. We are all of us very [4] fond of them, & I like the wild spots w[h]ere they are to be found, deep hollows in the woods & retired solitary forest scenes full of associations and melancholy rememberances of the past when the Indians chased the deer & buffalo through them, and of the poetry of Nature.

Now, when the flowers of spring & summer, the wild storms of winter, the birds & animals, come livingly to our mind as we gaze upon the grass that waves beneath their countless trunks, the very crush of leaves under our feet at this season is delightful to me & the streaming of sunshine through the leafless branches has its own peculiar beauty.

Harrison & Elizabeth [Alderson] are gone to Quarterly Meeting & I am alone with the children, but with four noisy merry little things with their many wants, their joys & troubles, I am never dull & then to fill up the time to snatch a few minutes to converse with thee & dear mother is such a pleasant change.

What a blessing it is to have dear mother still to write to & to receive her letters, so interesting & so full of good feelings & thoughts. I always feel grateful to a kind Providence for still sparing her when another letter arrives. Dear creature, I fear she too may have thought me negligent, but I shall try to write by this post. It is my greatest wish not to fail now in doing the utmost in my power, though that is small indeed, to contribute to her comfort, & I know she likes to hear from us. What a privilege you have who can see her from time to time.

Give my dear love to Daniel, [1] Mary, M. Ann, Charles, Alfred, Samuel and kiss the two little ones for their loving aunt, & with warm & true affection believe me, dear sister, to be ever thine, Emma A

Write soon; your letters are a source of extreme pleasure to all of us. My love to Cousin Lucy Bayliffe & to cousin Smith. We received his letter.

58. To Ann Botham, November 15 to 24, 1846[81]
11th mo 24

My beloved Mother, I begin to look longingly to the time when I may expect to receive one of thy ever welcome letters. The last mail only brought us a Friend, yet that was a pleasant assurance that thou wast well, as it was directed by thy own dear hand; but I want a letter now that will tell me more about thyself and all you dear ones in England, & I feel assured that the end of the month will bring me one.

My last little scrap would inform thee how we were then occupied. Since that time I have been favoured to regain my health & strength entirely & restored to the active duties of life with renewed desires more faithfully to fulfill them.

I have had a great loss to day in our good steady Dutch girl [Louisa] who has lived near two years with us &.was so trusty that I always felt I had a treasure in her; when almost all our friends & acquaintances were bothered with their servants, I used to rejoice over our good fortune. She was one of those that felt like an humble member in the family & now she is gone. She thought she would try the city, but I fancy she will have to try many places before she feels as much at home as she was with us. I am discouraged about trying another & think of seeing how we can get along without one; I dread common, vulgar girls amongst the children.

My great difficulty will be to find leisure to teach the children; it is so necessary to be systematic & so impossible when so many things require attention, but Elizabeth is helpful & Harrison is the best man in the world, doing a hundred things himself & putting up with anything or nothing as it is convenient: only give him his beloved tea & he never complains.

[November] 20. I am ashamed, dearest mother, in looking over my letter penned some days ago at this long & to thee uninteresting paragraph about our servants. It cannot, I am sure, be agreeable & only that my time is very limited I would begin another letter entirely. At the time it felt of importance &, like many other things which seem at the moment of absorbing interest, the day carried it away.

81. The first date in this letter, November 20, indicates that it had been started "some days" prior to that date. The date at the top of the letter, therefore, I take to have been added when the letter was finished, though its composition may have continued beyond that date.

So far we get on wonderfully well, but when the cold weather comes, I expect, shall soon tire. We have a man who can do many rough jobs for us & I enjoy, as I have often before done, our quietness.

Thou wouldst be ready to be angry with me, I fear, for not sending thee our friends' address in Philadelphia. I was very sorry when the letter was sent to recollect I had forgotten it but will try to add it in this.[82]

[2] A few first-days ago an event occurred which interested me much & perhaps it will thee. A woman Friend had a concern to hold a meeting with the chain gang in the prison; leave was cheerfully granted & she, accompanied by two strangers who chanced to be here, one a brother of L. M. Hoag, an old man of 60 who has been a minister ever since he was 11 years old, & some few friends besides, amongst whom was Harrison, went in the afternoon to the jail. They were taken into a large area surrounded by galleries; about 50 prisoners were assembled, some violent & dragging their long chains & heavy balls, (encumbered with which we have so often seen them toiling on the public roads beneath the fervid summer's sun); others were without these degrading fetters. At first H. said they looked careless, & some even laughed, but they soon became serious & they had a very good meeting, and at parting the poor fellows gathered round them & begged them to come again, thanking them for this visit.

What a blessing it is that from time to time the hearts of good men & women are turned towards even the very outcasts of society to yearn over & pray for the restoration of these poor benighted wanderers. Are not they influenced by the tender compassion of Him who came to seek & save that which was lost, & does not our Heavenly Father, who regards even the falling sparrow, thus evidence his parental care[?] Oh for another John Howard or Elizabeth Fry to give their whole lives & energies, aided by divine grace, to this work of mercy and love.

I am very sorry to hear of the failure of the potatoe crop again; it will be a severe loss to the poor & one which no foreign supplies can fully remedy. My heart often aches when I think of the poor enduring their many privations so patiently. We see so little poverty, especially in the country that I think it would be a comfort to have the opportunity of relieving the many wants of some \of the/ poor old destitute beings we used to know. How would the crumbs which fall from thousands of tables in this abounding country comfort & help them. This has been an abundant season, though the larger promise of fruit somewhat failed: a deal both of peaches & apples decayed as they ripened. Still, there is enough of these luxuries &, of the necessaries, a great abundance.

When I go into our cellar & see the piles of pumpkins & squashes, of beets & potatoes, [3] the barrels of apples, & our shelf of nice cheeses, I think how

82. Given in the margin: Wm Henry Bacon / ~~Carrier~~ Hat manufacturer / Philadelphia.

much cause there is for gratitude to a kind, good Providence for these, a small portion of his good gifts to us even, & the land is overflowing with His bounty. Yet ungrateful & unworthy, the nation is carrying on an unrighteous war & wasting its men & treasure in a contest, the very foundations of which is slavery. Poor Mildred Ratcliff used to say that a day of heavy retribution awaited the country for the treatment of the Indian & negroes.

I am very glad you have become acquainted with Loyd Garrison & Frederic Douglas; they are each a noble specimen of human nature and an honour to their country & race, and it comforts my heart to hear of those who boldly advocate the cause of philanthropy.

Elihu Burritt is another noble hearted American who is now in England. I hope you will become acquainted with him; he is a powerful advocate of temperance & peace & an avowed oponent of slavery. Surely the hand of the Lord may be seen in thus turning the hearts of great & good men to execute his righteous will in the earth. Are not these actively engaged in establishing his Kingdom, in pulling down the strongholds of sin & Satan?

Oh how thankful do I feel that dear Wm and Mary are enlisted into this glorious band, that they are not only great in the field of literature, but doubly great as instruments in promoting righteousness in the earth, of advancing the welfare & eternal interests of their fellow men.

Thomas & Sarah Frankland with their family have arrived after a most stormy passage. They were out in that terrible storm in which the Great Western was nearly lost; they described the scene & their situation as most awful. They have been to spend two days with us; it was very pleasant to renew their acquaintance and to hear their intelligent & interesting account of many things near & dear to us as English. ~~and~~ It makes my heart glow with pride to claim that privilege \that proud title/. There is much to deplore in the condition of the people, I know—much to make the heart sad—& yet the progress is onward \in England/; that dear little spot is the ark of the world: there the life-blood circulates which renovates & blesses the human family.

I know there are many great & good Americans, that the country is naturally the finest & most favoured [4] in the world, but there is a national cold heartedness & selfishness that sickens me. Shall I weary thee with this strain? And dost thou think me [a] smelfungus[83] & very disagreeable[?] Dearest mother, excuse me; I often long to be associated with those who hoe for others & are not absorbed in the narrow world of their own comforts & enjoyments. It probably is our own very limited sphere which makes me draw such conclusions.

83. The term "smelfungus" was coined by Laurence Sterne in an attack on Tobias Smollett in *A Sentimental Journey* (1768). By the early nineteenth century, the word had entered the English language as "smellfungus," "a discontented person; a grumbler, faultfinder." OED Online, s.v. "smellfungus, n.," accessed May 3, 2020, https://www-oed-com.pitt.idm.oclc.org/view/Entry/182548.

Tell dearest Mary I have sometimes thought a curious & interesting paper might be written called comparisons between the English & Americans in their customs & manners. If I were equal to it, I would try to do it for her; however I will sometime send you a few materials such as my small means of observation furnish \to/ which she can add & perhaps make an article for the People's Journal, in which, though I have not seen a single number yet, as their paper, I feel much interested.

How is dear Anna Mary? I often think of her as one of those gifted & lovely beings whose very name is delightful to dwell upon. How I should like to have one of her delightful letters; I know I do not deserve one, for I believe her last is unanswered, but tell her, though I am become a check-apron character, a very busy American housewife, yet I love the elegancies & refinements of literary life. [1] I would be glad if she will lift the veil & let me have a peep.

My dearest love to Wm, Mary & the dear family; how happy & thankful do I feel that thou hast such a sweet home with them. I often visit thee in thought in thy own beautiful and pleasant room.

I wrote to dear Anna a few days ago.

Farewell my endeared mother; Harrison's & the children's dear love to you all. We have just been to see Cousin Ann Shipley; she sends her love.

Thy most affectionate,

Emma

59. To Ann Botham, December 20, 1846
12 mo 20th 1846

My tenderly beloved Mother,
The year is fast drawing to a close, but I hope to be able to dispatch a letter to thee before it terminates, and yet my time is so fully occupied that I find it difficult to snatch even a few moments for thee.

It is more than a fortnight since I wrote these few lines & alas my letter, which I hoped to have sent by the 12th month packet, is yet unwritten. I have thought of thee daily, almost hourly, & it seemed as if my silence reproached me with the appearance at least of neglect; but, my precious mother, could thou understand how constantly my time is occupied in working for the family & at present in daily household duties, for we are at present without a girl, I am sure thou wouldst fully excuse me. (We have thought during the winter, when we are not liable to much company, as we have a man in the house who can do the roughest work, that we would try to save the expence of wages for a few months, as they are so high as to be a very serious item. The man & woman together would run away with near half our actual income. A man we must have for the farm, and now I am so much more accustomed to work, I do not find it a hardship as I used to do.[84]

84. There is no closing parenthesis in this paragraph.

My great trouble is that I cannot find as much time to write as I should like & the children's lessons are neglected, but we have a daughter of Thomas Frankland, a very nice girl just come from Ackworth, who has been with us some weeks & she hears them read & keeps them quiet & orderly for hours together by reading to them, and as she is young enough to be entirely under my control, I find it answer very well & my mind is easy on that point.[85] I believe it is a kindness to them to take her & it just supplies me with my most urgent want. So thou sees, dear mother, we are always cared for and I do hope to be able to write more frequently as the children's winter clothing is at last completed & I do not feel such a press of engagements as I had a few weeks ago.

Thou must excuse this long preamble & minute account of things, but to thee, dear mother, & to none other have I told our real motive. Some of our friends wonder at me and some may blame, but I am anxious to spare dear Harrison any unnecessary cares & he is very sensitive on these points, fearing to bring disgrace on his profession by going beyond his means. I often think of dear Father when I see his anxieties & hear his fears, but do not suppose we any of us lack comfort; we have plenty for that with care, & besides some thing to spare for others. I could not value our blessings if there was nothing to give & I will gladly forgo something myself for this. It is the richest attribute of wealth, the finest luxury of possession.

With us the winter is unusually mild; I hope it is so with you for thy sake & for the sake of the poor, half famished thousands who would feel their privations tenfold if to want be added an inclement winter. We often talk of them, and the children frequently ask when eating a good meal would not the poor Irish be glad of this? Anna Mary in her simplicity has a great fear of Famine coming here. She thinks, I suppose, it is some great fearful presence that in bodily form takes up its abode on the earth. Famine, thank God, we have no need to fear & yet I do think the accumulating sins of this country will certainly bring some heavy judgments upon us.

I heard a few days ago such a description of the barbarous nature of the Mexican war as makes one's blood curdle. It was the relation of a surgeon in the American army; he had returned on furlough & told a friend of ours. The Mexicans cut off every straggler from the camp, and should any of [2] the soldiers thus fall a victim to their excited animosity, the whole company to which they belonged sally forth and murder in cold blood every one who falls within their their range, men, women & children: thus perhaps fifty lives are sacrificed for one. He related that at Monterey, which the Americans have taken, a soldier \siezed/ a pig, killed it & was in the act of dressing it, when he was shot dead by an unknown hand. His company immediately went into the street & butchered forty persons in revenge. It is said that the climate is

85. Possibly Agnes Frankland (1830–1908), whose wedding to Samuel Haughton on April 26, 1849, Harrison and Elizabeth Alderson attended.

such that the men do not shave & that the army is assuming a frightfully neglected appearance, and, added to the brutalizing effects of a war accompanied with the utmost rapine & cruelty, sickness carries off hundreds in a very short time & destroys the health of more, so that those who have returned are gastly spectacles, the victims of vice & pestilence. This is no exagerated picture: I saw it in a speech of one of the commanders before Congress.

The war is becoming very unpopular; it is expensive & moreover very inglorious, but above all, to christian men and women especially hateful. Its very basis is slavery; to strengthen the slave interests it was commenced, & to seize Ahab-like on their neighbours' vinyard \is its second object/ and, oh, what an awful evil is slavery. I think my abhorrence of it & my prayer for its speedy removal daily increases. It seems as if nothing but the fiat of omnipotence could tear up its strongholds, and soften the hardened hearts of wicked men as to make them yield to the voice of justice & humanity.

Last night a Friend called upon us who has lived in a part of this state, Ohio, bordering upon Virginia, where the inhabitants are warm abolitionists & there occurred what has been the theme of the papers for many months, the "Parkersburgh affray,["] but \if/ should thou not have heard of this, I will tell thee as far as I myself know. The people had rendered themselves very offensive to their neighbours on the opposite shore of the river, for Parkersburgh is on or near the Ohio, by aiding their runaway slaves in their flight from bondage to liberty. The slaveholders vowed vengeance, but how to effect this without violating the constitution & the individual rights of each State, which is independent in itself, was the difficulty. However, traitors are not lacking in these days nor ever have been since Judas Iscariot, and one was found in this community—a Preacher who went over & contrived with some slaveholders to deliver his Friends into their hands in the very act of depriving them of their property. He arranged with some slaves to meet them on such a day & came & told the good people what a fine opportunity was at hand to exercise their philanthropy. They joyfully went in a body to the place agreed upon at the appointed time; the slaves were there & their masters also in ambush, who, when these worthy people were rejoicing over their oppressed fellow beings rising out of the galling tyranny in which their whole lives had been spent, when the Virginians rushed in upon them, a struggle ensued in which one fine fellow, a slave, made his escape, but the women and children with some of the Parkersburgh men were taken & carried away; the latter were lodged in prison [3] and, though they found they could not lawfully do any thing at them, and durst not use violence, yet they detained them 6 months to their great inconvenience & made their imprisonment as expensive as possible.

On one occasion the people of that neighbourhood were more successful. A party of escaped slaves, men, women & children, came & were kindly & promptly assisted on their northward journey, for, as Elihu Burritt beautifully has it, Heaven & Canada are the only hope of the slave on this side the Atlantic. Well these people were safely launched when about 8 of their oppressors arrived in hot pursuit. The accounts they received were so vague that they concluded the slaves were in this place & fixed upon the very house where they were concealed. Of course they were refused admittance, so they must go to the justice for warrants. He was tardy; a day passed, all which while the people were getting still farther away. At last the men came with loud boasts of vengeance & went blustering through the house, but no slaves were there & disappointed & bewildered they returned to their homes.

Let me tell thee, Friends are not the least active in this good work, though it is not an unfrequent question with some if it is quite right to do it & yet I do believe there are very few who would refuse to assist to the utmost the poor fugitive.

There has been a circular handed to Harrison from friends of Philadelphia who have formed a committee for raising funds & contributing in behalf of the poor famishing Irish. I am rejoiced that they are preparing warmly to sympathize & assist those who are so needy. We are blessed with abundance & have cause to consider & commiserate to such as are less favoured by Providence but perhaps quite as deserving. I will tell thee the success of this appeal.

Hast thou read the Journal of Maria Fox? We have been much pleased & I think I may say benefitted by its perusal. It is the record of self-sacrifice of a devoted christian, a most exemplary wife & mother, a woman of superior intellect & highly cultivated & refined mind. I often thought of thee, my beloved mother, & wished thou couldst read it. Indeed the book was more than commonly interesting to me from the idea that perhaps thou & others dear to me in England had perused its pages & been comforted & strengthened by its heavenly spirit \besides I think thou knew her as Maria Middleton/. I wish dear Anna would read it; I often thought of her as a kindred spirit with that sainted woman.

We had a most gratifying rememberance a few weeks ago from John Allen of Liskard, one of the London Committee, in a beautiful little case containing dried specimens of Cornish Heaths, most beautifully preserved & carrying my mind back to the lovely hills of England, so rich in their purple & yellow, so free & bright & carpeted with flowers, far fairer & dearer to me than \those of/ any other land. Besides the flowers there were packets of seeds, amongst the rest wild broom & furze; how I shall love to cultivate them here. [4] I wish dear Anna Mary would send me seed of the yellow primrose & wild daisy. I should also like a pressed specimen of each and seeds of the hone-bell.

You may think it strange, but as far as my observation goes, England is far more richly carpeted with lovely wildflowers than America. There is nothing here to compare to the hedge banks & hedges, the natural turf of heathery hills \of our own country,/ but I enclose you some seeds of our wild flowers.

Has the news reached you of the ungracious reception of Benjamin Sebohm at Philadelphia? He has been refused by two Monthly Meetings there leave to visit families, but he is an Englishman & prejudice is an eating canker: the Jews have no dealings with the Samaritans. I do expect those hot-headed partizans will be satisfied with nothing short of division & yet they divide for they know not what—a tradition, an idea, a construction of other men's faith—not for Gospel truth as in the Hicksite separation.

Thomas Frankland has got a situation with our good friends the Taylors; it is a comfortable living & they seem very gratified. Sarah says the kindness they have received since coming here is more like what we read of in books than a reality. Their son is an apprentice at 3 dollars a week; they have a lodger & his girls teach a school.

It is said that the inhabitants of the city of New York have subscribed most liberally for the relief of the Irish & have sent it to the committee of Friends in Dublin to be distributed by them. It is an honourable mark of confidence & I am glad of it as, from all we know & expect, it will be more impartially applied than if given to either of the two great religious parties in that country.

Thank thee, dearest mother, for thy kindness in sending the Friends. I am glad you like Elihu Burritt; he is a great favorite of mine. I had lately a little work of his given to me, 'Sparks from the Anvil,' an excellent collection.[86] I am looking daily for the parcel thou so kindly mentions: it seems long coming but I will not be anxious as I am sure it will arrive safely. I wish I could send thee something; I have some excellent dried pared peaches & some peach leather all of our own preparing waiting an opportunity of forwarding; I wish I could hear of one.

I am wearing thy beautiful poplin petticoat, looking so handsome since it was quilted. I wish I could send thee one and a comfort too; they would keep thee so warm by day & by night. But I have one great & constant comfort in the thought that thou lacks nothing to insure thy ease. May Heaven bless every one who promotes thy happiness. <*sealed*>

Dear love to all at Clapton & Woodside.

[1] We have the most changeable winter we ever experienced, sometimes excessively wet & warm & in the course of 24 hours the Thermometer below zero. I then rejoice thou art not here & yet we could make thee comfortable with an air-tight stove.

Farewell, my precious mother. Harrison, Elizabeth & the children desire their love.

Thine in warmest affection,

Emma.

86. Elihu Burritt, *Sparks from the Anvil* (Worcester, Mass.: Henry J. Howland, 1846), a popular collection of essays on various subjects, including peace, temperance, and abolition.

60. To Mary Howitt, November 29 to December 25, 1846
11. Mo 29

Our pleasant Indian Summer has been broken in upon by a most energetic visitation of winter: first rain, then snow, with cold biting winds and afterwards intense frost. When the ground became white with snow the children almost jumped for joy at the thought of the fine sleighing in prospect. They gathered handfuls of snow & eat it & extolled its amiable properties. Swallow's wing was brought out of the woodhouse into the kitchen to be ready for the morning light, but morning brought a day so cold & stormy that after two or three inefectual attempts they gave up & wished for the pleasant fine weather, & here it is again: the snow is gone in less than three days, & a sun bright & warm is cheering us with its genial beams.

Charles has now his daily task of husking and shelling corn: about half a bushel \of cobs/ a day is his task. Anna Mary usually helps him & after the chickens are fed & breakfast is over they sit down by the stove in the kitchen; then come lessons & in the afternoon we have a great piece of work in hand cutting & piecing carpet rags. Of this you know nothing, so I must tell you that rag carpetts are more or less made & used in every part of America. The rich have their kitchens \& often dining rooms/ spread with it; the farmers have their bedrooms & often every part of the house covered with it; in the country "imported carpets," as they are called, are a great & very uncommon luxury. Now, the making of these carpets is I think very curious. All kinds of rags are employed but usually kept apart; for instance, we tear up old woolen clothes in strips of about half an inch in width & each piece is sewed together & wound in balls about the size of a child's head. These make the best carpest, especially if they have a woolen warp or chain, but more commonly they are interspersed with cotton or linsey prepared in the same manner. We are cutting up a heterogeneous collection of rags, & the children sew them together. Cousin Charles & Marshall & Ella have helped to sew what they compute will make 70 yards of carpet. The effect of this kind of carpet is a confused mottle of all colours—red, grey, brown white & green or yellow—dashed in confused stripes, or sometimes they are dyed & wove in a regular stripe or plaid.

[November] 27 was Anna Mary's birth day. She is now 5 years old & yet, as she often says, cannot say her A. B. C. She has wonderful knowledge in hickory nuts, \candy/ apples, pears & peaches; she can chop wood & fetch in wood, milk Blackberry & even, when occasion requires, go up into the loft & give her hay. If any body wants any thing doing, Annie is the first called because she is always so willing. She loves work, active hand work—\one day she was found currying Farmer/—but to sew & read are rather too tame & still for her active spirit.

There are lights & shadows in people's minds & tempers as well as in life & nature, & this evening was a very dark one with poor Charley. Just before supper when all looked so cheerful & promised to be so happy, he behaved rudely to mother. He was required to speak more respectfully & on refusing was sent out of the room until he would comply. The tea went on tardily & g[l]oomily; even the currant cake did not taste as good as common when one so dear was absent. Annie and Agnes each made an excuse to go out to beg him just to say please & request to come in, but this once Charles was obstinate, whistled, & tried to appear quite indifferent. All ate very slowly, hoping he would submit, but at last the time of finishing did come & Charles was still outside the parlour door & had not had his supper. Never had he before been so long in overcoming himself and, as he continued to show a spirit of defiance, he was sent to bed and even there refused to speak to Father; so he was left to his own reflections & the effect of a night's rest, which restored him to his right mind & in the morning he very affectionately asked Father & Mother to excuse him.

Children feel unhappy \when/ naughty but they little know [2] the anguish and sorrow their perversity occasions ~~them &~~ their \Parents/. With ~~what a~~ saddened hearts, Charles' Father & mother sate down to talk over his conduct when the rest of the children were gone to bed & ~~how~~ his mother awoke in the morning with an undefined feeling of distress as if some great sorrow hung over the house. In these moments of depression when all efforts to disperse the gloomy clouds & to move the obdurate heart \are vain/ our only recourse seems to be to commend our unhappy children to the powerful operation of Divine Grace & to ask for fresh supplies of wisdom to so conduct ourselves before them & towards them that they may be won by kindness & love to choose the path of virtue & goodness, and often we are cheered by observing the struggle ~~between~~ against evil to see a better spirit take precedence & for a time dispel the darkness of temptation. So it was with Charles: through the next day he husked & shelled his daily task of corn, even alone in the corn crib, with cheerful compliance; sifted sand & put it upon the sweet potatoes that were yet uncovered & the dahlia & mexican vine roots; drew Alice about in the ~~sleigh~~ sled; mended the fire; read and wrote without a murmur; & was very kind to his sisters all day.

We have a very nice girl come to spend some time with us called Anna; she is old enough to have authority over the children & yet not too old to enjoy a game of play or to sit cracking nuts on the steps going into the barn yard or under the hay stack, and when tired of that she reads to them delightful stories and verses which sound even sweeter & pleasanter in the open air from her sweet voice. They sit down in a morning to lessons & work & Anna is their instructress.

First day, 12 mo. 6. The weather has been unusually wet. This morning we had soaking rain, so that only Father, Mother & Charles went to meeting. The mud road was in a sad state, full of deep holes, which made the carriage jolt terribly & half way up the horses legs in mud & water in others. As we rode along we met two little boys wading through the dirt \going to the cemetery/, one of them carrying a great red wooden cross on which was a name painted—possibly, we thought, that of their father or mother, & they, poor things, in their affection were going to erect it over their grave~~s~~.[87] There was something affecting in the thought of these two children, for they were quite small, setting out alone on this wet morning to perform this sacred duty & perhaps return weary, wet, & hungry to a solitary home where the kind mother who had cared for them & supplied all their wants was \~~perhaps~~/ no longer there to comfort & provide for them.

Mill Creek was overflowed like a river & the Ohio looked turbid & swollen with the heavy rains and was covered with driftwood, whilst men in small boats were up & down upon it, gathering up the logs & trunks of great trees that were floating down. When we came home Anna read the Story of Mill Hill to the children in Miss Sedgwic[k]'s beautiful Love Token.[88]

[December] 7th A wet day. In the morning Anna heard the children their lessons. Annie begins to show some capacity for the alphabet. Afternoon they adjourned into the kitchen after their lesson in Geography & cut & pieced carpet rags, read "Our Rover" & in the evening had a lamp at a side table and made spills.[89]

[December] 8. Charles shelled corn & Agnes made patchwork; began the Boys Country Book for the twentieth time; it is to the children always new & always delightful; sewed carpet rags again in the kitchen after dinner. In the evening at the side table played with letters, set each other words; Anna puzzled us all with upstairs. Another terribly wet day—we think there will be dreadful floods & impassible roads.

[December] 9th The carpet rags continue a very agreeable employment; this evening the children & Anna formed a nice group round the stove—sewing and, as reading would occupy some, one and all were very busy. They repeated verses & told tales & were as happy as could be.

[December] 10th Charles took Anna Mary's shoes to the shoe maker at Warsaw. In the evening he went with Henry to ~~spread~~ work in the meadow; whilst there, Charles Rittenbar came with a great stick to beat the cedar trees to frighten the \snow/ birds who were gone to roost in them. Charles told him not to do so; Henry desired him to go, but he only called them names & at last threw stones at them. Agnes is very busy preparing little Christmas presents: she has four spectacle wipers in hand & two view holders.[90]

[December] 10th The weather is again fine & today the children turned out once again to play out of doors. The old waggon has fallen to pieces at

87. Strict Quakers like the Aldersons would be unlikely to perform such rites of mourning, but Emma is no less moved by this show of devotion to a dead parent.
88. Sedgwick, *A Love Token for Children*, 78–136.
89. These may be the wooden pegs described in an undated portion of letter #61. *OED* gives as one definition of "spill" "A rod or stalk of wood, metal, etc." OED Online, s.v. "spill, n.2," accessed May 3, 2020, https://www-oed-com.pitt.idm.oclc.org/view/Entry/186631.
90. *OCO* says "kettle-holders" (285), but the manuscript is clear.

last, & so Charles brought out the wheelbarrow & put a \buffalo/ skin & a horse blanket in it to wrap up Alice. Anna held the shafts & the three children, tied to a long rope, pulled most lustily. They were a very picturesque company. Charles went with William to help to gather the corn, which is still standing out in the field; they bring it into \the barn/ & husk it at leisure.

This afternoon we were thrown into consternation by Henry returning with the horses all covered with mud & Ben quite lame. He had overturned on the hill & told that the waggon was lying in a hollow sadly broken & that a man had to come & cut the wheel before Ben's leg, which was caught in it, could be extracted. The poor horse was washed & \bathed with/ a strong application of vinegar & saltpetre.

[December] 11. This morning Ben seems so much better that we ventured to <*illegible*>. As we went down the hill we saw the poor broken waggon & were thankful that it had not rolled to the bottom of the steep declivity & that the horses escaped with their lives. Alice walks alone now to the great delight of the household.

12th mo. 20th. This is a week since our last date. Charles that day ~~Charles~~ was left in the city; he went after dinner, which we took at a friend's house, to take a walk with one of the ~~youths~~ sons & did not return before we left. They begged he might remain & thus unexpectedly he paid a visit of many days which, however, was not marked by much incident. His friends were very kind to him [and] took him about in the city. In one of their rambles they met a recruiting party; the officers asked his young friend, a find handsome youth, if he would go to Mexico; of course he declined. The war fever is happily over, but alas its direful work is going on in the invaded country & amongst the poor, deluded men who compose the American Army.

Charles learnt to play at draughts, became familiar with the Eolian Harp, saw many new books, amongst which 2 vols. of Hone's Every day book figured largely, & his mind is now full of its wild legends.[91] On his return he told them to a wondering auditon consisting of Agnes & Anna Mary, & even Henry, whilst they were together husking corn in the corn-crib, came in for a share of the marvelous.

The weather is now very severe & keeps us very close in the house. Charles & his sisters are very busy preparing their little christmas gifts. Agnes, with Anna's kind assistance, has completed many of hers, & Charles spends his evenings in making up neat bundles of spils which he intends to give to some of his kind friends; Anna Mary has managed to make one little bag, but she is "so tired" when she takes up a needle that she can accomplish very little, especially as this work is all free will or good for nothing.

91. William Hone, radical editor, journalist, and publisher, produced his miscellany *Every-Day Book* weekly from 1825 to 1827. Laurel Brake and Marysa Demoor, eds., *Dictionary of Nineteenth-Century Journalism* (London: The British Library, 2009), 287, 678.

There is a small family of young chickens which a silly hen has just brought out in the loft that greatly excite our sympathy; there are nine poor little things just come out of the shell in this inclement season. Charles feeds them daily, but the chance is that some morning we shall find them all frozen stiff, as was the case with some little pigs of William's last night; they had great difficulty in reviving them.

[December 21] Second day. Agnes gets on finely with her little presents. She has a view holder, 2 spectacle wipers, & a pin cushion completed. Anna is busy making aprons for her & Annie & her own little sister Fanny. This afternoon Father took us all to call upon a Friend in the country.

[4] [December 22] 3rd day. Charles went down with Father & Mother to the city; his object was to purchase a few presents for his sisters. His means were not large, being only 30 cents, & it was somewhat difficult to find gifts for so many with such a small sum. However, he managed to get a trumpet for Alice, a windmill for Agnes, & Queen Victoria nursing her baby for Annie. Mother was not forgotten: he spent 10 cents in a plaister of Paris Dove, which now ornaments her chimney piece & is highly prized as his gift. He brought home an invitation from cousin Elizabeth [Shipley Taylor] for sisters & he to spend Christmas day with her.

4th day [December] 23rd. Another journey to the city with Father in the waggon to bring up an air-tight[92] stove for the dining room. When there, Charles went with Father into the market to look at the beef show, and there they saw four bears, killed & ready for cutting up. They looked very strange with their large black paws left on & their great muzzles, & yet father said the flesh looked very fine resembling beautiful veal. \Venison/, oppossums, squirrels, wild turkeys &c. were also in the market in abundance.

[December] 25th. Charles went to help Wm & Henry to husk corn & then shelled his usual task with Anna Mary's assistance. The evening was very pleasantly spent in completing their presents. Charles has made a great quantity of spills which he ties up in little bundles as his gifts. Agnes made him & Anna Mary each a very pretty tricket bag,[93] & even Annie did her very best at sewing in making Father a cent bag.

As we were thus employed I heard the report of guns & pistols in the neighbourhood. The \children/ wished someone would come & shoot at our windows, & then we began to talk of that glorious music that the shepherds heard on the plains of Bethlehem 1846 years ago & the beautiful array of angels singing the sweetest song that ever greeted mortal ears and of the jour-

92. Instead of "air-tight," Mary Howitt gives, "Arnott," which was a popular and highly efficient "thermometer stove" developed by the physician and public health reformer Neil Arnott (1788–1874) around 1838. The importance of this stove was still recognized in 1854, when Arnott was awarded the Rumford medal by the Royal Society. If Howitt is correct, based either on surmise or on some missing communication from her sister, this would indicate that the Aldersons were using the very latest in heating technology (*ODNB*; *OCO*, 288).

93. The word should perhaps be "ticket," but the manuscript clearly says "tricket."

ney of the wondering enraptured men to behold the lovely baby & his mother at the inn. The children all wished they could have seen the heavenly host & heard their solemn anthem & then Charles began to repeat

"When Shepherds watched their flocks by night
All seated on the ground
The angel of the Lord came down
And glory shone around &c.["]

It was a wet drizzly evening & all feared it would be a wet day & that the visit to cousin Elizabeth, which depended upon the weather, must be given up. It was aranged that William & Joseph, who with their wives and children were going down to the city in their large covered waggon, should take them, but now another difficulty arose. Henry said they were going to set out at 7'oclock, & that of course would be too early. Perhaps he said this to frighten them & still their many enquiries.

Morning came at last. Charles was awake at 5 & his first query was if it was wet. So asked Agnes & Annie. No, it was only cloudy & windy but so warm that Father said it certainly would rain. However it did not, & as we sate at breakfast the sun began to shine through the bare leafless ~~cedar~~ \locust/ & catalpa trees; \they/ looked even beautiful, but far more so the green cedars & the turf & woods & blue hills in the distance. All was now bustle & excitement. William did not go till 9; there was plenty of time for dressing & even receiving their christmas gifts. The shoes and the hearth had been forgotten, but on the table in the dining room were laid, first, a hood, an apron, a book from Aunt, Queen Victoria, & the ticket bag for Annie; second, a hood, apron, brush & comb, book & windmill for Agnes; third, a pair of knit suspenders from cousin Elizabeth, a belt & book & ticket bag for Charles; fourth, a barking dog for Alice. The new hoods and aprons on & their own little presents in their hands, they set out & of course were the first arrival. Cousin Charles & Marshall came soon after & as soon as dinner was over the other company began to arrive.

61. To Mary Howitt, February 2, 1847

Part of Wm Charles' christmas was spent with his cousin Charles at Mount Auburn. The weather was very severe & the snow covered the ground, so they had \a/ fine time for sledding. Charles' sled was shod with iron & of course a first rate article & they had a deal of fun up & down the steep hill in the orchard. When tired of this, they got large pieces of bark & tied them on their feet for snow shoes or played at Mexicans & Americans. They laid themselves down upon the snow & printed it with their own figure & this was an army against which they went to war.

The old bleached tree at the end of the pasture, which we called the woodpecker's column & which was spared in the summer when they were clearing away the stumps & old wood because the woodpeckers had nests in it, was cut down a few days ago. Charles took his hatchet & went with Henry to fell it; when it was split up, they found it perforated in all parts with small holes, but in one place was a much larger one, the winter abode of a little squirril. The poor little creature of course was not there, but a nice bed of dry grass & three fine hickory nuts showed its wise forethought. The children almost cried when they thought how sadly it would grieve over its loss & how that cold, frosty night, it would have to seek another home in the fences or wood. Anna Mary was indignant whenever she thought of the robery & plunder.

Charles' kind friend Joseph Taylor gave him 6 nice young pigeons. They wanted feeding for a few days & he boiled them corn & then wheat, on which they thrive. Father & he spent a day in fixing up a place for them adjoining the hen house. They made three boxes & put up a partition between the hen house roof & the loft of the cart shed, which makes a fine place for them, & every morning Charles goes to feed them before breakfast & gives them a good supply of sand & water, for at present they are too young to come down & help themselves.

Louis Icle came to ask Charles to sell him a guinea hen; he has 5 and 2 males, so father gave him leave to part with one which, as it was not to be killed, Charles thought there could be no objection to; so this first piece of merchandise brought him 15 cents. Richard also brought up a little black puppy, which is a great favorite. There has been much discussion about its name; R[ichard] called it Colonel, but father thinks Wasp would be much better; Agnes says "peach Kernels & nut kernels are small things & puppy is a small thing & I think that name is much the best."

Charles was reckoning up his possessions this morning; he had, he said, 6 guinea fowls, 1 hen, 6 pigeons, 2 dogs, & as many rats & mice as he choose to claim.

The dismal accounts of scarcity in Ireland excite deep interest in the minds of the children. They often ask "would not the little children there be glad of this good dinner[?"] & one undertakes to lecture the other on any occasion of dissatisfaction with the sinfulness of ingratitude when so many would be thankful for such good porridge or nice bread. Charles sent his 15 cents, the proceeds of his guinea fowl, as a subscription; it was all he had except a long well hoarded English shilling, and as Agnes and Annie would not be behind, so Agnes gave 10 cents, which she had earned [2] by making 2 pillow cases, & Annie begged 5 cents from Father. They though[t] perhaps this 30 cents would buy three little Irish children a good meal each.

As whatever is peculiar in the country or manner of the people is interesting, the shoes worn ~~by~~ in America are worthy of notice. The large wooden shoes of the South of France & Germany are much used by the country people, that is the German portion of them. Then the common strong shoes are not sewed as in England, but pegged with small wooded pegs which, by the bye, are somewhat inconvenient in summer, for then the dryness contracts the leather & wood, & the pegs are apt to drop out & the shoes to ~~be~~ come to pieces.

A few evenings ago, our man was busy making pegs & mending his old shoes. Charles saw him & the idea occurred to him that he could make pegs too. He had seen in his frequent visits to the shoemaker the country boys bring little bundles of pegs which he bought from them & he thought he could likewise make pegs & sell them & have something more to give; so every spare half hour he has been cutting & shaping them out of the sugar wood or maple, which was recently brought home for fire wood. They are about half an inch long & formed like small, thick nail without heads. He has whittled & cut till his thumb is quite sore, but he is still very much bent on perseverance.

I have often mentioned Mill Creek & its dilapidated bridge. They are now erecting a new one; it is one of those large covered wood bridges which we see all over the country, formed of immense timbers, crossing & counter-crossing in the most elaborate & astonishing manner, a mystery of carpentry to an unpractised eye. The timbers are supported by arches, which spring from the buttments and extend to the roof through the whole structure. There are always two roads, one for going, the other for returning; within you see its construction, but without it is shingled & weather boarded & looks very ugly. We have seen these bridges of great extent over the Monongahela, Susqueannah, & other rivers. This at Mill Creek is a small one, but its progress has been a subject of deep interest to the children, I will try to get a sketch of one of these bridges to send you.[94]

Now dearest sister, I have a word to say to thee. Should thou in arranging this journal find it worth publishing, be so kind as not to give the real names of the grown persons at least. It would do as well to alter them & might be like telling tales. I have had much pleasure in writing it & had I had more time, but especially more ability, it might have been much more interesting, but I intend to continue it: two years thrown into one will be fuller of incident. I sent thee a description of our home: will this of our woods do? If it is not right nor what thou wishes, tell me.

I wish thou wouldst commence a juvenile paper promotive of the spirit of benevolence amongst the young—an Antislavery, Peace & Temperance Advocate. With thy capability & standing it must succeed. I think [of] the amount of good it would accomplish & almost envy thee the opportunity of doing so much good. I do not know but I believe such a thing is not in existence. If it is & is worthy, I should value it much in our Family, but I would like it best from thy hand. Do think of it & tell me when thou writes.

[3] One of our pleasantest & favorite resorts in spring & summer is Jack's wood. It is a little piece of the old forest which has been left uncleared for

94. In *OCO*, this description of covered bridges and the construction of the one at Mill Creek is worked into an account of the visit to Mill Creek bridge by Willie with his Uncle Cornelius on August 5 (187–188).

the purpose of supplying firewood to the possessor & is fast dwindling away as their needs require—from time to time a handsome hickory or sugar maple is felled & cut up & a bare ~~place~~ unsightly stump marks the place where it once beautified the earth & cast its refreshing shade on the flowery turf below. Last winter when the old \coloured/ man \Jack/ was sick & they were in low water, ~~the old woman~~ \his wife/ sold William some cords of wood & with great jealousy did we see him & Joseph go daily to this work of destruction. Never set your heart upon a tree or a pleasant bit of wood in America, for as sure as you begin to love it some one will \come with an axe &/ clear it away & either leave the trunks to rot or carry them off to cook dinners. How many a fine old forester have we seen so removed & as woods are becoming scarce in this immediate neighbourhood, how is the beauty of the country marred & a bare uninteresting surface remains.

Notwithstanding all the demands upon this little bit of wood, it is suprizing how much beauty & how great a variety of trees & plants are collected within its contracted limits. Its surface is broken into little hollows or dingles, which in spring are rich in flowers; there we find the blood root, the <~~Adamsonian~~> <*blank*>, the Solomon's seal of various kinds, Phlox, or Sweet William as it is here called, the lovely blue & white Collinsia anemone, violets \yellow, white & blue/ & the beautiful scarlet silene & many other flowers as the summer advances. Here are Hickory, Maple, Beech & Walnut & here have been the splendid American Linden, the Red bud or Judas Tree, the wild clamatis; sweet briar & American Hawthorn are its less aspiring denizens & there are thickets of ~~blackberry~~ brambles which produce the finest blackberries. In the Fall Hickory nuts, beech nuts & white walnuts or butter nuts attract children to its precincts & there amongst the rustling leaves they collect these woodland treasures or bring home perfect besoms of golden rod and Michaelmass daisy of various kinds. This wood is \the/ Southern boundary of our fields.

The wood on the right, that beautiful ascent covered with trees, is John's wood. It is a part of the pasture of the adjoining farm & has its own character. It is cut in two by a run which in winter is ~~almost~~ worthy of the name but in summer ~~its bed~~ is dry or nearly so, but amongst the loose stones & limestone which compose its bed we find various fosils—shells & corals and other specimens in mineralogy. The hill rises steeply from the run & its growth is principally Beech & Buckeye, a species of horse chesnut. The flowers here are fewer but in some respects peculiar: the tooth wort, a beautiful waxen like flower with extremely elegant leaves, the snake root & poke weed grow here, & here rabits, ground squirrils & snakes abound. The house on this farm is a log cabin, very picturesque with its log stable & sheds of various kinds, very comfortable as all such places are in winter, but in summer the marvel with people who live in more commodious houses is how any one can exist in such small, pent up, close places with such little windows & so few of them, with fire & beds & chairs & tables all in one room or at the most two, & yet thousands of families in America are happy in log cabins. Men of large estates who are magistrates & senators & judges are living or have lived in them. Our house stands on high ground in the middle of a field, planted with ornamental trees—Locust, Catalpa, Cedar & smaller shrubs. This field or lawn is not grazed on account of the trees, but the grass is cut twice a year. There is no enclosure to separate the house & field. An avenue of Locust, Catalpa, & Cedar [4] trees leads from the road to the house, & the flower beds are cut in the turf & the arbor stands upon it without interruption. At the back of the house is a large two storied piazza \shaded by a fine grape vine/ where in summer, when the sun does not shine too hot, we take our meals. If this is the case, we go to some shady spot on the grass under the trees. The wood house is near with its bird box on the roof where the blue birds come early in the spring & rear two or three broods during the summer. Beyond this is the barn yard fenced with a neat white paling, & below lies the kitchen garden. Below that on a fine slope hanging to the south east, the vinyard, waggon sheds, corn cribs, a new horse stable, carriage house, cowshed & many other useful buildings are in the barn yard.

There is a gentle rise from the vinyard to the \far/ meadow bounded by Jack's wood & here we watched with delight the beautiful Indian Corn from its first shooting from the ground to its maturity in autumn, its \broad/ green leaves waving in the summer's sun, its elegant crown & graceful tasseled ear, and along the fences of these fields we daily gathered in the season a rich treat of blackberries. The pasture lies on the right between these fields & John's wood & in a lane below the barn yard between the orchard & pasture, is the spring surrounded by 6 Locust trees ~~&~~ near \which/ grows a fine button wood tree. At the north west corner of the orchard near a grove of willow trees stands Wm's cottage. The house, you know, is white with green venetian shutters & in front, which is due east, is a handsome double storied porch or portico.

We shall, my beloved sister, send you some papers this mail. Tell dear mother not to take the Yearly Minutes in if they are costly. I should like to know how they act in order that we may send you pamphlets. If they go free, I shall copy thee some articles for your paper so good Philadelphia poetry. Harrison desires his dear love. Be sure to tell me if I have not met thy wishes: I will try to do better. Dearest love to Wm, Anna Mary, & the dear boys; also Miss Margaret.

Thy most affectionate sister,

Emma

62. To Mary Howitt, February 21 and October 7, 1847
2nd mo. 21st

Large flocks of pigeons begin to appear flying northward & they continue to increase daily; we hear the report of guns on every hand & so continuous is this shooting that Charles' remarks this morning the 25th that he thinks the very air in some places must smell of gun powder appears not exaggeration but probability.

[February] 30th.. The pigeons, which at first came with a steady flight from the south & steered northward, began in a few days to appear flying in a contrary direction. Father said that though the weather was still mild with us he doubted not they had met winter & were turning from it & it would doubtless be a severe "spell" yet & true enough we have had frost & snow & biting winds which make us retire to our warm stoves & betake to our double comforts, & ["]what will become of the poor pigeons[?"] is not an infrequent question with the children. They are gone into Kentucky where the weather is warmer & the woods more extensive than here, or perhaps they have gone farther south. The markets are filled with them & pigeons are [2] to be met with at every table; their price is 75 cents a dozen. The storm continued many days & during its continuance the large flocks seemed to have been broken & they came again in small flights & we no longer heard the rush of wings as we had done on their first appearance.

One of Charles' kind friends who has two of these \bird/ houses on his stable told him of the contest he had just been witnessing with much interest between the rival claimants. The blue birds had got possession of the boxes, a pair in each, & were very busy building when the martins arrived & his attention was drawn by a loud & angry chattering, the martins menacing, the blue birds defending. They sate on the roof all morning as if watching a chance of getting inside, but the others, contrary to their usual practice, kept close at home. The next day the martins, still more desperate, attacked the others & there was something like a battle for mastery; on the third day the blue birds disappeared, leaving their homes empty to the new comers. It was a result our friend regretted, but of course it was best to leave them to themselves, for to say who had enjoyed that <*letter broken off here*>

[1-*cross*] <10th mo 7th> the pigeons are now on their return: the children counted 15 flocks on their southbound journey. They have to day brought home a basket of wild grapes called chicken grapes but they are sour & want mellowing by the frost.

63. To Mary and Margaret Ann Harrison, March 20, 1847

Cedar Lodge 3rd mo 20.

My very dear Neices,
I have been pondering whether I should address my letter to you or your dear mother, but as I wrote last to her and am hoping every mail will bring me a reply I have concluded I will write to you this time, but let me tell you I could find in my heart to scold you for not writing oftener, you that have plenty of time and such fine subjects to talk about. You little know how I should delight to have a family chronicle of all your doings, something that from time to

time would give me such a telescopic view of the household that I should feel as if I had been paying you a visit. The very dresses you wear, the work you do, the books you read, the walks you take & the people you love best are all interesting to me. Men have studied the appearance & drawn maps of the Moon till many, I expect, feel as if they had travelled upon its surface, walked by its rivers & crossed its mountains, and I often think I see you in your pleasant garden or at your cheerful fireside, & was not that great Atlantic between us I should someday surprize you by paying you a visit. If I was rich the ocean should not stop me, for dear as all are here & dependent upon me, yet three months are soon gone & I could see you all, but most of all my own dear mother once again. However it is vain to speculate & wish, & dearly as I should love it I am too busy at home to be melancholy.

I do sometimes await with trembling anxiety the arrival of letters. We are so far seperated & life is so uncertain that I have felt a fear hang over me like a heavy cloud that some great sorrow was at hand. Perhaps it is wrong but the intimations of change so seldom reach us till all is over that I cannot help it.

The news of dear Joseph John Gurney's death came like a shock. The opposition that is felt towards him here has endeared him to me; besides I admire his works & love his character & I believe he has been a chosen instrument in diffusing gospel light & principles not only in our own society but through the christian world at large. He was a bright example of the ennobling enriching power of Divine Grace; in him the christian virtues shone forth brightly & he brought forth much fruit to the glory of the great Husbandman: his wealth, his talents, his strength were all offered upon the alter of dedication. At first when I thought of the loss sustained by the removal of Elizabeth Fry and J. J. G, I felt desponding & ready to question how it could be supplied, but when we remember the all-sufficiency of that Grace by which they and every christian are what they are, how all the gifts of the Spirit, all that men possess, are received from above, may we not reverently trust that [2] to the end of time such witnesses for God will not be wanting[?]

It has been a favourite study with me and one that I can recommend to you as confirmatory of our faith & productive of delightful emotions to observe that the genuine root of Christianity produces the same fruit under every name & circumstance: the biography of good men shows their parralel lives of experience. There is a beautiful individuality and a wonderful similarity, diverse & yet the same; they move on, and the nearer they approach the goal, the stronger becomes the resemblance. Not more uniform is Nature in her appointed course than are the operations of Divine grace on the heart of man, proving that God is no respecter of persons, that it is not the name, not the garb nor speech, but the heart which he regards. There it is that we have to mourn over present evil & infirmity, there to strive & war & weep & pray, there to deplore our coldness & deadness & utter impotency, & there to apply to the great Physician for healing & life & strength & to know, if ever it is our happy experience, his glorious kingdom set up & his reign established.

What an awful visitation is the famine prevailing in Ireland; it seems as if my thoughts were continually turning to the poor famishing, death stricken land. What will become of them if this state of things continues[?] There is a deal of sympathy felt throughout this country, and could they have the surplus food without the intervention of speculators, there is abundance to supply all their wants cheaply. But we have been very much concerned to hear the high price of provisions sent from America. Corn meal sells in Cincinnati market from 40 to 45 cents a bushel, the very best quality & there are upwards of 50 lbs in a bushel. This we consider very high, but could you have it at double that price it would be cheap & excellent food. Flour is now 5 dollars a barrel & sugar \70c a lb/, beef & pork \5c./ potatoes & every thing else in proportion.

The winter has been a very trying one, alternations of ~~heat~~ \mild/ & cold with an unusual quantity of rain. Our roads are almost impassable & so it is through Indiana, Illinois and Kentucky. About 3 weeks ago we felt sure spring was come. The pigeons came from the South, flying direct north in immense flocks, but after a day or two we observed them returning. Poor things, they flew eastward & westward, hither & thither as though they were bewildered but mainly south and your Uncle said they had met cold winter & we should have another blast & truly, a dismal time we have had: rains, winds, snow & sharp frost have made us retreat to our warm stoves, and poor little Alice stretches out her hands & says "coge, coge" in a most deplorable tone.

Again the "soft South wind begins to blow,"[95] and the children are all gone into the corn field to the great burning of corn stalks. You never see such bonfires in England; at first I used to think in the still warm spring evenings our neighbours' houses were on fire, but we have learnt to account for the great lights.

I have been looking out with some anxiety for a chance of sending you a nice collection of \seeds of/ native plants. Some I have gathered myself, but the principal part have been given me by a very dear friend who brought them from Philadelphia. I wish I knew how those fared I sent in your dear mother's letter; if they are charged double in consequence be sure to tell me. If not [3] I shall seldom send a letter without them.

A kind Friend, John Allen of Liskeard, one of the London committee sent me a small collection of English seeds amongst which \are/ the yellow Broom

95. Possibly a reference to Mary Howitt's "Migration of the Grey Squirrels," from *Sketches of Natural History* (London: Effingham Wilson, 1834), 61–66:

And the frosty plains like diamonds shone,
And the iced rocks also,
Like emeralds and like beryls clear,
Till the soft south wind did blow.

& Furze; I cannot tell you how I shall prize the plants if I can raise them. Do please send me the seed of the yellow primrose; it is so exquisitely beautiful, so delightful a memento of the lovely hedge banks & dingles of England & would be so rare that I should have quite a prize.

You would wonder to see how the single wall-flower is estimated here; they raise it in pots & sell it at a great price. I had once a plant given to me & the scent of that flower was English and carried me back to our own garden at Uttoxeter more than anything I have seen since I left.

Last week there were two Indian boys in the city from friends school. They are come to learn to farm & are placed with friends in the country. I heard \of/ a little trait of independence in one of them which I admire. He had a pony & thinking it unjust that anyone should be at expence for him when he had the means of paying, sold his horse & with the money furnished himself & paid his fare in the steam boat.

How is Aunt Mary Thompson[?] Give my love to her & tell her that the pretty pieces of silk she gave to Agnes at parting have been a delightful store & this christmas she made many little presents for her friends from them. Dear child, she is a sweet, tractable girl, one that tries to be good & has an inate love of neatness & order. She begins to write nicely & some-day I hope will send her cousin Agnes a note.

The subscription for Ireland from Cincinnati amounts to 10,000 dollars, and there is a society formed to prepare during the summer quilted peticoats & comforts, which are a most excellent kind of bed cover made of dark colored print, quilted or tacked with about 3 lbs of cotton batting, which \is/ cotton wool, between the two sides. With one blanket they make a bed warm & comfortable in very cold weather. I have supplied all our beds with them.

I wish you could see my handsome black poplin peticoat that dear grandmother sent me. I quilted it last summer & most delightful it is, but it makes me look as if I was in the fashion & wore a bustle. The ladies like that; they wear heaps of them & look magnificently portly. I have heard of them fainting under the weight of their clothes. I can believe it in warm weather. They are preposterously fashionable here and look like Parisien dolls.

Now I think I must tell you what a good tailor I am become. It is no more than most American wives & mothers do, but I make all your uncle's & Wm Charles' clothes. I have just completed 2 pair of pantaloons for Uncle & I do not think you could find them out.

Have you ever seen Whittier's poems? He writes beautifully & I think you, with \me,/ will admire him. I shall the first opportunity send you his volume, but I fear of no one going to England: many come but few return. If we lived in a Sea-port I expect it would be different.

The Franklands seem likely to get on comfortably: Thomas is in a situation & they have opened a school; their son is an aprentice in a Printer's ofice. In this country people have no premiums or aprentice fees to pay, but boys get wages from the first, what generally provide them with board & clothes. Uncle Harrison's nephew Richard has now 3 dollars a week but in the higher trades the wages are proportionally higher,

We have not heard any thing of your uncles or aunt Alice for a long time.[96] Alice wrote S. Frankland & seemed [4] much dissatisfied, but perhaps by this time she is better reconciled. One thing she will find, & that is the experience of all who come to America, that she must work. In this respect it is a land of equality: the poor that can work & will work find themselves benefitted. High pay & cheap living make a great and favourable contrast to England & America. A woman can get 75 cents a day for washing and from 50 to 75 cents a day for washing & ironing at home; girls get from 2 to 1 ½ dollars a week wages, and yet I do not think the people are more thrifty here than with you. To be sure, we never see rags nor pale faces, the result of want, but as uncle was remarking yesterday, a man of property had better stay in England unless he is willing to be a drudge. And if you have any family pride, this is not the land to preserve it: the work of leveling goes on & rich men's sons do not often maintain the ground their fathers occupied. Perhaps this is all right and just as it should be, but it robs society of all romance & makes a very homely commonplace nation of us.

I am more aristocratic than I used to be; I love family dignity and ancient greatness: the rich crust of antiquity is beautiful & England with its noble history, its castles, & its rich cathedrals, its venerable churches & wise & good men is dearer than ever to me, but most I love my country as the centre of benevolence & blessing to the whole world. They laugh at me and perhaps pity me but it is the poetry of my life to have been born in England.

Now you must write to me very often. You must have time, for I who have 6 to work for, children to teach, & often house work to do can write to you occasionally. I am very sorry I have not a letter for dear grandmother, but please send her this to read with my very dearest love.

Did I ever tell you that double letters, any thing under half an ounce, goes through our post now? So Harrison says it is in England; tell me if we are correct.

Give my love to Cousin L. Bayliffe. Uncle Harrison desires [1] me to give his love to you all. Little Anna Mary stands beside me & says give my love too. Dearest love to your Father & mother, brothers & sisters from your affectionate aunt,

Emma Alderson

[4] Remember me to Joseph Crossfield: I wish he would pay us another visit.

96. It is unclear what Alice she is referring to. Harrison's brother John was married to Alice Hunter (1788–1868), and they had a daughter, Alice (1818–1858), who married James Airey in England in 1840. Both of these women died in England, but they might have emigrated briefly in the 1840s.

64. To Ann Botham, March 1847[97]

I feel reluctant, my precious Mother, to let the mail leave without a word to thee & yet my time is so limited that I cannot undertake more than a half sheet, so I will not put thee to the expence of a letter. I shall send thee the Minutes of our Yearly Meeting as I doubt not they will be interesting to thee. The reports of the Indian Committee & that of the Free people of Color I am sure will please thee if thou hast not seen them & would not Wm & Mary like to insert them in their Journal. I think they are very valuable documents.

Oh my dearest mother, how do I wish I could see thee; it is a constant thought with me and I feel as if I could not give up the idea & hope of again beholding thy beloved countenance. People talk of time & distance wearing out love; it seems to me that thou art daily dearer to me; nay I believe I never loved any of you as I do now, nor felt how precious are the ties of family affection. I often wish I could make our children understand the greatness of their happiness whilst an undivided circle round their parents. The sight carries me back to those days when, in our home at Uttoxeter, we dwelt in peace & love.[98] Strange is it that the full sense of the privilege comes mostly too late, when the opportunity of joyfully [2] fulfilling our duty to Father, Mother, brother & sister is gone irretrievably. May God forgive those sorrowful shortcomings.

Thou wilt be glad to hear that a very lively interest is felt in Cincinnati on behalf of the suffering poor in Ireland. Public Meetings have been held in the city and handsome subscriptions raised. It was proposed to freight a ship with provisions & send it laden with the bounty of this large, rich city to Ireland. There is something beautiful to me in the idea; it would go like a messenger of Mercy ove[r] the mighty deep, a token of the love & charity of thousands. It is said throughout this Western community \in the interior/ where dollars are scarce, abundance of provisions would be gladly bestowed by the farmers could it only be got to the places from whence it might be shipped. The Friends in the country have sent messages to this effect to Friends here. All they want is the means of transport.

We have read with trembling, fearful foreboding for the future the harrowing accounts of the present state of the country. May God in his compassion be pleased to say it is enough. Oh, how dependent do these things make us feel. Should they continue another year, what may be the consequence[?] I look at the [3] sinfulness, the ingratitude, the hardened continuance in evil of this country & is seems to me that for these things an awful

97. The dating is uncertain for this letter. The promise to send Yearly Meeting minutes might suggest placement closer to the Yearly Meeting Alderson attended in 1845, but the reference to John Randolph places it in late 1846 at least. The mention of birds flying north suggests March.

98. Although there is no actual "sight" in this paragraph to which she could be referring, her use of the term may indicate the vividness of her mental image of her family.

visitation awaits us. Who knows how near famine is to our own door. This wickedest of all wicked wars still continues; slavery is dominant, pride & fulness of bread make men forgetful, & what can we expect? But the Almighty is very merciful & longsuffering.

I heard a little incident the other day that I think will please thee. When Lindley Murray Hoag was traveling in the South Carolina, I believe, he had public meetings & was most severe & uncompromising in his denunciation against slavery, yet he was followed from place to place & had large overflowing meetings. On one occasion he took his seat in an unusually large assembly; he felt, he said, the power of opposition so strong & his own weakness & helplessness so great that he was ready to sink under it, but he rose & told them that he \had/ left all that was near & dear to him, prepared to lay down his natural life should his master require it, and now if you are permitted to take it, I freely offer it up a sacrifice into your hands! He then went on & with unwonted authority preached the gospel & laid their sins as slaveholders before them till they wept, to use his own expression, under the rod [4] of the Master as children under the chastisement of an earthly parent. May we not hope, shall we not pray, that seed so sown may bring forth a goodly harvest. Many perhaps, like John Randolph, struggle with conscience through life & lie down to die, stung with bitter remorse.

Please, dearest mother, give my endeared love to Anna. I hope to hear soon from her; her letters are so sweet, so evince a mind redeemed & sanctified & set on better things, that they always do me good. I felt a little disappointed at not receiving one messenger of rememberance last mail except, my beloved mother, the British Friend, whose envelope told of thee, but time goes on rapidly & a few days bring letters again from England.

Harrison desires his dear love; he has been very unwell, but is now better. We have had a very mild winter & have early tokens of spring. The birds begin to fly northward in large flocks. The blue birds have begun to sing & build & the air is often very mild, but the season is wet. The children all send their dear love.

With every feeling of [1] tender affection, thy attached daughter,

Emma

Do not take the minutes if they charge high for them.

65. To Ann Botham, April 10 to 20, 1847
Cedar Lodge 4th mo 10th 184~~6~~7

My dearly beloved Parent,
I have of late found myself so unexpectedly surprized by the arrival of the time for dispatching letters that I have not been able to accomplish what I most desired: writing to thee, one of my pleasantest and best beloved employ, but this post I will take time by the forelock and keep a chronicle for thee of the events of the past & the coming fortnight, but first let me tell thee what

I am sure will please thee as it has done me: we have heard of the safety of the parcel thou sent by Wm Lloyd Garrison. I had begun to feel very anxious about it & wrote to him, but scarcely had my letter left when a lady of my acquaintance told me she had just received a letter from her mother in Boston requesting her to inform her of our residence & stating that a parcel or parcels were lying for us there. I assure thee I was very glad; I did not care having written to the great man, for perhaps I may get a letter from him in reply, but my anxiety was at rest about the main point.

I am constantly wishing I could hear of people going to England. I could find many things worth sending to you if there was only a private conveyance. I have a store of dried peaches in a bag which I cannot find in my heart to touch as they were marked off for thee, and perhaps I shall see them destroyed by worms before I can send them. When the warm weather comes it is surprising how immediately corruption commences: bread becomes ropy in two days; pies & custards mould in as short a time; moths eat our wollens; grubs breed in our dried fruit; roaches, ants, spiders & flies abound & yet it is glorious—such bright sunshine, so warm, so rich & redolent with life.

This has been a most rapid spring. The pigeons came a month ago & we all thought spring was certainly at hand, but we were all mistaken; the poor birds were sadly bewildered; they flew north, they flew south, and the driving storm followed them, and every body that owned a gun was out shooting. It is wonderful what a destruction there must have been, but their numbers were very great. The rush of their wings was like a great blast of strong wind, and flock after flock was going over throughout the day. Well, the cold weather continued till almost the end of 3rd month.

In three days the children brought in flowers, and now 10 days since we saw the first, they gather a great variety. The fruit trees are bursting into bloom; the fields are the richest green & the pale delicate lines of the maple are clearly discernible in the woods.

Harrison is very busy this spring. The farming on shares did not answer, as it seldom does, for though it took all the care & labour from him, he plainly saw the object of the men [2] was to get all they could out of the ground & do nothing, so that in time our fine rich fields would have been worked out & little worth. Besides they were very slovenly, allowing every thing to go out of repair & weeds to grow like forest trees to the deterioration even of the crops. So they are gone & we have an Irishman & his wife in the cottage. He is hired at 15 dollars a month & pasturage for a cow and the house to live in. His wife is a perfect jewel of an Irishwoman; her name is Biddy; she has a most goodnatured face & seems best pleased when she is obliging us. She washes for me and will come any hour of the day to help us, so that I consider her quite an acquisition. The children run down to see her & to hear her tell fairy tales, for she herself has seen fairies & sate under fairy trees & loves the saints & the virgin Mary as truly as any good catholic should. She has a lamp that came from Rome & has kissed a piece of the true cross & moreover has converted her husband to the true faith so thou mayst be sure she is a remarkable woman & yet she is not yet twenty two.

It would shock thy good Protestant heart to see how Romanism prevails here. There is a large new cathedral just completed & a bishop, an Irishman too, of the name of Purcell.[99] Then there is a Jesuit College, a very thriving establishment, where even protestant children are often sent & educated.[100] They are extending, and a school & church are to be erected this summer near us, nay two churches, and in the city German and English catholic churches are every where & always crowded to excess.[101] We pass one in going to meeting & the steps & doors are filled with kneeling worshipers. There are the Sisters of Charity with their orphan schools and the Jesuits as of old have many missionaries among the Indians. I heard of one who lately baptized 130 in one day—poor things, what a pity that when the light of christianity should break upon them it should shine so dimly.

But having rambled from Harrison & his farming I will now return. He is laying down the farmeadow, a field of about 10 acres, which was broken up & where they have raised potatoes & corn, in oats & Timothy. The oats are for this year's crop & the timothy a species of grass for permanent sod. It always sells well as hay & is a certain crop. Then they are going to plant about 3 acres in potatoes, & there is the vineyard to fix: the young vines want stakes & these have to be driven down very deep & *<illegible>* & strong wires, like what we had for clothes lines at Uttoxeter, run along in three or four heights for the vines to be trained to.

A farmer's life is a busy one & Harrison sometimes thinks he has not done wisely in engaging on so large a place. A very few acres would has supplied our wants & the capital invested would yield us a larger income without toil, but then the [3] place is so lovely, such a choice situation, so healthy & so retired & yet within the reach of good society that I feel we have much to make us thankful & to fill us with the idea that we are as happily circumstanced as in this world of light & shade we can ever hope to be. This is not our abiding place; therefore, if enabled by Divine Grace, & nothing short is

99. St. Peter in Chains was built in 1845. Bishop (later Archbishop) John Baptist Purcell (1800–1884) had taken on the direction of the diocese in 1833 and would oversee the greatest period of growth in the local church's history (John Henry Lamott, *History of the Archdiocese of Cincinnati, 1821–1921* [New York: Frederick Pustet, 1921], http://archive.org/details/historyofthearchoolamouoft, 70–85, 127).

100. The Athanaeum opened at Seventh and Sycamore Street in Cincinnati on October 17, 1831, under the direction of Bishop Fenwick. In 1840, after declining enrollments in the late 1830s, it was given by Bishop Purcell (Fenwick's successor) to the Society of Jesus (Jesuits) and renamed St. Xavier College (Gilbert Joseph Garraghan, *The Jesuits of the Middle United States*, vol. 3 [New York: American Press, 1938], 160–170, https://catalog.hathitrust.org/Record/006253812). Alderson's observation that the school admitted a large number of non-Catholic students is corroborated by Garraghan and contemporary observers.

101. It is unclear whether she means Anglo-Catholic (i.e., Anglican) churches or English-speaking Roman Catholic churches.

sufficient for this, faithfully to perform our allotted work in the day time we need not be so very anxious to have all things so wholly bright & smooth, as if earth were indeed heaven.

Thou art very kind, dearest mother, in sending us the British Friend. I like it much better than the London: it is much more spirited and a much abler paper. I have made enquiries & hope to meet with a bookseller in Philadelphia or New York who ~~takes~~ receives 'Howitt's Journal.' I feel an increased pleasure in it since it has become wholly Wm & Mary's. If you can send me an occasional weekly number, which as they are stamped, could be done on mail weeks, I should be glad of that if I cannot have the whole. I hope you do not think me covetous & exacting, but remember I am very much shut out from these things, and even a glimpse is refreshing & pleasant.

A Society has been formed in the city, Susanna Neville & Sarah Frankland at the head, to provide clothing for the coming winters to be sent to Ireland. Their principal object is to send quilted petticoats & comforts for beds. They have a large room & have set up 10 or a dozen quilting frames, and twice a week the ladies assemble to quilt. They beg old shirts, calico print, & cotton batting or wool as we call it & manufacture most excellent garments, which will I hope be a comfort to many a poor woman when they arrive at their destination. The subscription from Cincinnati amounted to 10,000 dollars, and there are provisions & other things sent liberally from the country. I do hope that the exertions that have been made will be productive of relief & that thousands who were miserable a few months ago, the victims of want & nakedness, are in comparative comfort.

What noble efforts Friends are making; people seem to have great confidence in them and little in any other class. Agnes has been practising a note to thee, and many a time has she written ["]My dear Grandmother,["] but though very desirous of writing, she has not yet accomplished anything good enough to be enclosed. She promises to make a good writer & is becoming useful to me with her needle. Anna Mary also is a clever sewer; she has learnt very quickly.

[April] 18. I have lately had a communication from one of my Friends in Philadelphia, which I will copy, as it contains the information thou kindly requests respecting the Journal.

"J. W. Moore, Chestnut Street Philadelphia and Wm Taylor & Co No 2 Aster House, New York are both agents for Howitts Journal, and if thou would write to thy sister requesting her to send thee through either of these gentlemen, they will receive it free of expence & forward to Cinti by mail."

Now if you still think it worth [4] while to be at so much trouble, I shall feel very grateful and should prefer its being sent to Philadelphia, as should there be any difficulty, we have friends & acquaintance there who would kindly see after it for me.

Since I wrote on the other page I have been myself at the Quilting rooms. I wished when there thou couldst take a peep at us. It was to me a beautiful scene of active benevolence, the room so large & unfurnished & \there were/ groups of ladies, some quilting, others putting into the frames, some engaged in running the seams or binding and finishing the peticoats which are excellent, warm garments. One poor old man brought a subscription of 10 cents; two little girls sent each 5 cents; a poor man brought a bundle of clothes, and the Irish draymen have offered to do all that they can gratis. It seems as if many hearts responded to the cry of the afflicted; it might comfort their sorrow stricken souls to know that in this distant land, all the time, all the means, and all the thoughts that can be spared from house duties are employed by many in their behalf. May the Lord reward them.

Last week we had a very pleasant visit from Cousin Ann Shipley. It is a great effort for her to leave home, but she came to spend the day with us. She desired her love to thee. Dear woman, she always brings her thimble with her that she may help me & often takes home work. How like my own dear mother.

I will tell thee as I hope thou wilt not attribute it altogether to egotism a little incident which pleased me at the time, though I do not wish it talked of. A Friend from the Indian settlement told me that the dear people there i[n] ~~return~~ gratitude for a very small kindness, had named one of the little Indian children after me. I should have felt the attention from any, but to have a little Indian namesake was more than common honour. I wish I could go to see them; they have my warmest interest & sympathy in [1] their life of self denial & devotedness.

I wish my paper was larger. Farewell, my most tenderly beloved mother; I cannot express the love I feel for you all. Harrison & the children's dear love,

Thy most affectionate daughter,

Emma.

My dear love to the good folks at Woodside. Need I say how welcome a letter will be? Tell Mary I want to hear from her. 4th mo. 20

66. To Ann Botham, May 23, 1847

Thy last letter bearing date the <*blank*> was truly acceptable, as are all thine, my tenderly beloved Mother, since which I have received a number of Howitts Journal, & accept my warmest thanks for it. I am sure I shall like it, although as it only came last night & we had company, I have only glanced at it: I have yet the pleasure of its perusal in store. I have just given it to Richard, who is come to spend his first day with us, to read on the piazza, while during the absence of the family at meeting, I spend an hour in writing to thee.

Our parcel sent by Wm L. Garrison is on its way; I hope to receive it before I close this. Thank thee, my kindest mother, for it & for the things thou so kindly hast in store for us. I hope thou dost not inconvenience thyself in any way, for delightful as every token of thy love is, could I think it deprived thee of the smallest comfort, it would make my heart ache and make me very miserable.

Oh how it would enhance all our blessings and enjoyments to me could I share them with thee & those I so tenderly love in England. Our fruits & vegetables, our dairy & poultry-yard would all be ten times more valuable to me could we only send you a portion. I sometimes think in these dear times perhaps you are subjected to privation [or] at all events know little of the abounding luxury we witness in this land, especially in country places. It seems to me that there their difficulty is to consume their abundance. As a person told Harrison whilst we were out lately on a little journey, they eat neither corn bread nor brown bread but take of the best of the land, the finest flour & butter & cream without stint.

Let me tell thee now I think of it, for I have often forgotten, that when you send parcels, if you would direct them to the care of Abraham M. Taylor & Co. Columbia Street Cincinnati, they will reach us without difficulty. We live in the country & are little known. Our friends the Taylors are an old established firm & well known in the commercial world, & for want of such an address, Lloyd Garrison was at a loss how safely to forward the parcel.

A few days since we returned from a Quarterly Meeting trip. We took our carriage & horses & Agnes & Anna-Mary & had a very pleasant journey, and as it may perhaps be interesting to thee, I will try to give thee a little account of it. Our Quarter as it is here called is always held at Waynesville, one of the oldest settlements in the country, a town about 36 miles from the city near the little Miami river. The road lies along the Miami Valley, a very fine, rich tract of country, where a great deal of Indian corn is raised [2] and sweet potatoes & melons for the Cincinnati market. Lebanon, the county town, stands in a very fertile part, & the scenery is really very beautiful, consisting of meadows, cornfields, pastures & woods. The pretty little town, with its court-house, prison & places of worship, which some of them can boast of a neat white wooden spire, the houses mostly white & interspersed with trees, really has a very handsome & unusually neat appearance, both as you approach it or when within its precincts.

We have some very kind friends [Evans] in the neighbourhood of Waynesveille who welcomed us with fine American hospitality. They and their place are my admiration; the family consists of father & mother & some grown up daughters who, simple & unpretending, are really very fine girls, both in the English & American sense of the word: we apply it to external appearance, they to character & conduct. The whole establishment is plump & well fed; there are the fattest pigs, the sleekest horses & oxen, the finest turkeys. Every thing about them is large & fat and comfortable as kindness can make them. The house stands on a steep hill over looking the Miami valley & river & is placed in a very commanding & beautiful situation. The rail-road is within sight, that rail road which is to bring us within two days journey of the lakes when completed.

On sixth day was held the select meeting & afterwards the African Committee sat. Harrison attended the former, but we missed the latter, which I should have liked to have met had we not made an engagement to go into the country. One subject which came before them was interesting: it related to a family who 3 years ago left North Carolina for Indiana. In crossing the Kentucky river, the ferry boat was upset & they lost their youngest child and their freedom papers, a sad loss to a coloured man in a slave state. Their means were exhausted & they remain somewhere in Kentucky, exposed to the barbarous liability of being seized, thrown into prison & sold to pay costs. A friend was appointed to go & search them out & if possible bring them to Cincinnati.

In the afternoon we went to Ceasar's Creek settlement, about 6 miles from Waynesville. A most secluded spot it is, consisting of fine farms belonging mostly to friends, and retaining much of the primitive character of early times. The woods are extensive, nay they are every where; all the rich cornfields & meadows are bounded by them & many a beautiful woodland scene did we witness through the openings. The road lay over a ridge still covered with the original forest, and would that I could give thee an idea of these woods at this season. The ashes & oaks & walnuts are various tints of pale brown, but the maple & buckeye are the richest—green rolling masses of umbrageous beauty—& within the depths of the wood & everywhere on its boundary lines are the dogwood, which attains the height of from 20 to 25 feet, white as though snow had fallen thick upon them & in beautiful contrast to their bloom. Here & there the pink Judas tree grew by their side; no human hand could have disposed them so tastefully, and now & then there were the American hawthorn and the curious stone-colored blossom of the wild plum to deversify the scene.

The friends we visited are plain, well to do people who came from Carolina [3] at the time of the Ohio mania, settled down in the woods & from a log cabin & small beginnings are grown wealthy, but they still live in a log house, manufacture their own clothes, soap, candles & sugar & are half a century behind the age in general enlightenment. They are, however, uncommonly kind & I enjoyed myself much. I went into their storeroom to see the sugar they made; this season it was about 17 cwt [i.e., 1,904 pounds] of very good quality, besides molasses.

We bought our year's supply at 9 cents a lb from them as we much prefer it, being free labor & a sort of market testimony which most understand of our feelings on the subject. The dear old man pointed to a heap of dried apples & said ["]those I call mine because I did them all myself, I shall give Emma some, not because she is poor, mind, but because I don't want her to forget me.["]

There are fine Sugar Camps here; the next neighbour made 2000 lbs this spring: it was considered a good season. I must not forget to tell thee that Charity Cook, of whom I have heard thee speak, lies buried in Caesar's Creek grave-yard.

Here, as at Westland, & indeed througout the country where we have been, the good people seem to have so much that they load their tables to excess. I will give thee a bill of fare of our supper & we were unexpected guests: there was fried ham & chipped beef, poached eggs, bread, sweet cakes, 2 kinds of pie, butter, cheese, stewed apples, preserves & cream, tea & coffee, all of the very best. The next morning was a repetition with the addition of most excellent hot buttered pikelets.

The Quarterly Meeting begins at 11, and the Indian Committee \sits/ before its commencement. I am sorry to say that dear, devoted missionary Thomas Wells is going to leave for the present. At least I am very much concerned, for I think he has given that establishment a character it never before possessed—that of a religious institution & I fear there are not many like him to supply the void.

There was a goodly company of strangers present at the meeting, being a committee sent to visit The Quarters. The meeting for business was opened with raised shutters & at the close they were again drawn up & they gave us some very good advice on the attendance of meetings, family government & the daily reading of the scriptures, all much needed I expect.

One subject that came before the men's meeting would have seemed strange at Liverpool or Manchester. It was a circumstantial detail of expences incurred in rescuing a poor woman & her family from the clutches of the Shakers. The Narrative was long & very singular. A man, a member of society either unable or unwilling longer to supply his family, removed himself & them to Union Village. He & the children were so well pleased that he left for Illinois to fetch another daughter but in the course of his journey was drowned & his wife, not so well satisfied as himself, refused to remain any longer, demanding her children; but they were refused & indeed declined to go. She then applied to Friends; they went & had interviews with the parties. The eldest girl was firm in her purpose, but they by threats got two younger children away. But strange to say at night, when lodging at a tavern, the elder of the two ran back to her old Friends. Again they were pursued & at last, being obstinate, the mother summoned the elder of the shakers & his company before the court at Lebanon & at last, by aid of the law, got her children & hastened out of the neighbourhood. It is a well known fact that once in, it is almost as difficult to get a child out of this settlement as a nun out of a nunnery.

Perhaps thou art not aware that Quarterly Meetings are usually held in this country on seventh day. It is an old custom & very inconvenient, so we determined to remain in the neighbourhood over 1st day & attend a little meeting called Turtle Creek about 6 miles on our way home. This is one of the "nooks of the world," doomed to comparative solitude by almost impassable roads.[102] We went to it by the Miami, whose banks, thickly wooded to the water's edge, are very picturesque. The little meeting-house stands within a most beautiful green enclosure of about half an acre, smooth and fine as the turf of a gentleman's lawn, studded over with noble sugar maple trees.

We walked about 1/2 mile from a friend's house to it through a wood & I was quite delighted with its quiet <beauty> and the perfect stillness, unbroken except by the notes of [4] innumerable birds, and to sit down with that little company carried me back to the bright & happy days of my childhood. I don't know why, but I never felt so like once again being in the little meeting at Uttoxeter. We had, I thought, to use a homely phrase, a good meeting. Dear Harrison dwelt warmly & largely on the consolations of the gospel, on the unutterable love of God in Jesus our Saviour and the privileges & blessedness of the fine christian: it seemed as if the bright sunshine without was but a trifle of the glorious rays of the Store of righteousness whose beams warmed & vivified & transmuted for a time our dark cloudy hearts. I thought of an expression of a friend in our previous Quarterly Meeting speaking of these small gatherings, "Friends,["] said he, "if the promise of our blessed Lord should then be fulfilled & he indeed condescend to be ~~amongst~~ amidst you, I consider that would be a great meeting compared with which all the pomp of courts, all the glories of national conventions, all the splendor of earthly potentates from under this influence would be a shadow, a bubble." We spent a very pleasant day amongst the kind Friends there and the next morning set forth home well satisfied with our ~~pleas~~ trip.

I must not forget one little trait of the American hospitality. The Friend at whose house we lodged sent his little boy, a fine lad of 10, to guide us to & from his house through the woods, & after we had left, we saw him running across the fields with a quantity of delicious sweet cakes which his wife had baked for us that morning to eat on our way home.

I intend to write regularly to thee every month and hope to hear from thee if it is not too great a task. It feels a sad blank when there is no letter from you when the mail arrives. I am much pleased with the Journal; we all think Engele a delightful story and the poetry, too, is very good.[103]

102. In 1835, *Tait's Edinburgh Magazine* published William Howitt's "Nooks of the World; or, A Peep into the Back Settlements of England," describing life in Derbyshire and Nottinghamshire. That article was reprinted along with a second chapter on the "nooks" of Yorkshire and Lancashire in Howitt's *Rural Life of England* (1838). Mary Howitt's *Autobiography* is apparently wrong in claiming that this material was published in *Douglas Jerrold's Shilling Magazine* (Howitt, *Autobiography*, 1:129).

103. Mary Howitt's "The Joy of Engele" appeared in *Howitt's Journal* 1, no. 16 (April 17, 1847) 223–224. It is a simple story about the seven-year-old daughter (Engele) of a poor German painter. She has sat for his paintings since she was born, first as the infant Jesus and later as various angels, but now she is too old to serve that purpose, and the painter longs for another baby. In the end, to everyone's joy, a new baby is born, and one of his paintings is bought by the king. The poetry in this issue includes translations by Mary Howitt of a German folk

I want to write to Mary. Give my dearest love to her; tell her I long for a letter. Harrison's dear love to thee and all the family. Farewell my best beloved mother. Thou and <*sealed*> my continual rememberances, with prayers to our Heavenly Father that he will bless & keep & comfort thee <*sealed*> to the end, and mayst thou partake largely of a sense of his great love & mercy in the dear Saviour.

Farewell, my precious mother. Pray, thy ever affectionate daughter,

Emma 5 mo 23

67. To Ann Botham, June to July 1847

My last letter began with announcing the news that our parcels sent by W. L. Garrison were at hand, and now my best beloved mother, let me tell thee in commencing this how greatly I feel obliged by their contents. The books are a real treasure to us all and the children are delighted with them. Many a pleasant reading have we already had in them. One day I told them if they said their lessons well I had a treat for them, to read a story from the People's Journal, "Oh,["] Wm Charles said, ["]that is a treat, the greatest I can have."[104]

To me they are deeply interesting as containing much valuable information & advocating the cause of suffering humanity. How thankful and how proud do I feel that Wm & Mary have joined the ranks of that noble army whose object is to destroy the strong holds of sin and Satan. Time was when they were silent on the great questions of Peace, Temperance & Slavery, but how powerfully & how well can they plead for virtue.

Tell Mary we have read her Thanksgiving Hymn for Labor again & again; Harrison is delighted with it & yesterday would try its effect upon Wm Charles. It is indeed a noble piece. I feel as if I wanted to make a kind of levee & call together a few of our choice friends to enjoy our treasure with us. I have marked pieces to read to such & such a one when I have opportunity.

I am also greatly obliged to thee for the cuffs; they are beautiful and, as thy work, invaluable. I gave, as thou requested, Elizabeth one pair & to two of my most particular friends each a pair. They seemed much gratified to receive anything of thy work & thought themselves especially honoured to be thus selected. One was Hannah Taylor, Joseph's sister, the beloved & only sister of six brothers & a most lovely woman. She keeps Abraham & Joseph's

song and "Little Viggo" by Hans Christian Andersen as well as the heavily Christian and pro-British "Farewell to Frederick Douglass, who Sailed from England for America, April 4, 1847, Easter Sunday" by M[ary] C[arpenter].

104. For about a year beginning in April 1846, William and Mary Howitt collaborated with John Saunders on the *People's Journal*, "one of the more sustained and successful journals of popular progress," until the journal failed, leading to a bitter falling-out between Saunders and the Howitts (Brian Maidment, "Howitt's Journal of Literature and Popular Progress [1847–1848]," in *Dictionary of Nineteenth-Century Journalism in Great Britain and Ireland*, ed. Laurel Brake and Marysa Demoor [London: Academia Press and the British Library, 2009], CD-ROM).

house & is a perfect specimen of female character: so kind, so gentle, so lady-like & yet with the simplicity of a little child that we all love her dearly. She is the children's model of all that is sweet & lovable. That family is remarkable. I often think, looking at our children, what a blessing it would be to see them growing in to men & women as excellent & honoured as they are.

Tell dearest Anna Mary I am extremely obliged for thy likeness. We think it is like thee but not such a perfect likeness as the one she kindly sent in a letter: that is a gem and has been universally admired. Joseph Taylor says it is a beautiful picture but not like thee: he is sure he seems to think he knows thee very well. It is a beautiful picture & reminds me of thee & I mean to have it framed.

Again I have to thank you for a \monthly/ number of Howitt's Journal \for April/. I have especial pleasure in this because it is altogether Wm & Mary's, and every word is good & sincere. I cannot look at John Saunders' name without repulsion & I abominate every thing that I fancy comes from his pen. One thing I think: Wm & Mary will never have any thing so low as the Tavern at [M]idnight in their journal. Every thing [2] I do not like I lay down to Mr. John Saunders.[105] I hope Wm did not suffer pecuniary loss by him, a good-for-nothing hypocrite.

Oh, if I could sketch or write, what delightful things I could send them. There is a deal that is picturesque & original in this land. The country, with its rural gatherings, and the city with its processions & suburban camp meetings, the pic nics and gay parties, the weddings & funerals are all characteristic—not at all English—as far as I know any thing of such matters. A cheerful enjoyment of flowers & fresh air & bright sunshine or rather green shade seems to constitute much of the pleasures of American life & it is very rational.

The people work hard behind the screen but <u>appear</u> to lead most indolent lives of perfect exemption from toil. I seldom go into a house where there are signs of sewing going forward; the parlor is all order, well dusted & beautifully arranged, but the lady is seldom there. She comes in soon, however, dressed as if she was expecting guests, but most probably she comes from her bed-room where she has been sewing, but from whence she brings no sign of her occupations: it often makes me think of James & Martha Astle. Then in summer evenings, the steps & areas of every good house \in the city/ are the resort of the family. Father & Mother & little children, gay young ladies & fashionable gentlemen often form beautiful & to me very interesting groups, each little circle absorbed in their own pleasant conversation & company. At first I thought it very odd & used to say what would they think in England of such a turnout, but it is common here & therefore well approved & besides, after being pent up in the close darkened rooms of the house \all

105. This is only the first of numerous diatribes by Alderson against John Saunders. See appendix 2, "Directory of Names."

day/, it is most refreshing to come out & enjoy the delicious evening air & fine moonlight in the soft shade of the Hielanthus & other trees that border the parapet & overshadow the little courts in this cheerful sociality.

A few weeks ago I was invited to join a party at the house of a lady in the country. It was the meeting of an anti slavery sewing society & to me a very interesting occasion. Their object is to provide clothing for poor runaway slaves, who often lurk about in the woods & through the country & are frequently discovered by their abject & miserable appearance. Of course this is composed of the red hot stigmatized abolitionists & a thing little known amongst friends ~~but~~ and a very questionable affair altogether, but I am perverse enough to have rather a peculiar pleasure in their society & to give a decided preference in my own mind to their proceedings. They told me with a kind of triumph of the arrival of two bands of runaways from Kentucky within the last few weeks, \each/ consisting of upwards of 20 persons. One gentleman lost 11 slaves & these were aided in their effort for liberty, clothed & helped forward on their northward route by the good abolitionists of Cincinnati.

A few days ago to my great joy I heard of an opportunity of sending a parcel to England; I hope it will prove a good one. I can judge better when I see the person, who is a stranger to me. I want [3] to send thee some dried fruits, a pair of Indian mocasins, a feather fan & some other trifles. I shall send thee a quilted peticoat for next winter, but not by this opportunity. I am going to do one in the very best style I am able, but that is far inferior to many. I have some India silk pongee by me for the purpose.

I am making a collection of the Forest treats of this neighbourhood for Wm, but at present it is not complete. I have found it a very interesting work; what I want is more time.

We continue American like to do without a servant, & with Biddy's assistance I get along very well but of course have no leisure. The small portion of spare time is fully occupied with sewing & teaching the children & when I can do this I feel quite satisfied, but alas company & occasionally a busy day break sadly into their regular instruction. I have been tailorin a good deal of late, making Harrison a light cloth summer coat & vest & clothes for Charley & am some-what proud of my exploits in that line. I sometimes wonder if Joseph Pedley would find \one/ out. One thing I have tried to avoid: not to forget the padding & stay tape.

6 mo 28th. We are in the midst of our hay harvest, & such beautiful weather we have that what is cut one day is housed the next & looks most excellently. Our crops this summer are hay, oats, & potatoes & I think the farm will do well. We have had rather a serious loss which makes us <*cut*> economical, but which a good season will repair <*cut*> loss through a mistake on the part of John Thwaite (but do not mention it) of one of our half year's remittances from England & as our Dutchmen grew nothing but weeds last summer, Harrison got a mere trifle from the land; but do not make thyself

uneasy: we have no lack of every comfort & a few months will make up the deficiency, only we have had to deny ourselves a few things I should have liked to have had. I believe I told thee all this before: if I did excuse me.

Tell dearest Anna with my most affectionate love I thank her for her letter & will answer it very shortly. She mentions her intentions of paying you a visit: what a happy meeting it will be; I am rejoiced when I think of it. I know how great a pleasure it will be to thee, my best beloved mother, & every thing that contributes to thy happiness is a source of rejoicing & comfort to my heart. I suppose it is because I have thought so much of you, but of late my dreams are vividly full of you. I have seemed to live with you in sleep & it was a pleasure to me when night came to lay my head on the pillow & resume my delightful visions.

7 mo 4th the famous 4th of July, the great national festival from one end of the United States to the other. It is the anniversary of the Declaration of Independence & the firing of cannon, guns & squibs, fireworks & processions sound on all sides & are seen everywhere in honour of the day.

Yesterday we had the most awful hailstorm I ever witnessed. The morning had been unusually hot & the storm came on very rapidly; the lumps of ice, [4] many of them, measured 2 inches round. The leaves of the grape vines, squashes & melons beets & those broad leaved plants are literally torn to pieces & it is doubtful with me if the plants can survive the destruction of the leaf. I could not help thinking of the Plague of Hail & what must have been its direful consequences: how it must have crushed & smitten the beautiful promises of the Egyptian summer.

I have been boiling the grapes which were cut with the hail as if they had been done with a knife, but as Harrison carefully picked them out, perhaps the clusters will not be worse for their thinning & we like the young green grapes preserved before the seed is hard. It reminds us more of gooseberry jam than anything else we get & as we have no gooseberries we are very glad of the substitute.

I had hoped, my beloved mother, to have sent this by the 1st of the month, but alas it is unfinished. However, it gives me an opportunity of thanking thee for thy ever acceptable, most welcome letters, which tells me thou art enjoying dear Anna's society and art in thy usual health, though not able to attend the Yearly Meeting. Hannah Taylor who is going East has kindly promised to see after the box thou mentions.

Dearest mother, how kind thou art. If I was not sure it gave thee great pleasure to oblige, I should get thee not to trouble thyself so much for us, but, my beloved mother, with a heart overflowing with gratitude, I accept these proofs of thy never failing & unwearied kindness with affection & joy.

I am hoping to be able to send thee a parcel shortly & if I like the medium I will enclose a very interesting & excellent work called Western Annals, a history of this part of America from the days of Soto, the first Europeans who crossed the wilderness & trod the shores of the Mississippi, to the present time.[106]

I have just received a letter from H. W. Moore stating the safe arrival of the parcel, so I shall shortly receive it. Thank thee again for its contents, & now my dearest mother, I must conclude this letter written at frequent & long intervals & requiring all thy kind consideration & allowance. Our united dear love to you all. With earnest desires that the soul sustaining [1] presence of the dear Saviour may be sensibly near to comfort & bless thee to the end of time, I am, my tenderly beloved parent, thy most affectionate daughter,

Emma.

The children beg their dear love. The Journal for May is come; thank you for it. Please just surround it with a wrapper. It is a great treasure.

68. To Mary Howitt, July 23, 1847
7th mo 23rd

My dearest Sister,
I have had a sheet in preparation for thee for the last two months & nothing but lack of time, which from the scarceness of thy letters I fancy thou also experiences, has prevented my completing & sending it. Yes, perhaps a little question as to its being altogether worth thy acceptance, but I will try to finish it & enclose it in this.

Thanks to the liberality of postmasters we are not quite so exact now respecting the bulk & contents of our letters; but let me not delay to express my great gratitude to you for a most unexpected pleasure in a parcel received a day or two since, containing the Homes & Haunts of the Poets & your Journals: how unlooked for & how kind. I had set down in my mind that when I was rich enough I would have Harper's edition of the former which is said to be unusually beautiful, but no American book can come up to our London editions & this is superlative: fit for Queen Victoria's tables & such a rich ~~treat~~ intellectual treat \within/. I have had many a peep & have been rewarding the children for a good lesson by turning over the pages, showing them the pictures & reading the poetry.

Do you know, a short time since, a friend sent me up two reviews of this book & taxed my good nature to the utmost to take it in good part & not to consider it an insult to have one of them laid before one, nay, thrust into my hand, with a request I would send it to you; this I positively declined, passing it off with contempt as a piece of low newspaper abuse in which personal

106. Probably James Perkins's account of Hernando de Soto in *Annals of the West, Embracing a Concise Account of Principal Events which Have Occurred in the Western States and Territories from the Discovery of the Mississippi Valley to the Year Eighteen Hundred and Forty Five* (Cincinnati: James R. Albach, 1846).

feeling was very visible. But what does this same officious person then propose? To send it on his own responsibility, so that if you do receive an Anti Slavery Standard with the Cincinnati postmark do not suppose we have had any hand in it; I find it somewhat difficult to love the man as well as I did before.

What has John Saunders been saying & doing to give occasion for the closing remarks that cut me most? It is so like an attack upon your character; do let the world know, if only giving the decision of the court, the real state of the case. I do not want you involved in a paper war but I want to see you vindicated. Thou canst not think, my dear Sister, what a treat the Journals are to me. I seem as if I now was acquainted with your literary career; I could understand what are the thoughts & interests that occupy your daily attention. I have great hopes that it will do much good.

Is there any thing I can possibly do for you. Thou knows my opportunities &, above [2] all my abilities are very limited, but are there any papers or any works I could send you that would be interesting? Do you get the National Era regularly?[107] As J. G. Whittier is \one of the/ editors, I fancy that it probably is an excellent Anti Slavery paper; if you do not, say so & we will subscribe for it & send it you. I have a parcel for dearest mother only waiting an opportunity for sending. I shall enclose a few mementos to you & dear Anna if I can get them ready.

I have just received a packet from a friend of Philadelphia containing dried specimens of many beautiful plants gathered near Mammoth Cave, the fall of Niagara & Trenton Falls in New York. How delightful are these surprises betokening the most kindly thoughts & rememberances in our dear absent friends. I think I never have felt the benevolence & tender beauty of flowers so much as of late; we cultivate & cherish them in our gardens with assiduous affection for the sake of those we love, we gather their beautiful blossoms & send them as love tokens hither & thither. Their value is tenfold if we think a few seeds will reach still more beloved & distant ones & be objects of their care for our sakes. We go into the deep recesses of the ancient forest on to the wild hills or by the solitary creeks & collect them that their forms may live & gladden the eyes of these dear ones.

Oh I wish I could give thee an idea of one species of lilly that grows wild in a most interesting locality: the largest cemetery belonging to this city. Its extent is about 150 acres & the primitive beauty of the place is as much as possible preserved; the upper end is rising ground covered with the softest turf interspersed with old & noble trees. I think I shall never forget the holy quiet which reigned there when we first visited it; it was on the occasion of the funeral of a friend. The grave was dug under one of the old forest trees &

107. John Greenleaf Whittier was associate editor of the abolitionist *National Era* (1847–1860) with Dr. Gamaliel Bailey as editor. The *National Era* serialized *Uncle Tom's Cabin* from June 1851 to April 1852.

as its broad shadow fell upon the green grass, so fresh & untroden in the warm sunshine of a May morning, I thought truly here was a realization of perfect peace in our last [3] resting place, such as Poets have pictured & men have sighed for but seldom realized; & then how sweetly did the hopes and joys of the christian, his blessing in life & his crown of rejoicing in death, seem in the awful stillness of Nature's great temple.

Yes, dear Sister, pure & excellent as are the gifts of God in Creation calling upon us for a never ending song of Thanksgiving & praise, they cannot fully satisfy the cravings of our human nature. Rather, I would say our affinity to the Eternal Fountain of all Good is shown by the longing of the Soul for higher & better things, an apetite & desire which none but He himself can satisfy and none but the pure in heart can possess. "Thy kingdom come": how full & comprehensive have those words often appeared to me, the very climax of our aim & hopes, & if happily by submission to the regulating enriching influences of that spirit so freely offered to all, we know the Redeemer to rule & reign in us, what a lustre & excellence will be added to every good by which we are surrounded: the mist of sin will be withdrawn; the light of Heaven ~~would~~ \will/ shine upon & brighten our path.

The flowers I spoke of are like a cluster of tiny tiger lillys and rise most elegantly amongst their long pale green leaves; they are found in profusion in a dingle in this beautiful spot where also grows the lovely Colinsia with its party colored flowers of bright blue & white petals. We have had a very cool summer, frequently broken with thunder showers which keep the ground moist & the country beautifully green. It is said the harvest prospects are very fine; for ourselves we never had such crops—all but fruit, the larger kinds, & that is a complete failure; we have scarcely a peach nor a bushel of apples in the orchard. What a comfort it is to hear such good accounts of the crops in Europe, and yet I tremble when I think of the precarious season & that the Autumn is often the most critical time.

What a desolated country Ireland must be; they are coming over by thousands to America, bringing fever & contagion with them. It is said [4] that at New York alone a thousand emigrants land daily, chiefly Irish, & that they are usually taken to the hospitals provided for them; some of the respectable inhabitants have fallen victims to the typhus or ship fever as it is here called. Some few have found their way to Cincinnati, & begging about the streets with their children in company, are a new feature here; their whole air & the very smell of their clothes brings old times very forcibly back to my mind.

Is dear Anna Mary still pursuing her studies at the academy[?] I am delighted to hear of her success; ask her with my dear love if she will not give me a peep into her studies in your drawing room. How I loved to read ["]the Turtle dove of Mount Carmel[."][108] I have seen you & your children for a day

108. This story was published by Mary Howitt in *The Poet's Children* (London: A. W. Bennet, 1863), 22–32. Apparently it was published earlier in either a book or a periodical.

at home. Wm Charles concluded he should watch the migration of the pigeons with a new interest another spring.

My most endeared love to our beloved mother I am looking with anxiety for a letter from her. Will not thou write, dearest sister? I long to have a letter from thee; I am ashamed of this shabby, worthless scrawl but thou canst scarcely imagine how little time I have for the arts.

Harrison's dear love to you; all the children run in saying "our love to aunt Mary & <grand>mother.["] Let dearest mother [1] read this; I have not time to write to her, which I always regret. Wet, wet, wet; this bids fair to be a wet summer in America: an anomaly in Nature. I should think the grapes are rotting on the vines. Farewell my best beloved sister; in the warmest affection to you all, thine,

Emma.

Please give my endeared love to Anna & her husband & family.

69. To Mary Howitt and Ann Botham, July 24, 1847

Thy letter, my tenderly beloved Sister, I received this day when at meeting & although I had one prepared ready for thee to leave for posting, I am determined to make a great effort to obtain all the information thou wishes respecting J. O. W.[109] The feeling that I have towards the man is not favourable; I know that he is connected with a party who by sober minded men are considered visionary men that neglect their own proper business to follow schemes & phantoms & he is one of those who, disowning the government, have refused to sanction its authority in everything so far as to dec[l]ine the usual forms of marriage.

Since we have been members of this meeting, a complaint has been made by some distant meeting against his wife for uniting herself to one not in membership & on enquiry it was found that they were not legally married at all, though considering themselves so. He is a great abolitionist & no worse for that in my opinion, but I am going down tomorrow to enquire farther and if I can get Harrison into the mind we will see him & talk with him if possible,—I would not for a great deal that your name should be connected even indirectly with any one who is mean or unworthy, & truly in this land there are many such, ready to make a prey of the trusting & upright.

Witness the \Ohio/ Phalanx which if I understand right was something on the plan of the Cooperative bands. It was composed of many sincere hearted individuals, one of whom was poor Thompson Harrison. He threw in his all, worked with unwearied zeal, endured the utmost privation even to shortness of bread because his heart was warm & his hopes ardent that in a few years there would be an oasis of independent happiness in a wilder-

109. John Otis Wattles. See appendix 2, "Directory of Names," for more information about this interesting and controversial individual.

ness world. He described the place as becoming bountiful as Eden under the united effort upwards of 100 men. The choicest fruit trees were planted, the most beautiful ornaments in the way of [2] flowers; shrubs & trees decorated & adorned the gardens & houses; cottages & workshops were rising up, giving an air of prosperity & comfort to the whole, when in less than a month the ~~whole~~ establishment was broken up by the perfidy of the President, a lawyer of Columbus who sought to get the whole into his possession & rob them of their rights.[110]

Poor T. left in disgust after trying for some days to stand against the tyrant & took away his wife & child in an old buggy with a lame horse—all he could obtain as his share out of the wreck. I have often wished I could get you the history of Thompson's experience there; it would be one of the most striking records of the day & his poor wife could tell a sad tale also. After all, bad men are the worst thorns & briars that sin has brought into the world.

Oh how my heart has ached for you in what you have suffered with that wretch Saunders. I have been cut to the quick by seeing how his statements have gained ground here. Is there no remedy? Perhaps it is best after giving a dignified reply to leave it. I thought & still think the world loves thee too well to believe all he dares to say. Never mind, dearest sister, if you find you cannot live in England come to America; I promise you a hearty welcome amongst a warm hearted people. You shall build a beautiful cottage upon our land; it would be quite a relief to divide the farm & then you will never know want nor fear it, for everybody that can work, either with hand or head, can get a most plentiful livelihood, & the dearest wish of my heart may yet be realized to see our beloved mother once under our roof. You could wrap her up in cotton wool & bring her quite safe. She must excuse my joking, but I get on stilts at the bare idea.

I shall certainly attend to thy request about additions for the children's book. There have been many little incidents which I have [3] thought of transcribing, but want of time has been my constant excuse & on the whole last year was a much more eventful one than this so far has been.

Did thou ever get the letter with the account of old Jack, his death & burial? As thou never mentioned it, I feared it did not reach thee. I am preparing a collection of Forest trees for William; the children are very hearty in the idea & bring me specimens whenever they can.

The remainder of this sheet I will devote to mother & give the results of my further investigations respecting J. O. Wattles on a slip of paper.[111]

I feel as if I had not said half I want to [4] nor a tythe of what I feel for you, but Oh how inadequate words are when the heart wants to unburden itself. I have taken comfort in the idea that you will perhaps come & live in

110. Elijah P. Grant. See pages 106–107.

111. This may be just the postscript to this letter. At any rate, no other report was saved with the letter.

the country & yet I should not like you to appear to run away from your enemy. No, dearest Mary, weather the storm & may the Almighty who knows your innocence support you & in the end vindicate your cause. Perhaps these cruel trials are permitted to teach hard but good lessons, to wean you from men & the world & purify your hearts that so, with a more single eye & purpose, you may persevere in the righteous cause you have undertaken, to advocate the cause of humanity & the progress of virtue. Take it as an evidence you are accepted apostles & will eventually be blessed. Let the spirit of that dear child animate you; kiss her ten times for me: she is a noble hearted little creature.

My dearest love to William & Anna Mary, yes to all; thy most affection & attach sister,

Emma.

See I have written this in less than an hour.

[3][112]
7 mo 24

My best beloved Mother,
Most gladly would I take a sheet & write a long letter to thee, but I know I have not time & this even is more than I calculated upon. I like to act upon impulse in such things & this day dear Mary's letter made my heart so full that I could not bear to let a whole fortnight pass before I told her how dear you all are to me & how much I too sympathise with you, for I know how thy kind heart will have participated in their trials & woes. Thou hast suffered with them in their anxieties & distresses; trust on dear mother: we have seen dark days & seen them pass away too; we have seen bad men triumph & the innocent bow their head in the storm & yet the hand of Providence was near to succour & his power was manifested to comfort & to bless.

God looks at \the/ heart, though men judge by the outward appearance, & in the end he will vindicate the upright & oppressed. This is a dark day & a heavy trial & that vile man's attempts to blight the fair reputation of Wm & Mary is the most grevious part of it, but Harrison says he is \in/ hopes his malignity is too barefaced to be successful.

I am looking out for a conveyance for my parcel but so far can hear of none; however, I hope to meet with someone who will undertake it.

Dear Wm's books came very safe and are a great prize. Tell dear Anna she must not think me unkind. I do not love her the less for delaying replying to her letter which was so truly acceptable.

Thomas Wells, the superintendent of the Shawnee School, has returned & with[out] him I fear the prosperity of the establishment will cease. He

112. In this letter to her mother, Alderson fills in whatever space remained from, and even over the top of, the first letter addressed jointly to her mother and sister.

brought with him four Indian children. I should much have liked to have had one of the girls in our family, but the reason I once mentioned to thee weighed with me.[113] One of the girls was the writer of the letter \of which/ I sent thee a copy.

Thomas was describing the difficulties with which they have to contend; there is an unconquerable tenacity in the Indian character: it seem impossible to make a permanent change in their habits. He had a while back great hopes of some who had become regular attenders at meeting and seemed so far broken off from their customs that at the approach of the spring dances which, [4] like all their dances, is a religious ceremony, he ventured to advise & exhort them not to join their people on the occasion. He appealed to their convictions & understandings, but this interference was so unpalatable that they went away, joined the *<blank>* & returned to their nation—that is, fell back into its wild practice & corrupt habits & superstition. To keep these poor children who have been 7 years under the care of Friends and are very promising from this influence, he has brought them amongst friends for a time at least.

His heart is all in this good work; he is going to pay a religious visit to the Indians in Canada & to visit the coming Yearly Meetings on their behalf. He is by trade a tailor & has taught the girls so well that he showed us a suit of their making, so neat & cleverly done that they appeared to equal man's work. He said he stipulated they should make the two boys & himself each a suit before they prepared for their own journey.

Harrison desires his dear love. Most affectionately, my beloved mother, thy attached daughter,

Emma

I am now down in the city & cannot hear much of this person but all I hear confirms our opinion of him. He is considered a well-intentioned man but very visionary, a man of no prosperity ~~but~~ and one who has not thriven in his own affairs. I leave it for you to judge if such a person is likely to carry out his scheme, however plausible, to advantage, but I will see him if possible & at all events enquire from other sources & write by the next mail.

Farewell my best beloved sister. Thine,

E. A.

70. To Anna Harrison, August 24, 1847

Cedar Lodge 8 mo 24th 1847

I am sure, my beloved Sister, thy last kind letter, which was so truly welcome, deserved an earlier reply & each post I have hoped to be able to write to thee; my only excuse is want of time. I have made a great effort to write to dearest mother every month & have so far been able of late to accomplish it, but that

113. See page 371.

I regard as a duty not to be neglected nor set aside by any thing. It is a pleasure & a privilege to keep up our correspondence & it now seems the only thing in my power left to me that I can do for her. I know she likes to hear from us, and it makes my heart very sad to think that she should ever expect a letter without receiving one.

I often thought of you during the time thou was visiting at Clapton, and I felt happy in the idea that you were so blessed in the society & love of each other. To dearest mother I knew it would be a more than ordinary pleasure: thy society was always & deservedly delightful to her & now that she is unable to travel I do hope thou wilt often go to see her. What a comfort to sit beside her & gaze upon her dear aged countenance & hear the sweet tones of her beloved voice. I can imagine what heavenly conversations you would have together when dear Wm & Mary had left you all alone to pursue their avocations. How thy heart, warm with love, would turn to the dear Saviour as the theme most acceptable & how the heart of the dear aged christian would glow with thanksgiving and, strengthened in the hopes & consolations of Christ, be animated to pursue in peace the remnant of that lengthened pilgrimage which ere long must terminate in a blissful eternity. We are all journeying onward toward the grave & Oh, that we may also be in a true heavenward course so that, though traversing lines widely seperated, we may meet at home at last in our Father's house.

I am sometimes startled when I recollect that I, who have always felt I had the heart & step of a girl, am in my forty first year and yet how little victory is gained over sin. How do the weakness & infirmity of nature bow beneath temptation. It is beautiful & animating to say & believe we can do all things through Christ which strengthens us, & it is distressing to reflect & to feel that daily do we go mourning because of the oppression of the enemy, that though we have year by year struggled & wept & prayed, we are not yet conquerors, that sin has still dominion over us.

I often wonder if thou or others that I know to be good christians are or ever were tried as I am. I think you cannot be because you have not such hard implacable hearts; the spirit of your great Redeemer reigns there more or less, & how could you feel obstinate dislike & repulsion to anyone?

But when I began I did not contemplate getting into this strain, and many other subjects perhaps more profitable are around me. Hast thou read the life of Sarah Martin?[114] It is a most beautiful & instructive memoir of a simple hearted, devoted christian, & how admirably does it illustrate that "the peace of God that passeth words" is the rich reward of perfect obedience. My heart is often thankful for such bright examples; they seem as living seals of the goodness and faithfulness of a covenant keeping God, blessed be his name. Through all generations witnesses are not wanting to declare his mercy &

114. Sarah Martin, *A Brief Sketch of the Life of the Late Miss Sarah Martin; of Great Yarmouth* (Yarmouth: C. Barber, Quay, 1844), https://books.google.com/books?id=bwBjAAAAcAAJ.

truth and to sing aloud of his salvation. To think of men & women with \enlarged/ capacities & extensive means wasting their time in folly or absorbed in their own selfish pursuit of gain or pleasure, whose hearts are cankered with disappointment & discontent because, like great sponges, they have absorbed all knowledge, all light, all good & the rich bounties of Providence & have not sought blessing in [2] diffusion, when the whole world around them is calling for help and if, like Sarah Martin, we really desired to do good, wide fields of usefulness & the Divine blessing would be at our right hand. Oh, dear Anna, let us try to train our children to enlist in that noble army which is now on the earth; let us endeavour to infuse a contempt of the mean & trifling things of time & noble & exalted views of the great end for which we have a being. Yes, if we can sow the seeds of the great principles of christian truth, which in God's own time will bring an abundant harvest, we shall not have lived in vain. To do my duty faithfully & well in the narrow sphere of my own household seems now to have taken place in my mind of every other feeling. I have lost, for the present it may be, my desire for foreign pleasures or other society & to live for these dear ones is all I want, to live for their present & eternal good, & may we receive wisdom from above to do this.

I am looking out anxiously for an opportunity of sending you a few trifles I have collected, principally \dry/ flowers, & I believe make much amusement to some of my acquaintance by my perpetual question ["]do you know of anyone going to England?["] However, love is strong & persevering & I shall go on till I succeed. I have tried long enough to find that there are few things I strongly set my heart upon accomplishing but I can sooner or later achieve it. I once heard a gentleman say "I never put my hand to a work but success attended me." Poor man, I thought, canst thou say that of thy soul's salvation? This I fear, in the multitude of worldly things prosperously accomplished, ~~I fear~~ he had neglected, & there, in the midst of every thing that could gratify & delight, he stood upon the brink of the grave, a poor, desolate creature: what a lesson to us all.

Thy account of Cousin Lucy Bayliffe & her family was very interesting to me & instructive also. I remember Alice—what a sweet girl she was & how kind to our children; they have yet play things that were her gift.[115] It has been my intention to send her a collection of Ohio shells, but she is gone & there must be a sad blank in her poor mother's heart; yet she can take comfort in the rememberance that one of her most precious jewels is safely deposited in the eternal casket, a treasure in Heaven made secure from all the changes & uncertainties of time. There \neither/ the rust of this world nor thief that would rob the soul of its blessing can penetrate.

115. Obituary of Alice Lucy Bayliffe. *Annual Monitor for 1848, or Obituary of the Members of the Society of Friends in Great Britain and Ireland, for the year 1847*, n.s., 6 (1847): 26, https://books.google.com/books?id=XFoEAAAAQAAJ.

Cousin Ann Shipley, who retains a most affectionate interest in her neice, shed tears in sympathy for her when I read thy beautiful account of her loss & resignation. Dear woman, hers is a tried course. I never saw a family so variously & continuously afflicted. It is often marvelous to me to reflect on the successive trials which we have seen dispensed to them, & a life of trial had been her portion previously. The one bright event, the comfort of dear cousin Ann's old age, was the marriage of her favourite granddaughter Elizabeth to one of our friends the Taylors, a very good & very rich man. But alas, this has been a cause of most intense sorrow, for in each of her confinements her mind has been affected. [3] The first child died when its poor mother was raving & lately she has had a little son, but [the] poor thing is again sorrowfully deranged, though we all hope it may not be as severe & protracted as the first. Pecuniary losses & common sickness, which they have likewise experienced, affect them little in comparison to this & cousin Ann's is a mind that feels it acutely,

Poor Susanna Neville is one, too, in whom I feel much interested; thou knows she lost her eldest daughter & now the little one, a sweet child, has a diseased spine & is become a cripple, lame & very crooked. She has a pale, delicate countenance with an amiable but painful expression. Susanna spent yesterday with us & brought her little Eliza, & our children endeavoured to subdue themselves into the quietness of their poor afflicted little friend, playing on the grass with their dolls & showing her pictures & consulting her wish & comfort in all things. We had been reading that beautiful story in the Journal, "Libby Marsh," & I think it prepared them to sympathize with Eliza & taught them the beauty of trying to please & bless the sufferers.[116]

Dear Mary has kindly sent me the Journals regularly & it is a great pleasure to possess & read it. I have long wanted some thing that connected me with the Literature of England & this is more than a common periodical. It familiarizes me with the pursuits & thoughts of our dear brother & sister & I am always more at Clapton when I read it than anywhere else.

But dear Anna, what is thy honest sentiment about association, with which they are so much taken? I cannot help connecting it in my mind with Owenism & infidelity & all the foreign efforts \by/ which men have sought to accomplish that which christianity can alone effect, social & moral reform. It has been tried & is still trying here. Thompson was in one of those establishments & as enthusiastic an admirer of the system as it was possible to be, one who was confident that when the world was right it would be resolved into universal association. Poor man, it robbed him of his all by inducing him to risk his all & then he & many others were the prey of a few bad men.

116. Novelist Elizabeth Gaskell's first publication, "Life in Manchester: Libbie Marsh's Three Eras" was published in *Howitt's Journal* (vol. 1 [1846]: 345) under the pseudonym Cotton Mather Mills.

All sober people here denounce it altogether as wild & visionary, but then Christ was rejected of the Scribes & Pharisees & all reform has been cried down by the prosperous & worldly minded & I am at a loss to decide. Tell me thine & Daniel's opinion, I am interested in the subject, now Wm & Mary's names are connected with it as its friends & advocates.

We have had a cool & rather wet summer & fruit is late & scarce. I do not think we shall have a melon in perfection before the frosts come. Still, in all substantial produce so far as it is collected, the crops are excellent & abundant. The cool season has suited the wheat, grass & oats; corn is not yet ripe but [4] I suppose is promising. There has been much planted in order to exportation but if the good accounts we hear are correct there will not be as much demand for it this year as last. I can never fancy that it will be popular in England when you can get good wheat flour, especially as you must receive it kiln dried & then I think it is spoiled.

We are very fond of corn bread, but we get the meal in perfection. I began this letter with something like a boast & the fate of the boaster is mine: I have no letter for dearest mother this month. Well beloved sister, send this poor uninteresting scrawl to her with nothing to recommend it but my most affectionate love & thanks for her parcel, which we have received & for which we are \all/ much obliged.

How beautiful is the persevering love & kindness of a mother.—give my dear love to Daniel & the dear children, especially Mary & Margaret Ann, who are much endeared to me by proving so great a comfort & assistance to thee. Dear girls, I often think of them & cannot help fancying them each busy & happy in the performance of their duty & the feeling that they are making thee happy. I used to admire the daughters of Alice Mason, who took the entire charge & labour of the house; & their mother who, when they were younger, had much to do, now lives the life of a lady in perfect ease & freedom from care.

I am trying to make our children useful & it is surprizing how much Agnes, who is not 8, can do & how much happier she is when she feels herself useful.

American life throws us upon our own resources & habit makes us easy in what at first was a hardship. I have not had any help besides a woman to wash for many months & yet with the children's assistance I can find leisure for many things which people with servants cannot think of. Depend upon it, servants are a great care as well as a great comfort & as grapes are sour when out of our reach, I have concluded the balance of comfort is in my favor.

Farewell, my precious sister; write soon to thy sincerely attached & very affectionate Emma.

Harrison & the children's dear love. Charles says do tell Sammy to come & see us & Agnes adds if I can get a chance I will go & see Aunt Anna next summer to get away from the musquitos & to pay a visit to my cousins & aunts & dear grandmother.

71. To Mary Howitt, October 1847

[3][117] I am going to try, my beloved Sister, to comply with thy request & give thee a few more materials to add to the children's journal of last year; I shall write without reference to dates & if thou thinks them interesting then thou canst use them as thou best approves.

One fine morning this Summer, Charles & I walked down to the city; as we went past Terry's woods we met a nice neat carriage, one of those called Harrison Waggons here. They are square bodied with upright posts at each corner & on each side so as to form the doors to which are attached black leather curtains that may be rolled up at pleasure & make a very ~~comfortable~~ airy vehicle in warm weather; or in wet & cold when closed all round & buttoned down tight to the body of the carriage, which is usually about a foot & a half high neatly panelled & painted, a very snug comfortable conveyance, & has altogether quite a respectable appearance. There are two seats & the inside is mostly well lined & cushioned.

This carriage was black & drawn by a good strong horse; in it sate our neighbour Jerry and his wife, the colored man who took old Jack's farm last summer; \they are evidently doing very well/. He stopped & as we were passing along with a nod of recognition, called out "Madam, Miss Jack's dead." What unexpected intelligence; we had not even known she was sick. Of course our enquiries were many as to her sickness, death & burial; she had been ill a week & had died that morning & they were going to bury her \in the wood/ beside her poor old man at 4 oclock in the afternoon. What a pity; we would have given anything to have been at the funeral, but could not give up our journey to the city.

Poor old people, childless & friendless, they lie side by side in a corner of their own wood & it is said their little property is passed into the hands of a lawyer who used to transact their business. The old lady made him a gift of it on her death bed because she had no one belonging to her & he had always been friendly, & in gratitude he has placed two white marble head stone over the grave of each one, inscribed ["]To the Memory of John Kett, who departed this life April 1846 aged more than one hundred years;" the other ["]In memory of Jane Kett &c. aged 76.["]

[1] I have told you of Muddy Creek & our pleasant rides through the wild scenery of the valley down which it flows on its way to the Ohio. We had a very pleasant pic nic there a few weeks ago; it was on a bright, warm day in August; the children had a little visitor, & accompanied by a very delightful, intellectual Friend of our own, we set out to take tea beneath the ancient forest trees in this sequestered spot.

117. This letter starts with the top three quarters of the third page before returning to the first page and then continuing on as usual.

On the 3rd of July[118] we had had a most violent storm which with us had been only a hurricane of wind breaking down trees & scattering branches in wild confusion, but it had been accompanied in its course in some neighbourhoods by most destructive hail & this region, about 2 miles south west of us, had been almost desolated. The cornfields looked most miserably; the broad leaves had been torn & split to ribbons & hung withered around the battered stems & dying husks which contained the half ripened but withered cobs. My heart ached for the inhabitants of the log cabins who were evidently poor &, having spent many a hard day in ploughing, planting & hoeing, were looking to this crop for food for their horses & pigs which constitute their chief wealth & for fattening which the corn is chiefly grown.

We stayed at the head of the Pawpaw wood to seek for its delicious fruit but found it still hard & unfit to eat, so we left them to be mellowed by the early frost & drove on to the favourite spot that mentally we chose for our rural feast. Green & beautiful were those noble trees that when last we saw them were arrayed in the glowing tints of autumn, & when we came to a broad green area ~~round which the~~ studded with fine buttonwood trees round the stream, bent enclosing it in its rocky arms, we concluded here we would alight & boil our kettle.

The packing of our carriage calculated to hold four, with 3 grown persons & 5 children besides baskets, kettle &c., had been a piece of great ingenuity & we were comforted to find on alighting that nothing was lacking to our comfort but a tin can to ladle water. The fire was lit after some difficulty & being reduced to the last match made it an operation of trembling anxiety, but the dry leaves smoked & then blazed most approvedly, & all hands were alert in gathering up dry sticks, of which \& logs/, however, there were enough to have cooked a dinner for an army, & soon we had a noble fire; & our kettle, filled from the clear stream, for—\here/ it does not at all deserve its appelation of muddy creek—suspended by a chain to an elevated log, sung & at length boiled.

The table cloth was spread on the green turf beneath a fine ~~buttonwood~~ \elm/ tree & the contents of the baskets spread; leaves of the buttonwood [2] & pawpaw supplied the place of plates & the ramblers who were seeking fossils in the creek or flowers in the woods were summoned to tea. The bright sun gilded the tops of the trees; the wild note of the cat bird & incessant chirp of the tree frog & grasshoppers gave life & enjoyment to the scene. We rolled a log for a seat for the older & more dignified part of the company; the children sate on the grass & enjoyed our tea most entirely. On one side, the ripple of the water & its rocky bank covered with dogwood & other trees, on

118. It is significant that Alderson has departed here from the Quaker system of assigning only numbers to the months and days of the week.

the other, the winding road & sloping bank wooded to its summit & a rustic wood bridge formed a scene for the pencil, highly picturesque & beautiful.

Little Alice danced with delight; her joy knew no bounds; she talked, laughed & rolled on the ground in extacies. The children took the infection & laughed till the woods rang again & we laughed in sympathy & then they bounded away to trace the course of the Creek beyond the pretty bridge & we beguiled the time with a pleasant tale till the cool breeze of evening warned us that we were 4 miles from home & the vision of sleepy children & an empty house rushed upon me; so we gathered up our things, not forgetting a few of those fine leaves that had served as plates for mementos of our pleasant evening in the woods &, calling the children, were soon on our homeward way. It was a charming ride; the west glowed with the rich light of the setting sun; then Venus shone forth gloriously & one little star after another appeared till the whole glory of the heavens was around us.

The children have two absorbing pets this summer. On the 4th of July, that great jubilee in America, Agnes had a noble present of a canary & cage. We had been out a ramble in the woods & on returning found the treasure hanging up in the piazza. A kind cousin, hearing of Agnes' great ~~wealth~~ happiness, sent Anna Mary a little mate for Dickey which, for its delicate form & the clear pale yellow of its feathers, is called primrose. Anna Mary had consoled herself in the want of a bird before this new pet arrived by the consideration that a nice wax doll just brought her from New York would never die as birds are sure to do sometime, and that should such catastrophe happen to Dickey, which however she hoped would not, she & her dolly would be at the funeral as chief mourners. The birds are a constant source of interest & are fed immediately after breakfast. Dickey begins to sing very beautifully, & he & Primrose chirp to each other the day through, & at night before going to bed they will see them brought in & safely placed under their musquito bar, for bird lovers have told them [3] that the musquitos bite & even cause the death of canaries. One of their friends also told them of a bird he knew who was strangled by spiders; one of these creatures spun its web so tightly round the neck of the bird as to kill it.

One morning when Anna Mary was feeding her bird, she left the cage door open and away went Primrose into the tall Locust Trees. Oh what a trouble[!] Anna Mary cried as if her heart would break. Charles ran to call the man, a goodnatured German, who was a great bird fancier; he never came in to his meals without looking at the fogels[119] [4] & now Barnard's ingenuity was put to the test. At first he hung Dicky & his cage up in the tree & \placed/ the other cage beside it, but Primrose was evidently delighted with liberty; she flew higher up & even into another tree and answered Dicky's chirp with one still louder. Time went on; Barnard could not stay; the bird seemed gone, & only now & then could we distinguish her voice when \at/

119. Presumably she means "*vogel*," German for "bird."

dinner time, Barnard, finding the "Canary fogel" still away, removed the cages from the tree to the top of an adjoining shed. In a short time Primrose came nearer, answering the other continually; then she was on a bough just above; now she was on Dicky's cage & the two birds seemed to be kissing each other through the wires. And now Barnard took his opportunity & slyly creeping up the the spot, placed the open door of the empty cage most cleverly over her & now it was closed & the poor, bird weary with its wanderings & hungry also, seemed as glad as we were to be at home again.

Few things have struck me more pleasantly than the bird houses so universally provided for the blue-birds & martins; there is a kindliness in the practice & it keeps alive a tenderness of feelings for these innocent familiar creatures that must have a beneficial influence on the heart. High up on the strong pole near the house or affixed to the roof are these little mansions, and in spring it is delightful to see the blue-bird~~s,~~ the earliest comer~~s~~ of the two, returning to its home & busied in repairing the old nest & preparing for the cares of the approaching season (see figure 32). They are a gentle lovely bird with a bright blue back & wings & cinnamon brown breast; but they are not always allowed to remain in quiet possession of their homes, for when the martin arrives he claims the place as his & the struggle is often continued for days, but usually the martin conquers & the poor blue-bird has to seek a new home.

72. To Ann Botham, October 9, 1847

I hope, my beloved mother, thou wilt not have thought me long in replying to thy two last, most welcome letters. Thou knows my time is limited and I have written to both Anna & Mary; since I addressed thee I hoped their letters would at least inform thee of our welfare & constant rememberance, & yet my precious mother, I never feel as if I had done right when I omit to write to thee, it is so great a pleasure & when thou assures me thou likes to receive my poor epistles & that they are a comfort to thee, I feel it a stimulus to exertion and a satisfaction to my own mind that it is painful to neglect.

Harrison has just returned from the Yearly Meeting & for thy sake I have wished I could have been there, but if he will do as he has just been observing he wishes, that is write to thee himself, I shall be content. I know he can send thee many interesting particulars and give thee much information on what came before them & the occur~~r~~ences of the time.

Lindley Murray Hoag was there; he is as you know a remarkable man & his labours were abundant & very extraordinary. It was with no common interest I met him as one who had so lately visited England & with whom you had felt pleased. He came up to see us on his way to the Yearly Meeting & is now in the city. We are hoping to see him tomorrow. He is going to settle at New York & commence a Free Labor Store but I can scarcely think it compatable with the will of Him who has so prepared & qualified him for usefulness that he should be long bound down to the counter & the routine of trade, even though in pursuing it he may be practically advocating great principles.

Thy parcel, dearest mother, came entirely safe, and accept our warmest \thanks for its/ contents. The socks are just what Harrison was wanting for fall wear & my handkerchiefs were most acceptable, not that I was really needing them, for thy <*torn*> kindness [h]as kept me well supplied, [2] but I have been weak enough to wish for some of these elegant small size which every body here wears. Indeed the people of this country are very dainty about this article: I see the very finest quality of French cambric in the hands of the Friends, but these that thou has so kindly sent are as fine as I desire & far more valuable to me than any other could be, hemmed by thy own dear fingers & Mary's marking: I look at them with great affection. The children were delighted with their comfortables[120] & very grateful to dear grandmother for \them/. They beg me to give their dear love. The purses also were much admired & both cousin Ann Shipley & Joseph Taylor were much pleased by thy rememberance of them & desired me to thank thee kindly.

I hope to forward my parcel in a few weeks; I have been busy during Harrison's absence in arranging the plants. Perhaps, dearest mother, thy peticoat may not be ready, for I am sorry to say I have not yet been able to commence quilting. This is the season when all good housewifes are busy preparing comforts, peticoats &c for the winter & every week I hope to begin but at present have not leisure, and the Friend whom I had calculated upon to assist me is sick & unable to work much.

I have just been putting our little Ann Alice to bed, and whilst undressing her the dear little creature clasped her hands together & exclaimed "Good Jesus bless little Alice." There was an earnestness & simplicity in the action & I thought thou wouldst be pleased with the incident. It seems to me to be the very model of a child's prayer.

Tell dearest Mary I have made frequent enquiry & find the Irish are not as numerous in Cincinnati as in the cities & towns near the coast & yet such [3] is the sickliness at New Orleans from the fevers prevalent at this season & from the diseases contracted during the voyage that numbers contrive to leave it & get into the country.[121] A short time ago a very decent man bearing all the marks of emaciation from sickness asked charity at our door. I asked him some particulars of his history: he had been a small farmer in the Co Galway, had had 4 acres for which he paid 30/ an acre &, to use his own expression, ["]the rent must be paid if there was not a rag left in the house,["] but he said Ireland was a beautiful country till the potatoe rot came & then

120. Although the *OED* does not recognize "comfortable" as a noun, *Webster's Revised Unabridged Dictionary* (1913) gives as one definition, "a stuffed or quilted coverlet for a bed; a comforter; a comfort." This is one example of an Americanism sent by Alderson but omitted by Howitt in *OCO*.

121. Yellow fever epidemics struck New Orleans and Mobile, Alabama, in the summer of 1847.

there was nothing but misery & starvation, so they scraped together all their little means & left the country with 6 children, 2 of whom died on board before landing. There were 600 emigrants \60 of whom died/ in the ship, & both he & his wife had the ship fever & then the common fever & ague \of this country/ & were now so weak as to be unable to work, but he began to feel stronger & was seeking work & [“]you know,[”] <wishe-*torn*> said he, [“]if I can get a dollar a day I can satisfy my family well, & my wife can soon work too.[”] What a change—he had probably overcalculated his earnings by 25 cents but his wife would be able, if willing, to get her 50 or even 75 cents \a day/ & where provisions are so cheap & good & clothing very moderate, their condition must be inferior from the miserable livelihood earned on his rackrent 4 acres. He said many others had come to Cincinnati, & probably they had, but at this season work is abundant & none need beg who are willing to labor, \so they are not conspicuous/.

I have been much interested by the progress of the Telegraph & its wonderful effects. It is now brought \from/ Boston to this city, a distance of near 1000 miles, & messages are transmitted \here/ from thence, New York & Philadelphia in a moment. I look at those wonderful wires on their high poles, carried over mountain, valley, wood & river & think of the mysterious agency employed that mocks time & distance until it appears, a type of angelic visitation, when the messenger of God, descending on the sunbeam, communicates his will to his favored servants.

Elizabeth has left us & again commenced a school in the city. I hope it may answer as I think both she & we are more comfortable when [4] separated. I am often sorry for her but it seems as if in our house she could not be content & comfortable & I feel as if it was another blessing in my overflowing cup to be relieved from this only drawback on our happiness.

Do you know much of this horrible war? It is a disgrace to the age & country, & the conduct of some of the volunteer companies is most disorderly & lawless at home. They are a nuisance in the neighbourhood where they are quartered. A friend told us that the fruit, chickens, pigs & even pantries were constantly robbed, & they scarcely felt safe in their house. Drunkenness & all kinds of disorder prevailed in the camp—what discipline! I suppose it is republican; one encampment we saw was more like a company of potters than a military body: no uniforms & the sentinels on guard in their artizan dresses looked a burlesque. On the whole affair, think of such an army let loose in an invaded country: it makes one tremble for the poor women & children who are always the greatest sufferers in times of war, & then their escapes expose these men to the direful effects of an unhealthy climate. Oh what a state to die in & should they return, what a corrupt mass thrown back into the community.

Hannah Taylor, who is here, desires her dear love to thee. She has been working a purse for thee which will of course come in thy parcel.

[1] [I] shall want to write again very soon; with dearest love to you all & most affectionate feelings to thee, my beloved mother, and thy attached & obliged daughter,

Emma

10 mo 9

Harrison sends his dear love. E[lizabeth Taylor]'s love also.

73. To Mary Howitt, November 23, 1847

In my last I told you of the dear little pet canary birds, & very little then did we anticipate the fearful catastrophe which was at hand. Dicky had become increasingly beautiful, the pride & delight of his little mistress & a very sweet songster. He, with his little wife Primrose, were fed punctually every morning & the cage decorated with Ailanthus leaves & \the scarlet/ trumpet flower till they looked like little bowers in Eden. We had a new treasure in a little playful kitten called Jessy, a very handsome but rather wild creature, an excellent mouser & like all other good cats a great lover of little birds—not, of course, for the great beauty of their plumage nor for the love of sweet music, but for the delicacy of their little tender bodies, which doubtless to a cat are a delicious morsel. She often eyed Dicky's cage with longing eyes &, strange to say, her example seemed to put unlawful thoughts in the head of the old yellow cat Shinken who, before her arrival, was never so much as suspected of such treason.

One fine autumn evening the birds were hanging as usual in the piazza & Agnes had been showing hers with great pride to the kind Friend from whom she had received him as a present; he thought he looked beautiful & did her care great credit. We had other company & the step ladder had been used for gathering grapes from the vine by the piazza & unfortunately left under the cage of Dicky, against which one of the Venetian doors leaned. Agnes' last request on going to bed was that the birds might be brought in & put under the musquito bar. Alas, it was forgotten; some hours elapsed & when brought in, no one noticed whether the birds were there or not. In the morning as usual Agnes went to look at hers and when she discovered the cage was empty, Dicky was not there. All was so silent & empty that it looked quite melancholy; we could all have cried with the poor child in sympathy for her great loss. When she was a little soothed she went to investigate & on the porch and amongst the grass at the foot of the vine she found some of his bright yellow feathers; these she carefully collected & folded up in paper, her only relic of the beloved favorite. Shinkin had surely done the mischief; he absented himself for two days & when he made his appearance had a skulking look like an old thief. Poor Primrose looked very sad & disconsolate; she sate for some days on her perch & did not even chirp; there was no one to answer her. We were afraid she too would die, but she has got up her spirits & Agnes pets & tends her; yet she thinks she shall never love any other bird like Dicky.

One day in coming up the hill, the children saw a sight which much delighted them; on a stone upon the bank below the road sate two young chippy monks side by side in the most affectionate manner as if they were holding a conversation about the beauty of the bright sunshine & the hickory & beech nuts they must lay up against winter, and consulting how best they might put in practice the many excellent lessons they had received from their \experienced/ parents on the necessity of forethought & provision. Perhaps we [2] were mistaken, but so we conjectured & so absorbed & happy did they seem that our presence disturbed them not & we had full opportunity of admiring them. They were not larger than small kittens & their bright brown fur & pale buff breasts looked wonderfully pretty as they sate side by side on their hind legs.

Wm Charles this Fall paid a visit to our good Friends the Evans's on the banks of the Little Miami \River/. I have told you of this family & their rural plenty before; they are a perfect specimen of country independence & comfort. The estate or plantation is large and has woods of great extent, upon it a fine sugar camp, a grist mill, tan yard & oil saw mill. The house is beautifully situated on a fine eminence overlooking the Miami valley & this prospect is diversified by fields & woods, hill & plain in beautiful variety.

The orchards are large & full of the finest fruit & they grow castor oil plants in large fields, broom corn & Indian corn; raise abundance of hops, turkey & chickens; make their own sugar, soap & candles; kill their own calves & sheep & live like princes. The wool of the sheep is either spun at home or sent to be manufactured for the use of the family to the Factory so that they seem to be a little world within themselves. They have two colored men whom they have raised from little boys & always treated with the utmost kindness & the family is often large from visitors & work hands as they are called, but the ~~household~~ domestic arrangements are all conducted by the excellent mother & three grown up daughters who, notwithstanding, have an air of refinement & improvement not common in the country.

When Charles arrived, they were busy raising a new frame house, and the next day he & the boys went with the colored men & the ox team to haul saw logs to the mill. There they found the pleasant sweet acorns of the pin oak, which resemble in flavor the hazel nut; the tree is a noble one with broad polished leaves similar in size & shape to those of the chestnut.[122] There were plenty of hickory & beech nuts; the little grey squirrils & the pretty brown chippy monks amused them with their actions. The day before, a fine large

122. Pin oak leaves do not resemble chestnut leaves, nor are their acorns good to eat, being very high in tannin. Alderson might be referring to the chestnut oak, whose leaves do resemble those of the chestnut and whose acorns, like those of the white oak, are low in tannin.

Figure 34. A sketch by William Charles Alderson, drawn on a loose piece of paper, which may have been enclosed in letter #73. In that letter, Alderson describes the drawing as depicting "an old tortoise & three young ones basking in the sunshine." Ht/7/1/80, Correspondence of Mary Howitt (1799–1888), Manuscripts and Special Collections, University of Nottingham.

oposom had been killed; it had somewhat the appearance of a young pig & is by some much esteemed for its flesh which is said to be good eating, but they are chiefly destroyed for their destructive qualities amongst the poultry. They make no resistance when attacked but lie down on the ground & pretend death.

Then the boys went down to the river by the mill race; they saw a sight that interested them much. They were fishing; William, the oldest boy, had caught a fine perch when he espied upon a log \under an old button wood tree/ in the water an old tortoise & three young ones basking in the sunshine.[123] The boys, as most other boys would do, threw little pieces of wood at them, when they all plunged into the water except one of the young ones who, less fearful than the rest, sate looking at them in apparent unconcern. Charles proposed to wade into the water & catch it but the other boys assured [3] him that he would soon repent as the tortoise has such strong teeth that they had known them to snap a hook in two. They abound in these waters; not far from here is a stream called Turtle Creek & on fine evenings you may see them running about on land enjoying a pleasant stroll.

In the evening the men took their guns into the woods & told the family they would shoot them a fine dish of squirrils for breakfast next morning. They would not let the boys go but they were in the orchard picking up pears & golden russets; they heard the guns go frap, frap & of course concluded they had met with plenty of game, but no such thing. They spent their shot & powder on a mark & only brought home one poor little grey squirrel. In the evenings the boys & men played in the kitchen at blind's mans buff or read by the large blazing fire of logs on the hearth the history [of] Big Foot & Little Foot: two Indian chiefs & their deadly encounters on the banks of the Ohio with one Adam Poe, an Irish settler.[124]

I wish I could give more particulars of this visit which really was an interesting \one/, but not being myself present I can only write the outline which Charles himself gave of it. The \three/ boys, William, George & Joseph [Evans], are thorough country boys: [they] go when there is a school in "session" to the district school &, when it is not taught, work on the farm or play as occasion may serve; they wear grey Kentucky jean clothes made in an old fashioned country style. William wished when he saw Wm Charles' full pantaloons his Father would let him have such; but despite their country air & manners they are fine intelligent boys, full of life & activity.

One day when cousin Isabella and a little English boy [Thomas] newly arrived in the country were visiting us, the children begged to have a fishing excursion & pic nic to Boldface Creek. So a quantity of pasties & some sandwiches were put into a basket which, as the oldest, was consigned to Isabella, who promised to act the part of mother on the occasion, & all agreed to be good & obedient to her authority. Charles took his long rod & new grass line which Joseph Taylor had lately given him. Agnes & Thomas had each as good a one as they could manufacture from sewing cotton & proposed cutting Pawpaw rods & in the woods & using them in preference to taking any from

123. See figure 34.

124. This is the frequently reprinted story of the settler Adam Poe and his fight with the Wyandot chief Big-Foot following some attacks on settlers along the Ohio River near Wheeling. The story varies from one publication to another, but it typically invokes the familiar stereotypes of the heroic settler locked in a heroic battle with the fierce but cowardly native.

home. Anna Mary was commissioned to take charge of a tin box containing shreds of dried beef for bait & a tin can to drink out of.

At 10 oclock we thought the dew would be sufficiently dried off the grass which, it being the month of October, was long & rank, and they were permitted to set out; the sun shone bright & warm and the shade of the trees in Jack's wood was very pleasant, but they lingered not here in Jack's, or more properly, Jerry's meadow where one of the tributaries of the little Creek runs along a grassy channel. The old white horse who seemed quietly grazing ran full speed after them to the great terror of the girls & exciting the courageous valor of the boys, who took up sticks to drive him away & sent him kicking up his heels [4] to the other end of the field. Perhaps the poor creature thought they were bringing him salt in that nice little basket, for presently they met Jerry's little daughter, a child of about 10 who with infinite good humour diverted them with her remarks; she has, as Annie said, the brightest pair of eyes & such white teeth & was so merry laughing & talking & jumped over the fences like a deer. When she left them she said, "I am the girl that looks after the cows," and bounded up into the wood.

Yes indeed; though she is, by the color of her skin & her strongly marked negro features, probably doomed to a life ~~of~~ sadden[ed] & darkened by a sense of degradation & contempt to bear with patience the scorn & hard names heaped upon her race until habit has so familiarized her with these things that they become the very element of her being, she is now beautiful & happy as childhood & good-humour can make her. There is something to me peculiarly interesting in coloured children: there is a thoughtful seriousness in their fine countenances which, however, can brighten up with the fullest expression of intelligence or become radiant with mirth & fun.

The children pursued their course \to/ where the little creek ran over its rocky bed; the valley is a wild & solitary place, shut in by hills on which grow Locust, Walnut & other trees; by the stream the Tulip Tree or Yellow Poplar, Willow & button-wood trees here & there overshadow ~~it~~ & make it very pretty. In the shallow parts they searched for fosil shells and coral for Isabella's brother Robert, who is quite a naturalist & has a drawer full of curiosities. At last they came to a sort of deep basin overhung with a broad, flat slab of limestone over which when the water is out there must be a splendid waterfall, to speak comparatively; this spot is by preeminence called by the children the Fish pond & here [1-*cross*] they commenced operations. Agnes' line lacked a float & Thomas fetched her a piece of rock; then she lost her lead & he would fix it. "But what with [?"] Why, he then brought a light rotton stick & who that looked at his merry eyes would wonder at the quiet fun that was ever bubbling up. They had many bites but some how or other could catch no fish: only one little white perch that kindly allowed itself to be drawn out of the water & was honored when they got home by having the whole frying pan to itself, wherein to be fried in solitary grandeur.

After a while Isabella thought it must be near dinner time; so judged all by their craving appetites, and therefore they pursued their course to the dining room, a beautiful little nook where the stream flowed through a narrow opening which, taking a bend, seemed to shut them in, & being overhung with small trees & bushes was quite picturesque. A broad, smooth floor of blue slaty rock then dry was the spot to spread the table, & here they laid out their dinner on \buttonwood/ leaves & made cups to drink out of from others: the tin can was too common. It was a merry dinner: oh, how good was the pumkin cheesecake & the apple pasties & how lovely the water that rippled in small fairy waves by them, & those pretty silver minnows, how they darted about, far prettier in the water than dangling & struggling on the hooks; & Isabella had a deal of [2-*cross*] trouble to keep her company within the bounds of propriety and at last ended by a merry threat: "Really, children, I must relinquish my authority if you are so wild."

At last their fun settled itself in trying to catch some minnows alive & to put them in the tin can & take them home to pet & tame. Charles said Frederic had fish in their cistern that were caught & put [there] last summer & why could not he have some also. They managed to secure about half a dozen & then proposed to return, only just take a run down the road which was near to see if the old log house that was burnt down, and finding it still uninhabited they came back. It was dusty & hot & one & all took off their shoes—stockings they had none—& \they/ waded in the pleasantly warm water, now & then stopping to admire some tiny waterfall, now to observe some rapids or search amongst the shalley, loose grey earth of which the bank was here & there composed to pick up some most beautifully minute & perfect specimens of shells.

They hoped to have brought the dinner basket home full of ripe pawpaws but only finding one cluster they thought themselves fortunate in meeting with a fine wild vine growing over a stump on which was an abundance of clusters of the small chicken grape; & laden with this new treasure, they returned to tea, [3-*cross*] there to rehearse the adventures of the day. There was one dash, however, to their joy: Anna had lost one of her shoes; they were new & she of course was in sad trouble, dreading reproof & perhaps correction. All said they were too tired to think of going back to seek it, but Charles kindly said he would go alone. So, getting a drink of water & a slice of bread & butter, he set out & before sunset came back with the lost shoe to the joy & comfort of all.

And now with dear love, farewell; thine beloved sister,

Emma.

I wrote to mother & sent my letter yesterday, 11th mo 22. [4] The enclosed sketch is one of W. C.'s efforts & sent with his dear love to Aunt Mary.

74. To Mary and William Howitt, December 1847

M. [&] W. Howitt,
I have intended to thank thee, my beloved Mary, for the two delightful treats which thy unexpected parcels afforded me. I had often inwardly regreted that our communications by that channel were so seldom. I love to be surprized into joy, and nothing affords me such lovely pleasure as hearing from my [2] dearly beloved A or M; and never, my sweet sister, omit writing when thou hast an opportunity.

I regret much the mental & bodily slavery which I have laboured under this after noon & which has bound me with a strong chain to my chair and book. Hogg's Winter Evening Tales fell in my way and this afternoon I have almost read myself stupid & frightened with the horrors of Welldean Hall.[125] It is this that compels me to scrawl only a very few lines on this scrap of paper.

I am glad A[lfred Alaric] Watts is not the [3] despicable man we have painted him; I think in future this shall be a warning to me to be more charitable and to look on the best side of men and their actions.

I have sent the baby linen. Take no thought of paying for any of the things; I intend to make them good. All but the flannel I can replace at no expense and only the sacrifice of a little time, so if thou sends aught for them I shall think thou wilt not be beholden to me for anything.

I have begged a few more papers & cut all out [4] that can possibly be of any use to thee. There is a deal I doubt not that thou wilt reject, but perhaps some may do.

The cap, dearest M, I meant for thee is [1-*cross*] thou thinks it worth keeping. Thou quite delights me with thy interesting notices of thy dear little lassie; it is what I have often wished thou wouldst remember. I wish, my love, I could come & spend a little time with you and personally testify how great my affection is for you; as it is I can only hope that every blessing will be yours & that sometime I may evince my love in something more than empty [2-*cross*] words.

Thank thee, love, for the Every Day books,[126] but why dost thou so often wish thou couldst send me something? Bless thee, Mary; I really want nothing that I can name, and were I put to my choice I had rather have one of thy letters full of affection & kindness than the most splendid present thou couldst send me.

[3-*cross*] With dearest love to you all, I remain thy affectionate sister,

Emma

Kennedy is actually no Physician. Pray do not get robbed if you can help it.

125. James Hogg (1770–1835), known for his gothic tales of otherworldly creatures prowling the hills of his native Scotland, published "Welldean Hall" as part of "Country Dreams and Apparitions" in *Tales and Sketches by the Ettrick Shepherd* (Glasgow: Blackie & Son, 1837), 190–274.
126. For more on William Hone's *Every-Day Book*, see page 401*n*91.

75. To Ann Botham and William Howitt [from Harrison Alderson], December 18, 1847

My beloved Mother,
I am ill qualified under existing circumstances to address thee, but feeling very unwilling the sorrowful tidings should reach thee, in the first instance at least, thro: any other channel, I sit down to make the attempt to communicate an account which has plunged me into the very depths of affection: my best beloved on earth, my greatest earthly treasure, the delight of my eyes, the solace and comfort of my life—she for whom I seemed very much to live, perhaps too much so—the mother and guardian of my precious children—has been suddenly taken from me, leaving me desolate, affected, almost crushed.

How unsearchable are His judgments, who has appointed, at least permitted it, and His ways past finding out! Such I have often felt and increasingly as time has rolled on and opportunities \have occurred/, and they have been many, of evidencing it; never was man more wonderfully blessed and provided for in a companion—in matters both temporal and spiritual. She was my helper and counselor; into her bosom I could ever without fear pour my sorrows and my complaints, and as often was I comforted and encouraged to pursue my course—to press on that way cast up for me—and now she is gone! What shall, what can I say! Thy judgments, O Lord, are indeed a great deep! Past, entirely beyond the reach and comprehension of finite men! For some wise purpose, we are bound to believe, this stroke of sore affliction has been permitted to fall upon us.

My precious little ones, what a loss is theirs! very partially if at all to be estimated by them, but which I, their poor father, feels in the fulness, and yet scarcely so—for it cannot be fully known but in the experience of days yet to come, every one of which will feelingly demonstrate their and my great loss. My precious Emma has left a name and a savour <u>here</u> which will, I believe, be long, very long remembered and felt: greatly was she beloved, and many were looking to her for peculiar usefulness in the Church, and she did indeed evidence a growing fitness and capacity to serve Him whom she loved, but it seems this growing fitness for service in the Church Militant was in reality a readiness for being joined to the Church triumphant.

But now I must return to the circumstances preceding and attending this solemn event. This day two weeks she was delivered of a little boy under circumstances more trying than has afore time been her lot—that is, more bodily distress ever—& persevered still. Her suffering was not particularly great but somewhat more protracted than usual for her. She was not at her full term, but the child was living and is doing well. In the night her breathing was considerably affected and I, for I remained with her thro the night, towards morning became anxious and sent off to the city for the Doctor: it was evident she was labouring under some affection of the chest. I ought to have mentioned that after rising in the morning she became affected with severe chill and I induced her to return to bed. She did so and soon after symptoms, tho: slight, of labor came on, but not, as I said before, being at her time, she thought and we hoped by keeping quiet these would go off; this, however, was not the case, and the little boy was born about three oclock in the afternoon.

When the dr. came he used such remedies as he deemed useful, and the complaint seemed to yield and she was considerably better the \two/ following days, and we quite hoped the complaint was effectually subdued, but fever and renewed symptoms of inflammation again appeared and were again apparently in good measure subdued but not eradicated. Thus we went on from day to day alternating between hope and fear, tho: I perhaps was the only one who had much fear at this stage, and indeed the doctor seemed to be encouraged and to speak encouragingly nearly to the last; indeed he did to the morning of the day preceding her death, but on that day in the afternoon I became increasingly anxious and my mind was filled with apprehension and consequently with distress; I had suffered a good deal in the fear how it might terminate some days before, being very sensitive and keenly alive to the most distant danger at these seasons of the trial of her strength.

That evening just alluded to, my dear friend Joseph W. Taylor, who was educated \for/ and, previous to coming to this city practised as a Physician, made his way to our home. I say made his way, for the ordinary course from this city was entirely cut off at this time \&/ is still by the overflowing of the waters of the Ohio and its turbulence—a distressing visitation—as well as by the \unprecedented heavy/ fall of snow, & he, on visiting dear E, entirely confirmed my apprehensions of her very critical situate.

Previous to his seeing her, way opened for our having some serious & deeply interesting conversation, when she communicated to me some of her feelings; alluding to her present critical situation, she told me she had anticipated some very serious visitation—that it was not unexpected by her—but could not then tell how it would issue. Remarking that we were in the hands of a wise & good providence, she told me hers was not a presumptuous hope but she believed that death would have nothing, nor the grave any victory, in her case. She said a passage of scripture had been for some time resting upon, and was a great stay & comfort to, her mind—"lead me to the Rock that is higher than I."[127] To this she clung as on this Rock she had built her every hope for eternity, and they that build here build safely—for behold I lay in Zion a stone—a chief corner stone—elect, precious—he that believeth in him shall not be confounded.[128] She further said that she had seemed to

127. "Hear my cry, O God; attend unto my prayer. / From the end of the earth will I cry unto thee, when my heart is overwhelmed: lead me to the rock that is higher than I" (Psalm 61:1–2, King James Version).
128. "Behold, I lay in Sion a chief corner stone, elect, precious: and he that believeth on him shall not be confounded" (1 Peter 2:6, King James Version).

have been hovering about the gate of death for some days; still, she felt there was one able, and if he saw meet, would raise her up again.

She endeavoured to comfort and encourage me to bear my affliction meetly—thou had, she said, <??> encourage[d] others, and now thou must teach by example. Seek then for full and perfect resignation to the divine will & remember thou had received a great commission & be engaged to fulfill it—or in words to this effect. It was to me and others around her bed, as it was to her, a great trial that, owing to the extreme soreness of her mouth: dear Lamb, from the free use of calomel,[129] she could converse very indifferently. She passed this fifth-day night pretty comfortably, sleeping generally; next morning she inclined to sleep and did so till symptoms of suffering and approaching dissolution manifested themselves; her breathing became very laboured and distressing, but notwtithstanding this she had at her own request considerable portions of Holy Scripture read to her, which seemed greatly to interest her—about this time and I believe throughout the day when not engaged in communicating as she could with us on matters of interest—in fervent supplicate—her lips moving and sometimes giving utterance with a few expressions.

About noon or perhaps a little after, she requested to have the children brought and all of them were introduced as opportunity offered. She spoke to and affectionately smiled upon & kissed them & addressed them as she <??> to all around, taking leave [with] great composure, expressing her affectionate sense of their kindness and attention now in her <??> especially and at other time—<??> had been shown her—a very touching and deeply affecting time. Some time after this she wished to speak to Mr. Taylor. He came. She she asked his opinion if at all better than when he saw her in the morn, he having been down into the city to bring up Elizabeth <Harrison/Shipley Taylor??> this sister—a very precious <bos??> of my beloved E's—and, being informed by him that there was no improvement, she with great distinctness of utterance and emphasis exclaimed "God's holy will be done." After this she became calm and she wished to be quiet—all by myself.

Dear Hannah Taylor who has been as a sister & <be beloved> E and <taken?> the letter <??> as <??> desires her kind love.[130]

129. Mercurous chloride, a purgative used from the sixteenth century until its toxicity was recognized.

130. Amice Lee renders this passage as "Dear Hannah Taylor has been as a sister to beloved E.—her brothers are as bone of my bone." Amice Macdonell Lee, *In Their Several Generations* (Plainfield, N.J.: Interstate, [1956?]), 24.

Epilogue

Emma Alderson's death, and that of her infant son Samuel (named after his grandfather), came as a blow to her mother, Ann Botham, who died a few months later, in May 1848. Other principal figures in this narrative and many of their descendants, however, lived long and productive lives. Through business, education, and public service, they left lasting contributions to the world. It is appropriate, therefore, to follow up on some of those lives in the years following the close of Emma's own life.

Cedar Lodge

The surviving Aldersons left Cincinnati in 1851, the children going off to boarding school and Harrison sailing for an extended visit to England. Sometime in the 1850s, Cedar Lodge was bought by the Sisters of Charity, who renamed the property "Cedar Grove" and moved onto the premises with the Mount St. Vincent Academy for girls. Classes were conducted in the Alderson home, which came to be called "the cradle." Later in the century, the school was renamed Seton High School, after Mother Seton, the founder of the order. Sadly, in the 1950s, the Aldersons' home was torn down to make room for a new three-story school building. The school is still in operation.

The Aldersons and Their Descendants

After Emma's and Samuel's deaths, Harrison Alderson (1800–1871) stayed on at Cedar Lodge for another four years, after which, following a year or so in England, he returned to America to settle in a home he called "The Cedars" in Burlington, New Jersey, the site of one of the first Quaker meetings in America and a stronghold of Orthodox Friends. Alderson distinguished himself sufficiently in the Burlington Monthly Meeting to be recognized at his death with a lengthy obituary in the British Friends' *Annual Monitor.*[1] Alice Ann Alderson, their only surviving

American-born child, had never been strong and so returned to England with Elizabeth Alderson soon after her mother's death. Alice Ann went to live with the Howitts and then with friends in Esher until 1855, when she succumbed to scarlet fever. The others apparently stayed with their father but were sent east to Philadelphia to attend nearby West-town Boarding School for brief periods: William Charles from 1850 to 1854 and his sisters from 1853 to 1855.[2] In 1853, Harrison moved to Burlington, New Jersey. Although he seems not to have risen to any great prominence in the Society of Friends, he maintained his membership and served from 1855 to 1867 as an officer of the Haverford School Association and the Corporation of Haverford College.[3] In 1871 he traveled with his younger daughter, Anna Mary, to England to visit his older daughter, Agnes, and her husband, Joseph Simpson, in Staffordshire, England, when he became ill and died at their home. Ironically, while Emma lay buried far away in Ohio, her husband was laid to rest in the cemetery of the Uttoxeter meeting-house beside Emma's father, Samuel Botham.[4]

Later pictures of William Charles show him sometimes with glasses and sometimes without, so apparently the troubles with his eyes that his mother wrote about never progressed to blindness. After graduating from Westtown in 1854, William Charles attended Haverford College for one year.[5] Little is known for certain about what he did from there, but according to his grandson, Edward Janeway, Alderson returned to the Midwest, working in coal and on the railroads, eventually becoming treasurer of the Ohio Valley Railroad. Janeway remembers his grandfather showing him "a watch that had been nicked by a bullet when somebody had tried to rob him of the payroll and all that."[6] According to one genealogist, Alderson was president of Grady Trading Company and treasurer of the Choctaw Oklahoma and Gulf Railroad and was honored for that work with the naming of the town of Alderson, Oklahoma.[7] In any case, in 1870, Alderson began a long career with Lehigh Valley Railroad,[8] married Eleanor Yarnall (who was from a family with deep roots in the Philadelphia Quaker community), and settled at Wynndown in Overbrook, just west of Philadelphia, where he would live the rest of his life. Other records from Haverford and Boyd's Blue Book Directory indicate that he may also have maintained a residence in the city at 228 South 3rd Street.

Alderson's boyhood love of the outdoors stayed with him throughout his life, and several pictures show him hunting and camping in the Adirondacks, where he became a founder and the first treasurer of the Adirondack Mountain Reserve, formed in 1887 to purchase land in the Adirondacks for protection against logging. The actions of the Adirondack Mountain Reserve ultimately helped make possible Adirondack State Park, one of the largest and most magnificent wilderness preserves in the eastern United States. The reserve itself continues its existence today as the Ausable Club.[9]

Eleanor and William Charles Alderson produced only one child, Eleanor Caroline Alderson (perhaps named after Caroline Shipley), but the couple adopted a second child, Lilian Cope Coale (sometimes "Lillian"; b. 1868), presumably in 1880 when she was left an orphan by the death of her father, William Ellis Coale Jr. (Her mother, Louisa Schmidt, had died in 1873.) Nothing is known about the circumstances of this adoption, but Eleanor may have been related through marriage to Lilian, whose uncle was Francis Cope Yarnall. By 1906, Lilian was still living with William Charles and Eleanor at Wynndown, but according to census records, one Lillian C. Alderson was living in Fairfield, Connecticut, in 1920, the same year she published a short article in *House and Garden*. Thus, there are no descendants of Emma and Harrison bearing the Alderson name. However, Eleanor Caroline Alderson and her husband, Theodore Caldwell Janeway, left a line of descendants, many of whom bear the memory of the Aldersons as a middle name. Among those grandchildren of William Charles was Edward G. Janeway, who served as a lieutenant commander in the Navy during World War II and later as a Republican state senator in Vermont. In the latter role, he broke ranks with the Republican Party to oppose the escalation of the war in Vietnam. As committed pacifists, Harrison and Emma might have been disturbed by their great-grandson's participation in war (or they might, like many Quakers, have accepted the necessity of that one), but they would have been pleased with his stand against the less defensible war in Southeast Asia.

Like her brother, Anna Mary (Nanny or Annie) Alderson married into a leading Quaker family from Philadelphia. In 1863, shortly before her twenty-second birthday, she wed William Wilberforce Wistar (1837–1866). It is unclear what relationship, if any, her husband had to the Wilberforce family (including the great abolitionist William Wilberforce), but the Wistars had been an important family among Philadelphia Quakers for several generations. William Wistar's early death left Anna Mary with only one child, Emma Alderson Wistar, named after her grandmother. The granddaughter married the Englishman John Shaw of Derbyshire in Philadelphia on April 23, 1889, and had one son, John Valentine Wistar Shaw, who went on to a remarkable career with the British Home Office, holding senior administrative posts in the Gold Coast, Sierra Leone, Palestine, Cyprus, and Trinidad between 1921 and 1950.[10]

Agnes Alderson married Joseph Simpson (the brother of Frederick Simpson, who married into the Shipley family) on September 15, 1870, and had seven children, two of them named after her parents, Emma and Harrison. Their grandson Joseph Simpson (1909–1968) rose through the ranks to become commissioner of the London Metropolitan Police, and in 1959 he was knighted as Knight Commander of the Order of the British Empire (*ODNB*). This Joseph Simpson's sister, Josephine (1904–1986), renewed the links between Emma and Harrison's descendants by marrying her second cousin (Anna Mary's grandson), John Valentine Wistar Shaw.

The Harrisons and Their Descendants

The business that Daniel Harrison started with his younger brother Smith Harrison and his former employee Joseph Crosfield thrived and soon moved from Liverpool to London. Daniel Harrison had been the leading force in the founding of the company, but his brother Smith (twenty-three years younger) had carried much of the weight.[11] Daniel's son Charles Harrison (b. 1830) became a partner in the firm in 1855, while Smith's son, John Mason Harrison, was taken into the partnership in 1878 and stayed until 1917.[12] Daniel's younger son Samuel (b. 1834) went to work for Harrisons and Crosfield, traveling to China at one point on business. The company survived and expanded into other areas, including wood, rubber, chemicals, and more. In the mid-1990s, the company turned its attention entirely to chemicals and changed its name to Elementis. Today Harrisons and Crosfield teas are available from a new company started by Al Sharif, who adopted the well-known name for its marketing value.[13]

Mary Harrison (1825–1898), the oldest of Anna's eight surviving children, never married, but throughout her life she maintained an emotionally intimate relationship with her Bavarian music teacher, Wilhelm Pranz, with whom she had studied as a teenager during an extended stay in Germany with her cousin Anna Mary Howitt. All her life, Mary Harrison suffered from some physical disability, which limited her participation in family events but did not dampen her energy for causes that she undertook. "If I had been a man," she wrote, "I could have succeeded in business."[14] In later years, she wrote a memoir of her life and that of her mother and had even secured a contract with John Ruskin's own publisher, but realizing that it would cover the same ground as Mary Howitt's projected autobiography, she pulled her publication in deference to her aunt. The memoir is still available in manuscript but has never been published.

Margaret Ann Harrison (1827–1899), Mary's sister and the younger of the two nieces with whom Emma Alderson corresponded, married Ellis Yarnall, who was from the same Philadelphia Quaker family as William Charles Alderson's wife, Eleanor Yarnall. Ellis Yarnall's parents had been active in the Society of Friends, but his generation had left to join the Episcopal Church. As of this writing, one of Anna Harrison's great-great-granddaughters lives in Maine with an oil portrait of Anna over the mantelpiece.

Agnes Harrison (1835–1925) and Annie Harrison (1841–1930) married two brothers, John and James Macdonell. Prior to her marriage, Agnes had lived for eight years with her sister Margaret Yarnall and brother-in-law Ellis in Philadelphia. The period of her stay, 1860–1868, included one of the most tumultuous periods in American history, and close to 100 letters from Agnes and Margaret to friends, family, and public figures back in England tell a poignant tale comparable to the one told in the letters of her aunt Emma Alderson twenty years earlier.[15] The Yarnall family was closely tied to the abolition movement, Ellis's aunt (his mother's sister) being Lucretia Mott, and one of his cousins having married the son of William Lloyd Garrison.[16] With public opinion in Britain on the side of the Confederacy, Agnes and Margaret found themselves busy promoting the cause of the Union and abolition. Their letters provided information and credibility to their sister Mary, who in 1864 was corresponding with a number of prominent English political and religious figures, including the Duke of Argyll, Edmund Pusey, and William Gladstone. The letters describe dinner at the home of secretary of state Seward and even a brief meeting with Abraham Lincoln. Agnes also wrote two novels, *For the King's Dues* (1874) and *Quaker Cousins* (1879), and an article-length biography of abolitionist and women's rights activist Lucretia Mott.[17]

Agnes Harrison's husband, John Macdonell (1845–1921), became a famous jurist, legal scholar, and reformer and the first dean of the faculty of law in the University of London. Macdonell was among the first to compile and use judicial statistics to assess the effectiveness of the judicial system and to propose reforms. He was knighted in 1903 and promoted to KBC in 1914. After World War I, Macdonell participated in the prosecution of German war criminals, helping to establish important precedent in international law.[18]

Among Agnes Harrison's daughters was Amice Macdonell, later Amice Lee, who preserved the letters in this collection and many others before they were turned over to the University of Nottingham. Her books, *In Their Several Generations* (a family biography) and *Laurels & Rosemary: The Life of William and Mary Howitt* (a biography of William and Mary Howitt), remain among the best published sources of information about the personal and family lives of the Howitts and their extended family. Without her work, my own would have been immensely more difficult.

In 1871, Annie Harrison married James Macdonell (1841–1879), a gifted journalist who had made an early name for himself in the radical and reformist press. Macdonell became chief foreign affairs writer for the *Times*, where his radicalism was tolerated, if not always appreciated. When he died unexpectedly shortly before his thirty-eighth birthday, Annie was left to complete and publish his collection of essays *France since the First Empire* (1879; *ODNB*). One of their children, Philip James Macdonell, combined the careers of his father and his uncle James Macdonell as a jurist and legal reformer. In 1900, he was called to the bar but instead went to South Africa as a war correspondent for the *Times*. By 1903, he had turned back to the law, and he ended up serving in colonial administrations in South Africa, Northern Rhodesia, Ceylon, and Trinidad and Tobago. He was knighted in 1925 (*ODNB*).

Perhaps the most interesting and accomplished of Anna's children was the youngest, Emma Lucy Harrison, born in 1844 and named after the aunt who had left for America before she was born. Although she dropped the name "Emma" early in life, Lucy Harrison finally fulfilled the dreams her aunt had had many years earlier of opening a school in Uttoxeter. Wealthier by far than her own parents had been and liberal enough to countenance such a move, Anna Harrison was able to send both Lucy and her sister Annie to Bedford College, a liberal, non-sectarian institution, in 1861. Lucy Harrison became adept at wood carving, which she taught for a few years at the Working Women's College in London.

When she was twenty-two, Lucy's short-term employment as a substitute for a sick teacher at the Bedford College School (a preparatory day school for girls) turned into a lifetime career. When the school was given up by Bedford College, it moved to Gower Street, where Harrison continued to teach and in 1875 became sole head of the school. She continued in that capacity for ten years, leaving a lasting impression on a generation of young women, including the poet Charlotte Mew and others who were later influential in the Bloomsbury Group. In 1885, poor health forced her to resign, but four years later she returned to education as headmistress of The Mount School, a Quaker boarding school for girls in York, where she stayed for the next twelve years. Joseph Rowntree, one of the leading liberal Quakers of the late nineteenth century and a member of the school committee that hired Lucy Harrison, reflected in 1915 that "there was with her the combination so rarely seen of gentleness and strength, of refinement and practical wisdom. All things which were beautiful and good seemed her natural habitude, and so a moral and intellectual atmosphere was created which must have influenced many lives."[19]

An active scholar as well as a teacher, Lucy Harrison edited a teaching edition of Edmund Spenser and published articles on Jane Austen, Shakespeare, Ann Radcliffe, John Woolman, Rabindranath Tagore, and others. In the years following her retirement from Bedford College, Harrison developed a committed long-term relationship with her successor, Amy Greener, who later joined her in Yorkshire and, after Harrison's death, published her papers as *A Lover of Books: The Life and Literary Papers of Lucy Harrison*. One chapter on "Three of Shakespeare's Women," with its survey of representations of women in literature, anticipates a similar survey in Virginia Woolf's *A Room of One's Own* (1929).[20] Harrison remained a Quaker all her life and was buried at the Friends meeting-house near her home in Bainbridge.

The Howitts and Their Descendants

Of all of Emma Alderson's relations and descendants, William and Mary Howitt left the most impressive legacy—by some estimates more than 170 books, including translations, young adult and children's literature, poetry, fiction, politics, and history. They corresponded with and visited most of the leading literary figures of their day, including William Wordsworth, Charles Dickens, William Makepeace Thackeray, Ralph Waldo Emerson, Harriet Beecher Stowe, Alfred Tennyson, and others. They promoted the work of women and working-class writers, including Elizabeth Gaskell, whose first venture into fiction, "The Three Eras of Libbie Marsh," was published in *Howitt's Journal*. Later William encouraged and assisted Gaskell with the publication of her first novel, *Mary Barton*.[21]

After leaving the Society of Friends in the 1840s (see page 16), the Howitts attended Unitarian and Anglican services but did not settle on any particular denomination before William's death in 1879. The Howitts' literary reputation skyrocketed from the late 1820s to the late 1840s, after which it mostly declined quickly, with the bankruptcy of *Howitt's Journal* in 1848. Still, they continued their writing and translating until the ends of their lives, with a steady stream of books and articles in Dickens's *Household Words*, *Tait's Edinburgh Magazine*, *Macmillan's Magazine*, *Harper's*, and elsewhere. William experienced a brief resurgence in his career when two years in Australia (1852–1854) led to the publication of five books on the subject, especially *Life, Labor, and Gold; or, Two Years in Victoria with Visits to Sidney and Van Diemen's Land* in 1855. The same year, his *Boy's Adventures in the Wilds of Australia, or Herbert's Journal* repeats the model of *Our Cousins in Ohio* with its narrative of life in a foreign land told from the point of view of a child. We get some idea of the Howitts' name recognition at least from a contemporary riddle, "what authors do you think of first when you see a burning library?" The answer was "Dickens, Howitt, Burns."[22] Later, they became deeply involved in the spiritualist movement that was then drawing people from all walks of life to table rappings, séances, and other forms of communion with the unseen world. However, there is some indication that the family was split for a time between William and Anna Mary's spiritualism and Mary and Margaret's skepticism.[23]

In 1869, the Howitts left England for what was to be a brief stay but turned out to last the rest of their lives. After traveling through Egypt, Palestine, Greece, Italy, Switzerland, and elsewhere, they and their daughter Margaret divided their lives between Rome in the winter and Dietenheim in the Tyrols of southern Germany during the summer. Throughout that time, the Howitts continued their literary output and their active correspondence with friends, literary acquaintances, and relatives back in England, much of which is now held by the University of Nottingham along with the correspondence in this book. In 1879, William died in Rome in the presence of Mary and their three surviving children and was buried there in the Protestant cemetery along with John Keats and the ashes of Percy Bysshe Shelley. Three years later, on May 26, 1882, Mary was quietly baptized into the Catholic Church, something she might not have done during the lifetime of William, who remained until his death staunchly anti-Catholic.[24] On January 10, 1888, just a year before her death, Mary was granted a private audience with Pope Leo XIII, an event she described in a letter to Father Paul Perkmann:

> I was unconscious of everything. A serene happiness, almost joy filled my whole being as I at once found myself on my knees before the Vicar of Christ. . . . All the time I did not know whether I was in the body or not. I knew afterwards that I felt unspeakably happy, and with a sense of unwillingness to leave. How long it lasted—perhaps a minute or so—I know not; but I certainly was lifted into a high spiritual state of bliss, such as I never had experience of before, and which now fills me with astonishment and deep thankfulness to recall. I woke in the stillness of last night with the sense of it upon me. It is wonderful. I hope I may never lose it.[25]

As far removed as the Roman Catholic Church may be from the austere Quakerism of her youth, Mary never lost her feeling for the simplicity and unadorned spirituality of Quakerism: even as she walked through the Vatican on her way to meet the Pope, she commented that nothing struck her "more than the wonderful simplicity of the apartments; all similar and wholly without ornament or costly show."[26] When she died on January 30, 1889, large numbers attended the Requiem Mass, after which, by special permission of the Cardinal Vicar of Rome, she was interred in the Protestant cemetery beside her husband.

The oldest by six years of the Howitts' surviving children, Anna Mary (1824–1884) seemed destined for a promising career as an artist and illustrator, collaborating on a number of books with her parents, including *Our Cousins*, for which she produced four illustrations (including the frontispiece; see figures 26–29). Between 1850 and 1851, Anna Mary spent a year with her friend Jane Benson studying under the painter and muralist Wilhelm von Kaulbach (1804–1874) at the Düsseldorf Academy in Munich, an experience detailed in her very successful *Art Student in Munich* (London, 1853).[27] A talented watercolorist, Anna Mary may not have benefited as much as she imagined from her time with Kaulbach, from whom she apparently "learned . . . to crowd Gargantuan canvases with Biblical and historical drama."[28] In 1856, her artistic career ended with what she hoped would be her greatest work to date, a biblical canvas of *Boadicea Brooding over Her Wrongs*. Howitt's close friend and women's rights activist Barbara Leigh Smith (later Bodichon) had sat for the painting, calling attention to the contemporary relevance of the material. In this way, as one recent critic has argued, "Anna Mary Howitt visually elided the contemporary activist with the warrior queen who defied and outwitted Roman imperialism. . . . For the community of women who recognised Barbara Bodichon's distinctive appearance, the painting articulated a feminist politics of visual representation."[29] Whatever meanings the painting held for that community of progressive women, it elicited a scathing review from John Ruskin, the most influential critic of the day. Most biographers have accepted Mary Howitt's claim that Ruskin's denunciation of her daughter's work "so crushed her sensitive nature as to make her yield to her bias for the supernatural, and withdraw from the ordinary arena of the fine arts."[30] She continued to do some professional work as an illustrator and, as an ardent spiritualist, to practice "automatic" drawing, but her career in the art world had indeed ended. Drawing on unpublished correspondence from the younger sister, Margaret Howitt, Linda H. Peterson has challenged this interpretation of events, treating Howitt's account of the situation with Ruskin as an attempt to deflect attention away from "an ideological rift within the family" over William and Anna Mary's growing interest in spiritualism.[31] In 1859, Anna Mary married Alfred Alaric Watts, with whom (in keeping with her family's history of literary collaboration) she published *Aurora* (1875), "a volume of spiritualized, latently spiritualistic poems."[32] In 1884, on a visit to her mother in her new villa near Meran in the Tyrol region of Italy, Anna Mary died of diphtheria.

When William Howitt traveled to Australia in 1852, accompanied by his two surviving sons, Alfred William (1830–1908) and Herbert Charlton (1838–1863), the three of them joined his brothers Richard (1799–1869) and Godfrey (1800–1864), a physician who had emigrated twelve years earlier. After two years and a serious illness that nearly took his life, William returned with Herbert Charlton, leaving Alfred William to work on his uncle's farm. The older son made his permanent home in Australia, where he distinguished himself as an explorer, civil servant, naturalist, and ethnographer, publishing dozens of articles and a book, *The Native Tribes of South-East Australia* (1904), on aboriginal culture.[33] In 1864, Howitt married Mary Robinson "Liney" Booth, with whom he had five children, the only grandchildren of William and Mary.

Like his cousin William Charles Alderson, with whom he had shared a boyhood correspondence, Herbert Charlton was an inveterate outdoorsman and longed for more adventure than he could find in England. Thus in 1860, he announced that he would spend the summer learning to farm with friends in Lincolnshire in preparation for emigration to New Zealand later that year. Charlton thrived in the new country, living with a collection of dogs, cats, and birds in a hut he had built himself outside of Christchurch. His hardihood and leadership ability were recognized, and he was soon leading exploring parties. In 1863, the government invited him to lead a party to mark out a route from Christchurch on the eastern shore to the goldfields on the western shore. Tragically, that June, he and two other men were in a canoe on Lake Bruner when a storm came up, presumably capsizing the canoe and drowning the men, none of whom was ever found.[34]

Margaret Howitt (1839–1930), or Maggie, as she was called, was the youngest of the Howitt children and the one to whom William Charles Alderson addressed his letters from America. Margaret spent much of her life caring for her parents, but she was nevertheless an accomplished author in her own right, if never as famous as her parents. Margaret spent a year from 1864 to 1865 with Fredrika Bremer in Sweden, where she perfected her Swedish. Out of that experience grew her first book, *Twelve Months with Fredrika Bremer in Sweden* (1866), based, like a number of other Howitt family publications, on personal correspondence between herself and Bremer. The following year, she published a novel, *Birds of a Feather; or, The Two Schoolboys.* After Mary Howitt's death, Margaret compiled and published her mother's autobiography, having recently completed a massive two-volume biography of the Nazarene artist Friederich Overbeck, which she wrote initially in English before translating it into German. After converting to Catholicism, Margaret turned to hagiography, first publishing a translation and abridgement from the Italian of a work on Saint Anastasia and later beginning a work on *God's Ambassadress: St. Bridget of Sweden*, which would be completed and published posthumously in 1947 by Sister Helen M. D. Redpath.[35] Margaret was the quieter and more conservative member of the family, resisting her father's radical republicanism as well as his and Anna Mary's experiments with spiritualism. After her mother's death, Margaret lived in Austria until, with the approach of World War I, she returned to England and Cornwall, where she lived to the age of ninety.

APPENDIX 1

Physical and Postal Attributes

What follows is a descriptive catalog of the letters, including the extent of each letter and whatever information appears on the address panels, where those exist. "Postmarks" include anything stamped on the paper. "Inscriptions" are those marks made by hand. All marks are in black ink unless otherwise indicated, with [R] for red or [B] for blue. I have done the best I can to record all details accurately, but many of the postmarks and inscriptions are worn and difficult to make out with certainty.

Alderson used a variety of different paper sizes, either folding them in half to create up to four pages on a single sheet or else treating a single sheet (even a very large sheet) as two pages. In some cases where there are six pages on two sheets, she has used both methods in a single letter. The address panel, where it exists, appears as a portion of one page, usually the last page, with Alderson's text covering most of the rest of that page (see figures 5, 7, 12). The age and condition of the paper has made it hard to give precise measurements: rounding to the quarter inch, as I have done, may suggest a greater degree of precision than can reliably be counted on. No effort was made to assess the type or quality of the paper, nor were any watermarks noticed.

Much might be learned from a close analysis of this material about the practice of sending and receiving letters, including the costs and the time elapsed from posting to delivery. A decrease in the time between American and English postmarks after the first years of the correspondence demonstrates the value of the newly introduced transatlantic steam packets. Several of the letters have been readdressed and sent on to new readers, illustrating the extended audience for immigrant writing. The remarkable appearance of postage stamps (Penny Reds) on some of the later letters marks one of the most important developments in nineteenth-century postal conventions and also illustrates the practice of forwarding, at a cost, a letter on to other potential readers.

Letter 1. Ht/7/5/8: 2 pp. 1 sheet: 4.75″×4.5″.

Letter 2. Ht/7/2/7. 8 pp. 2 sheets: 17″×20″.

Letter 3. Ht/7/4/8: 2 pp. 1 sheet: 9.75″×15″. Address: ~~Daniel Harrison / Temple Court / Liverpool~~ / Anna H. Readdressed: Ann Botham - / Care of Marg^{t} Abbott / Confectioners / Preston. Postmarks: PRESTON OC 25 1842; LIVERPOOL OC 28 1842 [R].

Letter 4. Ht/7/4/7: 4 pp. 1 sheet: 12.5″×14″. Address: Daniel Harrison / Temple Court / Liverpool / Old England / for A.B. & A.H. Postmarks: AMERICA L. Inscriptions: Paid 25d; to be forwarded by the first Packet; Boston Steam Packet; 'Oct 9 E Bethlehem Pa.'

Letter 5. Ht/7/4/1: 4 pp. 1 sheet: 12″×15.5″. Address: Daniel Harrison / Temple Place / Liverpool / Old England / D & A.H. Postmarks: BROWNSVILLE Pa DEC 20; AMERICA; PAID. Inscriptions: 8 9/4; 11 Month 30 42.

Letter 6. Ht/7/2/8: 4 pp. 1 sheet: 15″×15.5″. Address: Ann Botham / Margaret Abbott / Confectioner, Fisher Gate / Preston / Lancashire / Old England. Postmarks: AMERICA l.; PRESTON MR51843. Inscriptions: E. Bethlehem Pa / Feb 24; By first steam packet; Single Sheet; Paid 23—.

Letter 7. Ht/7/4/3: 4 pp. 1 sheet: 15″×15.5″. Address: Daniel Harrison / Temple Court / Liverpool / Old England / M & MA Harrison. Postmarks: AMERICA L. Inscriptions: Paid 25; Single Sheet; East Bethlehem Pa Mar 29 1847; By 1st steam packet. Notes: also includes "2 L" shapes on address panel.

Letter 8. Ht/7/2/9: 4 pp. 1 sheet: 11.75″×16″. Address: Danl Harrison / Temple Place / Liverpool / Old England. Postmarks: AMERICA L. Inscriptions: Paid; Paid 25; East Bethlehem Pa; April 19; Ann Botham; <2>.

Letter 9. Ht/7/2/10: 4 pp. 1 sheet: 16.5″×21.5″. Address: Ann Botham / Uttoxeter / Staffordshire / Old England. Postmarks: AMERICA L; Uttoxeter; JU 30 1843. Inscriptions: East Bethlehem Pa / May 30; By First Steam Packet; Paid 25.

Letter 10. Ht/7/4/2: 4 pp. 1 sheet: 16.75″×21.5″. Address: Danl Harrison / Temple Court / Liverpool / Old England/ D & A.H. Postmarks: JY 26 43 LIVERPOOL SHIP. Inscriptions: by the First Packet; 6 month 29.43; 8. Notes: includes floor plan of Aldersons' house.

Letter 11. Ht/7/2/11: 6 pp. 2 sheets: 16.5″×21″. Address: Ann Botham / Uttoxeter / Staffordshire / Old England. Postmarks: AMERICA L; UTTOXETER SP 14 1843; UTTOXETER OC 3 1843; Clapton No. 2D PAID [dark red]; A PAID 2 OCT 2 1843 [R]; BOSTON AUG 28 [R; appears to have been marked out with an ink scribble].

Letter 12. Ht/7/2/12: 4 pp. 1 sheet: 16.5″×21″. Address: Ann Botham / Uttoxeter / Staffordshire / Old England. Postmarks: 20 NO 43 LIVERPOOL SHIP; UTTOXETER NO 21 1843. Inscriptions:—; Single sheet.

Letter 13. Ht/7/1/62: 4 pp. 1 sheet: 16″×21″. Address: ~~Mary Howitt / Grange Upper Clapton / London / Old England~~. Readdressed: Mrs. Botham / Uttoxeter / Staffordshire. Postmarks: 20 NO 43 LIVERPOOL SHIP; UTTOXETER NO 28 1843; Clapton No 2D PAID; J PAID 27 NO 27 1843 [R]; 10 Fn 10 NO 21 1843 n [R]; J 21 NO 21 1843. Inscriptions: ~~Single~~; 9/7.

Letter 14. Ht/7/2/13: 4 pp. 1 sheet: 16″×20″. Address: Ann Botham / Uttoxeter / Staffordshire / Old England. Postmarks: Y 3 JA 3 1844 [R]; UTTOXETER JA 4 1844; SHIP LETTER. Notes: includes image of town crier with caption.

Letter 15. Ht/7/3/2: 4 pp. 1 sheet: 16.25″×18″. Address: Danl Harrison / ~~Temple Court / Liverpool / Old England / For Anna Harrison~~. Readdressed: Mrs [added in front of Danl Harrison] Price Street / Woodside / Birkenhead / Cheshire. Postmarks: Birkenhead JA 30 1844; 17 JA 44 LIVERPOOL SHIP; Clapton NO 2D PAID [R]; C PAID 29 JA 29 1844 [R]. Inscriptions: Paid.; 11 month 20 43.

Letter 16. Ht/7/2/14: 4 pp. 2 sheets: 5″×7″ and 7″×9″. Address: Ann Botham / Uttoxeter / Staffordshire / ~~Old England~~. Postmarks: UTTOXETER FE 27 1844; V PAID 5 MAR 5, 1844 [R]; UTTOXETER MR 6 1844 CLAPTON NO 1D PAID [dark red]; PORTSMOUTH SHIP LETTER. Inscriptions: ~~By the First Packet~~; Paid.

Letter 17. Ht/7/2/15: 4 pp. 1 sheet: 15″×19″. Address: Ann Botham / Uttoxeter / Staffordshire / England. Postmarks: 8 AP 44 LIVERPOOL SHIP; UTTOXETER AP 9 1844. Inscriptions: Single; <24>.

Letter 18. Ht/7/2/16: 4 pp. 1 sheet: 12.25″×16″. Address: Ann Botham / Uttoxeter / Staffordshire / Old England. Postmarks: 22 JU 44 LIVERPOOL SHIP; UTTOXETER JU 23 1844. Inscriptions: By the First Packet; Post Paid; 8; Per Pkt Ship Cambridge—1st June. Notes: "Plan of the City of Cincinnati" engraving on stationery.

Letter 19. Ht/7/2/17: 4 pp. 1 sheet: 12.25″×16″. Address: Ann Botham / Uttoxeter / Staffordshire / Old England. Postmarks: UTTOXETER JY 30 1844; 20 JY 44 LIVERPOOL SHIP. Inscription: 8. Notes: stationery is headed with engraving of "CINCINNATI. From mouth of Licking River Covington."

Letter 20. Ht/7/2/18: 4 pp. 1 sheet: 12.25″×16″. Address: Ann Botham / Uttoxeter / Staffordshire / Old England. Postmarks: UTTOXETER SP 13 1844; 12 SP 44 LIVERPOOL SHIP. Inscription: 8. Notes: view of Cincinnati engraving on stationery.

Letter 21. Ht/7/3/3: 4 pp. 1 sheet: 9.5×14.75. Address: Daniel Harrison / Temple Place / Liverpool / England / Anna Harrison. Postmark: 19 NO 44 LIVERPOOL SHIP. Inscription: <NH>. Note: includes sketch of "drinking gourd."

Letter 22. Ht/7/1/63: 4 pp. 1 sheet: 14″×19.5″. Address: ~~Mary Howitt / Upper Clapton / nr. London / England~~. Readdressed: Mrs Botham / Uttoxeter / Staffordshire. Postmarks: UTTOXETER DE 17 18; DE 44 LIVERPOOL SHIP; Clapton 2D PAID. A PAID 16 DE 16 1844 [R]; KH 5 DE 5 1844 [R]. Inscriptions: Paid; ~~8~~.

Letter 23. Ht/7/2/19: 4 pp. 1 sheet: 12.15″×18″. Address: Ann Botham / Uttoxeter / Staffordshire / England. Postmarks: PAID [R]; CINCINATTI O <??> [R]; UTTOXETER NO <??> 1844; AMERICA LIVERPOOL NO 29 1844. Inscriptions: By the First packet; 20; [indiscernible mark].

Letter 24. Ht/7/2/20: 4 pp. 1 sheet: 15″×19.5″. Address: Ann Botham / Uttoxeter / Staffordshire / Old England. Postmarks: UTTOXETER FE 3 1845; FE <??> 1845 LIVERPOOL SHIP. Inscriptions: P. Paid to Liverpool—; Per packet Stephen Whitney 11th Jan.

Letter 25. Ht/7/1/64: 4 pp. 1 sheet: 14.75″×19.5″. Address: Mary Howitt / Upper Clapton / nr. London. Postmarks: 26 MR 1845 LIVERPOOL SHIP; MZ 27 MR 27 1845 [R]. Inscriptions: By the First Packet; <??>.

Letter 26. Ht/7/2/21: 4 pp. 1 sheet: 15″×19.5″. Address: ~~Ann Botham / Uttoxeter / Staffordshire / England~~. Readdressed: Mrs. Harrison / Holt Hill / Birkenhead / Cheshire. Postmarks: UTTOXETER AP 12 1845; 11 AP 11 1845 [R]; Clapton NO <??>. PORTSMOUTH SHIP LETTER; IC 4 JU 4 1845; BIRKENHEAD JU 5 1845. Inscription: [indecipherable mark crossed out]. Notes: remnants of Penny Red stamp; indecipherable writing across the top of the address panel.

Letter 27. Ht/7/2/22: 4 pp. 1 sheet: 15″×19.5″. Address: Ann Botham / Uttoxeter / Staffordshire / England. Postmarks: 12 MAY 45 LIVERPOOL SHIP; PHILADELPHIA Pa. APR 15 [B]; UTTOXETER MY 14 1845; PAID [B] Inscriptions: By the first Packet via New York; 25 [B]; <24>.

Letter 28. Ht/7/2/23: 4 pp. 1 sheet: 15″×19.5″. Address: ~~Danl Harrison / Temple Place / Liverpool / for Ann Botham~~. Readdressed: Ann Botham / Balance Street / Uttoxeter / Staffordshire. Postmarks: BIRKENHEAD JU 15 1845; UTTOXETER JU 16 1845. Notes: two Penny Red stamps.

Letter 29. Ht/7/4/6: 4 pp. 1 sheet: 14″×19″. Address: William Howitt Esqr / The Elms, Clapton / nr London / England / for Anna Mary. Postmarks: 17 MY 1845 LIVERPOOL SHIP; NEW-YORK JUN 26 [R]; KS 18 JY 18 1845 [R]. Inscription: <??>.

Letter 30. Ht/7/3/4: 4 pp. 1 sheet: 14″×19″. Address: Anna Harrison / Danl Harrison / Temple Place / Liverpool. Inscriptions: Kindly conveyed by Francis Thompson; 7 mo 1845. Notes: includes calligraphic alphabet A-N on address panel.

Letter 31. Ht/7/2/24: 4 pp. 1 sheet: 15″×16″. Address: William Howitt / The Elms nr Clapton / London / England / for Ann Botham. Postmarks: CINCINNATI O. SEP 13 [R]; 15 OC 1845 LIVERPOOL SHIP; KR 16 OC 16 1845 [R]. Inscriptions: 10; 8.

Letter 32. Ht/7/5/5: 4 pp. 1 sheet: 12″×15.5″; continued on Ht/7/2/34: 4 pp. 1 sheet: 12″×15.5″.

Letter 33. Ht/7/2/26: 4 pp. 1 sheet: 12.5″×16″. Address: William Howitt / The Elms, Clapton / nr London / England / Ann Botham. Postmarks: YP 15 MR 15 1846 [R]; CINCINATTI O JAN <??> [R]. Inscriptions: Paid; By the first Steamer via Boston; 10 < 2>.

Letter 34. Ht/7/3/5: 4 pp. 1 sheet: 12.25″×16″. Address: Danl Harrison / Temple Place / Liverpool / for Anna. Inscriptions: indecipherable pencil writing, includes "Newport"; 11 mo 1845.

Letter 35. Ht/7/2/25: 4 pp. 1 sheet: 15″×16″. Address: William Howitt Esqr / Elms nr Clapton / nr London / Ann Botham. Postmarks: CINCINNATI O DEC 26 [R]; 5 A 1846 LIVERPOOL SHIP; KA 26 JA 26 1846 [R]. Inscriptions: 10; 8.

Letter 36. Ht/7/4/9: 4 pp. 1 sheet: 12.5″×16″. Address: William Howitt Esqr / Elms, Clapton / nr London / England. Postmarks: CINCINNATI O <??> [R]; IR 15 DE 15 1846 [R]. Inscriptions: By first Packet on Ship; 10; <2>.

Letter 37. Ht/18/1: 4 pp. 1 sheet: 10″×14″. Notes: image of a mouse.

Letter 38. Ht/18/2: 4 pp. 1 sheet: 12″×15.5″. Address: William Howitt / Elms, Clapton / nr London / England / For Charlton & Margaret. Postmarks: 27 FE 1846 LIVERPOOL SHIP; KO 28 FE 28 1846 [R]. Inscription: 8.

Letter 39. Ht/7/4/10: 4 pp. 1 sheet: 12.5″×16″; continued on Ht/7/1/65: 4 pp. 1 sheet: 12.25″×16″. Address: Mary Howitt / Elms Clapton / nr. London. Postmarks: CINCINNATI O MAR 23 [R]; 3 MAY 45 LIVERPOOL SHIP; AO 4 MY 1845 [R]; PAID [R]. Inscriptions: 10; &.

Letter 40. Ht/18/3: 4 pp. 1 sheet: 12.25″×16″.

Letter 41. Ht/7/2/27: 4 pp. 1 sheet: 12.5″×16″. Address: Ann Botham / William Howitt / Elms, Clapton / nr London. Postmarks: NEW-YORK APR 6 [R]; 6 MY 1846 LIVERPOOL SHIP; IT 7 MY 7 1846 [R]; star stamp. Inscription: 8.

Letter 42. Ht/18/4: 4 pp. 1 sheet: 12.25″×16″; continued on Ht/7/1/66: 2 pp. 1 sheet: 8″×12.25″. Address: Mary Howitt / The Elms Clapton / nr. London / England. Postmarks: CINCINNATI. O. APR 1 [R]; 5 MAY 1846 LIVERPOOL SHIP [R]; BS 6 MAY 6 1846 [R]; PAID [R]. Inscriptions: 10; M.&C.; 8.

Letter 43. Ht/7/1/67: 6 pp. 2 sheets: 12.25″×16″. Address: Mary Howitt / Elms Clapton / nr. London/ C&M. Postmarks: Philadelphia Pa. April 28 10 [B]; PA 15 MY 15 1846 [R]; PAID [B]. Inscriptions: 1.3 2;—; By the first ~~Packet~~ Steamer.

Letter 44. Ht/7/5/3: 2 pp. 1 sheet: 7.13″×12.25″; continued on Ht/7/1/69: 2 pp. 1 sheet: 7.13″×12.25″. Address: Mary Howitt / Elms, Clapton / nr. London / England. Postmarks: IA 15 JUL 15 1846 [R]. Inscription: <??>.

Letter 45. Ht/7/2/28: 6 pp. 2 sheets: 12.5″×16″. Address: Wm Howitt / Elms, Clapton / nr London / England / Ann Botham. Postmarks: 25 JY 1846 LIVERPOOL SHIP; AK 27 JY 27 1846 [R]. Inscription: 8.

Letter 46. Ht/7/5/4: 8 pp. 2 sheets: 13″×16″; continued on Ht/7/1/71: 4 pp. 1 sheet: 13″×16″. Address: Mary Howitt / Elms Clapton /nr. London / England. Postmarks: NEW-YORK JUL 15 5 PAID [R]; FP 1 AU 1 1846 [R]; indecipherable stamp [R]. Inscription: <??>.

Letter 47. Ht/7/1/68: 4 pp. 1 sheet: 12.5″×15.5″. Address: Mary Howitt / Elms Clapton / nr. London / England. Postmarks: Philadelphia Pa JUL 20 10 [B]; FZ 13 AU 13 1846 [R]; PAID [B]. Inscriptions: <2>; W [in red pencil].

Letter 48. Ht/7/3/6: 4 pp. 1 sheet: 12.5″×15.5″. Address: Danl Harrison / Temple Place / Liverpool / England / Anna Harrison. Postmarks: CINCINNATI O JUL 27 [R]; 21 AU 1848 LIVERPOOL SHIP; PAID [R]. Inscriptions: 10; 8; 8 mo 1846. Notes: also includes a sum of numbers.

Letter 49. Ht/7/2/29: 4 pp. 1 sheet: 12.5″×15.5″. Address: William Howitt Esqr / Elms, Clapton / nr London / England / for Ann Botham. Postmarks: PHILADELPHIA PA JUL 20 10 [B]; CZ 13 AU 13 1846 [R]; PAID [B]. Inscriptions: <2>; 8th Mo.; W [R pencil].

Letter 50. Ht/7/1/70: 4 pp. 1 sheet: 12.5″×15.5″. Address: Mary Howitt / Elms, Clapton / nr. London / England. Postmarks: CINCINNATI [R]; GEV 6 SP 28 1846 [R]; SHIP LETTER [R]; PAID [R]. Inscriptions: 10; 8.

Letter 51. Ht/7/1/73: 4 pp. 1 sheet: 12.5″×15″. Address: Mary Howitt / Elms Clapton / nr. London / England. Postmarks: CINCINNATI. O. SEP 4 [R]; AS 5 OC 5 1846 [R]; PORTSMOUTH SHIPLETTER; PAID [R]; <??> [R]. Inscriptions: 10; 8.

Letter 52. Ht/7/5/1: 4 pp. 1 sheet: 12.25″×15″; continued on Ht/7/1/74: 4 pp. 1 sheet: 12.25″×15″. Address: Mary Howitt / Elms Clapton / nr. London / England. Postmarks: CINCINNATI. O. SEP 28 [R]; AR 3 NO 3 1846 [R]; KINGSBRIDGE/SHIPLETTER; PAID [R]. Inscriptions: ~~20~~; <??>.

Letter 53. Ht/7/2/30: 4 pp. 1 sheet: 12.25″×15.5″. Address: William Howitt / Elms, Clapton / nr London / England / Ann Botham. Postmarks: CINCINNATI O SEPT 23 [R]; AR 3 NO 3 1846 [R]; KINGSBRIDGE SHIP LETTER; PAID [R]. Inscriptions: 8; 10.

Letter 54. Ht/7/2/31: 4 pp. 1 sheet: 12.5″×15.5″. Address: Ann Botham / William Howitt Esqr / Elms, Clapton / nr London / England. Postmarks: SHIP LETTER [R]; GEN6 SP 28 1846 [R]; CINCINNATI O AUG 30 [R]; PAID [R]. Inscriptions: [three unidentifiable marks].

Letter 55. Ht/7/1/75: 6 pp. 2 sheets: 12.25″×15.5″. Address: Mary Howitt / Elms, Clapton / nr. London / England. Postmarks: CINCINNATI. O. OCT 25 [R]; LYMINGTON SHIP I.RE; LYMINGTON JA 2 1847; LH JA 3 1847 [R]; PAID [R]. Inscription: <??>.

Letter 56. Ht/7/5/6: 2 pp. 1 sheet: 7.75″×12.25″; continued on Ht/7/1/76: 4 pp. 1 sheet: 7.75″×12.25″. Address: Mary Howitt / Elms Clapton / nr. London / England. Postmarks: 29 DE 1846 LIVERPOOL SHIP: GAN 3 DECEMBER 30, 1846; GA 30 DE 30 1846 [R]; <??>; PAID [R]. Inscriptions: <??>; By the first Packet; 20.

Letter 57. Ht/7/3/7: 4 pp. 1 sheet: 12.5″×15.5″. Address: Daniel Harrison & Co / Temple Place / Liverpool / England / Anna Harrison. Postmarks: AMERICA LIVERPOOL DE 1 1846; CINCINNATI O NO 22 [R]; PAID [R]. Inscriptions: 1st Steamer via Boston; Au^{t} 1845 [B].[1]

Letter 58. Ht/7/2/32: 4 pp. 1 sheet: 12.25″×15.5″. Address: Ann Botham / Wm Howitt / Elms, Clapton / nr London / England. Postmarks: CINCINNATI O <??> [R]; AQ 1 JAN 1 1847 [R]; SHIP LETTER; PAID [R]. Inscriptions: By the first Packet; 8; 10.

Letter 59. Ht/7/2/33: 4 pp. 1 sheet: 7″×12.25″. Address: Ann Botham / Wm Howitt / Elms, Clapton / nr London / England. Postmarks: CINCINNATI O JAN 22 [R];16 FE LIVERPOOL SHIP <??> 1847; PAID [R]; AE 17 FE 17 1847 [R]. Inscriptions: 8; 10.

Letter 60. Ht/7/5/2: 4 pp. 1 sheet: 12.25″×15.5″.

Letter 61. Ht/7/1/77: 4 pp. 1 sheet: 12.5″×15.75″. Address: Mary Howitt / Elms Clapton / nr. London / England. Postmarks: CINCINNATI O FEB 2 <8> [R]; MARCH <??> 1847 [R]; SHIPLETTER; PAID [R]. Inscriptions: 8; 10.

Letter 62. Ht/7/5/7: 2 pp. 1 sheet: 5.5″×8″. Notes: documented as incomplete.

Letter 63. Ht/7/4/4: 4 pp. 1 sheet: 12.25″×15.5″. Address: Danl Harrison & Co / Temple Place / Liverpool / England / For Mary & Margaret Ann. Postmarks: 26 AP 1847 LIVERPOOL SHIP; CINCINNATI O MAR 23 [R]; PAID [R]. Inscriptions: 10; 8. April 1847.

Letter 64. Ht/7/2/35: 4 pp. 1 sheet: 7″×10″.

Letter 65. Ht/7/2/36: 4 pp. 1 sheet: 12.25″×15.5″. Address: Ann Botham / Wm Howitt / Elms Clapton / nr London / England. Postmarks: CINCINNATI O APR 2<??> [R]; SHIP LETTER; AL 27 MY 27 1847 [R]; PAID [R]. Inscriptions: 8; ~~10~~.

Letter 66. Ht/7/2/37: 4 pp. 1 sheet: 12.25″×15.5″. Address: Wm Howitt / Ann Botham / Elms Clapton / nr London / England. Postmarks: 3 AN 3 JU 29 1847 [R]; CINCINANTI O MAY 24 [R]; SHIP LETTER [R]; PAID [R]; HM 29 JU 29 1847 [R]; <??>; <??>. Inscriptions: 10; 8.

Letter 67. Ht/7/2/38: 4 pp. 1 sheet: 12.25″×14.25″. Address: Ann Botham / Wm Howitt / Elms, Clapton / nr London / England. Postmarks: CINCINNATI O JUL 9 10 [R]; AD 7 AU 7 1847 [R]; SHIP LETTER KINGSBRIDGE; PAID [R]. Inscription: 8.

Letter 68. Ht/7/1/78: 4 pp. 1 sheet: 13″×16″. Address: Mary Howitt / Elms Clapton / nr. London / England. Postmarks: CINCINNATI O JUL 26 [R]; HB 14 AU 14 1847 [R]; 3 AN3 AU 14 1847 [R]; PAID [R]. Inscriptions: 20; <21>; By the first packet.

Letter 69. Ht/7/2/39: 4 pp. 1 sheet: 12.5″×16″. Address: Ann Botham / Elms, Clapton / nr London / England. Postmarks: CINCINNATI O JU 26 10 [R]; SHIP LETTER; AP 31 AU 31 1847 [R]; PAID [R]. Inscription: 8. Notes: consists of two separate letters: one to mother, one to Mary Howitt.

Letter 70. Ht/7/3/8: 4 pp. 1 sheet: 15″×19.5″. Address: Danl Harrison & Co / Temple Place / Liverpool / England / Anna Harrison. Postmarks: CINCINNATI O AUG 26 [R]; 25 SP 1847 LIVERPOOL SHIP; PAID [R]. Inscriptions: 20; <??>; 8 mo 1847.

Letter 71. Ht/7/1/79: 4 pp. 1 sheet: 12.5″×16″. Address: Mary Howitt / Elms, Clapton / nr. London / England. Postmarks: <??> October 10 10 [R]; FO 29 OC 29 1847 [R]; PAID [R]; <??>; <??>. Inscriptions: 1st Steamer via Boston; <2>. Notes: illustration of bluebird houses.

Letter 72. Ht/7/2/40: 4 pp. 1 sheet: 13″×16″. Address: Ann Botham / Wm Howitt / Elms, Clapton / nr London / England. Postmarks: CINCINNATI OCT 10 10 [R]; FJ 29 OCT 29 1847 [R]; PAID [R]. Inscriptions: 1st Steamer via Boston; By the first Packet; <2>.

Letter 73. Ht/7/1/80: 4 pp. 1 sheet: 12.5″×16″. Address: Mary Howitt / Elms Clapton / nr. London / England. Postmarks: CINCINNATI O NOV 25 10 [R]; AP 30 DE 30 1847 [R]; SHIP LETTER PLYMOUTH; PAID. Note: includes sketch of tortoises.

Letter 74. Ht/7/1/81: 4 pp. 1 sheet: 5″×8″.

Letter 75. Ht/7/8/3: 4 pp. 1 sheet: 10″×16″. Address: Ann Botham / William Howitt / The Elms / nr Clapton ~~Clapham~~ / near London. Postmarks: FE 17 JAN 17 1848 [R]; JA 17 1848 [R]; CINCINNATI O DEC 24 10 [R]; PAID [R]; <??>; <??>. Inscriptions: By 1st Steamer; <2>.

APPENDIX 2

Directory of Names

Many of the names in a collection of personal correspondence will forever remain obscure. This directory includes some basic biographical information about everyone for whom information could be located. Where an individual's name changed through marriage, she is listed under whatever name was used during the period of 1842 to 1847. Alternate names and spellings are given in parentheses with name-equivalents from *Our Cousins in Ohio* (*OCO*) in italics along with the page numbers from the first London edition of that book. Due to the frequency of their appearance, no page numbers are given for members of the immediate family or for Richard Alderson, Elizabeth Alderson, Mary Crehoe, William, Joseph, or the Ketts. At the end, I have also listed place names that were changed in *Our Cousins*. All names for which no additional information can be given are omitted. For more information about Aldersons, Howitts, and Harrisons, see the epilogue. For many of the better-known names, I have given relatively little information, trusting that readers can look up information themselves online, in the *Oxford Dictionary of National Biography* (*ODNB*), *American National Biography Online* (*ANBO*), *Encyclopaedia Britannica*, or elsewhere.

Adams, John Quincy (1767–1848). Sixth president of the United States (1825–1829); visited Cincinnati in October 1843, a few months after the Aldersons' arrival.

Albright, Thomas (ca. 1781–1848). Emigrated from England in the early 1840s; wife, Sarah, died 1844; father of Agnes (b. ca. 1831); Thomas died at his home in Hannibal, Missouri, February 20, 1848.[1]

Alderson, Agnes (1839–1925; *Florence*). Oldest surviving daughter of Harrison and Emma; returned to England in 1860.

Alderson, Alice Ann (Annie; 1844–ca. 1855; *Cornelia, Nelly*). Youngest daughter of Harrison and Emma; at the time of her death, she was living with her aunt Anna Harrison in Surrey, England.

Alderson, Ann. Wife of Ralph Alderson; American born; had one daughter by a previous marriage and another with Ralph. After the death of Ralph, she lived for a time with Harrison and Emma.

Alderson, Anna Mary (Nanny; 1841–1934; *Anna, Nanny*). Second surviving daughter of Harrison and Emma; returned to England in the 1850s.

Alderson, Elizabeth (1808–1853). Harrison's sister; emigrated with Emma and Harrison in 1843 but returned to England shortly before her death.

Alderson, Mary. Daughter of Ralph and Ann.

Alderson, Ralph (1796–1843). Harrison's brother, in 1842 residing in Beallsville, Pennsylvania; married to American-born Ann; in 1843, after Ralph's death, Ann moved to Cincinnati to join her brother-in-law's family.

Alderson, Richard (1828–1889; *Cousin Michael*). Son of Harrison's brother Daniel and Mary Speight; emigrated with Emma and Harrison in 1843 and died in Kenosha, Wisconsin.

Alderson, Samuel Botham (1847–1848). Infant son of Harrison and Emma; his birth was followed by fatal complications for his mother.

Alderson, William Charles (1837–1914; *William, Willy*). Second child (first surviving child) of Harrison and Emma.

Allen, John (1790–1859). Born and died in Liskeard, Cornwall; an Elder and an active member of Bible, antislavery, and peace societies. Allen was one of a delegation (along with George Stacey and William and Josiah Forster) sent from London Yearly Meeting in 1845 to urge the return of the "Anti-Slavery Friends," led by Charles Osborn and Levi Coffin, to the main body of Orthodox Friends.[2] Allen published various pamphlets and books on baptism, church and state, and peace; also published a local history of Liskeard.[3]

Annie (*Julia 59–61*). Elizabeth Shipley's servant.

Astle, Martha (b. ca. 1799). English friend of the Bothams; forbidden to wear fancy clothes by their strict Quaker father, the Botham sisters sewed frocks for Martha (who was not good at sewing), vicariously experiencing through her the social life they were denied;[4] James Astle might have been her brother.

Bales, Thomas (probably d. 1801, *"an old 'ministering Friend'"* [29–31]). Minister from North Carolina; in 1782 became one of the first Quaker emigrants to settle in Ohio.[5] Howitt expands on Alderson's own account of Bales.

Barbauld, Anna Laetitia (1743–1825). Poet, educator, essayist, and literary critic with liberal Unitarian religious views; associated at the end of her life with a circle of radical intellectuals (*ODNB*).

Basset, Johnathan. Patternmaker; according to the 1850 Cincinnati directory, lived about 1.5 miles southeast of Cedar Lodge near the Ohio River on Broadway Street near what is now East Liberty Street.[6]

Bates, Elisha (1781–1861). Member of Short Creek Monthly Meeting of Ohio Yearly Meeting from 1817 and a minister from 1822. Bates opposed Elias Hicks and went on to take an ultra-Orthodox (evangelical) position in support of Isaac Crewdson and the "Beaconite" movement in Manchester, England. Bates is reported to have been the first Quaker minister to receive water baptism and was disowned by American Friends in 1837. He joined the Methodists and became a minister of that denomination until his membership was revoked there, too. Later in life he resumed attendance at Short Creek Monthly Meeting but did not seek to restore his membership.[7]

Bayliffe, Alice Lucy (1833–1847), daughter of Edward Bayliffe (1793–1855) and Lucy Lythall Bayliffe (1792–1852), granddaughter of Mary Shipley Bayliffe (1752–1792). Died at age fourteen on April 1, 1847, in Birkenhead, England (Obituary of Alice Lucy Bayliffe, *Annual Monitor for 1848, or Obituary of the Members of the Society of Friends in Great Britain and Ireland, for the Year 1847*, n.s., 6 [1848]).

Bayliffe, Lucy (1792–1852; see Bayliffe, Alice Lucy above). Anna Harrison's youngest daughter was named Emma Lucy Harrison, after Emma Alderson and Lucy Bayliffe.[8]

Bell, Mary and Dorothy. Girlhood friends of the Botham sisters, who were impressed with the Bells' learning, sophistication, and generosity in lending them literature, including, according to Mary Howitt, "the first novel we ever read."[9]

Bemoe, John (b. ca. 1825; *in OCO* 86–87; last name given only in the English editions). Seminole, educated in Philadelphia and converted to Christianity; returned to Seminoles ca. 1846. No other information available.

Benezet, Anthony (1713–1784). Educator and abolitionist, friend of John Woolman. Benezet was born in St. Quentin, France, but fled Huguenot persecution to Rotterdam, London (where he became a Quaker), and then Philadelphia in 1731. Benezet taught in Germantown and at William Penn Charter School (for 12 years) but then dedicated his life to bringing education to those who might not otherwise receive it, including girls, African Americans, and low-income white children. With Woolman, Benezet let Philadelphia Yearly Meeting to make any dealing in slaves grounds for disownment and in 1775 became the first president of the Society for the Relief of Free Negroes Unlawfully Held in Bondage, which later became the Pennsylvania Society for the Abolition of Slavery. Benezet was influential with abolition movements worldwide.[10]

Bonsal, Jane (b. ca. 1834; *Felicia Bower*). From Cincinnati, friend of the Alderson children; probably a misspelling of Bonsall, an extended Quaker family from Pennsylvania.

Botham, Charles (1808–1825). Emma Alderson's only brother and the youngest of the four children; ran away to sea and died from an injury incurred during his first voyage.

Bragg, Thomas and Alice (or Annie). Immigrants to Cincinnati; Thomas Bragg was brother of Rebecca Martindale; Alice Bragg was sister of William Boodle; nothing more is known of them.

Burritt, Elihu (1810–1879). Non-Quaker evangelist, temperance advocate, abolitionist, and reformer; published the *Christian Citizen*, a weekly reformist newspaper, 1844–1851; in June 1846 founded League of Universal Brotherhood, strongly supported by Quakers, to promote world peace and universal brotherhood; as postal reformer, advocated penny postage for overseas letters as a means of promoting world peace (*ANBO*).

Clay, Henry (1777–1852). Senator from Kentucky, secretary of state under John Quincy Adams, unsuccessful presidential candidate in 1832 (National Republican Party) and 1844 (Whig Party).

Cloud, Joseph (1742–1816). Orthodox Quaker minister, among the founders of the Miami Monthly Meeting of Indiana Yearly Meeting. From 1802 to 1804, he traveled, visiting meetings in England, Scotland, Ireland, and Wales. During that time he may have met Ann Botham, whom Alderson thanks for an account of his life.[11]

Cook, Charity (1774–1835). Quaker minister from Bush River in Newberry County, South Carolina; traveled extensively in America, Britain, and the continent, including Germany, where she was jailed for holding a Quaker meeting; later moved to Caesar's Creek in Ohio.

Cope, Thomas Pim (probably 1768–1854). Philadelphia Quaker merchant, very active in civic affairs as, for example, President of Board of Trade and the Mercantile Library, member of Philadelphia City Council, Pennsylvania legislature, and the convention to amend Pennsylvania's constitution (1837). Helped create Fairmount Park and build a water supply for Philadelphia from the Schuylkill River. Established a packet line between Philadelphia and Liverpool, including the *Shenandoah*, on which the Aldersons sailed to America. Mentioned by Alderson for his assistance conveying letters and parcels between Aldersons and family in England. Cope's grandson Thomas Pim Cope (1823–1900) was employed in and later assumed ownership of the elder Cope's business.[12]

Corder, Susanna (1787–1864). Quaker minister, elder, biographer, and progressive educator; author of *Life of Elizabeth Fry* (1853) and other books on Friends, education, and women's ministry. She was first a teacher at Suire Island School in Ireland until 1824, when she joined other Friends in establishing a new Quaker school for girls in Stoke Newington (now in the London borough of Hackney). Corder was among those who signed the letter disowning John Wilkinson for his outspoken participation in the Beaconite schism in Manchester, led by Isaac Crewdson.[13]

Crehoe, Mary (*Madame Leonard*). The name also appears as Creole, and on the plot map it appears as Crehore just west of Cedar Lodge on the road to Warsaw; husband James Crehoe has no equivalent in *OCO*; no additional information is known (see figures 18 and 10).

Crewdson, Isaac (1780–1844). Staunchly evangelical Quaker; published *A Beacon to the Society of Friends* (1835), criticizing Friends for placing the authority of the inner light above the authority of the scripture. The following year he resigned from the Society of Friends to form the Free Evangelical Friends in Manchester, also known as the Beaconites. Unlike more moderate evangelical Friends, Crewdson urged and practiced water baptism. The group dispersed into other denominations after Crewdson's death (*ODNB*).

Crosfield, George (erroneously spelled Crossfield; 1785–1847). Father of Joseph Crosfield; Conservative English Quaker; close friend, supporter, and correspondent with John Wilbur, the most famous of those who opposed the evangelical teachings of Joseph John Gurney. His work, *Some Letters to Friends on some of the Primitive Doctrines of Christianity* (1832) became a seminal work for Conservative Friends. Crosfield's name appears as one of the witnesses on the Aldersons' marriage certificate.[14]

Crosfield, Joseph (erroneously spelled Crossfield; 1821–1879). Son of George Crosfield (1785–1847) and nephew of Joseph Crosfield (1792–1844); employed by Daniel Harrison in the firm of Harrison and Waterhouse; later a partner with Daniel and Smith Harrison in Harrisons and Crossfield; also a Quaker minister, who traveled in the United States in 1845 and 1865.

Douglas, Cornelius (1798–1885). Quaker minister from Vassalboro Monthly Meeting in Maine; attended 1845 Indiana Yearly Meeting; in 1846 moved with wife Phebe and two children (Lydia and Mary) to Springfield, Ohio, and then to Richmond, Indiana, in 1847, where he oversaw Friends Boarding School (later Earlham College) for six months; in 1850 moved to Kansas City, where he succeeded Thomas Wells as superintendent of the Shawnee Mission School.[15]

Douglass, Frederick (1818–1895). Escaped slave and leader in the American abolition movement; autobiography published in 1845; publisher of antislavery *North Star* (beginning 1847).

Driesbach, "Herr" Jacob (1807–1877; in *OCO 269*). From upstate New York, billed as "the unrivalled animal Subduer," was the most famous lion tamer in the United States in the 1849s. Performed around Europe and the United States from 1830 to 1854; said to be the first to perform with a tame leopard.

Ecroyd, Ann (1780–1859). Quaker philanthropist and elder from Marsden in northeast Lancashire.[16]

Emlen, Sara[h] (ca. 1787–1849). Wife of James Emlen; member of Birmingham and (formerly) Chester Monthly Meeting. As a minister of the Society of Friends, she traveled throughout Britain and Ireland in 1844.[17]

Evans, Joseph (b. 1840), George (b. 1838), and William (b. 1834). Sons of Thomas Evans (1791–1852) and Elizabeth Robinson (b. 1802); friends of William Charles, living in Waynesville, Ohio. Thomas and, later, Joseph chaired the Earlham College Board of Trustees.[18]

Evans, William. This is likely the prominent Philadelphia minister (1787–1867), who, along with his father, Jonathan, led the evangelical movement in Philadelphia Yearly Meeting. Not surprisingly, the two were among the fiercest critics of Elias Hicks.[19]

Far, Thomas, Emma, Robert, Eliza, Alice, Henry, Elizabeth, Edward, Mary, and Isabella. Fellow passengers on the *Shenandoah*.

Fish, Susan (1830–1871). Fish was left an orphan when her parents, Abigail Sanford and William Fish, died in 1832 and 1833. Fish attended the Friends' Shawnee Mission School near Kansas City and in 1847 married Lauren Baldwin Maltbie of Warren, Ohio.[20]

Flower, Eliza. Possibly (1803–1846) the radical Unitarian composer and domestic partner of the minister William James Fox, who traveled in circles that included Mary Howitt. Flower left no writings about life in America, as suggested by the one reference in these letters. The two might have been introduced by Howitt, but their religious differences would have created difficulty for Alderson. Another possibility is Eliza Julia Flower (1792?–1862), wife of George Flower, who (along with Morris Birkbeck) was instrumental in establishing two English settlements in Illinois, along the lines of Robert Owen's New Harmony community across the river in Indiana, during the second through fourth decades of the nineteenth century. Nothing of E. J. Flower's was published during Alderson's lifetime, and there is no other indication of her having known Alderson.[21]

Forster, Josiah (1782–1870). One of the leading members of London and Middlesex Quarterly Meeting, especially in relation to Friends in other countries, serving for more than fifty years on the London Yearly Meeting committee appointed to correspond with Friends abroad. Later (1853–4), he formed one of a delegation (including his brother William) to present an address from London to the president of the United States on the subject of slavery (*DQB*).

Forster, William (ca. 1786–1854). Quaker minister from about the age of twenty-one; born in Tottenham, near London, he lived in Norwich (1837–1854) and Bridport in Dorset (1816–1837). In 1843 cofounded the *Friend*, a more evangelical alternative to the new *British Friend* recently begun in Glasgow. Beginning in 1820, he frequently made religious visits to North American meetings, spending a total of more than five years on such trips. On his last visit to America he became ill and died in Tennessee at the age of 70. See Allen, John, above.[22]

Fox, Maria (1793–1844). English Quaker minister whose life, travels, and ministry are recounted in *Memoirs of Maria Fox* (London, 1846).

Frankland, Agnes (1830–1908). Born in Liverpool to Thomas and Sarah Frankland. Harrison and Elizabeth Alderson attended her marriage to Samuel Murphy Haughton in 1849.

Frankland, Thomas (b. 1799) and Sarah (née Greenwood) (1808–1868). Emigrated to Cincinnati from the north of England around 1846. Thomas was a Quaker minister and drysalter (a dealer in various chemical goods), but was disowned at some point by the Society of Friends;[23] Sarah was a minor poet and editor, best known for her anthology *Literary Leaves* (1838), which includes several poems by the Howitts (as would have been expected at that time). Although Thomas spoke out at 1836 London Yearly Meeting against the Gurneyite push for scriptural authority, Alderson demonstrates a strong affection for this couple.[24]

Friar, Ellen. Fellow passenger on the *Shenandoah*.

Fry, Elizabeth Gurney (1780–1845). English Quaker minister and prison reformer; sister of Joseph John Gurney (*ODNB*).

Gillingham, Francis. Abolitionist from Massachusetts; nothing more is known.

Graham, Sylvester (1794–1851). Presbyterian minister turned temperance and nutrition activist; promoted vegetarianism and the consumption of fresh vegetables, fruits, and whole grains as physiological and spiritual imperatives (*ANBO*).

Griffith, Amos (ca. 1794–1871) and Edith (ca. 1801–1873). Orthodox Friends in Pennsylvania, associated with Ohio Yearly Meeting. Members of Westland Monthly Meeting, the Griffiths seem to have attended Pike Run Meeting for Worship, a subordinate meeting to Westland Monthly Meeting and, according to various sources, more specifically with Westland and Redstone Monthly Meetings and Pike Run Meeting (overseen by Westland Monthly Meeting). Jacob Griffith, perhaps Amos's father, had been instrumental in purchasing the land for the Westland meetinghouse in 1797. In the 1850s, when the meeting ceased, the Griffith family were the only remaining members.[25] In 1854, they and their four children (George, Mary, Amos, and Edith) transferred from Westland Monthly Meeting to Redstone Monthly Meeting. At her death, Edith was a Minister of Short Creek Monthly Meeting in Ohio.[26]

Gurney, Joseph John (1788–1847). English banker and Quaker minister; principal leader of the evangelical movement among Quakers, beginning with London Yearly Meeting's epistle of 1836. His ministry during a prolonged tour of the United States led to the second major split in American Friends, between the so-called Orthodox or Gurneyites and the Conservatives or Wilburites (see page 110).

Harrison, Anna Botham (1797–1882). Eldest daughter of Samuel and Ann Botham; married to Harrison, Daniel (1795–1873), lived in Liverpool during Alderson's time in America.

Harrison, Daniel (1795–1873). Husband of Anna Botham Harrison, first cousin to Harrison Alderson. Daniel Harrison's name appears as one of the witnesses on the Aldersons' marriage certificate.

Harrison, John (1796–1852). No clear relationship to Daniel Harrison (Alderson's brother-in-law through her sister Anna and Harrison Alderson's cousin). A friend and supporter of John Wilbur, who writes fondly of him and includes some of his correspondence in his Journal. Harrison published a *Vindication of the Society of Friends against the Calumnies of Apostates and False Brethren* (1839), condemning Elisha Bates, John Wilkinson, and others among Isaac Crewdson's Beaconite movement. Although no great supporter of the Beaconites, Alderson would not have appreciated his and Caleb Haworth's tract (reprinted from the Philadelphia *Friend*) asking the question "Is it Proper to Call the Holy Scriptures 'the Word of God,'" in which they suggested that to do so verged on idolatry.[27]

Harrison, Margaret Ann (1827–1899). Second of Daniel and Anna's eight children.

Harrison, Mary (1825–1898). Daniel and Anna's eldest child.

Harrison, Richard (1807–ca. 1863). Daniel Harrison's brother; emigrated ca. 1846 to Ohio with wife and children; thought to have died fighting for the Union in the Civil War.

Harrison, Thompson (Cousin Thompson; b. 1813; *Cousin Israel Hopper 213–214*). Daniel Harrison's brother; around 1823 emigrated to America, where he worked for abolition with William Lloyd Garrison; later fell on hard times and then lost what he had left through his involvement with the Fourierist Ohio Phalanx; moved to Louisiana and became a supporter of the Confederacy. In *OCO*, Howitt omits the account of his financial ruin in the Ohio Phalanx, related elsewhere in Alderson's letters. His character's name is curiously similar to Isaac Hopper, a Hicksite and abolitionist who was disowned by his meeting in 1841 for taking too prominent a role in non-Quaker abolition movements.[28]

Hart, Thomas (d. 1813). Uttoxeter banker and Quaker (and sympathizer with the French Revolution), noted by Howitt for his ideas on the second coming and a utopian "new day of human brotherhood."[29]

Harvey, Jesse (1808–1848) and Elizabeth Burgess (1801–1888). Orthodox Friends, originally from North Carolina and Virginia, respectively. Founders of (among other educational ventures) the Harveysburg Free Black School in 1831 with financial support of Grove Monthly Meeting. Jesse was a physician and the brother of William Harvey, who laid out the village in 1828 and for whom it was named. Elizabeth was the principal teacher in the school, which continued until 1909, when it was absorbed by the Massie Township school system. According to some sources, the school was opened at the request of a Southern planter, Stephen Wall, who wanted to give his mixed-race children a decent education. In 1847, Jesse Harvey moved west to superintend the Quaker Shawnee Mission School near Kansas City, about which Alderson frequently writes. After her husband's death, Elizabeth stayed on for two years as superintendent before returning to Ohio.[30]

Haworth, Caleb (1792–1879). Appears to have been a supporter of John Wilbur and opponent of Joseph John Gurney. From Marsden, attended Ackworth School until 1809 (Ackworth School Catalogue). See John Harrison.

Haynes, Eli and Phoebe. Brownsville, Pennsylvania, Friends, formerly from Maine. In 1815, Eli was a teacher in 1815 in Bridgeport, a borough just west of Brownsville on the Monongahela River.[31]

Henry, the Dutchman (*Bernard, the German Labourer 205–207, 210, 259, 282, 288, 290, 294*).

Hilles, David (1785–1837). Son of William Hilles and Rebecca Pugh; married Hannah Dingee (ca. 1783–1837) in 1811; family split by the Hicksite-Orthodox schism. At the 1828 Redstone Quarterly Meeting, where the separation took place, David Hilles became the first men's clerk of Ohio Yearly Meeting (Hicksite), but he was disowned a few years later for disorderly conduct.[33] The events described by Alderson must have taken place sometime after this disownment.

Hoag, Elizabeth. See Meader, John.

Hoag, Lindley Murray (1808–1880). Highly active American Quaker minister, influential in the growth of Quakerism in Norway; later settled in Iowa; sister of Elizabeth Meader and son of Quaker minister Joseph Hoag (1762–1846). In 1831, Hoag married another Quaker minister, Hulda Varney, who died in 1843. He traveled for religious purposes over much of the United States and Europe. He helped establish and was a member for much of his life of Rocksylvania Monthly Meeting in Iowa Falls.[34]

Hodgson, Thomas (1800–1869). English acquaintance (especially, perhaps, of the Harrisons) from Lancaster whose brother visited the Aldersons in Philadelphia soon after their arrival. The Hodgsons' father and his brothers reportedly moved to Lancaster after being expelled from home for having joined the Society of Friends.[35]

Howard, John (1726?–1790). British philanthropist and prison reformer, a non-Quaker dissenter without strong ties to any particular denomination; worked to provide salaries for jailers, who until that time had relied on fees from inmates, a practice that frequently kept individuals in jail even after an acquittal if they could not pay these sometimes exorbitant fees (*ODNB*).

Howitt, Alfred William (1830–1908). William and Mary's oldest surviving son; in 1852 traveled with his father and brother to Australia, where he lived for the rest of his life, making important contributions to the fields of anthropology and geology.

Howitt, Anna Mary (1824–1884). William and Mary's older daughter, an artist; later married Alfred Alaric Watts; produced four illustrations (including the frontispiece) for the English editions of *OCO*. See figures 26–29.

Howitt, Claude Middleton (1833–1844). William and Mary's second son, whose painful death stemming from a seemingly insignificant injury a year earlier in Europe led to a great deal of anguish and self-reflection on the part of his mother.[36]

Howitt, Godfrey (1800–1864). Physician and youngest brother of William Howitt; emigrated to Australia; married Phoebe Bakewell (1806–1864).

Howitt, Herbert Charlton (1838–1863). William and Mary's youngest son; in 1860 emigrated to New Zealand, where he drowned three years later exploring the interior of the country.

Howitt, Margaret Anastasia (1839–1930). William and Mary's younger daughter, who later edited her mother's autobiography. Margaret and Herbert are the principal characters in Mary Howitt's *The Children's Year.*

Howitt, Mary Botham (1799–1888). Sister of Emma Alderson; prolific translator, poet, and author, mostly of books for children and young people; translated Fredrika Bremer and Hans Christian Andersen.

Howitt, William (1792–1879). Husband of Mary Howitt; prolific author of books on politics, religion, natural history, history, and more; publisher and editor of the *People's Journal* and then *Howitt's Journal.*

Hubbard, Jeremiah (1775–1848). Clerk of North Carolina Yearly Meeting for sixteen years and agent in the founding of New Garden Friends boarding school, with would later become Guilford College; Hubbard moved in 1837 to the vicinity of Richmond, Indiana. Some sources assign Hubbard Cherokee ancestry through his maternal grandmother, but the claim has been formally denied by the Cherokee Nation. Hubbard is most famous for having accompanied Chief Ross and a Cherokee delegation to Washington, D.C., to meet with President Andrew Jackson.[37]

Hudson (Mr.) (*Mr. Henderson 89, 114*). The "coloured preacher" who gave the sermon at Dr. Jack's funeral. A Baptist minister by the name of Henderson (no first name) is listed in the 1825 Cincinnati directory;[32] no such individual is noted in the 1850 directory.

Hughes, Gideon (d. 1852). Quaker and successful businessman from New Lisbon, Ohio; in 1808 constructed one of the first furnaces in Ohio for smelting iron, the remains of which are still visible at Boy Scout Camp McKinley; elected to board of directors for Columbiana Bank of New Lisbon in 1814. Hughes served in Ohio State Senate from 1821 to 1823. Around 1830, financial problems forced him out of business, and he moved to Lebanon, Ohio, where he joined the Shakers.[38]

Icles, Louis. Friend of William Charles, son of the Aldersons' butcher and veterinarian. The 1850 Cincinnati directory gives a Charles Icles as a resident of Western Avenue.[39]

Isabella (no surname; *Henrietta 239–243*). Newly arrived from England with her brother, Thomas (*Frank*).

Jack (Dr. & Mrs.). See Kett.

John (*Carl, Old Carl 93–94, 98*). German neighbor and laborer who sometimes worked for the Aldersons.

Jones, Ann (née Burgess; 1774–1846). With husband, George (d. 1841), among the most forceful English proponents of evangelicalism to visit meetings in America. So confrontational was their approach when they visited in 1826 that they sometimes almost provoked riots and at least once drew the police.[40] Later, the couple provoked the ire of Orthodox Friends, including Joseph John Gurney, with accusations that they encouraged "carnal wisdom" and "head knowledge, . . . despising Christ in his inward and spiritual appearance."[41]

Jones, Eli (1807–1890) and Sybil (1808–1873); Quaker ministers, born in Maine, traveled extensively in Europe, North America, Africa, and the Middle East; founded schools in Ramallah, Palestine, and Brummana, Lebanon, which are still open today.[42]

Joseph (no surname; *Heinrich*). brother of William (*Eberhard*); no surname is given.

Kennerley, Thomas and Harriet. English Friends; Thomas died in 1844.

Kenoba (in *OCO 86–87*). Seminole chief, according to Alderson; no other information available.

Kett, Jane (Mrs. Jack; d. 1847). Wife of John Kett.

Kett, John (Dr. Jack; d. 1847). Physician and former slave; friend and neighbor of the Aldersons.

King, Lucia B. Girl at Shawnee Mission school, whose letter Alderson transcribed for Ann Botham.

Lee, Ann (1736–1784). Leader of the American Shaker movement; born in Manchester, emigrated to the Albany, New York, area in 1774 following a mystical experience telling her to do so.

Lybrook, Jacob (1787–1869), Justice of the Peace, Wayne County, Indiana. The Aldersons stayed with him, his wife, Elizabeth Crawford Lybrook (1790–1894), and daughter, Maria (1826–1905), on their way to Indiana Yearly Meeting in Richmond, Indiana, in 1845. The Lybrook family were not Moravians, as Alderson asserts, but Dunkers (another offshoot of the German Pietist movement of the 1690s) and were among the founders of Upper Four Mile Church of the Brethren. Their home would have been a convenient stopping place, located as it was on the Ohio-Indiana border along the Boston Pike (now Indiana 227), which was the main stagecoach road between Richmond and Hamilton, Ohio. Alderson exaggerates the rusticity of their home, which was in fact a relatively new two-story brick building.[43]

Lyndon, Ann. The Botham sisters' maternal grandfather, Charles Wood, married Jemima Brownrigg, widow of Roger Lyndon, captain of the slave ship *Dolphin*. Lyndon's sons, Roger and George, would therefore be Ann Botham's half-brothers; the Ann mentioned here may be a daughter or granddaughter of one of them.[44]

Martin, Sarah (1791–1843). English seamstress noted for her work in prisons, mainly in Yarmouth, delivering sermons, advocating for prisoners' needs, and giving instruction in reading, writing, and simple vocational skills. She also superintended classes for pauper children and factory women (*ODNB*).

Mason, Alice Alderson (1789–1862). The oldest of Harrison's 14 siblings, married to William Mason (1775–1855), with whom she emigrated from Yorkshire; friends of the Aldersons in Westland, Pennsylvania.

Mason, Elizabeth (1823–1892; *Cousin Margaret 87–88, 111, 125–126, 128, 131–132, 147, 164*). The daughter of Alice and William Mason, she visited the Aldersons in Cincinnati for about two months from the middle of April, 1846.

Meader, John (1797–1860). Married to Elizabeth Hoag (sister of Lindley Murray Hoag); both were recorded ministers of Sandwich Monthly Meeting of New England Yearly Meeting and traveled extensively in Quaker missionary work.[45]

Morgan, Ephraim (1790–1873) and family. Friends of the Aldersons, living about a mile east of Cedar Lodge on 6th Street between John and Smith, according to the 1850 Cincinnati directory.[46] Ephraim Morgan was not born a Quaker, but he married Charlotte Anthony, the daughter of one of the founders of Cincinnati Monthly Meeting and joined the Society of Friends in 1823, after which he became one of its most active and influential members. His firm, Morgan, Lodge, Fisher and L'Hommedieu, published *Liberty Hall* and then the *Cincinnati Daily Gazette* until he left the firm in opposition to their policy of running advertisements for the return of runaway slaves. He then formed his own publishing business, mostly putting out religious and educational books, including *The Missouri Harmony*, which is still used today for shape-note singing.[47]

Mulgrew, Marshall (*Eugene Munro 10, 275*). See Stewart, Ella.

Neave, Hannah. Possibly Hannah (née Shipley; 1772–1848) of Manchester, married to John Neave (1764–1832). Relationship to Ann Shipley is unknown, but Emma reports correspondence between Hannah Neave and Ann Botham about the declining health of the former.[48]

Nevill, Joseph and Susanna (Alderson appears to spell this name "Neville"). Active members of Cincinnati Friends Meeting; moved there in July 1843 with their three children, at least two of whom died within the next few years. Joseph Nevill is listed in the 1850 Cincinnati directory as agent for the American Live Stock Insurance Companies and, with "Sons & Co.," of the Great Western Land and Emigration Office.[49]

Ord, S. Perhaps Sarah Satterthwaite Ord (1788–1867). Originally from Preston in Lancashire, Ord returned to Preston after the death of her husband, William Ord, in 1832. In 1837 she was recorded a minister of Preston Monthly Meeting, to which Emma and Harrison both belonged until their departure for America (*DQB*).

Osborn, Charles (1775–1850). Quaker minister, founder of the Tennessee Manumission Society, and publisher of the first American abolitionist newspaper, the *Philanthropist* (commenced 1816, sold to Elisha Bates in 1822[50]); disqualified from service by Indiana Yearly Meeting and later disowned by Birch Lake Monthly Meeting in 1844 for his leadership in the Anti-Slavery Friends.[51]

Passmoor (Squire) (*Squire Peacham 42–43*). Shoemaker turned magistrate; no other information available. A William Passmore appears in the 1850 Cincinnati directory in connection with James and Co. (stereotypers) at 167 Walnut Street.[52]

Pease, John (1797–1868). An active traveling minister from Darlington, Lancashire. From 1825 until his death, he undertook forty-six official ministerial journeys through England, the Channel Islands, France, Germany, and the United States, where he resided from 1843 to 1845 (*DQB*). At the end of that time, he published an "Address to Friends in America," in which he urged strict religious discipline and adherence to Friends practices. In a comment clearly directed at Charles Osborn and the Anti-Slavery Friends, Pease acknowledged the value of working for social reform along with other denominations, but warned that such work must be viewed as the fruit of, not a substitute for, Christian devotion. "Great should be the care of our beloved young Friends not to indulge in the smallest departure from a conscientious adherence to all our peculiar doctrines, views, and practices."[53]

Pipe, Humphrey. Attorney, "the first to use an eyeglass in Uttoxeter"; the Bothams' family friend, who loaned them Dugdale's *Monasticon* and Camden's *Britannia*.[54]

Purcell, John Baptist (1800–1884). Born in Mallow County, Ireland; bishop (later archbishop) of Cincinnati diocese (later archdiocese) beginning in 1833 (*ANBO*).

Ratcliff, Mildred (ca. 1772–1847). Raised a Baptist in Virginia, Ratcliff became a Quaker and then a recorded minister in 1803. Married to Harrison Ratcliff. The *Friend* represents her as a fierce opponent of Elias Hicks: "Dwelling near the Divine life, she was quick of discernment, and early sounded the alarm, when infidelity was making its insidious inroads in our religious Society, by the views promulgated by Elias Hicks and his adherents."[55] She was a member of Short Creek Monthly Meeting in Ohio before moving to Brownsville, Pennsylvania. Although Alderson speaks approvingly of her, Ratcliff inveighed against the evangelical teachings of the Orthodox Joseph John Gurney, whose views Alderson shared. Many years later, an incident was still recalled in which one Mildred Radcliff (likely a misspelling of Ratcliff) "once expressed herself in the Yearly Meeting of Philadelphia nearly as follows: 'I had rather be an Indian—the attention of the meeting was at the time directed to this people—than one of those in this highly favored city, who are neglecting their privileges, in that awfully approaching period that fast maketh haste.'"[56]

Rittenbar, Charley (*Martin Brandenburg*). A neighborhood bully.

Rogers, Isabella (*Milicent Benson 10, 62, 83*). Probably born ca. 1830, based on a record of 1848 graduates from Wesleyan Female College of Cincinnati; cousin of the Aldersons, living in Cincinnati, with brother Robert.

Sarah (*Sarah 83*). Isabella Rogers's servant, formerly a slave.

Saunders, John (1811–1895). English writer, editor, and publisher; first collaborated with William Howitt in 1840. On April 11, 1846, Saunders and the Howitts entered into a partnership to produce the *People's Journal*, a reform-minded miscellany of literary, historical, scientific, geographical, and political articles aimed at a middle- and working-class readership. The failure of the journal a year later led to a complicated lawsuit and a bitter debate between the two men, publicized on both sides of the Atlantic. In January 1847, well before the actual demise of the journal, the Howitts had begun their own *Howitt's Journal* along much the same lines, but that lasted only a year and a half. Settlement of the lawsuit and the affairs of the *People's Journal*, according to William Howitt, cost him close to £4,000, most of which was paid to Saunders.[57]

Seebohm, Benjamin (1798–1871). Born in Germany; became a Quaker and at age 17 moved to England, where he became a minister and, by the 1840s, a Gurneyite leader; married fellow minister Esther Wheeler. From 1846 to 1851, he joined Robert Lindsey in visiting most of the Quaker meetings in America. Seebohm edited the Friends' *Annual Monitor* from 1852 to 1863 and later wrote biographies of notable Friends Stephen Grellet and William Forster.[58] For a full account of the visit to 966 meetings for worship in America (including, perhaps, the resistance that Alderson alludes to her reference to Seebohm), see Lindsey, Robert.[59]

Shillitoe, Thomas (1754–1836). Quietist Quaker minister; moved to Ohio in 1826. According to Abbott et al., he was "the key opponent of Elias Hicks and a major precipitating factor in the Great Separation of 1827–1828,"[60] yet (perhaps anticipating the Wilburite movement of the 1840s) he was also an opponent of Joseph John Gurney, whose writings he denounced as "not sound Quaker principles," adding that "they have done great mischief in our Society."[61]

Shipley, Ann (1760–1854; *unnamed Hutchinson matriarch*). First cousin to Emma Alderson's father, Samuel Botham, and mother figure to the Aldersons in Cincinnati. In July 1779 she had eloped with her first cousin, Morris Shipley (1754–1795), who had been visiting from Philadelphia where he had been living, and were married in Gretna Green. Historians have generally followed Mary Howitt's account of their expulsion from the Society of Friends in February 1780 as having been due to the Quaker prohibition against cousins marrying, but the situation may have been aggravated by the fact that she was already pregnant with William. In any case, the following August they were readmitted, presumably after a public acknowledgement of their transgression, as was the common practice. Sometime later, Morris returned to Pennsylvania, where Ann joined him in 1794. Sometime after Morris's death, she was recorded as a minister in Oswego Monthly Meeting and traveled extensively in that capacity, including to Ohio. In 1834, she moved to Cincinnati. In *OCO*, this "old relation" (*59, 61, 270*), the Hutchinsons' "venerable old mother," is said to remind the Alderson children of their own "beloved old grandmother in England" (*10*), a comment Alderson makes repeatedly about Ann Shipley in her letters. Mary Howitt incorrectly gives her year of death as 1843.[62]

Shipley, Caroline (1822–1896). Daughter of William Shipley and Phebe Comstock Shipley. Alderson describes her as a "suffering invalid," "confined to her room & often to her bed," but she apparently rallied and lived unmarried to a respectable age.

Shipley, Charles (*Henry Munro 10, 156–157, 275, 293*). Son of Thomas C. Shipley and Mary Emily McMillan (deceased); good friend and distant cousin to William Charles Alderson; see also Ella Stewart and Marshall Mulgrew.

Shipley, Elizabeth (Cousin Elizabeth; 1826–1855; *Christina 10, 59–61, 155, 199, 201–203, 237, 270–271, 280, 287, 293*). Granddaughter of Ann Shipley and daughter of William and Phebe Comstock Shipley; married James Taylor in 1844. Their fourth daughter, born in 1853, was named Emma Alderson Taylor.[63] Elizabeth Shipley was a favorite of the Alderson children. The character of "Christina" is more fully developed and fictionalized in *OCO*, including her courtship and marriage with "Uncle Cornelius," who otherwise corresponds more closely to James Taylor's brother Joseph.

Shipley, Phebe (Comstock; sometimes misspelled "Phoebe" or "Pheobe"; (ca. 1783–1863). Widow of William Shipley, mother of eight (sources vary in the exact number), living with her mother-in-law, Ann Shipley; grandmother to Charles Shipley. Phebe Shipley was an elder of Cincinnati Monthly Meeting and among the group to welcome the Aldersons formally when they arrived.

Shipley, Thomas C. (1807–1864). Son of William and Phebe Comstock Shipley; widower of Mary Emily McMillan (1813–1843); father of Charles Shipley; and partner in Ogborn, Shipley & Co., dealer in "trimmings and fancy goods" in Cincinnati.[64]

Smith, George and Ruth. Leading members of Westland Monthly Meeting in Pennsylvania. George's father, Abraham, was one of three men who purchased the land to build the meeting house in 1792. Westland Meeting operated until April 21, 1864, when its members were transferred to Salem Monthly Meeting in Ohio.[65]

Solo, David. Warsaw, Ohio, butcher with son John.

Stacey, George (1786–1857; spelled "Stacy" by Alderson). Chemist and leading Friend in London Yearly Meeting (clerk 1838–1849). Published works on abolition, pacifism, and evangelical Christianity, which were translated into several European languages during his lifetime. See Allen, John, above regarding 1845 visit to Indiana Yearly Meeting. The following year Stacey attended Philadelphia Yearly Meeting during the peak of the Gurneyite-Wilburite controversy (*DQB*).

Stewart, Ella (*Ada Munro 10, 15, 275*). One of three "motherless children" (along with Charles Shipley and Marshall Mulgrew) who lived with the Shipleys (the "Hutchinsons" in *OCO*). There is no evidence in the correspondence that Stewart and Mulgrew were related, although Howitt gives them a common surname.

Stubbs, Rev. Jonathan (d. ca. 1811). Friend of Samuel Botham; fictionalized as "Parson Goodman" in Mary Howitt's *Two Apprentices*; married to Ann Stubbs.

Sylvester, Dorothy. Ann Wood's Anglican sister; lived for a brief but very happy time with Ann and Emma in Uttoxeter; her lively and sociable demeanor left a lasting impression on Emma after the severity of her father's Quaker household.

Taylor, Abraham (1795–1873; *David Hutchinson 10,*), James (1801–1885), Hannah (1808–1889; *Aunt Hutchinson 10, 270*), and Joseph (1810–1880; *Uncle Cornelius 10, 27–29, 61, 107, 135, 152–155, 159, 187, 193, 199, 260, 268–271, 280, 291–293*; see figure 31 for portrait). Daughter and three of the four sons of Edward Taylor (1763–1835) and Sarah Merritt (1765–1832), prominent Friends from Monmouth County, New Jersey, near Philadelphia. Abraham had emigrated to Cincinnati in 1825 and began a tanning business under the name A. M. Taylor and Company at 20–24 West 2nd.[66] Joseph, with training as an apothecary and a medical degree from University of Pennsylvania, was practicing medicine in New Jersey; James was running a school. In 1835, both brothers joined Abraham in the business. Hannah joined them by 1843. They were the Aldersons' closest friends in Cincinnati, and Joseph attended Emma at her death. In *OCO*, "Uncle Cornelius," who most closely approximates Joseph, marries "Christina" (Elizabeth Shipley); in reality, it was James whom she married on October 24, 1844. Joseph's will provided for the establishment of what would become Bryn Mawr College.[67]

Taylor, Elizabeth. See Shipley, Elizabeth.

Thomas (no surname; *Frank 239–240, 242*). Newly arrived from England with his sister, Isabella ("Henrietta").

Thompson, John (1807–1898). First cousin to Daniel Harrison (on his mother's side); his first wife, Mary Spencer, died in July 1843, about a year after the birth of their only child, also named John Thompson.

Thompson, Mary. Perhaps a sister of Margaret Harrison (née Thompson), Daniel Harrison's mother.

Thwaite, John and Lucy (ca. 1801–1852). Friends in England; John assisted the Aldersons with transatlantic financial matters. John's name appears as one of the witnesses on the Aldersons' marriage certificate.

Townsend, Ann (ca. 1778–1859). Cincinnati Friend with whom Elizabeth Alderson boarded; listed at Longworth Avenue in the 1850 Cincinnati directory.[68] Widow of William Townsend and member of Plainfield Monthly Meeting in Hendricks County, Indiana, at her death.[69]

Tuke, James Hack (1819–1896). Yorkshire Quaker, active with Friends' Foreign Mission Association and Friends' Central Education Board; best known for his work on famine relief in Ireland. In 1845, Tuke, Joseph Crosfield, and William Forster visited Alderson during a tour of the United States, during which Tuke visited asylums for the insane for the benefit of The Retreat, an asylum he managed that had been started by his grandfather in York. He also collected information on American educational institutions, which he presented in 1846 and 1853 at the Friends' Educational Society (*ODNB*).

Warder, Bessie (1841–1912; *Nelly Hutchinson 136–137*) and Hannah (or Anna; 1837–1903) Warder (*Susan Hutchinson 10*). Friends of the Alderson children, living in Cincinnati by 1846; a third sister, Jane (1839–1879), may correspond with either "Kitty" or "Sophia Hutchinson" in *OCO*. Another Bessie Warder, whom the Aldersons visited in Philadelphia, may have been their mother, Elizabeth (1817–1891); otherwise there is no mention of their parents, though their father, John A. Warder, had moved to Cincinnati from Alabama in 1837 to establish a medical practice.[70] Although these Hutchinsons and those we can identify with the Shipley family are somehow related in *OCO*, I have not found any genealogical link between the Warders and Shipleys.

Wattles, John Otis (1809–1859). Abolitionist, spiritualist, temperance and women's rights advocate, communitarian, and founder of several utopian communities. Wattles lived in Cincinnati at various times, including a period beginning in late 1844 or early 1845 after the collapse of the Prairie Home Community near West Liberty, Ohio. Alderson would have embraced some of his causes but have found insurmountable difficulties with others, especially his belief in utopian and communitarian enterprises and his affiliation (though he was not a Quaker himself) with Hicksite Friends. In 1849, a school that Wattles had founded was suspected of embracing principles of "free love" (*ANBO*). *Howitt's Journal* took an interest in Wattles's work with the cooperative movement and published several letters or extracts of letters between Wattles and Goodwyn Barmby of the Co-Operative League.

Webster, Delia (1817–1903). A teacher at Lexington Female Academy; became the first woman to go to prison for abolitionist activities when, in September 1844, she and Calvin Fairbank rescued Lewis Hayden and his family from slavery in Kentucky and brought them to Ohio to meet up with the Underground Railroad.[71]

Wells, Thomas (1799–1879) and Hannah (d. 1862). English Quaker missionaries and superintendents at the Shawnee Mission School just south of Kansas City until July 1847. Thomas Wells was born into a Methodist family in Tewksbury, England, but joined the Society of Friends in 1815 and in 1827 emigrated to Philadelphia, where he was acknowledged as a minister in 1834. After Hannah's death, Thomas returned to England and visited every Monthly Meeting in England and Ireland.[72]

West, Captain James. Captain of the *Shenandoah*, a temperance ship, which made at least fourteen voyages between Liverpool and Philadelphia from 1839 to 1845.

Whittier, John Greenleaf (1807–1892). American Quaker (Hicksite) poet, abolitionist, and journalist from near Haverhill, Massachusetts. Whittier's reputation as a poet and intellectual grew as support for abolition became more mainstream in the 1850s, but before that time (the period during which Alderson would have known of him), he had been an outspoken advocate for abolition in both his poetry and prose. In 1840, his belief in the efficacy of the legislative process led him to separate from William Lloyd Garrison and found the Liberty Party(*ANBO*). Rufus Jones describes him as having been "without any question, the most influential Friend who worked for the liberation of slaves and for the destruction of the system."[73]

Wilbur, John (1774–1856). Quaker minister from Rhode Island, whose rejection of Gurneyite evangelical Quakerism led to the second major split in the Society of Friends in the nineteenth century. Although he was disowned by New England Yearly Meeting in 1843, Wilburite Friends continued to exercise a strong minority position.

William (*Eberhard*). A tenant farmer employed by the Aldersons; brother of Joseph (*Heinrich*); no surname is given.

Winn, Thomas. Philadelphia merchant and brassfounder, receiver of letters and parcels from England directed to Aldersons.[74] His wife, Annabella (ca. 1817–1908), originally from Newport Monthly Meeting in Rhode Island, was a Quaker minister who traveled with her husband to Iowa for several years in the 1850s.[75]

Woolman, John (1720–1772). Quaker abolitionist who traveled through the colonies, often staying with slaveholders while advocating abolition. Woolman also visited Native American communities in an effort to learn more about them and to alleviate if possible the conflict between them and the European settlers. His "Plea for the Poor" (published posthumously) called attention to the suffering caused by wide economic disparities. "Woolman is thought by many to be the central figure of 18th-century Quaker faith and social reform."[76]

PLACE NAMES

John's Wood (*Diedrich's Wood*). Wood north of Cedar Lodge.

Mount Auburn (*Mount Vernon*). The home of the Taylors and, later, of Ann Shipley and her family, located just north of Cincinnati (now part of the city), though Emma Alderson gives its location as east of the city. Joseph and Susanna Nevill also moved to Mount Auburn in 1844.

Warsaw (*Athens*). A small village half a mile west of Cedar Lodge.

Westland (*Fairland 87, 147*). A Quaker settlement about four miles west of Brownsville, Pennsylvania, and the location of the first Friends meeting west of the Alleghenies; home of the Aldersons during the winter of 1842–1843. See pages 47–49 for more details.

Notes

PREFACE

1. Howard Brinton, *Friends for 350 Years: The History and Beliefs of the Society of Friends since George Fox started the Quaker Movement*, updated by Marjorie Hope Bacon (Wallingford, Penn: Pendle Hill Publications, 2002) 133.

INTRODUCTION

1. Richard's age of fourteen, according to the passenger list, confirms he was the son of Daniel Alderson (1790–1831) and Mary Speight and not Harrison's other nephew Richard (1787–1855), son of John Alderson (1787–1855).
2. Ben J. Wattenberg, ed., *The Statistical History of the United States, from Colonial Times to the Present* (New York: Basic Books, 1976), 106, https://books.google.com/books?id=3lLAUYpTDzAC.
3. Charlotte Erickson, *Invisible Immigrants: The Adaptation of English and Scottish Immigrants in Nineteenth-Century America* (Coral Gables, Fla.: University of Miami Press, 1972), 22–23; and William E. Van Vugt, ed., *British Immigration to the United States, 1776–1914* (London: Pickering & Chatto, 2009), 1:xv.
4. Charlotte Erickson, "Emigration from the British Isles to the U.S.A. in 1841: Part I. Emigration from the British Isles," *Population Studies* 43, no. 3 (November 1989): 363, http://www.jstor.org/stable/2174006.
5. Although some of the texts included here are more journalistic, with daily dated entries, and others more epistolary, any clear distinction between letters and journals is difficult to make. Even those written in a more epistolary style may have multiple dates, indicating their composition over several weeks. For that reason, I use the terms "letters" or "correspondence" interchangeably to refer to all of the texts written by Alderson for her family's consumption back in England.
6. See pages 271–279 for a more detailed analysis of the production of *Our Cousins* and appendix 2, "Directory of Names," at the end of this volume for an identification of the semi-fictional characters of *Our Cousins* with their originals in Alderson's letters.
7. See pages 271-279 for a more detailed analysis of the production of *Our Cousins* and appendix 2, "Directory of Names," at the end of this volume for an identification of the semi-fictional characters of *Our Cousins* with their originals in Alderson's letters.

8. According to Google Books' Ngram Viewer, the number of published references to Mary Howitt peaked between 1846 and 1847 (https://books.google.com/ngrams).

9. Amice Macdonell Lee, "Emma Botham Alderson 1806–1847," in *In Their Several Generations* (Plainfield, N.J.: Interstate, [1956?]), 105–125 (hereafter cited as *ITSG*).

10. Jennifer Sinor, *The Extraordinary Work of Ordinary Writing: Annie Ray's Diary* (Iowa City: University of Iowa Press, 2002), 16.

11. I use the term "frontier" somewhat loosely. By 1842, the frontier might more properly be said to have reached the Mississippi River on the western side of Illinois. Cincinnati had grown rapidly into a thriving city, the sixth largest in the United States. Yet Alderson's frequent accounts of westward travelers or those returning from the frontier represent Cincinnati as something of a western outpost of the settled United States. Riots and vigilantism in the summer of 1841, just two years before the Aldersons' arrival, further reveal the residual frontier character of that city. Thus, for Alderson and others, the experience of living in Cincinnati was an experience of living on the border between civilization and frontier as well as on that other even less settled border between North and South.

12. Emma Alderson to Mary Howitt, 6 May [1836], Ht/7/1/33, Correspondence of Mary Howitt (1799–1888), Manuscripts and Special Collections, University of Nottingham (hereafter cited as Howitt Corr., UNMSC).

13. William E. Van Vugt, *Britain to America: Mid-Nineteenth-Century Immigrants to the United States* (Urbana: University of Illinois Press, 1999), 133.

14. Van Vugt, *British Immigration to the United States*, xiii.

15. Richard T. Vann and David Edward Charles Eversley, *Friends in Life and Death: The British and Irish Quakers in the Demographic Transition, 1650–1900* (Cambridge: Cambridge University Press, 1992), 122.

16. For an authoritative account of the Quaker schisms of the first half of the nineteenth century, see Thomas D. Hamm, *The Transformation of American Quakerism: Orthodox Friends, 1800–1907* (Bloomington: Indiana University Press, 1988), 15–35. See also Thomas D. Hamm, "Hicksite, Orthodox, and Evangelical Quakerism, 1805–1887," in *The Oxford Handbook of Quaker Studies*, ed. Stephen W. Angell and Pink Dandelion (Oxford: Oxford University Press, 2013), 63–71; and Carole Dale Spencer, "Quakers in Theological Context," in *Oxford Handbook of Quaker Studies*, 146–148.

17. Elizabeth Isichei, *Victorian Quakers* (London: Oxford University Press, 1970), 111–112.

18. The Monthly Meeting is the smallest administrative unit of Quakers, meeting monthly for business and weekly or more often for worship. Each Monthly Meeting sent representatives to the Quarterly Meeting, or "Quarter," which in turn sent representatives to the Yearly Meeting. The larger bodies issued "queries" regarding the corporate life of its Monthly Meetings and their members and might serve as a board of appeal in such matters as membership or disownment. Monthly Meetings furnished replies to the queries but in general were free to act with more autonomy than individual congregations in most Christian denominations. The practice of Quarterly Meeting has largely been discontinued, as have the formal replies to Yearly Meeting queries. In theory, the Yearly Meetings all acted with the same level of authority; in practice, the word of London Yearly Meeting exercised at least an informal supervision over other Yearly Meetings, as we see in the visit by four weighty London Friends to address the Anti-Slavery Friends' separation of 1843. For more about this event, see pages 113–114.

19. George Fox, *The Journal of George Fox*, ed. John L. Nickalls (Cambridge: Cambridge University Press, 1952), 11; emphasis added.

20. See Margaret H. Bacon, *The Quiet Rebels: The Story of the Quakers in America* (New York: Basic Books, 1969), esp. 160–161. For a more recent and nuanced assessment of how

Quaker women in both their public and private capacities helped to define Quaker practice and the polity of the Quaker community internationally, see Naomi Pullin, *Female Friends and the Making of Transatlantic Quakerism, 1650–1750* (Cambridge: Cambridge University Press, 2018).

21. Mary Howitt, *Mary Howitt: An Autobiography*, ed. Margaret Howitt (London: W. Isbister, 1889), 1:3–4.

22. M. B. Rowlands, "Wood, William (1671–1730)," in *ODNB*. January 3, 2008, https://doi.org/10.1093/ref:odnb/29898.

23. Howitt, *Autobiography*, 1:14.

24. Christine MacLeod, *Inventing the Industrial Revolution: The English Patent System, 1660–1800* (Cambridge: Cambridge University Press, 2002), 179.

25. Considering the date of his death in October 1774, Wood could not, as Howitt maintains, have been a supporter of George Washington during the American War of Independence (see Howitt, *Autobiography*, 1:19; and *ITSG*, 22). His letters, however, do indicate support for the American cause.

26. Nigel Aston, "Horne, George (1730–1792)," in *ODNB*, September 23, 2004, https://doi.org/10.1093/ref:odnb/13789.

27. Howitt, *Autobiography*, 1:30.

28. Howitt, 1:45.

29. Howitt, 1:47.

30. Howitt, 1:45.

31. Howitt, 1:59.

32. *ITSG*, 111.

33. Emma Alderson to Mary Howitt, n.d. Ht/7/1/51, Howitt Corr., UNMSC. The phrase "rin wood" may mean "run, or go, mad." *Oxford English Dictionary (OED)* gives "wood" as an archaic adjective with a variety of meanings, including "out of one's mind" as well as "going beyond all reasonable bounds; utterly senseless; extremely rash or reckless." Oxford English Dictionary, s.v. "wood, adj., n.2, and adv." OED Online, Oxford University Press, accessed March 12, 2020, https://www-oed-com.pitt.idm.oclc.org/view/Entry/230008. The letter is undated, but Lee plausibly identifies it with the years immediately following Mary's and Anna's marriages. *OED* defines "a chip in porridge" as "an addition which does neither good nor harm, a thing of no moment." OED Online, s.v. "porridge, n," accessed March 12, 2020, https://www-oed-com.pitt.idm.oclc.org/view/Entry/148081.

34. *ITSG*, 107.

35. *ITSG*, 106.

36. Howitt, *Autobiography*, 1:189–194.

37. Emma Alderson to Mary Howitt, 10 January 1828, Ht/7/1/25, Howitt Corr., UNMSC.

38. *ITSG*, 109.

39. *ITSG*, 109–110.

40. Obituary of Ann Botham, *British Friend* 6, no. 5 (May 1848): 140, http://books.google.com/books?id=gjcrAAAAYAAJ.

41. *ITSG*, 111.

42. Helen E. Roberts, *Researching Yorkshire Quaker History: A Guide to Sources* (Hull: University of Hull Brynmor Jones Library, 2007), 70, http://www.hullhistorycentre.org.uk/research/research-guides/PDF/Researching-Yorkshire-Quaker-History.pdf.

43. Except as a more recent innovation among some American Quakers, ministers in the Society of Friends have always been unpaid, though they have, during some periods, been formally recognized by their meetings and even given financial support to pursue

missionary or other religious activity. The term "ministry" or "vocal ministry" refers to the spontaneous delivery of messages received through the divine workings of the inner light.

44. *ITSG*, 80–81.

45. *ITSG*, 167.

46. Howitt, *Autobiography*, 2:43.

47. Emma Alderson to Mary Howitt, 6 May [1836], Ht/7/1/33, Howitt Corr., UNMSC. See Elias Hicks and Isaac Crewdson in appendix 2, "Directory of Names."

48. *ITSG*, 112.

49. Ancestry, *England, Select Deaths and Burials, 1538–1991*, Ancestry.com.

50. Emma Alderson to Mary Howitt, n.d. [5 May 1837 from postmark], Ht/7/1/39, Howitt Corr., UNMSC.

51. Emma Alderson to Mary Howitt, n.d. [5 May 1837 from postmark], Ht/7/1/36, Howitt Corr., UNMSC.

52. *ITSG*, 164.

53. Howitt, *Autobiography*, 1:297.

54. Howitt, 1:323–324.

55. Charlotte Erickson, *Leaving England: Essays on British Emigration in the Nineteenth Century* (Ithaca, N.Y.: Cornell University Press, 1994), 52–59.

56. David A. Gerber, *Authors of Their Lives: The Personal Correspondence of British Immigrants to North America in the Nineteenth Century* (New York: New York University Press, 2006), 80–81.

57. Erickson, *Leaving England*, 239n1.

58. *ITSG*, 169, 55.

59. Michel Foucault, "What Is an Author?," in *The Foucault Reader*, ed. Paul Rabinow (New York: Pantheon Books, 1984), 108.

60. Gerber, *Authors of Their Lives*, 117.

61. Elizabeth Heckendorn Cook, *Epistolary Bodies: Gender and Genre in the Eighteenth-Century Republic of Letters* (Stanford, Calif.: Stanford University Press, 1996), 6.

62. See Gerber's chapter "Traditions of Inquiry" in his *Authors of Their Lives* (33–56) for a detailed critical history of scholarship on immigrant correspondence.

63. William I. Thomas and Florian Znaniecki, *The Polish Peasant in Europe and America*, ed. Eli Zaretsky, 5 vols. (Urbana: University of Illinois Press, 1984).

64. See, for example, Olga Kenyon, ed., *800 Years of Women's Letters* (Boston: Faber and Faber, 1993); Marcia J. Heringa Mason, ed., *Remember the Distance that Divides Us: The Family Letters of Philadelphia Quaker Abolitionist and Michigan Pioneer Elizabeth Margaret Chandler, 1830–1842* (East Lansing: Michigan State University Press, 2004); and Elizabeth C. Goldsmith, ed., *Writing the Female Voice: Essays on Epistolary Literature* (Boston: Northeastern University Press, 1989).

65. Amanda Gilroy and W. M. Verhoeven, *Epistolary Histories: Letters, Fiction, Culture* (Charlottesville: University Press of Virginia, 2000), 1.

66. Charles T. Davis and Henry Louis Gates Jr., eds., *The Slave's Narrative* (New York: Oxford University Press, 1985), xi.

67. Davis and Gates, xii.

68. Christina Marsden Gillis, *The Paradox of Privacy: Epistolary Form in "Clarissa"* (Gainesville: University Presses of Florida, 1984), 2.

69. Bakhtin writes that "the novel can be defined as a diversity of social speech types (sometimes even diversity of languages) and a diversity of individual voices, artistically organized." M. M. Bakhtin, *The Dialogic Imagination: Four Essays*, ed. Michael

Holquist, trans. Caryl Emerson and Holquist (Austin: University of Texas Press, 1981), 262.

70. James How, *Epistolary Spaces: English Letter-Writing from the Foundation of the Post Office to Richardson's "Clarissa"* (Burlington, Vt.: Ashgate, 2003), 5.

71. How, 7.

72. Benedict Anderson, *Imagined Communities: Reflections on the Origin and Spread of Nationalism*, rev. ed. (London: Verso, 2016), 24–26.

73. Sinor, *Extraordinary Work*, 110–111.

74. How, *Epistolary Spaces*, 8.

75. Cook, *Epistolary Bodies*, 29.

76. Cook, 169–171.

77. Linda H. Peterson, "Collaborative Life Writing as Ideology: The Auto/biographies of Mary Howitt and Her Family," *Prose Studies: History, Theory, Criticism* 26, no. 1–2 (2003): 185.

78. Peterson, 184.

79. Gerber, *Authors of Their Lives*, 128.

80. Gerber, 155.

81. Gerber, 159.

82. Gerber, 57.

83. Gerber, 156.

84. Linda H. Peterson, "Mother-Daughter Productions: Mary Howitt and Anna Mary Howitt in *Howitt's Journal*, *Household Words*, and Other Mid-Victorian Publications," *Victorian Periodicals Review* 31, no. 1 (Spring 1998): 35.

85. Mary Howitt, *The Children's Year* (London: Longman, Brown, Green, and Longmans, 1847), v.

86. *OCO*, preface.

87. Peterson, "Collaborative Life Writing," 180.

88. David A. Gerber, "Moving Backward and Moving On: Nostalgia, Significant Others, and Social Reintegration in Nineteenth-Century British Immigrant Personal Correspondence," *History of the Family* 21, no. 3 (2015): 294, http://dx.doi.org/10.1080/1081602X.2015.1089413.

89. J. B., "Cheap Postage in Britain," *Constitution* (Middletown, Conn.), July 5, 1848, America's Historical Newspapers, 2.

90. With no international agreements on postage, the rates could vary widely depending on the shipping line and other factors. One writer reported costs ranging from sixteen pence to two shillings for the transatlantic journey ("Postage," *Emancipator and Free American*, August 31, 1843). Additional charges would be levied for transit to and from the ports of departure and arrival. The equivalency is based on the prices given in Alderson's letter to her mother of October 28, 1846, and an exchange rate of $4.85 to £1. ("Computing 'Real Value' over Time with a Conversion between U.K. Pounds and U.S. Dollars, 1791 to Present," MeasuringWorth, Lawrence H. Officer and Samuel H. Williamson, 2019, accessed May 19, 2019, https://www.measuringworth.com/calculators/exchange/result_exchange.php.

91. Even such seminal collections and analyses of immigrant writing as Charlotte Erickson's *Invisible Immigrants* and Thomas and Znaniecki's *The Polish Peasant in Europe and America* draw very selectively on passages to support the authors' narratives and forgo any clear statement of editorial principles.

92. Mary-Jo Kline and Susan Holbrook Perdue, *A Guide to Documentary Editing*, 3rd ed. (Charlottesville: University of Virginia Press, 2008), 211.

93. Elizabeth Cleghorn Gaskell, *The Letters of Mrs. Gaskell*, ed. J. A. V. Chapple and Arthur Pollard (Cambridge, Mass.: Harvard University Press, 1967).

94. For more detail on this portion of the correspondence, see page 272.

PART I — LEAVING HOME: THE *SHENANDOAH*, ACROSS THE ALLEGHENIES, THE FIRST WINTER

1. "Emigration.-Comforts on the Voyage, & c.," *Times* (London), March 6, 1835, http://tinyurl.galegroup.com/tinyurl/AHF4w9.

2. Godfrey T. Anderson, "The Captain Lays Down the Law," *New England Quarterly* 44, no. 2 (June 1971): 305–309, https://doi.org/10.2307/364532.

3. Chris J. Lewie, *Two Generations on the Allegheny Portage Railroad: The First Railroad to Cross the Allegheny Mountains* (Shippensburg, Pa.: Burd Street, 2001), 6–7. See also Francis P. Boscoe, "A Project of Doubtful Utility: Measuring Legislative Opposition to the Pennsylvania Canal," *Political Geography* 19, no. 8 (November 2000): 998–999, https://doi.org/10.1016/S0962-6298(00)00039-1; and William Bender Wilson, *History of the Pennsylvania Railroad Company, with Plan of Organization, Portraits of Officials and Biographical Sketches* (Philadelphia: Henry T. Coates, 1895), 1:95–150, https://books.google.com/books?id=qj9N-eWi71YC.

4. Jesse L. Hartman, "The Portage Railroad National Historic Site and the Johnstown Flood Memorial," *Pennsylvania History* 31, no. 2 (April 1964): 145, https://www.jstor.org/stable/27770249.

5. Wilson, *Pennsylvania Railroad Company*, 105.

6. Hartman, "Portage Railroad," 145.

7. Charles Dickens, *American Notes for General Circulation* (London: Chapman and Hall, 1850), 102.

8. The phrase "Preparative Meeting" can have slightly different meanings, but it is most often used, as it is in this context, to denote an individual congregation subordinate to a Monthly Meeting. Thus, a single Monthly Meeting might oversee several Preparative Meetings. As the membership of a Preparative Meeting grew, it might be elevated to the status of Monthly Meeting (Thomas Hamm, e-mail message to author, May 23, 2019).

9. Levinus K. Painter, "The Rise and Decline of Quakerism in the Monongahela Valley," *Bulletin of Friends' Historical Association* 45, no. 1 (1956): 25. See also James L. Burke and Donald E. Bensch, "Mount Pleasant and the Early Quakers of Ohio," *Ohio History* 83, no. 4 (Autumn 1974): 223, https://resources.ohiohistory.org/ohj/; and "Ohio Yearly Meeting," Quaker Chronicle, updated April 26, 2017, http://www.quaker-chronicle.info/meetings.php?meetingID=1.

10. For good, brief discussions of the Hicksite-Orthodox split, see Thomas D. Hamm, *The Quakers in America* (New York: Columbia University Press, 2003), 39–43; and Hamm, "Hicksite, Orthodox, and Evangelical Quakerism, 1805–1887," in *The Oxford Handbook of Quaker Studies*, ed. Stephen W. Angell and Pink Dandelion (Oxford: Oxford University Press, 2013), 64–71. For a fuller treatment of the split, see H. Larry Ingle, *Quakers in Conflict: The Hicksite Reformation* (Wallingford, Pa.: Pendle Hill, 1998). For a sociohistorical analysis of the separation, see Robert. W. Doherty, *The Hicksite Separation: A Sociological Analysis of Religious Schism in Early Nineteenth Century America* (New Brunswick, N.J.: Rutgers University Press, 1967).

11. The earliest certificate of removal on record for Westland Monthly Meeting is for a John Smith, coming from Fairfax, Virginia, in 1785 (Stephen Beauregard Weeks, *Southern Quakers and Slavery: A Study in Institutional History* [Baltimore: Johns Hopkins Press, 1896], 249). When Quakers moved from one meeting to another, their old meeting issued

them a "certificate of removal." That certificate testified to the spiritual and financial soundness of the individual or family in question and assured the new meeting that these were indeed members in good standing.

12. Rufus Jones records that between 1793 and 1811, 104 individuals were disowned in Redstone Monthly Meeting alone for "marriage contrary to discipline"—in other words, for marriage to a non-Friend or according to the practices of another denomination. Rufus M. Jones, *The Later Periods of Quakerism*, 2 vols. (London: Macmillan, 1921), 1:396.

13. Flannel-kicking was a highly social event in which quantities of newly woven flannel doused with soapy water were kicked and beaten to thicken it and prepare it to be stitched into clothing. One nineteenth-century family historian describes it as follows: "soapsuds as hot as the boys could possibly bear it, was poured on the flannel, then the fun commenced in earnest, every one kicking the pile of flannel for dear life, the boys laughing and yelling, the girls screaming, and the soap suds splattering and squirting." Sara Jane Harris Keifer, *Genealogical and Biographical Sketches of the New Jersey Branch of the Harris Family, in the United States* (Madison, Wis.: Democratic Printing Company, 1888), 345 and *passim*.

14. Francis D. Nichol, *The Midnight Cry: A Defense of the Character and Conduct of William Miller and the Millerites* (Washington, D.C.: Review and Herald, 1945), 158.

15. David L. Rowe, "Millerites: A Shadow Portrait," in *The Disappointed: Millerism and Millenarianism in the Nineteenth Century*, 2nd ed., ed. Ronald L. Numbers and Jonathan M. Butler (Knoxville: University of Tennessee Press, 1993), 7.

16. Francis D. Nichol's defensive history of the Millerites argues that much of what was attributed to them was fabricated. For a more scholarly assessment, see the essays collected in Ronald L. Numbers and Jonathan M. Butler, eds., *The Disappointed: Millerism and Millenarianism in the Nineteenth Century*, 2nd ed. (Knoxville: University of Tennessee Press, 1993).

17. Donald K. Yeomans, *Comets: A Chronological History of Observation, Science, Myth, and Folklore* (New York: Wiley, 1991), 179.

18. Numbers and Butler, *The Disappointed*, 13.

19. Thompson appears in *OCO* as Cousin Israel Hopper, but only as an adventurer; the financial difficulties are never mentioned. Mary Howitt *Our Cousins in Ohio* (London: Darton, 1849), 213–214.

20. A search for "Mary Howitt" on https://books.google.com/ngrams/ shows a peak in number of references in the years 1846 and 1847.

PART II — A HOME OF THEIR OWN: FIRST YEARS AT CEDAR LODGE

1. Louis C. Hunter, *Steamboats on the Western Rivers: An Economic and Technological History* (Cambridge, Mass.: Harvard University Press, 1949), 481–498. Hunter reports at this time "as many as two hundred steamboat arrivals annually at Pittsburgh from points above on" the Monongahela (44).

2. Hunter, 381.

3. Hunter, 403.

4. Charles Dickens, *American Notes for General Circulation* (London: Chapman and Hall, 1850), 107. Statistics are hard to come by, but one congressional report estimated close to 2,000 deaths in steamboat accidents prior to 1840, mostly from fires and explosions (Hunter, *Steamboats*, 277–278).

5. Hunter, *Steamboats*, 490.

6. Andrew F. Smith, *The Tomato in America: Early History, Culture, and Cookery* (Urbana: University of Illinois Press, 2001), 35.

7. Charles Darwin, *The Origin of Species by Means of Natural Selection, or the Preservation of Favoured Races in the Struggle for Life*, 6th ed. (London: Murray, 1872), 429. Some readers may be more familiar with the phrase "an entangled bank," used in earlier editions of the *Origin*.

8. Pierre Bourdieu, *Distinction* (Cambridge, Mass: Harvard University Press, 1984), 466.

9. Carl Guarneri, *The Utopian Alternative: Fourierism in Nineteenth-Century America* (Ithaca, N.Y.: Cornell University Press, 1991), 7.

10. Guarneri, 18–19.

11. Guarneri, 408.

12. Guarneri, 160.

13. Two causes that Guarneri cites are the return of American prosperity in the 1850s and the diversion of reformist energies toward other movements, especially abolition (Guarneri, 10).

14. Sterling F. Delano, *Brook Farm: The Dark Side of Utopia* (Cambridge, Mass.: Belknap, 2004), 362.

15. Guarneri, *Utopian Alternative*, 10.

16. Judith Johnston, *Victorian Women and the Economies of Travel, Translation and Culture, 1830–1870* (London: Routledge, 2016), 151–170.

17. Mary Howitt, *Mary Howitt: An Autobiography*, ed. Margaret Howitt (London: W. Isbister, 1889), 2:17–18.

18. Linda H. Peterson, "Collaborative Life Writing as Ideology: The Auto/biographies of Mary Howitt and Her Family," *Prose Studies: History, Theory, Criticism* 26, no. 1–2 (2003): 180.

19. Mary Howitt, *Our Cousins in Ohio* (London: Darton, 1849), 18–21.

20. Details about the Aldersons' involvement with the Society of Friends, when not drawn from Emma's letters, come from the minutes of Cincinnati Monthly, Miami Quarterly, and Indiana Yearly Meetings, held in the Quaker Rare Collection at Watson Library, Wilmington College, Ohio.

21. Information on Steer, Morgan, and Crossman, as well as additional background on Cincinnati Monthly Meeting, comes from Sabrina Darnowsky, *Friends Past and Present: The Bicentennial History of Cincinnati Friends Meeting (1815–2015)* (self-pub., CreateSpace, 2015), esp. 23–63, 80.

22. See pages 113–114 for a discussion of this separation.

23. Peter Pugh, *Great Enterprise: A History of Harrisons and Crosfield* (London: Harrisons and Crosfield, 1990), 4–9.

24. See pages 113–114, where Alderson expresses surprise at Daniel Harrison's "wonderful change of feeling" about Joseph Crosfield.

25. Pugh, *Great Enterprise*, 10.

26. Amice Macdonell Lee, *In Their Several Generations* (Plainfield, N.J.: Interstate, [1956?]), 170–171, 322.

27. Howitt, *Autobiography*, 1:47.

28. William Howitt and Mary Howitt, *The Desolation of Eyam: The Emigrant, a Tale of the American Woods; And Other Poems* (London: Wightman and Cramp, 1827).

29. Howitt, *Autobiography*, 1:48.

30. Howitt, 1:259.

31. Howitt, 1:292.

32. Vanessa Morton, "Quaker Politics and Industrial Change c. 1800–1850" (PhD thesis, Open University, 1988), 95.

33. Thomas D. Hamm, "Hicksite, Orthodox, and Evangelical Quakerism, 1805–1887," in *The Oxford Handbook of Quaker Studies*, ed. Stephen W. Angell and Pink Dandelion (Oxford: Oxford University Press, 2013), 68.

34. Howitt, *Autobiography*, 1:188.

35. "The Indiana Separation of 1842 and the Limits of Quaker Anti-Slavery," *Quaker History* 89, no. 1 (Spring 2000): 13. (Jordan incorrectly gives 1844 as the year the delegation from London YM visited Indiana.)

36. Rufus M. Jones, *The Later Periods of Quakerism*, 2 vols. (London: Macmillan, 1921), 2:587–94.

37. For the fullest treatment of this separation, see Ryan P. Jordan, *Slavery and the Meetinghouse* (Bloomington: Indiana University Press, 2007). See Elizabeth Cazden, "Quakers, Slavery, Anti-slavery, and Race," in Stephen W. Angell and Pink Dandelion, eds., *The Oxford Handbook of Quaker Studies* (Oxford: Oxford University Press, 2013), 357. (Cazden is in error here in asserting that Joseph John Gurney was part of the delegation from London YM.)

38. I have one of the anonymous reviewers of this book's manuscript to thank for the idea that Alderson's reticence about Quakerism might have masked some dissatisfaction with the Society of Friends.

39. Emma Alderson to Mary Howitt, 6 May 1836, Ht/7/1/33, Howitt Corr., UNMSC. See Elias Hicks and Isaac Crewdson in appendix 2, "Directory of Names."

PART III — THE FINAL YEARS

1. "Meeting Minutes, 1834–41," Nonconformist Registers of the Central Library, Liverpool, 510. I am indebted to Christopher Stokes for sharing this information with me in an e-mail exchange, June 13–19, 2019.

2. *A Report of the Proceedings of the Yearly Meeting of the Society of Friends* [. . .]; *To Which Is Added the Quakers' Yearly Epistle for 1836* (London: John Stephens, 1836), 16, https://books.google.com/books?id=j8wsAAAAYAAJ.

3. Nikki Marie Taylor, *Frontiers of Freedom: Cincinnati's Black Community, 1802–1868* (Athens: Ohio University Press, 2005), 4–5.

4. Taylor, 50, 117.

5. Taylor, 122.

6. Taylor, 126.

7. Charles Bowen, "American Colonization Society," in *The American Almanac and Repository of Useful Knowledge for the Year 1834* (Boston: Charles Bowen, 1835), 92–94, https://books.google.com/books?id=G6wkAQAAMAAJ.

8. Hugh A. Garland, *The Life of John Randolph of Roanoke*, 13th ed. (New York: D. Appleton, 1874), 2:266, http://books.google.com/books?id=q1eqAAAAIAAJ.

9. Taylor, *Frontiers of Freedom*, 78.

10. Taylor, 210.

11. "Another Mob in Cincinnati," *Philanthropist*, October 8, 1839, America's Historical Newspapers.

12. Lydia Mott, sister-in-law to Lucretia Mott (1793–1880), was active throughout her life as an abolitionist, reformist, and women's rights advocate.

13. Taylor, *Frontiers of Freedom*, 128, 131. For a description of all three orphanages, see Charles Frederic Goss, *Cincinnati, the Queen City, 1788–1912* (Chicago: S. J. Clarke, 1912), http://books.google.com/books?id=HxIWAAAAYAAJ.

14. Thomas D. Hamm, *The Quakers in America* (New York: Columbia University Press, 2003), 169. For an account emphasizing the harmonious relationships between

Quakers and Native Americans, see Margaret H. Bacon, *The Quiet Rebels: The Story of the Quakers in America* (New York: Basic Books, 1969), 47–49, 152–160.

15. Mary Howitt, *Mary Howitt: An Autobiography*, ed. Margaret Howitt (London: W. Isbister, 1889), 2:48; *Our Cousins in Ohio* (London: Darton, 1849), preface.

16. Obituary of Harrison Alderson, *The Annual Monitor for 1872, or Obituary of the Members of the Society of Friends in Great Britain and Ireland, for the Year 1871* (1871), 5, https://books.google.com/books?id=jLoNAAAAYAAJ.

17. Jennifer Sinor, *The Extraordinary Work of Ordinary Writing: Annie Ray's Diary* (Iowa City: University of Iowa Press, 2002), 198.

18. *OCO*, preface.

19. Linda H. Peterson, "Collaborative Life Writing as Ideology: The Auto/biographies of Mary Howitt and Her Family," *Prose Studies: History, Theory, Criticism* 26, no. 1–2 (2003): 184.

20. Jude Piesse, "Dreaming across Oceans: Emigration and Nation in the Mid-Victorian Christmas Issue," *Victorian Periodicals Review* 46, no. 1 (Spring 2013): 44, https://doi.org/10.1353/vpr.2013.0003.

21. Cornelia Meigs, *What Makes a College? A History of Bryn Mawr* (New York: Macmillan, 1956), 6–22.

22. Harrison's statement that "She passed this fifth-day night pretty comfortably" would suggest that Emma died on Friday (sixth-day), December 17. Lee's account, based on Anna Harrison's journals, is otherwise consistent with Harrison Alderson's letter but gives the date as December 16. Amice Macdonell Lee, *In Their Several Generations* (Plainfield, N.J.: Interstate, [1956?]), 174. I conclude that Harrison's reference to "fifth-day night" reflects either a mental lapse on his part (understandable under the circumstances) or a reference to the night *preceding* fifth day.

23. An abbreviated account of Alderson's death and her sister's journal appears in Amice Macdonell Lee, *Laurels & Rosemary: The Life of William and Mary Howitt* (London: Oxford University Press, 1955), 177–178.

EPILOGUE

1. Obituary of Harrison Alderson, *Annual Monitor for 1872, or Obituary of the Members of the Society of Friends in Great Britain and Ireland, for the Year 1871*, n.s., 30 (1871): 1–12, https://books.google.com/books?id=jLoNAAAAYAAJ.

2. Richard Scott (Alderson Family History Society), e-mail with author, August 8, 2008; "Boys' Register, 1835–1875," "Girls' Register, 1835–1883," Esther Duke Archives, Westtown School, Westtown, Pa. Now officially "Westtown School" (no hyphen), this Quaker boarding school was opened in 1799.

3. *Biographical Catalogue of the Matriculates of Haverford College: Together with Lists of the Members of the College Faculty and the Managers, Officers and Recipients of Honorary Degrees, 1833–1922* (Philadelphia, 1922), xv, accessed April 15, 2020, https://catalog.hathitrust.org/Record/009574168.

4. Amice Macdonell Lee, *In Their Several Generations* (Plainfield, N.J.: Interstate, [1956?]), 125 (hereafter cited as *ITSG*).

5. *Biographical Catalogue of the Matriculates of Haverford College*, 82.

6. Elsie Janeway Apthorp, *Elinor & Edward Janeway* (Privately printed, 2005), 132–133.

7. Based on personal e-mails from Richard Scott, August 20, 2008, and various articles by Jim Cross in the *Alderson Family History Society Newsletter*, vols. 38, 47, and 48. I am indebted to Jo Skelton and others from the Alderson Family History Society for providing me with copies of these articles.

8. T. Addison Busbey, ed., *The Biographical Directory of the Railway Officials of America* (Chicago: Railway Age, 1906), 6–7, http://books.google.com/books?id=c8ApAAAAYAAJ.

9. Apthorp, *Elinor & Edward Janeway*, 22.

10. "Papers of Sir John Valentine W. Shaw," Bodleian Archives and Manuscripts, Oxford University, Accessed April 15, 2020, https://archives.bodleian.ox.ac.uk/repositories/2/resources/1495.

11. *ITSG*, 214.

12. Peter Pugh, *Great Enterprise: A History of Harrisons and Crosfield* (London: Harrisons and Crosfield, 1990), 16–17.

13. Al Sharif, e-mail with author.

14. *ITSG*, 209.

15. *ITSG*, 233. She later published extracts of these letters as "America Then and Now: Recollections of Lincoln," *Contemporary Review* 111, no. 617 (May 1917), 562–569.

16. *ITSG*, 246.

17. Agnes Macdonell, "Lucretia Mott," *Macmillan's Magazine* 43, no. 258 (April 1881) 452–460.

18. Kirsten Sellars, "Trying the Kaiser: The Origins of International Criminal Law," in *Historical Origins of International Criminal Law*, vol. 1, ed. Morten Bergsmo, Cheah Wui Ling, and Yi Ping (Brussels: Torkel Opsahl Academic EPublisher, 2014), 196–198, https://www.legal-tools.org/doc/cdda84/pdf/.

19. Quoted in Lucy Harrison, *A Lover of Books: The Life and Literary Papers of Lucy Harrison, Written and Arranged by Amy Greener* (London: J. M. Dent, 1916), 41.

20. Lucy Harrison, *A Lover of Books*, 22, 25, 40–41, 143-160.

21. The best biography of William and Mary Howitt remains Carl Woodring, *Victorian Samplers: William and Mary Howitt* (Lawrence: University of Kansas Press, 1952). Amice Macdonell Lee, *Laurels & Rosemary: The Life of William and Mary Howitt* (London: Oxford University Press, 1955), by their great-niece, draws on a great deal of material held within the family. Howitt's own *Autobiography*, on which both of these biographies draw heavily, is, of course, a wealth of information. More contemporary biographies include several books privately published by Joy Dunicliff of Uttoxeter, including *Quaker to Catholic: Mary Howitt, Lost Author of the 19th Century* (McMinnville, Tenn.: St. Clair, 2010) and *Traveller on the Hill-Top: Mary Howitt, the Famous Victorian Authoress* (Leek, UK: Churnet Valley Books, 1998).

22. Woodring, *Victorian Samplers*, 153.

23. Linda H. Peterson, "Collaborative Life Writing as Ideology: The Auto/biographies of Mary Howitt and Her Family," *Prose Studies: History, Theory, Criticism* 26, no. 1–2 (2003): 189–190.

24. Woodring, *Victorian Samplers*, 210–212.

25. Mary Howitt, *Mary Howitt: An Autobiography*, ed. Margaret Howitt (London: W. Isbister, 1889), 2:355–356.

26. Howitt, 2:354.

27. Woodring, *Victorian Samplers*, 164–165.

28. Woodring, 171.

29. Deborah Cherry, "Women Artists and the Politics of Feminism 1850–1900," in *Women in the Victorian Art World*, ed. Clarissa Campbell Orr (Manchester, UK: Manchester University Press, 1995), 58.

30. Howitt, *Autobiography*, 2:117. Lee, for example, writes that Ruskin's "cruel words . . . struck the death blow to Annie's career as an artist" (*Laurels & Rosemary*, 217).

31. Peterson, "Collaborative Life Writing," 190.

32. Woodring, *Victorian Samplers*, 212.

33. W.E.H. Stanner, "Howitt, Alfred William (1830–1908)," in *Australian Dictionary of Biography*, online ed. (National Centre of Biography, Australian National University, 2006), http://www.adb.online.anu.edu.au/biogs/A040489b.htm.

34. Lee, *Laurels & Rosemary*, 37–41, 231.

35. Woodring, *Victorian Samplers*, 223.

APPENDIX 1 — PHYSICAL AND POSTAL ATTRIBUTES

1. I have no explanation for the incongruity of this date in relation to the other postal marks and the contents of the letter. The transcriptions have been double-checked and appear to be accurate.

APPENDIX 2 — DIRECTORY OF NAMES

1. Obituary of Thomas Albright, *Friends' Review* 1, no. 34 (May 13, 1848): 539, https://books.google.com/books?id=JoArAAAAYAAJ.

2. Rufus M. Jones, *The Later Periods of Quakerism*, 2 vols., (London: Macmillan, 1921), 2:589–594.

3. *Dictionary of Quaker Biography*, Haverford College Quaker Collection, Haverford, Pa.; hereafter cited as *DQB*.

4. Amice Macdonell Lee, *In Their Several Generations* (Plainfield, N.J.: Interstate, [1956?]), 75–76 (hereafter cited as *ITSG*).

5. Charles Frederick Holder, *The Quakers in Great Britain and America: The Religious and Political History of the Society of Friends from the Seventeenth to the Twentieth Century* (New York: Neuner, 1913), 54.

6. Williams Directory Company, *Williams' Cincinnati Directory and Business Advertiser, for 1850–51* (Cincinnati, Ohio: C. S. Williams—College Hall, 1850), 29, https://books.google.com/books?id=353NAAAAMAAJ.

7. *ANBO*; Anna Braithwaite Thomas, "The Beaconite Controversy," *Bulletin of Friends' Historical Society* 4, no. 2 (1912); H. Larry Ingle, *Quakers in Conflict: The Hicksite Reformation* (Wallingford, Pa.: Pendle Hill, 1998), 231–234.

8. Obituary of Lucy Bayliffe, *Annual Monitor for 1854, or Obituary of the Members of the Society of Friends in Great Britain and Ireland, for the Year 1853*, n.s., 12 (1853): 11, https://books.google.com/books?id=FAAqAAAAYAAJ; *ITSG*, 168.

9. Mary Howitt, *Mary Howitt: An Autobiography*, ed. Margaret Howitt (London: W. Isbister, 1889), 1:106–107.

10. *ANBO*; Maurice Jackson, *Let This Voice Be Heard: Anthony Benezet, Father of Atlantic Abolitionism* (Philadelphia: University of Pennsylvania Press, 2010).

11. Nikki Marie Taylor, *Frontiers of Freedom: Cincinnati's Black Community, 1802–1868* (Athens: Ohio University Press, 2005), 18–31; "A Testimony of Miami Monthly Meeting of Friends, Concerning Joseph Cloud," *Friend* 5, no. 39 (1832): 310–311.

12. "Cope Family Papers," Historical Society of Pennsylvania, 2003, accessed June 19, 2019, https://hsp.org/sites/default/files/mss/finding_aid_1486_cope.pdf.

13. *DQB*; *ODNB*; Obituary of Susanna Corder, *Annual Monitor for 1865, or Obituary of the Members of the Society of Friends in Great Britain and Ireland, for the year 1864*, 23 n.s. (1864), 42–51.

14. Margery Post Abbott, Mary Ellen Chijioke, Pink Dandelion, and John William Oliver Jr., *The A to Z of the Friends (Quakers)* (Lanham, Md.: Scarecrow Press, 2006), 66.

15. Joshua Lufkin Douglas, *The Douglas Genealogy: the Descendants of John Douglas of Middleborough, Massachusetts* (Bath, Maine: Sentinel and Times Pub. Co., 1890), 65–66.

16. Obituary of Ann Ecroyd, *Annual Monitor for 1860, or Obituary of the Members of the Society of Friends in Great Britain and Ireland, for the Year 1859*, n.s., 18 (1859): 87–88, https://books.google.com/books?id=n1oEAAAAQAAJ; Sara Horrell, Jane Humphries, and Hans-Joachim Voth, "Stature and Relative Deprivation: Fatherless Children in Early Industrial Britain," *Continuity and Change* 13, no. 1 (May 1998): 75.

17. Obituary of Sarah Emlen, *Friends' Review* 2, no. 46 (August 4, 1849): 728, https://books.google.com/books?id=2sZLAAAAMAAJ.

18. Karen Campbell, "The Evans Family of Waynesville," *Quaker Genealogy in Southwest Ohio* (blog), September 7, 2005, http://qugenswohio.blogspot.com/2005/09/evans-family-of-waynesville.html. Also from e-mail message from Matt Engel to author, December 17, 2008.

19. William Wade Hinshaw, *Encyclopedia of American Quaker Genealogy* (Baltimore: Genealogical Publishing, 1969), 2:704; Ingle, *Quakers in Conflict*, 22.

20. *ODNB*, "Maltbie Genealology," *"Old Northwest" Genealogical Quarterly* 9 (1906): 314–325, https://books.google.com/books?id=-EM9AQAAMAAJ.

21. Janet R. Walker and Richard W. Burkhardt, *Eliza Julia Flower: Letters of an English Gentlewoman; Life on the Illinois-Indiana Frontier, 1817–1861* (Muncie, Ind: Ball State University, 1991).

22. *DQB*; Obituary of William Forster, *Annual Monitor for 1855, or Obituary of the Members of the Society of Friends in Great Britain and Ireland, for the Year 1854*, n.s., 13 (1854): 48, https://books.google.com/books?id=e1oEAAAAQAAJ.

23. Charles E. G. Pease, "The Descendants of Ralph Small," Pennyghael.org.uk, November 20, 2015, http://www.pennyghael.org.uk/Small.pdf; Christopher Stokes, "Lost Poets #4: Sarah Frankland," *Maddalo: Thoughts of Some Description* (blog), August 14, 2018, http://maddalo.blogspot.com/2018/08/lost-poets-4-sarah-frankland.html.

24. "London Yearly Meeting, 1836," *Journal of the Friends Historical Society* 2, no. 12 (1920): 86, https://archive.org/stream/journaloffriends1718frie/journaloffriends1718frie_djvu.txt.

25. Consistent information about the hierarchy of meetings, their dates, and memberships is difficult to obtain. In various yearly meeting minutes, Quaker journals, and local histories, Edith Griffith is identified with Westland, Redstone, and Salem Monthly Meetings, with Pike Run Meeting for Worship in southwest Pennsylvania, and with Short Creek Monthly Meeting of Indiana Yearly Meeting in Ohio. My information is based largely on Boyd Crumrine, *History of Washington County, Pennsylvania: With Biographical Sketches of Many of Its Pioneers and Prominent Men* (Philadelphia: L. H. Everts, 1882), https://books.google.com/books?id=7jxbQDo2BigC, with additional data from Quaker Chronicle, http://www.quaker-chronicle.info/index.php.

26. Earle R. Forrest, *History of Washington County Pennsylvania* (Chicago: S. J. Clarke, 1926), 592. "Correspondence," *Friends' Review; a Religious, Literary and Miscellaneous Journal* (1847–1894) 26, no. 30 (March 15, 1873), https://search-proquest-com.pitt.idm.oclc.org/docview/91125056.

27. [John Harrison], "Is It Proper to Call the Holy Scriptures 'the Word of God'?," *Friend* (Philadelphia) 6, no. 25 (March 30, 1833): 197–198; Henry Ecroyd Smith, *Annals of Smith of Cantley, Balby, and Doncaster, County York* (Yorkshire, UK: Hills, 1878), 301, http://books.google.com/books?id=nSkAAAAAQAAJ.

28. Hugh Barbour and J. William Frost, *The Quakers* (New York: Greenwood, 1988), 333–334.

29. Howitt, *Autobiography*, 1:7, 38.

30. Thomas D. Hamm, April Beckman, Florio Marissa, Kirsti Giles, and Marie Hopper, "'A Great and Good People': Midwestern Quakers and the Struggle against Slavery," *Indiana*

Magazine of History 100, no. 1 (2004): 15–16; "History," Village of Harveysburg, accessed April 13, 2020, http://www.villageofharveysburg.org/history; "Elizabeth B. Harvey," Ohio History Central, accessed April 13, 2020, https://ohiohistorycentral.org/w/Elizabeth_B._Harvey.

31. John Percy Hart and W. H. Bright, eds., *Hart's History and Directory of the Three Towns, Brownsville, Bridgeport, West Brownsville* (Cadwallader, Pa.: J. P. Hart, 1904), 347, https://books.google.com/books?id=NJhAAAAAYAAJ.

32. Harvey Hall, *The Cincinnati Directory for 1825* (Cincinnati, Ohio: Samuel J. Browne, 1825), 109, https://www.cincinnatilibrary.org/citydirectory/CincinnatiDirectory_1825.pdf.

33. *Historic Atlas of Ohio Yearly Meeting: An Illustrated Documentation of the History of the Ohio Quakers from Their Earliest Meetings to Their Bicentennial in 2013* (Barnesville: Ohio Yearly Meeting of Friends, 2012), 32; Hilles family information is from "Descendants of David Hilles, Generation No. 3," Genealogy.com, accessed June 10, 2019, https://www.genealogy.com/ftm/h/i/l/William-C-Hilles/GENE60-0003.html.

34. *History of Hardin County, Iowa* (Springfield, Ill.: Union, 1883), 755–757, https://books.google.com/books?id=WHBHAQAAMAAJ.

35. John H. Nodal, *The Bibliography (Biographical and Topographical) of Ackworth School* (Manchester, UK: F. Nodal, 1889), 14, http://books.google.com/books?id=yeoBAAAAYAAJ.

36. See Linda H. Peterson, "Collaborative Life Writing as Ideology: The Auto/biographies of Mary Howitt and Her Family," *Prose Studies: History, Theory, Criticism* 26, no. 1–2 (2003): 179–180.

37. Algie I. Newlin, "Hubbard, Jeremiah," in *Dictionary of North Carolina Biography*, ed. William S. Powell (Chapel Hill: University of North Carolina Press, 1988), https://www.ncpedia.org/biography/hubbard-jeremiah.

38. Horace Mack, *History of Columbiana County, Ohio: With Illustrations and Biographical Sketches of Some of Its Prominent Men and Pioneers* (Philadelphia: D. W. Ensign, 1879), 102, 108, https://books.google.com/books?id=OeA4AQAAMAAJ.

39. Williams Directory Company, 144.

40. Ingle, *Quakers in Conflict*, 34–35, 161–162, 209.

41. Jones, *Later Periods*, 1:509; *A Report of the Proceedings of the Yearly Meeting of the Society of Friends,* [. . .] *To Which Is Added the Quakers' Yearly Epistle for 1836* (London: John Stephens, 1836), 14, https://books.google.com/books?id=j8wsAAAAYAAJ.

42. Khalil Totah, "Quakerism in Palestine," *Bulletin of Friends Historical Association* 26, no. 2 (1937): 79–82, https://www.jstor.org/stable/41944049; "Biographical Note," in *Eli and Sybil Jones Family Papers, 1830–1890 (MC.1009.A): Finding Aid Prepared by Mary A. Crauderueff* (Haverford, Pa.: Quaker & Special Collections, Haverford College, December 2015), 4, https://library.haverford.edu/finding-aids/files/1009A.pdf.

43. Merle C. Rummel, e-mail with author, March 31, 2020; Rummel, "Four Mile Church—200th Anniversary Presentation on the First 100 Years," accessed March 30, 2020, https://www.cob-net.org/docs/bl/four-mile-presentation.pdf

44. Howitt, *Autobiography*, 1:16–17.

45. Obituary of John Meader, *American Annual Monitor for 1862, or Obituary of the Members of the Society of Friends in America, for the Year 1861* 5 (1862): 119–151, https://books.google.com/books?id=JHcUZy-8tH4C; "Glossary," Josiah Parker Papers, Earlham College Friends Collection and College Archives, accessed June 9, 2019, https://exhibits.earlham.edu/exhibits/show/parker/glossary/macy-overman.

46. Williams Directory Company, 195.

47. Sabrina Darnowsky, *Friends Past and Present: The Bicentennial History of Cincinnati Friends Meeting (1815–2015)* (self-pub., CreateSpace, 2015), 16–17; Allen D. Carden, *The Missouri Harmony, or a Collection of Psalm and Hymn Tunes, and Anthems: An Introduction to the Grounds and Rudiments of Music* (Lincoln: University of Nebraska Press, 1994).

48. Charles E. G. Pease, "The Descendants of Moses Neave," Pennyghael.org.uk, November 21, 2015, http://www.pennyghael.org.uk/Neave.pdf.

49. Williams Directory Company, 21, 115.

50. James L. Burke and Donald E. Bensch, "Mount Pleasant and the Early Quakers of Ohio," *Ohio History* 83, no. 4 (Autumn 1974), 247.

51. Thomas D. Hamm, *The Transformation of American Quakerism: Orthodox Friends, 1800–1907* (Bloomington: Indiana University Press, 1988), 32–33; "Glossary," Josiah Parker Papers.

52. Williams Directory Company, 211.

53. John Pease, *Address of John Pease to Friends in America* (New York: Egbert, Hovey & King, 1845), 9, https://books.google.com/books?id=xN-mdRIjMvsC.

54. Howitt, *Autobiography*, 1:63, 107.

55. Obituary of Mildred Ratcliff, *Friend* 20, no. 19 (January 30, 1847), 44, https://books.google.com/books?id=9ylHAQAAMAAJ.

56. "A Testimony in Philadelphia Yearly Meeting," *Friend: A Religious and Literary Journal* 56, no. 4 (September 2, 1882): 27, https://books.google.com/books?id=cTxHAQAAMAAJ.

57. Carl Woodring, *Victorian Samplers: William and Mary Howitt* (Lawrence: University of Kansas Press, 1952), 127–129.

58. Obituary of Benjamin Seebohm, *Annual Monitor for 1872, or Obituary of the Members of the Society of Friends in Great Britain and Ireland, for the Year 1871*, n.s., 30 (1871), 210–229, https://books.google.com/books?id=jLoNAAAAYAAJ&dq.

59. For a highly sympathetic account of Seebohm's travels in America, see Robert Lindsey, *Travels of Robert and Sarah Lindsey* (London: Samuel Harris, 1886), https://books.google.com/books?id=HlcHeoMG4NEC, 11–53; for a summary of the trip see page 50. For a more critical account of the objections raised by his visits to Philadelphia meetings, see William Hodgson, *The Society of Friends in the Nineteenth Century: A Historical View of the Successive Convulsions and Schisms Therein During That Period* (Philadelphia: Sherman, 1876), 2:112–117, https://books.google.com/books?id=Yg3yaEZlVzoC.

60. Abbott et al., *A to Z*, 261–262.

61. Quoted in Thomas D. Hamm, "Hicksite, Orthodox, and Evangelical Quakerism, 1805–1887," in *The Oxford Handbook of Quaker Studies*, ed. Stephen W. Angell and Pink Dandelion (Oxford: Oxford University Press, 2013), 70–71.

62. Howitt, *Autobiography*, 1:4.

63. William Shipley Taylor and J. Gurney Taylor, *Family Record of the Descendants of Dr. Edward Taylor to December 1953* (Milwaukee: J. G. Taylor, 1954), 28, https://books.google.com/books?id=4QoIAwAAQBAJ.

64. Williams Directory Company, 207, 245.

65. Bob Closson and Mary Closson, *Abstracts of Washington County, Pennsylvania Willbooks 1–5, 1776–1841* (Apollo, Pa.: Closson Press, 1995), 107.

66. Williams Directory Company, 266.

67. Quaker Rare Collection at Watson Library, Wilmington College, Ohio; "Abraham Merritt Abram Taylor," Ancestry, accessed April 19, 2020, https://www.ancestry.com/family-tree/person/tree/319873/person/110045623566/facts.

68. Williams Directory Company, 272.

69. Obituary of Ann Townsend, *Friends Journal* 12 (June 11, 1859): 634, American Periodicals.

70. "Anna Aston Warder," Ancestry, accessed April 19, 2020, https://www.ancestry.com/family-tree/person/tree/66537868/person/46183858722/facts; Warder-Haines papers (1789–1854, bulk 1822–1854), Clements Library, University of Michigan, accessed April 19, 2020, https://quod.lib.umich.edu/c/clementsead/umich-wcl-M-2911war?view=text.

71. Randolph Paul Runyon, *Delia Webster and the Underground Railroad* (Lexington: University Press of Kentucky, 1999).

72. *DQB*; Obituary of Thomas Wells, *Annual Monitor for 1880, or Obituary of the Members of the Society of Friends in Great Britain and Ireland, for the Year 1879*, n.s., 38 (1879): 173–179, https://books.google.com/books?id=67kNAAAAYAAJ.

73. Jones, 2:580.

74. *Philadelphia Directory for the Year 1840* (Philadelphia: A. M'Elroy, 1840), 277, https://books.google.com/books?id=O6J4AAAAMAAJ.

75. Obituary of Annabella E. Winn, *Friend: A Religious and Literary Journal* 83, no. 5 (August 5, 1909): 34, https://books.google.com/books?id=6T1HAQAAMAAJ.

76. Abbott et al., *A to Z*, 306–307.

Bibliography

Abbott, Margery Post, Mary Ellen Chijioke, Pink Dandelion, and John William Oliver Jr. *The A to Z of the Friends (Quakers).* Lanham, Md.: Scarecrow Press, 2006.

Allen, Theodore W. *The Invention of the White Race. Vol. 1, Racial Oppression and Social Control.* London: Verso Books, 1994.

American National Biography Online. New York: Oxford University Press, 2000–. https://www.anb.org/.

Anderson, Benedict. *Imagined Communities: Reflections on the Origin and Spread of Nationalism.* Rev. ed. London: Verso, 2016.

Anderson, Godfrey T. "The Captain Lays Down the Law." *New England Quarterly* 44, no. 2 (June 1971): 305–309. https://doi.org/10.2307/364532.

Apthorp, Elsie Janeway. *Elinor & Edward Janeway.* Privately printed, 2005.

Bacon, Margaret H. *The Quiet Rebels: The Story of the Quakers in America.* New York: Basic Books, 1969.

Bakhtin, M. M. *The Dialogic Imagination: Four Essays.* Edited by Michael Holquist. Translated by Caryl Emerson and Holquist. Austin: University of Texas Press, 1981.

Barbour, Hugh, and J. William Frost. *The Quakers.* New York: Greenwood, 1988.

"Biographical Note." In *Eli and Sybil Jones Family Papers, 1830–1890 (MC.1009.A): Finding Aid Prepared by Mary A. Crauderueff,* 4. Haverford, Pa.: Quaker & Special Collections, Haverford College, December 2015. https://library. haverford.edu/finding-aids/files/1009A.pdf.

Boscoe, Francis P. "A Project of Doubtful Utility: Measuring Legislative Opposition to the Pennsylvania Canal." *Political Geography* 19, no. 8 (November 2000): 997–1011. https://doi.org/10.1016/S0962-6298(00)00039-1.

Bowen, Charles. "American Colonization Society." In *The American Almanac and Repository of Useful Knowledge for the Year 1834,* 92–94. Boston: Charles Bowen, 1835. https://books.google.com/books?id=G6wkAQAAMAAJ.

Brake, Laurel and Marysa Demoor, eds. *Dictionary of Nineteenth-Century Journalism.* London: The British Library, 2009.

Bremer, Frederika [*sic*]. *The Home; or, Family Cares and Family Joys.* Translated by Mary Howitt. 2 vols. London: Longman, Brown, Green, and Longmans, 1843.

———. *The Neighbours: A Story of Every-Day Life.* Translated by Mary Howitt. 2 vols. London: Longman, Brown, Green, and Longmans, 1842.

———. *The President's Daughters: Including Nina.* Translated by Mary Howitt. 3 vols. London: Longman, Brown, Green, and Longmans, 1843. https://books.google.com/books?id=QFhVAAAAYAAJ.

Burke, James L., and Donald E. Bensch. "Mount Pleasant and the Early Quakers of Ohio." *Ohio History* 83, no. 4 (Autumn 1974): 220–255.

Burritt, Elihu. *Sparks from the Anvil.* Worcester, Mass.: Henry J. Howland, 1846,

Busbey, T. Addison, ed. *The Biographical Directory of the Railway Officials of America.* Chicago: Railway Age, 1906.

Campbell, Karen. "The Evans Family of Waynesville." *Quaker Genealogy in Southwest Ohio* (blog), September 7, 2005. http://qugenswohio.blogspot.com/2005/09/evans-family-of-waynesville.html.

Carden, Allen D. *The Missouri Harmony, or a Collection of Psalm and Hymn Tunes, and Anthems; An Introduction to the Grounds and Rudiments of Music.* Lincoln: University of Nebraska Press, 1994.

Cazden, Elizabeth. "Quakers, Slavery, Anti-slavery, and Race," in *The Oxford Handbook of Quaker Studies.* Edited by Stephen W. Angell and Pink Dandelion. 345-362. Oxford: Oxford University Press, 2013.

Cherry, Deborah. "Women Artists and the Politics of Feminism 1850–1900." In *Women in the Victorian Art World*, edited by Clarissa Campbell Orr, 49–69. Manchester, UK: Manchester University Press, 1995.

Closson, Bob, and Mary Closson. *Abstracts of Washington County, Pennsylvania Will-books 1–5, 1776–1841.* Apollo, Pa.: Closson Press, 1995.

Coffin, Levi. *Reminiscences of Levi Coffin, the Reputed President of the Underground Railroad.* Cincinnati, Ohio: Western Tract Society, 1876. https://books.google.com/books?id=fS4OAAAAIAAJ.

Coggeshall, William T. *The Poets and Poetry of the West.* Columbus, Ohio: Follett, Foster and Col, 1860. https://books.google.com/books?id=QotDhcgByroC.

Cook, Elizabeth Heckendorn. *Epistolary Bodies: Gender and Genre in the Eighteenth-Century Republic of Letters.* Stanford, Calif.: Stanford University Press, 1996.

"Cope Family Papers." Historical Society of Pennsylvania, 2003. Accessed June 19, 2019. https://hsp.org/sites/default/files/mss/finding_aid_1486_cope.pdf.

"Correspondence." *Friends' Review: A Religious, Literary and Miscellaneous Journal* 26, no. 30 (March 15, 1873): 475.

Crumrine, Boyd, ed. *History of Washington County, Pennsylvania: With Biographical Sketches of Many of Its Pioneers and Prominent Men.* Philadelphia: L. H. Everts, 1882. https://books.google.com/books?id=7jxbQDo2BigC.

Darnowsky, Sabrina. *Friends Past and Present: The Bicentennial History of Cincinnati Friends Meeting (1815–2015).* Self-published, CreateSpace, 2015.

Darwin, Charles. *The Origin of Species by Means of Natural Selection, or the Preservation of Favored Races in the Struggle for Life.* London: John Murray, 1872.

Davis, Charles T., and Henry Louis Gates Jr., eds. *The Slave's Narrative.* New York: Oxford University Press, 1985.

Delano, Sterling F. *Brook Farm: The Dark Side of Utopia.* Cambridge, Mass.: Belknap, 2004.

"Descendants of David Hilles, Generation No. 3." Genealogy.com. Accessed June 10, 2019. https://www.genealogy.com/ftm/h/i/l/William-C-Hilles/GENE60-0003.html.

Dickens, Charles. *American Notes for General Circulation.* London: Chapman and Hall, 1850.

Dix, John Ross [A Cosmopolitan, pseud.]. "Pen and Ink Sketches of Popular Persons and Places." *Boston Daily Atlas* 64 (September 13, 1845). Nineteenth-Century U. S. Newspapers.

Doherty, Robert. W. *The Hicksite Separation: A Sociological Analysis of Religious Schism in Early Nineteenth Century America.* New Brunswick, N.J.: Rutgers University Press, 1967.

Dunicliff, Joy. *Quaker to Catholic: Mary Howitt, Lost Author of the 19th Century.* McMinnville, Tenn.: St. Clair, 2010.

———. *Traveller on the Hill-Top: Mary Howitt, the Famous Victorian Authoress.* Leek, UK: Churnet Valley, 1998.

Elliott, Errol T. *Quakers on the American Frontier: A History of the Westward Migrations, Settlements, and Developments of Friends on the American Continent.* Richmond, Ind.: Friends United Press, 1969.

Emancipator (Boston). "John Randolph's Slaves." 11, no. 12 (July 15, 1846): 48. America's Historical Newspapers.

Emancipator and Free American (Boston). "Postage." August 31, 1843. America's Historical Newspapers.

Emancipator and Free American (Boston). "The Press and the Mob." 8, no. 17 (August 24, 1843): [65]. America's Historical Newspapers.

Erickson, Charlotte. "Emigration from the British Isles to the U.S.A. in 1841: Part I. Emigration from the British Isles." *Population Studies* 43, no. 3 (November 1989): 347–367.

———. *Invisible Immigrants: The Adaptation of English and Scottish Immigrants in Nineteenth-Century America.* Coral Gables, Fla.: University of Miami Press, 1972.

———. *Leaving England: Essays on British Emigration in the Nineteenth Century.* Ithaca, N.Y.: Cornell University Press, 1994.

Forrest, Earle R. *History of Washington County, Pennsylvania.* Chicago: S. J. Clarke, 1926.

Foucault, Michel. "What Is an Author?" In *The Foucault Reader*, edited by Paul Rabinow, 101–120. New York: Pantheon Books, 1984.

Fox, George. *The Journal of George Fox.* Edited by John L. Nickalls. Cambridge: Cambridge University Press, 1952.

Frémont, John Charles. *Narrative of the Exploring Expedition to the Rocky Mountains in the Year 1842.* Washington, D.C.: Taylor, Wilde, 1840. https://books.google.com/books?id=AyoUAAAAYAAJ.

"Garden Gossip." *The Florist and Pomologist, and Suburban Gardener.* August 1884. 127–128. https://www.biodiversitylibrary.org/item/272732.

Garland, Hugh A. *The Life of John Randolph of Roanoke.* 13th ed. New York: D. Appleton, 1874. http://books.google.com/books?id=q1eqAAAAIAAJ.

Garraghan, Gilbert Joseph. *The Jesuits of the Middle United States.* New York: American Press, 1938.

Gaskell, Elizabeth Cleghorn *The Letters of Mrs. Gaskell.* Edited by J.A.V. Chapple and Arthur Pollard. Cambridge, Mass.: Harvard University Press, 1967.

———. [Cotton Mather Mills, pseud.]. "Life in Manchester: Libbie Marsh's Three Eras." *Howitt's Journal* 1 (1846): 310–313, 334–336, 345–347.

Gerber, David A. *Authors of Their Lives: The Personal Correspondence of British Immigrants to North America in the Nineteenth Century.* New York: New York University Press, 2006.

———. "Moving Backward and Moving On: Nostalgia, Significant Others, and Social Reintegration in Nineteenth-Century British Immigrant Personal Correspondence." *History of the Family* 21, no. 3 (2015): 291–314.

Gillis, Christina Marsden. *The Paradox of Privacy: Epistolary Form in "Clarissa."* Gainesville: University Presses of Florida, 1984.

Gilroy, Amanda, and W. M. Verhoeven. *Epistolary Histories: Letters, Fiction, Culture.* Charlottesville: University Press of Virginia, 2000.

"Glossary." Josiah Parker Papers. Earlham College Friends Collection and College Archives. Accessed June 9, 2019. https://exhibits.earlham.edu/exhibits/show/parker/glossary/macy-overman.

Goldsmith, Elizabeth C., ed. *Writing the Female Voice: Essays on Epistolary Literature.* Boston: Northeastern University Press, 1989.

Goodrich, Samuel Griswold [Peter Parley, pseud.]. *A Grammar of Modern Geography.* London: Thomas Tegg, 1838.

———. *Tales about Animals.* London: Thomas Tegg, 1838.

Goss, Charles Frederic. *Cincinnati, the Queen City, 1788–1912.* Chicago: S. J. Clarke, 1912.

Graham, Sylvester. *A Treatise on Bread and Bread-Making.* Boston: Light & Stearns, 1837.

Guarneri, Carl. *The Utopian Alternative: Fourierism in Nineteenth-Century America.* Ithaca, N.Y.: Cornell University Press, 1991.

Hall, Harvey. *The Cincinnati Directory for 1825.* Cincinnati, Ohio: Samuel J. Browne, 1825. https://www.cincinnatilibrary.org/citydirectory/CincinnatiDirectory_1825.pdf.

Hamm, Thomas D. *Earlham College: A History, 1847–1997.* Bloomington: Indiana University Press, 1997.

———. "Hicksite, Orthodox, and Evangelical Quakerism, 1805–1887." In *The Oxford Handbook of Quaker Studies*, edited by Stephen W. Angell and Pink Dandelion, 63–77. Oxford: Oxford University Press, 2013.

———. "History." Earlham College. 2010. https://earlham.edu/about/campus-history/history/.

———. *The Quakers in America.* New York: Columbia University Press, 2003.

———. *The Transformation of American Quakerism: Orthodox Friends, 1800–1907.* Bloomington: Indiana University Press, 1988.

Hamm, Thomas D., April Beckman, Florio Marissa, Kirsti Giles, and Marie Hopper. "'A Great and Good People': Midwestern Quakers and the Struggle against Slavery." *Indiana Magazine of History* 100, no. 1 (2004): 3–25.

Harrison, Edward. *The Extraordinary Case of Sarah Hawkes: One of Extreme Deformity, Cured by a Method Founded upon Simple Principles.* London: Joseph Robins, 1832.

[Harrison, John]. "Is It Proper to Call the Holy Scriptures 'the Word of God'?" *Friend: A Religious and Literary Journal* 6, no. 25 (March 30, 1833): 197–198.

Harrison, Lucy. *A Lover of Books: The Life and Literary Papers of Lucy Harrison, Written and Arranged by Amy Greener.* London: J. M. Dent, 1916.

Hart, John Percy, and W. H. Bright, eds. *Hart's History and Directory of the Three Towns, Brownsville, Bridgeport, West Brownsville.* Cadwallader, Pa.: J. P. Hart, 1904. https://books.google.com/books?id=NJhAAAAAYAAJ.

Hartman, Jesse L. "The Portage Railroad National Historic Site and the Johnstown Flood Memorial." *Pennsylvania History* 31, no. 2 (April 1964): 138–156.

Hinshaw, William Wade. *Encyclopedia of American Quaker Genealogy.* 7 vols. Baltimore: Genealogical Publishing, 1969.

Historic Atlas of Ohio Yearly Meeting: An Illustrated Documentation of the History of the Ohio Quakers from Their Earliest Meetings to Their Bicentennial in 2013. Barnesville: Ohio Yearly Meeting of Friends, 2012.

"History." Village of Harveysburg. Accessed April 13, 2020, http://villageofharveysburg.org/history.

History of Hardin County, Iowa. Springfield, Ill.: Union, 1883. https://books.google.com/books?id=WHBHAQAAMAAJ.

Hodgson, William. *The Society of Friends in the Nineteenth Century: A Historical View of the Successive Convulsions and Schisms Therein during That Period.* 2 vols. Philadelphia: Sherman, 1876. https://books.google.com/books?id=Yg3yaEZlVzoC.

Hogg, James. "Welldean Hall." In *Tales and Sketches by the Ettrick Shepherd*, 190–274. Glasgow: Blackie & Son, 1837.

Holder, Charles Frederick. *The Quakers in Great Britain and America: The Religious and Political History of the Society of Friends from the Seventeenth to the Twentieth Century*. New York: Neuner, 1913.

Horrell, Sara, Jane Humphries, and Hans-Joachim Voth. "Stature and Relative Deprivation: Fatherless Children in Early Industrial Britain." *Continuity and Change* 13, no. 1 (May 1998): 73–115.

How, James. *Epistolary Spaces: English Letter-Writing from the Foundation of the Post Office to Richardson's "Clarissa."* Studies in Early Modern English Literature. Burlington, Vt.: Ashgate, 2003.

Howitt, Mary. *The Author's Daughter: A Tale*. Boston: Waite, Peirce, 1845.

———. *Birds and Flowers and Other Country Things*. [London]: J. Green, 1837.

———. *The Children's Year*. London: Longman, Brown, Green, and Longmans, 1847.

———. *Hymns and Fire-Side Verses*. London: Darton and Clark, 1839.

———. *Mary Howitt: An Autobiography*. Edited by Margaret Howitt. 2 vols. London: W. Isbister, 1889.

———. *My Own Story; or, The Autobiography of a Child*. New York: D. Appleton, 1844.

———. *No Sense Like Common Sense; or, Some Passages in the Life of Charles Middleton, Esq*. London: Thomas Tegg, 1843.

———. *Our Cousins in Ohio*. London: Darton, 1849.

———. *Our Cousins in Ohio*. New York: Collins & Brother, 1849.

———. *Sketches of Natural History*. London: Effingham Wilson, 1834.

———. *Strive and Thrive: A Tale*. London: Thomas Tegg, 1840.

———. *The Two Apprentices: A Tale for Youth*. London: Thomas Tegg, 1844.

Howitt, Richard. *Australia: Historical, Descriptive, and Statistic; with an Account of a Four Years' Residence in That Colony*. London: Longman, Brown, Green, and Longmans, 1845.

———. *Impressions of Australia Felix, during Four Years' Residence in That Colony* . London: Longman, Brown, Green, and Longmans, 1845.

Howitt, William. *The Boy's Country-Book: Being the Real Life of a Country Boy, Written by Himself*. London: Longman, Orme, Brown, Green, and Longmans, 1839.

———. *The Life and Adventures of Jack of the Mill*. London: Longman, Brown, Green, and Longmans, 1844.

———. *The Rural and Domestic Life of Germany*. London: Longman, Brown, Green, and Longmans, 1842.

———. *The Student-Life of Germany: From the Unpublished ms. of Dr. Cornelius; Containing nearly Forty of the Most Famous Student Songs, with the Original Music, Adapted to the Piano Forte*. London: Longman, Brown, Green, and Longmans, 1841.

———. *Visits to Remarkable Places: Old Halls, Battle Fields, and Scenes Illustrative of Striking Passages in History and Poetry*. 2nd series. London: Longman, Brown, Green, and Longmans, 1842.

Howitt, William, and Mary Howitt. *The Desolation of Eyam: The Emigrant, a Tale of the American Woods; And Other Poems*. London: Wightman and Cramp, 1827. https://books.google.com/books?id=j7wkAAAAMAAJ.

———. *Howitt's Journal*. Vol. 3. London: William Lovett, 1848.

Hugill, Stan. *Shanties from the Seven Seas: Shipboard Work-Songs and Songs Used as Work-Songs from the Great Days of Sail*. 2nd ed. London: Routledge & Kegan Paul, 1984.

Hunter, Louis C. *Steamboats on the Western Rivers: An Economic and Technological History*. Cambridge, Mass.: Harvard University Press, 1949.

"Infamous." *Daily Atlas* (Boston), August 8, 1843.

Ingle, H. Larry. *Quakers in Conflict: The Hicksite Reformation.* Wallingford, Pa.: Pendle Hill, 1998.

Isichei, Elizabeth. *Victorian Quakers.* London: Oxford University Press, 1970.

J.B. "Cheap Postage in Britain." *Constitution* (Middletown, Conn.). July 5, 1848. America's Historical Newspapers, 2.

Jackson, Maurice. *Let This Voice Be Heard: Anthony Benezet, Father of Atlantic Abolitionism.* Philadelphia: University of Pennsylvania Press, 2010.

"John Randolph's Emancipated Slaves," *Friend* 19, no. 43 (July 7, 1846): 343.

Johnston, Judith. *Victorian Women and the Economies of Travel, Translation and Culture, 1830–1870.* London: Routledge, 2016.

Jones, Rufus M. *The Later Periods of Quakerism.* 2 vols. London: Macmillan, 1921.

Jordan, Ryan. *Slavery and the Meetinghouse.* Bloomington: Indiana University Press, 2007.

Keifer, Sara Jane Harris. *Genealogical and Biographical Sketches of the New Jersey Branch of the Harris Family, in the United States*, Madison, Wis: Democratic Printing Company, 1888. https://catalog.hathitrust.org/Record/008912921

Kenyon, Olga, ed. *800 Years of Women's Letters.* Boston: Faber and Faber, 1993.

Kirkland, Caroline M. *Forest Life.* 2 vols. London: Longman, Brown, Green, and Longmans, 1842.

———. *A New Home—Who'll Follow? Or, Glimpses of Western Life.* New York: C. S. Francis, 1839.

Kline, Mary-Jo, and Susan Holbrook Perdue. *A Guide to Documentary Editing.* 3rd ed. Charlottesville: University of Virginia Press, 2008.

Klopfenstein, Carl G. "The Removal of the Wyandots from Ohio." *Ohio Historical Quarterly* 66, no. 2 (April 1957): 119–136.

Knight, Charles, ed. *Mind amongst the Spindles: A Selection from the Lowell Offering; A Miscellany Wholly Composed by the Factory Girls of an American City.* London: Charles Knight, 1844.

Krummacher, F. W. *Elijah the Tishbite.* London: Religious Tract Society, 1836.

Lamott, John Henry. *History of the Archdiocese of Cincinnati, 1821–1921.* New York: Frederick Pustet, 1921.

Lee, Amice Macdonell. *In Their Several Generations.* Plainfield, N.J.: Interstate, [1956?].

———. *Laurels & Rosemary: The Life of William and Mary Howitt.* London: Oxford University Press, 1955.

Lewie, Chris J. *Two Generations on the Allegheny Portage Railroad: The First Railroad to Cross the Allegheny Mountains.* Shippensburg, Pa.: Burd Street, 2001.

Lindsey, Robert. *Travels of Robert and Sarah Lindsey.* London: Samuel Harris, 1886. https://books.google.com/books?id=HlcHeoMG4NEC.

"London Yearly Meeting, 1836." *Journal of the Friends Historical Society* 17, no. 3 (1920): 82–89. https://archive.org/details/journaloffriends1718frie.

Mack, Horace. *History of Columbiana County, Ohio: With Illustrations and Biographical Sketches of Some of Its Prominent Men and Pioneers.* Philadelphia: D. W. Ensign, 1879. https://books.google.com/books?id=OeA4AQAAMAAJ.

MacLeod, Christine. *Inventing the Industrial Revolution: The English Patent System, 1660–1800.* Cambridge: Cambridge University Press, 2002.

Maidment, Brian. "Howitt's Journal of Literature and Popular Progress (1847–1848)." In *Dictionary of Nineteenth-Century Journalism in Great Britain and Ireland*, edited by Laurel Brake and Marysa Demoor. London: Academia Press and the British Library, 2009. CD-ROM.

"Maltbie Genealogy." *"Old Northwest" Genealogical Quarterly* 9 (1906): 314–325. https://books.google.com/books?id=-EM9AQAAMAAJ.

Mason, Marcia J. Heringa, ed. *Remember the Distance that Divides Us: The Family Letters of Philadelphia Quaker Abolitionist and Michigan Pioneer Elizabeth Margaret Chandler, 1830–1842*. East Lansing: Michigan State University Press, 2004.

Meigs, Cornelia. *What Makes a College? A History of Bryn Mawr*. New York: Macmillan, 1956.

Merle d'Aubigné, J. H. *History of the Reformation of the Sixteenth Century: from Its Commencement until the Days of Calvin* (New York: The American Tract Society), 1835.

[Mogridge, George]. *Thoughts for the Thoughtful, by Old Humphrey*. London: Religious Tract Society, 1841. https://books.google.com/books?id=ZBh6ZK_O_xAC.

Morton, Vanessa. "Quaker Politics and Industrial Change c. 1800–1850." PhD thesis, Open University, 1988.

NaNations. "Wyandot Indian Tribe." Accessed March 16, 2020. http://www.nanations.com/wyandot/history.htm.

Nelson, Bruce. *Irish Nationalists and the Making of the Irish Race*. Princeton, N.J.: Princeton University Press, 2012.

Newlin, Algie I. "Hubbard, Jeremiah." In *Dictionary of North Carolina Biography*, edited by William S. Powell. Chapel Hill: University of North Carolina Press, 1988.

Newton, John. *Cardiphonia; or, The Utterance of the Heart; In the Course of a Real Correspondence*. London: J. Buckland and J. Johnson, 1781.

Nichol, Francis D. *The Midnight Cry: A Defense of the Character and Conduct of William Miller and the Millerites*. Washington, D.C.: Review and Herald, 1945.

Nodal, John H. *The Bibliography (Biographical and Topographical) of Ackworth School*. Manchester, UK: F. Nodal, 1889. http://books.google.com/books?id=yeoBAAAAYAAJ.

Numbers, Ronald L., and Jonathan M. Butler, eds. *The Disappointed: Millerism and Millenarianism in the Nineteenth Century*. 2nd ed. Knoxville: University of Tennessee Press, 1993.

Obituary of Alice Lucy Bayliffe. *Annual Monitor for 1848, or Obituary of the Members of the Society of Friends in Great Britain and Ireland, for the year 1847*, n.s., 6 (1847): 26. https://books.google.com/books?id=XFoEAAAAQAAJ.

Obituary of Ann Botham. *British Friend* 6, no. 5 (May 31, 1848): 140. http://books.google.com/books?id=gjcrAAAAYAAJ.

Obituary of Ann Ecroyd. *Annual Monitor for 1860, or Obituary of the Members of the Society of Friends in Great Britain and Ireland, for the Year 1859*, n.s., 18 (1859): 87–88. https://books.google.com/books?id=n1oEAAAAQAAJ.

Obituary of Ann Townsend. *Friends Journal* 12 (June 11, 1859): 634.

Obituary of Annabella E. Winn. *Friend: A Religious and Literary Journal* 83, no. 5 (August 5, 1909): 34.

Obituary of Benjamin Seebohm. *Annual Monitor for 1872, or Obituary of the Members of the Society of Friends in Great Britain and Ireland, for the year 1871*, n.s., 30 (1871): 210–229. https://books.google.com/books?id=jLoNAAAAYAAJ&dq.

Obituary of Harrison Alderson. *Annual Monitor for 1872, or Obituary of the Members of the Society of Friends in Great Britain and Ireland, for the year 1871*, n.s., 30 (1871): 1–12. https://books.google.com/books?id=jLoNAAAAYAAJ.

Obituary of John Meader. *American Annual Monitor for 1862, or Obituary of the Members of the Society of Friends in America* 5 (1862): 119–151. https://books.google.com/books?id=JHcUZy-8tH4C.

Obituary of Lucy Bayliffe. *Annual Monitor for 1854, or Obituary of the Members of the Society of Friends in Great Britain and Ireland, for the Year 1853*, n.s., 12 (1853): 11. https://books.google.com/books?id=FAAqAAAAYAAJ.

Obituary of Mildred Ratcliff. *Friend: A Religious and Literary Journal* 20, no. 19 (January 30, 1847): 152. https://books.google.com/books?id=9ylHAQAAMAAJ.

Obituary of Sarah Emlen. *Friends' Review: A Religious, Literary and Miscellaneous Journal* 2, no. 46 (August 4, 1849): 728. https://books.google.com/books?id=2sZLAAAAMAAJ.

Obituary of Susanna Corder. *Annual Monitor for 1865, or Obituary of the Members of the Society of Friends in Great Britain and Ireland, for the year 1864*, n.s., 23 (1864), 42–51. https://www.google.com/books/edition/The_Annual_Monitor/LwEqAAAAYAAJ.

Obituary of Thomas Albright. *Friends' Review: A Religious, Literary and Miscellaneous Journal* 1, no. 34 (May 13, 1848): 539. https://books.google.com/books?id=JoArAAAAYAAJ.

Obituary of Thomas Wells. *Annual Monitor for 1880, or Obituary of the Members of the Society of Friends in Great Britain and Ireland, for the Year 1879*, n.s., 38 (1879), 173–179. https://books.google.com/books?id=67kNAAAAYAAJ.

Obituary of William Forster. *Annual Monitor for 1855, or Obituary of the Members of the Society of Friends in Great Britain and Ireland, for the Year 1854*, n.s., 13 (1854): 48. https://books.google.com/books?id=e10EAAAAQAAJ.

Officer, Lawrence H., and Samuel H. Williamson. "Computing 'Real Value' over Time with a Conversion between U.K. Pounds and U.S. Dollars, 1791 to Present." MeasuringWorth, 2019. Accessed May 19, 2019. https://www.measuringworth.com/calculators/exchange/result_exchange.php.

"Ohio Yearly Meeting." Quaker Chronicle. Updated April 26, 2017. http://www.quaker-chronicle.info/meetings.php?meetingID=1.

Oxford Dictionary of National Biography. Online ed. New York: Oxford University Press, 2004–. https://www.oxforddnb.com/.

Painter, Levinus K. "The Rise and Decline of Quakerism in the Monongahela Valley." *Bulletin of Friends' Historical Association* 45, no. 1 (Spring 1956): 24–29.

Park, Mungo. *Travels in the Interior Districts of Africa: Performed under the Direction and Patronage of the African Association, in the Years 1795, 1796, and 1797*. London: W. Bulmer, 1799. https://catalog.hathitrust.org/Record/008697840.

Pease, Charles E. G. "The Descendants of Moses Neave." Pennyghael.org.uk, November 21, 2015, http://www.pennyghael.org.uk/Neave.pdf.

———. "The Descendants of Ralph Small." Pennyghael.org.uk, November 20, 2015. http://www.pennyghael.org.uk/Small.pdf.

Pease, John. *Address of John Pease to Friends in America*. New York: Egbert, Hovey & King, 1845. https://books.google.com/books?id=xN-mdRIjMvsC.

Peterson, Linda H. "Collaborative Life Writing as Ideology: The Auto/biographies of Mary Howitt and Her Family." *Prose Studies: History, Theory, Criticism* 26, no. 1–2 (2003): 176–195.

———. "Mother-Daughter Productions: Mary Howitt and Anna Mary Howitt in *Howitt's Journal, Household Words*, and Other Mid-Victorian Publications." *Victorian Periodicals Review* 31, no. 1 (Spring 1998): 31–54.

Phelps, Almira Hart Lincoln. *Familiar Lectures on Botany*. Hartford, Conn.: H. and F. J. Huntington, 1829. https://books.google.com/books?id=9WYXAAAAYAAJ.

Philadelphia Directory for the Year 1840. Philadelphia: A. M'Elroy, 1840. https://books.google.com/books?id=O6J4AAAAMAAJ.

Philanthropist. "Another Mob in Cincinnati." October 8, 1839. America's Historical Newspapers.

Piesse, Jude. "Dreaming across Oceans: Emigration and Nation in the Mid-Victorian Christmas Issue." *Victorian Periodicals Review* 46, no. 1 (Spring 2013): 37–60. https://doi.org/10.1353/vpr.2013.0003.

Pitcairn, David. *Perfect Peace: Letters-Memorial of the Late John Warren Howell, Esq., of Bath, M.R.C.S.* London: J. H. Jackson, 1844.

Prison Discipline Society. "Nineteenth Annual Report of the Board of Managers of the Prison Discipline Society, Boston, May, 1844." In *Reports of the Prison Discipline Society, Boston.* Vol. 2, *1836–1845*, 331–446. Boston: T. R. Marvin, 1855. http://books.google.com/books?id=-b8JAAAAIAAJ.

Pugh, Peter. *Great Enterprise: A History of Harrisons and Crosfield.* London: Harrisons and Crosfield, 1990.

Pullin, Naomi. *Female Friends and the Making of Transatlantic Quakerism, 1650–1750.* Cambridge: Cambridge University Press, 2018.

"Remarkable Dreams: Warnings and Providences." *Howitt's Journal* 3, no. 61–65 (1848): 136–139, 157–158, 173–174, 203–206.

A Report of the Proceedings of the Yearly Meeting of the Society of Friends [. . .] *To Which Is Added the Quakers' Yearly Epistle for 1836.* London: John Stephens, 1836. https://books.google.com/books?id=j8wsAAAAYAAJ.

Roberts, Helen E. *Researching Yorkshire Quaker History: A Guide to Sources.* Hull: University of Hull Brynmor Jones Library, 2007.

Rollins, Ron. "Living with History: Letter from Springboro." *Ohio Magazine* (August 2006), 15–16.

Rowe, David L. "Millerites: A Shadow Portrait." In *The Disappointed: Millerism and Millenarianism in the Nineteenth Century*, 2nd ed., edited by Ronald L. Numbers and Jonathan M. Butler, 1–16. Knoxville: University of Tennessee Press, 1993.

Rummel, Merle C. "Four Mile Church—200th Anniversary Presentation on the First 100 Years." Accessed March 30, 2020. https://www.cob-net.org/docs/bl/four-mile-presentation.pdf.

Runyon, Randolph Paul. *Delia Webster and the Underground Railroad.* Lexington: University Press of Kentucky, 1999.

Sedgwick, Catherine Maria. "The Widow Ellis and Her Son Willie: Overcome Evil with Good" in *Love Token for Children: Designed for Sunday-School Libraries.* New York: Harper & Brothers, 1838. 9-33.

Sellars, Kirsten. "Trying the Kaiser: The Origins of International Criminal Law." In *Historical Origins of International Criminal Law.* Vol. 1, edited by Morten Bergsmo, Cheah Wui Ling, and Yi Ping, 195–211. Brussels: Torkel Opsahl Academic EPublisher, 2014.

Sinor, Jennifer. *The Extraordinary Work of Ordinary Writing: Annie Ray's Diary.* Iowa City: University of Iowa Press, 2002.

Smith, Andrew F. *The Tomato in America: Early History, Culture, and Cookery.* Urbana: University of Illinois Press, 2001. https://books.google.com/books?id=e82QWB89_sIC.

Smith, Henry Ecroyd. *Annals of Smith of Cantley, Balby, and Doncaster, County York.* Yorkshire, UK: Hills, 1878. http://books.google.com/books?id=nSkAAAAAQAAJ.

Speckter, Otto. *The Child's Picture and Verse Book.* Translated by Mary Howitt. London: Longman, Brown, Green, and Longmans, 1844. https://books.google.com/books?id=nA5mAAAAcAAJ.

Spencer, Carole Dale. "Quakers in Theological Context." In *The Oxford Handbook of Quaker Studies*, edited by Stephen W. Angell and Pink Dandelion, 143–157. Oxford: Oxford University Press, 2013.

Stanner, W.E.H. "Howitt, Alfred William (1830–1908)." In *Australian Dictionary of Biography*. Online ed. National Centre of Biography, Australian National University, 2006. http://www.adb.online.anu.edu.au/biogs/A040489b.htm.

Stokes, Christopher. "Lost Poets #4: Sarah Frankland." *Maddalo: Thoughts of Some Description* (blog), August 14, 2018. http://maddalo.blogspot.com/2018/08/lost-poets-4-sarah-frankland.html.

Taylor, Nikki Marie. *Frontiers of Freedom: Cincinnati's Black Community, 1802–1868*. Athens: Ohio University Press, 2005.

Taylor, William Shipley, and J. Gurney Taylor. *Family Record of the Descendants of Dr. Edward Taylor to December 1953*. Milwaukee: J. G. Taylor, 1954. https://books.google.com/books?id=4QoIAwAAQBAJ.

"A Testimony in Philadelphia Yearly Meeting." *Friend: A Religious and Literary Journal* 56, no. 4 (September 2, 1882): 27. https://books.google.com/books?id=cTxHAQAAMAAJ.

"A Testimony of Miami Monthly Meeting of Friends, Concerning Joseph Cloud." *Friend: A Religious and Literary Journal* 5, no. 39 (1832): 310–311.

Thomas, Anna Braithwaite. "The Beaconite Controversy." *Bulletin of Friends' Historical Society* 4, no. 2 (1912): 70–81.

Thomas, William I., and Florian Znaniecki. *The Polish Peasant in Europe and America*. Edited by Eli Zaretsky. 5 vols. Urbana: University of Illinois Press, 1984.

Times (London). "Emigration.—Comforts on the Voyage, &c." March 6, 1835. http://tinyurl.galegroup.com/tinyurl/AHF4w9.

Tonna, Charlotte Elizabeth. *Principalities and Powers in Heavenly Places*. London: R. B. Seeley and W. Burnside, 1842.

Totah, Khalil. "Quakerism in Palestine." *Bulletin of Friends Historical Association* 26, no. 2 (1937): 79–86.

Van Vugt, William E. *Britain to America: Mid-Nineteenth-Century Immigrants to the United States*. Urbana: University of Illinois Press, 1999.

———, ed. *British Immigration to the United States, 1776–1914*. 4 vols. London: Pickering & Chatto, 2009.

Vann, Richard T., and David Edward Charles Eversley. *Friends in Life and Death: The British and Irish Quakers in the Demographic Transition, 1650–1900*. Cambridge: Cambridge University Press, 1992.

"Varieties of Yellow Indian Corns." *California Culturist: A Journal of Agriculture, Horticulture, Mechanism and Mining* (April 1859): 461–466. https://books.google.com/books?id=exQLAAAAIAAJ.

Walker, Janet R., and Richard W. Burkhardt. *Eliza Julia Flower: Letters of an English Gentlewoman; Life on the Illinois-Indiana Frontier, 1817–1861*. Muncie, Ind: Ball State University, 1991.

Waterton, Charles. *Wanderings in South America, the North-West of the United States, and the Antilles: In the Years 1812, 1816, 1820, and 1824*. London: J. Mawman, 1825. https://books.google.com/books?id=vTXdbQztxDQC.

Wattenberg, Ben J., ed. *The Statistical History of the United States, from Colonial Times to the Present*. New York: Basic Books, 1976. https://books.google.com/books?id=3lLAUYpTDzAC.

Weeks, Stephen Beauregard. *Southern Quakers and Slavery: A Study in Institutional History*. Baltimore: Johns Hopkins Press, 1896.

White, Joseph M. "Cincinnati's German Catholic Life: A Heritage of Lay Participation." *U.S. Catholic Historian* 12, no. 3 (1994): 1–16.

Whittier, John Greenleaf. *Moll Pitcher: A Poem*. Boston: Carter and Hendee, 1832.

Wiley & Putnam's Emigrant's Guide: Comprising Advice and Instruction in Every Stage of the Voyage to America. London: Wiley & Putnam, 1845. https://books.google.com/books?id=qmsFAAAAQAAJ.

Williams Directory Company. *Williams' Cincinnati Directory and Business Advertiser, for 1850–51*. Cincinnati, Ohio: C. S. Williams—College Hall, 1850. https://books.google.com/books?id=353NAAAAMAAJ.

Wilson, William Bender. *History of the Pennsylvania Railroad Company, with Plan of Organization, Portraits of Officials and Biographical Sketches*. 2 vols. Philadelphia: Henry T. Coates, 1895. https://books.google.com/books?id=qj9N-eWi71YC.

Woodring, Carl. *Victorian Samplers: William and Mary Howitt*. Lawrence: University of Kansas Press, 1952.

Wordsworth, William and Samuel Taylor Coleridge. *Lyrical Ballads, with a Few Other Poems*. London: J. & A. Arch, 1798.

Yeomans, Donald K. *Comets: A Chronological History of Observation, Science, Myth, and Folklore*. New York: Wiley, 1991.

Youngs, Benjamin Seth. *The Testimony of Christ's Second Appearing: Containing a General Statement of All Things Pertaining to the Faith and Practice of the Church of God in this Latter Day*. 3rd ed. Union Village, OH: B. Fisher and A. Burnett, 1823. https://books.google.com/books?id=5FYoAAAAYAAJ.

Index

Notes: Page references in *italics* refer to illustrative matter. Individual items indexed under broad categories (e.g. fabrics, flowers and flowering shrubs, Quaker meetings, transportation, trees) are not generally indexed as separate entries. Misspellings, alternate spellings, and mis-namings are given parenthetically in quotation marks. With the exception of *Our Cousins in Ohio*, books by William and Mary Howitt and Fredrika Bremer are listed with their authors; others are indexed by title.

Abbreviations: EBA (Emma Botham Alderson), ABH (Anna Botham Harrison), MBH (Mary Botham Howitt), MM (Monthly Meeting), QM (Quarterly Meeting), YM (Yearly Meeting)

About the Editor and Author

Donald Ingram Ulin lives in Allegany, New York, with a family that includes four goats and a dog named Emma, after the author of these letters. He is associate professor and director of English at the University of Pittsburgh at Bradford and has published articles on a wide variety of topics, including literary pedagogy, Charles Darwin, film adaptations of *Huckleberry Finn,* and the nineteenth-century invention of an English countryside.

Emma Botham Alderson (1806–1847) was a Quaker woman who immigrated to Ohio from Liverpool, England, in 1842, with her husband and other family members. She was the sister of popular English poet and author Mary Howitt.